A SH

A Shorter Welsh Dictionary

Geiriadur Bach Gomer

D. Geraint Lewis

Including a collection of phrases and idioms by /
Yn cynnwys casgliad o ymadroddion a
phriod-ddulliau gan

Berwyn Prys Jones

Gomer

Cyflwynedig i Jonathan a Caroline

First impression – 2005

ISBN 1 84323 099 2

Printed in Wales at
Gomer Press, Llandysul, Ceredigion SA44 4JL

Contents / Cynnwys

Preface

This book is an attempt to bridge the gap between those pocket dictionaries, which contain both Welsh/English and English/Welsh vocabularies, and the large, comprehensive dictionary of the Welsh Academy. The basis for this expansion from a pocket dictionary to a Shorter dictionary was the administrative and educational terms which I had gathered for departmental use here in Ceredigion County Council. However, I decided to exclude the more specialist terms and sometimes short-lived acronyms from the field of education.

The result is a more comprehensive general vocabulary than would normally be contained in a standard pocket dictionary, without straying into those specialised fields where specific lists of terms already exist.

I had hoped to contain a fuller vocabulary from the field of Information Technology and Computer Science, but there is a surprising lack of consensus in this field at present.

There exists no obvious bilingual gazetteer of the names of countries and so I have included an appendix of countries in both Welsh/English and English/Welsh.

I count myself fortunate indeed, to have received Berwyn Prys Jones' permission to include his list of idiomatic phrases collected over many years as a professional translator.

It is worth mulling over these examples of the translator's art, to see how a master craftsman analyses and solves the problems presented by the original phrases. Berwyn mentions elsewhere that a translator's nose can sometimes be too close to the page, but here one sees the sinewy style of a translator who is completely at home in the two languages in which he works.

My thanks are also due to Dr Telfryn Pritchard, who, in reading the original text, not only unpicked inconsistencies of style, but also rescued me from many errors and pitfalls.

My gratitude to these two gentlemen is great, as it is to Gomer Press for their diligence, but any faults that remain are entirely my own.

Rhagair

Dyma gais i lenwi'r bwlch rhwng y geiriaduron bach, sy'n cynnig geirfaoedd Cymraeg/Saesneg, Saesneg/Cymraeg, a geiriadur mawr, cynhwysfawr yr Academi.

Sylfaen y gwaith ehangu oedd cynnwys mwy o eirfa'n ymwneud â Gweinyddiaeth ac Addysg ar gyfer yr adran hon yng Nghyngor Sir Ceredigion, ond rhag ei orbwyso, tynnais ymaith y llu o acronymau a thermau arbenigol ym myd addysg.

Y canlyniad yw ei fod yn cynnwys geirfa gyffredinol ehangach na'r geiriaduron bach, ond heb fentro i mewn i feysydd arbenigol lle y ceir casgliadau o dermau eisoes.

Fy ngobaith oedd cynnwys rhestr fwy cyflawn o eirfa Technoleg Gwybodaeth a Chyfrifiadura, ond does dim llawer o gytundeb yn y maes – o wefan, i safwe, neu hyd yn oed ynglŷn â'r 'e-byst' cyffredin!

Rwy'n cynnwys rhestr o Enwau Gwledydd Cymraeg/Saesneg a Saesneg/Cymraeg gan nad oes rhestrau tebyg ar gael yn hylaw, a bûm yn ddigon ffodus i dderbyn caniatâd Berwyn Prys Jones i gynnwys y rhestr o ymadroddion y mae ef wedi'u casglu dros gyfnod hir o gyfieithu proffesiynol.

Mae'n werth craffu ar yr enghreifftiau hyn i weld sut y mae meistr ar y grefft yn dadansoddi ac yn ateb y problemau a geir yn yr ymadroddion gwreiddiol. Mae Berwyn yn sôn mewn man arall fod trwyn y cyfieithydd weithiau'n gallu bod yn rhy agos at y papur, ond gwelir yma ymateb rhywiog cyfieithydd sy'n adnabod i'r dim deithi'r ddwy iaith y mae'n ymwneud â nhw.

Rhaid diolch hefyd i Dr Telfryn Pritchard a ddarllenodd y testun gwreiddiol gan nid yn unig ei gysoni, ond hefyd fy achub rhag llawer camgymeriad a llithriad.

Mae fy nyled yn fawr i'r ddau fonheddwr, ac i Wasg Gomer am ei gofal arferol wrth fy ngwaith, ond eiddo i mi yw pob llithriad a bai a erys.

D. Geraint Lewis

Terms and Abbreviations

English / Saesneg

auto. – automobile
bot. – botany
chem. – chemistry
comptr – computer
elec. – electricity
fig. – figurative
fin. – finance
geol. – geology
geom. – geometry
gram. – grammar
journ. – journalism
phil. – philosophy
math. – mathematics
mech. – mechanics
mech. eng. – mechanical engineering
med. – medicine
mus. – music
naut. – nautical
pers. – personal
photo. – photography
phys. – physiology
pol. – politics
tex. – texture
typ. – typology

Welsh / Cymraeg

enw – noun
hwn – masculine noun
hon – feminine noun
hyn – plural noun
be – berfenw / infinitive
berf – verb
ans – ansoddair / adjective
adf – adferf / adverb
ardd – arddodiad / preposition
cysyllt – cysylltair / conjunction
byrfodd – abbreviation
llu – lluosog

A

a (no Welsh equivalent) 'a book' = ***llyfr***
abacus *enw* ***abacws*** *hwn*
abandon *enw* (gaiety) ***afiaith*** *hwn*
abandon *be* (leave) ***gadael***, ***rhoi'r gorau i***
abandoned *ans* ***unig***
abase *be* ***darostwng***
abash *be* ***cywilyddio***
abate *be* ***gostegu***, ***lleddfu***, ***lleihau***
abatement *enw* ***lleihad*** *hwn*
abattoir *enw* ***lladd-dy*** *hwn*
abbess *enw* ***abades*** *hon*
abbey *enw* ***abaty*** *hwn*
abbot *enw* ***abad*** *hwn*
abbreviate *be* ***cwtogi***, ***talfyrru***
abbreviation *enw* ***byrfodd***, ***talfyriad*** *hwn*
ABC (alphabet) *enw* ***yr wyddor*** *hon*
abdicate *be* ***ymddiswyddo***; (responsibility) ***ymwrthod â***; (the throne) ***ymddiorseddu***
abdomen *enw* ***bol***, ***bola*** *hwn*
abduct *be* ***cipio***, ***herwgipio***
abductor *enw* ***cipiwr***, ***herwgipiwr*** *hwn*
aberrant *ans* ***cyfeiliornus***
aberration *enw* ***cyfeiliornad*** *hwn*
abet *be* ***cefnogi***
abeyance *enw* ***oediad*** *hwn*
  fall into a~ ***dod i ben***
  in a~ ***heb ei benderfynu***
  put in a~ ***rhoi o'r neilltu***
abhor *be* ***ffieiddio***
abhorrence *enw* ***atgasedd*** *hwn*
abhorrent *ans* ***atgas***, ***ffiaidd***
abide *be* (live) ***trigo***; (put up with) ***goddef***
  a~ by ***parchu***, ***glynu wrth***
  can't a~ ***methu goddef***
abiding *ans* ***arhosol***, ***parhaol***, ***safadwy***
ability *enw* ***dawn*** *hwn/hon*, ***gallu*** *hwn*
ab initio *adf* ***o'r dechrau***
abject *ans* ***distadl***; ***truenus***
abjectness *enw* ***dinodedd*** *hwn*
abjure *be* ***ymwrthod â***
ablaze *adf* ***yn wenfflam***
able *ans* ***atebol***, ***galluog***
able (to be) *be* ***gallu***, ***medru***
able-bodied *ans* ***cydnerth***, ***heb anabledd***
ably
  a~ assisted by ***gyda chymorth glew***
abnegation *enw* ***ymwadiad*** *hwn*
abnormal *ans* ***anghyffredin***, ***anarferol***
aboard *adf* ***ar fwrdd***
abode *enw* ***annedd*** *hwn/hon*, ***trigfan*** *hon*
abolish *be* ***diddymu***, ***dileu***
abolition *enw* ***diddymiad***, ***dilead*** *hwn*
abominable *ans* ***atgas***, ***ffiaidd***

a

abominate *be* ***ffieiddio***
abomination *enw* ***ffieidd-dra*** *hwn*
aboriginal *ans* ***cynfrodorol***
aborigines *enw* ***cynfrodorion*** *hyn*
abort *be* ***erthylu***
abortion *enw* ***erthyliad*** *hwn*
abortive *ans* ***seithug***
abound *be* ***heigio***
examples a~ ***enghreifftiau lu***
abounding *ans* ***llawn***, ***cyforiog***
about *ardd* (referring to) ***am***, ***ar***, ***ynghylch***, ***ynglŷn â*** (surrounding) ***o amgylch***, ***ar hyd a lled***, ***o gwmpas***; (approximately) *adf* ***oddeutu***, ***rhyw***, ***tua***
a~ to begin ***ar ddechrau***
above *ardd* ***uwch***, ***uwchben***, ***uwchlaw***; *adf* ***fry***
a~ all ***yn anad dim***, ***yn bwysicach na dim***
as a~ ***fel y nodwyd uchod***
level 3 or a~ ***lefel 3 neu uwch***
above board *ans* ***agored***, ***(g)onest***
abrade *be* ***treulio***
abrasion *enw* ***crafiad***, ***ysgraffiniad*** *hwn*
abrasive *ans* ***crafog***
abreast *adf* ***ochr yn ochr***
to keep a~ of ***cael gwybod yn gyson am***
abridge *be* ***talfyrru***, ***crynhoi***
abridged *ans* ***talfyredig***, ***cryno***
abridgement *enw* ***talfyriad*** *hwn*
abroad *adf* ***dramor***
from a~ ***o wlad/wledydd d/tramor***
abrogate *be* ***dileu***
abrogation *enw* ***diddymiad*** *hwn*
abrupt *ans* ***disymwth***, ***swta***, ***sydyn***
abruptness *enw* ***sydynrwydd*** *hwn*
abscess *enw* ***casgliad***, ***cornwyd*** *hwn*
abscond *be* ***dianc***
absence *enw* ***absenoldeb***, ***absenoliad*** *hwn*
in the a~ of ***yn absenoldeb***, ***yn niffyg***
absent *ans* ***absennol***
absent *be* ***cadw draw***
absentee *enw* ***absenolwr***
absenteeism *enw* ***absenoliaeth*** *hon*
absent-minded *ans* ***anghofus***
absolute *ans* ***absoliwt***, ***hollol***, ***eithaf***
a~ order ***gorchymyn diamod*** *hwn*
a~ zero ***sero absoliwt*** *hwn*
absolutely *adf* ***yn hollol***, ***bost***, ***gorn***, ***i'r dim***
absolution *enw* ***maddeuant*** *hwn*
absolutism *enw* ***unbennaeth*** *hon*
absolve *be* ***rhyddhau***
absorb *be* ***amsugno***, ***llyncu***
absorbent *ans* ***amsugnol***
absorbing *ans* (interesting) ***cyfareddol***
absorption *enw* ***amsugniad*** *hwn*
abstain *be* ***ymatal***, ***ymwrthod***

abstemious *ans* ***cymedrol***

abstention *enw* ***ymataliad*** *hwn*

abstinence *enw* ***dirwest*** *hwn*

abstinent *ans* ***cymedrol***

abstract *ans* ***haniaethol***

abstract *enw* (summary) ***crynodeb*** *hwn*

abstract *be* (extract) ***echdynnu***, ***tynnu***; (steal) ***dwyn***

abstracted *ans* ***a'i feddwl yn bell***; ***wedi'i echdynnu***

abstraction *enw* ***haniaeth*** *hwn/hon*; ***echdyniad*** *hwn*

abstruse *ans* ***astrus***

abstruseness *enw* ***cymhlethdod*** *hwn*

absurd *ans* ***gwirion***, ***hurt***, ***abswrd***

absurdity *enw* ***gwiriondeb***, ***hurtrwydd***, ***dwli*** *hwn*

abundance *enw* ***digonedd*** *hwn*, ***toreth*** *hon*

abundant *ans* ***lluosog***, ***toreithiog***

abuse *enw* ***camddefnydd*** *hwn*, ***camdriniaeth*** *hon*

abuse *be* ***camddefnyddio***; (physical) ***cam-drin***; (verbal) ***difenwi***, ***difrïo***

abusive *ans* ***difrïol***, ***sarhaus***

abut *be* ***ffinio***

abysmal *ans* ***affwysol***

abyss *enw* ***(g)agendor*** *hwn/hon*

acacia *enw* ***acesia*** *hwn*

academic *ans* ***academaidd***, ***academig***

academy *enw* ***academi*** *hon*

accede *be* ***cydsynio***, ***cytuno***

accelerate *be* ***cyflymu***

acceleration *enw* ***cyflymiad*** *hwn*

accelerator *enw* (general) ***cyflymydd***; (car) ***sbardun*** *hwn*

accent *enw* ***acen*** *hon*

accent *be* ***acennu***

accentuate *be* ***acennu***, ***pwysleisio***
the problem is a~d ***mae'r broblem yn waeth yn/mewn***

accept *be* ***arddel***, ***derbyn***

acceptable *ans* ***cymeradwy***, ***derbyniol***

acceptance *enw* ***derbyniad*** *hwn*

accepted *ans* (usual) ***arferol***

access *enw* ***mynediad*** *hwn*

access *be* ***cael gafael ar***; ***cael mynediad i***

accessibility *enw* ***hygyrchedd*** *hwn*
for easier a~ ***er hwylustod***

accessible *ans* ***hygyrch***, ***wrth law***

accession *enw* ***esgyniad*** *hwn*

accessory *enw* ***ychwanegiad***; (to a crime) ***cefnogwr*** *hwn*

accident *enw* ***damwain*** *hon*

accidental *ans* ***damweiniol***

accidental *enw* (music) **hapnod** *hwn*

acclaim *enw* ***canmoliaeth***, ***cymeradwyaeth*** *hon*

acclaim *be* ***cymeradwyo***

acclamation *enw* ***bonllef*** *hon*
endorsed with a~ ***cymeradwyo'n frwd***

acclimatize *be* ***cynefino***

a

acclimatized *ans* ***cynefin***
acclivity *enw* ***rhiw*** *hon*
accolade *enw* ***anrhydedd***, ***canmoliaeth*** *hon*
accommodate *be* ***lletya***, ***rhoi lle i***, ***cynnwys***
to a~ gradually (to a situation) ***ymgyfarwyddo'n raddol***
to a~ (customers) ***bodloni dymuniadau***
accommodating *ans* ***caredig***
accommodation *enw* ***llety*** *hwn*, ***ystafelloedd*** *hyn*
accompaniment *enw* (music) ***cyfeiliant*** *hwn*
accompanist *enw* ***cyfeilydd*** *hwn*
accompany *be* (music) ***cyfeilio***; (keep company) ***hebrwng***
accompanied by ***ynghyd â***
accompanying *ans* ***cysylltiedig***
accomplice *enw* ***cynorthwyydd*** *hwn*
accomplish *be* ***cyflawni***
accomplished *ans* (skilled) ***medrus***
accomplishment *enw* (skill) ***camp*** *hon*; (completion) ***cyflawniad*** *hwn*
accord *enw* ***cytundeb***, ***unfrydedd*** *hwn*
of their own a~ ***o'u pen a'u pastwn eu hunain***
out of a~ with ***heb fod yn gydnaws â***
accord *be* ***cytuno***, ***gweddu i***; ***caniatáu***, ***rhoi***
accordance
in a~ with ***yn unol â***
accordingly *adf* ***felly***
according to *adf* ***yn ôl***
accordion *enw* ***acordion*** *hwn*
accost *be* **cyfarch**
account *enw* (bank) ***cyfrif***; (report) ***adroddiad***, ***hanes*** *hwn*
a~ rendered ***cyfrif a roddwyd***
by all a~ ***yn ôl pob sôn***
on that a~ ***o'r herwydd***
account *be* ***rhoi cyfrif***
hold to a~ ***gwneud yn atebol***
to a~ for ***(bod/sydd) i gyfrif am***
accountability *enw* ***atebolrwydd***, ***cyfrifoldeb*** *hwn*
accountable *ans* ***atebol***, ***cyfrifol***
accountancy *enw* ***cyfrifyddiaeth*** *hon*
accountant *enw* ***cyfrifydd*** *hwn*
accounting *be* ***cyfrifo***
accoutre *be* ***gwisgo***
accredit *be* ***achredu***
accredited *ans* ***achrededig***
accretion *enw* ***croniant*** *hwn*
accrual *enw* ***croniad*** *hwn*
accrue *be* ***deillio***, ***cronni***, ***ennill***
accumulate *be* ***crynhoi***, ***casglu***; ***cynyddu***
accumulation *enw* ***crynhoad*** *hwn*
accumulative *ans* ***cynyddol***
accuracy *enw* ***cywirdeb*** *hwn*
accurate *ans* ***cywir***
accursed *ans* ***melltigedig***, ***ysgymun***

accusation *enw* ***cyhuddiad*** *hwn*
accuse *be* ***cyhuddo***
accused *enw* ***cyhuddedig*** *hwn*
accustom *be* ***arfer***, ***cyfarwyddo***
accustomed *ans* ***cynefin***, ***cyfarwydd***
 to become a~ ***cynefino â***
ace *enw* ***as*** *hon*
acerbic *ans* ***crafog***; ***sur***
acerbity *enw* ***chwerwder*** *hwn*
ache *enw* ***cur*** *hwn/hon*, ***poen*** *hwn*
ache *be* ***brifo***, ***gwynegu***
achieve *be* ***cyflawni***, ***cael y maen i'r wal***
achievement *enw* ***cyflawniad*** *hwn*, ***camp***, ***gorchest*** *hon*; ***cyrhaeddiad***
aching *ans* ***poenus***
acid *ans* ***sur***
 the a~ test ***y prawf mawr/allweddol*** *hwn*
acid *enw* ***asid*** *hwn*
acidity *enw* ***asidedd*** *hwn*
acknowledge *be* ***arddel***, ***cydnabod***, ***cyfarch***
acknowledged *ans* ***cydnabyddedig***
acknowledgement *enw* ***cydnabyddiaeth*** *hon*
acme *enw* ***brig***, ***uchafbwynt*** *hwn*
acne *enw* ***plorynnod*** *hyn*
acorn *enw* ***mesen*** *hon*
acoustic *ans* ***acwstig***
acoustics *enw* ***acwsteg*** *hon*
acquaint *be* ***hysbysu***
 to become a~ed with ***ymgyfarwyddo â***
acquaintance *enw* (person) ***cydnabod*** *hwn*; (knowledge of) ***adnabyddiaeth*** *hon*
acquiesce *be* ***cydsynio***
acquiescent *ans* ***cydsyniol***; ***ufudd***
acquire *be* ***cael***, ***ennill***, ***caffael***; ***codi***; ***denu***; ***magu (blas)***
acquired *ans* ***caffaeledig***
acquisition *enw* ***caffaeliad*** *hwn*
acquisitive *ans* ***barus***
acquit *be* ***cael yn ddieuog***
acre *enw* ***cyfair*** *hwn/hon*, ***erw*** *hon*
acrid *ans* ***chwerw***
acrimonious *ans* ***chwerw***
acrimony *enw* ***chwerwedd***, ***drwgdeimlad*** *hwn*
acrobat *enw* ***acrobat*** *hwn*
acrobatics *enw* ***campau acrobatig*** *hyn*
acronym *enw* ***acronym*** *hwn*
across *adf* ***ar draws***, ***ledled***
acrostic *enw* ***acrostig*** *hwn*
act *be* ***actio***; ***gweithredu***
act *enw* (play) ***act*** *hon*; (law) ***deddf*** *hon*
acting *ans* ***gweithredol***, ***dros dro***
action *enw* ***gweithred*** *hon*; (court) ***achos*** *(hwn)*
 bring an a~ ***dwyn achos***
 in a~ ***wrth fy (dy, ei etc.) ngwaith***, ***ar waith***
 take a~ ***mynd ati***, ***gweithredu***
 take no a~ ***gwneud dim***

action-packed *ans* ***llawn cyffro***
action plan *enw* ***cynllun gweithredu*** *hwn*
activate *be* ***cychwyn***, ***rhoi ar waith***
active *ans* ***gweithgar***; ***heini***, ***sionc***; (functional) ***gweithredol***
actively considering ***wrthi'n ystyried***
activity *enw* ***gweithgaredd***, ***gweithgarwch*** *hwn*
Act of Union (1536) ***y Ddeddf Uno***
actor *enw* ***actor*** *hwn*
actress *enw* ***actores*** *hon*
Acts (Book of) ***Llyfr yr Actau***
actual *ans* ***gwir***, ***go iawn***; ***ei hun***
a~ cost *enw* ***gwir gost*** *hon*
actuality *enw* ***gwirionedd*** *hwn*, ***ffaith*** *hon*
actually *adf* ***mewn gwirionedd***, ***a dweud y gwir***
acuity *enw* ***craffter*** *hwn*
acumen *enw* ***craffter*** *hwn*
acute *ans* ***llym***; ***difrifol***
AD *byrfodd* ***OC (Oed Crist)***
adage *enw* ***dywediad*** *hwn*
adamant *ans* ***diysgog***, ***hollol bendant***
Adam's apple *enw* ***afal breuant*** *hwn*
adapt *be* ***addasu***
adaptability *enw* ***y gallu i ymaddasu***, ***hyblygrwydd*** *hwn*
adaptable *ans* ***cymwysadwy***, ***addasadwy***, ***hyblyg***
adaptation *enw* ***cyfaddasiad***, ***addasiad*** *hwn*
adapter *enw* ***addasydd*** *hwn*
add *be* ***ychwanegu***
add up *be* (sums) ***adio***
addendum *enw* ***atodiad*** *hwn*
adder *enw* ***gwiber*** *hon*
addict *enw* ***dibynnwr*** *hwn*
addict *be* ***caethiwo***
addicted *ans* ***yn gaeth i***
addiction *enw* ***caethineb***, ***gorddibyniaeth*** *hon*
addictive *ans* ***caethiwus***
addition *enw* ***ychwanegiad*** *hwn*
in a~ ***ar ben hynny***
additional *ans* ***ychwanegol***
additionality *enw* ***ychwanegoldeb*** *hwn*
additive *enw* ***ychwanegyn*** *hwn*
addled *ans* (egg) ***clonc***, ***clwc***; (brain) ***dryslyd***
address *enw* (letter) ***cyfeiriad*** *hwn*; (speech) ***anerchiad*** *hwn*
address *be* (speech) ***annerch***; (a letter) ***cyfeirio***; (problems) ***rhoi sylw i***, ***ystyried***
adept *ans* ***deheuig***
to be a~ at ***bod â'r ddawn i***
adequacy *enw* ***digonolrwydd*** *hwn*
adequate *ans* ***digonol***, ***digon da***
adhere *be* ***glynu wrth***
adherent *enw* ***canlynwr***, ***cefnogwr*** *hwn*
adherence *enw* ***ymlyniad*** *hwn*
adhesion *enw* ***ymlyniad*** *hwn*
adhesive *enw* ***glud*** *hwn*
adhesive *ans* ***gludiog***, ***adlynol***

ad hoc *ans* ***ad hoc***, ***unswydd***
adieu *ebychiad* ***ffarwél! yn iach!***
adipose *ans* ***brasterog***
adjacent *ans* ***cyfagos***
adjective *enw* ***ansoddair*** *hwn*
adjoin *be* ***bod yn gyfagos***
adjourn *be* ***gohirio***, ***torri***
adjournment *enw* ***gohiriad*** *hwn*
adjudge *be* ***dyfarnu***
adjudicate *be* ***beirniadu***, ***dyfarnu***
adjudication *enw* ***beirniadaeth*** *hon*, ***dyfarniad*** *hwn*
adjudicator *enw* ***beirniad*** *hwn*
adjunct *enw* ***atodiad*** *hwn*
adjure *be* ***annog***, ***cymell***; ***ymbil***
adjust *be* ***addasu***, ***cymhwyso***
adjustable *ans* ***modd i'w (h)addasu***
adjustment *enw* ***addasiad*** *hwn*
ad lib *adf* ***yn fyrfyfyr***
administer *be* ***gweinyddu***, ***rheoli***
to a~ a test ***gosod prawf***
administration *enw* ***gweinyddiaeth*** *hon*
administrative *ans* ***gweinyddol***
administrator *enw* ***gweinyddwr*** *hwn*, ***gweinyddwraig*** *hon*
admirable *ans* ***campus***
admiral *enw* ***llyngesydd*** *hwn*
admiration *enw* ***edmygedd*** *hwn*
admire *be* ***edmygu***
admirer *enw* ***edmygydd*** *hwn*
admissible *ans* ***derbyniol***, ***derbyniadwy***
admission *enw* (confession) ***cyfaddefiad*** *hwn*; (entrance) ***mynediad*** *hwn*; (acceptance) **derbyn**
admit *be* (confess) ***cyfaddef***, ***cyffesu***; (allow in) ***derbyn***
to a~ blame ***syrthio ar fy*** (***dy, ei etc.) mai***
admittance *enw* ***mynediad*** *hwn*
admittedly *adf* ***rhaid cyfaddef***, ***mae'n wir***
admonish *be* ***ceryddu***
admonition *enw* ***cerydd*** *hwn*
ad nauseam *adf* ***hyd syrffed***
ado *enw* ***helynt*** *hon*, ***lol*** *hwn*
adolescence *enw* ***llencyndod*** *hwn*
adolescent *enw* ***llanc*** *hwn*, ***llances*** *hon*
adopt *be* ***mabwysiadu***, ***derbyn***
to a~ a style ***arfer arddull***
adoption *enw* ***mabwysiad*** *hwn*
adoptive *ans* ***mabwysiol***
adorable *ans* ***swynol***
adoration *enw* ***addoliad*** *hwn*
adore *be* ***addoli***, ***dwlu ar***
adorn *be* ***addurno***, ***gwisgo***, ***harddu***
adornment *enw* ***addurniad*** *hwn*
adrift *adf* ***yn rhydd***
adroit *ans* ***deheuig***
adulation *enw* ***gweniaith*** *hon*
adult *enw* ***oedolyn***
a~ learners ***oedolion sy'n ddysgwyr***
adult *ans* ***mewn oed***
adulterate *be* ***llygru***
adulterer *enw* ***godinebwr*** *hwn*

a

adultery *enw* ***godineb*** *hwn*
advance *be* ***symud ymlaen***; ***cynnig***; ***hybu***
a~ notice ***rhybudd ymlaen llaw*** *hwn*
a~ payment ***blaendal*** *hwn*
advanced *ans* ***uwch***
a~ in years ***mewn gwth o oedran***
advantage *enw* ***mantais*** *hon*
this could, with a~, be ***mantais fyddai***
use to a~ ***defnyddio'n bwrpasol***
advantageous *ans* ***llesol***, ***manteisiol***
advent *enw* ***dyfodiad*** *hwn*
Advent *enw* ***Adfent*** *hwn*
adventitious *ans* ***damweiniol***, ***annisgwyl***
adventure *enw* ***antur***, ***anturiaeth*** *hon*
adventurer *enw* ***anturiwr***, ***anturiaethwr*** *hwn*
adventuress *enw* ***anturiaethwraig*** *hon*
adventurous *ans* ***anturus***
adverb *enw* ***adferf*** *hwn/hon*
adversarial *ans* ***ymosodol***
adversary *enw* ***gwrthwynebydd***, ***gwrthwynebwr*** *hwn*
adverse *ans* ***croes***
a~ inference ***casgliad gwrthwynebus*** *hwn*
adversity *enw* ***adfyd***, ***caledi*** *hwn*
advert *enw* ***hysbýs*** *hon*
advertise *be* ***hysbysebu***, ***tynnu sylw at***
advertisement *enw* ***hysbyseb*** *hon*
advertiser *enw* ***hysbysebwr*** *hwn*
advertising *be* ***hysbysebu***
advice *enw* ***cyngor***, ***cyfarwyddyd*** *hwn*
your Council's a~ ***sylwadau'ch Cyngor***
advisability *enw* ***doethineb***, ***priodoldeb*** *hwn*
advisable *ans* ***doeth***
if a~ ***os hynny sydd orau***
advise *be* ***cynghori***; (inform) ***hysbysu***, ***rhoi gwybod am/i***
you should be a~d ***dylech wybod***
advisedly *adf* ***yn fwriadol***
adviser *enw* ***ymgynghorwr***, ***ymgynghorydd*** *hwn*
advisory *ans* ***ymgynghorol***
advocacy *enw* ***eiriolaeth*** *hon*; (function of advocate) ***adfocatiaeth*** *hon*
advocate *enw* (lawyer) ***adfocad***; ***cefnogwr*** *hwn*
advocate *be* ***pledio***, ***argymell***, ***dadlau o blaid***
aegis *enw* ***nawdd*** *hwn*
aeon *enw* ***oes*** *hon*
aerial *enw* ***erial*** *hwn/hon*
aerial *ans* ***o'r awyr***, ***yn yr awyr***
aerobic *ans* ***aerobig***
aerodrome *enw* ***maes awyr*** *hwn*

aeroplane *enw* ***awyren*** *hon*
aerosol *enw* ***chwistrell*** *hon*, ***erosol*** *hwn*
aesthetic *ans* ***esthetig***
afar *ans* ***hirbell***
affability *enw* ***hynawsedd*** *hwn*
affable *ans* ***hynaws***
affair *enw* ***mater*** *hwn*; ***carwriaeth*** *hon*
affect *be* ***effeithio***
affectation *enw* ***mursendod*** *hwn*
affected *ans* ***mursennaidd***
affection *enw* ***hoffter***, ***anwylder*** *hwn*
affectionate *ans* ***cynnes***, ***serchog***, ***annwyl***
affidavit *enw* ***affidafid*** *hwn*
affiliate *be* ***derbyn yn aelod***, ***ymgysylltu â***
affiliation *enw* ***cysylltiad*** *hwn*
affinity *enw* ***cydnawsedd*** *hwn*
affirm *be* ***cadarnhau***; (law) ***haeru***, ***dwys-haeru***
affirmation *enw* ***cadarnhad***, ***datganiad***, ***dwys-haeriad*** *hwn*
affirmative *ans* ***cadarnhaol***
affix *be* ***glynu***
afflict *be* ***cystuddio***, ***blino***, ***amharu ar***
affliction *hwn* ***cystudd*** *hwn*
affluence *enw* ***cyfoeth***, ***golud*** *hwn*
affluent *ans* ***goludog***
afford *be* ***fforddio***
afforest *be* ***coedwigo***
affray *enw* ***ysgarmes*** *hon*
affront *enw* ***sarhad*** *hwn*
affront *be* ***sarhau***
  they were a~ed by ***fe'u digiwyd gan***
afield
  further a~ ***tu hwnt***, ***ymhellach oddi cartref***
aflame *adf* ***ar dân***
afloat *adf* ***ar wyneb y dŵr***
afoot *adf* ***ar droed***
afraid *ans* ***ofnus***
afraid (**to be**) *be* ***ofni***
afresh *adf* ***o'r newydd***
after ardd ***ar ôl***
after *adf* ***wedyn***
  a~ a while ***ymhen amser***
  to be a~ someone ***bod am waed***
after all *adf* ***wedi'r cyfan***
afterbirth *enw* ***brych***, ***garw*** *hwn*
after-effect *enw* ***ôl-effaith*** *hon*
aftermath *enw* ***canlyniad*** *hwn*; (crops) ***adladd*** *hwn*
  in the a~ of ***yn sgil***
afternoon *enw* ***prynhawn*** *hwn*
afters *enw* ***pwdin*** *hwn*
afterward(s) *adf* ***wedyn***
again *adf* ***eto***, ***drachefn***
  yet again ***eto fyth***
against ardd ***yn erbyn***
  to decide a~ ***penderfynu peidio â***
  to go a~ ***tynnu'n groes i***
agape *adf* ***yn gegrwth***
age *enw* (how old) ***oedran*** *hwn*; (period) ***oes*** *hon*
  come of a~ ***ennill eu plwyf***

take a~s ***cymryd hydoedd***
with a~ ***wrth heneiddio***
age *be* ***heneiddio***
aged *ans* ***oedrannus***
aged *enw* (the elderly) ***henoed*** *hyn*
ageing *be* ***heneiddio***
ageless *ans* ***bytholwyrdd***
agency *enw* ***asiantaeth*** *hon*
agenda *enw* ***agenda*** *hon*
agent *enw* ***asiant***, ***cynrychiolydd*** *hwn*
age-old *ans* **hen**, **hen**
ages *enw* ***oesoedd*** *hyn*
agglomerate *be* ***pentyrru***
aggrandisement *enw* ***dyrchafiad*** *hwn*
aggravate *be* ***gwneud yn waeth***, ***gwaethygu***
aggregate *enw* ***cyfanswm***, ***crynswth*** *hwn*
aggregate *be* ***crynhoi***, ***cyfansymio***
aggression *enw* ***gormes*** *hwn*
aggressive *ans* ***ymosodol***
aggressor *enw* ***ymosodwr*** *hwn*
aggrieve *be* ***tramgwyddo***
aggrieved *ans* ***dig***, ***blin***, ***crac***
aghast *ans* ***syn***
agile *ans* ***gwisgi***, ***sionc***
agility *enw* ***sioncrwydd*** *hwn*
agitate *be* ***cynhyrfu***, ***cyffroi***
agitated *ans* ***cynhyrfus***, ***cyffrous***
agitation *enw* ***cynnwrf*** *hwn*
agitator *enw* ***cynhyrfwr*** *hwn*, ***cynhyrfwraig*** *hon*
aglow *adf* ***yn tywynnu***
agnostic *ans* ***agnostig***
ago *adf* ***yn ôl***
agog *ans* ***ar bigau drain***
agonised:agonising *ans* ***ingol***
agony *enw* ***gwewyr***, ***ing*** *hwn*
agrarian *ans* ***amaethyddol***
agree *be* ***cytuno***
agreeable *ans* ***dymunol***
agreed *ans* ***cytûn***
agreement *enw* ***cytundeb*** *hwn*
agricultural *ans* ***amaethyddol***
agriculture *enw* ***amaethyddiaeth*** *hon*
ague *enw* ***cryd*** *hwn*
ahead *adf* ***o flaen***, ***sydd i ddod***
aid *be* ***cynorthwyo***
aid *enw* ***cymorth*** *hwn*
aide *enw* ***cynorthwyydd*** *hwn*
aide-memoire *enw* ***cymorth cof*** *hwn*
aids *enw* ***cymhorthion*** *hyn*
AIDS *enw* ***AIDS***
ail *be* ***clafychu***
ailment *enw* ***anhwyldeb*** *hwn*
aim *be* ***anelu***
to a~ at ***ceisio***
aim *enw* ***amcan***, ***nod*** *hwn*
aims and objectives ***nodau ac amcanion*** *hyn*
aimless *ans* ***diamcan***
air *enw* (sky) ***awyr***; (tune) ***alaw*** *hon*
air *be* (clothes) ***caledu***, ***crasu***; (opinion) ***gwyntyllu***
airbase *enw* ***gorsaf awyr*** *hon*
airborne *ans* ***hedegog***

air-conditioned *ans* ***wedi'i (h)aerdymheru***
air conditioning *enw* ***system aerdymheru*** *hon*
aircraft *enw* ***awyren*** *hon*
aired *ans* ***cras***
airfield *enw* ***maes glanio***
airforce *enw* ***awyrlu*** *hwn*
airily *adf* ***yn ysgafn***
airless *ans* ***diawyr***, ***diawel***, ***trymaidd***, ***clòs***
airlift *be* ***cludo mewn awyren***
airline *enw* ***cwmni hedfan*** *hwn*
airliner *enw* ***awyren deithwyr*** *hon*
airport *enw* ***maes awyr*** *hwn*
air raid *enw* ***cyrch awyr*** *hwn*
airship *enw* ***awyrlong*** *hon*
airsickness *enw* ***salwch awyr*** *hwn*
airstrip *enw* ***llain lanio*** *hon*
air terminal *enw* ***terfynell***, ***terfynfa*** *hon*
airtight *ans* ***aer-dynn***, ***aerglos***
airworthiness *enw* ***addasrwydd i hedfan*** *hwn*
airworthy *ans* ***addas i hedfan***
aisle *enw* ***eil***, ***ale*** *hon*
ajar *ans* ***cilagored***
a.k.a. ***enw arall ar***
akin *ans* ***yn perthyn***, ***yn debyg***
alack *ebychiad* ***gwaetha'r modd***
alacrity *enw* ***sioncrwydd*** *hwn*
alarm *enw* (warning) ***rhybudd*** *hwn*; (fear) ***dychryn*** *hwn*; (device) ***larwm*** *hwn/hon*
alarm *be* ***dychryn***
to be alarmed ***cael braw***
alarm clock *enw* ***cloc larwm*** *hwn*
alarmist *enw* ***codwr bwganod*** *hwn*
alas *adf* ***ysywaeth***
albeit *cysyllt* ***er***, ***er hynny***
album *enw* ***albwm*** *hwn*
albumen *enw* ***gwynwy*** *hwn*
alcohol *enw* ***alcohol*** *hwn*
alcoholic *ans* ***meddwol***
alcoholic *enw* (person) ***alcoholig*** *hwn*
alder *enw* ***gwern***, ***gwernen*** *hon*
alderman *enw* ***henadur*** *hwn*
ale *enw* ***cwrw*** *hwn*
alert *enw* ***rhybudd*** *hwn*
alert *ans* ***gwyliadwrus***, ***effro***
alert *be* ***rhybuddio***, ***tynnu sylw***
alertness *enw* ***gwyliadwriaeth*** *hon*
algae *enw* ***algae:algâu*** *hyn*
algebra *enw* ***algebra*** *hwn*
alien *ans* ***estron***, ***dieithr***
alienate *be* ***dieithrio***
alienation *enw* ***dieithrwch***, ***ymddieithrwch*** *hwn*
alight *ans* (fire) ***ynghynn***, ***ar dân***
alight *be* (descend) ***disgyn***
align *be* ***alinio***, ***ymochri***
to a~ standards ***cysoni***
aligned *ans* ***ymochrol***
alignment *enw* ***aliniad***, ***ymochredd*** *hwn*
alike *ans* ***tebyg***
alimentary canal *enw* ***pibell fwyd*** *hon*
alive *ans* ***byw***

alkali *enw* ***alcali*** *hwn*
all *ans* ***holl***, ***oll***, ***i gyd***
a~ day ***drwy'r dydd***
on a~ fours ***ar fy (dy, ei etc.) mhedwar***
a~ in ***wedi ymlâdd***
a~ in a~ ***ar y cyfan***
a~ over the place ***ar draws ac ar hyd***
a~ round ***ym mhob ffordd***
a~ the money ***pob ceiniog goch***
a~ the time ***drwy'r amser***
a~ three ***ill tri***
a~ time (low) ***(yn is) nag erioed o'r blaen***
a~ too familiar ***hen gyfarwydd***
a~ too soon ***rhy gynnar o lawer***
do a~ one can ***gwneud eich gorau glas***
for a~ I know ***hyd y gwn i***
for a~ time ***am byth***
in no time at a~ ***mewn dim o dro***
not at a~ well ***dim hanner da***
of a~ things ***o bopeth dan haul***
allay *be* ***lliniaru***
to a~ the possibility ***osgoi'r posibilrwydd***
allegation *enw* ***haeriad***, ***honiad*** *hwn*
allege *be* ***haeru***
alleged *ans* ***honedig***
allegiance *enw* ***teyrngarwch*** *hwn*
allegory *enw* ***alegori*** *hon*
all-embracing *ans* ***hollgynhwysfawr***
allergy *enw* ***alergedd*** *hwn*
alleviate *be* ***lliniaru***
alley *enw* ***ale*** *hon*
alliance *enw* ***cynghrair*** *hwn/hon*
allied *ans* ***perthynol***
alliteration *enw* ***cyflythreniad***, ***cyseinedd*** *hwn*
all-night *ans* ***drwy'r nos***
allocate *be* ***dosrannu***, ***dyrannu***
allocation *enw* ***dyraniad*** *hwn*
allot *be* ***pennu***
allotment *enw* (share) ***cyfran*** *hon*; (garden) ***llain o ardd***, ***rhandir*** *hwn*
all-out *ans* ***gorau glas***
all over *adf* (end) ***drosodd***; (everywhere) ***dros y lle***
allow *be* ***caniatáu***
allowance *enw* ***lwfans*** *hwn*
to make a~s for ***bod yn drugarog***, ***cymryd i ystyriaeth***
alloy *enw* ***aloi*** *hwn*
all-purpose *ans* ***at bob diben***
all right *adf* ***yn iawn***
all-rounder *enw* (person) ***amryddawn*** *hwn*
all-time *ans* ***erioed***
allude *be* ***crybwyll***, ***cyfeirio***
allure *enw* ***hudoliaeth*** *hon*
allure *be* ***hudo***
alluring *ans* ***hudolus***
allusion *enw* ***cyfeiriad*** *hwn*
allusive *ans* ***awgrymog***
alluvium *enw* ***tir gwaddod***, ***llifwaddod*** *hwn*

ally *enw* ***cynghreiriad*** *hwn*
ally *be* ***cynghreirio***
almanac *enw* ***almanac*** *hwn*
almighty *ans* (God) ***hollalluog***; (huge) ***aruthrol***
almond *enw* ***almon*** *hwn/hon*
almost *adf* ***bron***
  a~ at once ***mewn dim o dro***
  a~ total lack of ***prin bod unrhyw***
alms *enw* ***cardod*** *hwn*, ***elusen*** *hon*
aloft *adf* ***fry***
alone *ans* ***unig***
  leave a~ ***gadael yn llonydd***
  this a~ ***hyn ynddo'i hun***
along *adf* ***ymlaen***
along *ardd* ***ar hyd***
  a~ the lines that ***i'r perwyl***
alongside *adf/ardd* ***ochr yn ochr***
aloof *adf* ***o hyd braich***
aloof *ans* ***ffroenuchel***
aloud *adf* ***yn uchel***
alp *enw* ***alp*** *hwn*, ***ffridd*** *hon*
alphabet *enw* ***(yr) wyddor*** *hon*
alphabetical *ans* ***yn nhrefn yr wyddor***
alpine *ans* ***alpaidd***
already *adf* ***yn barod***, ***eisoes***
alsatian *enw* ***bleiddgi*** *hwn*
also *adf* ***hefyd***
altar *enw* ***allor*** *hon*
alter *be* ***newid***
alteration *enw* ***newid*** *hwn*
altercation *enw* ***ffrae*** *hon*
alternate *ans* ***bob yn ail***
alternating *ans* (electricity) ***eiledol***
alternative *enw* ***dewis (arall)*** *hwn*
  there's no a~ ***does dim dewis***
alternative *ans* ***amgen***, ***gwahanol***, ***arall***
  a~ technology ***technoleg amgen*** *hon*
alternator *enw* ***eiliadur*** *hwn*
although *cysyllt* ***er***
altimeter *enw* ***altimedr*** *hwn*
altitude *enw* ***uchder*** *hwn*
alto *enw* ***alto*** *hwn/hon*
altogether *adf* ***i gyd***, ***yn llwyr***
  a~ different ***cwbl wahanol***
aluminium *enw* ***alwminiwm*** *hwn*
always *adf* ***bob amser***, ***yn wastad***
a.m. *adf* ***y bore***
AM *byrfodd* ***Aelod o'r Cynulliad (AC)***
am (I am) *berf* ***wyf***
amalgamate *be* ***uno***, ***cyfuno***
amalgamation *enw* ***cyfuniad*** *hwn*
amass *be* ***cronni***
amateur *enw* ***amatur*** *hwn/hon*
amateur: amateurish *ans* ***amaturaidd***
amatory *ans* ***carwriaethol***
amaze *be* ***rhyfeddu***, ***synnu***
amazed *ans* ***syn***
amazement *enw* ***syndod*** *hwn*
amazing *ans* ***rhyfeddol***
ambassador *enw* ***llysgennad*** *hwn*
amber *enw* ***ambr*** *hwn*
ambidextrous *ans* ***deheuig â dwy law***

a

ambience *enw* ***awyrgylch*** *hwn*
ambiguity *enw* ***amwysedd*** *hwn*
ambiguous *ans* ***amwys***
ambit *enw* ***cwmpas, maes*** *hwn*
ambition *enw* ***uchelgais*** *hwn/hon*
ambitious *ans* ***uchelgeisiol***
ambivalent *ans* ***amwys***
amble *be* ***cerdded yn hamddenol***
ambulance *enw* ***ambiwlans*** *hwn*
ambulate *be* ***cerdded***
  a~ory therapy ***therapi cerdded*** *hwn*
ambush *enw* ***cudd-ymosodiad***, ***rhagod*** *hwn*
ameliorate *be* ***lleddfu***, ***gwella***
amelioration *enw* ***gwelliant*** *hwn*
amen *enw* ***amen*** *hwn*
amenable *ans* ***parod***, ***bodlon***, ***hydrin***
amend *be* ***gwella***, ***diwygio***, ***newid***
amended *ans* ***diwygiedig***
amendment *enw* ***gwelliant***, ***newidiad*** *hwn*
amends *enw* ***iawn*** *hwn*
amenities *enw* ***mwynderau*** *hyn*; (education/leisure) ***adnoddau***, ***darpariaethau*** *hyn*
America *enw* ***yr Amerig*** *hon*
American *ans* ***Americanaidd***
amiability *enw* ***hawddgarwch*** *hwn*
amiable *ans* ***hawddgar***
amicable *ans* ***cyfeillgar***
amid(st) *ardd* ***ymhlith***
amiss *ans* ***ar gam***, ***o chwith***, ***o'i le***
amity *enw* ***cyfeillgarwch*** *hwn*
ammeter *enw* ***amedr*** *hwn*
ammunition *enw* ***ffrwydron***, ***bwledi*** *hyn*
amnesia *enw* ***anghofrwydd*** *hwn*
amnesty *enw* ***amnest*** *hwn*
amoeba *enw* ***amoeba*** *hwn*
among(st) *ardd* ***ymysg***
  a~ other examples ***mae enghreifftiau eraill yn cynnwys***
amorous *ans* ***cariadus***, ***carwriaethol***
amount *enw* ***swm*** *hwn*
  considerable a~ ***cryn dipyn***
  increasing a~ ***mwy a mwy***
  large a~ ***llawer***
  limited a~ ***rhywfaint***, ***hyn a hyn***
  this a~ ***cymaint â hyn***, ***cyn lleied â hyn***
  vast a~ ***toreth***
amount to *be* ***dod i***
amour *enw* ***serch*** *hwn*
ampere (electricity) *enw* ***amper*** *hwn*
amphibian *enw* ***amffibiad*** *hwn*
amphibious *ans* ***amffibiaidd***
amphitheatre *enw* ***amffitheatr*** *hon*
ample *ans* ***digonol***
amplifier *enw* (photo.) ***chwyddwr***; (sound) ***uchelseinydd***
amplify *be* (photo.) ***chwyddo***; (sound) ***cynyddu***; (expand) ***ymhelaethu***
amplitude *enw* ***amlder*** *hwn*
ampoule *enw* ***ffiol*** *hon*
amputate *be* ***trychu***
amputation *enw* ***trychiad*** *hwn*

amuse *be* ***difyrru***, ***diddanu***
amusement *enw* ***difyrrwch***, ***digrifwch*** *hwn*
amusing *ans* ***digrif***, ***doniol***
an gw. **'a'**
anachronism *enw* ***camamseriad*** *hwn*
anaemia *enw* ***diffyg gwaed*** *hwn*
anaesthetic *enw* ***anesthetig*** *hwn*
anaesthetist *enw* ***anesthetydd*** *hwn*
anagram *enw* ***anagram*** *hwn*
analgesic *enw* ***poenladdwr*** *hwn*
analogy *enw* ***cyfatebiaeth*** *hon*
analogous *ans* ***cydweddu â***
analyse *be* ***dadansoddi***
analysis *enw* ***dadansoddiad*** *hwn*
in the final a~ ***yn y pen draw***
analyst *enw* ***dadansoddwr*** *hwn*
analytical *ans* ***dadansoddol***
anarchic *ans* ***anarchaidd***
anarchism *enw* ***anarchiaeth*** *hon*
anarchy *enw* ***anarchiaeth*** *hon*
anathema *enw* ***anathema*** *hwn*
going there was a~ ***arswydwn rhag***
anatomical *ans* ***anatomegol***
anatomy *enw* ***anatomeg*** *hon*
ancestor *enw* ***hynafiad*** *hwn/hon*
ancestry *enw* ***llinach*** *hon*
anchor *enw* ***angor*** *hwn*
anchor *be* ***angori***
anchorage *enw* ***angorfa*** *hon*
anchovy *enw* ***brwyniad*** *hwn*
ancient *ans* ***hynafol***
a~ history ***hen***, ***hen hanes*** *hwn*
ancient monuments *enw* ***henebion*** *hyn*
anecdotal *ans* ***hanesiol***, ***storïol***
ancillary *ans* ***cynorthwyol***, ***ategol***
and *cysyllt* ***a:ac***
anecdote *enw* ***hanesyn*** *hwn*, ***stori*** *hon*
anemone *enw* ***blodyn y gwynt*** *hwn*
anew *adf* ***o'r newydd***
angel *enw* ***angel*** *hwn*, ***angyles*** *hon*
anger *enw* ***dicter*** *hwn*
anger *be* ***cythruddo***, ***codi gwrychyn***
angle *enw* (geometry) ***ongl*** *hon*
angle *be* (fish) ***pysgota***
angler *enw* ***genweiriwr***, ***pysgotwr*** *hwn*
Anglicize *be* ***Seisnigo***, ***Seisnigeiddio***
angling *be* ***pysgota***
anglophile *enw* ***seisgarwr*** *hwn*
anglophobic *ans* ***gwrth-Seisnig***
Anglo-Welsh *ans* ***Eingl-Gymreig***
angry *ans* ***dig***
anguish *enw* ***ing*** *hwn*
angular *ans* ***onglog***
animadversion *enw* ***beirniadaeth*** *hon*
animal *enw* ***anifail*** *hwn*
animal husbandry *be* ***magu anifeiliaid***
animate *be* ***bywhau***
animated *ans* ***bywiog***
animation *enw* ***animeiddiad*** *hwn*

a

animosity *enw* ***atgasedd*** *hwn*
aniseed *enw* ***anis*** *hwn*
ankle *enw* ***migwrn*** *hwn*, ***ffêr*** *hon*
annals *enw* ***cofnodion*** **(blwyddyn)** *hyn*
anneal *be* ***caledu***, ***tymheru***
annex *be* ***atodi***
annexe *enw* ***atodiad*** *hwn*
annihilate *be* ***difodi***, ***dinistrio***
annihilation *enw* ***difodiad*** *hwn*
anniversary *enw* ***pen blwydd*** *hwn*
  100th a~ ***canmlwyddiant*** *hwn*
Anno Domini *enw* ***Oed Crist*** *hwn*
annotate *be* ***gwneud nodiadau***
annotated *ans* ***gyda sylwadau priodol ar***, ***anodedig***
annotation *enw* ***nodiadau*** *hyn*
announce *be* ***cyhoeddi***, ***datgan***
announcement *enw* ***cyhoeddiad*** *hwn*
announcer *enw* ***cyhoeddwr*** *hwn*
annoy *be* ***cythruddo***, ***tynnu blewyn o drwyn***, ***codi gwrychyn***
annoyance *enw* ***dicter*** *hwn*
annoyed *ans* ***dig***, ***penwan***
annual *ans* ***blynyddol***
annuity *enw* ***blwydd-dal*** *hwn*
annul *be* ***diddymu***
annular *ans* ***cylchol***
annunciation *enw* ***cyfarchiad*** *hwn*
anoint *be* ***eneinio***, ***iro***
anomalous *ans* ***anarferol***, ***afreolaidd***
anomaly *enw* ***anghysonder*** *hwn*
anon. *byrfodd* ***dienw***
anonomie *enw* ***anobaith*** *hwn*
anonymity *enw* ***anhysbysrwydd*** *hwn*
anonymous *ans* ***dienw***
anorak *enw* ***anorac*** *hwn/hon*
A.N.Other ***Ann Hysbys***
another *ans* ***arall***
answer *be* ***ateb***
answer *enw* ***ateb*** *hwn*
answerable *ans* ***atebol***
ant *enw* ***morgrugyn*** *hwn*
antacid *enw* ***gwrthasid*** *hwn*
antagonism *enw* ***gelyniaeth*** *hon*
antagonist *enw* ***gwrthwynebydd*** *hwn*
antagonize *be* ***digio***
Antarctic *ans/enw* ***Antarctig*** *hon*
antecedent *enw* ***rhagflaenydd*** *hwn*
  a~ to the research ***cefndir yr ymchwil***
antecedent *ans* ***blaenorol***
antedate *be* ***rhagddyddio***
antediluvian *ans* ***henffasiwn***
antelope *enw* ***gafrewig*** *hon*
ante meridian *adf* ***y bore***
antenna *enw* ***teimlydd*** *hwn*
anterior *ans* ***blaenorol***; ***pen blaen***
anthem *enw* ***anthem*** *hon*
anthology *enw* ***blodeugerdd*** *hon*
anthracite *enw* ***glo caled:glo carreg*** *hwn*
anthropology *enw* ***anthropoleg*** *hon*
anti *ardd* ***yn erbyn***
anti- *rhag* ***gwrth-***

anti-aircraft *ans* ***gwrthawyrennol***
antibiotic *enw* ***gwrthfiotig*** *hwn*
anticipate *be* ***achub y blaen***, ***rhagweld***
anticipation *enw* ***edrych ymlaen***, ***disgwyl***
anticlockwise *ans* ***gwrthglocwedd***
antics *enw* ***stranciau*** *hyn*
anti-discriminatory *ans* ***gwrthwahaniaethol***
antidote *enw* ***gwrthwenwyn, gwrthgyffur*** *hwn*
antifreeze *enw* ***gwrthrewydd*** *hwn*
antihero *enw* ***gwrtharwr*** *hwn*
antipathy *enw* ***gelyniaeth*** *hon*
anti-personnel *ans* ***lladd pobl***
antiquarian *enw* ***hynafiaethydd*** *hwn*
antiquated *ans* ***hynafol***
antiques *enw* ***hynafion*** *hyn*
antiquity *enw* ***cynfyd*** *hwn*
antirrhinum *enw* (bot.) ***trwyn y llo*** *hwn*
antiseptic *ans* ***antiseptig***
antisocial *ans* ***gwrthgymdeithasol, anghymdeithasol***
antithesis *enw* (contrast) ***gwrthgyferbyniad*** *hwn*; (the opposite) ***y gwrthwyneb*** *hwn*
antler *enw* ***corn carw*** *hwn*
anus *enw* ***rhefr*** *hwn*
anvil *enw* ***einion*** *hon*
anxiety *enw* ***pryder*** *hwn*
anxious *ans* ***pryderus***
any *ans* ***unrhyw***, ***dim***
a~ old how ***rywsut rywfodd***
as good as a~ ***cystal â dim***
a~ number ***amryw byd o***
anybody *rhag* ***rhywun***, ***unrhyw un***, ***neb***
anyhow *adf* ***beth bynnag***, ***rywsut rywsut***
any more *adf* ***ragor***, ***mwyach***
anyone = **anybody**
anything *rhag* ***rhywbeth***, ***unrhyw beth***, ***dim***
anyway = **anyhow**
anywhere *adf* ***rhywle***, ***unrhyw le***, ***unman***, ***unlle***
AOB *byrfodd* ***UFA (Unrhyw Fater Arall)***
apace *adf* ***yn gyflym***
apart *adf* ***ar wahân***
drift a~ ***pellhau***
fall a~ ***syrthio'n ddarnau***
apartheid *enw* ***apartheid*** *hwn*
apartment *enw* ***fflat*** *hon*
apathetic *ans* ***di-hid***, ***difater***
apathy *enw* ***difaterwch***, ***difrawder*** *hwn*
ape *enw* ***epa*** *hwn*
ape *be* ***efelychu***
aperture *enw* ***agen*** *hon,* ***twll*** *hwn*; (photo.) ***agorfa*** *hon*
apex *enw* (triangle) ***apig*** *hon*; (mountain) ***copa*** *hwn/hon;* (career) ***uchafbwynt***, ***brig*** *hwn*
aphid *enw* ***llysleuen*** *hon*
aphorism *enw* ***dywediad*** *hwn*
apiece *adf* ***yr un***, ***bobo***

a

aplomb *enw* ***hunanfeddiant*** *hwn*
apocalypse *enw* ***datguddiad*** *hwn*
apolitical *ans* ***anwleidyddol***, ***amhleidiol***
apologize *be* ***ymddiheuro***
apology *enw* ***ymddiheuriad*** *hwn*
apoplectic *ans* ***candryll***
apostle *enw* ***apostol*** *hwn*
apostolic *ans* ***apostolaidd***
apostrophe *enw* ***collnod*** *hwn*
appal *be* ***brawychu***, ***codi arswyd***
appalling *ans* ***echrydus***
apparatus *enw* ***offer*** *hyn*, ***cyfarpar*** *hwn*
apparel *enw* ***gwisg*** *hon*, ***dillad*** *hyn*
apparent *ans* ***amlwg***, ***ymddangosiadol***
become a~ ***dod i'r amlwg***
more a~ than real ***addo mwy na ellir ei gyflawni***
no a~ difficulty ***yn ddigon diffwdan***
apparently *adf* ***yn ôl pob golwg***, ***mae'n debyg***
apparition *enw* ***drychiolaeth*** *hon*
appeal *be* ***apelio***
appeal *enw* ***apêl*** *hon*
appealing *ans* ***apelgar***, ***atyniadol***
appear *be* ***ymddangos***, ***dod i'r golwg***
appearance *enw* ***ymddangosiad*** *hwn*, ***golwg*** *hon*, ***pryd a gwedd***; (design) ***diwyg*** *hwn*
appease *be* ***cymodi***, ***tawelu***
appeasement *enw* ***cymod*** *hwn*
appellant *enw* ***apelydd*** *hwn*
appellation *enw* ***teitl*** *hwn*
append *be* ***atodi***
appendage *enw* ***atodiad***, ***ychwanegiad***, ***atodyn*** *hwn*, ***cynffon*** *hon*
appendix *enw* (document) ***atodiad*** *hwn*; (body) ***coluddyn crog*** *hwn*
appertain *be* ***perthyn***; ***gweddu***
appetite *enw* ***archwaeth***, ***awydd***, ***chwant*** *hwn*
appetizing *ans* ***blasus***
applaud *be* ***cymeradwyo***
applause *enw* ***cymeradwyaeth*** *hon*
apple *enw* ***afal*** *hwn*
apple-tree *enw* ***coeden afalau*** *hon*
appliance *enw* ***teclyn*** *hwn*, ***dyfais*** *hon*
applicable *ans* ***perthnasol***
applicant *enw* ***ymgeisydd*** *hwn*
application (of paint etc.) ***taenu***, ***rhoi ar***; (effort) ***ymroddiad*** *hwn*; (request) ***cais*** *hwn*
applied *ans* ***cymhwysol***
apply *be* (seek) ***cynnig***; (adjust, use) ***cymhwyso***, ***defnyddio***; (strive) ***ymroi***, ***gweithredu***
to a~ a standard ***defnyddio safon***
to a~ pressure ***rhoi pwysau ar***
appoint *be* ***penodi***
appointed *ans* ***penodedig***
appointee *enw* ***y sawl a benodwyd***
appointer *enw* ***penodwr*** *hwn*

appointment *enw* (post) ***penodiad*** *hwn*; (doctor's) ***wedi trefnu i weld***; (tryst) ***oed***; (meeting) ***apwyntiad*** *hwn*
apportion *be* ***rhannu***, ***dyrannu***
apposite *ans* ***addas***
appraisal *enw* ***gwerthusiad*** *hwn*
appraise *be* ***pwyso a mesur gwerth***, ***gwerthuso***
appreciable *ans* ***sylweddol***
without any a~ change ***heb fawr o newid***
appreciate *be* ***bod yn ymwybodol o***, ***ymdeimlo â***, ***gwerthfawrogi***
appreciation *enw* ***gwerthfawrogiad*** *hwn*
appreciative *ans* ***gwerthfawrogol***
apprehend *be* ***dal***
apprehension *enw* ***ofn***, ***pryder*** *hwn*
apprehensive *ans* ***ofnus***, ***pryderus***
apprentice *enw* ***prentis*** *hwn*
apprenticeship *enw* ***prentisiaeth*** *hon*
apprise *be* ***rhoi gwybod***
approach *enw* ***ffordd o fynd ati***, ***ymagwedd*** *hon*
approach *be* ***dynesu***, ***nesáu***, ***tynnu at***
to a~ someone with a view to ***mynd ar ofyn***
to a~ a task ***mynd ati***
approachable *ans* (place) ***hygyrch***, ***hawdd mynd ato***, ***hawdd ei gyrraedd***; (person) ***agos-atoch***, ***hawdd siarad ag e***
approbation *enw* ***cymeradwyaeth*** *hon*
appropriate *ans* ***addas***, ***priodol***
appropriate *be* ***meddiannu***, ***clustnodi***, ***neilltuo***
approval *enw* ***cymeradwyaeth*** *hon*
approve *be* ***cymeradwyo***
approved *ans* ***cymeradwy***
approximately *adf* ***fwy neu lai***, ***tua***
approximation *enw* ***brasamcan*** *hwn*
apricot *enw* ***bricyllen*** *hon*
April *enw* ***Ebrill*** *hwn*
apron *enw* ***brat*** *hwn*, ***ffedog*** *hon*
apt *ans* (appropriate) ***priodol***; (tends to) ***chwannog***
aptitude *enw (fitness)* ***cymhwyster***, ***addasrwydd*** *hwn*; (ability) ***dawn*** *hon*; (propensity) ***tuedd*** *hon*, ***tueddiad*** *hwn*
aquaculture *enw* ***dyfrdyfu***
aqualung *enw* ***tanc anadlu*** *hwn*
aquaplane *be* ***sglefrio ar ddŵr***
aquarium *enw* ***acwariwm*** *hwn*
aquatic *ans* ***dyfrol***
aqueduct *enw* ***traphont ddŵr*** *hon*
aqueous *ans* ***dyfrllyd***
aquiline *ans* ***fel eryr***
arable *ans* ***âr***
arbiter *enw* ***beirniad***, ***canolwr*** *hwn*
arbitrary *ans* ***mympwyol***
arbitrary units ***unedau gwneud*** *hyn*
arbitrate *be* ***cymrodeddu***, ***cyflafareddu***; ***canoli***, ***dyfarnu***, ***penderfynu***

a

arbitration *enw* ***cyflafareddiad*** *hwn*
go to a~ ***mynd gerbron canolwr***
arbitrator *enw* ***cymrodeddwr***, ***cyflafareddwr***, ***canolwr*** *hwn*
arboreal *ans* ***y coed***, ***coediol***
arc *enw* ***arc*** *hwn*
arcade *enw* ***arcêd*** *hon*
arch *enw* ***bwa*** *hwn*, ***pont*** *hon*
arch *be* ***pontio***
archaeological *ans* ***archaeolegol***
archaeology *enw* ***archaeoleg*** *hon*
archaic *ans* ***hynafol***
archaism *enw* ***ymadrodd hynafol*** *hwn*
archangel *enw* ***archangel*** *hwn*
archbishop *enw* ***archesgob*** *hwn*
archdruid *enw* ***archdderwydd*** *hwn*
arched *ans* ***bwaog***
archer *enw* ***saethydd*** *hwn*
archery *enw* ***saethyddiaeth*** *hon*
archipelago *enw* ***ynysfor*** *hon*
architect *enw* ***pensaer*** *hwn*
architecture *enw* ***pensaernïaeth*** *hon*
archival *ans* ***archifyddol***
archival staff ***staff yr archifau***
archive *enw* ***archif*** *hwn*
a~ administration ***archifyddiaeth*** *hon*
archway *enw* ***porth bwaog*** *hwn*
Arctic *enw* ***Yr Arctig*** *hwn*
ardent *ans* ***selog***, ***brwd***, ***angerddol***, ***taer***
ardour *enw* ***angerdd***, ***brwdfrydedd*** *hwn*
arduous *ans* ***llafurus***, ***beichus***
area *enw* ***ardal*** *hon*, ***darn tir*** *hwn*; (maths) ***arwynebedd*** *hwn*; (experience) ***maes*** *hwn*
arguable *ans* ***dadleuol***
arguably *adf* ***efallai***
argue *be* ***dadlau***
to a~ for ***dadlau o blaid***
argument *enw* ***dadl*** *hon*
argumentative *ans* ***dadleugar***
arid *ans* ***cras***, ***diffrwyth***
aridity *enw* ***craster*** *hwn*
aright *adf* ***yn gywir***, ***yn iawn***
arise *be* ***codi***, ***cyfodi***
arising from ***yn codi o***, ***oherwydd***
as the need a~s ***yn ôl y galw***
if the need a~s ***pe bai/ os bydd angen***
when the need a~s ***pan fo angen***
aristocracy *enw* ***pendefigaeth*** *hon*
aristocrat *enw* ***pendefig*** *hwn*
aristocratic *ans* ***pendefigaidd***
arithmetic *enw* ***rhifyddeg*** *hon*
ark *enw* ***arch*** *hon*
arm *enw* ***braich*** *hon*
arm *be* ***arfogi***
armada *enw* ***llynges ryfel*** *hon*
armament *enw* ***arfogaeth*** *hon*
armband *enw* ***rhwymyn braich*** *hwn*
armchair *enw* ***cadair freichiau*** *hon*
armed *ans* ***arfog***
armful *enw* ***coflaid*** *hon*
armhole *enw* ***twll braich*** *hwn*
armistice *enw* ***cadoediad*** *hwn*

armour *enw* ***arfwisg*** *hon*
armoured *ans* ***arfog***
armourer *enw* ***arfogwr*** *hwn*
armoury *enw* ***arfdy*** *hwn*
  linguistic a~ ***cronfa ieithyddol*** *hon*
armpit *enw* ***cesail*** *hon*
arms *enw* ***arfau*** *hyn*
army *enw* ***byddin*** *hon*
aroma *enw* ***perarogl***, ***persawr*** *hwn*
aromatic *ans* ***peraroglus, persawrus***
around ardd ***o gwmpas***
  a~ the country ***ar hyd a lled y wlad***
  from a~ the world ***o bedwar ban byd***
  lying a~ ***gorwedd ar hyd y lle***
  winter's a~ the corner ***mae'r gaeaf ar ein gwarthaf***
arouse *be* (from sleep) ***deffro***, ***dihuno***; (feelings) ***cynhyrfu***, ***codi***, ***ennyn***
arraign *be* ***ymosod ar***
arrange *be* ***trefnu***, ***gosod mewn trefn***
arrangement *enw* ***trefniant*** *hwn*
arrant *ans* ***llwyr***, ***hollol***
array *enw* ***rhestr*** *hon,* ***rhesi*** *hyn*; ***arddangosfa*** *hon*; ***casgliad*** *hwn*
  an a~ of new courses ***amryw byd o gyrsiau newydd***
  a rich a~ ***amrywiaeth cyfoethog*** *hwn*
arrears *enw* ***ôl-ddyled*** *hon*
arrest *be* ***dal***, ***arestio***
arrival *enw* ***dyfodiad*** *hwn*
  on a~ ***ar ôl cyrraedd***
arrive *be* ***cyrraedd***
  to a~ at a consistent interpretation ***cytuno ar ddehongliad***
  to a~ at a solution ***dod o hyd i ateb***
arrogance *enw* ***haerllugrwydd***, ***balchder*** *hwn*
arrogant *ans* ***haerllug***, ***balch***, ***mawreddog***
arrow *enw* ***saeth*** *hon*
arrowhead *enw* ***blaen saeth*** *hwn*
arse *enw* ***tin*** *hon*
arsenal *enw* ***arfdy*** *hwn*
arson *be* ***llosgi bwriadol***
art *enw* ***celfyddyd*** *hon*
  the a~ of ***cyfrinach*** *hon*
  a work of a~ ***campwaith*** *hwn*
art gallery *enw* ***oriel*** *hon*
artery *enw* ***rhydweli*** *hon*
artful *ans* ***cyfrwys***
arthritis *enw* ***gwynegon*** *hyn*
article *enw* ***erthygl*** *hon*
articulate *be* ***ynganu***, ***lleisio***, ***rhoi mewn geiriau***
articulate *ans* ***croyw***, ***rhugl***
articulated *ans* (e.g. lorry) ***cymalog***
articulation *enw* ***ynganiad*** *hwn*
artifice *enw* ***ystryw, gallu*** *hwn*
artificial *ans* ***ffug***, ***gosod***
artillery *enw* ***magnelau*** *hyn*
artisan *enw* ***crefftwr*** *hwn*

artist *enw* ***artist***, ***arlunydd*** *hwn*
artistic *ans* ***celfydd***
artistry *enw* ***celfyddyd*** *hon*, ***cywreinwaith*** *hwn*
artless *ans* (unskilled) ***anghelfydd***; (simple) ***syml***, ***di-lol***; (guileless) ***diniwed***
as *cysyllt* ***fel***, ***mor – â***
  a~ above ***fel y nodwyd uchod***
  a~ appropriate ***fel y bo'n briodol***
  a~ are those ***felly hefyd y rhai***
  a~ best they can ***orau y gallant***
  a~ directed by ***yn unol â***
  a~ expected ***cystal/cynddrwg â'r disgwyl***
  a~ necessary ***yn ôl y galw***
  a~ of the end of May ***o ddiwedd Mai ymlaen***
  a~ yet ***hyd yn hyn***, ***hyd yma***
  a~ planned ***yn unol â'r cynllun***
  a~ such ***fel y cyfryw***
  a~ though ***fel pe***
  important a~ these are ***er pwysiced yw'r rhain***
  tell it a~ it is ***gair o brofiad***
asbestos *enw* ***asbestos*** *hwn*
ascend *be* ***dringo***, ***esgyn***
ascendancy *enw* ***goruchafiaeth*** *hon*
ascendant *ans* ***esgynnol***
ascension *enw* ***esgyniad*** *hwn*
ascent *enw* ***esgyniad*** *hwn*
ascertain *be* ***canfod***, ***darganfod***
ascetic *ans* ***meudwyaidd***
ascribe *be* ***priodoli***, ***tadogi***
  to a~ to a level ***rhoi***, ***dyfarnu***
ash *enw* (tree) ***onnen*** *hon*; (dust) ***lludw*** *hwn*
ashamed *ans* ***â chywilydd***
ashen *ans* ***gwelw***
ashore *adf* ***ar y lan***
ashtray *enw* ***blwch llwch*** *hwn*
aside *enw* ***rhywbeth wrth fynd heibio*** *hwn*
aside *adf* ***o'r neilltu***
  aside from ***heblaw am***
asinine *ans* ***asynnaidd***, ***twp***
ask *be* ***gofyn***, ***holi***
askance *adf* ***yn gam***
  to look a~ ***drwgdybio***
askew *adf* ***ar dro***, ***yn gam***
aslant *adf* ***ar oleddf***, ***ar ogwydd***
asleep *adf* ***ynghwsg***
asparagus *enw* ***merllys*** *hyn*
aspect *enw* ***gwedd*** *hon*
asperity *enw* ***llymder*** *hwn*
aspersion *enw* ***sen*** *hon*, ***anfri*** *hwn*
asphyxiate *be* ***mygu***
asphyxiation *enw* ***mogfa*** *hon*
aspirant *enw* ***ymgeisydd*** *hwn*
aspiration *enw* ***dyhead*** *hwn*, ***uchelgais*** *hwn/hon*
aspire *be* ***dyheu***
  to a~ to ***anelu at***
ass *enw* ***asen*** *hon*, ***asyn*** *hwn*
assail *be* ***ymosod***
assailant *enw* ***ymosodwr*** *hwn*
assassin *enw* ***llofrudd*** *hwn*
assassinate *be* ***llofruddio***

assault *enw* ***ymosodiad*** *hwn*
assault *be* ***ymosod***
assay *enw* ***prawf*** *hwn*
assemble *be* (people) ***casglu ynghyd***, ***ymgynnull***; (objects) ***crynhoi/casglu ynghyd***; ***rhoi rhywbeth at ei gilydd***, ***adeiladu***
assembly *enw* ***cynulliad*** *hwn*, ***cymanfa*** *hon*; (school) ***gwasanaeth*** *hwn*
Assembly (National) *enw* ***Cynulliad Cenedlaethol*** *hwn*
Assembly Member *enw* ***Aelod o'r Cynulliad*** *hwn*
assent *enw* ***cydsyniad*** *hwn*
assent *be* ***cydsynio***
assert *be* ***mynnu***, ***mynegi***, ***arddel***
assertion *enw* ***honiad*** *hwn*
assertive *ans* ***haerllug***; ***pendant***, ***di-droi'n-ôl***
assess *be* ***asesu***, ***pwyso a mesur***
assessment *enw* ***asesiad*** *hwn*
assessor *enw* ***aseswr*** *hwn*
assets *enw* ***asedau*** *hyn*
asseverate *be* ***tyngu, taeru***
assiduous *ans* ***diwyd***
assign *be* ***neilltuo, pennu***; (law) ***aseinio***
assignation *enw* ***oed*** *hwn*
assignment *enw* ***gorchwyl*** *hwn*, ***aseiniad*** *hwn*
assimilate *be* ***cymathu***
assist *be* ***cynorthwyo***
assistance *enw* ***cymorth*** *hwn*
without a~ ***ohonynt eu hunain***
assistant *enw* ***cynorthwy-ydd*** *hwn*
assistant *ans* ***cynorthwyol***
assizes *enw* ***brawdlys*** *hwn/hon*
associate *be* ***cysylltu***
to be a~ed with ***bod yn gysylltiedig â***
associate *enw* ***cydymaith*** *hwn*
association *enw* ***cymdeithas*** *hon*
assonance *enw* ***cyseinedd*** *hon*
assorted *ans* ***cymysg***
assortment *enw* ***cymysgedd*** *hwn/hon*
assuage *be* ***lleddfu***, ***lliniaru***
assume *be* ***rhagdybio***, ***cymryd yn ganiataol***
assuming that ***a bwrw bod***
to a~ responsibilty for ***mynd yn gyfrifol am***
to a~ the chairmanship ***ymgymryd â'r gadeiryddiaeth***
the role to be a~d by ***y rôl sydd i'w harfer gan***
assumption *enw* ***rhagdybiaeth*** *hon*
it is a safe a~ that ***mae'n deg casglu bod***
assurance *enw* ***sicrwydd***, ***hyder*** *hwn*; (finance) ***aswiriant*** *hwn*
assure *be* ***sicrhau***
assured *ans* ***dibetrus***, ***sicr***
please rest assured that ***gallaf eich sicrhau bod***
assuredly *adf* ***yn bendifaddau***
assuredness *enw* ***hunanhyder*** *hwn*

a

asterisk *enw* ***seren*** *hon*
asteroid *enw* ***asteroid*** *hwn*
asthma *enw* ***y fogfa*** *hon*, ***asthma*** *hwn*
astir *ans* ***ar gerdded***, ***ar waith***; ***yn gyffro i gyd***
astonish *be* ***rhyfeddu***, ***syfrdanu***
astonished *ans* ***syn***
astonishment *enw* ***syndod*** *hwn*
astound *be* ***syfrdanu***
astounding *ans* ***syfrdanol***
astray *adf* ***ar gyfeiliorn, ar ddisberod***
astride *adf* ***ar gefn, bagl o boptu***
astrologer *enw* ***sêr-ddewin*** *hwn*
astrology *enw* ***sêr-ddewiniaeth*** *hon*
astronaut *enw* ***gofodwr*** *hwn*, ***gofodwraig*** *hon*
astronomer *enw* ***seryddwr*** *hwn*, ***seryddwraig*** *hon*
astronomical *ans* ***seryddol***; ***aruthrol***
astronomy *enw* ***seryddiaeth***
astute *ans* ***craff***
asunder *adf* ***ar wahân***
asylum *enw* (mental health) ***gwallgofdy*** *hwn*; (refuge) ***noddfa*** *hon*
asymetrical *ans* ***anghymesur***
at ardd ***am***, ***ar***, ***yn***
  at a glance ***cipolwg***; ***ar amrantiad***
atheism *enw* ***anffyddiaeth*** *hon*
atheist *enw* ***anffyddiwr*** *hwn*, ***anffyddwraig*** *hon*
athlete *enw* ***mabolgampwr*** *hwn*, ***mabolgampwraig*** *hon*, ***athletwr*** *hwn*, ***athletwraig*** *hon*
athlete's foot ***tarwden y traed*** *hon*, ***derweinyn y traed*** *hwn*
athletic *ans* ***athletaidd***
athletics *enw* ***athletau***, ***mabolgampau*** *hyn*
athwart *adf* ***ar draws***
atishoo *ebychiad* ***tisian***, ***tisiw***
atlas *enw* ***atlas*** *hwn*
atmosphere *enw* ***awyrgylch***; (air) ***atmosffer*** *hwn*
atmospherics *enw* ***atmosffereg*** *hon*
atoll *enw* ***atol*** *hon*
atom *enw* ***atom*** *hwn/hon*
atomic *ans* ***atomig***
atone *be* ***talu iawn***
atonement *enw* ***iawn*** *hwn*
atop *ardd* ***ar ben***
atrocious *ans* ***erchyll***
atrocity *enw* ***erchylltra*** *hwn*
atrophy *be* ***gwywo***
attach *be* ***atodi***
attachment *enw* (device) ***atodyn***; (closeness) ***ymlyniad*** *hwn*
attack *be* ***ymosod***
attack *enw* ***ymosodiad*** *hwn*
attacker *enw* ***ymosodwr*** *hwn*, ***ymosodwraig*** *hon*
attacking *ans* ***ymosodol***
attain *be* ***cyrraedd***, ***ennill***

to a~ potential ***gwireddu potensial/addewid***
attainable *ans* ***yn ymarferol bosibl***
attainment *enw* ***cyrhaeddiad*** *hwn*
attempt *be* ***ceisio***, ***rhoi cynnig ar***
attempt *enw* ***ymdrech***, ***ymgais*** *hwn/hon*
attend *be* (be present) ***mynychu***, ***bod yn bresennol***; (serve) ***gweini***; ***rhoi sylw***
a~ to an incident ***cael eich galw i ddigwyddiad***
attendance *enw* ***presenoldeb*** *hwn*; (service) ***gwasanaeth*** *hwn*
attendance allowance *enw* (care) ***lwfans gweini/presenoldeb*** *hwn*
attendant *enw* ***gweinydd*** *hwn*, ***gweinyddes*** *hon*
attendant *ans* ***ynghlwm wrth***
a~ on ***ynghlwm wrth***
attendee *enw* ***un oedd/sydd yn bresennol***
attender *enw* ***mynychwr*** *hwn*
attention *enw* ***sylw*** *hwn*
a~ to detail ***ymboeni am fanylion***, ***manylder***
for the a~ of ***i gael sylw***
for your a~ ***i chi roi eich sylw iddo***
attentive *ans* ***astud***, ***sylwgar***
attenuate *be* ***gwanhau***, ***teneuo***
attest *be* ***tystio***, ***ardystio***
attic *enw* ***croglofft***, ***atig*** *hon*
attire *enw* ***gwisg*** *hon*
attire *be* ***gwisgo***
attitude *enw* ***agwedd*** *hon*
attorney *enw* ***twrnai*** *hwn*
Attorney-General ***y Twrnai Cyffredinol*** *hwn*
attract *be* ***denu***
they were a~ed to the idea ***apeliodd y syniad atynt***
attraction *enw* ***atyniad*** *hwn*
attractive *ans* ***atyniadol***, ***deniadol***
to make a~ ***harddu***
attribute *enw* ***priodoledd*** *hwn*
attribute *be* ***priodoli***
attune *be* ***ymgyfarwyddo***, ***ymglywed â***
atypical *ans* ***annodweddiadol***
auburn *ans* ***(gwallt) coch***
auction *enw* ***arwerthiant*** *hwn*
auctioneer *enw* ***arwerthwr*** *hwn*
audacious *ans* ***beiddgar***, ***haerllug***
audacity *enw* ***beiddgarwch***, ***haerllugrwydd*** *hwn*
audible *ans* ***clywadwy***
audience *enw* ***cynulleidfa*** *hon*
audio cassette *enw* ***casét sain*** *hwn*
audio-conferencing *enw* ***clyw-gynadledda***
audio typist *enw* ***clyw-deipydd (-es)*** *hwn (hon)*
audio-visual *ans* ***clyweled***
audit *enw* ***archwiliad*** *hwn*
audit *be* ***archwilio***
Audit Commission *enw* ***Comisiwn Archwilio*** *hwn*
audited *ans* ***archwiliedig***
audition *enw* ***clyweliad*** *hwn*

auditor *enw* ***archwilydd*** *hwn*
auditory *ans* ***clywedol***
auger *enw* ***taradr***, ***ebill*** *hwn*
augment *be* ***cynyddu***
augur be ***argoeli***
augury *enw* ***argoel*** *hon*
August *enw* ***Awst*** *hwn*
aunt *enw* ***modryb*** *hon*
aura *enw* ***awyrgylch***; ***gwawl*** *hwn*
aural *ans* ***clywedol***
au revoir *ebychiad* ***tan y tro nesaf***, ***yn iach***, ***ffarwél***
aurora borealis ***goleuni'r Gogledd*** *hwn*
auspices *enw* ***nawdd*** *hwn*; ***cylch awdurdod***
auspicious *ans* ***addawol***
austere *ans* ***llym***
authentic *ans* ***dilys***
authenticate *be* ***dilysu***, ***cadarnhau dilysrwydd***
authenticity *enw* ***dilysrwydd*** *hwn*
author *enw* ***awdur*** *hwn*, ***awdures*** *hon*
authorise *be* ***awdurdodi***
authorised *ans* ***awdurdodedig***
authoritarian *ans* ***awdurdodus***
authoritative *ans* ***awdurdodol***
authority *enw* ***awdurdod*** *hwn*
autism *enw* ***awtistiaeth*** *hon*
autobahn *enw* ***traffordd*** *hon*
autobiographical *ans* ***hunangofiannol***
autobiography *enw* ***hunangofiant*** *hwn*
autocracy *enw* ***unbennaeth*** *hon*
autocrat *enw* ***teyrn***, ***unben*** *hwn*, ***unbennes*** *hon*
autocratic *ans* ***unbenaethol***
autograph *enw* ***llofnod*** *hwn*
autograph *be* ***llofnodi***
automate *be* ***awtomeiddio***
automatic *ans* ***awtomatig***
automobile *enw* ***modur*** *hwn*
autonomous *ans* ***hunanlywodraethol***, ***awtonomaidd***
autonomy *enw* ***hunanlywodraeth*** *hon*, ***rhyddid*** *hwn*
autopsy *enw* ***awtopsi*** *hwn*
autumn *enw* ***hydref*** *hwn*
autumnal *ans* ***hydrefol***
auxiliary *ans* ***cynorthwyol***, ***ategol***
avail *enw* ***budd*** *hwn*
  of/to no a~ ***ofer***, ***waeth imi fod yn siarad â'r wal ddim***
available *ans* ***ar gael***
  become a~ ***dod yn rhydd***, ***bod o fewn cyrraedd***, ***bod at wasanaeth***, ***dod i law***
avalanche *enw* ***eirlithriad*** *hwn*
avarice *enw* ***trachwant***, ***cybydd-dod*** *hwn*
avaricious *ans* ***trachwantus***, ***cybyddlyd***
avenge *be* ***dial***
avenue *enw* ***coedlan***, ***lôn/rhodfa goed***; (street) ***rhodfa*** *hon*
  a~s of experience ***meysydd profiad*** *hyn*

aver *be* ***taeru***
average *enw* ***cyfartaledd*** *hwn*
average *ans* ***cyffredin, cymedrol, normal***
averse *ans* ***yn erbyn***
aversion *enw* ***atgasedd***, ***casbeth*** *hwn*
avert *be* ***troi heibio***, ***osgoi***
aviation *be* ***hedfan***
avid *ans* ***awchus***
 a~ readers ***darllenwyr mawr/brwd*** *hyn*
avocation *enw* ***hobi*** *hwn*
avoid *be* ***gochel***, ***osgoi***
 just a~ed ***ond y dim i***
avow *be* ***addef***
await *be* ***aros***, ***disgwyl***
awake *be* ***deffro***, ***dihuno***
awake *adf* ***ar ddi-hun***, ***yn effro***
award *be* ***dyfarnu***
award *enw* (adjudication) ***dyfarniad*** *hwn*; (prize) ***gwobr*** *hon*; (monetary) ***dyfarndal*** *hwn*
aware *ans* ***ymwybodol***
 to be a~ of ***sylweddoli***
 to be fully a~ ***gwybod yn iawn***
 to make a~ ***rhoi gwybod***
awareness *enw* ***ymwybyddiaeth*** *hon*
 to have an a~ of ***bod yn effro i***
 to maintain an a~ ***bod yn gyson ymwybodol***
awash *ans* ***yn nofio***
away *adf* ***i ffwrdd***, ***ymaith***
 to keep/stay away ***cadw draw***
awe *enw* ***parchedig ofn*** *hwn*
awestruck *ans* ***wedi'i arswydo***
awful *ans* ***ofnadwy***, ***dychrynllyd***, ***arswydus***
awhile *adf* ***dro***, ***am ychydig***
awkward *ans* ***lletchwith***, ***trwsgl***, ***yn fodiau i gyd***
 a~ person ***un sy'n tynnu'n groes***
awkwardness *enw* ***lletchwithdod*** *hwn*
awl *enw* ***ebill*** *hwn/hon*
awning *enw* ***adlen*** *hon*
awry *ans* ***o chwith***
axe *enw* ***bwyall:bwyell*** *hon*
axiom *enw* ***gwireb*** *hon*
axis *enw* ***echelin*** *hon*
axle *enw* ***echel*** *hon*
azure *ans* ***asur***

b

B

baa *be* ***brefu***
babble *be* ***baldorddi***
babbler *enw* ***baldorddwr*** *hwn*
babe, **baby** *enw* ***baban*** *hwn*
baboon *enw* ***babŵn*** *hwn*
baby *enw* ***babi*** *hwn*
babyhood *enw* ***babandod*** *hwn*
babyish *ans* ***babïaidd***
babysit *be* ***gwarchod***
babysitter *enw* ***gwarchodwr*** *hwn*
bachelor *enw* ***hen lanc*** *hwn*
bacillus *enw* ***basilws*** *hwn*
back *enw* ***cefn*** *hwn*; (games) ***cefnwr*** *hwn*
back *adf* ***yn ôl***
  b~ to b~ ***gefn gefn***
back *be* (support) ***cefnogi***; (reverse) ***bacio***
backache *enw* ***cefn tost***, ***poen yn y cefn*** *hwn*
back-bench *ans* ***mainc gefn***
backbite *be* ***lladd ar***
backbone *enw* ***asgwrn cefn*** *hwn*
backchat *be* ***ateb yn ôl***
backdate *be* ***ôl-ddyddio***
back down *be* ***tynnu yn ôl***
backer *enw* ***cefnogwr*** *hwn*, ***cefnogwraig*** *hon*
background *enw* ***cefndir*** *hwn*
background *ans* ***cefndirol***
backhand *enw* ***trawiad gwrthlaw*** *hwn*
backhander *enw* ***cildwrn*** *hwn*
backing *enw* ***cefnogaeth*** *hon*
backlash *enw* ***adlach*** *hon*
backlog *enw* ***gwaith (sydd) wedi pentyrru*** *hwn*, ***tagfa*** *hon*
backmost *ans* ***pellaf yn ôl***
back number *enw* ***ôl-rifyn*** *hwn*
back out *be* ***tynnu allan***
back payment *enw* ***ôl-daliad*** *hwn*
backside *enw* ***pen-ôl*** *hwn*, ***tin*** *hon*
backslide *be* ***gwrthgilio***, ***dirywio***
backstage *adf* ***yng nghefn y llwyfan***
backstreet *enw* ***stryd gefn*** *hon*
backstroke *enw* ***dull cefn*** *hwn*
back-up *enw* ***cefnogaeth*** *hon*
  b~ and support ***cymorth ategol ac ymarferol*** *hwn*
backward *ans* ***araf***
backwards *adf* ***yn ôl***
backwater *enw* ***merddwr*** *hwn*
backyard *enw* ***iard gefn***, ***milltir sgwâr*** *hon*
bacon *enw* ***cig moch*** *hwn*
bacterium *enw* ***bacteriwm*** *hwn*
bad *ans* ***drwg***, ***sâl***, ***gwael***
  b~ language ***iaith aflednais*** *hon*
badge *enw* ***bathodyn*** *hwn*
badger *enw* ***mochyn daear***, ***pryf llwyd*** *hwn*
badger *be* ***plagio***
badinage *enw* ***smaldod*** *hwn*
badinage *be* ***pryfocio***
badly *adf* ***yn wael***

b~ wrong ***(rhywbeth) mawr o'i le***
shaking b~ ***crynu'n ofnadwy***
badness *enw* ***drygioni*** *hwn*
baffle *be* ***drysu***
bag *enw* ***bag***, ***cwd***, ***cwdyn*** *hwn*
bagful *enw* ***cydaid*** *hwn*
baggage *enw* ***paciau*** *hyn*
our own personal b~ ***ein sgrepan/stôr ein hunain o ragfarnau/brofiadau***
baggy *ans* ***llac***
bagpipes *enw* ***pibau*** *hyn*
bail *enw* (cricket) ***caten*** *hon*; (court) ***mechnïaeth*** *hon*
bailey *enw* **beili** *hwn*
bailiff *enw* ***beili*** *hwn*
bail out *be* (water) ***disbyddu***
bait *enw* ***abwyd*** *hwn*
bake *be* ***crasu***, ***pobi***
baked *ans* ***cras***, ***pob***
bakehouse *enw* ***popty*** *hwn*
baker *enw* ***pobydd***
bakery *enw* ***popty*** *hwn*
bakestone *enw* ***gradell*** *hon*
baking *enw* ***pobiad*** *hwn*
baking powder *enw* ***powdr codi*** *hwn*
balance *enw* ***cydbwysedd*** *hwn*; (scale) ***clorian*** *hon*; (financial) **gweddill** *hwn*
on b~ ***o bwyso a mesur***
in the b~ ***yn y fantol***
balance *be* ***cydbwyso***; (budget) ***mantoli***
balanced *ans* ***cytbwys***
b~ budget ***cyllideb fantoledig*** *hon*
balance sheet *enw* ***mantolen*** *hon*
balcony *enw* ***balconi*** *hwn*
bald *ans* ***moel***
balderdash *enw* ***rwtsh*** *hwn*
baldly *adf* (speech) ***yn ddi-flewyn ar dafod***, ***yn blwmp ac yn blaen***
baldness *enw* ***moelni*** *hwn*
bale *enw* (hay) ***bwrn*** *hwn*
balk *be* ***nogio***, ***jibo***
ball *enw* ***pêl***, ***pelen*** *hon*; ***dawns*** *hon*
ballad *enw* ***baled*** *hon*
ballad-monger *enw* ***baledwr*** *hwn*
ball-bearing *enw* ***pelferyn*** *hwn*
ballerina *enw* ***dawnswraig fale*** *hon*
ballet *enw* ***bale***, ***ballet*** *hwn*
balloon *enw* ***balŵn*** *hwn/hon*
balloonist *enw* ***balwnydd*** *hwn*
ballot *enw* ***pleidlais bapur*** *hon*, ***balot*** *hwn*
ballot *be* ***pleidleisio***
balm, **balsam** *enw* ***balm***, ***lles*** *hwn*
balmy *ans* ***balmaidd***
bamboo *enw* ***bambŵ*** *hwn*
bamboozle *be* ***twyllo***
ban *enw* ***gwaharddiad*** *hwn*
ban *be* ***gwahardd***
banal *ans* ***ystrydebol***, ***di-fflach***
banana *enw* ***banana*** *hon*
to go b~s ***mynd yn lloerig***
band *enw* ***band*** *hwn*

b

bandage *enw* ***rhwymyn*** *hwn*
bandage *be* ***rhwymo***
bandit *enw* ***gwylliad*** *hwn*
bando *enw* ***bando*** *hwn*
bane *enw* ***pla*** *hwn*
bandy-legged *ans* ***coesgam***
bang *enw* ***ergyd*** *hwn/hon*
bang *be* ***taro***
bangle *enw* ***breichled*** *hon*
bang on *ebychiad* ***i'r dim***
banish *be* ***alltudio***
banishment *enw* ***alltudiaeth*** *hon*
banister *enw* ***canllaw*** *hwn*
banjo *enw* ***banjô*** *hwn*
bank *enw* (river) ***glan***, ***torlan*** *hon*; (money) ***banc*** *hwn*; (stock) ***cronfa*** *hon*
bank *be* ***bancio***
to b~ on ***dibynnu ar***
banker *enw* ***banciwr*** *hwn*
bank holiday *enw* ***gŵyl banc*** *hon*
banknote *enw* ***arian papur*** *hwn*
bank rate *enw* ***cyfradd banc*** *hon*
bankrupt *enw* ***methdalwr*** *hwn*
bankruptcy *enw* ***methdaliad*** *hwn*
banned *ans* ***gwaharddedig***
banner *enw* ***baner*** *hon*
bannock *enw* ***bara ceirch*** *hwn*
banns *enw* ***gostegion*** *hyn*
banquet *enw* ***gwledd*** *hon*
bantam *enw* ***bantam*** *hwn*
bantamweight *enw* ***pwysau bantam*** *hyn*
banter *enw* ***cellwair*** *hwn*
banter *be* ***cellwair***
baptism *enw* ***bedydd*** *hwn*
Baptist *enw* ***Bedyddiwr*** *hwn*, ***Bedyddwraig*** *hon*
baptize *be* ***bedyddio***
bar *enw* ***bar*** *hwn*
bar *be* ***bario***, ***bolltio (drws)***; ***rhwystro***
barb *enw* ***adfach*** *hwn*
barbarian *enw* ***barbariad*** *hwn*
barbarity *enw* ***barbareiddiwch*** *hwn*
barbarous *ans* ***barbaraidd***
barbecue *enw* ***barbeciw*** *hwn*
barbed wire *enw* ***weiren bigog*** *hon*
barber *enw* ***barbwr*** *hwn*
bard *enw* ***bardd*** *hwn*
bardic *ans* ***barddol***
bare *ans* ***noeth***, ***diaddurn***
bare *be* ***dinoethi***
bareback *ans* ***digyfrwy***
barefoot(ed) *ans* ***troednoeth***
barely *adf* ***prin***, ***cwta***
bareness *enw* ***moelni*** *hwn*
bargain *enw* ***bargen*** *hon*
bargain *be* ***bargeinio***
barge *enw* (boat) ***ysgraff*** *hon*
barge *be* ***gwthio***
baritone *enw* ***bariton*** *hwn*
bark *enw* (tree) ***rhisgl*** *hwn*; (dog) ***cyfarthiad*** *hwn*
bark *be* ***cyfarth***
b~ up the wrong tree ***mynd ar y trywydd anghywir***
barley *enw* ***haidd***, ***barlys*** *hwn*
barman *enw* ***barmon*** *hwn*

barmy *ans* ***gwallgof***
barn *enw* ***ysgubor*** *hon*
barnacle *enw* ***gwyran*** *hwn/hon*
barn dance *enw* ***twmpath (dawns)*** *hwn*
barnstorming *ans* ***ysgubol***
barnyard *enw* ***ydlan*** *hon*
barometer *enw* ***baromedr*** *hwn*
baron *enw* ***barwn*** *hwn*
baroness *enw* ***barwnes*** *hon*
barrack *be* ***heclan***
barracks *enw* ***barics*** *hyn*
barrage *enw* ***argae***, ***cob***, ***morglawdd*** *hwn*
barrel *enw* ***casgen*** *hon*
barren *ans* ***diffrwyth***, ***diffaith***
barricade *enw* ***gwrthglawdd*** *hwn*
barrier *enw* ***rhwystr*** *hwn*
barrister *enw* ***bargyfreithiwr*** *hwn*, ***bargyfreithwraig*** *hon*
barrow *enw* ***berfa*** *hon*
barrowful *enw* ***llond berfa***, ***berfáid*** *hon*
bartender *enw* ***barmon*** *hwn*
barter *be* ***ffeirio***, ***trwco***
base *enw* ***sylfaen***, ***sail*** *hon*
  b~ line ***llinell waelod*** *hon*
  client b~ ***cronfa o gwsmeriaid***
  home b~ ***man sefydlog***, ***cartref***
base *be* ***sylfaenu***
  class ~d ***ar raddfa dosbarth***
  b~d on ***ar sail***, ***yn seiliedig ar***
baseball *enw* ***pêl-fas*** *hon*
baseless *ans* ***di-sail***
baseline *enw* ***llinell sylfaen***, ***sail*** *hon*
basement *enw* ***llawr isaf*** *hwn*
bash *be* ***cledro***, ***dilorni***
  to have a b~ ***rhoi tro ar***, ***mentro***
bashful *ans* ***swil***
basic *ans* ***sylfaenol***; (chem.) ***basig***
basically *adf* ***yn y bôn***
basin *enw* ***basn:basin*** *hwn*
basis *enw* ***sail*** *hon*
  on a county-wide b~ ***ledled y sir***
  on an individual b~ ***fesul unigolyn***
  on a quarterly b~ ***bob chwarter***
  on a rota b~ ***yn ôl trefn rota***
  on the b~ that ***am/gan fod***
bask *be* ***torheulo***
basket *enw* ***basged*** *hon*, ***cawell*** *hwn*
basketball *enw* ***pêl-fasged*** *hon*
basketful *enw* ***basgedaid*** *hon*
basket maker *enw* ***basgedwr*** *hwn*
bass *enw* (music) ***bas*** *hwn*; (fish) ***draenog y môr***
bassoon *enw* ***baswn*** *hwn*
bastard *enw* ***bastard*** *hwn*
baste *be* (cookery) ***seimio***, ***iro***; (needlework) ***brasbwytho***, ***tacio***
bastion *enw* ***cadarnle*** *hwn*
bat *enw* (mammal) ***ystlum*** *hwn*; (games) ***bat*** *hwn*
  off their own b~ ***ohonynt eu hunain***
bat *be* ***batio***
batch *enw* ***ffyrnaid*** *hon*, ***swp*** *hwn*
bated *ans* (breath) ***gan ddal fy (dy, ei etc.) anadl***

b

bated *enw* ***bath*** *hwn*
bathe *be* ***ymdrochi***
bather *enw* ***trochwr*** *hwn*
bathing suit *enw* ***gwisg nofio*** *hon*
bathroom *enw* ***ystafell ymolchi*** *hon*
baths *enw* ***pwll nofio*** *hwn*
bathtub *enw* ***twba*** *hwn*
baton *enw* ***baton*** *hon*
bats *ans* ***gwallgof***
batsman *enw* ***batiwr*** *hwn*
battalion *enw* ***bataliwn*** *hwn*
batten *enw* ***astell*** *hon*
batter *be* ***curo, dyrnu, pwyo***
batter *enw* (cookery) ***cytew*** *hwn*
battered *ans* (beaten) ***ysig***
battery *enw* ***batri*** *hwn*
  b~ of techniques ***nifer fawr o amrywiol dechnegau***
battle *enw* ***brwydr*** *hon*
battle *be* ***brwydro***
battlefield *enw* ***maes y gad*** *hwn*
battleship *enw* ***llong ryfel*** *hon*
batty *ans* ***gwallgof***
bauble *enw* ***tegan*** *hwn*
baulk *be* ***nogio***, ***jibio***
bawdy *ans* ***anweddus***
bawl *be* ***crochlefain***
bay *enw* ***bae*** *hwn*; (in a building) ***llecyn*** *hwn*
bay *be* (wolf) ***udo***
bayonet *enw* ***bidog*** *hwn/hon*
bazaar *enw* ***basâr*** *hwn*
be *be* ***bod***
beach *enw* ***traeth*** *hwn*
beacon *enw* ***coelcerth*** *hon*
bead *enw* ***glain*** *hwn*
beady *ans* ***treiddgar***, ***llygad barcud***
beak *enw* ***pig*** *hon*
beaker *enw* ***bicer*** *hwn*
beam *enw* (building) ***trawst***; (ray) ***pelydryn*** *hwn*
beam *be* ***tywynnu***
bean *enw* ***ffeuen*** *hon*
beans (broad) *enw* ***ffa*** *hyn*
bear *enw* ***arth*** *hon*
bear *be* ***dwyn***, ***goddef***
  b~ a grudge ***dal dig***
  b~ down (draw near) ***dynesu***; (bring pressure to bear; e.g. 'costs') **ceisio lleihau**
  b~ examination ***dal dŵr***
  b~ on ***ymwneud â***
  b~ out ***cadarnhau***
  b~ the marks ***bod ag ôl***
  b~ with us ***byddwch yn amyneddgar***
  bring to b~ ***rhoi ar waith***
  I can't b~ them ***maen nhw'n dân ar fy nghroen***
  this does not b~ thinking about ***thâl hi ddim i feddwl amdano***
bearable *ans* ***goddefadwy***
beard *enw* ***barf*** *hwn*
bearded *ans* ***barfog***
bearer *enw* ***cludwr*** *hwn*
bearing *enw* (mechanical) ***beryn*** *hwn*; (posture) ***ymarweddiad*** *hwn*

have a b~ on ***mae a wnelo â*****,** ***ymwneud â***
beast *enw* ***bwystfil*** *hwn*
beastly *ans* ***bwystfilaidd***
beat *be* ***curo***
beat *enw* ***curiad*** *hwn*
beaten *ans* (metal) ***curedig***; (defeated) ***wedi'i drechu***
beatific *ans* ***gwynfydedig***
beating *enw* (of wings, heart etc.) ***curiad*** *hwn*; (thrashing) ***curfa***, ***cweir***, ***crasfa***, ***cosfa*** *hon*
Beatitudes *enw* ***Gwynfydau*** *hyn*
beautiful *ans* ***hardd***, ***prydferth***
beautify *be* ***harddu***, ***prydferthu***
beauty *enw* ***harddwch***, ***prydferthwch***, ***tegwch*** *hwn*
beaver *enw* ***afanc*** *hwn*
beaver away *be* ***pydru arni***
because *ardd* ***oherwydd***, ***o achos***
because *cysyllt* ***gan***
beckon *be* ***amneidio***
become *be* ***dod***; (suit) ***gweddu***
becoming *ans* ***gweddus***
bed *enw* ***gwely*** *hwn*
bedclothes *enw* ***dillad gwely*** *hyn*
bedeck *be* ***addurno***
bedevil *be* ***plagio***, ***chwarae'r diawl â***
bedfellow *enw* ***cywely*** *hwn*
bedlam *enw* ***fel ffair***
bedpan *enw* ***padell wely*** *hon*
bedraggled *ans* ***caglog***; ***aflêr***, ***anniben***
bedridden *ans* ***gorweiddiog***
bedroom *enw* ***ystafell wely*** *hon*
bedside *enw* ***erchwyn*** *hwn/hon*
bedspread *enw* ***cwrlid*** *hwn*
bee *enw* ***gwenynen*** *hon*
beech *enw* ***ffawydden*** *hon*
beechmast *enw* ***cnau ffawydd*** *hyn*
beef *enw* ***cig eidion*** *hwn*
to b~ up ***cryfhau***
beefburger *enw* ***eidionyn*** *hwn*
beehive *enw* ***cwch gwenyn*** *hwn*
been *bf* ***wedi bod***
beer *enw* ***cwrw*** *hwn*
beeswax *enw* ***cwyr***
beet *enw* ***betys*** *hyn*
beetle *enw* ***chwilen*** *hon*
beetroot *enw* ***betys coch*** *hyn*
befall *be* ***digwydd***
befit *be* ***gweddu***
before *adf* ***o'r blaen***, ***cyn***
long b~ ***ymhell cyn hynny***
b~ long ***cyn bo hir***
before ardd ***o flaen***, ***gerbron***, ***ger fy (dy***, ***ei etc.) mron***
beforehand *adf* ***ymlaen llaw***
until shortly b~ ***tan ychydig cyn hynny***
befuddle *be* ***mwydro***
beg *be* ***ymbil***; (for money) ***cardota***
beggar *enw* ***cardotyn*** *hwn*
begin *be* ***dechrau***, ***cychwyn***
to b~ with ***cam cyntaf*** *hwn*
beginner *enw* ***dechreuwr*** *hwn*, ***dechreuwraig*** *hon*
beginning *enw* ***dechreuad*** *hwn*
begone *ebychiad* ***ymaith! i ffwrdd!***

b

begrudge *be* ***gwarafun***
beguile *be* ***hudo***
beguiling *ans* ***hudol***
behalf (on behalf of) *enw* ***ar ran***
behave *be* ***ymddwyn***
behaviour *enw* ***ymddygiad*** *hwn*
Behaviour Support Plan ***Cynllun Cynnal Ymddygiad*** *hwn*
behavioural *ans* ***ymddygiadol***
behead *be* ***dienyddio***
behest *enw* ***gorchymyn***, ***cais*** *hwn*
behind *adf* ***ar ôl***
behind *ardd* ***tu ôl***, ***tu cefn***
  the principle b~ this ***yr egwyddor sy'n sail i***
behold *ebychiad* ***wele!***
beholden *ans* ***dyledus***
being *enw* ***bod*** *hwn*, ***bodolaeth*** *hon*
belated *ans* ***diweddar***, ***hwyr***
belay *be* ***sicrhau***, ***clymu***
belch *be* ***pecial***, ***torri gwynt***
belfry *enw* ***clochdy*** *hwn*
belie *be* (contradict) ***gwrth-ddweud***; (misrepresent) ***camliwio***; (disguise) ***cuddio***
belief *enw* ***cred*** *hon*
  in the b~ that ***gan gredu***
  it is their firm b~ ***credant yn bendant taw/mai***
  sad beyond b~ ***mwy trist na thristwch***
believable *ans* ***credadwy***
believe *be* ***credu***, ***coelio***
believer *enw* ***crediniwr*** *hwn*, ***credinwraig*** *hon*, ***credadun*** *hwn*
belittle *be* ***bychanu***
bell *enw* ***cloch*** *hon*
belle *enw* ***meinwen*** *hon*
bellicose *ans* ***cecrus***
belligerent *ans* ***cwerylgar***, ***rhyfelgar***
bellow *be* ***rhuo***, ***bugunad***
bellow *enw* ***bugunad*** *hwn*
bellows *enw* ***megin*** *hon*
belly *enw* ***bol:bola*** *hwn*
bellyache *enw* ***poen yn y bol***, ***bola tost*** *hwn*
bellyful *enw* ***llond bol***
belong *be* ***perthyn***
belongings *enw* ***meddiannau*** *hyn*, ***eiddo*** *hwn*
beloved *ans* ***annwyl***, ***hoff***
beloved *enw* ***cariad*** *hwn*
below *adf* ***oddi tanodd***, ***islaw***
below *ardd* ***tan***, ***dan***
belt *enw* ***gwregys*** *hwn*; (land) ***llain***, ***ardal*** *hon*; (clout) ***clatsien***, ***wad*** *hon*
belt *be* ***clatsio***, ***bwrw***, ***waldio***, ***hemio***
  to **b~ along** ***rhuthro***
  b~ up! ***cau dy geg!***
bemoan *be* ***galarnadu***
bemused *ans* ***syn***
bench *enw* ***mainc*** *hon*
benchmark *enw* ***meincnod*** *hwn*
benchmarking *be* ***meincnodi***
bend *be* ***plygu***
bend *enw* ***tro*** *hwn*
beneath *adf* ***oddi tanodd***

beneath *ardd* ***tan***, ***dan***
benediction *enw* **bendith** *hon*
benefactor *enw* ***cymwynaswr*** *hwn*, ***cymwynaswraig*** *hon*
beneficent *ans* ***bendithiol***
beneficial *ans* ***buddiol***, ***llesol***
benefit *enw* ***budd***, ***budd-dâl***, ***buddiant*** *hwn*
  b~ in kind ***budd cyfatebol*** *hwn*
  the b~ of their experience ***ffrwyth eu profiad***
  perceived b~ ***mantais amlwg*** *hon*
benefit *be* ***elwa***, ***bod ar fy (dy***, ***ei etc.) ennill***
benefits *enw* ***buddiannau*** *hyn*
benevolence *enw* ***cymwynasgarwch*** *hwn*
benevolent *ans* ***cymwynasgar***
benign *ans* ***tirion***; (medical) ***diniwed***
bent *ans* ***cam***, ***crwca***
benumb *be* ***merwino***, ***sythu***
bequeath *be* ***cymynnu/ cymynroddi***, ***ewyllysio***
bequest *enw* ***cymynrodd*** *hon*
berate *be* ***dweud y drefn***, ***difrïo***
bereavement *enw* ***profedigaeth*** *hon*
berries *enw* ***aeron*** *hyn*
berserk *ans* ***gwyllt***
berth *enw* (ship) ***angorfa*** *hon*; (bed) ***gwely*** *hwn*
beseech *be* ***deisyf***, ***erfyn***
beset *be* ***amgylchynu***
  b~ by fears ***cael eich poeni gan ofnau***
beside *ardd* ***gerllaw***, ***yn ymyl***
  to be b~ themselves ***yn lloerig***
besides *ardd* ***yn ogystal***, ***heblaw***
besiege *be* ***gwarchae***
besmirch *be* ***pardduo***
bespoke *ans* ***at y pwrpas***, ***pwrpasol***
best *ans* ***gorau***
  all the b~ ***pob hwyl!***
  b~ of friends ***cyfeillion pennaf***
  how b~ to ***sut orau y mae***
  in the b~ interest ***er lles***
  it's b~ if ***y drefn orau yw***
  of the b~ quality ***o'r radd flaenaf***
  they are b~ avoided ***gorau oll os gellir eu hosgoi***
  they are past their b~ ***maent wedi gweld eu dyddiau gorau***
  to get the b~ of ***er mwyn elwa ar***
  to the b~ effect ***manteisio i'r eithaf ar***
  to the b~ of their ability ***hyd eithaf eu gallu***
best *be* ***cael y gorau ar***
bestial *ans* ***ffiaidd***, ***bwystfilaidd***
bestir *be* ***ystwyrian***
best man *enw* ***gwas priodas*** *hwn*
bestow *be* ***cyflwyno***, ***rhoi***
bestrew *be* ***gwasgaru***
bet *enw* ***bet*** *hon*
  your best b~ ***fyddai ddoethaf***

b

bet *be* ***betio***, ***mentro***
I bet – ***mentra i –***
betray *be* ***bradychu***
betrayal *enw* ***brad***, ***bradychiad*** *hwn*
betroth *be* ***dyweddïo***
better *ans* ***gwell***
b~ safe than sorry ***gwell gofalu na difaru***
b~ suited ***mwy addas***
getting b~ ***bod ar wellhad***
much b~ than ***yn frenin wrth***
to get the b~ of ***trechu***
better *adf* ***yn well***
betting *enw* ***hapchwarae*** *hwn*
between ardd ***rhwng***
b~ now and – ***o hyn tan***
bevel *enw* ***befel*** *hwn*
beverage *enw* ***diod*** *hon*
bevy *enw* ***haid*** *hon*
beware *be* ***gochel***
but b~ there will be ***ond cofiwch –***
bewilder *be* ***drysu***, ***mwydro***
bewildered *ans* ***ffrwcslyd***
bewilderment *enw* ***dryswch***, ***penbleth*** *hwn*
bewitch *be* ***rheibio***, ***swyno***, ***hudo***
bewitching *ans* ***hudol***
beyond ardd ***tu hwnt***
biannual *ans* ***chwemisol***, ***hanner blynyddol***
bias *enw* ***gogwydd*** *hwn*, ***rhagfarn*** *hon*
Bible *enw* ***Beibl*** *hwn*
Biblical *ans* ***Beiblaidd***
bibliography *enw* ***llyfryddiaeth*** *hon*
bicentenary *enw* ***daucanmlwyddiant*** *hwn*
bicker *be* ***cecran***
bicycle *enw* ***beic***, ***beisicl*** *hwn*
bid *be* ***cynnig***
bid *enw* ***cynnig*** *hwn*
bidding *enw* ***gorchymyn*** *hwn*
bide *be* ***aros***, ***disgwyl***
biennial *ans* ***bob yn ail flwyddyn***
bier *enw* ***elor*** *hon*
big *ans* ***mawr***
bigger *ans* ***mwy***
big-head *enw* ***person mawreddog***, ***tipyn o feddwl ynddo***, ***fi fawr***, ***pen bach*** *hwn*
big mouth *enw* ***hen geg*** *hon*
bigot *enw* ***rhywun llawn rhagfarn***
bigoted *ans* ***cul***
bigwig *enw* ***pwysigyn*** *hwn*
bike *enw* ***beic*** *hwn*
bikini *enw* ***bicini*** *hwn*
bilateral *ans* ***dwyochrog***
bilberries *enw* ***llus*** *hyn*
bile *enw* ***bustl*** *hwn*
bilingual *ans* ***dwyieithog***
bilingualism *enw* ***dwyieithrwydd*** *hwn*
bill *enw* (payment) ***bil***; (Parliament) ***mesur*** *hwn*; (beak) ***pig*** *hon*
to fit the b~ ***taro deuddeg***
billet *enw* ***llety*** *hwn*
billhook *enw* ***bilwg*** *hwn*
billiards *enw* ***biliards*** *hwn*

billion *enw* ***biliwn*** *hon*
billow *be* ***tonni***
billy goat *enw* ***bwch gafr*** *hwn*
bimonthly *ans* ***deufisol***
bin *enw* ***bin*** *hwn*
binary *ans* ***deuaidd***
  b~ digit ***did*** *hwn*
bind *be* ***rhwymo***
binder *enw* ***rhwymwr*** *hwn*
binding *ans* ***ymrwymol***
binge *enw* ***sbri*** *hon*
  b~ing ***llowcio a chyfogi***
binoculars *enw* ***gwydrau*** *hyn*
biochemistry *enw* ***biocemeg*** *hon*
biodiversity *enw* ***bioamrywiaeth*** *hon*
biographer *enw* ***cofiannydd*** *hwn*
biography *enw* ***cofiant*** *hwn*
biological *ans* ***biolegol***
biologist *enw* ***biolegydd*** *hwn*
biology *enw* ***bioleg*** *hon*
bipartisan *ans* ***dwybleidiol***
biped *ans* ***deudroed***
birch *enw* ***bedwen*** *hon*
bird *enw* ***aderyn*** *hwn*
bird-catcher *enw* ***adarwr*** *hwn*
birdie *enw* (golf) ***pluen*** *hon*
biro *enw* ***biro*** *hwn*
birth *enw* ***genedigaeth*** *hon*
  a south Walian by b~ ***brodor o'r de***
  from b~ to death ***o'r crud i'r bedd***
birth certificate *enw* ***tystysgrif geni*** *hon*
birth control *enw* ***atal cenhedlu***
birthday *enw* ***pen blwydd*** *hwn*
  it's their birthday ***mae'n ben blwydd arnynt***
birthmark *enw* ***man geni*** *hwn*
biscuit *enw* ***bisgïen*** *hon*
bisect *be* ***rhannu'n ddwy***
bisexual *ans* ***deuryw***, ***deurywiol***
bishop *enw* ***esgob*** *hwn*
bishopric *enw* ***esgobaeth*** *hon*
bison *enw* ***bual***, ***beison*** *hwn*
bit *enw* ***tamaid*** *hwn*; (horse) ***genfa*** *hon*; (drill) ***ebill*** *hwn/hon*; (computer) ***did*** *hwn*
  b~ by b~ ***ychydig ar y tro***, ***fesul darn***, ***fesul tamaid***
  in b~s ***yn deilchion***
bitch *enw* ***gast*** *hon*
bitchy *ans* ***llawn gwenwyn***
bite *be* ***cnoi***, ***brathu***
bite *enw* ***cnoad***, ***brathiad*** *hwn*
  intellectual b~ ***miniogrwydd deallusol*** *hwn*
biting *ans* ***yn brathu***, ***brathog***
bitter *ans* ***chwerw***
  to regret bitterly ***difaru'n ofnadwy***
  to oppose bitterly ***gwrthwynebu'n chwyrn***
bittern *enw* ***aderyn y bwn*** *hwn*
bitterness *enw* ***chwerwder*** *hwn*
bitty *ans* ***tameidiog***
biweekly *ans* ***bob yn ail wythnos***, ***pythefnosol***
bizarre *ans* ***od***, ***rhyfedd***

b

blab *be* ***clapian***, ***clepian***
black *ans* ***du***
black (skinned) *ans* ***croenddu***
blackberries *enw* ***mwyar duon*** *hyn*
blackberry *be* ***mwyara***
blackbird *enw* ***aderyn du*** *hwn*, ***mwyalchen*** *hon*
blackboard *enw* ***bwrdd du*** *hwn*
blackcurrants *enw* ***cwrens duon*** *hyn*
blacken *be* ***duo***, ***pardduo***
blackguard *enw* ***dihiryn*** *hwn*
blackhead *enw* ***pendduyn*** *hwn*
blackleg *enw* ***bradwr*** *hwn*
blackmail *enw* ***blacmêl*** *hwn*
blackness *enw* ***düwch*** *hwn*
blackout *enw* ***blac-owt*** *hwn*
blacksmith *enw* ***gof*** *hwn*
black spot *enw* ***man peryglus*** *hwn*
blackthorn *enw* ***draenen ddu*** *hon*
bladder *enw* ***pledren*** *hon*
blade *enw* ***llafn*** *hwn*; (grass) ***llafn***, ***glaswelltyn*** *hwn*
blame *be* ***beio***, ***bwrw'r bai ar***
blame *enw* ***bai*** *hwn*; ***ar – mae'r bai***
blameless *ans* ***di-fai:difai***
blanch *be* ***gwynnu***
bland *ans* ***mwyn***, ***di-flas***, ***digymeriad***
blandish *be* ***gwenieithio***
blank *ans* ***gwag***
  my mind went b~ ***aeth yn nos arnaf***
  to refuse point-b~ ***gwrthod yn lân***
blanket *enw* ***carthen*** *hon*
blank verse *enw* ***mesur di-odl*** *hwn*
blare *be* ***rhuo***
blarney *enw* ***gweniaith*** *hon*
blasé *ans* ***di-hid***
blaspheme *be* ***cablu***
blasphemy *enw* ***cabledd*** *hwn*
blast *enw* ***ffrwydrad*** *hwn*
blast *be* ***ffrwydro***
blatant *ans* ***eofn***, ***haerllug***; ***amlwg***, ***agored***
blaze *be* ***fflamio***
blaze *enw* ***tanllwyth*** *hwn*
bleach *enw* ***cannydd*** *hwn*
bleach *be* ***cannu***
bleak *ans* ***llwm***
  b~ future ***dyfodol du*** *hwn*
bleakness *enw* ***moelni*** *hwn*
bleary *ans* ***molog***
bleat *enw* ***bref*** *hon*
bleat *be* ***brefu***, ***dolefain***
bleed *be* ***gwaedu***
  to b~ them dry ***eu godro'n sych***
bleep *be* ***bipian***
blemish *be* ***llychwino***
blemish *enw* ***nam***, ***brycheuyn***, ***mefl*** *hwn*
blench *be* ***gwingo***
blend *be* ***ymdoddi***, ***cyfuno***
blend *enw* ***cyfuniad*** *hwn*
blender *enw* ***hylifydd*** *hwn*
bless *be* ***bendithio***
blessed *ans* ***bendigaid***
  of b~ memory ***coffa da am***, ***o barchus goffadwriaeth***

blessing *enw* ***bendith*** *hon*
blight *be* ***difetha***
blight *enw* ***malltod*** *hwn*
blind *ans* ***dall***
  a b~ alley ***mynd i'r gors***
  b~ obedience ***ufudd-dod digwestiwn*** *hwn*
blind *be* ***dallu***
blind *enw* (window) ***bleind*** *hwn*
blindfold *enw* ***mwgwd*** *hwn*
blindfold *be* ***mygydu***
blindness *enw* ***dallineb*** *hwn*
blinkered *ans* ***unllygeidiog***
bliss *enw* ***gwynfyd*** *hwn*
blissful *ans* ***dedwydd***
blister *enw* ***chwysigen***, ***pothell*** *hon*
blistering *ans* ***deifiol***
  b~ attack ***ymosodiad deifiol*** *hwn*
blithe *ans* ***nwyfus***
blitz *enw* ***cyrch (awyr)*** *hwn*
blizzard *enw* ***storm o eira*** *hon*
bloated *ans* ***chwyddedig***
bloater *enw* ***pennog coch*** *hwn*
blob *enw* ***smotyn*** *hwn*
block *enw* ***bloc*** *hwn*
block *be* ***blocio***, ***rhwystro***
blockade *be* ***gwarchae***
blockage *enw* ***tagfa*** *hon*
blockhead *enw* ***clwpa*** *hwn*
bloke *enw* ***boi*** *hwn*
blond *ans* ***pryd golau***
blood *enw* ***gwaed*** *hwn*
bloodbath *enw* ***cyflafan*** *hon*
blood donor *enw* ***rhoddwr gwaed*** *hwn*
blood group *enw* ***grŵp gwaed*** *hwn*
blood pressure *enw* ***pwysedd gwaed*** *hwn*
blood relation *enw* ***perthynas drwy waed*** *hwn/hon*
bloodstream *enw* ***llif gwaed*** *hwn*
bloodthirsty *ans* ***yn awchu am waed***
blood transfusion *enw* ***trallwysiad gwaed*** *hwn*
blood vessel *enw* ***pibell waed*** *hon*
bloody *ans* ***gwaedlyd***
bloom *be* ***blodeuo***; (fig.) ***ffynnu***
bloom *enw* ***blodyn***; (person) ***gwrid*** *hwn*
  in b~ ***yn ei flodau***
blossom *enw* ***blodeuyn*** *hwn*
blossom *be* ***blodeuo***
blot *be* ***blotio***
blot *enw* ***blotyn du*** *hwn*
  b~ out efforts ***llethu ymdrechion***
blotting paper *enw* ***papur sugno*** *hwn*
blotto *ans* ***meddw gaib***
blouse *enw* ***blows:blowsen*** *hon*
blow *be* ***chwythu***
blow *enw* ***ergyd*** *hwn/hon*
  a mortal b~ ***taro yn ei dalcen***
blow up *be* ***ffrwydro***
blower *enw* ***chwythwr*** *hwn*
blubber *enw* ***bloneg morfil*** *hwn*
bludgeon *enw* ***pastwn*** *hwn*
bludgeon *be* ***pastynu***

b

blue *ans* ***glas***
b~ chip company ***cwmni o'r radd flaenaf***
out of the b~ ***yn gwbl annisgwyl/ddirybudd***
bluebells *enw* ***clychau'r gog*** *hyn*
bluebottle *enw* ***cleren las*** *hon*
blueness *enw* ***glesni*** *hwn*
blueprint *enw* ***cynddelw*** *hon*, ***glasbrint*** *hwn*, ***canllawiau*** *hyn*
blues *enw* ***y felan*** *hon*
bluff *be* ***blyffio***
blunder *enw* ***camgymeriad*** *hwn*
blunt *ans* ***pŵl***, ***di-awch***; ***plaen***, ***swta***, ***di-lol***
blunt *be* ***pylu***
bluntness *enw* ***pylni*** *hwn*
blur *enw* ***aneglurder*** *hwn*
blur *be* ***cymylu***
blurb *enw* ***broliant*** *hwn*
blush *enw* ***gwrid*** *hwn*
blush *be* ***gwrido***
bluster *be* ***ffromi***
boar *enw* ***baidd*** *hwn*
board *enw* ***bwrdd*** *hwn*, ***astell***, ***bord*** *hon*; (food) ***prydau*** *hyn*
get on b~ a train ***mynd ar y trên***
on b~ ***yn y car/cerbyd***
take on b~ ***mabwysiadu***; ***cymryd i ystyriaeth***
on b~ ship ***ar fwrdd llong***
boarder *enw* ***lletywr*** *hwn*
boarding house *enw* ***llety*** *hwn*
boarding school *enw* ***ysgol breswyl*** *hon*
boast *be* ***ymffrostio***, ***brolio***
boast *enw* ***ymffrost*** *hwn*, ***bost*** *hon*
boastful *ans* ***ymffrostgar***
boat *enw* ***cwch***, ***bad*** *hwn*
bode *be* ***argoeli***
bodice *enw* ***bodis*** *hwn*
bodily *ans* ***corfforol***
body *enw* ***corff*** *hwn*
bodywork *enw* ***corff*** *hwn*
boffin *enw* ***gwyddonydd*** *hwn*
bog *enw* ***cors***, ***siglen*** *hon*
bogey *enw* ***bwci*** *hwn*
boggle *be* ***arswydo***
boggy *ans* ***corsiog***
bogus *ans* ***ffug***
boil *be* ***berwi***
what it all b~s down to ***swm a sylwedd y peth***
boil *enw* ***cornwyd*** *hwn*
boiler *enw* ***boeler*** *hwn*
boiling *ans* ***berwedig***
b~ hot water ***dŵr berw*** *hwn*
boiling point *enw* ***berwbwynt*** *hwn*
boisterous *ans* ***hoenus***, ***swnllyd***
bold *ans* ***beiddgar***, ***eofn***
boldness *enw* ***beiddgarwch***, ***ehofndra*** *hwn*
bole *enw* ***bôn*** *hwn*
bolster *enw* ***gobennydd*** *hwn*
bolster *be* ***atgyfnerthu***, ***rhoi hwb i***
bolt *enw* ***bollt:bollten*** *hon*
shot its b~ ***wedi chwythu ei blwc***
bolt *be* (lock) ***bolltio***; (plants) ***hadu***; (run) ***rhuthro (ymaith)***, ***dianc***

bomb *enw* ***bom*** *hwn/hon*
bomb *be* ***bomio***
bombard *be* ***bombardio***, ***peledu***
bombastic *ans* ***chwyddedig***, ***llawn gwynt***
bona fide *ans* ***dilys***
bond *enw* ***rhwymyn*** *hwn*; (finance) **bond** *hwn*
bond *be* ***cyplysu***, ***cysylltu***
bondage *enw* ***caethwasiaeth*** *hon*
bone *enw* ***asgwrn*** *hwn*
  b~ of contention ***asgwrn y gynnen***
bonfire *enw* ***coelcerth*** *hon*
bonkers *ans* ***gwallgof***, ***boncyrs***
bonnet *enw* ***boned*** *hon*
bonus *enw* ***bonws*** *hwn*
bony *ans* ***esgyrnog***
boo *be* ***bwio***
booby trap *enw* ***magl*** *hon*
book *enw* ***llyfr*** *hwn*
book *be* ***bwcio***; (ticket) ***codi***
bookcase *enw* ***cwpwrdd llyfrau*** *hwn*
book-keeper *enw* ***cyfrifydd*** *hwn*
  book-keeping ***cadw cyfrifon***
booklet *enw* ***llyfryn*** *hwn*
bookseller *enw* ***llyfrwerthwr*** *hwn*, ***llyfrwerthwraig*** *hon*
bookstore *enw* ***siop lyfrau*** *hon*
bookworm *enw* ***llyfrbryf*** *hwn*
boom *enw* ***dwndwr*** *hwn*
boom *be* ***mae tipyn o fynd/mynd mawr ar***
boomerang *enw* ***bwmerang*** *hwn*
boon *enw* ***bendith*** *hwn*; ***caffaeliad mawr***
boor *enw* ***taeog*** *hwn*
boorish *ans* ***anfoesgar***
boost *enw* ***hwb*** *hwn*
boost *be* ***hybu***, ***rhoi hwb i***
boot *enw* (shoe) ***esgid*** *hon*; (car) ***cist*** *hon*
booth *enw* ***bwth*** *hwn*, ***stondin*** *hon*
booty *enw* ***ysbail*** *hon*
border *enw* ***ffin*** *hon*
border *be* ***ffinio***
borderline *ans* ***ymylol***
bore *be* (hole) ***tyllu***; (tire) ***llethu***
bore *enw* ***bôr*** *hwn*
boredom *enw* ***diflastod*** *hwn*
boring *ans* ***diflas***, ***undonog***, ***syrffedus***
born *ans* ***genedigol***
borough *enw* ***bwrdeistref*** *hon*
borrow *be* ***benthyca***
borrowed *ans* ***benthyg***
borrower *enw* ***benthycwr*** *hwn*
bosom *enw* ***mynwes*** *hon*
boss *enw* ***meistr***, ***giaffer*** *hwn*
boss-eyed *ans* ***llygatgam***
botanic(al) *ans* ***botanegol***
botanist *enw* ***botanegydd*** *hwn*
botany *enw* ***botaneg***, ***llysieueg*** *hon*
botch *enw* ***cawl*** *hwn*
botch *be* ***cawlio***
both *rhag* ***y ddau***, ***y ddwy***, ***ill dau/dwy***
bother *enw* ***ffwdan*** *hwn*

b

bother *be* ***poeni***, ***trafferthu***
bottle *enw* ***potel*** *hon*
bottle *be* ***potelu***
to b~ things up ***cadw'r cyfan iddynt eu hunain***
bottleneck *enw* ***tagfa (draffig)*** *hon*
bottle-opener *enw* ***teclyn agor poteli*** *hwn*
bottom *enw* ***gwaelod***, ***pen ôl*** *hwn*
bottomless *ans* ***diwaelod***
bough *enw* ***cangen*** *hon*
boulder *enw* ***clogfaen*** *hwn*
bounce *enw* ***sbonc*** *hon*
bounce *be* ***sboncio***
bound *be* ***llamu***
bound *enw* ***llam*** *hwn*; (boundary) ***ffin*** *hon*
their greed knows no b~ ***does dim pall/pen draw ar eu trachwant***
bound *ans* (book) ***rhwymedig***
boundary *enw* ***ffin*** *hon*, ***terfyn*** *hwn*
boundless *ans* ***diderfyn***
bounds *enw* ***cyffiniau*** *hyn*
bounteous *ans* ***hael***, ***haelionus***
bountiful *ans* ***haelionus***, ***hael***
bouquet *enw* ***tusw*** *hwn*
bout *enw* (boxing) ***gornest*** *hon*; (coughing) ***pwl*** *hwn*
bow *be* ***moesymgrymu***
bow *enw* ***bwa*** *hwn*
bow tie *enw* ***dici bô*** *hwn*
bowdlerize *be* ***glastwreiddio***
bowels *enw* ***perfedd***, ***perfeddion*** *hyn*
bowl *enw* ***dysgl***, ***powlen*** *hon*
bowl *be* ***bowlio***, ***powlio***
bow-legged *ans* ***coesgam***
bowler *enw* ***bowliwr*** *hwn*
box *be* (sport) ***paffio***
box *enw* ***blwch*** *hwn*
b~ office ***swyddfa docynnau*** *hon*
boxer *enw* ***paffiwr*** *hwn*, ***paffwraig*** *hon*
Boxing Day *enw* ***Gŵyl San Steffan*** *hon*
boy *enw* ***bachgen*** *hwn*
boycott *be* ***boicotio***
boyfriend *enw* ***cariad***, ***sboner*** *hwn*
boyhood *enw* ***bachgendod*** *hwn*
boyish *ans* ***bachgennaidd***
bra *enw* ***bra***, ***bronglwm*** *hwn*
brace *enw* (carpenter's) ***carn-tro*** *hwn*
bracelet *enw* ***breichled*** *hon*
braces *enw* ***bresys*** *hyn*
bracing *ans* ***iachus***
bracken *enw* ***rhedyn*** *hyn*
bracket *enw* ***bach*** *hwn*
brackish *ans* ***hallt***
bradawl *enw* ***mynawyd*** *hwn*
brag *be* ***brolio***
braggart *enw* ***broliwr*** *hwn*
braid *enw* ***pleth*** *hon*
braid *be* ***plethu***
braille *enw* ***braille*** *hwn*
brain *enw* ***ymennydd*** *hwn*
brainchild *enw* ***syniad*** *hwn*

brainstorming *be* ***gwyntyllu syniadau***, ***pentyrru syniadau***
brainwave *enw* ***fflach o weledigaeth*** *hon*
brainy *ans* ***peniog***
brake *enw* ***brêc*** *hwn*
brake *be* ***brecio***
bramble *enw* ***drysïen*** *hon*
branch *enw* ***cangen*** *hon*
to b~ out in new directions ***torri cwysi newydd***
brand *enw* ***gwneuthuriad***, ***brand*** *hwn*
brand *be* ***llosgnodi***
to be b~ed as liars ***cawsant yr enw o fod yn gelwyddgwn***
brandish *be* ***chwifio***
brand new *ans* ***newydd sbon***
brandy *enw* ***brandi*** *hwn*
brash *ans* ***hyf***, ***digywilydd***
brass *enw* ***pres*** *hwn*
brass band *enw* ***band pres*** *hwn*
brassed off *ans* ***wedi cael llond bol***
brassiere *enw* ***bronglwm*** *hwn*
brat *enw* ***crwtyn*** *hwn*, ***croten*** *hon*, ***cythraul bach*** *hwn*
bravado *enw* ***ymffrost*** *hwn*
brave *ans* ***dewr***, ***gwrol***
brave *be* ***wynebu***
bravery *enw* ***dewrder***, ***gwroldeb*** *hwn*
braves *enw* ***dewrion*** *hyn*
brawl *enw* ***ffrwgwd*** *hwn*
brawl *be* ***ffraeo***, ***ymrafael***
brawny *ans* ***cyhyrog***
bray *be* ***nadu***
braze *be* ***sodro â phres***
brazen *ans* ***digywilydd***
breach *enw* (gap) ***adwy*** *hon*; ***tor (cyfraith/ddisgyblaeth)*** *hwn*
breach *be* ***bylchu***, ***torri***
breach of duty *enw* ***tordyletswydd*** *hwn*
bread *enw* ***bara*** *hwn*
breadcrumbs *enw* ***briwsion*** *hyn*
breadth *enw* ***lled*** *hwn*
break *be* ***torri***
to b~ away from ***dianc rhag***
to b~ down ***diffygio***, ***methu'n llwyr***
to b~ down barriers ***dileu ffiniau***
to b~ the mould ***torri tir newydd***
break *enw* ***toriad*** *hwn*, ***egwyl*** *hon*
breakdown *enw* (figures) ***dosraniad*** *hwn*; (health) ***gwaeledd nerfol*** *hwn*
breaker *enw* ***caseg fôr***, ***gwaneg*** *hon*
breakfast *enw* ***brecwast*** *hwn*
breakfast *be* ***brecwasta***
breakneck *ans* ***fel cath i gythraul***
breakthrough *enw* ***datblygiad allweddol/arloesol*** *hwn*
breakwater *enw* ***morglawdd*** *hwn*
breast *enw* ***bron***, ***mynwes*** *hon*
breastbone *enw* ***cledr y ddwyfron*** *hon*

b

breath *enw* ***anadl*** *hon*
breathalyse *be* ***profi anadl***
breathe *be* ***anadlu***
breather *enw* ***saib*** *hwn*
breathless *ans* ***â'm gwynt yn fy nwrn***
breathtaking *ans* ***syfrdanol***
breeches *enw* ***llodrau*** *hyn*
breed *enw* ***brid*** *hwn*, ***gwaedoliaeth*** *hon*
breed *be* ***bridio***, ***magu***
breeder *enw* ***bridiwr***, ***magwr*** *hwn*, ***bridwraig***, ***magwraig*** *hon*
breeding *enw* ***magwraeth*** *hon*
brethren *enw* ***brodyr*** *hyn*
breeze *enw* ***awel*** *hon*
breezy *ans* ***gwyntog***; (lighthearted) ***hwyliog***
brevity *enw* ***byrder:byrdra*** *hwn*
  the need for b~ ***yr angen i fod yn gryno***
brew *be* ***bragu***, ***macsu***; ***bwrw ffrwyth***
brewer *enw* ***bragwr*** *hwn*
brewery *enw* ***bragdy*** *hwn*
briars *enw* ***drysi*** *hyn*
bribe *enw* ***cildwrn*** *hwn*, ***llwgrwobr*** *hon*
bribe *be* ***llwgrwobrwyo***
bribery *enw* ***llwgrwobrwyaeth*** *hon*
bric-a-brac *enw* ***petheuach***, ***trugareddau*** *hyn*
brick *enw* ***bricsen*** *hon*
brick *be* ***bricio***
bricklayer *enw* ***briciwr*** *hwn*
bride *enw* ***priodferch:priodasferch*** *hon*
bridegroom *enw* ***priodfab: priodasfab*** *hwn*
bridesmaid *enw* ***morwyn briodas*** *hon*
bridge *enw* ***pont*** *hon*
bridge *be* ***pontio***
bridle *enw* ***ffrwyn*** *hon*
brief *enw* ***briff***, ***cyfarwyddyd*** *hwn*
brief *ans* ***byr***, ***cwta***
  a b~ history of ***crynodeb o hanes***
  in b~ ***hynny yw***, ***mewn gair***
brief *be* ***briffio***
briefing *enw* ***cyfarwyddyd*** *hwn*, ***rhagdrafodaeth*** *hon*
brigade *enw* ***brigâd*** *hon*
brigand *enw* ***gwylliad*** *hwn*
bright *ans* ***disglair***
brighten *be* ***goleuo***, ***gloywi***
brightness *enw* ***gloywder*** *hwn*
brilliance *enw* ***disgleirdeb: disgleirder*** *hwn*
brilliant *ans* ***disglair***, ***llachar***
brim *enw* ***ymyl*** *hwn/hon*
brimming *ans* ***yn llawn i'r ymylon***
  b~ with confidence ***yn byrlymu o hyder***
brindled *ans* ***brith***
brine *enw* ***dŵr hallt***, ***heli*** *hwn*
bring *be* ***dod â***, ***dwyn***
brink *enw* ***ymyl y dibyn*** *hwn*
  on the b~ of ***ar drothwy***, ***ar fin***
briny *enw* ***heli*** *hwn*

brisk *ans* ***sionc***, ***heini***
briskness *enw* ***sioncrwydd*** *hwn*
bristle *enw* ***gwrychyn*** *hwn*
bristle *be* ***codi gwrychyn***
brittle *ans* ***brau***
broach *be* ***agor***
broad *ans* ***eang***, ***llydan***, ***bras***
broad beans *enw* ***ffa*** *hyn*
broadly *adf* ***yn fras***, ***i gryn raddau***
broad-minded *ans* ***eangfrydig***
broadcast *enw* ***darllediad*** *hwn*
broadcast *be* ***darlledu***
broadcaster *enw* ***darlledwr*** *hwn*, ***darlledwraig*** *hon*
broaden *be* ***ehangu***, ***lledu***
broadness *enw* ***ehangder***, ***lled*** *hwn*
broccoli *enw* ***blodfresych y gaeaf*** *hyn*, ***brocoli*** *hwn*
brochure *enw* ***pamffled: pamffledyn*** *hwn*
broken *ans* ***wedi torri***
broker *enw* ***brocer*** *hwn*
brolly *enw* ***ymbarél*** *hwn/hon*
bronchitis *enw* ***bronceitus*** *hwn*
bronze *enw* ***efydd*** *hwn*
brooch *enw* ***broets*** *hon*, ***tlws*** *hwn*
brood *be* ***gori***; ***pendroni***
brood *enw* ***nythaid*** *hon*
broody *ans* ***clwc***, ***gorllyd***
brook *enw* ***nant*** *hon*
broom *enw* (brush) ***ysgub*** *hon*; (flowers) ***banadl*** *hyn*
broth *enw* ***cawl***, ***potes*** *hwn*
brother *enw* ***brawd*** *hwn*
brother-in-law *enw* ***brawd-yng-nghyfraith*** *hwn*
brotherhood *enw* ***brawdoliaeth*** *hon*
brotherly *ans* ***brawdol***
brow *enw* ***ael*** *hon*
brown *ans* ***brown***
browned off *ans* ***wedi syrffedu***
browse *be* ***pori***
bruise *enw* ***clais*** *hwn*
bruise *be* ***cleisio***
brunt *enw* ***baich*** *hwn*
brush *enw* ***brws*** *hwn*
brush *be* ***ysgubo***, ***brwsio***
brushwood *enw* ***prysgwydd*** *hyn*
brusque *ans* ***swta***
brutal *ans* ***ciaidd***, ***creulon***
brutality *enw* ***creulondeb: creulonder*** *hwn*
brute *enw* ***bwystfil*** *hwn*
  b~ strength ***nerth bôn braich***
  nasty, brutish and short ***byr***, ***brwnt a brau***
bubble *enw* ***swigen***, ***cloch ddŵr*** *hon*
bubble *be* ***byrlymu***
buccaneer *enw* ***môr-leidr*** *hwn*
buck *enw* (deer) ***bwch*** *hwn*
buck *be* ***gwingo***; ***tasgu***
  b~ the trend ***mynd yn groes i'r duedd***
  b~ up ***sirioli drwyddo***
bucket *enw* ***bwced*** *hon/hwn*
buckle *enw* ***bwcl*** *hwn*
busk *ans* ***gwladaidd***
bud *enw* ***eginyn***, ***blaguryn*** *hwn*

bud *be* ***egino***, ***blaguro***
Buddhism *enw* ***Bwdïaeth: Bwdistiaeth*** *hon*
buddy *enw* ***partner*** *hwn*
budge *be* ***symud***
budgerigar *enw* ***bwji*** *hwn*
budget *enw* ***cyllideb*** *hon*
budgetary *ans* ***cyllidebol***
buff *be* ***caboli***
buffalo *enw* ***byfflo*** *hwn*
buffoon *enw* ***hwlpyn gwirion*** *hwn*
buffet *enw* ***pryd bys a bawd***, ***bwffe*** *hwn*
bug *enw* ***lleuen*** *hon*; (computer) ***byg*** *hwn*
build *be* ***codi***, ***adeiladu***
 to b~ into ***ymgorffori***
 to b~ on contacts ***meithrin cysylltiadau pellach***
 to b~ up descriptions ***graddol lunio***
 to b~ up knowledge of ***crynhoi gwybodaeth***
 to b~ up sets of books ***cynnull setiau o lyfrau***
 to b~ up their confidence ***meithrin eu hyder***
builder *enw* ***adeiladydd*** *hwn*
building *enw* ***adeilad*** *hwn*
bulb *enw* ***bwlb*** *hwn*
bulge *be* ***chwyddo***
bulge *enw* ***chwydd*** *hwn*
bulk *enw* ***crynswth***, ***swmp*** *hwn*
bulky *ans* ***swmpus***, ***llwythog***
bull *enw* ***tarw*** *hwn*
bulldozer *enw* ***tarw dur*** *hwn*
bullet *enw* ***bwled*** *hwn/hon*
bulletproof *ans* ***atal bwledi***
bulletin *enw* ***bwletin***, ***hysbysiad*** *hwn*
bullfinch *enw* ***coch y berllan*** *hwn*
bullock *enw* ***bustach*** *hwn*
bullring *enw* ***talwrn teirw*** *hwn*
bully *enw* ***bwli*** *hwn*
bully *be* ***bwlio***, ***gormesu***
bulrushes *enw* ***brwyn*** *hyn*
bum *enw* ***pen ôl*** *hwn*
bumble *be* ***stablad***
bump *enw* ***clonc*** *hon*
bump *be* ***cnocio***
bumper *enw* (car) ***bymper*** *hwn*
 b~ season ***tymor llwyddiannus dros ben***
bumpkin *enw* ***llabwst***, ***llo*** *hwn*
bumptious *ans* ***hunanbwysig***
bumpy *ans* ***anwastad***
bun *enw* ***bynnen*** *hon*
bunch *enw* ***cwlwm***, ***tusw*** *hwn*
bunch *be* ***crynhoi***
bundle *enw* ***bwndel***, ***swp*** *hwn*
bundle *be* ***bwndelu, sypynnu***
bungle *be* ***gwneud cawl o***
bungle *enw* ***stomp*** *hwn/hon*
bunk *enw* ***gwely bach*** *hwn*
 to b~ down ***mynd i'r gwely***
 to b~ off ***diflannu***
bunting *enw* ***baneri*** *hyn*
buoy *enw* ***bwi*** *hwn*
buoyancy *enw* ***hynofedd*** *hwn*
buoyant *ans* ***hynawf***, ***yn nofio***

a b~ market ***marchnad lewyrchus*** *hon*
burble *be* ***byrlymu***
burden *enw* ***baich*** *hwn*
burdened *ans* ***llwythog***
burdensome *ans* ***beichus***
burdock *enw* ***cacamwci*** *hwn*
bureau *enw* ***biwro*** *hwn/hon*
bureaucracy *enw* ***biwrocratiaeth*** *hon*
bureaucrat *enw* ***biwrocrat*** *hwn*
burgeon *be* ***cynyddu***
burglar *enw* ***lleidr*** *hwn*
burgle *be* ***lladrata***
burial *enw* ***claddedigaeth*** *hon*
burly *ans* ***cydnerth***
burn *be* ***llosgi***
to b~ up ***llosgi'n ulw***
burn *enw* ***llosgiad*** *hwn*
burning *ans* ***tanbaid***, ***llosg***
burnish *be* ***gloywi***
burp *be* ***torri gwynt***, ***pecial***
burrow *enw* ***twll*** *hwn*
burrow *be* ***cloddio***, ***turio***
bursary *enw* ***ysgoloriaeth*** *hon*
burst *be* ***byrstio***
bursting *ans* ***methu byw yn eu crwyn***
b~ with ***yn byrlymu o***
bury *be* ***claddu***
bus *enw* ***bws*** *hwn*
bush *enw* ***perth*** *hon*, ***llwyn*** *hwn*
business *enw* ***busnes*** *hwn*
to go about their b~ ***mynd o gwmpas eu pethau***
to go out of b~ ***mynd i'r wal***
businesslike *ans* ***di-lol***
businessman *enw* ***dyn busnes*** *hwn*
businesswoman *enw* ***gwraig fusnes*** *hon*
busk *be* ***chwarae'n ddifyfyr***
bus stop *enw* ***arhosfan*** *hon*
bust *enw* ***penddelw*** *hon*
bustle *enw* ***ffrwst***, ***bwrlwm*** *hwn*
busy *ans* ***prysur***
busybody *enw* ***busnesyn*** *hwn*
but *cysyllt* ***ond***
butcher *enw* ***cigydd*** *hwn*
butcher *be* ***bwtsiera***
butler *enw* ***trulliad*** *hwn*
butt *be* ***cornio***, ***topi***
butt *enw* ***cyff*** *hwn*
butter *enw* ***menyn:ymenyn*** *hwn*
butterfly *enw* ***glöyn byw***, ***pilipala*** *hwn*, ***iâr fach yr haf*** *hon*
buttermilk *enw* ***llaeth enwyn*** *hwn*
buttock *enw* ***boch tin*** *hwn*
button *enw* ***botwm*** *hwn*
button *be* ***botymu***
buttoned *ans* ***botymog***
buttonhole *enw* ***twll botwm***, ***rhwyllyn*** *hwn*
buy *be* ***prynu***
buyer *enw* ***prynwr*** *hwn*, ***prynwraig*** *hon*
buxom *ans* ***llond ei chroen***
buzz *enw* ***su*** *hwn/hon*, ***cyffro*** *hwn*, ***gwefr*** *hon*
buzz *be* ***suo***

buzzard *enw* ***bwncath*** *hwn*
buzzword *enw* ***bwncath*** *hwn*
by ardd ***wrth***; ***gan***; ***erbyn***
  b~ and large ***at ei gilydd***, ***ar y cyfan***
  b~ the way ***gyda llaw***
  drop b~ drop ***fesul diferyn***
  side b~ side ***ochr yn ochr***
  step b~ step ***gam wrth gam***
by-election *enw* ***is-etholiad*** *hwn/hon*
bygone *ans* ***gynt***
by-law *enw* ***is-ddeddf*** *hon*
bypass *enw* ***ffordd osgoi*** *hon*
by-product *enw* ***isgynnyrch*** *hwn*
byre *enw* ***beudy*** *hwn*
byte *enw* ***talp*** *hwn*
byword *enw* ***dihareb*** *hon*

C

cab *enw* ***cab*** *hwn*
cabal *enw* ***clic*** *hwn*
cabbage *enw* ***bresychen*** *hon*
cabin *enw* ***caban*** *hwn*
cabinet *enw* ***cabinet*** *hwn*
cable *enw* ***cebl*** *hwn*
cache *enw* ***celc*** *hwn*
cachet *enw* ***nod amgen*** *hwn*
cackle *be* ***clochdar***
cackle *enw* ***clegar*** *hwn*
cacophony *enw* ***mwstwr*** *hwn*
cactus *enw* ***cactws*** *hwn*
cad *enw* ***cnaf*** *hwn*
cadaver *enw* ***celain*** *hon*
caddie *enw* ***cadi*** *hwn*
cadence *enw* ***diweddeb*** *hon*
cadge *be* ***begian***
caesura *enw* ***gorffwysfa*** *hon*
café *enw* ***caffe*** *hwn*
cage *enw* ***caets***, ***cawell*** *hwn*
cagey *ans* ***cyndyn***, ***gofalus***
cairn *enw* ***carn:carnedd*** *hon*
cajole *be* ***cocsio***
cake *enw* ***teisen*** *hon*
calamitous *ans* ***trychinebus***
calamity *enw* ***trychineb*** *hwn/hon*
calcify *be* ***calcheiddio, ymgaregu***
calcium *enw* ***calsiwm*** *hwn*
calculable *ans* ***mesuradwy***
calculate *be* ***bwrw cyfrif***, ***cyfrifo***
calculation *enw* ***cyfrif*** *hwn*
calculator *enw* ***cyfrifiannell*** *hwn*
calendar *enw* ***calendr*** *hwn*
calf *enw* (animal) ***llo*** *hwn/hon*; (leg) ***croth y goes*** *hon*
calibre *enw* ***calibr*** *hwn*
high c~ students ***myfyrwyr disglair*** *hyn*
call *be* ***galw***
c~ed ***o'r enw***
call *enw* ***galwad*** *hon*
there is no c~ for ***nid oes angen***
calligraphy *enw* ***caligraffi*** *hwn*, ***llythrennu'n gain***
calling *enw* ***galwedigaeth*** *hon*
callous *ans* ***didrugaredd***, ***dienaid***
callousness *enw* ***caledwch*** *hwn*
callow *ans* ***cyw***; ***dibrofiad***
callus *enw* ***corn*** *hwn*
calm *enw* ***tawelwch*** *hwn*
calm *ans* ***tawel***
calm *be* ***tawelu***
to c~ down ***pwyllo***, ***ymbwyllo***
calorie *enw* ***calori*** *hwn*
calumny *enw* ***enllib*** *hwn*
cam *enw* ***cam*** *hwn*
camaraderie *enw* ***cwmnïaeth*** *hon*
camel *enw* ***camel*** *hwn*
camera *enw* ***camera*** *hwn*
in c~ ***yn y dirgel***
camouflage *enw* ***cuddliw*** *hwn*
camp *enw* ***gwersyll*** *hwn*
camp *be* ***gwersylla:gwersyllu***
campaign *enw* ***ymgyrch*** *hwn/hon*
campaign *be* ***ymgyrchu***

C

campaigner *enw* ***ymgyrchydd*** *hwn*
camper *enw* ***gwersyllwr*** *hwn*, ***gwersyllwraig*** *hon*
campsite *enw* ***gwersyllfa*** *hon*
campus *enw* ***campws*** *hwn*
camshaft *enw* ***camwerthyd*** *hon*
can *be* (to be able) ***gallu***
can *enw* ***bocs***, ***can*** *hwn*
can-opener *enw* ***agorwr caniau*** *hwn*
canal *enw* ***camlas*** *hon*
canary *enw* ***caneri*** *hwn*
cancel *be* ***canslo***, ***diddymu***
cancer *enw* ***cancr***, ***canser*** *hwn*
candid *ans* ***agored***, ***didwyll***
candidate *enw* ***ymgeisydd*** *hwn*
  main c~ ***ceffyl blaen*** *hwn*
candidature *enw* ***ymgeisyddiaeth*** *hon*
candle *enw* ***cannwyll*** *hon*
candlestick *enw* ***canhwyllbren*** *hwn*
candour *enw* ***didwylledd*** *hwn*
cane *enw* ***corsen***, ***gwialen*** *hon*
canker *enw* ***cancr*** *hwn*
cannibal *enw* ***canibal*** *hwn*
cannibalism *enw* ***canibaliaeth*** *hon*
cannon *enw* ***canon*** *hwn*, ***magnel*** *hon*
canny *ans* ***craff***, ***hirben***
canoe *enw* ***canŵ*** *hwn*
canon *enw* ***canon*** *hwn*
  in c~ ***y naill ar ôl y llall***
canopy *enw* ***canopi*** *hwn*
cant *be* ***gwyro***
cantankerous *ans* ***cecrus***, ***cynhennus***
canteen *enw* ***cantîn***, ***ffreutur*** *hwn*
canter *be* ***rhygyngu***
cantor *enw* ***codwr canu*** *hwn*
canvas *enw* ***cynfas*** *hwn/hon*
canvass *be* ***canfasio***
canyon *enw* ***ceunant*** *hwn*
cap *enw* ***cap:capan*** *hwn*
  to go c~ in hand ***mynd ar ofyn***
capability *enw* ***gallu*** *hwn*
capable *ans* ***galluog***, ***abl***
capacious *ans* ***cynhwysfawr***
capacity *enw* ***maint***, ***gallu*** *hwn*; ***swyddogaeth*** *hon*
  in a personal c~ ***fel unigolyn***
  to their full c~ ***hyd eu heithaf***
  seating c~ of 50 ***a seddau i 50***
cape *enw* (cloak) ***mantell*** *hon*; (land) ***penrhyn*** *hwn*
caper *be* ***prancio***
capital *ans* ***prif***
capital *enw* ***cyfalaf*** *hwn*
capital punishment *enw* ***y gosb eithaf*** *hon*
capitalism *enw* ***cyfalafiaeth*** *hon*
capitalist *enw* ***cyfalafwr*** *hwn*, ***cyfalafwraig*** *hon*
capitalize *be* ***elwa***
capitation *enw* ***(arian) y pen***
capitulate *be* ***ildio***
capping *be* ***capio***
caprice *enw* ***mympwy*** *hwn*
capricious *ans* ***mympwyol***, ***oriog***
capsize *be* ***dymchwel***
capsule *enw* ***capsiwl*** *hwn*
captain *enw* ***capten*** *hwn*

caption *enw* ***capsiwn, egluryn*** *hwn*; (screen) ***pennawd*** *hwn*
captivate *be* ***swyno***, ***cyfareddu***
captivating *ans* ***cyfareddol***, ***swynol***
captivation *enw* ***cyfaredd*** *hon*
captive *enw* ***carcharor*** *hwn*
captivity *enw* ***caethiwed*** *hwn*
capture *be* ***dal***; ***crisialu***
to c~ the imagination/interest ***tanio***, ***cyffroi***
car *enw* ***car*** *hwn*
carapace *enw* ***cragen*** *hon*
caravan *enw* ***carafán*** *hon*
carbohydrate *enw* ***carbohydrad*** *hwn*
carbon *enw* ***carbon*** *hwn*
carbuncle *enw* ***cornwyd*** *hwn*
carburettor *enw* ***carburedr*** *hwn*
carcass *enw* ***corff*** *hwn*
card *enw* ***carden*** *hon*, ***cerdyn*** *hwn*
cardboard *enw* ***cardfwrdd*** *hwn*
cardinal *ans* ***prif***
cardinal *enw* ***cardinal*** *hwn*
care *enw* ***gofal*** *hwn*
without a c~ in the world ***heb boen/un gofal yn y byd***
care *be* ***gofalu, poeni***
all they c~ about – ***yw'r cyfan iddynt***
those you c~ about ***anwyliaid***
to c~ little for ***malio botwm corn***, ***hidio'r un ffeuen/daten am***
career *enw* ***gyrfa*** *hon*
carefree *ans* ***di-hid***, ***didaro***
careful *ans* ***gofalus***
careless *ans* ***diofal***, ***esgeulus***
carelessness *enw* ***esgeulustod***, ***diofalwch*** *hwn*
caress *enw* ***anwes*** *hwn*
caress *be* ***anwesu***
caretaker *enw* ***gofalwr*** *hwn*, ***gofalwraig*** *hon*
cargo *enw* ***cargo***, ***llwyth*** *hwn*
caricature *enw* ***gwawdlun*** *hwn*
carnage *enw* ***cyflafan*** *hon*
carnal *ans* ***cnawdol***
carnation *enw* ***ceian*** *hon*
carnival *enw* ***cárnifal*** *hwn*
carnivore *enw* ***cigysydd*** *hwn*
carnivorous *ans* ***cigysol***
carol *enw* ***carol*** *hon*
carouse *be* ***cyfeddach***, ***gloddesta***
carousel *enw* ***ceffylau bach*** *hyn*; (projector) ***carwsél*** *hwn*
car park *enw* ***maes parcio*** *hwn*
carpenter *enw* ***saer coed*** *hwn*
carpentry *enw* ***gwaith coed*** *hwn*
carpet *enw* ***carped*** *hwn*
carpet *be* ***carpedu***
carriage *enw* ***cerbyd*** *hwn*
carrier *enw* ***cludydd*** *hwn*
carrots *enw* ***moron*** *hyn*
carry *be* ***cario***, ***cludo***, ***dwyn***; (a motion) ***cymeradwyo***
cart *enw* ***trol*** *hon*
cart *be* ***cartio***
carthorse *enw* ***ceffyl gwedd*** *hwn*
cartilage *enw* ***madruddyn*** *hwn*

C

cartoon *enw* ***cartŵn*** *hwn*
cartoonist *enw* ***cartwnydd*** *hwn*
cartridge *enw* ***cartrisen*** *hon*
carve *be* ***naddu***, ***cerfio***
carved *ans* ***cerfiedig***
carving *enw* ***cerfiad*** *hwn*
cascade *enw* ***rhaeadr*** *hon*
cascade *be* ***rhaeadru***
case *enw* (court) ***achos***; (bag) ***cas:casyn*** *hwn*
as is the c~ with ***fel sy'n digwydd yn achos***
it remains the c~ ***y ffaith amdani yw***
this being the c~ ***felly***
to know if this is the c~ ***gwybod ai felly mae***
cash *enw* ***arian parod*** *hwn*
cashier *enw* ***ariannydd*** *hwn*
casing *enw* ***cragen*** *hon*, ***casyn*** *hwn*
casino *enw* ***casino*** *hwn*
cask *enw* ***casgen*** *hon*
casket *enw* ***blwch*** *hwn*
casserole *enw* ***caserol*** *hwn*
cassette *enw* ***casét*** *hwn*
cassette player *enw* ***chwaraewr casetiau*** *hwn*
cassock *enw* ***casog*** *hon*
cast *enw* (theatre) ***cast*** *hwn*
cast *be* ***bwrw***
to c~ an idea in the form of ***cyflwyno syniad ar ffurf***
caste *enw* ***cast***, ***dosbarth*** *hwn*
castellated *ans* ***castellog***
castigate *be* ***cystwyo***
cast iron *enw* ***haearn bwrw*** *hwn*
castle *enw* ***castell*** *hwn*
cast-offs *enw* ***sborion*** *hyn*
castrate *be* ***disbaddu***, ***ysbaddu***
castration *enw* ***disbaddiad*** *hwn*
casual *ans* ***damweiniol***, ***anffurfiol***
to the c~ observer ***ar yr olwg gyntaf***
cat *enw* ***cath*** *hon*
catacomb *enw* ***mynwent danddaearol*** *hon*
catalogue *enw* ***catalog*** *hwn*, ***rhestr*** *hon*
catalyst *enw* ***catalydd*** *hwn*
catapult *enw* ***blif*** *hwn*, ***ffon dafl*** *hon*
cataract *enw* (waterfall) ***rhaeadr***; (eye) ***pilen*** *hon*
catastrophe *enw* ***trychineb*** *hwn/hon*
catch *be* ***dal***
catch *enw* ***dalfa*** *hon*
catch-all *ans* ***dal-popeth***, ***cynhwysfawr***
catching *ans* ***heintus***
catchment area *enw* ***dalgylch*** *hwn*
catchphrase *enw* ***ymadrodd bachog*** *hwn*
catchword *enw* ***slogan*** *hwn/hon*
catchy *ans* ***bachog***, ***trawiadol***
catechism *enw* ***holwyddoreg*** *hon*
categorical *ans* ***pendant***
categorize *be* ***categoreiddio***
category *enw* ***dosbarth***, ***categori*** *hwn*

cater *be* ***arlwyo***
caterers *enw* ***arlwywyr*** *hyn*
catering *enw* ***arlwyaeth*** *hon*
caterpillar *enw* ***lindys*** *hwn*
cathedral *enw* ***eglwys gadeiriol***, ***cadeirlan*** *hon*
catholic *ans* ***catholig***
catkins *enw* ***cynffonau ŵyn bach*** *hyn*
catnap *enw* ***cyntun*** *hwn*
cattle *enw* ***gwartheg*** *hyn*
caucus *enw* ***cawcws*** *hwn*, ***carfan*** *hon*
caul *enw* ***breithell*** *hon*
cauldron *enw* ***crochan*** *hwn*
cauliflower *enw* ***blodfresychen*** *hon*
causation *enw* ***achosiaeth*** *hon*
cause *enw* ***achos*** *hwn*
  in the common c~ ***er lles pawb***
cause *be* ***achosi***
causeway *enw* ***sarn*** *hon*
caustic *ans* ***brathog***; (chem.) ***ysol, costig***
cauterize *be* ***serio***
caution *enw* ***pwyll***, ***gofal*** *hwn*
  a word of c~ ***gair i gall***
caution *enw* (warning) ***rhybudd*** *hwn*
caution *be* ***rhybuddio***
cautious *ans* ***gofalus***, ***gwyliadwrus***
cavalcade *enw* ***gorymdaith*** *hon*
cavalry *enw* ***gwŷr meirch*** *hyn*
cave *enw* ***ogof*** *hon*
cavern *enw* ***ceudwll*** *hwn*
cavil *be* ***pigo bai***
cavity *enw* ***ceudod*** *hwn*
cavort *be* ***llamsachu***
cease *be* ***peidio***, ***darfod***
ceaseless *ans* ***di-baid***
cedars *enw* ***cedrwydd*** *hyn*
cede *be* ***ildio***
ceiling *enw* ***nenfwd*** *hwn*
  up to a c~ of ***hyd at derfyn***
celebrate *be* ***dathlu***, ***canu clodydd***
celebrated *ans* ***enwog***, ***nodedig***
celebration *enw* ***dathliad*** *hwn*
celebrities *enw* ***enwogion*** *hyn*
celerity *enw* ***cyflymder*** *hwn*
celery *enw* ***helogan*** *hon*
celestial *ans* ***nefol***
celibate *ans* ***diwair***, ***dibriod***
cell *enw* ***cell*** *hon*
cellar *enw* ***seler*** *hon*
cello *enw* ***soddgrwth*** *hwn*
celluloid *enw* ***seliwloid*** *hwn*
Celsius *ans* ***canradd***
Celtic *ans* ***Celtaidd***
cement *enw* ***sment*** *hwn*
cement *be* ***smentio***; ***cydio'n dynn yn ei gilydd***
cemetery *enw* ***mynwent*** *hon*
censure *enw* ***cerydd*** *hwn*
censure *be* ***ceryddu***
cenotaph *enw* ***cofadail*** *hon*
censor *enw* ***sensor*** *hwn*
censorship *enw* ***sensoriaeth*** *hon*
censure *be* ***ceryddu***
census *enw* ***cyfrifiad*** *hwn*

C

centaur *enw* ***dynfarch*** *hwn*
centenary *enw* **canmlwyddiant** *hwn*
centigrade *ans* ***canradd***
centimetre *enw* ***centimetr*** *hwn*
centipede *enw* ***cantroed*** *hwn*
central *ans* ***canolog***
centralize *be* ***canoli***
centre *enw* (building) ***canolfan*** *hwn/hon*; (middle) ***canol*** *hwn*
centre *be* ***canoli***
centre of gravity *enw* ***craidd disgyrchiant*** *hwn*
centrifugal *ans* ***allgyrchol***
centurion *enw* ***canwriad*** *hwn*
century *enw* ***canrif*** *hon*
ceramic *ans* ***ceramig***
ceramics *enw* ***cerameg*** *hon*
cereal *enw* ***grawnfwyd*** *hwn*
cerebral *ans* ***ymenyddol***
ceremonial *ans* ***defodol***, ***seremonïol***
ceremony *enw* ***defod***, ***seremoni*** *hon*
certain *ans* ***sicr***, ***siŵr***, ***diamau***
certainly *adf* ***yn sicr***, ***yn bendant***; ***wrth gwrs***
certainty *enw* ***sicrwydd*** *hwn*
certificate *enw* ***tystysgrif*** *hon*
certification *enw* ***ardystiad*** *hwn*
certify *be* ***tystio***, ***ardystio***
certitude *enw* ***sicrwydd*** *hwn*
cessation *enw* ***diwedd***, ***terfyn*** *hwn*
chafe *be* ***rhwbio***
chaff *enw* ***us*** *hyn*
chaffinch *enw* ***ji-binc***, ***asgell arian*** *hon*
chagrin *enw* ***siom*** *hwn/hon*
chain *enw* ***cadwyn*** *hon*
chain *be* ***cadwyno***
chair *enw* ***cadair*** *hon*
chair *be* ***cadeirio***
chairman *enw* ***cadeirydd*** *hwn*
chairperson *enw* ***cadeirydd*** *hwn*
chalice *enw* ***caregl*** *hwn*
chalk *enw* ***sialc*** *hwn*
  by a long chalk ***o ddigon***, ***o bell ffordd***
challenge *enw* ***her*** *hon*
challenge *be* ***herio***
challenger *enw* ***heriwr*** *hwn*
challenging *ans* (questioning) ***herfeiddiol***; (full of challenges) ***llawn her***
chamber *enw* ***siambr*** *hon*
chameleon *enw* ***camelion*** *hwn*
champ *be* ***cnoi***
champion *enw* ***pencampwr*** *hwn*, ***pencampwraig*** *hon*; ***pleidiwr*** *hwn*, ***hyrwyddwr*** *hwn*
champion *be* ***amddiffyn***
champion *be* ***dadlau'n gryf o blaid***; ***hyrwyddo defnydd***
championship *enw* ***pencampwriaeth*** *hon*
chance *enw* ***hap***, ***damwain*** *hon*, ***siawns*** *hwn/hon*; (opportunity) ***cyfle***, ***gobaith*** *hwn*, ***siawns*** *hwn/hon*
  there's little c~ ***go brin y bydd***

to take a c~ ***mentro***
chance *be* (happen) ***digwydd***; (risk) ***mentro***
if you c~ to see him ***os digwyddwch ei weld***
to c~ it ***ei mentro hi***
chancel *enw* ***cangell*** *hon*
chancellor *enw* ***canghellor*** *hwn*
change *be* ***newid***
things have c~d considerably ***bu tro ar fyd***
change *enw* ***newid*** *hwn*
changeable *ans* ***cyfnewidiol***
changeless *ans* ***digyfnewid***
channel *enw* ***sianel*** *hon*
channel *be* ***sianelu***
chant *enw* ***salm-dôn*** *hon*
chant *be* ***llafarganu***
chaos *enw* ***anhrefn*** *hon*
chaotic *ans* ***anhrefnus***, ***cawl gwyllt***
chapel *enw* ***capel*** *hwn*
chaplain *enw* ***caplan*** *hwn*
chapter *enw* ***pennod*** *hon*
char *enw* (fish) ***torgoch*** *hwn*
char *be* ***golosgi***
character *enw* (person) ***cymeriad*** *hwn*; (symbol, letter etc.) ***nod*** *hwn*; (nature) ***cymeriad*** *hwn*, ***nodwedd*** *hon*
the c~ of the work ***natur y gwaith***;
characteristic *ans* ***nodweddiadol***
characteristics *enw* ***nodweddion*** *hyn*
characterize *be* ***cymeriadu***
characterless *ans* ***digymeriad***
charcoal *enw* ***golosg***, ***sercol*** *hwn*
charge *be* (price) ***codi***; (attack) ***hyrddio***; (command) ***siarsio***; (responsibility) ***rhoi cyfrifoldeb i***; (crime) ***cyhuddo***
to be firmly in c~ ***bod â'r awennau'n dynn yn eu dwylo***
charge *enw* (price) ***pris***, ***tâl*** *hwn*
free of c~ ***am ddim***, ***yn ddi-dâl***; (assault) ***rhuthr***, ***ymosodiad*** *hwn*; (court) ***cyhuddiad*** *hwn*
charge nurse *enw* ***prif weinydd*** *(hwn)*/***prif weinyddes*** *(hon)* ***nyrsio***
charges *enw* (price) ***codiannau***; (allegations) ***cyhuddiadau*** *hyn*
charisma *enw* ***carisma*** *hwn*
charismatic *ans* ***carismataidd***, ***cyfareddol***
charitable *ans* ***elusennol***
charity *enw* ***elusen*** *hon*
charm *enw* ***swyn*** *hwn*
keep the c~ of the original ***cadw apêl y gwreiddiol***
charm *be* ***swyno***
charming *ans* ***swynol***
chart *enw* ***siart*** *hon*
chart *be* ***siartio***, ***olrhain***
charter *enw* ***siarter***, ***breinlen*** *hon*
charter *be* ***llogi***
chary *ans* ***cyndyn***
chase *be* ***hela***, ***ymlid***
chase *enw* ***helfa*** *hon*
chasm *enw* ***(g)agendor*** *hwn/hon*

C

chassis *enw* ***ffrâm*** *hon*
chaste *ans* ***diwair***
chastise *be* ***cosbi***, ***cystuddio***
chastisement *enw* ***cosbedigaeth*** *hon*
chastity *enw* ***diweirdeb*** *hwn*
chat *be* ***sgwrsio***
chat *enw* ***sgwrs*** *hon*
chatter *enw* (persons) ***mân siarad, cleber*** *hwn*; (birds) ***clegar***, ***trydar***, ***cogor***
chatter *be* (persons) ***clebran***; (birds) ***clegar***, ***trydar***, ***cogor***
chatterbox *enw* ***cloncen*** *hon,* ***clebryn*** *hwn,* ***clebren*** *hon*
chatty *ans* ***siaradus***
chauffeur *enw* ***gyrrwr*** *hwn*
chauffeuse *enw* ***gyrwraig*** *hon*
chauvinist *enw* ***siofinydd*** *hwn*
cheap *ans* ***rhad***
  c~ crack ***rhyw sylw ceiniog a dimai***
cheapen *be* ***gostwng (pris/gwerth)***
cheat *be* ***twyllo***
cheat *enw* ***twyllwr*** *hwn*, ***twyllwraig*** *hon*
check *be* ***gwirio***, ***bwrw golwg dros***
  c~ for ***chwiliwch am***
  c~ it out ***holwch***, ***ewch i weld***
  c~ with them ***eu holi***
  please c~ the following ***a yw'r canlynol yn gywir?***
check *enw* ***gwiriad*** *hwn*
  c~s and balances ***rhwystrau a gwrthbwysau*** *hyn*
checklist *enw* ***rhestr gyfeirio*** *hon*
check-up *enw* ***archwiliad*** *hwn*
cheek *enw* (face) ***boch*** *hon*; (impoliteness) ***haerllugrwydd*** *hwn*
  he's got a c~ ***mae wyneb gydag e***
cheer *enw* ***bonllef***, ***cymeradwyaeth*** *hon*
cheer *be* ***bloeddio***
cheerful *ans* ***siriol***, ***llon***
cheerfulness *enw* ***sirioldeb*** *hwn*
cheers! *ebychiad* ***hwyl! iechyd da!***
cheese *enw* ***caws*** *hwn*
chef *enw* ***pen-cogydd*** *hwn*
chemical *enw* ***cemegyn*** *hwn*
chemical *ans* ***cemegol***
chemist *enw* ***cemegydd***, ***fferyllydd*** *hwn*
chemistry *enw* ***cemeg*** *hon*
cheque *enw* ***siec*** *hon*
chequered *ans* ***brith***
cherish *be* ***anwylo***, ***coleddu***
cherry *enw* ***ceiriosen*** *hon*
chess *enw* ***gwyddbwyll*** *hon*
chest *enw* ***brest*** *hon*; (box) ***cist*** *hon*
chestnut *enw* ***castan*** *hon*
chew *be* ***cnoi***
chicanery *enw* ***twyll*** *hwn*
chick *enw* ***cyw*** *hwn*
chicken *enw* ***cyw iâr***, ***ffowlyn*** *hwn*
chicken-pox *enw* ***brech yr ieir*** *hon*
chide *be* ***ceryddu***
chief *ans* ***prif***

chief *enw* ***pennaeth*** *hwn*
  Chief Examiner *Prif Arholwr*
chieftain *enw* ***pennaeth*** *hwn*
chilblains *enw* ***cibwst*** *hon*, ***llosg eira, maleithau*** *hyn*
child *enw* ***plentyn*** *hwn*
  a true c~ of the soil *hen ŷd y wlad*
child abuse *be* ***cam-drin plant***
childbirth *enw* ***genedigaeth*** *hon*
childcare *enw* ***gofal plant*** *hwn*
  childcare assistant *cynorthwy-ydd gofal plant* *hwn*
  childcare worker *gweithiwr gofal plant* *hwn*
child-centred *ans* ***plentyn ganolog***
child detention *enw* ***cadw plant i mewn***
child guidance *enw* ***cyfarwyddo plant***
childhood *enw* ***plentyndod*** *hwn*
childish *ans* ***plentynnaidd***
childminder *enw* ***gwarchodwr plant*** *hwn*
children *enw* ***plant*** *hyn*
child with a statement *enw* ***plentyn ar ddatganiad*** *hwn*
chill *enw* ***oerfel, annwyd*** *hwn*
chill *be* ***oeri***
chilling *ans* ***iasoer***
chilly *ans* ***oeraidd***
chimney *enw* ***simdde:simnai*** *hon*
chimney stack *enw* ***corn simne*** *hwn*
chimpanzee *enw* ***tsimpansî*** *hwn*
chin *enw* ***gên*** *hon*
chink *enw* ***agen*** *hon*
chinwag *be* ***sgwrsio***
chip *be* ***naddu***
chip *enw* ***sglodyn*** *hwn*
chippings *enw* ***graean*** *hyn*
chirp *be* ***trydar***
chirpy *ans* ***sionc***
chisel *enw* ***cŷn*** *hwn*, ***gaing*** *hon*
chivalry *enw* ***sifalri*** *hwn*
chloride *enw* ***clorid*** *hwn*
chlorine *enw* ***clorin*** *hwn*
chock *enw* ***lletem*** *hon*
chocolate *enw* ***siocled*** *hwn*
choice *enw* ***dewis*** *hwn*; ***amrywiaeth*** *hon*
choice *ans* ***amheuthun***; ***dethol***
choir *enw* ***côr*** *hwn*
choke *enw* (car) ***tagydd*** *hwn*
choke *be* ***tagu***
choose *be* ***dewis***, ***dethol***
  to choose from *dewis o blith*
chop *be* ***torri***
chop *enw* (meat) ***golwyth*** *hwn*
choral *ans* ***corawl***
chord *enw* ***cord*** *hwn*
chore *enw* ***gorchwyl*** *hwn*, ***tasg*** *hon*
chorus *enw* ***cytgan*** *hon*, ***corws*** *hwn*
christen *be* ***bedyddio***
christening *enw* ***bedydd*** *hwn*
Christian *ans* ***Cristnogol***
Christian *enw* ***Cristion*** *hwn*
Christmas *enw* ***Nadolig*** *hwn*

Christmas Eve *enw* ***Noswyl y Nadolig*** *hon*
chromosome *enw* ***cromosom*** *hwn*
chronic *ans* ***cronig***, ***di-baid***
chronicle *enw* ***cronicl*** *hwn*
chronicle *be* ***croniclo***
chronicler *enw* ***croniclydd***, ***cofiadur*** *hwn*
chronological *ans* ***cronolegol***
chronology *enw* ***cronoleg*** *hon*
chronometer *enw* ***amserydd*** *hwn*
chrysalis *enw* ***chwiler*** *hwn*
chubby *ans* ***llond ei groen***
chuck *be* ***rhoi ffling***
chuckle *enw* ***chwerthiniad bach*** *hwn*
chum *enw* ***mêt***, ***cyfaill*** *hwn*
chump *enw* ***hurtyn*** *hwn*
chunk *enw* ***talp***, ***cwlffyn*** *hwn*
church *enw* ***eglwys*** *hon*
churlish *ans* ***anfoesgar***, ***sarrug***
churn *enw* (for turning) ***buddai*** *hon*; (milk-can) ***can llaeth*** *hwn*
churn *be* ***corddi***
chute *enw* ***llithren*** *hon*
chutney *enw* ***catwad*** *hwn*
cider *enw* ***seidr*** *hwn*
cigar *enw* ***sigâr*** *hon*
cigarette *enw* ***sigarét*** *hon*
cinder *enw* ***colsyn***, ***marworyn*** *hwn*
cinema *enw* ***sinema*** *hwn*
cinematics *enw* ***sinemateg*** *hon*
cinnamon *enw* ***sinamon*** *hwn*
circa *ardd* ***tua***
circle *enw* ***cylch*** *hwn*
circle *be* ***cylchu***
circuit *enw* ***cylchdaith***; (electrical) ***cylched*** *hon*
circuitous *ans* ***trofaus***
circular *ans* ***crwn***
circular *enw* (letter) ***cylchlythyr*** *hwn*
circulate *be* ***cylchredeg***
circulation *enw* ***cylchrediad*** *hwn*
 circulation spaces ***mannau tramwy***
circumcise *be* ***enwaedu***
circumference *enw* ***cylchedd*** *hwn*
circumflex *enw* ***to bach*** *hwn*
circumnavigation *enw* ***mordaith (o gwmpas)*** *hon*
circumscribed *ans* ***cyfyng***
circumspect *ans* ***gochelgar***
circumspection *enw* ***gochelgarwch***, ***pwyll*** *hwn*
circumstance *enw* ***amgylchiad*** *hwn*
circumvent *be* ***osgoi***, ***twyllo***
circus *enw* ***syrcas*** *hon*
cirque *enw* ***peiran*** *hwn*
cistern *enw* ***tanc dŵr*** *hwn*
citadel *enw* ***caer ddinesig*** *hon*
cite *be* ***gwysio***; ***dyfynnu***, ***cyfeirio at***
citizen *enw* ***dinesydd*** *hwn*
Citizens' Advice Bureau *enw* ***Canolfan Gynghori*** *hon*
citizenship *enw* ***dinasyddiaeth*** *hon*
city *enw* ***dinas*** *hon*
civic *ans* ***dinesig***

civil *ans* ***sifil***
civilian *enw* ***dinesydd (preifat)*** *hwn*
civility *enw* ***gwarineb*** *hwn*
civilization *enw* ***gwareiddiad*** *hwn*
civilize *be* ***gwareiddio***
civilized *ans* ***gwâr***
claim *be* ***hawlio***, ***honni***
claim *enw* ***cais***; ***honiad*** *hwn*
c~ to fame ***dyma'u camp fwyaf nodedig***
claimant *enw* ***hawliwr***, ***hawlydd*** *hwn*
clamber *be* ***dringo***
clamorous *ans* ***croch***
clamour *enw* ***twrw, dadwrdd*** *hwn*; ***holl alw***
clamp *enw* ***clamp*** *hwn*
clamp *be* ***clampio***
clan *enw* ***llwyth*** *hwn*
clandestine *ans* ***dirgel***
clank *enw* ***clonc*** *hwn*
clap *be* ***curo dwylo***
clapper *enw* (bell) ***tafod*** *hwn*
claptrap *enw* ***ffregod*** *hon*, ***dwli*** *hwn*
clarification *enw* ***eglurhad*** *hwn*
points requiring c~ ***pwyntiau aneglur*** *hyn*
clarify *be* ***egluro***, ***gloywi***, ***dangos yn fwy eglur***
clarinet *enw* ***clarinét*** *hwn*
clarity *enw* ***eglurder***, ***gloywder*** *hwn*
clash *be* ***gwrthdaro***
clasp *enw* ***clesbyn*** *hwn*
clasp *be* ***gwasgu'n dynn***
class *enw* ***dosbarth*** *hwn*
top class ***o'r radd flaenaf***
class *be* ***dosbarthu***
classic(al) *ans* ***clasurol***
classics *enw* ***clasuron*** *hyn*
classification *enw* ***dosbarthiad*** *hwn*
classify *be* ***dosbarthu***
classroom *enw* ***ystafell ddosbarth*** *hon*
clatter *be* ***clindarddach***
clatter *enw* ***twrw*** *hwn*
clause *enw* ***cymal*** *hwn*
clavicle *enw* ***pont yr ysgwydd*** *hon*
claw *enw* ***crafanc*** *hon*
clawback *be* ***adfachu***
clay *enw* ***clai*** *hwn*
clean *ans* ***glân***
clean *be* ***glanhau***
cleaner *enw* ***glanhawr*** *hwn*, ***glanhawraig*** *hon*
cleaning *enw* ***glanhad:glanheuad*** *hwn*
cleanliness *enw* ***glanweithdra: glendid*** *hwn*
cleanse *be* ***glanhau***
clear *ans* ***clir***, ***eglur***
clear *be* ***clirio***
clear-cut *ans* ***hollol glir***
clearing *enw* ***llannerch*** *hon*
clearing house *enw* ***cyfnewidfa*** *hon*
cleave *be* ***hollti***

cleave to *be* ***ymlynu (wrth)***
cleaver *enw* ***twca*** *hwn*
cleft *enw* ***hollt*** *hon*
clemency *enw* ***trugaredd*** *hon/hwn*
clement *ans* ***tirion***
clench *be* ***cau***, ***clensio***, ***gwasgu***
clergy *enw* ***offeiriaid*** *hyn*
clergyman *enw* ***clerigwr*** *hwn*
clerical *ans* ***clerigol***
clerk *enw* ***clerc*** *hwn*
clever *ans* ***craff***; ***medrus***, ***peniog***
cleverness *enw* ***clyfrwch*** *hwn*
cliché *enw* ***ystrydeb*** *hon*
click *be* ***clicio***
click *enw* ***clic*** *hwn*
client *enw* ***cwsmer***, ***cleient*** *hwn*
cliff *enw* ***clogwyn*** *hwn*
climate *enw* ***hinsawdd*** *hon*
climatic *ans* ***hinsoddol***
climax *enw* ***anterth***, ***uchafbwynt*** *hwn*
climb *be* ***dringo***
climber *enw* ***dringwr*** *hwn*
cling *be* ***glynu***
clinic *enw* ***clinig*** *hwn*
clinical *ans* ***clinigol***
clip *enw* (film) ***pwt*** *hwn*; (slap on the ear) ***bonclust*** *hwn*, ***clusten*** *hon*
clip *be* (fasten) ***clipio***, ***cydio***; (shear/cut) ***cneifio***, ***tocio***, ***clipio***
clique *enw* ***ciwed*** *hon*
cloak *enw* ***clogyn***, ***mantell*** *hon*
cloak *be* ***taflu mantell dros***
cloakroom *enw* ***ystafell gotiau*** *hon*
clock *enw* ***cloc*** *hwn*
clockwise *ans* ***clocwedd***
clockwork *enw* ***clocwaith*** *hwn*
  work like c~ ***rhedeg fel wats***
clod *enw* ***tywarchen*** *hon*
clog *enw* ***clocsen*** *hon*
clog *be* **arafu**, **tagu**
cloister *enw* ***clas***, ***clwysty*** *hwn*
close *be* ***cau***
close *enw* ***diwedd*** *hwn*
  draw to a c~ ***dirwyn i ben***
close *ans* (distance) ***agos***; (in relation to) ***clòs***, ***tynn***; (weather) ***mwll***, ***trymaidd***, ***clòs***
  keep a close eye on ***cadw llygad barcud ar***
closed *ans* ***ar gau***
closeness *enw* (physical) ***agosrwydd*** *hwn*; (intimacy) ***agosatrwydd***
clot *enw* (blood) ***tolch***, ***tolchen*** *hon*
clot *be* ***ceulo***, ***tolchennu***
cloth *enw* ***brethyn***, ***lliain*** *hwn*
clothe *be* ***dilladu***
clothes *enw* ***dillad*** *hyn*
clothing *enw* ***gwisg*** *hon*
cloud *enw* ***cwmwl*** *hwn*
cloud *be* ***cymylu***
cloudy *ans* ***cymylog***
clout *enw* ***bonclust*** *hwn*, ***cernod*** *hon*
clove *enw* (garlic) ***ewin*** *hwn/hon*
clover *enw* ***meillion*** *hyn*
clown *enw* ***clown*** *hwn*

club *enw* ***pastwn***; (institution) ***clwb*** *hwn*
club *be* ***pastynu***
cluck *be* ***clegar***
clue *enw* ***cliw*** *hwn*
  they haven't a c~ ***maent yn gwbl ddi-glem***
clueless *ans* ***di-glem***
clumsiness *enw* ***lletchwithdod*** *hwn*
clumsy *ans* ***lletchwith***, ***trwsgl***, ***afrosgo***
  c~ child syndrome *enw* ***syndrom plentyn afrosgo*** *hwn*
cluster *enw* ***clwstwr***, ***cwlwm*** *hwn*
cluster *be* ***clystyru***
clutch *enw* ***cydiwr***, ***clyts*** *hwn*
clutch *be* ***gafael***
clutter *enw* ***annibendod*** *hwn*
coach *enw* (bus) ***coets*** *hon*; (trainer) ***hyfforddwr*** *hwn*, ***hyfforddwraig*** *hon*
coach *be* ***hyfforddi***
coagulate *be* ***ceulo***
coal *enw* ***glo*** *hwn*
coalesce *be* ***ymdoddi***
coalfield *enw* ***maes glo*** *hwn*
coalition *enw* ***clymblaid*** *hon*
coal-mine *enw* ***pwll glo*** *hwn*, ***glofa*** *hon*
coarse *ans* ***garw***; ***aflednais***
coast *enw* ***arfordir*** *hwn*
coastal *ans* ***arfordirol***
coastguard *enw* ***gwyliwr y glannau*** *hwn*
coat *enw* ***cot***, ***côt*** *hon*
coating *enw* ***cot***, ***côt***, ***haen*** *hon*
coax *be* ***perswadio***
cobbler *enw* ***crydd*** *hwn*
cobweb *enw* ***gwe pry copyn*** *hon*
cock *enw* ***ceiliog*** *hwn*
  c~ and hen (brickwork) ***dafad ac oen***
cockabundy *enw* ***coch y bonddu*** *hwn*
cockatoo *enw* ***cocatŵ*** *hwn*
cockcrow *enw* (sound) ***caniad ceiliog***; (morning) ***glas y dydd*** *hwn*
cockerel *enw* ***ceiliog*** *hwn*
cockles *enw* ***cocos***, ***rhython*** *hyn*
cockpit *enw* ***talwrn*** *hwn*
cockscomb *enw* ***crib ceiliog*** *hwn*
cocky *ans* ***larts***, ***ewn***, ***hyf***, ***talog***
cocoa *enw* ***coco*** *hwn*
coconut *enw* ***cneuen goco*** *hon*
cocoon *enw* ***cocŵn*** *hwn*
cod *enw* ***penfras*** *hwn*
code *enw* ***cod*** *hwn*
code *be* ***codio***
code of conduct *enw* ***cod ymddygiad*** *hwn*
code of practice *enw* ***cod ymarfer*** *hwn*
codpiece *enw* ***balog*** *hwn*
co-educational *ans* ***cydaddysgol***
coerce *be* ***gorfodi***
coercion *enw* ***gorfodaeth*** *hon*
coexist *be* ***cyd-fyw***
coexistence *enw* ***cydfodolaeth*** *hon*

coffee *enw* ***coffi*** *hwn*
coffer *enw* ***coffr*** *hwn/hon*
coffin *enw* ***arch*** *hon*
cog *enw* ***cocsyn*** *hwn*, ***cocsen*** *hon*, ***dant*** *hwn*
cogency *enw* ***grym***, ***argyhoeddiad*** *hwn*
cogent *ans* ***grymus***, ***cryf***
cogitate *be* ***synfyfyrio***
cognate *ans* ***cytras***
cognisance *enw* ***gwybyddiaeth*** *hon*
to take c~ of ***cymryd i ystyriaeth***
cognition *enw* ***gwybyddiaeth*** *hon*
cognitive *ans* ***gwybyddol***
cogwheel *enw* ***olwyn gocos*** *hon*
cohabit *be* ***cyd-fyw***, ***byw tali***
cohabitation *be* ***cyd-fyw***
cohere *be* ***cydlynu***
coherence *enw* ***cydlyniad*** *hwn*
coherent *ans* (logical) ***yn dal dŵr***, ***rhesymegol***; (of parts) ***cydlynol***; (of language) ***dealladwy***
cohesion *enw* ***cydlyniad*** *hwn*
cohesive *ans* ***ymlynol***
cohort *enw* ***carfan*** *hon*
coil *enw* ***torch*** *hon*
coil *be* ***torchi***
coin *enw* ***darn arian*** *hwn*
coin *be* ***bathu***
coincide *be* ***cyd-daro***, ***cyd-ddigwydd***
coincidence *enw* ***cyd-ddigwyddiad*** *hwn*
coitus *enw* ***cyfathrach rywiol*** *hon*
coke *enw* ***golosg*** *hwn*
colander *enw* ***colandr*** *hwn*, ***hidl*** *hon*
cold *ans* ***oer***
cold *enw* (weather) ***oerfel***; (illness) ***annwyd*** *hwn*
collaborate *be* ***cydweithio***
collaboration *enw* ***cydweithrediad*** *hwn*
in c~ with ***ar y cyd â***
collaborative *ans* ***cydweithredol***
collage *enw* ***gludlun***, ***gludwaith*** *hwn*
collapse *enw* ***cwymp*** *hwn*
collapse *be* ***dymchwelyd***, ***syrthio***, ***mynd â'i ben iddo***, ***mynd i'r gwellt***
collapsible *ans* ***plygadwy***
collar *enw* ***coler*** *hon/hwn*
collarbone *enw* ***pont yr ysgwydd*** *hon*
collate *be* ***coladu***
collateral *ans* ***cyfochrog***
colleague *enw* ***cydweithiwr*** *hwn*, ***cydweithwraig*** *hon*
collect *be* ***casglu***, ***hel***
collection *enw* **casgliad** *hwn*
collective *ans* ***cyd-***
c~ agreement ***cydgytundeb*** *hwn*
c~ bargaining ***cydfargeinio*** *hwn*
c~ leadership ***cydarweinyddiaeth*** *hon*
c~ listening ***gwrando torfol*** *hwn*

c~ responsibility *cydgyfrifoldeb* hwn
c~ worship *cydaddoliad* hwn
collector *enw* ***casglwr***, ***casglydd*** *hwn*
college *enw* ***coleg*** *hwn*
collegiality *enw* ***colegoldeb*** *hwn*; ***cydymdrechu'n gytûn***
collegiate *ans* ***colegol***
collide *be* ***gwrthdaro***
collie *enw* ***ci defaid*** *hwn*
collier *enw* ***glöwr*** *hwn*
colliery *enw* ***glofa*** *hon*, ***pwll glo*** *hwn*
collision *enw* ***gwrthdrawiad*** *hwn*
colloquial *ans* ***llafar***
colloquialism *enw* ***ymadrodd llafar***, ***gwerinair*** *hwn*
collude *be* ***cynllwynio***, ***cydgynllwynio***
collusion *enw* ***cydgynllwyn*** *hwn*
collusive *ans* ***cydgynllwyngar***
colon *enw* ***colon*** *hwn*
colonel *enw* ***cyrnol*** *hwn*
colonial *ans* ***trefedigaethol***, ***gwladychol***
colonize *be* ***gwladychu***
colony *enw* ***gwladfa***, ***trefedigaeth*** *hon*
colossal *ans* ***enfawr***
colour *enw* ***lliw*** *hwn*
colour *be* ***lliwio***
colour-blind *ans* ***dall i liwiau***
colour blindness *enw* ***dallineb lliw*** *hwn*
coloured *ans* ***lliw***
colourful *ans* ***lliwgar***
colourless *ans* ***di-liw***
colt *enw* ***ebol***, ***swclyn*** *hwn*
column *enw* ***colofn*** *hon*
columnist *enw* ***colofnydd*** *hwn*
coma *enw* ***côma*** *hwn*
comatose *ans* ***swrth***, ***mewn côma***
comb *enw* ***crib*** *hon/hwn*
comb *be* ***cribo***
combat *enw* ***gornest*** *hon*
combat *be* ***ymladd yn erbyn***, ***mynd i'r afael â***
combatant *enw* ***ymladdwr*** *hwn*
combination *enw* ***cyfuniad*** *hwn*
combine *be* ***cyfuno***; ***priodi***
combine harvester *enw* ***combein*** *hwn*
combustible *ans* ***hylosg***
combustion *enw* ***hylosgiad*** *hwn*
come *be* ***dod:dyfod***
c~ across ***taro ar***
c~ along ***dewch ymlaen***, ***dewch atom***
c~ Friday ***erbyn dydd Gwener***, ***ddydd Gwener***
c~ to realise ***dechrau sylweddoli***
c~ to that ***petai'n dod i hynny***
c~ up with an idea ***meddwl am syniad***
in years to c~ ***ymhen blynyddoedd***
when it c~s to ***pan ddaw hi'n fater o***

C

comedian *enw* ***digrifwr*** *hwn*
comedienne *enw* ***digrifwraig*** *hon*
comedy *enw* ***comedi*** *hon*
comely *ans* ***gosgeiddig***
comet *enw* ***comed***, ***seren gynffon*** *hon*
comfort *enw* ***cysur*** *hwn*
  from the c~ of your own home ***heb symud cam oddi cartref***
comfort *be* ***cysuro***
comfortable *ans* ***cyfforddus***
comforting *ans* ***cysurlon***, ***llawn cysur***
comic(al) *ans* ***digrif***, ***smala***
comma *enw* ***atalnod*** *hwn*
command *be* ***gorchymyn***
command *enw* ***gorchymyn*** *hwn*
  c~ word ***gair gorchmynnol*** *hwn*
commander *enw* ***comander*** *hwn*
commandment *enw* ***gorchymyn*** *hwn*
commemorate *be* ***coffáu***
commemoration *enw* ***coffâd*** *hwn*
commemorative *ans* ***coffa***, ***dathliadol***
commence *be* ***cychwyn***, ***dechrau***
commencement *enw* ***dechreuad*** *hwn*; ***dechrau***
commend *be* ***cyflwyno***, ***cymeradwyo***
commendable *ans* ***canmoladwy***, ***cymeradwy***
commendation *enw* ***cymeradwyaeth*** *hon*
commensurate *ans* ***cymesur***
  c~ with ***o'r un safon â***
comment *enw* ***sylw*** *hwn*
comment *be* ***gwneud sylw***
commentary *enw* (observation) ***sylwebaeth*** *hon*; (Biblical) ***esboniad*** *hwn*
commentator *enw* ***sylwebydd*** *hwn*
commerce *enw* ***masnach*** *hon*
commercial *ans* ***masnachol***
commiserate *be* ***cydymdeimlo***
commiseration *enw* ***cydymdeimlad*** *hwn*
commission *enw* ***comisiwn*** *hwn*
commission *be* ***comisiynu***, ***dirprwyo***
commit *be* (crime) ***cyflawni***; (send) ***traddodi***; (oneself) ***ymrwymo***; (resources) ***clustnodi***, ***addo***
commitment *enw* ***ymrwymiad*** *hwn*
committed *ans* ***ymrwymedig***, ***ymroddgar***
committee *enw* ***pwyllgor*** *hwn*
commodious *ans* ***helaeth***
common *ans* ***cyffredin***
  c~ knowledge ***fe ŵyr pawb***
  c~ sense ***synnwyr cyffredin*** *hwn*
  c~ speech ***iaith gyffredin*** *hon*
common *enw* ***comin***, ***cytir*** *hwn*
commonality *enw* ***pwrpas cyffredin***, ***tir cyffredin*** *hwn*
commonly *adf* ***yn gyffredin***
commonplace *ans* ***cyffredin***
Commonwealth *enw* ***Cymanwlad*** *hon*

commotion *enw* ***cyffro***, ***cynnwrf*** *hwn*
communicable *ans* ***mynegadwy***; ***heintus***
communicate *be* ***cyfathrebu***; ***cyfleu***
communion *enw* ***cymundeb*** *hwn*
communism *enw* ***comiwnyddiaeth*** *hon*
communist *enw* ***comiwnydd*** *hwn*
communist *ans* ***comiwnyddol***
community *enw* ***cymuned*** *hon*
Communities First ***Cymunedau'n Gyntaf***
community *ans* ***cymunedol***
commutable *ans* ***newidiadwy***
commute *be* ***cymudo***
commuter *enw* ***cymudwr*** *hwn*
compact *enw* ***cytundeb*** *hwn*
compact *ans* ***cryno***
compact disc *enw* ***cryno-ddisg*** *hwn*
companion *enw* ***cydymaith***, ***cymar*** *hwn*
c~ document/volume ***chwaer ddogfen/gyfrol*** *hon*
c~ teaching ***addysgu cefnogol***
companionable *ans* ***cyfeillgar***
companionship *enw* ***cwmni*** *hwn*
company *enw* ***cwmni*** *hwn*
comparability *enw* ***cymaroldeb*** *hwn*
comparable *ans* ***hafal***
comparative *ans* ***cymharol***
compare *be* ***cymharu***
comparison *enw* ***cymhariaeth*** *hon*
it does not bear c~ with ***nid yw'n dal cannwyll i***
compass *enw* (pair of compasses) ***cwmpas*** *hwn*; (navigation) ***cwmpawd*** *hwn*
compassion *enw* ***tosturi*** *hwn*
compassionate *ans* ***tosturiol***, ***trugarog***
compatibility *enw* ***cydnawsedd***, ***cyfaddasrwydd*** *hwn*
compatible *ans* ***cydnaws***, ***cyfaddas***
compatriot *enw* ***cydwladwr*** *hwn*
compel *be* ***gorfodi***, ***cymell***
compendium *enw* ***crynhoad*** *hwn*
compensate *be* (finance) ***digolledu***; (make amends) ***gwneud iawn am***
compensation *enw* ***iawndal*** *hwn*
compère *enw* ***arweinydd*** *hwn*
compete *be* ***cystadlu***, ***ymgiprys am***
competence *enw* ***gallu***, ***cymhwysedd*** *hwn*
competent *ans* (qualified) ***cymwys***; (skilful) ***galluog***, ***medrus***, ***deheuig***
competition *enw* ***cystadleuaeth*** *hon*
competitive *ans* ***cystadleuol***
competitor *enw* ***cystadleuydd*** *hwn*
compile *be* ***casglu***
compiler *enw* ***casglwr*** *hwn*
complacency *enw* ***hunanfoddhad***, ***hunanfodlonrwydd*** *hwn*

C

complacent *ans* ***hunanfoddhaus***, ***hunanfodlon***
complain *be* ***achwyn***, ***grwgnach***, ***cwyno***
complaint *enw* ***cwyn*** *hon*
  c~s procedure ***trefn gwyno*** *hon*
complement *enw* ***llawnder***, ***cyflawnder*** *hwn*
  full c~ ***nifer (l)lawn***
complement *be* ***cyflenwi***, ***cwblhau***, ***ategu***
complementary *ans* ***cyflenwol***, ***ategol***
complete *ans* ***cyflawn***
  c~ and utter hypocrisy ***rhagrith noeth*** *hwn*
  c~ master ***meistr corn*** *hwn*
  in c~ agreement with ***cytuno i'r carn***
complete *be* ***gorffen***, ***cwblhau***; (form) ***llenwi***
completely *adf* ***yn llwyr***
  almost c~ ***o fewn y dim i***
  c~ dead ***yn farw gorn***
  c~ inadequate ***yn gwbl annigonol***
  to disappear c~ ***diflannu o'r tir***
  to wear away c~ ***treulio'n ddim***
completion *enw* ***cwblhad*** *hwn*
  c~ date ***dyddiad cwblhau*** *hwn*
complex *ans* ***cymhleth***, ***astrus***
complexion *enw* ***pryd*** *hwn*, ***gwedd*** *hon*
complexity *enw* ***cymhlethdod*** *hwn*
compliance *enw* ***ufudd-dod***, ***cydsyniad*** *hwn*
compliance *enw* ***cydymffurfio***
compliant *ans* ***ufudd***
complicate *be* ***cymhlethu***
complicated *ans* ***cymhleth***
complication *enw* ***cymhlethdod*** *hwn*
complicity *enw* ***rhan***, ***cyfranogaeth*** *hon*
compliment *enw* (praise) ***canmoliaeth***, ***teyrnged*** *hon*; (greetings) *cyfarchion*
  c~ slip ***slip cyfarch*** *hwn*
compliment *be* ***canmol***, ***llongyfarch***
comply *be* ***ufuddhau***, ***cydsynio***, ***cydymffurfio***
component *enw* ***cydran*** *hon*
compose *be* ***cyfansoddi***
composed *ans* ***hunanfeddiannol***
composer *enw* ***cyfansoddwr*** *hwn*, ***cyfansoddwraig*** *hon*
composite *ans* ***cyfansawdd***, ***cyfun***
composition *enw* (music) ***cyfansoddiad***; (construction) ***gwneuthuriad***; (essay) ***traethawd*** *hwn*
compost *enw* ***gwrtaith***, ***compost*** *hwn*
composure *enw* ***hunanfeddiant*** *hwn*
compound *ans* ***cyfansawdd***
compound *enw* ***cyfansoddyn*** *hwn*
comprehend *be* ***amgyffred***

comprehensible *ans* ***dealladwy***
comprehension *enw* ***dirnadaeth*** *hon*, ***amgyffred*** *hwn*
comprehensive *ans* ***cynhwysfawr***; (school) ***cyfun***
compress *be* ***cywasgu***
compressor *enw* ***cywasgydd*** *hwn*
comprise *be* ***cynnwys***
compromise *enw* ***cyfaddawd*** *hwn*
compromise *be* ***cyfaddawdu***
  c~ the credibility of ***tanseilio hygrededd***
  c~ the quality of ***amharu ar ansawdd***
compulsion *enw* ***gorfodaeth*** *hon*
compulsory *ans* ***gorfodol***
compute *be* ***bwrw cyfrif***
computer *enw* ***cyfrifiadur*** *hwn*
computerize *be* ***cyfrifiaduro***
computer science *enw* ***cyfrifiadureg*** *hon*
computing *be* ***cyfrifiaduro***
comrade *enw* ***cydymaith***, ***cymrawd*** *hwn*
comradeship *enw* ***brawdoliaeth*** *hon*
concave *ans* ***ceugrwm***
conceal *be* ***cuddio***, ***celu***
concealment *enw* ***cuddio***, ***celu***
concede *be* ***ildio***
conceit *enw* ***hunan-dyb*** *hwn/hon*, ***balchder*** *hwn*
conceited *ans* ***hunandybus***
conceivable *ans* ***dichonadwy***; ***gellir dychmygu***
  every c~ aspect ***pob agwedd dan haul***
conceive *be* (pregnant) ***beichiogi***; ***dychmygu***
concentrate *be* (the mind) ***canolbwyntio***; (location) ***canoli***
  c~ attention on ***hoelio sylw ar***
concentrated *ans* (e.g. acid) ***crynodedig***
concentration *enw* ***crynodiad*** *hwn*
concentric *ans* ***cydganolog***
concept *enw* ***cysyniad*** *hwn*
conception *enw* ***syniad***; ***beichiogiad*** *hwn*
conceptualize *be* ***cysyniadoli***
concern *be* ***ymwneud â***
  as far as I'm c~ed ***o'm rhan i***
concern *enw* (worry) ***pryder***, ***gofal***; ***busnes***, ***consýrn*** *hwn*
  cause for c~ ***achos/testun pryder*** *hwn*
concerning ardd ***ynglŷn â***
concert *enw* ***cyngerdd*** *hwn/hon*
concerted *ans* ***ar y cyd***
concertina *enw* ***consertina*** *hwn*
concerto *enw* ***concerto*** *hwn*
concession *enw* ***goddefiad***, ***consesiwn*** *hwn*
conciliate *be* ***cymodi***
conciliation *enw* ***cymod*** *hwn*
conciliator *enw* ***cymodwr*** *hwn*
conciliatory *ans* ***cymodlon***
concise *ans* ***cryno***
conclude *be* ***casglu***, ***terfynu***
  and to c~ ***ac i gloi***

c~ inquiries ***cwblhau ymholiadau***
to be c~ed ***dod i ben***
conclusion *enw* ***casgliad***; (end) ***diweddglo*** *hwn*
conclusive *ans* ***terfynol***
concoct *be* ***llunio***, ***dyfeisio***
concoction *enw* ***cymysgwch*** *hwn*
concord *enw* ***cytgord*** *hwn*
concordance *enw* (harmony) ***cytgord***; (index) ***mynegai*** *hwn*
concordat *enw* ***cytundeb*** *hwn*
concrete *enw* ***concrit*** *hwn*
concrete *ans* (definite) ***pendant***; (gram./phil.) ***diriaethol***
concur *be* ***cyd-weld***, ***cydsynio***
concurrence *enw* ***cydsyniad*** *hwn*
concurrent *ans* ***cyfredol***, ***cydredol***, ***cydgyfredol***
concussion *enw* ***ysgytwad*** *hwn*; (med.) ***cyfergyd*** *hwn/hon*
condemn *be* ***condemnio***, ***collfarnu***
condemnation *enw* ***condemniad*** *hwn*, ***collfarn*** *hon*
condensation *enw* ***cyddwysedd*** *hwn*
condense *be* ***cywasgu***; ***cyddwyso***
condescend *be* ***ymostwng***
condescending *ans* ***nawddogol***, ***nawddoglyd***
condiments *enw* ***y confennau: cynfennau*** *hyn*
condition *be* ***cyflyru***
condition *enw* (state) ***cyflwr*** *hwn*; ***amod*** *hwn/hon*
c~ precedent ***rhagamod*** *hwn/hon*
c~ subsequent ***ôl-amod*** *hwn/hon*
conditional *ans* ***amodol***
condole *be* ***cydymdeimlo***
condolence *enw* ***cydymdeimlad*** *hwn*
condom *enw* ***condom*** *hwn*
condone *be* ***esgusodi***, ***derbyn***
conducive *ans* ***ffafriol***
conduct *enw* ***ymddygiad***, ***ymarweddiad*** *hwn*
conduct *be* (lead) ***arwain***; (oneself) ***ymddwyn***; (business) ***cynnal***
conduction *enw* ***dargludiad*** *hwn*
conductor *enw* (music) ***arweinydd***; (heat) ***dargludydd*** *hwn*
conduit *enw* (elec.) ***sianel***; (means) ***cyfrwng*** *hwn*
cone *enw* ***côn*** *hwn*
confectionery *enw* (sweets) ***melysion***, ***teisennau*** *hyn*
confederation *enw* ***cynghrair*** *hwn*
confer *be* ***ymgynghori***; (bestow) ***cyflwyno***
conference *enw* ***cynhadledd*** *hon*
confess *be* ***cyffesu***, ***cyfaddef***
confession *enw* ***cyfaddefiad*** *hwn*, ***cyffes*** *hon*
confidant *enw* ***cyfaill mynwesol*** *hwn*
confide *be* ***ymddiried***
confidence *enw* ***hyder*** *hwn*, ***ymddiriedaeth***, ***ffydd*** *hon*

confident *ans* ***hyderus***
confidential *ans* ***cyfrinachol***
confidentiality *enw* ***cyfrinachedd*** *hwn*
confine *be* ***cyfyngu***
confines *enw* ***ffiniau*** *hyn*
confinement *enw* ***caethiwed*** *hwn*
confirm *be* ***cadarnhau***; (church) ***conffirmio***
confirmation *enw* ***cadarnhad*** *hwn*
confiscate *be* ***cymryd oddi ar***
conflagration *enw* ***coelcerth*** *hon*
conflict *enw* ***gwrthdrawiad*** *hwn*
conflict *be* ***gwrthdaro***
to be in c~ with ***tynnu'n groes i***, ***bod yn groes i***
conflicting *ans* ***anghyson***, ***croes***
confluence *enw* ***aber***, ***cymer*** *hwn*
conform *be* ***cydymffurfio***, ***cydweddu***
conformity *enw* ***cydymffurfiad*** *hwn*
confound *be* ***drysu***
confront *be* ***wynebu***, ***bod wyneb yn wyneb â***
confrontation *be* ***gwrthdaro***
confrontational *ans* ***ymosodol***
confuse *be* ***cymysgu***, ***drysu***
confusion *enw* ***dryswch*** *hwn*, ***anhrefn*** *hon*
congeal *be* ***ceulo***
congenial *ans* ***cydnaws***, ***at eu dant***
congenital *ans* ***cynhenid***
congestion *enw* (med.) ***gorlawnder***, ***caethder*** *hwn*; (traffic) ***tagfa*** *hon*
congratulate *be* ***llongyfarch***
congratulations *enw* ***llongyfarchiadau*** *hyn*
congregate *be* ***casglu***, ***ymgynnull***
congregation *enw* ***cynulleidfa*** *hon*
congress *enw* ***cyngres*** *hon*, ***cynulliad*** *hwn*
congruent *ans* ***cyfath***
these things are not c~ with our beliefs ***nid yw'r pethau hyn yn gydnaws â'n credoau ni***
congruity *enw* ***cyfaddasrwydd*** *hwn*
congruous *ans* ***addas***
conifer *enw* ***coniffer*** *hwn/hon*, ***conwydden*** *hon*
conjecture *be* ***tybio***, ***dyfalu***
conjugal *ans* ***priodasol***
conjugate *be* (gram.) ***rhedeg***; (science) ***cydgysylltu***, ***ymgyfuno***
conjunction *enw* ***cysylltiad***; ***cysylltair*** *hwn*
in c~ with ***ar y cyd â***
conjuncture *enw* ***achlysur*** *hwn*
conjure *be* ***consurio***
conjuror *enw* ***consuriwr*** *hwn*
conker *enw* ***castan*** *hon*
connect *be* ***cysylltu***, ***cydio***
connection *enw* ***cysylltiad*** *hwn*
connive *be* ***cynllwynio***, ***cydgynllwynio***
connoisseur *enw* ***arbenigwr*** *hwn*, ***arbenigwraig*** *hon*
conquer *be* ***gorchfygu***, ***goresgyn***

C

conqueror *enw* ***gorchfygwr***, ***goresgynnwr*** *hwn*
conquest *enw* ***goresgyniad***, ***gorchfygiad*** *hwn*
consanguinity *enw* ***perthyn trwy waed***
conscience *enw* ***cydwybod*** *hon*
conscientious *ans* ***cydwybodol***
conscious *ans* ***ymwybodol***
consciousness *enw* ***ymwybyddiaeth*** *hon*
consecrate *be* ***cysegru***
consecration *enw* ***cysegriad*** *hwn*
consecutive *ans* ***olynol***, ***o'r bron***
consensual *ans* ***cydsyniol***
consensus *enw* ***consenswS***, ***cytundeb cyffredinol*** *hwn*
consent *enw* ***caniatâd*** *hwn*
consent *be* **caniatáu**, ***cydsynio***
consequence *enw* ***canlyniad*** *hwn*
of no c~ ***nid yw o bwys***
consequent *ans* ***canlynol***, ***dilynol***, ***yn sgil hynny***
conservation *enw* ***cadwraeth***, ***gwarchodaeth*** *hon*
conservative *ans* ***ceidwadol***
conservative *enw* ***ceidwadwr*** *hwn*
conservatory *enw* ***tŷ gwydr*** *hwn*, ***ystafell wydr*** *hon*
conserve *be* ***cadw***, ***gwarchod***
consider *be* ***ystyried***
considerable *ans* ***sylweddol***
a c~ distance ***bellter ffordd***
c~ efforts ***ymdrechu'n lew***
considerate *ans* ***ystyriol***, ***meddylgar***
consideration *enw* ***ystyriaeth*** *hon*
to show c~ ***bod yn ystyriol***
considered *ans* ***ystyrlon***, ***cytbwys***
it is our c~ opinion that ***credwn yn bendant fod***
consign *be* ***anfon***
consignment *enw* ***cyflenwad*** *hwn*
consist *be* ***cynnwys***
consistency *enw* ***cysondeb***; (texture) ***ansawdd*** *hwn*
consistent *ans* ***cyson***
consistent with ***cyd-fynd â***
consolation *enw* ***cysur*** *hwn*
console *be* ***cysuro***
consolidate *be* ***atgyfnerthu***, ***cyfnerthu, cadarnhau***; (settle) ***caledu***, ***sefydlogi***
consolidation *enw* ***cadarnhad***, ***cyfnerthiad*** *hwn*
consonance *enw* ***cyseinedd***, ***cytseinedd*** *hwn*; (agreement) ***cytundeb, cytgord***
consonant *enw* ***cytsain*** *hon*
consonant *ans* ***cyson***, ***yn unol â***
to be c~ with ***cyd-fynd â***
conspicuous *ans* ***amlwg***
consort *enw* ***cymar*** *hwn/hon*
consort *be* ***cyfeillachu***
consortium *enw* ***consortiwm***, ***cyfungorff*** *hwn*
conspicuous *ans* ***amlwg***
conspiracy *enw* ***cynllwyn*** *hwn*
conspirator *enw* ***cynllwyniwr*** *hwn*

conspire *be* ***cynllwynio***
constancy *enw* ***cysondeb, sefydlogrwydd, sadrwydd*** *hwn*
constant *ans* ***cyson, di-dor, di-baid***
constellation *enw* ***cytser*** *hwn*
consternation *enw* ***syndod*** *hwn*
constipated *ans* ***rhwym***
constipation *enw* ***rhwymedd*** *hwn*
constituency *enw* ***etholaeth*** *hon*
constituent *enw* ***etholwr*** *hwn*, ***etholwraig*** *hon*; (part) ***cyfansoddyn*** *hwn*
constituent *ans* ***cyfansoddol***
  c~ part ***rhan gyfansoddol, rhan hanfodol*** *hon*
constitute *be* ***gwneud, creu***
  this would c~ a change ***byddai hyn gyfystyr â newid***
  to c~ good cause for ***golygu bod achos da i***
constitution *enw* ***cyfansoddiad*** *hwn*
constitutional *ans* ***cyfansoddiadol***
constrain *be* ***gorfodi; cyfyngu***
constrained *ans* ***cyfyngus, wedi'i gyfyngu***
constraint *enw* ***cyfyngiad*** *hwn*
constrict *be* ***cywasgu***; (med.) ***culhau***
construct *be* ***adeiladu, llunio***
construction *enw* ***adeilad, adeiladwaith, lluniad*** *hwn*
constructive *ans* ***adeiladol***
construe *be* ***dehongli, deall***
consul *enw* ***conswl*** *hwn*
consult *be* ***ymgynghori, troi at***
consultant *enw* ***ymgynghorydd*** *hwn*
consultation *enw* ***ymgynghoriad*** *hwn*
consultative *ans* ***ymgynghorol***
consumable *ans* ***bwytadwy, treuliedig***
consumables *enw* ***defnyddiau bwytadwy/traul*** *hyn*
consume *be* ***bwyta, llyncu, difa, dihysbyddu***
consumer *enw* ***prynwr, defnyddiwr*** *hwn*, ***prynwraig, defnyddwraig*** *hon*
consummate *be* ***cyflawni***
consummate *ans* ***cyflawn***
  c~ musician ***cerddor o'i gorun i'w sawdl***
consumption *enw* ***traul*** *hon*; (TB) ***darfodedigaeth*** *hwn*
contact *enw* ***cysylltiad; cyffyrddiad*** *hwn*
  first point of c~ ***cysylltwch yn gyntaf â***
contagious *ans* ***heintus***
contain *be* ***cynnwys***
  to c~ a fire ***cyfyngu ar dân***
container *enw* ***cynhwysydd*** *hwn*
contaminate *be* ***llygru, heintio***
contamination *enw* ***llygredd*** *hwn*
contemplate *be* ***ystyried, myfyrio***
contemplation *enw* ***myfyrdod*** *hwn*
contemporary *ans* ***cyfoes***

C

contemporaries *enw* ***cyfoedion*** *hyn*
contempt *enw* ***dirmyg*** *hwn*
contemptible *ans* ***gwarthus***, ***cywilyddus***
contemptuous *ans* ***dirmygus***
contend *be* ***ymryson***, ***dadlau***
content *ans* ***bodlon***
content *enw* ***cynnwys*** *hwn*
contention *enw* (dispute) ***cynnen*** *hon*; (claim) ***honiad, haeriad*** *hwn,* ***dadl*** *hon*
contentious *ans* ***cynhengar***, ***dadleuol***
a c~ issue ***pwnc llosg*** *hwn*
contentment *enw* ***bodlonrwydd*** *hwn*
contents *enw* ***cynnwys*** *hwn*
contest *be* ***herio***, ***ymryson***
contest *enw* ***gornest*** *hon*
contestant *enw* ***cystadleuydd*** *hwn*
context *enw* ***cyd-destun*** *hwn*
contextual *ans* ***mewn cyd-destun***
continent *enw* ***cyfandir*** *hwn*
continental *ans* ***cyfandirol***
c~ Europe ***ar dir mawr Ewrop***
contingency *enw* ***digwyddiad annisgwyl/ ar hap***, ***hapddigwyddiad*** *hwn*
contingency *ans* ***wrth gefn***, ***annisgwyl***
contingent *enw* ***mintai*** *hon*
continual *ans* ***parhaus***
continuation *enw* ***parhad*** *hwn*
continue *be* ***parhau***
continuity *enw* ***parhad***, ***dilyniant*** *hwn*
continuous *ans* ***parhaol***, ***di-dor***
c~ writing ***ysgrifen glwm*** *hon*
contort *be* ***ystumio***
contortion *enw* ***dirdyniad*** *hwn*
contour *enw* ***cyfuchlinedd*** *hwn*
contraband *enw* ***eitemau gwaharddedig*** *hyn*
contraception *enw* ***atal cenhedlu***
contraceptive *enw* ***dyfais atal cenhedlu*** *hon*
contract *be* ***cyfamodi***, ***contractio***; (muscle) ***cyfangu***
contract *enw* ***cytundeb, cyfamod*** *hwn*
contraction *enw* ***cyfangiad*** *hwn*
contract out *be* ***ymryddhau o gontract***
contractual *ans* ***cytundebol***
contradict *be* ***gwrth-ddweud***
contradiction *enw* ***gwrthddywediad*** *hwn*
contradictory *ans* ***yn gwrth-ddweud***
contraption *enw* ***dyfais*** *hon*
contrary *ans* ***croes***
contrary *enw* ***gwrthwyneb*** *hwn*
contrast *enw* ***gwrthgyferbyniad*** *hwn*
by c~ ***ar y llaw arall***
in c~ to ***yn wahanol i***
in marked c~ to ***yn wahanol iawn i***
contrast *be* ***cyferbynnu***

contravene *be* ***torri deddf/rheol***
contribute *be* ***cyfrannu***
contribution *enw* ***cyfraniad*** *hwn*
contributor *enw* ***cyfrannwr*** *hwn*
contributory *ans* ***cyfrannol***
contrite *ans* ***edifar***, ***edifeiriol***
contrition *enw* ***edifeirwch*** *hwn*
contrivance *enw* (device) ***dyfais*** *hwn*; (ability to devise) ***dyfeisgarwch*** *hwn*; (deceit) ***twyll*** *hwn*, ***dichell*** *hon*
contrive *be* ***dyfeisio, llunio, mynd ati***; ***cynllunio***, ***trefnu***; ***llwyddo***
control *enw* ***rheolaeth*** *hon*
  to lose control ***colli arnynt eu hunain***
  to take c~ of ***cymryd yr awenau***
control *be* ***rheoli***, ***cadw trefn***
controlled *ans* ***graddol***; ***trefnus***
controversial *ans* ***dadleuol***
  a c~ issue ***pwnc llosg*** *hwn*
controversy *enw* ***dadl*** *hon*
conundrum *enw* ***pos*** *hwn*
contusion *enw* ***clais*** *hwn*
conurbation *enw* ***cytref*** *hon*
convalesce *be* ***cryfhau***, ***gwella***
convalescent *ans* ***ymadfer***
convection *enw* ***darfudiad*** *hwn*
convene *be* ***galw***, ***cynnull***
convener *enw* ***cynullydd*** *hwn*
convenience *enw* ***cyfleustra*** *hwn*
  I enclose an envelope for your c~ ***amgaeaf amlen i chi ei defnyddio***
convenient *ans* ***cyfleus***
convent *enw* ***cwfaint*** *hwn*
convention *enw* ***confensiwn*** *hwn*; ***cynhadledd*** *hon*
conventional *ans* ***confensiynol***
converge *be* ***cydgyfarfod***; ***heigio***
convergence *enw* ***cydgyfeiriant*** *hwn*
convergent *ans* ***cydgyfeiriol***
conversant *ans* ***hyddysg***, ***cyfarwydd***
  to become c~ with ***ymgyfarwyddo â***
  to be thoroughly c~ with ***wedi hen arfer â***
conversation *enw* ***sgwrs***, ***ymgom*** *hon*
converse *be* ***sgwrsio***, ***ymddiddan***
conversely *adf* ***ar y llaw arall***
conversion *enw* (religious) ***tröedigaeth*** *hon*; (change) ***trawsnewid***, ***cyfnewid***; (rugby) ***trosiad*** *hwn*
conversion *enw* ***tröedigaeth*** *hon*
convert *be* ***troi***, ***trosi***
convex *ans* ***amgrwm***
convey *be* ***trosglwyddo***, ***cludo***, ***cyfleu***
  please c~ these to your wife ***rhowch/cyflwynwch y rhain i'ch gwraig***
conveyance *enw* ***cludiad***; ***trosglwyddiad*** *hwn*
conveyancing *be* ***trosglwyddo (eiddo)***
convict *enw* ***carcharor*** *hwn*

C

convict *be* ***dyfarnu'n euog***
conviction *enw* ***argyhoeddiad*** *hwn*; (court) ***collfarn*** *hon*
convince *be* ***argyhoeddi***
c~d ***argyhoeddedig***, ***hollol bendant***
convincing *ans* ***argyhoeddiadol***
convivial *ans* ***llawen***, ***siriol***
conviviality *enw* ***miri*** *hwn*
convoke *be* ***cydgynnull***
convoy *enw* ***gosgordd*** *hon*
convulse *be* ***dirdynnu***
convulsion *enw* ***dirdyniad*** *hwn*
convulsive *ans* ***dirdynnol***
cook *enw* ***cogydd*** *hwn*, ***cogyddes*** *hon*
cook *be* ***coginio***
cooker *enw* ***popty*** *hwn*, ***ffwrn*** *hon*
cookery *enw* ***coginio***
cool *ans* ***oeraidd***, ***llugoer***, ***claear***
keep c~ ***gan bwyll***
cool *be* ***oeri***
to c~ down ***oeri'n raddol***; ***pwyllo***
coolness *enw* ***oerni*** *hwn*
coop *enw* ***cwb*** *hwn*
cooperate *be* ***cydweithio***
cooperation *enw* ***cydweithrediad*** *hwn*
cooperative *ans* ***cydweithredol***, ***parod i gydweithredu***
co-opt *be* ***cyfethol***
co-opted *ans* ***cyfetholedig***
coordinate *be* ***cydlynu***, ***cydgysylltu***; ***cydweddu***
coordination *enw* ***cydgordiad***, ***cydlynedd*** *hwn*
coordinator *enw* ***cydlynydd***, ***cydgysylltydd*** *hwn*
coot *enw* ***cwtiar:cotiar*** *hon*
cope *be* ***ymdopi***, ***ymgodymu â***
c~ with demands ***ceisio cwrdd â gofynion***
c~ with pupils ***rheoli disgyblion***
c~ with stress ***dal y pwysau***
copious *ans* ***helaeth***
to weep c~ly ***wylo'n hidl/lli***
copper *enw* (metal) ***copor***, ***copr***; (police) ***y glas*** *hwn*
coppice *enw* ***prysglwyn*** *hwn*, ***prysgoed*** *hyn*
copulate *be* ***cnuchio***, ***cyplu***
copy *enw* ***copi*** *hwn*
copy *be* ***copïo***, ***dynwared***; ***anfon copi o lythyr at***
copyright *enw* ***hawlfraint*** *hon*
coracle *enw* ***cwrwg:cwrwgl*** *hwn*
coral *enw* ***cwrel*** *hwn*
cord *enw* ***corden*** *hon*
cordial *ans* ***calonnog***, ***gwresog***
corduroy *enw* ***melfaréd*** *hwn*
core *enw* ***calon*** *hon*, ***craidd*** *hwn*
c~ skills ***medrau craidd*** *hyn*
corgi *enw* ***corgi*** *hwn*
cork *enw* ***corcyn*** *hwn*
cork *be* ***corcio***
corkscrew *enw* ***corcsgriw*** *hwn*
cormorant *enw* ***mulfran*** *hon*
corn *enw* ***llafur***, ***ŷd*** *hwn*
cornea *enw* ***cornbilen*** *hon*

corner *enw* ***cornel*** *hwn,* ***congl*** *hon*
to fight your c~ ***ymladd dros eich safbwynt***
winter's just round the c~ ***mae'r gaeaf ar ein gwarthaf***
cornerstone *enw* ***conglfaen*** *hwn*
cornet *enw* ***cornet*** *hwn*
cornflakes *enw* ***creision ŷd*** *hyn*
corollary *enw* ***canlyneb*** *hon*
with the c~ that ***gan gydnabod ar yr un pryd fod***
corona *enw* ***corongylch*** *hwn*
coronation *enw* ***coroni***
coroner *enw* ***crwner*** *hwn*
corporate *ans* ***corfforaethol***
c~ identity ***hunaniaeth gorfforaethol*** *hon*
c~ responsibility ***cydgyfrifoldeb*** *hwn*
c~ worship ***cydaddoliad*** *hwn*
corporation *enw* ***corfforaeth*** *hon*
corps *enw* ***corfflu*** *hwn*
corpse *enw* ***corff*** *hwn,* ***celain*** *hon*
corpulent *ans* ***tew, llond ei groen***
correct *be* ***cywiro***
correct *ans* ***cywir***
correction *enw* ***cywiriad*** *hwn*
correctness *enw* ***cywirdeb*** *hwn*
correlate *be* ***cydberthyn***
correlation *enw* ***cydberthynas*** *hon*
correspond *be* ***gohebu; cyfateb***
correspondence *enw* (likeness) ***cyfatebiaeth***; (letters) ***gohebiaeth*** *hon*
c~ course ***cwrs drwy'r post*** *hwn*
correspondent *enw* ***llythyrwr*** *hwn,* ***llythyrwraig*** *hon*
corridor *enw* ***coridor*** *hwn*
corrie *enw* ***peiran*** *hwn*
corroborate *be* ***cadarnhau, cydategu***
corroborative *ans* ***ategol***
corrode *be* ***rhydu, cyrydu***
corrosion *enw* ***rhwd, cyrydiad*** *hwn;* ***traul*** *hon*
corrosive *ans* ***difaol***
corrugated *ans* ***rhychiog***
corrupt *be* ***llygru***
corrupt *ans* ***llwgr, llygredig***
corruptible *ans* ***llygradwy***
corruption *enw* ***llygredd*** *hwn*
corruptor *enw* ***llygrwr*** *hwn*
corsair *enw* ***môr-leidr*** *hwn*
coruscate *be* ***tanbeidio***
cosmetic *ans* ***cosmetig***
cosmic *ans* ***cosmig***
cosmonaut *enw* ***gofodwr*** *hwn*
cosmopolitan *ans* ***aml-hiliol***
cosmos *enw* ***cosmos*** *hwn*
cosset *be* ***maldodi***
cost *enw* ***cost*** *hon,* ***pris*** *hwn*
at all c~s ***doed a ddelo***
cost *be* ***costio***
costing *enw* ***prisiad*** *hwn*
costly *ans* ***drud, drudfawr***
costume *enw* ***gwisg*** *hon*
cosy *ans* ***clyd***
coterminous *ans* ***yn rhannu'r un ffiniau***
cottage *enw* ***bwthyn*** *hwn*

C

cotton *enw* ***cotwm*** *hwn*
cotton wool *enw* ***gwlân cotwm*** *hwn*
couch *be* (express) ***mynegi***, ***geirio***
couch *enw* ***soffa*** *hon*
cough *enw* ***peswch*** *hwn*
cough *be* ***peswch:pesychu***
council *enw* ***cyngor*** *hwn*
counsel *enw* ***cyngor***; ***bargyfreithiwr, cwnsler*** *hwn*
counsel *be* ***cynghori***
counsellor *enw* ***cynghorydd*** *hwn*
count *be* ***cyfrif***
count *enw* (title) ***iarll*** *hwn*
countenance *enw* ***wynepryd*** *hwn*
countenance *be* ***ystyried***, ***caniatáu***
counter *enw* ***cownter*** *hwn*; ***ateb*** *hwn*
counteract *be* ***gwrthweithio***
counter-allegation *enw* ***gwrth-honiad*** *hwn*
counter-attack *be* ***gwrthymosod***
counterbalance *be* ***gwrthbwyso***
counterclockwise *ans* ***gwrthglocwedd***
counterfeit *be* ***ffugio***
counterfeit *ans* ***ffug***
counterfoil *enw* ***bonyn*** *hwn*
counter-melody *enw* ***cyfalaw*** *hon*
counterpane *enw* ***cwrlid*** *hwn*
counterpart *enw* ***un sy'n cyfateb*** *hwn/hon*; ***cymrodor***, ***cyfatebydd*** *hwn*
counter-proposal *enw* ***gwrthgynnig*** *hwn*
countersign *be* ***cydlofnodi***
countersignature *enw* ***cydlofnod*** *hwn*
countersink *be* ***gwrthsoddi***
countless *ans* ***dirifedi***
countrified *ans* ***gwladaidd***
country *enw* ***gwlad*** *hon*
country *ans* ***gwledig***
countryman *enw* ***gwladwr***, ***gwerinwr*** *hwn*
countryside *enw* ***gwlad*** *hon,* ***cefn gwlad*** *hwn*
county *enw* ***sir***, ***swydd*** *hon*
county-wide *adf* ***sirol***, ***ledled y sir***
couple *enw* ***cwpl*** *hwn*, ***deuddyn*** *hyn*
couple *be* ***cyplysu***, ***uno***
couplet *enw* ***cwpled*** *hwn*
coupon *enw* ***cwpon***, ***tocyn*** *hwn*
courage *enw* ***dewrder***, ***gwrhydri*** *hwn*
  to summon up enough c~ to ***magu digon o blwc i***
courageous *ans* ***dewr***, ***gwrol***
courier *enw* ***negesydd***, ***brysgennad*** *hwn*
course *enw* ***cwrs*** *hwn*
  in due c~ ***yn y man***
  as a matter of c~ ***fel rhan o'r drefn***
  c~ of events ***yr hyn sy'n digwydd***
  c~ of study ***cwrs astudio*** *hwn*

crash c~ *cwrs carlam* *hwn*
in c~ of preparation *ar y gweill*
in the c~ of their work *wrth wneud eu gwaith*
on course *yn dilyn y llwybr cywir*, *yn dilyn y llwybr iawn*
a sensible c~ of action *ffordd ddoeth o weithredu*
court *enw* ***llys*, *cwrt*** *hwn*
court *be* ***canlyn*, *caru***
to c~ danger *mentro*, *chwarae â thân*
courteous *ans* ***cwrtais*, *boneddigaidd***
courtesy *enw* ***cwrteisi*, *boneddigeiddrwydd*** *hwn*
courthouse *enw* ***llys*** *hwn*
courtroom *enw* ***cwrt*** *hwn*
courtship *enw* ***carwriaeth*** *hon*
courtyard *enw* ***cwrt*** *hwn*
cousin *enw* ***cefnder*** *hwn*, ***cyfnither*** *hon*
cove *enw* ***cilfach*** *hon*
covenant *enw* ***cyfamod*** *hwn*
cover *enw* ***gorchudd*** *hwn*; (lid) ***caead*** *hwn*; (book) ***clawr*** *hwn*; (mech. eng.) ***amgaead*** *hwn*; (shelter) ***cysgod*** *hwn*, ***lloches*** *hon*
cover *be* ***gorchuddio*; *clorio***; (range) ***cwmpasu***
they will c~ the whole of Wales *gweithredu ledled Cymru*; *o ben bwygilydd*
to be c~ed by *dod o dan*
to c~ the costs *talu'r costau*
coverage *enw* ***ymdriniaeth*** *hon*
covered pedestrian link *enw* ***rhodfa dan do*** *hon*
coverlet *enw* ***cwrlid*** *hwn*
covert *ans* ***cudd*, *dirgel***
cover-up *be* ***cuddio***
covet *be* ***chwennych:chwenychu***
covetous *ans* ***ariangar***
cow *enw* ***buwch*** *hon*
coward *enw* ***llwfrgi*** *hwn*
cowardice *enw* ***llwfrdra*** *hwn*
cowboy *enw* ***cowboi*** *hwn*
cow-collar *enw* ***aerwy*** *hwn*
cowl *enw* ***cwcwll*** *hwn*
cowpat *enw* ***gleuen*, *gleuad*** *hon*
cowshed *enw* ***beudy*** *hwn*
cowslips *enw* ***briallu Mair*** *hyn*
coy *ans* ***swil***
coyness *enw* ***swildod*** *hwn*
crab *enw* ***cranc*** *hwn*
crack *enw* (sound) ***clec*** *hon*; (split) ***crac*** *hwn*, ***hollt*** *hon*
crack *be* ***cracio*, *hollti***
c~ down on *cosbi'n llym*
c~ on *bwrw arni gyda'r gwaith*
c~ up *colli arnynt eu hunain*
cracking *ans* (idea) ***godidog*, *rhagorol***
crackle *be* ***clecian***
cradle *enw* ***crud*** *hwn*
craft *enw* ***crefft*** *hon*
craftsman *enw* ***crefftwr*** *hwn*
craftsmanship *enw* ***crefftwaith*** *hwn*

C

crafty *ans* ***cyfrwys***
crag *enw* ***craig*** *hon*
cram *be* ***stwffio***, ***gwthio***
cramp *enw* ***cwlwm gwythi*** *hwn*
cramp *be* ***llesteirio***
cranberries *enw* ***llugaeron*** *hyn*
crane *enw* ***craen*** *hwn*; (bird) ***garan*** *hon/hwn*
cranium *enw* ***penglog*** *hon*
crank *enw* ***cranc*** *hwn*
crankshaft *enw* ***crancwerthyd*** *hon*
cranny *enw* ***hollt*** *hwn/hon*
crap *enw* ***cachu***, ***cachiad*** *hwn*; (nonsense) ***rwtsh*** hwn
crap *be* ***cachu***
crash *be* ***gwrthdaro***; ***mynd i'r gwellt***
crash *enw* ***gwrthdrawiad***, ***twrw*** *hwn*
crate *enw* ***crât***, ***cawell*** *hwn*
crater *enw* ***crater***, ***ceudwll*** *hwn*
crave *be* ***erfyn***, ***crefu***, ***dyheu am***
  to c~ attention ***ysu am gael sylw***
craven *ans* ***llwfr***
craw *enw* ***crombil*** *hwn*
crawl *be* ***cropian***, ***ymlusgo***
crayon *enw* ***creon*** *hwn*
craze *enw* ***chwilen***, ***ffasiwn*** *hon*
craziness *enw* ***gwallgofrwydd***, ***ffolineb*** *hwn*
crazy *ans* ***gwallgof***, ***hurt***
  to be c~ about ***dwlu ar***
creak *be* ***gwichian***
cream *enw* ***hufen*** *hwn*
creamery *enw* ***hufenfa*** *hon*
crease *enw* ***plygiad***, ***crych*** *hwn*; (cricket) ***crîs*** *hwn*
create *be* ***creu***
creation *enw* ***cread*** *hwn*, ***creadigaeth*** *hon*
creative *ans* ***creadigol***
creature *enw* ***creadur*** *hwn*
crèche *enw* ***meithrinfa*** *hon*
credence *enw* ***cred***, ***coel*** *hon*
credibility *enw* ***hygrededd*** *hwn*
credible *ans* ***credadwy***
credit *enw* ***coel*** *hon*; ***clod*** *hwn/hon*
credit card *enw* ***cerdyn credyd*** *hwn*
creditable *ans* ***canmoladwy***
creditor *enw* ***credydwr*** *hwn*
credo *enw* ***credo*** *hwn*
credulous *ans* ***hygoelus***
creed *enw* ***credo*** *hon*
creek *enw* ***cilfach*** *hon*
creep *be* ***cropian***, ***sleifio***
cremate *be* ***llosgi***, ***amlosgi***
cremation *enw* ***amlosgiad*** *hwn*
crematorium *enw* ***amlosgfa*** *hon*
crescent *enw* ***cilgant*** *hwn*
cress *enw* ***berwr*** *hyn*
crest *enw* ***crib*** *hwn*; ***arfbais*** *hon*
crevasse *enw* ***crefas, (g)agendor*** *hwn*, ***hafn*** *hon*
crevice *enw* ***agen***, ***hollt*** *hon*
crew *enw* ***criw*** *hwn*
crib *enw* ***preseb*** *hwn*
crick *enw* ***cric*** *hwn*
cricket *enw* ***criced*** *hwn*
crime *enw* ***trosedd*** *hwn*

criminal *ans* ***troseddol***
c~ justice ***cyfiawnder troseddol*** *hwn*
criminal *enw* ***troseddwr*** *hwn*, ***troseddwraig*** *hon*
cringe *be* ***gwingo***; ***ymgreinio***
cripple *enw* ***crupl***, ***efrydd*** *hwn*
crisis *enw* ***argyfwng*** *hwn*
c~ management ***rheoli argyfwng***
crisp *ans* ***crimp***
criterion *enw* ***maen prawf*** *hwn*
critic *enw* ***beirniad*** *hwn*
critical *ans* ***beirniadol***; (crucial) ***allweddol***, ***hanfodol***; (maths and physics) ***critigol***; (of crisis) ***argyfyngus***
criticize *be* ***beirniadu***
to be severely c~d ***bod dan yr ordd***
criticism *enw* ***beirniadaeth*** *hon*
croak *be* ***crawcian***
crochet *be* ***crosio***
crockery *enw* ***llestri*** *hyn*
crocodile *enw* ***crocodeil*** *hwn*
crocus *enw* ***saffrwm*** *hwn*
croft *enw* ***tyddyn*** *hwn*
crofter *enw* ***tyddynwr*** *hwn*
crony *enw* ***hen ffrind*** *hwn*
cronyism *enw* ***ffrindgarwch*** *hwn*
crook *enw* ***ffon fugail*** *hon*; (criminal) ***dihiryn*** *hwn*
crooked *ans* ***cam***
crop *enw* ***cnwd*** *hwn*
the next c~ of students ***y to nesaf o fyfyrwyr***
to c~ up ***codi'i ben***
crop *be* ***tocio***, ***torri'n fyr/gwta***
cross *enw* ***croes*** *hon*
cross *be* ***croesi***
to c~ out ***tynnu llinell drwy***
cross *ans* ***croes***, ***blin***, ***crac***
cross-border *ans* ***trawsffiniol***
crossbow *enw* ***bwa croes*** *hwn*
cross-country *ans* ***traws gwlad***
cross-cutting issue *enw* ***mater trawsbynciol*** *hwn*
cross-examine *be* ***croesholi***
cross-eyed *ans* ***llygatgam***
crossing *enw* ***croesfan*** *hon/hwn*
cross-reference *enw* ***croesgyfeiriad*** *hwn*
crossroad *enw* ***croesffordd*** *hon*
cross section *enw* ***croestoriad*** *hwn*
crossword *enw* ***croesair*** *hwn*
crotch *enw* ***fforch***; ***ffwrch*** *hon*
crotchety *ans* ***pigog***
crouch *be* ***cyrcydu***, ***cwtsio***
crow *enw* ***brân*** *hon*
crowd *enw* ***torf***, ***tyrfa*** *hon*
crowd *be* ***tyrru***; ***llwytho***
crown *enw* ***coron*** *hon*
crown *be* ***coroni***
crucial *ans* ***hanfodol***
crucifix *enw* ***croes*** *hon*
crucify *be* ***croeshoelio***
crude *ans* ***amrwd***
cruel *ans* ***creulon***, ***brwnt***
cruelty *enw* ***creulondeb*** *hwn*

C

cruise *enw* ***mordaith*** *hon*
crumb *enw* ***briwsionyn*** *hwn*
crumble *be* ***briwo***, ***briwsioni***, ***syrthio'n ddarnau***
crumbly *ans* ***briwsionllyd***
crunch *be* ***crensian***
crunch *enw* ***pwynt tyngedfennol*** *hwn*
crumpled *ans* ***crych***
crush *be* ***gwasgu***, ***mathru***
crust *enw* (bread) ***crwstyn*** *hwn*; ***cramen*** *hon*
crustaceans *enw* ***cramenogion*** *hyn*
crutch *enw* ***ffon fagl*** *hon*
crux *enw* ***craidd*** *hwn*
cry *be* (weep) ***crïo, llefain***; (call) ***galw***
  cry wolf ***codi bwganod***
cry *enw* ***cri***, ***llef*** *hon*
crystal *enw* ***grisial:crisial*** *hwn*
  c~ clear ***mor glir â hoel ar bost***
crystalline *ans* ***grisialaidd: crisialaidd***
crystallize *be* ***crisialu***
cub *enw* ***cenau*** *hwn*
cube *enw* ***ciwb*** *hwn*
cubit *enw* ***cufydd*** *hwn*
cuckoo *enw* ***cwcw***, ***cog*** *hon*
cucumber *enw* ***ciwcymber: cucumer*** *hwn*
cuddle *be* ***cofleidio***, ***anwesu***
cudgel *enw* ***pastwn*** *hwn*
cue *enw* (theatre) ***ciw*** *hwn*; (billiards) ***ffon*** *hon*
cuff *enw* (garment) ***torch llawes*** *hon*; (blow) ***clowten*** *hon*
  off the c~ ***ffwrdd â hi***
culinary *ans* ***coginiol***
culminate *be* ***cyrraedd ei anterth***
culmination *enw* ***penllanw***, ***uchafbwynt*** *hwn*
culpable *ans* ***ar fai***
culprit *enw* ***troseddwr*** *hwn*, ***troseddwraig*** *hon*
cult *enw* ***cwlt*** *hwn*
cultivate *be* ***meithrin***, ***trin***
cultivation *enw* ***trin tir***
cultural *ans* ***diwylliadol***, ***diwylliannol***
  c~ heritage ***treftadaeth ddiwylliannol*** *hon*
culture *enw* ***diwylliant*** *hwn*; ***meddylfryd***
  c~ shock ***sioc i'r system***
cumbersome *ans* ***trwsgl***, ***afrosgo***
cumulative *ans* ***cynyddol***, ***cronnol***, ***cronnus***
cunning *ans* ***cyfrwys***
cup *enw* ***cwpan*** *hwn/hon*
cupidity *enw* ***gwanc*** *hwn*
cupboard *enw* ***cwpwrdd*** *hwn*
curate *enw* ***ciwrad*** *hwn*
curator *enw* ***curadur***, ***ceidwad*** *hwn*
curb *enw* ***atalfa*** *hon*
curb *be* ***ffrwyno***
curdle *be* ***cawsu***
curds *enw* ***ceulon*** *hyn*
cure *enw* ***iachâd*** *hwn*
cure *be* ***gwella***; (ham) ***halltu***

curiosity *enw* ***chwilfrydedd*** *hwn*
curious *ans* ***chwilfrydig***
curl *enw* ***modrwy*** *hon*
curl *be* ***modrwyo*, *cyrlio*, *cwrlo***
curlew *enw* ***gylfinir*** *hwn*
curly *ans* ***cyrliog*, *modrwyog***
currants *enw* ***cwrens*** *hyn*
currency *enw* ***arian treigl/breiniol*** *hwn*
current *ans* ***cyfredol***
  c~ affairs ***materion/pynciau'r dydd*** *hyn*
current *enw* ***cerrynt*** *hwn*
curriculum *enw* ***cwricwlwm*, *maes llafur*** *hwn*
curry *enw* ***cyrri*** *hwn*
curse *be* ***melltithio***
curse *enw* ***melltith*** *hwn*
cursory *ans* ***brysiog*; *cwta***
curt *ans* ***cwta*, *swta***
curtail *be* ***cwtogi***
curtain *enw* ***llen*** *hon*
curtsy *be* ***moesymgrymu***
curve *be* ***gwyro*, *troi***
curve *enw* ***tro*** *hwn*
cushion *enw* ***clustog*** *hon*
cushion *be* ***lliniaru***
cusp *enw* ***corn*** *hwn*
custard *enw* ***cwstard*** *hwn*
custodian *enw* ***ceidwad*** *hwn*
custom *enw* ***arfer*** *hwn/hon*
customary *ans* ***arferol***
customer *enw* ***cwsmer*** *hwn*
customised *ans* ***pwrpasol***
customs *enw* ***tollau*** *hyn*
customs officer *enw* ***swyddog y tollau*** *hwn*
cut *be* ***torri***
  to c~ a whole scene ***hepgor golygfa gyfan***
  to have one's work c~ out ***talcen caled***
cut *enw* ***toriad*** *hwn*
cutback *enw* ***cwtogiad*** *hwn*
cute *ans* ***ciwt***
cuticle *enw* ***pilen*** *hon*
cutlery *enw* ***cyllyll a ffyrc*** *hyn*
cutting *enw* ***toriad*** *hwn*
cutting *ans* ***miniog*, *llym***; (remark) ***brathog***
  c~-edge *enw* (blade) **min** *hwn*; *ans* ***diweddaraf un***
cycle *enw* ***cylch*; *beic*** *hwn*
cycle *be* ***seiclo***
cyclic *ans* ***cylchol***
cycling *be* ***beicio***
cyclist *enw* ***beiciwr*** *hwn*, ***beicwraig*** *hon*
cygnet *enw* ***cyw alarch*** *hwn*
cylinder *enw* ***silindr*** *hwn/hon*
cylindrical *ans* ***silindrog***
cymbal *enw* ***symbal*** *hwn*
cynic *enw* ***sinig*** *hwn*
cynical *ans* ***sinigaidd***
cynicism *enw* ***siniciaeth*** *hon*
cyst *enw* ***coden*** *hon*
cytoplasm *enw* ***sytoplasm*** *hwn*

d

D

dab *enw* (fish) ***lleden*** *hon*
dab *be* ***dabio***
dabble *be* ***ymhél â***
dachshund *enw* ***brochgi*** *hwn*
dad(dy) *enw* ***dad***, ***dat***, ***dada*** *hwn*
daffodil *enw* ***cenhinen Bedr*** *hon*
daft *ans* ***gwirion***, ***twp***
dagger *enw* ***dagr*** *hwn*
daily *ans* ***beunyddiol***, ***dyddiol***, ***o ddydd i ddydd***
daintiness *enw* ***lledneisrwydd*** *hwn*
dainty *ans* ***llednais***, ***del***
dairy *enw* ***llaethdy*** *hwn*
dais *enw* ***llwyfan*** *hwn/hon*
daisy *enw* ***llygad y dydd*** *hwn*
dale *enw* ***dyffryn*** *hwn*; ***dôl*** *hon*
dally *be* ***ymdroi***
dam *enw* ***argae*** *hwn*, ***cronfa ddŵr*** *hon*
dam *be* ***cronni***
damage *enw* ***difrod***, ***niwed*** *hwn*
damage *be* ***niweidio***
damages *enw* ***iawndal*** *hwn*
damn *be* ***damnio***
damnation *enw* ***damnedigaeth*** *hon*
damp *enw* ***lleithder*** *hwn*
damp *ans* ***llaith***
dampen *be* ***gwlychu***
to d~ enthusiasm ***lladd ysbryd***
damsel *enw* ***bun*** *hon*
damsons *enw* ***eirin duon*** *hyn*
dance *enw* ***dawns*** *hon*
dance *be* ***dawnsio***
dancer *enw* ***dawnsiwr*** *hwn*, ***dawnswraig*** *hon*
dandelion *enw* ***dant y llew*** *hwn*
dandle *be* ***dandwn***
dandruff *enw* ***cen*** *hwn*
dandy *enw* ***coegyn*** *hwn*
danger *enw* ***perygl*** *hwn*
dangerous *ans* ***peryglus***
dangle *be* ***hongian***
dank *ans* ***llaith***
dapper *ans* ***twt***, ***trwsiadus***
dappled *ans* ***brith***
dare *be* ***meiddio***, ***mentro***
I d~ say ***digon posibl***
daring *ans* ***beiddgar***
dark *ans* ***tywyll***
dark *enw* ***tywyllwch*** *hwn*
darken *be* ***tywyllu***
darkness *enw* ***tywyllwch*** *hwn*
darling *ans* ***annwyl***
you're a real d~ ***rwyt ti'n werth y byd***
darling *enw* ***cariad*** *hwn*
darn *be* ***brodio***
dart *enw* ***dart*** *hwn*
dart *be* ***gwibio***
dash *be* ***rhuthro***
dashing *ans* ***nwyfus***
data *enw* ***data*** *hyn*
d~ processing ***prosesu data***
d~ transmission ***trawsyrru data***
database *enw* ***cronfa ddata*** *hon*
date *enw* ***dyddiad*** *hwn*; (fruit)

datysen *hon*; (appointment) ***oed*** *hwn*
date *be* ***dyddio***
to d~ from ***mynd yn ôl i***
to up-d~ ***diweddaru***
dated *ans* ***wedi dyddio***, ***dyddiedig***; ***hen***
daughter *enw* ***merch*** *hon*
daunt *be* ***danto***, ***dantio***
dauntless *ans* ***eofn***
dawdle *be* ***tindroi***, ***loetran***
dawn *enw* ***gwawr*** *hon*
dawn *be* ***gwawrio***
day *enw* ***dydd***, ***diwrnod*** *hwn*
in this d~ and age ***yn y byd sydd ohoni***
daylight *enw* ***golau dydd*** *hwn*
daze *be* ***syfrdanu***
dazed *ans* ***syfrdan***
dazzle *be* ***dallu***
deacon *enw* ***blaenor***, ***diacon*** *hwn*
deacones *enw* ***diacones*** *hon*
dead *ans* ***marw***
deaden *be* ***lladd***
deadline *enw* ***dyddiad cau*** *hwn*
deadlock *enw* ***anghytundeb llwyr*** *hwn*
deadly *ans* ***marwol***, ***angheuol***
deaf *ans* ***byddar***, ***trwm fy (dy, ei etc.) nghlyw***
deafen *be* ***byddaru***
deafening *ans* ***byddarol***
deafness *enw* ***byddardod*** *hwn*
deal *enw* ***dêl*** *hon*
a good d~ of ***llawer***
a great d~ of ***cryn lawer***
deal *be* ***delio***, ***ymdrin â***
dealer *enw* ***masnachwr*** *hwn*
dean *enw* ***deon*** *hwn*
dear *ans* ***annwyl***; ***drud***
to hold d~ ***coleddu***
dearness *enw* ***anwyldeb*** *hwn*
dearth *enw* ***prinder*** *hwn*
death *enw* ***marwolaeth*** *hon*
d~ certificate ***tystysgrif marwolaeth*** *hon*
d~ penalty ***y gosb eithaf*** *hon*
debar *be* ***atal***
debase *be* ***diraddio***, ***darostwng***
debasement *enw* ***darostyngiad*** *hwn*
debatable *ans* ***dadleuol***
that's d~ ***mater o farn yw hynny***
debate *enw* ***dadl*** *hon*
debate *be* ***dadlau***
debilitate *be* ***gwanhau***, ***gwanio***
debilitating *ans* ***gwanychol***, ***niweidiol***
debit *enw* ***debyd*** *hwn*
debriefing *enw* ***ôl-drafodaeth*** *hon*
debris *enw* ***gweddillion***, ***malurion*** *hyn*; ***rwbel*** *hwn*
debt *enw* ***dyled*** *hon*
debtor *enw* ***dyledwr*** *hwn*
debug *be* ***dadfygio***
decade *enw* ***degawd*** *hwn*
decadence *enw* ***dirywiad*** *hwn*, ***dirywiaeth*** *hon*
decaffeinated *ans* ***digaffein***
decamp *be* ***ymadael***
decant *be* ***arllwys***

d

decay *be* ***dadfeilio***; ***pydru***
deceased *ans* ***ymadawedig***, ***diweddar***
deceit *enw* ***twyll*** *hwn*
deceitful *ans* ***twyllodrus***
deceive *be* ***twyllo***
decelerate *be* ***arafu***
December *enw* ***Rhagfyr*** *hwn*
decency *enw* ***gwedduster*** *hwn*
decent *ans* (seemly) ***gweddus***, ***gweddaidd***, ***parchus***; (satisfactory) ***purion***, ***gweddol***
decentralize *be* ***datganoli***
decentralized *ans* ***datganoledig***
deception *enw* ***twyll*** *hwn*
deceptive *ans* ***twyllodrus***
decide *be* ***penderfynu***
deciduous *ans* ***collddail***
decimal *ans* ***degol***
decimate *be* ***degymu***; ***difrodi***
decipher *be* ***datrys***
decision *enw* ***penderfyniad*** *hwn*
decisive *ans* ***penderfynol***; ***terfynol***
 this vote will be d~ ***y bleidlais hon fydd yn torri'r ddadl***
deck *enw* ***bwrdd*** *hwn*
deck *be* ***addurno***
declaim *be* ***llefaru***; ***traethu***
declaration *enw* ***datganiad*** *hwn*
declare *be* ***datgan***
 d~ an interest ***mynegi budd***, ***datgan diddordeb***
 the d~d strategy was ***y strategaeth a arddelid***
decline *enw* ***dirywiad*** *hwn*
 in d~ ***ar drai***
decline *be* ***ymwrthod â***, ***gwrthod***; ***edwino***, ***crebachu***
decode *be* ***datrys***, ***datgodio***
decompose *be* ***dadelfennu***; ***pydru***
decontaminate *be* ***dadlygru***
decontrol *be* ***dadreoli***
decorate *be* ***addurno***
decoration *enw* ***addurn***, ***addurniad*** *hwn*
decorative *ans* ***addurniadol***
decorous *ans* ***parchus***, ***propor***
decorousness *enw* ***urddas***, ***parchusrwydd*** *hwn*
decorum = ***decorousness***
decoy *enw* ***abwyd***, ***llith*** *hwn*
decrease *be* ***lleihau***
decree *enw* ***gorchymyn***, ***archddyfarniad*** *hwn*
decree *be* ***gorchymyn***, ***dyfarnu***
decrepit *ans* ***musgrell***
decry *be* ***bychanu***
dedicate *be* ***cysegru***; ***neilltuo***
 d~d network ***rhwydwaith pwrpasol*** *hwn*
dedication *enw* ***cysegriad***; ***cyflwyniad***; ***ymroddiad*** *hwn*
deduce *be* ***casglu***
 to d~ a meaning from ***dyfalu ystyr o***
deduct *be* ***tynnu allan***
deed *enw* ***gweithred*** *hon*
deem *be* ***ystyried***, ***cyfrif***
deep *ans* ***dwfn***
deepen *be* ***dyfnhau***, ***dwysáu***

deepness *enw* ***dyfnder*** *hwn*
deer *enw* ***carw*** *hwn*
deface *be* ***difwyno***
de facto ***mewn ffaith***
defamation *enw* ***enllib*** *hwn*
defamatory *ans* ***enllibus***, ***difenwol***
defame *be* ***difenwi***
default *enw* ***diffyg*** *hwn*
  by d~ ***drwy ddiffyg ystyriaeth***
defeat *enw* ***gorchfygiad*** *hwn*
defeat *be* ***gorchfygu***, ***bod yn drech na***
defecate *be* ***cachu***
defect *enw* ***nam***, ***diffyg*** *hwn*
defect *be* ***gadael***, ***gwrthgilio***
defective *ans* ***diffygiol***
defence *enw* ***amddiffyniad*** *hwn*
defend *be* ***amddiffyn***
defendant *enw* ***diffynnydd*** *hwn*
defensive *ans* ***amddiffynnol***
defer *be* ***gohirio***; ***ildio***
  d~ to ***ildio***
deference *enw* ***parch*** *hwn*
defiance *enw* ***herfeiddiwch***
  in d~ of ***er gwaethaf***
defiant *ans* ***herfeiddiol***
deficiency *enw* ***diffyg*** *hwn*
deficient *ans* ***diffygiol***, ***yn eisiau***
deficit *enw* ***diffyg*** *hwn*
defile *be* ***halogi***
define *be* ***diffinio***
definite *ans* ***pendant***
  the only d~ thing we know ***yr unig beth a wyddom i sicrwydd***
definition *enw* ***diffiniad*** *hwn*
  by d~ ***wrth reswm***
definitive *ans* ***terfynol***, ***diffiniol***
deflate *be* ***torri crib***; ***datchwyddo***
deflation *enw* (economic) ***datchwyddiant*** *hwn*
deflationary *ans* ***datchwyddol***
deflator *enw* (economic) ***datchwyddydd*** *hwn*
deflect *be* ***gwyro***
deflection *enw* ***gwyriad*** *hwn*
deform *be* ***anffurfio***
deformity *enw* ***anffurfiad*** *hwn*
defraud *be* ***twyllo***
defrost *be* ***dadrewi***
deft *ans* ***deheuig***
defunct *ans* ***wedi dod i ben***
defy *be* ***herio***
degenerate *be* ***dirywio***, ***dadfeilio***
degenerate *ans* ***dirywiedig***
degeneration *enw* ***dirywiad*** *hwn*
degradation *enw* ***diraddiad*** *hwn*
degrade *be* ***diraddio***
degree *enw* ***gradd*** *hon*
  d~ of satisfaction ***pa mor fodlon***
  this d~ of ***cymaint â hyn***
  to some d~ ***yn lled***, ***i raddau***
dehumanize *be* ***dad-ddyneiddio***
dehydration *enw* ***dadhydradedd*** *hwn*; ***colli gormod o ddŵr***
deify *be* ***dwyfoli***
deign *be* ***ymostwng***
deity *enw* ***duwdod*** *hwn*
dejected *ans* ***digalon***
dejection *enw* ***digalondid*** *hwn*
delay *enw* ***oediad*** *hwn*

with the minimum d~ ***yn ddioed*****,** ***yn ddiymdroi***
delay *be* ***oedi***
d~ing tactic ***tacteg ohirio*** *hon*
delectable *ans* ***hyfryd***
delectation *enw* ***pleser*** *hwn*
delegate *enw* ***cynrychiolydd*****,** ***cynadleddwr*** *hwn*
delegate *be* ***dirprwyo***
delegated *ans* ***dirprwyedig***
delegation *enw* ***dirprwyaeth*** *hon*
delete *be* ***dileu***
deleterious *ans* ***andwyol*****,** ***niweidiol***
to have a d~ effect ***amharu ar***
deliberate *be* ***ystyried*****,** ***trafod***
deliberate *ans* ***pwyllog*****;** ***bwriadol***
deliberation *enw* ***ystyriaeth*** *hon*
with sufficient d~ ***yn ddigon bwriadus***
delicacy *enw* ***danteithfwyd*****;** ***meinder*** *hwn*
delicate *ans* (finely beautiful) ***cywrain***; (health) ***eiddil*****,** ***gwanllyd***; (touch) ***ysgafn*****,** ***tyner***
d~ situation ***sefyllfa anodd*** *hon*
delicious *ans* ***amheuthun***
delight *enw* ***hyfrydwch*****;** ***pleser o'r mwyaf*** *hwn*
delight *be* ***swyno***
delighted *ans* ***wrth eich bodd***
delightful *ans* ***hyfryd***
delineate *be* ***dylunio***
delinquency *enw* ***tramgwydd*** *hwn*
delinquent *enw* ***troseddwr*****,** ***delincwent*****,** ***tramgwyddwr*** *hwn*
delinquent *ans* ***tramgwyddus***
delirious *ans* ***gorffwyll***
deliver *be* ***dosbarthu*****,** ***traddodi***
to d~ a better future ***sicrhau gwell dyfodol***
to d~ on its promises ***cadw at ei (g)air***
to d~ positive returns ***esgor ar ganlyniadau***
to d~ the goods ***bod cystal â'i (g)air***
delivery *be* ***trosglwyddo*****;** ***traddodi***
dell *enw* ***pant*** *hwn*
delta *enw* ***delta*** *hwn*
delude *be* ***twyllo***
deluge *enw* ***dilyw*** *hwn*
delusion *enw* ***twyll*****,** ***camargraff*** *hwn*; ***breuddwyd gwrach (wrth ei hewyllys)*** *hwn*
delve *be* ***ymbalfalu*****;** ***mynd ar eu trywydd***
demand *enw* ***galw*** *hwn*
by popular d~ ***ar gais y bobl***
on d~ ***yn ôl y galw***
demand *be* ***galw ar*****,** ***hawlio*****,** ***mynnu*****;** ***rhaid wrth***
demanding *ans* ***yn gofyn llawer gan*****,** ***anodd***
demarcate *be* ***gwahanu***
demean *be* ***ymostwng*****,** ***iselhau***
demeanour *enw* ***ymarweddiad*** *hwn*
demented *ans* ***gwallgof***
demise *enw* ***diwedd*** *hwn*; ***darfod (am)***

democracy *enw* ***democratiaeth*** *hon*
democratic *ans* ***democrataidd***
democratize *be* ***democrateiddio***
demolish *be* ***dymchwel: dymchwelyd***, ***chwalu***
demolition *enw* ***dymchweliad*** *hwn*
demon *enw* ***cythraul*** *hwn*
demoniacal *ans* ***cythreulig***
demonstrable *ans* ***dangosadwy***; ***amlwg***, ***eglur***
demonstrate *be* ***arddangos***; ***amlygu***; (protest) ***gwrthdystio***
demonstration *enw* ***arddangosiad***; ***gwrthdystiad*** *hwn*
demonstrator *enw* ***arddangoswr***; ***gwrthdystiwr*** *hwn*, ***gwrthdystwraig*** *hon*
demoralize *be* ***digalonni***, ***gwangalonni***; ***llethu ysbryd***
demote *be* ***diraddio***
demotivate *be* ***lladd pob awydd***, ***llethu pob cymhelliant***
demur *be* ***gwrthwynebu***
demure *ans* ***swil***
demystify *be* ***chwalu dirgelion***
den *enw* ***ffau***, ***gwâl*** *hon*
denial *enw* ***gwrthodiad***, ***gwadiad*** *hwn*
denigrate *be* ***difenwi***, ***pardduo***, ***dilorni***
denims *enw* ***dillad denim*** *hyn*
denizens *enw* ***trigolion*** *hyn*
denomination *enw* ***enwad*** *hwn*
denote *be* ***dynodi***
denouement *enw* ***diweddglo*** *hwn*
denounce *be* ***lladd ar***, ***condemnio***
denunciation *enw* ***condemniad*** *hwn*
dense *ans* ***dwys***, ***tew***
density *enw* ***dwysedd*** *hwn*
dent *enw* ***tolc*** *hwn*
dent *be* ***tolcio***
dentist *enw* ***deintydd*** *hwn*, ***deintyddes*** *hon*
dentistry *enw* ***deintyddiaeth*** *hon*
dentures *enw* ***dannedd gosod/ dodi*** *hyn*
denunciation *enw* ***condemniad*** *hwn*
denude *be* ***dinoethi***
deny *be* ***gwadu***
  to d~ them the right ***eu hamddifadu o'r hawl***
deodorant *enw* ***diaroglydd*** *hwn*
depart *be* ***ymadael***
  to d~ from the usual arrangement ***peidio â dilyn y drefn arferol***
department *enw* ***adran*** *hon*
departure *enw* ***ymadawiad*** *hwn*
  a new d~ ***datblygiad newydd*** *hwn*
  a radical d~ ***mae hyn yn dra gwahanol***
depend *be* ***dibynnu***
dependability *enw* ***dibynadwyaeth*** *hon*
dependable *ans* ***dibynadwy***, ***sad***
dependant *enw* ***dibynnydd*** *hwn*

dependent *ans* ***dibynnol***
depict *be* ***darlunio***
deplorable *ans* ***alaethus***, ***gwarthus***
deploy *be* ***trefnu***, ***lleoli***; ***cyflwyno***; ***defnyddio***
deplore *be* ***gresynu wrth/at***
depopulate *be* ***diboblogi***
depopulated *ans* ***wedi('i) d(d)iboblogi***
deport *be* ***alltudio***
deportation *enw* ***caethglud***, ***alltudiaeth*** *hon*
deportment *enw* ***ymddygiad***, ***ymarweddiad*** *hwn*
depose *be* ***disodli***
deposit *enw* ***ernes*** *hon*; (papers) ***adnau*** *hwn*
deposit *be* ***dyddodi***; ***gosod***
deposition *enw* ***diorseddiad***, ***diswyddiad*** *hwn*; (geol.) ***dyddodiad*** *hwn*
depot *enw* ***gorsaf***, ***storfa*** *hon*
deprave *be* ***llygru***
depravity *enw* ***llygredd*** *hwn*
deprecate *be* ***lladd ar***
depreciate *be* ***dibrisio***
depreciation *enw* ***dibrisiad*** *hwn*
depredation *enw* ***anrhaith*** *hon*, ***difrod*** *hwn*
depress *be* ***gwasgu***, ***dirwasgu***
depressed *ans* ***digalon***, ***di-hwyl***; (economic) ***dirwasgedig***
depressing *ans* ***heb fod yn codi calon dyn***
depression *enw* (physical) ***pant***; (economic) ***dirwasgiad***; (weather) ***diwasgedd***; (mental) ***iselder*** *hwn*
deprivation *enw* ***amddifadedd***, ***diffyg*** *hwn*
deprive *be* ***amddifadu***
deprived *ans* ***difreintiedig***
depth *enw* ***dyfnder*** *hwn*
in d~ ***yn fanwl***
deputation *enw* ***dirprwyaeth*** *hon*
depute/deputize *be* ***dirprwyo***
deputy *enw* ***dirprwy*** *hwn*
deranged *ans* ***wedi drysu***, ***gorffwyll***; ***colli arnynt eu hunain***
deregulate *be* ***dadreoleiddio***
deregulation *enw* ***dadreolaeth*** *hon*
derelict *ans* ***wedi'i esgeuluso***
d~ land ***tir diffaith***
derestrict *be* ***datgyfyngu***
deride *be* ***gwatwar***, ***gwawdio***
derision *enw* ***gwawd***, ***dirmyg*** *hwn*
derivative *ans* ***yn dynwared***
derive *be* ***deillio***
derogation *enw* ***rhan-ddirymiad*** *hwn*
derogatory *ans* ***dirmygus***, ***difrïol***
descant *enw* ***cyfalaw*** *hon*
descend *be* ***disgyn***
descendant *enw* ***disgynnydd*** *hwn*
descent *enw* ***disgyniad*** *hwn*
describe *be* ***disgrifio***; ***cwmpasu***
description *enw* ***disgrifiad*** *hwn*
descriptive *ans* ***disgrifiadol***
descriptor *enw* ***disgrifydd*** *hwn*

desecrate *be* ***halogi***
desert *enw* ***anialwch***, ***diffeithwch*** *hwn*
desert *be* ***cefnu ar***
desertion *enw* ***gwrthgiliad*** *hwn*
deserve *be* ***haeddu***, ***teilyngu***
design *be* ***cynllunio***, ***dylunio***
  designed to ***yn anelu at***
designate *be* ***enwebu***, ***pennu***, ***dynodi***
designate *ans* ***darpar***
designated *ans* ***dynodedig***, ***penodedig***
designation *enw* ***enwebiad***; ***penodiad***; ***teitl*** *hwn*
desirability *enw* ***dymunoldeb*** *hwn*; ***pa mor ddymunol***
desirable *ans* ***dymunol***, ***dewisol***; ***mawr ei angen***
desire *enw* ***awydd*** *hwn*, ***ysfa*** *hon*
desire *be* ***dymuno***, ***deisyfu***
desist *be* ***ymatal rhag***
desk *enw* ***desg*** *hon*
desktop *enw* (publishing) ***pen bwrdd*** *hwn*; (computer screen) ***bwrdd gwaith*** *hwn*
desolate *ans* ***unig***, ***anghyfannedd***
despair *enw* ***anobaith***, ***digalondid*** *hwn*
despair *be* ***anobeithio***, ***digalonni***
despairing *ans* ***diobaith***
desperate *ans* ***enbyd***; ***byrbwyll***; ***taer***
  they are d~ ***mae hi wedi mynd i'r pen arnynt***
desperation *enw* ***enbydrwydd*** *hwn*
despicable *ans* ***ffiaidd***, ***gwarthus***
despise *be* ***dirmygu***, ***wfftio***
despite *ardd* ***er gwaethaf***
despondency *enw* ***digalondid*** *hwn*
despondent *ans* ***digalon***
despot *enw* ***unben*** *hwn*
dessert *enw* ***melysfwyd***, ***pwdin*** *hwn*
destination *enw* ***pen y daith***, ***cyrchfan*** *hwn*
destiny *enw* ***tynged***, ***ffawd*** *hon*
destitute *ans* ***amddifad***; ***anghenus***; ***ar y clwt***
destitution *enw* ***tlodi***, ***cyni*** *hwn*
destroy *be* ***dinistrio***, ***difa***, ***dryllio***
destroyed *ans* ***drylliedig***
destruction *enw* ***dinistr***, ***distryw*** *hwn*
detach *be* ***datod***, ***gwahanu***, ***datgysylltu***
detachable *ans* ***datodadwy***
detail *enw* ***manylyn*** *hwn*
detail *be* ***manylu***
  d~ed nature ***manylder*** *hwn*
detain *be* ***cadw***
detect *be* ***canfod***, ***synhwyro***
  to d~ a note of ***clywed tinc o***
detection *enw* ***darganfyddiad*** *hwn*
detective *enw* ***ditectif*** *hwn*
detention *enw* ***carchariad***, ***ataliad*** *hwn*
deter *be* ***cadw rhag***, ***rhwystro***
detergent *enw* ***glanedydd*** *hwn*

deteriorate *be* ***dirywio***, ***gwaethygu***; (health) ***gwaelu***
deterioration *enw* ***dirywiad*** *hwn*
determination *enw* ***penderfyniad*** *hwn*
determine *be* ***penderfynu***, ***pennu***
determined *ans* ***penderfynol***
d~ effort ***ymdrech lew*** *hon*
detest *be* ***casáu***, ***ffieiddio***
detestable *ans* ***ffiaidd***
detonate *be* ***tanio***
detonation *enw* ***taniad, ffrwydrad*** *hwn*
detonator *enw* ***taniwr, ffrwydryn*** *hwn*
detour *enw* ***dargyfeiriad*** *hwn*
detract *be* ***tynnu wrth***, ***tynnu oddi ar***
detriment *enw* ***anfantais*** *hon*
to the d~ of ***ar draul***; ***amharu ar***
detrimental *ans* ***niweidiol***, ***andwyol***
devalue *be* ***gostwng mewn gwerth***
devastate *be* ***difrodi***, ***anrheithio***, ***gwneud drwg mawr***
devastating *ans* ***enbyd***, ***arswydus***
d~ experience ***profiad ysgytwol*** *hwn*
devastation *enw* ***difrod***, ***distryw*** *hwn*
develop *be* ***datblygu***
development *enw* ***cynnydd***, ***datblygiad*** *hwn*; ***twf*** *hwn*
deviant *ans* ***gwyrdroëdig***
deviate *be* ***gwyro***, ***cyfeiliorni***
deviation *enw* ***gwyriad*** *hwn*
device *enw* ***dyfais*** *hon*
devil *enw* ***diafol*** *hwn*
devious *ans* ***troellog***; (sly) ***cyfrwys***, ***ystrywgar***
devise *be* ***dyfeisio***
d~ terms ***bathu termau***
of their own d~ing ***o'u pen a'u pastwn eu hunain***
devoid *ans* ***amddifad***
devolution *enw* ***datganoli***
devolve *be* ***datganoli***
devolved *ans* ***datganoledig***
devote *be* ***cysegru***, ***rhoi***
d~ ***oneself ymroi***
devoted *ans* ***ffyddlon***; ***ymroddedig***
devotion *enw* ***ymroddiad*** *hwn*
devour *be* ***traflyncu***
devout *ans* ***duwiol***
dew *enw* ***gwlith*** *hwn*
dexterity *enw* ***deheurwydd*** *hwn*
dexterous *ans* ***deheuig***
diabetes *enw* ***y clefyd melys*** *hwn*
diabolic *ans* ***cythreulig***, ***dieflig***
diaeresis *enw* ***didolnod*** *hwn*
diagnose *be* ***ceisio canfod***
diagnosis *enw* ***barn feddygol*** *hon*
diagnostic *ans* ***diagnostig***
diagonal *ans* ***lletraws***
diagram *enw* ***diagram***, ***darlun*** *hwn*
dial *enw* ***deial*** *hwn*
dialect *enw* ***tafodiaith*** *hon*
dialogue *enw* ***ymddiddan*** *hwn*, ***ymgom***, ***sgwrs*** *hon*

diameter *enw* ***diamedr, trawsfesur*** *hwn*
diametrically (opposed) *adf* ***cwbl groes***, ***yn llwyr yn erbyn***, ***hollol wrthgyferbyniol***
diamond *enw* ***diemwnt*** *hwn*
diaphragm *enw* ***llengig*** *hwn*
diarrhoea *enw* ***dolur rhydd*** *hwn*
diary *enw* ***dyddiadur*** *hwn*
diatribe *enw* ***pregeth*** *hon*
dice *enw* ***dis*** *hwn*
dictate *be* ***arddweud***; ***deddfu***
the size of the rooms d~ the number of staff
mae maint yr ystafelloedd yn cyfyngu ar nifer y staff
to be d~d to ***bod ar drugaredd***
dictator *enw* ***unben*** *hwn*, ***unbennes*** *hon*
diction *enw* ***geirio***
dictionary *enw* ***geiriadur*** *hwn*
dictum *enw* ***dywediad*** *hwn*
diddle *be* ***twyllo***
die *be* ***marw***
diet *enw* ***diet*** *hwn*
diet *be* **colli** ***pwysau***
differ *be* ***gwahaniaethu***, ***amrywio***
beg to d~ ***anghytuno***
difference *enw* ***gwahaniaeth*** *hwn*
different *ans* ***gwahanol***
differential *enw* (gear) ***differyn*** *hwn*
differentiate *be* ***gwahaniaethu***
differentiated *ans* ***gwahaniaethol***
differentiation *enw* ***gwahaniaethiad*** *hwn*
difficult *ans* ***anodd***
I found it d~ to go there ***Yr oedd yn dipyn o dreth arnaf i***
what is d~ is ***y gamp yw***
difficulty *enw* ***anhawster***, ***trafferth*** *hwn*
it is with no little d~ ***nid ar chwarae bach y mae***
dig *be* ***palu***, ***cloddio***
digest *be* ***treulio***; ***ymgyfarwyddo***
digestion *enw* ***traul*** *hon*
digestive *ans* ***treuliadol***
digit *enw* ***bys***, ***digid*** *hwn*
digital *ans* ***digidol***
dignified *ans* ***urddasol***
dignity *enw* ***urddas*** *hon*
digress *be* ***crwydro***
digression *enw* ***crwydrad*** *hwn*
dilapidated *ans* ***wedi mynd â'i ben iddo***
dilate *be* ***lledu***
dilemma *enw* ***penbleth*** *hon/hwn*, ***cyfyng-gyngor*** *hwn*
diligence *enw* ***diwydrwydd***, ***dycnwch*** *hwn*
diligent *ans* ***diwyd***, ***dygn***
dilly-dally *be* ***llusgo traed***; ***sefyllian, tin-droi***
dilute *be* ***glastwreiddio***; ***gwanychu***
dim *ans* ***gwan***, ***pŵl***
dim *be* ***pylu***
dimension *enw* ***maintioli***, ***dimensiwn*** *hwn*
diminish *be* ***lleihau***, ***gostwng***; ***pylu***

d

diminutive *ans* ***bychan***
dimple *enw* ***pannwl*** *hwn*
dimwit *enw* ***twpsyn*** *hwn*
din *enw* ***mwstwr*** *hwn*
dine *be* ***ciniawa***
dingy *ans* ***di-raen***
dinner *enw* ***cinio*** *hwn*
dinosaur *enw* ***deinosor*** *hwn*
diocese *enw* ***esgobaeth*** *hon*
dip *enw* ***pant*** *hwn*
dip *be* ***trochi***, ***dipio***; ***gostwng***
diploma *enw* ***tystysgrif*** *hon*, ***diploma*** *hwn/hon*
diplomat *enw* ***diplomat*** *hwn*
diplomatic *ans* ***diplomataidd***, ***diplomyddol***
dire *ans* ***enbyd***, ***dybryd***
direct *ans* ***uniongyrchol***
direct *be* ***cyfeirio***
direction *enw* ***cyfarwyddyd***; ***cyfeiriad*** *hwn*; ***trywydd*** *hwn* **to point you in the right d~** ***eich gosod ar ben ffordd***
directive *enw* ***gorchymyn***, ***cyfarwyddyd*** hwn; (fin.; comptr.) ***cyfarwyddeb*** *hon*
directly *adf* ***yn syth***
director *enw* ***cyfarwyddwr*** *hwn*, ***cyfarwyddwraig*** *hon*
directorate *enw* ***cyfadran*** *hon*
directory *enw* ***cyfeirlyfr***, ***cyfarwyddiadur*** *hwn*
dirge *enw* ***galarnad*** *hon*
dirk *enw* ***dagr*** *hon*
dirt *enw* ***baw***, ***budreddi*** *hwn*
dirty *ans* ***brwnt***, ***budr***
disability *enw* ***anabledd*** *hwn*
disable *be* ***analluogi***
disabled *ans* ***anabl***
disadvantage *enw* ***anfantais*** *hon*
disadvantage *be* ***rhoi dan anfantais***; ***amharu ar***
disadvantaged *ans* ***dan anfantais***
disaffected *ans* ***anniddig***, ***anystywallt***, ***wedi'u dadrithio***
disaffection *enw* ***anfodlonrwydd*** *hwn*
disagree *be* ***anghytuno***, ***anghydweld***
disagreeable *ans* ***annymunol***, ***annifyr***
disagreement *enw* ***anghydfod***, ***anghytundeb*** *hwn*
disallow *be* ***gwrthod***, ***peidio â chaniatáu***
disappear *be* ***diflannu***
disappearance *enw* ***diflaniad*** *hwn*
disapplication *enw* ***datgymhwysiad*** *hwn*
disappoint *be* ***siomi***
disappointment *enw* **siom** *hon/hwn*
disapprobation *enw* ***anghymeradwyaeth*** *hon*
disapproval *enw* ***anghymeradwyaeth*** *hon*
disapprove *be* ***anghymeradwyo***
disarm *be* ***diarfogi***
disarray *enw* ***anhrefn*** *hon*

disassociate *be* ***ymddieithrio oddi wrth***
disaster *enw* ***trychineb*** *hon/hwn*
disastrous *ans* ***trychinebus***
disband *be* ***chwalu***
disbar *be* ***diarddel***
disbelief *enw* ***anghrediniaeth*** *hon*
disburse *be* ***talu, gwario (o gronfa)***
disbursement *enw* ***dostaliad*** *hwn*
disc *enw* ***disg*** *hwn/hon*
discard *be* ***taflu, diosg, rhoi o'r neilltu***
discern *be* ***canfod, dirnad***
discernible *ans* ***hyd y gellir gweld***
discerning *ans* ***craff***
discharge *enw* ***dadlwythiad; tywalltiad;*** (pus) ***crawn;*** (duty) ***diswyddiad, rhyddhad; cyflawniad*** *hwn*
discharge *be* ***dadlwytho, tywallt, gollwng; crawni; diswyddo, rhyddhau; cyflawni***
disciple *enw* ***disgybl*** *hwn*
disciplinary *ans* ***disgyblaethol***
d~ action ***camau disgyblu*** *hyn*
discipline *enw* ***disgyblaeth*** *hon*
discipline *be* ***disgyblu***
disclaim *be* ***gwadu***
discomfiture *enw* ***annifyrrwch, embaras*** *hwn*
disconcert *be* ***taflu (rhywun) oddi ar ei echel***
disclose *be* ***dadlennu, datgelu***
disclosure *enw* ***dadleniad, datguddiad*** *hwn*
disco *enw* ***disgo*** *hwn*
discolour *be* ***troi lliw, llychwino***
discomfort *enw* ***anesmwythder, anesmwythyd*** *hwn*
disconnect *be* ***datgysylltu***
disconsolate *ans* ***digysur; galarus***
discontent *enw* ***anfodlonrwydd, anniddigrwydd*** *hwn*
discontented *ans* ***anniddig, anfodlon***
discontinue *be* ***rhoi terfyn ar***
discontinuity *enw* ***diffyg parhad*** *hwn*
discontinuous *ans* ***digyswllt***
discord *enw* ***anghytgord*** *hwn*
discount *enw* ***gostyngiad, disgownt*** *hwn*
discount *be* ***rhoi disgownt; diystyru***
discourage *be* ***anghymeradwyo; digalonni***
to d~ teachers from ***peri i athrawon ymatal rhag***
to d~ weeds ***atal chwyn***
discouragement *enw* ***digalondid*** *hwn;* ***anghymeradwyaeth*** *hon*
discourse *enw* ***ymddiddan*** *hwn,* ***trafodaeth*** *hon*
discourteous *ans* ***anghwrtais***
discourtesy *enw* ***diffyg cwrteisi*** *hwn*
discover *be* ***darganfod***
now you can d~ for yourself ***ewch ati nawr i weld sut mae***
discovery *enw* ***darganfyddiad*** *hwn*

discredit *be* ***difrïo***, ***tanseilio***
discreet *ans* ***cynnil***; ***pwyllog***
discrepancy *enw* ***anghysondeb***, ***gwahaniaeth*** *hwn*
discrete *ans* ***ar wahân***
discretion *enw* ***barn*** *hon*, ***synnwyr***, ***doethineb*** *hwn*
to have d~ to ***bod yn rhydd i***
discretionary *ans* ***diamod***, ***dewisol***
discriminate *be* ***gwahaniaethu***
discrimination *enw* ***anffafriaeth***; ***ffafriaeth*** *hon*; ***chwaeth*** *hon*
discursive *ans* ***cwmpasog***
discuss *be* ***trafod***
discussion *enw* ***trafodaeth*** *hon*
disdain *enw* ***dirmyg*** *hwn*
disdain *be* ***dirmygu***
disdainful *ans* ***dirmygus***
disease *enw* ***clefyd*** *hwn*
disembark *be* ***glanio***
disembowel *be* ***diberfeddu***
disembroil *be* ***datrys***
disempower *be* ***dwyn grym oddi ar***
disenchant *be* ***dadrithio***
disenchanted *ans* ***dadrithiedig***
disencumber *be* ***ysgafnhau baich***
disenfranchise *be* ***difreinio***, ***dadfreinio***
disenfranchised *ans* ***difreintiedig***
disengage *be* ***rhyddhau***, ***datgysylltu***
disengaged *ans* ***wedi'i ymddieithrio***
disentangle *be* ***datod***, ***datglymu***
disestablish *be* ***datgysylltu***, ***dadsefydlu***
disfigure *be* ***anharddu***, ***hagru***
disgrace *enw* ***anfri***, ***gwarth*** *hwn*
disgrace *be* ***dwyn anfri ar***
disgraceful *ans* ***gwarthus***
disgruntled *ans* ***blin***
disguise *enw* ***cuddwisg*** *hon*
disguise *be* ***cuddio***
disgust *enw* ***ffieidd-dod***, ***diflastod*** *hwn*
disgust *be* ***mae'n troi ar(naf)***
dish *enw* ***dysgl*** *hon*
dishearten *be* ***digalonni***
dishes *enw* ***llestri*** *hyn*
dishevelled *ans* ***aflêr***
dishonest *ans* ***anonest***
dishonesty *enw* ***anonestrwydd*** *hwn*
dishonour *enw* ***amarch*** *hwn*
dishonour *be* ***amharchu***
disillusion *be* ***dadrithio***
disillusioned *ans* ***dadrithiedig***, ***siomedig***, ***colli ffydd yn***
disincentive *enw* ***maen tramgwydd*** *hwn*
disinclined *ans* ***amharod***
disinfect *be* ***diheintio***
disinfectant *enw* ***diheintydd*** *hwn*
disingenuous *ans* ***ffuantus***
disinherit *be* ***diarddel***
disintegrate *be* ***chwalu***
disinterested *ans* ***diduedd***; ***difater***
disjointed *ans* ***tameidiog***
disk *enw* ***disg*** *hwn/hon*

dislike *enw* ***atgasedd*** *hwn*
they are d~d ***nid oes fawr o neb yn eu hoffi***
dislike *be* ***casáu***
dislocate *be* ***datgymalu***
dislocation *enw* ***datgymaliad*** *hwn*
dislodge *be* ***symud***, ***rhyddhau***
disloyal *ans* ***annheyrngar***
dismal *ans* ***dilewyrch***
dismantle *be* ***dinoethi***; ***datgymalu***
dismay *enw* ***siom*** *hwn/hon*, ***gofid*** *hwn*
dismember *be* ***datgymalu***
dismiss *be* ***diswyddo***; ***wfftio***, ***diystyru***
dismissal *enw* ***diswyddiad*** *hwn*
dismount *be* ***disgyn***
disobedience *enw* ***anufudd-dod*** *hwn*
disobedient *ans* ***anufudd***
disobey *be* ***anufuddhau***
disorder *enw* ***anhrefn*** *hon*
disorderly *ans* ***anhrefnus***, ***afreolus***
disorientate *be* ***drysu***
disown *be* ***gwadu***
disparage *be* ***dibrisio***, ***bychanu***, ***dilorni***, ***lladd ar***
disparaging *ans* ***dilornus***
disparate *ans* ***gwahanol***, ***amrywiol***
disparity *enw* ***anghyfartaledd***, ***gwahaniaeth***, ***anghysondeb*** *hwn*
dispatch *be* ***anfon***
dispassionate *ans* ***pwyllog***, ***dideimlad***; ***diduedd***, ***gwrthrychol***
dispel *be* ***chwalu***; ***dileu***
dispensable *ans* ***diangen***, ***afraid***
dispensary *enw* ***fferyllfa*** *hon*
dispensation *enw* ***gollyngiad*** *hwn*; ***caniatâd*** *hwn*
dispense *be* ***dosbarthu***, ***gweinyddu***; ***anwybyddu***
disperse *be* ***chwalu***, ***gwasgaru***
dispirited *ans* ***digalon***, ***â'i ben yn ei blu***
displace *be* ***disodli***
display *enw* ***arddangosfa*** *hon*
display *be* ***arddangos***
to d~ care ***arfer gofal***
displease *be* ***digio***
displeased *ans* ***anfodlon***, ***anfoddog***
displeasure *enw* ***anfodlonrwydd*** *hwn*
disposal *enw* ***gwarediad*** *hwn*
the money at my d~ ***yr arian sydd gennyf***
to put at the d~ of ***rhoi at wasanaeth***
dispose *be* ***cael gwared ar***
disposition *enw* ***anian*** *hwn/hon*
disprove *be* ***gwrthbrofi***
disputatious *ans* ***dadleugar***
dispute *enw* ***cynnen***, ***dadl*** *hon*, ***anghydfod*** *hwn*
dispute *be* ***dadlau***; ***herio***
disqualification *enw* ***diarddeliad***, ***gwaharddiad*** *hwn*

disqualify *be* ***diarddel***, ***datgymhwyso***, ***anghymhwyso***
disquiet *enw* ***anesmwythyd***, ***anniddigrwydd*** *hwn*
disregard *enw* ***difaterwch***, ***esgeulustod***
disregard *be* ***anwybyddu***, ***diystyru***
disreputable *ans* ***anghlodwiw***, ***gwarthus***
disrepute *enw* ***anfri*** *hwn*
disrespect *enw* ***diffyg parch*** *hwn*
disrespectful *ans* ***amharchus***
disrupt *be* ***tarfu ar***, ***aflonyddu***
disruptive *ans* ***aflonyddgar***, ***anystywallt***
disruptiveness *enw* ***aflonyddwch*** *hwn*
dissatisfaction *enw* ***anfodlonrwydd*** *hwn*
dissatisfied *ans* ***anfodlon***
dissect *be* ***dyrannu***
dissemble *be* ***celu***
disseminate *be* ***lledaenu***
dissension *enw* ***anghytundeb***, ***anghydfod*** *hwn*
Dissent *enw* ***Anghydffurfiaeth***, ***Ymneilltuaeth*** *hon*
dissent *be* ***dadlau â***
Dissenter *enw* ***Anghydffurfiwr*** *hwn*, ***Anghydffurfwraig*** *hon*
dissenting *ans* ***anghytûn***
dissertation *enw* ***traethawd*** *hwn*
disservice *enw* ***anghymwynas*** *hwn*
dissident *enw* ***gwrthwynebydd***, ***anghydffurfiwr*** *hwn*
dissimilar *ans* ***annhebyg***
dissimilarity *enw* ***annhebygrwydd*** *hwn*
dissimulate *be* ***celu***
dissipate *be* ***gwasgaru***, ***chwalu***
dissipation *enw* ***gwasgariad*** *hwn*; ***afradlonedd*** *hwn*
dissociate *be* ***datgysylltu***
dissolute *ans* ***afrad***, ***ofer***
dissolution *enw* ***diddymiad*** *hwn*
dissolve *be* ***toddi***
dissonance *enw* ***anghyseinedd*** *hwn*
dissonant *ans* ***amhersain***
dissuade *be* ***cymell rhag***, ***darbwyllo rhag***
distance *enw* ***pellter*** *hwn*
  d~ learning ***dysgu o bell***
distance *be* ***pellhau***, ***ymbellhau***
distant *ans* ***pell***
distaste *enw* ***diflastod*** *hwn*
distasteful *ans* ***annymunol***, ***di-chwaeth***
distend *be* ***chwyddo***
distil *be* ***distyllu***
distinct *ans* ***eglur***; ***gwahanol***
distinction *enw* ***gwahaniaeth***; ***anrhydedd*** *hwn*
  of some d~ ***pur arbennig***
  to make a d~ between ***gwahaniaethu rhwng***
  to serve with d~ ***rhoi gwasanaeth rhagorol***
distinctive *ans* ***nodweddiadol***; ***gwahanol***; ***trawiadol***

distinguish *be* ***gwahaniaethu***, ***dynodi'r gwahaniaeth***
distinguishable *ans* ***gwahanadwy***
distort *be* ***ystumio***, ***llurgunio***
distortion *enw* ***gwyrdroad***, ***llurguniad*** *hwn*
distract *be* ***tynnu sylw***; ***colli golwg ar***
distracted *ans* ***synfyfyriol***; ***dryslyd***
distress *enw* ***gofid*** *hwn*
distribute *be* ***dosbarthu***, ***rhannu***
distribution *enw* ***dosraniad*** *hwn*
district *enw* ***ardal*** *hon*
distrust *enw* ***drwgdybiaeth*** *hon*
distrust *be* ***drwgdybio***
disturb *be* ***tarfu***, ***aflonyddu ar***; ***torri ar draws***
disturbance *enw* ***cynnwrf*** *hwn*
  d~ allowance ***lwfans tarfu*** *hwn*
disturbed *ans* ***aflonydd***, ***afreolaidd***; ***anniddig***, ***pryderus***
disunite *be* ***gwahanu***
disuse *enw* ***diffyg defnydd*** *hwn*
disused *ans* ***heb ei (d)defnyddio***
ditch *enw* ***ffos*** *hon*
ditch *be* ***cael gwared ar***
dither *be* ***petruso***, ***tin-droi***
dive *be* ***plymio***
diver *enw* ***deifiwr***, ***trochiwr***, ***trochwr*** *hwn*
diverge *be* ***ymwahanu***; ***dargyfeirio***
divergence *enw* ***gwahaniaeth*** *hwn*
divergent *ans* ***gwahanol***, ***ymwahanol***
diverse *ans* ***gwahanol***
diversify *be* ***arallgyfeirio***
diversion *enw* ***dargyfeiriad*** *hwn*
diversity *enw* ***amrywiaeth*** *hon/hwn*
divert *be* ***dargyfeirio***
divest *be* ***dihatru***
divide *be* ***rhannu***
dividers *enw* ***cwmpas*** *hwn*
divination *enw* ***darogan***
divine *ans* ***dwyfol***
divinity *enw* ***duwdod*** *hwn*
divisible *ans* ***rhanadwy***
division *enw* ***rhaniad***, ***ymraniad*** *hwn*
  d~ of opinion ***gwahaniaeth barn*** *hwn*
divorce *enw* ***ysgariad*** *hwn*
divorce *be* ***ysgaru***
  to be d~d from ***bod heb gysylltiad â***
divorced *ans* ***ysgar***
divulge *be* ***datgelu***, ***dadlennu***
dizziness *enw* ***pendro*** *hon*
dizzy *ans* ***penysgafn***, ***penfeddw***
do *be* ***gwneud***
  after all is said and done ***wedi'r cyfan***
  do call ***galwch***, ***da chi***
  done for ***wedi canu ar***
  dos and don'ts ***pethau i'w gwneud ac i beidio â'u gwneud***
  half-done ***ar ei hanner***
  to do well ***cael hwyl arni***
  to do with ***ymwneud â***
do-it-yourself *enw* ***o'th waith dy hun***

d

docile *ans* ***dof***
dock *enw* ***doc*** *hwn*; (plant) ***tafolen*** *hon*
doctor *enw* ***meddyg***; (academic) ***doethur*** *hwn*
doctrine *enw* ***athrawiaeth***, ***dysgeidiaeth*** *hon*
document *enw* ***dogfen*** *hon*
document *be* ***cofnodi***
documentary *ans* ***dogfennol***
documentation *enw* ***dogfennaeth*** *hon*
dodder *be* ***gwegian***
dodge *be* ***ochrgamu***; ***osgoi***
dodgy *ans* ***amheus***
dodo *enw* ***dodo*** *hwn*
doe *enw* ***elain***, ***ewig*** *hon*
dog *enw* ***ci*** *hwn*
dogfight *enw* ***ysgarmes*** *hon*
dogfish *enw* ***morgi, penci*** *hwn*
dogged *ans* ***dygn***
doggerel *enw* ***cerddi talcen slip*** *hyn*
dogmatic *ans* ***dogmataidd***
dogsbody *enw* ***gwas bach*** *hwn*
dole *enw* ***dôl*** *hwn*
dole *be* ***dosrannu***
doll *enw* ***dol:doli*** *hon*
dollar *enw* ***doler*** *hon*
dollop *enw* ***talp*** *hwn*
dolmen *enw* ***cromlech*** *hon*
dolorous *ans* ***prudd***
dolphin *enw* ***dolffin*** *hwn*, ***môr-hwch*** *hwn/hon*
dolt *enw* ***twpsyn*** *hwn*
domain *enw* ***tiriogaeth*** *hon*; ***parth*** *hwn*
d~ name ***enw parth*** *hwn*
dome *enw* ***cromen*** *hon*
domestic *ans* ***teuluol***, ***teuluaidd***
domesticate *be* ***hyweddu***, ***cartrefoli***
domesticity *enw* ***bywyd cartref*** *hwn*
domicile *enw* ***cartref*** *hwn*
domiciliary *ans* ***cartref***
dominance *enw* ***goruchafiaeth*** *hon*
dominant *ans* ***mwyaf blaenllaw***, ***blaenaf***, ***pennaf***, ***amlycaf***
dominate *be* ***tra-arglwyddiaethu***
dominating *ans* ***llywodraethol***
domination *enw* ***goruchafiaeth***, ***tra-arglwyddiaeth*** *hon*
domineer *be* ***gormesu***
domino *enw* ***domino*** *hwn*
don *be* ***gwisgo***
donate *be* ***rhoi:rhoddi***
donation *enw* ***rhodd*** *hon*
done gw. **'do'**
donkey *enw* ***asyn***, ***mul*** *hwn*
d~'s years ***oes mul*** *hwn*
donnish *ans* ***academaidd***
donor *enw* ***rhoddwr*** *hwn*, ***rhoddwraig*** *hon*
don't *gorchymyn* ***paid***
doom *enw* ***tranc*** *hwn*
d~ and gloom ***gofid a gwae***
they are d~ed ***mae hi wedi canu arnynt***
Doomsday *enw* ***Dydd y Farn*** *hwn*

door *enw* ***drws*** *hwn*
doorman *enw* ***porthor*** *hwn*
doorstep *enw* ***trothwy*** *hwn*
doorway *enw* ***drws***, ***porth*** *hwn*
dormant *ans* ***ynghwsg***
dormitory *enw* ***ystafell gysgu*** *hon*
dormouse *enw* ***pathew*** *hwn*
dosage *enw* ***dogn*** *hwn*
dose *enw* ***dogn*** *hwn*
dose *be* ***dogni***
dossier *enw* ***ffeil*** *hon*
dot *enw* ***dot:dotyn*** *hwn*
dot *be* ***dotio***
dote *be* ***dwlu***, ***dotio***
dotty *ans* ***penchwiban***, ***gwirion***
double *ans* ***dwbl***, ***dwywaith***
double *be* ***dyblu***
double room *enw* ***ystafell ddwbl*** *hon*
double-dealing *enw* ***chwarae'r ffon ddwybig*** *hon*
doubt *enw* ***amheuaeth*** *hon*
  in d~ ***yn y fantol***
  there's no d~ ***heb os nac onibai***; ***yn gwbl bendant***
doubt *be* ***amau***
doubtful *ans* ***amheus***
doubtless *adf* ***diau***; ***mae'n siŵr***
dough *enw* ***toes*** *hwn*
doughnut *enw* ***toesen*** *hon*
doughty *ans* ***glew***, ***dewr***
dour *ans* ***cyndyn***, ***llym***
douse *be* ***trochi***; ***diffodd***
dove *enw* ***colomen*** *hon*
dovecot *enw* ***colomendy*** *hwn*
dowdy *ans* ***didoreth***, ***di-raen***
dowel *enw* ***hoelbren*** *hwn*
down *enw* ***manblu*** *hyn*
down *be* ***llorio***; ***llyncu***
down *adf* ***i lawr***, ***i waered***; *ans* ***digalon***; *ardd* ***i lawr***
  blown d~ ***chwythu i'r llawr***
  cool d~ ***oeri graddol***; ***pwyllo***
  deep d~ ***yn y bôn***
  looking back d~ the years ***edrych dros ysgwydd y blynyddoedd***
  when they are d~ ***pan fyddant ar eu gwendid***
down-and-out *enw* ***caridým*** *hwn*
downcast *ans* ***penisel***
downfall *enw* ***cwymp*** *hwn*
downgrade *be* ***israddio***
downhearted *ans* ***digalon***, ***isel ei ysbryd***
downhill *enw* ***goriwaered*** *hwn*; *adf* ***ar i waered***
downright *ans* ***hollol***
downs *enw* ***twyni*** *hyn*
downside *enw* ***gwendid***, ***diffyg*** *hwn*
downstairs *adf* ***lawr llawr***
downtrodden *ans* ***dan orthrwm***
downturn *enw* ***dirywiad*** *hwn*
downward *adf* ***i waered***; ***o'r brig i'r bôn***
dowry *enw* ***gwaddol*** *hwn*
dowse *be* ***dewinio dŵr***
doyen *enw* ***hynafgwr*** *hwn*
doze *be* ***hepian***, ***pendwmpian***

d

dozen *enw* ***dwsin*** *hwn*
drab *ans* ***di-liw***, ***di-fflach***
draconian *ans* ***llym***, ***llethol***
draft *enw* ***drafft*** *hwn/hon*
draft *be* ***drafftio***
draftsman *enw* ***drafftsmon*** *hwn* (**drafftsmyn**)
drag *be* ***llusgo***
dragon *enw* ***draig*** *hon*
dragonfly *enw* ***gwas-y-neidr*** *hwn*
drain *enw* ***cwter***, ***ffos***, ***draen*** *hon*
  to be a d~ on ***bod yn faich/dreth ar***
drain *be* ***draenio:traenio***
drainage *enw* ***draeniad***; (sewer) ***carthffosiaeth*** *hon*
drake *enw* ***barlat***, ***marlat*** *hwn*
drama *enw* ***drama*** *hon*
dramatic *ans* ***dramataidd: dramatig***
dramatist *enw* ***dramodydd*** *hwn*
dramatize *be* ***dramateiddio***
drape *be* ***gorchuddio***
drastic *ans* ***eithafol, llym***
  d~ overhaul ***ailwampio'n llwyr***
draught *enw* ***drafft*** *hwn*
draughty *ans* ***drafftiog***
draw *be* ***tynnu***
  to d~ a distinction ***gwahaniaethu***
  to d~ a lesson from ***dysgu gwers oddi wrth***
  to d~ a response ***ennyn ymateb***
  to d~ closer ***dynesu***, ***closio***
  to d~ out ***amlygu***; ***tynnu sylw***
  to d~ to a close ***dirwyn i ben***
drawback *enw* ***anfantais*** *hon*
drawer *enw* ***drâr:drôr*** *hwn/hon*
drawing *enw* ***llun:lluniad*** *hwn*
drawing room *enw* ***parlwr*** *hwn*
dread *enw* ***arswyd*** *hwn*
dread *be* ***arswydo***, ***dychryn***
dreadful *ans* ***arswydus***, ***erchyll***
dream *enw* ***breuddwyd*** *hwn/hon*
  d~ job ***swydd ddelfrydol*** *hon*
dream *be* ***breuddwydio***
dreamer *enw* ***breuddwydiwr*** *hwn*
dreary *ans* ***diflas***
dregs *enw* ***gwaddod***, ***sorod*** *hyn*
drench *be* ***trochi***, ***gwlychu***; ***drensio***
dress *enw* ***gwisg***, ***ffrog*** *hon*
dress *be* ***gwisgo***
  dressing up ***gwisgo'n ffansi***
dresser *enw* ***dresel***, ***seld*** *hon*
dressy *ans* ***trwsiadus***
dribble *be* ***driblo:driblan***
driblet *enw* ***diferyn*** *hwn*
drift *be* ***drifftio***; (snow) ***lluwchio***
driftwood *enw* ***broc môr*** *hwn*
drill *enw* ***dril*** *hwn*
drill *be* ***tyllu***
drink *enw* ***diod*** *hon*
drink *be* ***yfed***; ***diota***, ***llymeitian***
drinkable *ans* ***yfadwy***
drinker *enw* ***yfwr***, ***llymeitiwr*** *hwn*
drip *enw* ***diferyn*** *hwn*
drip *be* ***diferu***
dripping *enw* ***toddion*** *hyn*
dripping *ans* ***diferol***
drive *be* ***gyrru***

drive *enw* (in car) ***tro*** *hwn*; (mech.) ***gyriant*** *hwn*; (of person) ***mynd***, ***egni*** *hwn*; (campaign) ***ymgyrch***, ***ymdrech*** *hon*
whist d~ ***gyrfa chwist*** *hon*
drivel *enw* ***glafoerion*** *hyn*; ***dwli*** *hwn*, ***lol*** *hon*
drivel *be* ***glafoerio***
driver *enw* ***gyrrwr*** *hwn*, ***gyrwraig*** *hon*
driving licence *enw* ***trwydded yrru*** *hon*
drizzle *enw* ***glaw mân*** *hwn*
droll *ans* ***doniol***, ***ysmala***
dromedary *enw* ***dromedari*** *hwn*
drone *be* ***grwnan***
drone *enw* ***gwenynen segur/ ormes*** *hon*; ***bygegyr*** *hwn*; (sound) ***grŵn***, ***sŵn*** *hwn*
droop *be* ***pendrymu***, ***diffygio***
drooping *ans* ***llipa***
drop *enw* ***dafn***, ***diferyn*** *hwn*
drop *be* ***cwympo***, ***gollwng***
d~ out ***ymgilio***, ***cilio***
drop kick *enw* ***cic adlam*** *hon*
droplet *enw* ***defnyn*** *hwn*
drops *enw* ***dafnau***, ***diferion*** *hyn*
dross *enw* ***sorod*** *hyn*, ***gwaddod*** *hwn*
drought *enw* ***sychder:sychdwr*** *hwn*
drover *enw* ***porthmon*** *hwn*
drown *be* ***boddi***
drowse *be* ***pendwmpian***
drowsiness *enw* ***syrthni*** *hwn*
drowsy *ans* ***cysglyd***, ***swrth***
drub *be* ***cledro***, ***curo***
drug *enw* ***cyffur*** *hwn*
drug *be* ***drygio***
druid *enw* ***derwydd*** *hwn*
drum *enw* ***drwm*** *hwn*
drum *be* ***drymio***
drumer *enw* ***drymiwr*** *hwn*
drunk *ans* ***meddw***
drunkard *enw* ***meddwyn*** *hwn*
drunkenness *enw* ***medd-dod*** *hwn*
dry *ans* ***sych***
dry *be* ***sychu***
dryer *enw* ***sychwr*** *hwn*
dryness *enw* ***sychder***, ***crasder*** *hwn*
dual *ans* ***deuol***
dub *be* (knight) ***urddo***; (leather) **iro**, **dwbio**; (T.V. voice) ***trosleisio***
dubious *ans* ***amheus***, ***drwgdybus***
duchess *enw* ***duges*** *hon*
duchy *enw* ***dugiaeth*** *hon*
duck *enw* ***hwyaden*** *hon*
duck *be* ***plygu pen***; (in water) ***trochi***; (avoid) ***osgoi***
duct *enw* ***dwythell*** *hon*
dud *ans* ***diwerth***
due *ans* ***dyladwy***
d~ to ***yn codi o***, ***i'w briodoli i***
in d~ course ***maes o law***
duel *enw* ***gornest***, ***cyfranc*** *hon*
dues *enw* ***dyledion*** *hyn*
duet *enw* ***deuawd*** *hwn*
duffer *enw* ***llo***, ***twpsyn*** *hwn*
duke *enw* ***dug*** *hwn*

dukedom *enw* ***dugiaeth*** *hon*
dull *ans* ***twp***; ***afloyw***, ***pŵl***
dumb *ans* ***mud***
dumbfound *be* ***syfrdanu***
dummy *enw* ***teth*** *hon*
dump *enw* ***tomen*** *hon*
dump *be* ***gollwng***
dumpling *enw* ***twmplen*** *hon*
dumps *enw* ***gwaelodion*** *hyn*
dumpy *ans* ***tew***
dun *ans* ***llwyd***
dunce *enw* ***twpsyn*** *hwn*
dune *enw* ***twyn (tywod)*** *hwn*
dung *enw* ***tail*** *hwn*, ***tom:dom*** *hon*
dungeon *enw* ***dwnsiwn*** *hwn*
dunghill *enw* ***tomen*** *hon*
dunk *be* ***dowcio***
dupe *be* ***twyllo***
duplicate *be* ***dyblygu***
duplicates *enw* ***dyblygion*** *hyn*
duplicity *enw* ***dichell*** *hon*
durability *enw* ***gwydnwch: gwytnwch*** *hwn*, ***hirhoedledd*** *hwn*
durable *ans* ***gwydn***, ***parhaol***
duration *enw* ***parhad***, ***hyd*** *hwn*; ***ystod*** *hon*
duress *enw* ***gorfodaeth*** *hon*
during *ardd* ***yn ystod***, ***trwy gydol***
dusk *enw* ***cyfnos***, ***gwyll*** *hwn*
dusky *ans* ***tywyll***
dust *enw* ***llwch*** *hwn*
dust *be* ***tynnu llwch***
dustcart *enw* ***lorri ludw*** *hon*
duster *enw* ***clwt***, ***clwtyn*** *hwn*
dust jacket *enw* ***siaced lwch*** *hon*
dusty *ans* ***llychlyd***
dutiful *ans* ***ufudd***
duty *enw* ***dyletswydd*** *hon*
dwarf *enw* ***corrach*** *hwn*, ***coraches*** *hon*
dwell *be* ***byw, preswylio***, ***trigo***; (remain) ***aros***, ***sefyll***, ***oedi***
dwelling *enw* ***anheddle*** *hwn*, ***preswylfa*** *hon*
dwindle *be* ***lleihau***, ***prinhau***
dye *be* ***llifo***, ***lliwio***
dye *enw* ***llifyn***, ***lliwur*** *hwn*
dying *ans* ***yn marw***, ***bron â marw***
dynamic *ans* ***deinamig***, ***egnïol***
dynamism *enw* ***bywiogrwydd*** *hwn*
dynasty *enw* ***llinach*** *hon*

E

each *rhag* ***pob***
eager *ans* ***awyddus***
eagerness *enw* ***awydd***, ***awch*** *hwn*
eagle *enw* ***eryr*** *hwn*
eagle-eyed *ans* ***â llygaid barcud***
ear *enw* ***clust*** *hwn/hon*; (of corn) ***tywysen*** *hon*
earache *enw* ***pigyn clust*** *hwn*
ear drum *enw* ***pilen y glust*** *hon*
earl *enw* ***iarll*** *hwn*
early *ans* ***cynnar***
  an e~ reply ***ateb buan*** *hwn*
  an e~ start ***cychwyn ben bore***
  the e~ hours ***oriau mân y bore*** *hyn*
earmark *be* ***clustnodi***
earn *be* ***ennill***
earnest *ans* **o** ***ddifrif***, ***taer***
  they e~ly hope ***eu gobaith didwyll yw***
earnings *enw* ***enillion*** *hyn*
earring *enw* ***clustdlws*** *hwn*
earshot *enw* ***clyw*** *hwn*
earth *enw* ***daear*** *hon*; (soil) ***pridd*** *hwn*
earth *be* ***daearu***; (garden) ***priddo***
  E~ Sciences ***y Gwyddorau Daear***
  Planet E~ ***y Ddaear***
  to promise the e~ ***addo môr a mynydd***
  what on e~ ***beth yn y byd mawr?***
earthen *ans* ***pridd***
earthly *ans* ***daearol***
earthquake *enw* ***daeargryn*** *hwn/hon*
earthwork *enw* ***gwrthglawdd*** *hwn*
earthworm *enw* ***abwyd***, ***abwydyn***, ***mwydyn***, ***pryf genwair*** *hwn*
earwig *enw* ***chwilen glust*** *hon*
ease *be* ***lleddfu***, ***esmwytho***; ***hwyluso***
  to put someone at their e~ ***gwneud iddynt deimlo'n gartrefol***
easement *enw* ***hawddfraint*** *hon*
easily *adf* ***yn rhwydd***, ***yn hawdd***, ***yn hwylus***
easiness *enw* ***rhwyddineb*** *hwn*
east *enw* ***dwyrain*** *hwn*
Easter *enw* ***y Pasg*** *hwn*
eastern *ans* ***dwyreiniol***
easy *ans* ***rhwydd***, ***hawdd***; (comfortable) ***esmwyth***; ***didrafferth***, ***diffwdan***
  no e~ task ***nid ar chwarae bach y mae***
  take it e~ ***gan bwyll bach***, ***gofal piau hi***
eat *be* ***bwyta***
eaves *enw* ***bargod***, ***bondo*** *hwn*
eavesdrop *be* ***clustfeinio***
ebb *enw* ***trai*** *hwn*
ebb *be* ***treio***
ebony *enw* ***eboni*** *hwn*

e

ebullience *enw* ***nwyf*** *hwn*, ***hoen*** *hon*
ebullient *ans* ***nwyfus***, ***hoenus***
EC *byrfodd* ***Comisiwn Ewropeaidd***
eccentric *ans* ***ecsentrig***, ***hynod***, ***od***
eccentricity *enw* ***hynodrwydd***, ***odrwydd*** *hwn*
ecclesiastical *ans* ***eglwysig***
echo *enw* ***adlais*** *hwn*, ***atsain*** *hon*
echo *be* ***adleisio***, ***atseinio***
eclipse *enw* ***diffyg***, ***eclips*** *hwn*
ecology *enw* ***ecoleg*** *hon*
e-commerce *enw* ***e-fasnach*** *hon*
economic *ans* ***economaidd***
economical *ans* ***cynnil***, ***darbodus***
economics *enw* ***economeg*** *hon*
economist *enw* ***economydd:*** ***economegydd*** *hwn*
economize *be* ***cynilo***, ***cwtogi***, ***arbed***
economy *enw* ***economi*** *hwn/hon*
  in the interest of e~ ***rhag bod yn wastraffus***
ecstasy *enw* ***perlewyg*** *hwn*
ecstatic *ans* ***llesmeiriol***
ecumenical *ans* ***eciwmenaidd***
eczema *enw* ***ecsema*** *hwn*
eddy *be* ***chwyrlïo***
edge *enw* ***min***, ***awch*** *hwn*; **ymyl** *hwn/hon*
  a competitive e~ ***mantais gystadleuol*** *hon*
  at the leading e~ ***ar flaen y gad***
edgy *ans* ***ar bigau drain***
edible *ans* ***bwytadwy***
edict *enw* ***gorchymyn*** *hwn*
edifice *enw* ***adeiladwaith*** *hwn*
edify *be* ***goleuo***
edit *be* ***golygu***
edition *enw* ***argraffiad*** *hwn*
editor *enw* ***golygydd*** *hwn*
educate *be* ***addysgu***
education *enw* ***addysg*** *hon*
educational *ans* ***addysgiadol***
educationist *enw* ***addysgwr*** *hwn*
EEC *enw* ***y Gymuned Economaidd Ewropeaidd*** *hon*
eel *enw* ***llysywen*** *hon*
eerie *ans* ***iasol***
efface *be* ***dileu***
effect *enw* ***effaith*** *hon*
  to good/great e~ ***yn effeithiol***
  to the best e~ ***manteisio i'r eithaf***
  to such e~ ***i gymaint graddau***
  with immediate e~ ***ar unwaith***
effect *be* ***effeithio***; ***gweithredu***
  to e~ improvements ***sicrhau gwelliannau***
effective *ans* ***effeithiol***
effectiveness *enw* ***effeithiolrwydd*** *hwn*
effectuate *be* ***cyflawni***
effeminate *ans* ***merchetaidd***
effervesce *be* ***byrlymu***
effervescence *enw* ***bwrlwm*** *hwn*
efficacious *ans* ***rhinweddol***
efficacy *enw* ***effeithiolrwydd*** *hwn*

efficiency *enw* ***effeithlonrwydd*** *hwn*
efficient *ans* ***effeithlon***
effigy *enw* ***delw*** *hon*
effort *enw* ***ymdrech*** *hwn/hon*
to make every e~ ***gwneud eich gorau glas***
with minimum e~ ***yn ddidrafferth***
effortless *ans* ***diymdrech***
effrontery *enw* ***digywilydd-dra*** *hwn*
e.g. *talfyriad* ***e.e.***
egalitarian *ans* ***cydraddol***
egg *enw* ***wy*** *hwn*
ego *enw* ***yr hunan***, ***ego*** *hwn*
ego(t)istical *ans* ***myfïol***
eggshell *enw* ***masgl wy***, ***plisgyn wy*** *hwn*
eiderdown *enw* ***cwrlid plu*** *hwn*
eight *rhifol* ***wyth***
eighteen *rhifol* ***deunaw***
eighteenth *ans* ***deunawfed***
eighth *ans* ***wythfed***
eightieth *ans* ***pedwar ugeinfed***
eighty *rhifol* ***pedwar ugain***, ***wyth deg***
eisteddfod *enw* ***eisteddfod*** *hon*
either *cysyllt* ***naill ai***, ***un ai***; *adf* ***ychwaith***
eject *be* ***bwrw/taflu allan***
ejection *enw* ***diarddeliad***, ***tafliad allan*** *hwn*
elaborate *be* ***manylu***, ***ymhelaethu***
elaborate *ans* ***cymhleth***; ***cywrain***
elapse *be* ***mynd heibio***
elastic *enw* ***lastig*** *hwn*
elastic *ans* ***ystwyth***, ***hydwyth***
elate *be* ***codi calon***
elated *ans* ***uwch ben eich digon***
elbow *enw* ***penelin*** *hwn/hon*
elder *enw* (man) ***hynafgwr*** *hwn*; (tree) ***ysgawen*** *hon*
elder *ans* ***hŷn***
elderly *ans* ***oedrannus***
elderly mentally infirm ***henoed llesg eu meddwl***
eldest *ans* ***hynaf***
elect *be* ***ethol***
elect *ans* ***darpar***
election *enw* ***etholiad*** *hwn*
electioneering *be* ***lecsiyna***
elector *enw* ***etholwr*** *hwn*
electoral *ans* ***etholiadol***
electorate *enw* ***etholaeth*** *hon*; ***pleidleiswyr*** *hyn*
electric(al) *ans* ***trydanol***
electrician *enw* ***trydanwr*** *hwn*
electricity *enw* ***trydan*** *hwn*
electrify *be* ***trydanu***, ***gwefreiddio***
electrode *enw* ***electrod*** *hwn*
electromagnetic *ans* ***electromagnetig***
electron *enw* ***electron*** *hwn*
electronic *ans* ***electronig***
electronics *enw* ***electroneg*** *hon*
elegance *enw* ***ceinder***, ***syberwyd*** *hwn*
elegant *ans* ***cain***, ***syber***
elegy *enw* ***marwnad*** *hwn*

e

element *enw* ***elfen*** *hon*
elementary *ans* ***elfennol***
elephant *enw* ***eliffant*** *hwn*
elephantine *ans* ***eliffantaidd***
elevate *be* ***dyrchafu***
elevated *ans* ***dyrchafedig***
elevation *enw* ***dyrchafiad*** *hwn*
eleven *rhifol* ***un ar ddeg***
elevenses *enw* ***te deg*** *hwn*
eleventh *ans* ***unfed ar ddeg***
elf *enw* ***pwca*** *hwn*
elicit *be* ***denu***; ***cael gan***
eligibility *enw* ***cymhwyster*** *hwn*
eligible *ans* ***cymwys***
to be eligible to ***bod ar dir i***
eliminate *be* ***dileu***
elite *ans* ***o'r radd flaenaf***
elk *enw* ***elc*** *hwn*
ellipse *enw* ***elips*** *hwn*
elm *enw* ***llwyfen*** *hon*
elocution *enw* ***llafareg:llefareg, areithyddiaeth*** *hon*, ***siarad cyhoeddus***
elocutionist *enw* (teacher) ***llafaregydd, athro llefaru***; (speaker) ***areithydd, adroddwr*** *hwn*, ***adroddwraig*** *hon*
elongate *be* ***estyn***, ***ymestyn***, ***hwyhau***
elongation *enw* ***estyniad***, ***ymestyniad*** *hwn*
elope *be* ***ffoi***, ***dianc***
eloquence *enw* ***huodledd*** *hwn*
eloquent *ans* ***huawdl***
else *adf/ans* ***arall***, ***amgen***
or e~ ***neu***
elsewhere *adf* ***rhywle arall***
elucidate *be* ***egluro***
elude *be* ***osgoi***
elusive *ans* ***anodd cael gafael ar***, ***anodd dod o hyd i***
emaciated *ans* ***llwglyd***, ***esgyrnog***
e-mail *enw* ***e-bost*** *hwn*
e-mail *be* ***e-bostio***
emanate *be* ***deillio***
emancipate *be* ***rhyddfreinio***
emancipation *enw* ***rhyddfreiniad*** *hwn*
emasculate *be* ***ysbaddu***; ***gwanhau***
embankment *enw* ***clawdd***, ***morglawdd*** *hwn*
embargo *enw* ***embargo***, ***gwaharddiad*** *hwn*
embark *be* ***cychwyn***, ***dechrau***
embarkation *enw* ***esgyniad***, ***dechreuad*** *hwn*
embarrass *be* ***codi cywilydd***, ***gwneud yn swil***
embarrassment *enw* ***cywilydd*** *hwn*
embassy *enw* ***llysgenhadaeth*** *hon*
embed *be* ***ymgorffori***; ***gwreiddio***
deeply e~ded ***wedi ennill eu plwyf***; ***bod â'u gwreiddiau'n ddwfn yn***
embellish *be* ***addurno***
embellishment *enw* ***addurn*** *hwn*
ember *enw* ***marworyn*** *hwn*
embezzle *be* ***dwyn***, ***embeslo***
embezzlement *enw* ***lladrad***, ***embeslad*** *hwn*

embitter *be* ***chwerwi***
emblem *enw* ***arwyddlun*** *hwn*
embodiment *enw* ***ymgorfforiad*** *hwn*
embody *be* ***ymgorffori***
embrace *be* ***cofleidio***, ***anwesu***, ***croesawu***; ***cynnwys***
  to e~ developments ***coleddu datblygiadau***
  to e~ broad issues ***rhychwantu materion eang***
embrasure *enw* ***bwlch*** *hwn*
embrocation *enw* ***eli*** *hwn*
embroider *be* ***brodio***
embroidery *enw* ***brodwaith*** *hwn*
embryo *enw* ***rhith***, ***embryo*** *hwn*
embryonic *ans* (fig.) ***cychwynnol***
emend *be* ***diwygio***, ***cywiro***
emerald *enw* ***emrallt*** *hwn*
emerge *be* ***ymddangos***; ***codi o***
  emerging issues ***materion sydd ar y gweill***
emergency *enw* ***argyfwng*** *hwn*
emergency *ans* ***brys***
emergency exit *enw* ***allanfa frys*** *hon*
emigrant *enw* ***ymfudwr*** *hwn*
emigrate *be* ***ymfudo***
emigration *enw* ***ymfudiad*** *hwn*
eminence *enw* ***amlygrwydd*** *hwn*
eminent *ans* ***amlwg***
emissary *enw* ***cennad*** *hon*
emission *enw* ***gollyngiad*** *hwn, be* ***gollwng***
emit *be* ***gollwng***
emollient *enw* ***eli*** *hwn*
emolument *enw* ***tâl*** *hwn*
emotion *enw* ***teimlad***, ***emosiwn*** *hwn*
emotional *ans* ***dan deimlad***, ***emosiynol***
emotive *ans* ***synhwyrus***; ***yn ennyn teimladau cryf(ion)***
empathy *enw* ***empathi*** *hwn*
emperor *enw* ***ymherodr*** *hwn*
emphasis *enw* ***pwyslais*** *hwn*
emphasize *be* ***pwysleisio***; ***tanlinellu pwysigrwydd***
emphatic *ans* ***pendant***
empire *enw* ***ymerodraeth*** *hon*
employ *be* ***cyflogi***; ***defnyddio***
employee *enw* ***gweithiwr*** *hwn*, ***gweithwraig*** *hon*, ***cyflogai*** *hwn*
employer *enw* ***cyflogwr***, ***cyflogydd*** *hwn*
employment *enw* ***cyflogaeth*** *hon*
empower *be* ***galluogi***, ***awdurdodi***
empress *enw* ***ymerodres*** *hon*
emptiness *enw* ***gwacter*** *hwn*
empty *ans* ***gwag***
empty *be* ***gwagio***
empty-handed *ans* ***gwaglaw***
emulate *be* ***efelychu***
emulsify *be* ***emwlseiddio:emwlsio***
emulsion *enw* ***emwlsiwn*** *hwn*
enable *be* ***galluogi***
enact *be* ***deddfu***
enamel *enw* ***enamel***, ***owmal*** *hwn*
enamour *be* ***ennyn serch***, ***swyno***
encamp *be* ***gwersyllu***

e

encampment *enw* ***gwersyll*** *hwn*
encapsulate *be* ***crisialu***
encase *be* ***cau mewn***
enchant *be* ***cyfareddu***, ***hudo***
enchanter *enw* ***swynwr*** *hwn*
enchanting *ans* ***cyfareddol***
enchantment *enw* ***hudoliaeth*** *hon*
encircle *be* ***amgylchynu***
enclave *enw* ***llecyn*** *hwn*
enclose *be* ***amgáu***
enclosed *ans* ***amgaeëdig***
enclosure *enw* ***cae***, ***lloc*** *hwn*; ***dogfen amgaeëdig*** *hon*
encode *be* ***codio***
encomium *enw* ***molawd*** *hwn*
encompass *be* ***cwmpasu***, ***rhychwantu***
encounter *enw* ***cyfarfod*** *hwn*; ***cysylltiad*** *hwn*
encounter *be* ***cyfarfod***; ***wynebu***
encourage *be* ***cefnogi***, ***hybu***; ***cymell***, ***annog***
encouragement *enw* ***cefnogaeth***; ***anogaeth*** *hon*
encouraging *adf* ***yn codi calon***, ***yn galondid***
encroach *be* ***tresmasu***; ***ymledu i***
encrusted *ans* ***cramennog***
encumbrance *enw* ***maen melin*** *hwn*
encyclical *enw* ***cylchlythyr*** *hwn*
encyclopaedia *enw* ***gwyddoniadur*** *hwn*
end *enw* ***diwedd***, ***terfyn***; ***pen*** *hwn*
  for years on e~ ***am flynyddoedd bwygilydd***
  in at the deep e~ ***mentro i'r dwfn***
  in the e~ ***ymhen hir a hwyr***
  there was no e~ to ***doedd dim pall ar***
  to this e~ ***i'r perwyl hwn***
end *be* ***diweddu***, ***terfynu***, ***darfod***
  this e~ed in ***diwedd hyn fu***
  to e~ in failure ***mynd i'r gwellt***
endanger *be* ***peryglu***
endearing *ans* ***annwyl***
endeavour *enw* ***ymgais***, ***ymdrech*** *hwn/hon*
  best e~ ***gorau glas***
endeavour *be* ***ymdrechu***
ending *enw* (gram.) ***terfyniad*** *hwn*
endless *ans* ***di-ben-draw***
endorse *be* (cheque etc.) ***arnodi***, ***ardystio***; (support) ***cymeradwyo***, ***cefnogi***; (confirm) ***ategu***, ***cadarnhau***
endorsement *enw* ***arnodiad*** *hwn*; ***cefnogaeth*** *hon*
endow *be* ***cynysgaeddu***, ***breintio***
end-product *enw* ***canlyniad***; ***ffrwyth*** *hwn*
endurable *ans* ***dioddefadwy***, ***goddefadwy***
endurance *enw* ***dycnwch:*** ***dygnwch***, ***dioddefgarwch*** *hwn*
endure *be* ***dioddef***, ***goddef***; ***parhau***
enemy *enw* ***gelyn*** *hwn*
energetic *ans* ***egnïol***, ***llawn egni***
energy *enw* ***egni***, ***ynni*** *hwn*; (power) ***ynni***

enervate *be* ***gwanychu, llesgáu***
enfeeble *be* ***gwanychu, llesgáu***
enfold *be* ***lapio***
enforce *be* ***gorfodi***
enfranchise *be* ***rhyddfreinio***
engage *be* ***cyflogi; cysylltu***
  actively e~d in ***wrthi***
  to e~ in behaviour which ***ymddwyn mewn ffordd***
  to e~ in conversation ***eu cynnwys yn y sgwrs***
  to e~ in discussion/debate ***trafod/dadlau***
  to e~ interest ***ennyn diddordeb***
  to e~ with a work of art ***mynd i'r afael â gwaith celf***
  to e~ the imagination ***tanio'r dychymyg***
engaged *ans* ***wedi dyweddïo***
engagement *enw* ***dyweddïad*** *hwn*
engaging *ans* ***atyniadol, apelgar***
engender *be* ***peri, ennyn; codi diddordeb***
engine *enw* ***peiriant*** *hwn*, ***injan*** *hon*
engineer *enw* ***peiriannydd*** *hwn*
engineering *enw* ***peirianneg*** *hon*
English *enw* ***Saesneg*** *hon*
English *ans* ***Seisnig***; (language) ***Saesneg***
Englishman *enw* ***Sais*** *hwn*
Englishwoman *enw* ***Saesnes*** *hon*
engrave *be* ***ysgythru***
engraving *enw* ***ysgythriad*** *hwn*
engross *be* ***ymgolli***
engrossing *ans* ***yn hoelio sylw***
engulf *be* ***traflyncu***
enhance *be* ***mireinio; gwella; cryfhau***
enigma *enw* ***dirgelwch*** *hwn*, ***enigma*** *hon*
enjoy *be* ***mwynhau, cael blas***; (possess) ***meddu ar, dod i'm rhan***
  she e~ed good health during her life ***daeth iechyd da i'w rhan drwy'i hoes***
enjoyable *ans* ***dymunol, hyfryd***
enjoyment *enw* ***mwynhad*** *hwn*
enlarge *be* ***mwyhau, ehangu, chwyddo, helaethu***
  to e~ upon ***ymhelaethu***
enlargement *enw* ***mwyhad, estyniad*** *hwn*
enlightened *ans* ***goleuedig***
enlist *be* ***listio, ymrestru***
  to e~ the help of ***sicrhau cefnogaeth***
enliven *be* ***bywhau, bywiogi, bywiocáu***
enmesh *be* ***rhwydo***
enmity *enw* ***gelyniaeth*** *hon*
ennoble *be* ***urddo***
enormity *enw* ***anferthedd, aruthredd*** *hwn*; (of crime) ***enbydrwydd***
enormous *ans* ***anferth, aruthrol, enfawr***
enough *adf* ***digon***
enquire *be* ***holi, ymholi***

enquiry *enw* ***ymholiad*** *hwn*
enrage *be* ***cynddeiriogi***
enrapture *be* ***cyfareddu***
enrich *be* ***cyfoethogi***; ***bod ar fy (dy, ei etc.) ennill***
enrol *be* ***cofrestru***, ***ymrestru***
ensconce *be* ***ymsefydlu***
enshrine *be* ***ymgorffori***
enshroud *be* ***gorchuddio***
enslave *be* ***caethiwo***
ensnare *be* ***maglu***
ensue *be* ***dilyn***
ensure *be* ***sicrhau***, ***gofalu bod***
entail *be* ***golygu***
entangle *be* ***drysu***
enter *be* ***mynd/dod i mewn***
  e~ into a new phase ***cychwyn ar gyfnod newydd***
  e~ into correspondence ***gohebu***
enterprise *enw* ***menter*** *hon*
  e~ initiative ***menter fentro*** *hon*
enterprising *ans* ***mentrus***
entertain *be* ***difyrru***, ***diddanu***
entertainer *enw* ***diddanwr*** *hwn*
entertaining *ans* ***difyr***
entertainment *enw* ***adloniant*** *hwn*
enthuse *be* ***cyffroi***, ***ennyn brwdfrydedd***
enthusiasm *enw* ***brwdfrydedd*** *hwn*
enthusiast *enw* ***rhywun brwdfrydig*** *hwn*
enthusiastic *ans* ***brwd***, ***brwdfrydig***
entice *be* ***hudo***
entire *ans* ***cyfan***, ***holl***
  the e~ course is ***mae'r cwrs drwyddo draw***
entirety *enw* ***crynswth*** *hwn*
  the programme in its e~ ***rhaglen gyfan*** *hon*
  in their e~ ***ar eu hyd***
entitle *be* ***bod â hawl***
  entitled ***a elwir yn***
entity *enw* ***endid*** *hwn*
entomb *be* ***daearu***, ***claddu***
entourage *enw* ***gosgordd*** *hon*
entrails *enw* ***ymysgaroedd*** *hyn*
entrance *enw* ***mynediad*** *hwn*, ***mynedfa*** *hon*
entrance *be* ***swyno***
entrant *enw* ***ymgeisydd***; ***newyddian*** *hwn*
entrap *be* ***maglu***
entreat *be* ***ymbil***, ***erfyn***
entreaty *enw* ***deisyfiad*** *hwn*
entrench *be* ***ymsefydlu***
entrepreneur *enw* ***mentrwr*** *hwn*
entrust *be* ***ymddiried***
entry *enw* ***mynediad*** *hwn*; (competition) ***cynnig*** *hwn*
entwine *be* ***ymgordeddu***
enumerate *be* ***rhifo***, ***cyfrif***
enunciate *be* (pronounce) ***cynanu***, ***ynganu***, ***geirio***; (state) ***datgan***, ***mynegi***
enunciator *enw* ***datganwr*** *hwn*
envelop *be* ***amgáu***, ***gorchuddio***
envelope *enw* ***amlen*** *hon*
envious *ans* ***eiddigeddus***, ***cenfigennus***

environment *enw* ***amgylchedd***, ***amgylchfyd*** *hwn*
environmental *ans* ***amgylcheddol***
environs *enw* ***cyffiniau*** *hyn*, ***libart*** *hwn*
envisage *be* ***gweld***, ***dychmygu***
envoy *enw* ***cennad*** *hon*
envy *enw* ***cenfigen*** *hon*, ***eiddigedd*** *hwn*
envy *be* ***cenfigennu***, ***eiddigeddu***
ephemeral *ans* ***byrhoedlog***
epic *ans* ***epig***
epidemic *enw* ***haint*** *hwn/hon*
epidermis *enw* ***glasgroen*** *hwn*
epigram *enw* ***epigram*** *hwn*
epilepsy *enw* ***epilepsi*** *hwn*
epileptic *ans* ***epileptig***
epilogue *enw* ***epilog*** *hwn*
Epiphany *enw* ***yr Ystwyll*** *hwn*
episcopal *ans* ***esgobol***
episode *enw* ***pennod*** *hon*
epistle *enw* ***epistol***, ***llythyr*** *hwn*
epitaph *enw* ***beddargraff*** *hwn*
epitomize *be* ***crynhoi***, ***ymgorffori***
epoch *enw* ***oes*** *hon*
equable *ans* ***gwastad***, ***cyfartal***
equal *ans* ***cydradd***, ***cyfartal***, ***hafal***; ***yr un faint o***; ***llawn cymaint***
e~ opportunities ***cyfleoedd cyfartal*** *hyn*
equality *enw* ***cydraddoldeb***, ***cyfartalwch*** *hwn*
equalize *be* ***cydraddoli***, ***dod yn gyfartal***
equanimity *enw* ***pwyll***, ***tawelwch meddwl*** *hwn*
equate *be* ***hafalu***, ***cymharu***; ***cyfateb***
to e~ to ***bod yn gyfystyr/ gymesur â***
equation *enw* ***hafaliad*** *hwn*
equator *enw* ***cyhydedd*** *hwn*
equidistant *ans* ***cytbell***
equilibrium *enw* ***cydbwysedd*** *hwn*
equinox *enw* ***cyhydnos*** *hon*
equipment *enw* ***cyfarpar*** *hwn*
equitable *ans* ***teg***
equivalent *ans* ***cyfwerth***
equivocal *ans* ***amwys***, ***amhendant***
equivocate *be* ***anwadalu***, ***bod yn amwys***
era *enw* ***cyfnod*** *hwn*
eradicate *be* ***cael gwared â***
eradication *enw* ***dilead***, ***difodiant*** *hwn*
erase *be* ***dileu***
eraser *enw* ***dilëwr*** *hwn*
ere *ardd* ***cyn***
erect *ans* ***talsyth***, ***union***
erect *be* ***codi***
erection *enw* ***codiad*** *hwn*
ergo *adf* ***felly***, ***o ganlyniad***
ermine *enw* ***carlwm*** *hwn*
erode *be* ***erydu***
erotic *ans* ***erotig***
err *be* ***cyfeiliorni***
errand *enw* ***neges*** *hon*
errant *ans* ***crwydrol***; ***cyfeiliornus***
erratic *ans* ***afreolaidd***, ***eratig***

e

erratum *enw* ***gwall*** *hwn*
erroneous *ans* ***anghywir***
error *enw* ***gwall***, ***camgymeriad*** *hwn*
in e~ ***ar gam***
erudite *ans* ***dysgedig***
erupt *be* ***echdorri***
eruption *enw* ***echdoriad***; ***tarddiant*** *hwn*
escalate *be* ***dwysáu***, ***cynyddu***
escapade *enw* ***pranc*** *hwn*; ***helyntion*** *hyn*
escape *enw* ***dihangfa*** *hon*
escape *be* ***dianc***; ***cael eich traed yn rhydd***
escarpment *enw* ***tarren*** *hon*
eschew *be* ***gochel***, ***osgoi***
escort *enw* ***gosgordd*** *hon*; ***hebryngwr*** *hwn*
escort *be* ***hebrwng***
escutcheon *enw* ***arfbais*** *hon*
esoteric *ans* ***cyfrin:cyfriniol***; (unintelligible) ***astrus***, ***tywyll***
especial *ans* ***arbennig***
espionage *be* ***ysbïo***
esplanade *enw* ***rhodfa lan môr*** *hon*
espouse *be* ***pledio***, ***arddel***
esq. *talfyriad* ***ysw.***
essay *enw* ***traethawd*** *hwn*
essay *be* ***rhoi cynnig ar***
essence *enw* ***hanfod***, ***craidd*** *hwn*
time is of the e~ ***amser sy'n hollbwysig yn awr***; ***rhaid taro tra bo'r haearn yn boeth***
essential *ans* ***hanfodol***
establish *be* ***gwreiddio***; ***sefydlu***, ***gosod***
establishment *enw* ***sefydliad*** *hwn*
estate *enw* ***stad:ystâd*** *hon*
esteem *enw* ***edmygedd***, ***parch*** *hwn*
esteem *be* ***edmygu***, ***parchu***
esthetic *ans* ***esthetaidd***, ***esthetig***
estimable *ans* ***cymeradwy***
estimate *be* ***amcangyfrif***
estimation *enw* ***barn*** *hon*, ***tyb*** *hwn/hon*
estrange *be* ***dieithrio***
estuary *enw* ***aber*** *hwn/hon*, ***moryd*** *hon*
etc. *talfyriad* ***ayyb***
etch *be* ***ysgythru***
etching *enw* ***ysgythriad*** *hwn*
eternal *ans* ***tragwyddol***
eternity *enw* ***tragwyddoldeb*** *hwn*
ethical *ans* ***moesegol***
ethics *enw* ***moeseg*** *hon*
ethnic *ans* ***ethnig***
ethnicity *enw* ***ethnigrwydd*** *hwn*
ethnological *ans* ***ethnolegol***
e~ studies ***astudiaethau gwerin*** *hyn*
ethos *enw* ***ethos*** *hwn*
etiolate *be* ***gwelwi***
etiquette *enw* ***cwrteisi*** *hwn*, ***safon ymddygiad*** *hon*
eucharist *enw* ***y cymun*** *hwn*
eulogize *be* ***moli***, ***canu mawl***
eulogy *enw* ***molawd*** *hwn*

euphonious *ans* ***persain***
euphony *enw* ***perseinedd*** *hwn*
euphoria *enw* ***perlesmair*** *hwn*
euro *enw* ***ewro*** *hwn*
European *ans* ***Ewropeaidd***
evacuate *be* ***gwacáu***, ***gwagio***
evacuation *enw* ***gwacâd*** *hwn*
evade *be* ***osgoi***, ***gochel***
evaluate *be* ***pwyso a mesur***, ***gwerthuso***; ***arfarnu***
evanescent *ans* ***darfodedig***
evangelical *ans* ***efengylaidd***
evangelist *enw* ***efengylwr***, ***efengylydd*** *hwn*
evaporate *be* ***anweddu***
evaporation *enw* ***anweddiad*** *hwn*
evasion *enw* ***gocheliad*** *hwn*
evasive *ans* ***gochelgar***
eve *enw* ***noswyl*** *hon*
even *ans* ***gwastad***, ***llyfn***; ***cyfartal***; ***teg***
  e~ handed ***teg***
  to get e~ ***talu'r pwyth yn ôl***
even *adf* ***hyd yn oed***
  e~ so ***er hynny***
evening *enw* ***noswaith*** *hon*, ***min nos*** *hwn*
evenness *enw* ***gwastadrwydd*** *hwn*
evensong *enw* ***gosber*** *hwn/hon*
event *enw* ***digwyddiad*** *hwn*
  after the e~ ***yn ddiweddarach***
  in any e~ ***'ta p'un***
eventide *enw* ***diwedydd***, ***diwetydd*** *hwn*
eventful *ans* ***cyffrous***
eventuality *enw* ***digwyddiad posibl***, ***posibilrwydd*** *hwn*
eventually *adf* ***ymhen hir a hwyr***
ever *adf* ***byth***, ***erioed***
evergreen *ans* ***bythwyrdd***, ***bytholwyrdd***
everlasting *ans* ***bythol***, ***tragwyddol***
evermore *adf* ***byth bythoedd***
every *ans* ***pob***
  e~ effort ***gorau glas***
  e~ one of them ***pob copa walltog***
everybody *rhag* ***pawb***
everyday *adf* ***bob dydd***
everything *rhag* ***popeth***
everywhere *adf* ***pobman***
evict *be* ***troi allan***
evidence *enw* ***tystiolaeth*** *hon*
  to be much in e~ ***bod yn amlwg iawn***
evident *ans* ***amlwg***
evil *enw* ***drwg*** *hwn*
evil *ans* ***drwg***
evince *be* ***amlygu***
eviscerate *be* ***diberfeddu***
evocative *ans* ***atgofus***, ***adleisiol***
evoke *be* ***galw***, ***dwyn (atgofion)***; ***cyfleu***
evolution *enw* ***esblygiad*** *hwn*
evolve *be* ***esblygu***
ewe *enw* ***hesbin***, ***hesben*** *hon*
ewer *enw* ***ystên*** *hon*, ***piser*** *hwn*
exacerbate *be* ***gwneud yn waeth***, ***ffyrnigo***

exact *ans* ***manwl gywir***; ***i drwch y blewyn***
at that e~ moment ***ar y gair***
exact *be* ***hawlio***
exacting *ans* (person) ***llym***, ***gormesol***; (work) ***gormesol***
exactness *enw* ***manwl gywirdeb*** *hwn*
exaggerate *be* ***gor-ddweud***
exaggeration *enw* ***gormodiaith*** *hon*
exalt *be* ***gogoneddu***, ***clodfori***
exaltation *enw* ***gorfoledd*** *hwn*
exalted *ans* ***gogoneddus***
examination *enw* ***arholiad***, ***archwiliad*** *hwn*
to bear e~ ***dal dŵr***
examine *be* ***archwilio***, ***astudio***; ***arholi***
example *enw* ***enghraifft*** *hon*
exasperate *be* ***gwaethygu***; ***cynddeiriogi***
excavate *be* ***cloddio***, ***tyllu***
excavation *enw* ***cloddfa*** *hon*
exceed *be* ***bod/mynd yn fwy na***, ***mynd ymhellach na***, ***mynd dros***
to e~ a target ***curo targed***
excel *be* ***rhagori***
excellence *enw* ***rhagoriaeth*** *hon*, ***godidowgrwydd*** *hwn*; ***y safon uchaf un***
excellent *ans* ***rhagorol***, ***ardderchog***, ***godidog***; ***tan gamp***
except *ardd* ***ac eithrio***, ***heblaw***
except *be* ***eithrio***
exception *enw* ***eithriad*** *hwn*
exceptionable *ans* ***annerbyniol***
exceptional *ans* ***eithriadol***
excerpt *enw* ***detholiad*** *hwn*
excess *enw* ***gormodedd*** *hwn*
excessive *ans* ***gormodol***, ***eithafol***
exchange *enw* ***cyfnewidfa*** *hon*
exchange *be* ***cyfnewid***
exchange rate *enw* ***cyfradd gyfnewid*** *hon*
Exchequer *enw* ***y Trysorlys*** *hwn*
excise *enw* ***toll*** *hon*
excise *be* ***torri allan***, ***trychu***
excitable *ans* ***gwyllt***, ***hawdd ei gynhyrfu***
excite *be* ***cynhyrfu***
excited *ans* ***cynhyrfus***, ***llawn cynnwrf***
excitement *enw* ***cyffro***, ***cynnwrf*** *hwn*
exciting *ans* ***cyffrous***, ***cynhyrfus***
exclaim *be* ***ebychu***
exclamation *enw* ***ebychiad*** *hwn*
exclude *be* ***cau/cadw/gadael allan***; ***eithrio***; (prevent) ***gwahardd***; (expel) ***diarddel***
excluded *ans* ***eithriedig***
excluding *ardd* ***ac eithrio***, ***heblaw am***, ***oni bai am***
exclusion *enw* ***gwaharddiad*** *hwn*; ***gan anwybyddu***
exclusive *ans* ***cyfyngedig***; ***llwyr-gyfyngedig***

excommunicate *be* ***ysgymuno***
excoriate *be* ***blingo***
excrement *enw* ***carthion*** *hyn*
excreta *enw* ***carthion*** *hyn*
excrete *be* ***ysgarthu***, ***tomi***, ***teilo***
excruciating *ans* ***dirdynnol***
exculpate *be* ***esgusodi***
excursion *enw* ***gwibdaith*** *hon*
excusable *ans* ***esgusadwy***
excuse *enw* ***esgus*** *hwn*
an e~ for ***bod yn esgus dros***
excuse *be* ***esgusodi***
execrable *ans* ***melltigedig***
execrate *be* ***melltithio***
execute *be* ***dienyddio***; ***cyflawni***
execution *enw* ***dienyddiad***; ***gweithrediad*** *hwn*
executioner *enw* ***dienyddiwr*** *hwn*
executive *enw* ***gweithredwr*** *hwn*
executive *ans* ***gweithredol***
executor *enw* ***ysgutor*** *hwn*
exemplar *enw* ***enghraifft batrymol*** *hon*
exemplary *ans* ***canmoladwy***, ***penigamp***
exemplify *be* ***enghreifftio***; ***amlygu***; ***gosod esiampl***
exempt *ans* ***rhydd***, ***wedi'ch esgusodi, wedi'i eithrio/ heithrio/'u heithrio***
exempt *be* ***eithrio***, ***rhyddhau***, ***esgusodi***
exemption *enw* ***rhyddhad*** *hwn*, ***rhyddhau***, ***esgusodi***
exercise *enw* ***arfer***, ***ymarfer*** *hwn/hon*; ***gwaith*** *hwn*
exercise *be* ***arfer***, ***ymarfer***
e~ care ***bod yn ofalus***
e~ influence ***dylanwadu***
e~ pressure ***dwyn pwysau***
exert *be* ***gweithredu***, ***ymdrechu***
to **e~ pressure** ***rhoi pwysau***
exertion *enw* ***ymdrech*** *hon*
ex gratia *adf/ans* ***fel (mater o) ffafr***
exhale *be* ***anadlu allan***, ***gollwng***
exhaust *be* ***dihysbyddu:disbyddu***
exhaust *enw* ***nwy llosg***, ***mwg*** *hwn*
exhausted *ans* ***lluddedig***
exhaustion *enw* ***lludded*** *hwn*
exhaustive *ans* ***trwyadl***, ***trylwyr***
the list is not e~ ***nid yw'r rhestr yn cynnwys popeth***
the ideas are not e~ ***nid yw'n ymdrin â phob posibilrwydd***
exhibit *be* ***arddangos***
exhibition *enw* ***arddangosfa*** *hon*
exhilarating *ans* ***bywiocaol***, ***gwefreiddiol***
exhilaration *enw* ***gorfoledd*** *hwn*, ***hoen*** *hwn/hon*
exhort *be* ***annog***
exhume *be* ***datgladdu***
exigency *enw* ***angen brys*** *hwn*
exiguous *ans* ***prin***, ***pitw***
exile *enw* ***alltudiaeth*** *hon*; ***alltud*** *hwn/hon*
to go into e~ ***troi'n alltud***
exile *be* ***alltudio***
exist *be* ***bodoli***; ***a geir***

e

existence *enw* ***bodolaeth*** *hon*
existent *ans* ***sydd ohoni***
exit *enw* ***allanfa*** *hon*
exit *be* ***ymadael***
exodus *enw* ***ymadawiad*** *hwn*
ex officio *adf/ans* ***yn rhinwedd ei swydd***
exonerate *be* ***esgusodi, rhyddhau (o fai)***
exoneration *enw* ***rhyddhad*** *hwn*
exorbitant *ans* ***afresymol***, ***gormodol***
exorcize *be* ***bwrw allan***
exotic *ans* ***dieithr***, ***lliwgar***
expand *be* (to make larger) ***ehangu***, ***helaethu***, ***chwyddo***; (to grow larger) ***ymehangu***, ***ymestyn***, ***tyfu***, ***chwyddo***
expanse *enw* ***ehangder*** *hwn*
expansion *enw* ***ehangiad***, ***twf*** *hwn*
expatriate *enw* ***alltud*** *hwn*
expatriate *be* ***alltudio***
expect *be* ***disgwyl***
expectant *ans* ***disgwylgar***
expectation *enw* ***disgwyliad***, ***disgwyl*** *hwn*
expediency *enw* ***hwylustod***, ***cyfleustra*** *hwn*
expedient *ans* ***hwylus***, ***cyfleus***
expedite *be* ***hwyluso***, ***prysuro***
expedition *enw* ***cyrch*** *hwn*; ***ymdaith*** *hon*
expeditious *ans* ***buan***; ***prydlon***, ***diymdroi***; ***rhwydd***, ***hwylus***
expel *be* ***diarddel***
expend *be* ***gwario***, ***treulio***
expendable *ans* ***hepgoradwy***; ***diwerth***, ***dibwys***
expenditure *enw* ***gwariant*** *hwn*
expense *enw* ***traul***, ***cost*** *hon*
  to charge e~s ***codi treuliau***
  even at the e~ of ***hyd yn oed os collir/ar draul***
expensive *ans* ***drud***, ***costus***
experience *enw* ***profiad*** *hwn*
experience *be* ***profi***
experiential *ans* ***drwy brofiad***
experienced *ans* ***profiadol***
experiment *enw* ***arbrawf*** *hwn*
experiment *be* ***arbrofi***
experimental *ans* ***arbrofol***
expert *ans* ***arbenigol***, ***medrus***
expert *enw* ***arbenigwr*** *hwn*, ***arbenigwraig*** *hon*
expertise *enw* ***gwybodaeth arbenigol***, ***dawn arbennig*** *hon*
expiate *be* ***gwneud iawn am***
expiration *enw* ***diwedd*** *hwn*
expire *be* ***darfod***, ***gorffen***, ***dod i ben***
expiry *enw* ***diwedd***, ***terfyn***
explain *be* ***egluro***, ***esbonio***
explanation *enw* ***eglurhad***, ***esboniad*** *hwn*
explanatory *ans* ***esboniadol***
explicable *ans* ***egluradwy***
explicate *be* ***egluro***
explicit *ans* ***croyw***, ***diamwys***; ***yn blwmp ac yn blaen***
  to make e~ ***manylu***

explode *be* ***ffrwydro***; ***dryllio***
exploit *enw* ***camp***, ***gorchest*** *hon*
exploit *be* ***defnyddio***; ***camddefnyddio***; ***manteisio'n llawn ar***
exploration *enw* ***archwiliad***, ***ymchwiliad*** *hwn*
exploratory *ans* ***archwiliadol***
explore *be* ***archwilio***, ***ymchwilio***, ***fforio***
explorer *enw* ***fforiwr*** *hwn*
explosion *enw* ***ffrwydrad*** *hwn*, ***tanchwa*** *hon*
explosive *enw* ***ffrwydryn*** *hwn*
explosive *ans* ***ffrwydrol***, ***tanbaid***, ***gwyllt***
export *be* ***allforio***
exports *enw* ***allforion*** *hyn*
  e~ trade ***masnach allforio*** *hon*
exportation *enw* ***allforio***
exporter *enw* ***allforiwr*** *hwn*
expose *be* ***dinoethi***, ***datguddio***
  to be e~d to ***dod wyneb yn wyneb â***
exposition *enw* ***eglurhad***, ***esboniad***, ***dehongliad*** *hwn*
expostulate *be* ***protestio***
exposure *enw* ***datguddiad***, ***dinoethiad*** *hwn*; (geol.) ***brigiad*** *hwn*
expound *be* ***traethu***, ***egluro***
express *enw* ***trên cyflym*** *hwn*
express *be* ***mynegi***
  this e~es itself in ***mae hyn i'w weld yn***
express *ans* ***unswydd***, ***penodol***; ***cyflym***, ***brys***
expression *enw* ***mynegiant*** *hwn*; ***ymadrodd***, ***dywediad*** *hwn*; (on the face) ***golwg*** *hon*
expressionless *ans* ***digyffro***, ***difynegiant***
expressive *ans* ***llawn mynegiant***, ***mynegiannol***
expropriate *be* ***difeddiannu***
expulsion *enw* ***diarddeliad*** *hwn*
expunge *be* ***dileu***
expurgate *be* ***sensro***
exquisite *ans* ***cain***, ***cyfewin***, ***cywrain***
extant *ans* ***yn goroesi***
extempore *ans* ***ar y pryd***, ***difyfyr***, ***o'r frest***
extemporize *be* ***siarad/chwarae yn ddifyfyr***
extend *be* ***estyn***, ***ehangu***, ***ymestyn***
  to e~ good practice ***lledaenu arfer da***
  to e~ the readership ***cynyddu nifer y darllenwyr***
extension *enw* ***estyniad*** *hwn*
extensive *ans* ***eang***, ***helaeth***
extent *enw* ***hyd a lled***; ***graddau*** *hyn*
extenuate *be* ***lleddfu***, ***lleihau***
exterior *ans* ***allanol***
exterminate *be* ***difodi***, ***difa***
external *ans* ***allanol***
extinct *ans* ***wedi darfod***, ***diflanedig***

e

extinction *enw* ***diwedd***, ***tranc*** *hwn*
extinguish *be* ***diffodd***
extinguisher *enw* ***diffoddydd*** *hwn*
extirpate *be* ***difa***
extol *be* ***clodfori***
extort *be* ***mynnu trwy orfodaeth***, ***cribddeilio (arian)***
extortion *enw* ***cribddeiliaeth*** *hon*
extra *ans* ***ychwanegol***
extract *enw* ***detholiad*** *hwn*
extract *be* ***echdynnu***, ***tynnu***
extraction *enw* ***tyniad*** *hwn*; (family) ***cyff*** *hwn*, ***hil*** *hon*
extra-curricular *ans* ***allgyrsiol***
extradite *be* ***estraddodi***
extraneous *ans* ***allanol***, ***estron***
extraordinary *ans* ***anarferol***, ***arbennig iawn***
extraterrestrial *ans* ***allfydol***
extravagance *enw* ***gormodedd***, ***rhysedd*** *hwn*
extravagant *ans* ***afradlon***
extreme *ans* ***eithafol***, ***pellaf***; ***hynod***
extremism *enw* ***eithafiaeth*** *hon*
extremist *enw* ***eithafwr*** *hwn*, ***eithafwraig*** *hon*
extremity *enw* ***cwr pellaf***, ***eithaf*** *hwn*
extricate *be* ***rhyddhau***, ***datod***
extrinsic *ans* ***allanol***
extrovert *ans* ***allblyg***
exuberance *enw* ***afiaith*** *hwn*, ***hwyl*** *hon*
exuberant *ans* ***afieithus***
exude *be* ***byrlymu***; ***bod yn gyforiog o***
exult *be* ***gorfoleddu***
eye *enw* ***llygad*** *hwn*
eye *be* ***llygadu***
to keep a sharp e~ on ***cadw llygad barcud ar***
eyeball *enw* ***pelen y llygad*** *hon*
eyebrow *enw* ***ael*** *hon*
eyelash *enw* ***blewyn (amrant)*** *hwn*
eyelid *enw* ***amrant***, ***clawr y llygad*** *hwn*
eye-opener *enw* ***agoriad llygad*** *hwn*
eyesight *enw* ***golwg*** *hwn*
eyewitness *enw* ***llygad-dyst*** *hwn*
eyrie *enw* ***nyth eryr*** *hwn/hon*

F

fable *enw* ***chwedl*** *hon*
fabric *enw* (tex.) ***defnydd***; (of building) ***adeiladwaith***; (of stone) ***gwead*** *hwn*
fabricate *be* ***llunio***; ***ffugio***
fabrication *enw* ***ffugiad***, ***anwiredd*** *hwn*
fabulous *ans* ***chwedlonol***; ***aruthrol***, ***gwych***
facade *enw* ***wyneb***, ***ffasâd*** *hwn*; ***rhyw lun/esgus o***
face *enw* ***wyneb*** *hwn*
f~ like a fiddle ***wyneb fel wythnos wlyb***
face *be* ***wynebu***
facecloth *enw* ***gwlanen*** *hon,* ***clwt(yn) 'molchi*** *hwn*
facelift *enw* ***newid golwg/diwyg***
facet *enw* ***ochr***, ***agwedd*** *hon*
facetious *ans* ***ffraeth***, ***cellweirus***
facile *ans* ***arwynebol***
facilitate *be* ***hyrwyddo***, ***hwyluso***
facilitator *enw* ***hwyluswr*** *hwn*
facility *enw* ***rhwyddineb***; ***cyfleuster*** *hwn*; ***dawn*** *hon*
facing *ans* ***yn wynebu***, ***gyferbyn â***
facsimile *enw* ***adlun*** *hwn*
fact *enw* ***ffaith*** *hon*
in f~ ***yn wir***
the f~ of the matter is ***y gwir amdani yw***
to know for a f~ ***gwybod i sicrwydd***
faction *enw* ***carfan*** *hon*
factor *enw* ***ffactor*** *hwn/hon*
factory *enw* ***ffatri*** *hon*
factual *ans* ***ffeithiol***
faculty *enw* (capability) ***cynneddf*** *hon*; (department) ***cyfadran*** *hon*
fad *enw* ***mympwy*** *hwn,* ***chwiw*** *hon*
fade *be* ***pylu***, ***edwino***
faeces *enw* ***ysgarthion*** *hyn*
faggot *enw* ***ffagotsen*** *hon*
fail *be* ***methu***
failure *enw* ***methiant*** *hwn*
to end in f~ ***mynd i'r gwellt***
faint *enw* ***llewyg*** *hwn*
faint *be* ***llewygu***
faint *ans* ***gwan***, ***aneglur***
fair *ans* ***teg***, ***golau***
f~ comment ***sylw teg*** *hwn*
f~ play ***chwarae teg*** *hwn*
to be f~ ***er tegwch***
fair *enw* ***ffair*** *hon*
fairies *enw* ***tylwyth teg*** *hyn*
fairness *enw* ***tegwch*** *hwn*
fairy tale *enw* ***stori hud a lledrith*** *hon*
faith *enw* ***ffydd*** *hon*
faithful *ans* ***ffyddlon***
faithless *ans* ***di-ffydd***
fake *ans* ***ffug***
fake *be* ***ffugio***
falcon *enw* ***gwalch*** *hwn*
fall *enw* ***cwymp*** *hwn*
fall *be* ***cwympo***, ***syrthio***

to f~ due ***mae'n daladwy***
to f~ into a category ***perthyn i gategori***
to f~ short ***bod yn llai na***
to f~ through ***mynd i'r gwellt***
to f~ to ***dod i ran***
fallacious *ans* ***cyfeiliornus***
fallacy *enw* ***cam-dyb*** *hwn/hon,* ***camsyniad*** *hwn*
fallible *ans* ***ffaeledig***
fallout *enw* (phys.) ***alldafliad*** *hwn*
fallow *ans* ***braenar***
fallow *be* ***braenaru***
falls *enw* ***rhaeadr*** *hon*
false *ans* ***camarweiniol, ffug***; ***ar gam***, ***twyllodrus***
falsehood *enw* ***anwiredd*** *hwn*
false alarm *enw* ***braw di-sail*** *hwn*
false teeth *enw* ***dannedd dodi***, ***dannedd gosod*** *hyn*
falsify *be* ***ffugio***
falter *be* ***petruso***, ***pallu***; ***baglu***
fame *enw* ***enwogrwydd*** *hwn*
familial *ans* ***teuluaidd***; (med.) ***etifeddol***
familiar *ans* ***cyfarwydd***, ***cynefin***
familiarity *enw* ***cynefindra*** *hwn,* ***adnabyddiaeth*** *hon*
familiarize *be* ***cynefino***
family *enw* ***teulu*** *hwn*
famine *enw* ***newyn*** *hwn*
famish *be* ***llwgu***
famished *ans* ***ar eich cythlwng***
famous *ans* ***enwog***
fan *enw* ***edmygydd*** *hwn*; ***gwyntyll*** *hwn*
fan *be* ***gwyntyllu***, ***megino***
fanatic *enw* ***penboethyn*** *hwn*
fancy *enw* ***dychymyg*** *hwn*
fancy *be* ***ffansïo***
fang *enw* ***dant*** *hwn*
fantastic *ans* ***ffantastig***, ***anhygoel***
fantasy *enw* ***dychymyg*** *hwn,* ***ffantasi*** *hwn/hon*
far *adf* ***ymhell***, ***yn bell***; *ans* ***pell***
f~ and away ***o gryn dipyn***
f~ better ***anrhaethol well***
f~ from easy ***ymhell o fod yn hawdd***
f~ off places ***pellafoedd (byd)***
f~ reaching ***pellgyrhaeddol***
f~ superior ***tra rhagori***
f~ too common ***yn rhy gyffredin o lawer***
f~ too little ***heb roi hanner digon***
few and f~ between ***prin***
farce *enw* ***ffars*** *hon*
fare *be* ***dod ymlaen***
to f~ badly ***dioddef***
to f~ well ***cael hwyl arni***
fare *enw* ***pris***, ***tâl*** *hwn;* ***bwyd, lluniaeth*** *hwn*
farewell *enw* ***ffarwél*** *hwn/hon*
far-fetched *ans* ***annhebygol***
farm *enw* ***fferm*** *hon*
farm *be* ***ffermio***
farmer *enw* ***ffermwr*** *hwn,* ***ffermwraig*** *hon*

farmhand *enw* ***gwas fferm*** *hwn*
farmhouse *enw* ***ffermdy*** *hwn*
farming *enw* ***amaethyddiaeth*** *hon*, ***amaeth*** *hwn*
farmland *enw* ***tir amaeth*** *hwn*
farmyard *enw* ***buarth*** *hwn*
farrago *enw* ***cawdel*** *hwn/hon*
farrier *enw* ***ffariar***, ***ffarier*** *hwn*
fart *enw* ***rhech*** *hon*
fart *be* ***rhechian***
fascia *enw* ***wynebfwrdd*** *hwn*
fascinate *be* ***hudo***, ***swyno***; ***mynd â bryd***
fascination *enw* ***cyfaredd*** *hon*; ***diddordeb ysol*** *hwn*
fascism *enw* ***ffasgiaeth*** *hon*
fascist *enw* ***ffasgydd*** *hwn*
fascist *ans* ***ffasgaidd***
fashion *enw* ***ffasiwn*** *hwn/hon*
fashion *be* ***llunio***, ***saernïo***
fashionable *ans* ***ffasiynol***
fast *ans* ***cyflym***; ***tynn***, ***sownd***
  fast asleep ***cysgu'n drwm***
fast *be* ***ymprydio***
fast *enw* ***ympryd*** *hwn*
fasten *be* ***sicrhau***, ***clymu***
fast food *enw* ***bwyd parod*** *hwn*
fastidious *ans* ***cysetlyd***
fast-track *ans* ***trac-cyflym***, ***carlam***
fast tracking *enw* ***dull carlam*** *hwn*
fat *ans* ***tew***, ***bras***
fat *enw* ***saim***, ***braster*** *hwn*
fatal *ans* ***angheuol***, ***marwol***
fatality *enw* ***marwolaeth*** *hon*
fate *enw* ***ffawd***, ***tynged*** *hon*
fateful *ans* ***tyngedfennol***
fathead *enw* ***penbwl*** *hwn*
father *enw* ***tad*** *hwn*
father *be* (a child) ***cenhedlu***
fatherhood *enw* ***tadolaeth*** *hon*
father-in-law *enw* ***tad-yng-nghyfraith*** *hwn*
fatherly *ans* ***tadol***
fathom *enw* ***gwrhyd*** *hwn*
fathom *be* (naut.) ***plymio***; ***amgyffred***, ***dirnad***
fatigue *enw* ***blinder***, ***lludded*** *hwn*
fatigue *be* ***blino***, ***lluddedu***
fatten *be* ***pesgi***
fatuous *ans* ***gwirion***, ***ffôl***
fault *enw* ***bai***, ***nam***; (geol.) ***ffawt*** *hwn*
fault *be* ***gweld bai ar***
faultless *ans* ***di-fai***
faulty *ans* ***diffygiol***, ***a nam arno***
favour *enw* ***cymwynas*** *hon*
  in your f~ ***bydd o'th blaid/o'ch plaid***
  to find f~ ***apelio at***
  to gain f~ ***dod yn boblogaidd***
favour *be* ***ffafrio***
favourable *ans* ***ffafriol***
favourite *enw* ***ffefryn*** *hwn*
favourite *ans* ***hoff***
favouritism *enw* ***ffafraeth***, ***ffafriaeth*** *hon*
fawn *enw* (deer) ***elain***, ***ewig*** *hon*; (colour) ***llwydfelyn*** *hwn*
fawn *be* (of deer) ***llydun***; (grovel)

cynffonna; (flatter) ***seboni, gwenieithio***
fax *enw* ***ffacs*** *hwn/hon*
fax *be* ***ffacsio***
fealty *enw* ***teyrngarwch*** *hwn*
fear *enw* ***ofn***, ***braw*** *hwn*
fear *be* ***ofni***
fearful *ans* ***ofnus***
fearless *ans* ***di-ofn***, ***eofn***
feasibility *enw* ***dichonolrwydd***, ***ymarferoldeb*** *hwn*
to discuss the f~ of ***trafod pa mor ymarferol bosibl fyddai***
feasible *ans* ***posibl***, ***dichonadwy***, ***ymarferol***
feast *enw* ***gwledd***, ***arlwy***; ***gŵyl*** *hon*
feast *be* ***gwledda***
feat *enw* ***camp***, ***gorchest*** *hon*
feather *enw* ***pluen*** *hon*
feathery *ans* ***pluog***
feature *enw* ***nodwedd*** *hon*
feature *be* ***dangos***, ***amlygu***, ***rhoi sylw i***; (newspaper etc.) ***ysgrif nodwedd***, ***rhaglen nodwedd*** *hon*
February *enw* ***Chwefror*** *hwn*
feckless *ans* ***didoreth***
fecund *ans* ***ffrwythlon***
federal *ans* ***ffederal***
federalism *enw* ***ffederaliaeth*** *hon*
fed up *ans* ***wedi syrffedu***
fee *enw* ***ffi*** *hon*, ***tâl*** *hwn*
feeble *ans* ***gwan***, ***eiddil***, ***gwachul***, ***tila***, ***llesg***
feebleness *enw* ***eiddilwch***, ***gwendid***, ***llesgedd*** *hwn*
feed *enw* ***porthiant***, ***ymborth*** *hwn*
feed *be* ***bwydo***, ***porthi***
feed-back *enw* ***adborth*** *hwn*
f~ sessions ***cyfarfodydd i rannu profiad***
feel *be* ***teimlo***, ***clywed***; ***cyffwrdd***
to f~ pain ***clywed poen***
to gain a f~ for ***magu dirnadaeth o***
please f~ free to ***croeso i chi***
feeler *enw* ***teimlydd*** *hwn*
feeling *enw* ***teimlad*** *hwn*
feign *be* ***ffugio***, ***esgus***
felicitate *be* **llongyfarch**
felicitations *enw* ***llongyfarchiadau*** *hyn*
fell *enw* ***rhos*** *hon*
fell *be* ***llorio, cymynu (coeden)***
fellow *enw* (companion) ***cymar***, ***cydymaith*** *hwn*
f~ worker ***cydweithiwr*** *hwn*
poor f~ ***druan ag ef***
fellowship *enw* ***cyfeillach***, ***cymdeithas*** *hon*; (of university) ***cymrodoriaeth*** *hon*
felon *enw* ***troseddwr*** *hwn*
felony *enw* ***trosedd*** *hwn*
female *enw* ***benyw*** *hon*
feminine *ans* ***benywaidd***
feminism *enw* ***ffeministiaeth*** *hon*
fen *enw* ***ffen, morfa*** *hwn*
fence *enw* ***ffens*** *hon*
fence *be* ***ffensio***; ***cleddyfa***

fencer *enw* ***ffensiwr***; ***cleddyfwr*** *hwn*
fend *be* (shot etc.) ***cadw (ergyd) draw***
to f~ for oneself ***gofalu amdanoch eich hun***
fender *enw* ***ffendar*** *hon*
ferment *enw* ***eples***, ***lefain*** *hwn*; ***eplesiad***, ***gwaith***; (excitement) ***cynnwrf***, ***cyffro*** *hwn*
ferment *be* ***eplesu***, ***gweithio***; ***cynhyrfu***
ferns *enw* ***rhedyn*** *hyn*
ferocious *ans* ***ffyrnig***
ferocity *enw* ***ffyrnigrwydd*** *hwn*
with unusual f~ ***yn anarferol o chwyrn***
ferret *enw* ***ffured*** *hon*
ferret *be* ***ffureta***
ferry *enw* ***fferi*** *hon*
fertile *ans* ***ffrwythlon***, ***toreithiog***
fertility *enw* ***ffrwythlondeb*** *hwn*
fertilize *be* ***ffrwythloni***; (manure) ***gwrteithio***, ***achlesu***
fertilizer *enw* ***gwrtaith***, ***achles*** *hwn*
fervent *ans* ***brwd***, ***brwdfrydig***, ***taer***, ***selog***
fervour *enw* ***brwdfrydedd*** *hwn*, **sêl** *hon*
fester *be* ***crawni***, ***gori***
festival *enw* ***gŵyl*** *hon*
festive *ans* ***llawen***, ***llawn hwyl***
fetch *be* ***cyrchu***, ***ymofyn***
fetching *ans* ***deniadol***
fête *enw* ***garddwest*** *hon*; ***ffair*** *hon*
fête *be* (an event) ***dathlu***; (a person) ***anrhydeddu***
fetid *ans* ***drewllyd***
fetlock *enw* ***egwyd*** *hon*, ***swrn*** *hwn*; ***cudyn*** *hwn*
fetter *enw* ***llyffethair***, ***hual*** *hwn*
fetter *be* ***llyffetheirio***, ***hualu***
feud *enw* ***cynnen*** *hon*, ***ymrafael*** *hwn*
feudal *ans* ***ffiwdal***
fever *enw* ***twymyn*** *hon*
feverish *ans* ***a gwres arno***
few *ans* ***ychydig***, ***ambell***
a f~ words about ***gair neu ddau am***
f~ if any ***prin – os oes rhai o gwbl***
f~ in number ***prin***
fiancé(e) *enw* ***dyweddi*** *hwn/hon*
fiasco *enw* ***ffiasgo*** *hwn/hon*
fib *enw* ***anwiredd*** *hwn*
fibre *enw* ***ffibr*** *hwn*
fickle *ans* ***anwadal***, ***oriog***
fiction *enw* ***ffuglen*** *hon*
fact not f~ ***ffaith nid ffwlbri***
fictional *ans* ***mewn ffuglen***
fictitious *ans* ***dychmygol***
fiddle *enw* (mus.) ***ffidl***, ***ffidil***, ***crwth***; (swindle) ***twyll***
face like a f~ ***wyneb fel wythnos wlyb***
fiddle *be* ***ffidlan***; ***ffidlo***
fiddler *enw* ***ffidlwr***, ***crythor*** *hwn*; ***twyllwr*** *hwn*
fidelity *enw* ***ffyddlondeb*** *hwn*

f

fidget *be* ***gwingo**, **bod yn aflonydd***
don't f~ ***bydd yn llonydd***
fidgety *ans* ***aflonydd***
fiduciary *ans* ***ymddiriedol***
field *enw* ***cae**, **maes** hwn*
to have a f~ day ***cael modd i fyw***
field *be* ***maesu***
fielder *enw* ***maeswr** hwn*
field mouse *enw* ***llygoden y maes** hon*
fieldwork *enw* ***gwaith maes** hwn*
fiend *enw* ***cythraul** hwn, **cythreules** hon*
fiendish *ans* ***cythreulig***
fierce *ans* ***ffyrnig**, **milain**, **chwyrn***
fierceness *enw* ***ffyrnigrwydd** hwn*
fiery *ans* ***tanbaid**, **tanllyd***
fife *enw* ***pib** hon*
fifteen *rhifol* ***pymtheg***
fifteenth *ans* ***pymthegfed***
fifth *ans* ***pumed***
fiftieth *ans* ***hanner canfed***
fifty *rhifol* ***hanner cant**, **pum deg***
fig *enw* ***ffigysen** hon*
fight *enw* ***brwydr** hon*
fight *be* ***ymladd**, **brwydro***
to f~ your corner ***ymladd dros eich safbwynt***
fighter *enw* ***ymladdwr** hwn, **ymladdwraig** hon*
figurative *ans* ***ffigurol***
figure *enw* ***ffurf** hon, **ffigur** hwn*
f~ of speech ***troad ymadrodd** hwn, **ffordd o siarad** hon*
figure *be* ***bod yn amlwg yn/mewn***
file *enw* (office, comptr) ***ffeil** hon*; (tool) ***ffeil**, **rhathell** hon*
file *be* ***ffeilio**, **llyfnhau***
fill *be* ***llanw:llenwi***
filly *enw* ***eboles** hon*
film *enw* ***haen**; **ffilm** hon*
film *be* ***ffilmio***
filter *enw* ***hidlen** hon*
filter *be* ***hidlo***
filth *enw* ***budreddi**, **mochyndra** hwn*
filthy *ans* ***mochynnaidd***
fin *enw* ***asgell** hon*
final *ans* ***olaf**, **terfynol***
a f~ reminder ***i'ch atgoffa cyn cloi***
final *enw* ***rownd derfynol** hon*
finalize *be* ***cwblhau***
finance *enw* ***cyllid**, **arian** hwn*
finance *be* ***cyllido, ariannu***
financial *ans* ***ariannol**, **cyllidol***
financier *enw* ***ariannwr** hwn, **arianwraig** hon*
find *be* ***darganfod**; **cael/dod o hyd i**; **cael (bod)***
find *enw* ***darganfyddiad** hwn*
finding *enw* ***canfyddiad**, **darganfyddiad** hwn*
findings *enw* ***casgliadau** hyn*
fine *ans* ***cain**, **cywrain**; **mân***
fine *enw* ***dirwy** hon*
fine *be* ***dirwyo***
fine *adf* ***(OK) iawn***
finesse *enw* ***cynildeb**, **craffter** hwn*
finger *enw* ***bys** hwn*

finger *be* ***byseddu***
fingernail *enw* ***ewin*** *hwn/hon*
fingerprints *enw* ***olion bysedd*** *hyn*
fingertip *enw* ***blaen bys*** *hwn*
  at his f~s ***ar flaen ei fysedd***
finicky *ans* ***cysetlyd***
finish *be* ***gorffen, cwblhau***
finish *enw* ***gorffeniad*** *hwn*
finished *ans* ***gorffenedig, ar ben***
  they are f~ ***mae wedi canu arnynt***
fir (tree) *enw* ***ffynidwydden*** *hon*
fire *enw* ***tân*** *hwn*
  f~ alarm ***cloch dân*** *hon,* ***larwm tân*** *hwn*
  f~ engine ***injan dân*** *hon*
  f~ escape ***dihangfa dân*** *hon*
  f~ extinguisher ***diffoddydd tân*** *hwn*
  f~ station ***gorsaf dân*** *hon*
fire *be* ***tanio***
firearm *enw* ***dryll*** *hwn*
fireman *enw* ***dyn tân*** *hwn*
fireplace *enw* ***lle tân*** *hwn*
fireproof *ans* ***gwrthdan***
firewall *enw* (computer) ***llen dân*** *hon*
firework *enw* ***tân gwyllt*** *hwn*
firm *ans* ***cadarn, ffyrf; pendant***
firm *enw* ***cwmni*** *hwn*
firmament *enw* ***ffurfafen*** *hon*
firmness *enw* ***cadernid*** *hwn*
first *ans* ***cyntaf***
  at f~ ***i gychwyn, ar y dechrau***
  at f~ hand ***(gweld) dros fy hun***
  f~ and foremost ***yn gyntaf oll***
first aid *enw* ***cymorth cyntaf*** *hwn*
firstborn *ans* ***cyntaf-anedig***
first-class *ans* ***rhagorol, di-ail***
first cousin *enw* ***cefnder*** *hwn,* ***cyfnither*** *hon*
first-hand *ans* ***uniongyrchol***
first-rate *ans* ***o'r radd flaenaf***
fiscal *ans* ***cyllidol***
fish *enw* ***pysgodyn*** *hwn*
fish *be* ***pysgota***
fisherman *enw* ***pysgotwr*** *hwn*
fisherwoman *enw* ***pysgotwraig*** *hon*
fishery *enw* ***pysgodfa*** *hon*
fishy *ans* ***amheus***
  something f~ ***drwg yn y caws***
fishing *enw* ***pysgota***
fission *enw* ***ymhollti***
fissure *enw* ***hollt, agen*** *hon*
fist *enw* ***dwrn*** *hwn*
fistful *enw* ***llond dwrn, dyrnaid*** *hwn*
fisticuffs *enw* ***dyrnu***
fit *ans* ***ffit, heini***
  fighting f~ ***iach fel y gneuen***
  to see f~ ***gweld y ffordd yn glir i***
fit *enw* ***pwl*** *hwn;* **ffit** *hon*
fit *be* ***ffitio, gweddu***
  to f~ the bill ***taro deuddeg***
fitness *enw* ***ffitrwydd; addasrwydd*** *hwn*
fitter *enw* ***ffitiwr*** *hwn*
fitting *ans* ***addas, gweddus***

f

fittings *enw* ***ffitiadau*** *hyn*
five *rhifol* **pump**
fix *enw* (predicament) ***helbul*** *hwn,* ***trafferth*** *hon,* **penbleth** *hwn/hon,* ***cyfyng-gyngor*** *hwn*; (dose of drug) ***pigiad*** *hwn,* **dos** *hwn/hon*; (swindle) ***twyll*** *hwn*
fix *be* ***sicrhau***, ***gosod***
f~ a date ***pennu dyddiad***
fixation *enw* ***obsesiwn*** *hwn*
fixed *ans* ***sefydlog***
fizz(le) *be* ***hisian***
fizzy *ans* ***byrlymog***
fjord *enw* ***ffiord*** *hwn*
flabbergasted *ans* ***cegrwth***
flab *enw* ***bloneg*** *hwn*
flabby *ans* ***llipa***
flaccid *ans* ***llipa***
flag *enw* ***baner*** *hon*
flag *be* ***fflagio***; ***gwanhau, llesgáu***
flagrant *ans* ***amlwg, eglur***
flail *enw* ***ffust*** *hon*
flail *be* ***ffusto***; ***dyrnu***
flair *enw* ***dawn*** *hon*
flake *enw* ***pluen*** *hon*; (of metal etc.) ***fflacsen, fflawen*** *hon*; ***cen*** *hwn*
flake *be* ***caenu***; ***pluo***; ***fflochennu***
flamboyant *ans* ***tanbaid***, ***lliwgar***
flame *enw* ***fflam*** *hon*
flammable *ans* ***hylosg***
flank *enw* ***ystlys*** *hon*
f~ forward ***blaenasgellwr*** *hwn*
flannel *enw* ***gwlanen*** *hon*
flap *enw* (of envelope etc.) ***llabed*** *hon*; (of wing) ***curiad*** *hwn*; (panic) ***ffwdan*** *hon,* ***helynt*** *hwn/hon*
flare *enw* ***fflach*** *hon*
flare *be* ***ffaglu***, ***fflachio***
flash *enw* ***fflach*** *hon*
flash *be* ***fflachio***
flashy *ans* ***rhodresgar***
flask *enw* ***fflasg*** *hon*
flat *ans* ***fflat***, ***gwastad***
flat *enw* (music) ***meddalnod*** *hwn*; (apartment) ***fflat*** *hwn*
flats *enw* (land) ***gwastadeddau*** *hyn*
flatten *be* ***gwastatu:gwastatáu***
flatter *be* ***gwenieithio***
flattery *enw* ***sebon*** *hwn*, ***gweniaith*** *hon*
flatulence *enw* ***gwynt*** *hwn*
flaunt *be* ***gwneud yn fawr***
flavour *enw* ***blas***, ***sawr*** *hwn*
flavour *be* ***blasu***
flaw *enw* ***nam***, ***diffyg*** *hwn*; ***gwendid*** *hwn*, ***mefl*** *hon*
flawed *ans* ***diffygiol***
flax *enw* ***llin*** *hwn*
flay *be* ***blingo***
flea *enw* ***chwannen*** *hon*
fleck *enw* ***smotyn***, ***brychni*** *hwn*
fleck *be* ***britho***, ***brychu***
fledgling *enw* ***cyw*** *hwn*, ***cywen*** *hon*
flee *be* ***dianc***, ***ffoi***
fleece *enw* ***cnu*** *hwn*
fleece *be* ***cneifio***; (duped) ***blingo***, ***pluo***
fleet *ans* ***chwim***
fleet *enw* ***llynges*** *hon*

fleeting *ans* ***brysiog***, ***diflanedig***
flesh *enw* ***cnawd*** *hwn*
flex *enw* ***fflecs*** *hwn*
flex *be* ***ystwytho***
flexibility *enw* ***hyblygrwydd*** *hwn*
flexible *ans* ***hyblyg***, ***ystwyth***
flexitime *enw* ***oriau hyblyg*** *hyn*
flick *enw* ***trawiad*** *hwn*; ***clec*** *hon*
flicker *be* ***neidio***, ***fflachio***; ***gwibio***
flies *enw* (of trousers) ***balog*** *hwn/hon*, ***copish*** *hwn*
flight *enw* ***ehediad***, ***hediad*** *hwn*
    in f~ ***ar ffo***
flighty *ans* ***penchwiban***
flimsy *ans* ***tila***, ***bregus***
flinch *be* ***cilio***, ***syflyd***; ***gwingo***
fling *be* ***taflu***, ***lluchio***
flint *enw* ***callestr*** *hon*
flip *enw* ***fflipen*** *hon*; ***chwifiad*** *hwn*; ***tro hwn***
    f~ side ***y tu chwith***, ***y cefn*** *hwn*
    f~ chart ***siart droi*** *hon*
flippant *ans* ***gwamal***, ***ysgafala***
flipper *enw* ***asgell*** *hon*
flirt *enw* ***merchetwr*** *hwn*, ***hoeden*** *hon*
flirt *be* ***fflyrtian***
flirtation *enw* ***cyboli***
flit *be* ***gwibio***
float *be* ***nofio***, ***arnofio***
flock *enw* ***praidd*** *hwn*, ***diadell*** *hon*
flock *be* ***heidio***, ***tyrru***
floe *enw* ***ffloch*** *hwn*
flog *be* ***fflangellu***
flood *enw* ***llif***, ***dilyw*** *hwn*
flood *be* ***boddi***
floodgate *enw* ***fflodiart***, ***llifddor*** *hon*
floodlight *enw* ***llifolau*** *hwn*
floods *enw* ***llifogydd*** *hyn*
flood tide *enw* ***llanw*** *hwn*
floor *enw* ***llawr*** *hwn*
floor *be* ***llorio***
flop *enw* ***methiant*** *hwn*
flop *be* ***methu***; ***syrthio'n fflemp***
floppy *ans* ***llipa***
    f~ disc ***disg hyblyg*** *hwn/hon*
flora *enw* ***planhigion*** *hyn*
floral *ans* ***blodeuog***
florid *ans* ***blodeuog***, ***gwritgoch***
florist *enw* ***gwerthwr blodau*** *hwn*; ***siop flodau*** *hon*
flotsam *enw* ***broc môr*** *hwn*
flounder *be* ***ymdrybaeddu***; (in speech) ***colli'ch trywydd***; (of horse) ***tindaflu***, ***gwingo***
flour *enw* ***blawd***, ***fflŵr*** *hwn*
flourish *be* ***ffynnu***
    to finish with a f~ ***gorffen mewn ffordd drawiadol***
flourishing *ans* ***llewyrchus***, ***ffyniannus***
flout *be* ***wfftio***
flow *enw* ***llif***, ***llanw*** *hwn*
flow *be* ***llifo***, ***ffrydio***
flow chart *enw* ***siart lif*** *hon*
flower *enw* ***blodyn:blodeuyn*** *hwn*
flower *be* ***blodeuo***
flowering *ans* ***blodeuog***, ***blodeuol***, ***yn ei flodau***

flowery *ans* ***blodeuog***
flowing *ans* ***llaes***, ***yn llifo***
flu *enw* ***ffliw*** *hwn*
fluctuate *be* ***amrywio***
fluctuation *enw* ***amrywiad*** *hwn*
fluency *enw* ***llithrigrwydd*** *hwn*
fluent *ans* ***rhugl***, ***rhwydd***
fluff *enw* ***blew***, ***blewiach*** *hyn*
fluffy *ans* ***gwlanog***
fluid *enw* ***hylif*** *hwn*
f~ ounce ***owns lifyddol*** *hon*
fluid *ans* ***ansicr***, ***yn llifo***
the situation remains f~ ***gallai'r sefyllfa newid eto***
fluke *enw* ***lwc mwnci:lwc mul***, ***ffliwcen*** *hon*
flummox *be* ***drysu***
flunk *be* ***methu***
fluoride *enw* ***fflẅorid*** *hwn*
fluorine *enw* ***fflẅorin*** *hwn*
flurry *enw* ***cwthwm***, ***hwrdd*** *hwn*; ***ffrwst*** *hwn*, ***ffwdan*** *hwn*
flush *enw* ***rhuthr dŵr*** *hwn*; (of emotions) ***hwrdd***, ***pwl*** *hwn*; (blush) ***gwrid***, ***cochni***, ***gwres*** *hwn*; (abundance) ***toreth*** *hon*, ***cnwd*** *hwn*; (cards) ***rhesaid*** *hon*
flush *be* ***golchi***, ***glanhau***; (comptr.) ***gwacáu***
to f~ a fox ***codi cadno***
flush *be* ***gwrido***; ***tynnu dŵr***
flushed *ans* ***gwridog***
fluster *be* ***drysu***, ***hurtio***; ***cynhyrfu***
flute *enw* ***ffliwt***, ***chwibanogl*** *hon*
flutter *be* (wings) ***ysgwyd***, ***curo (adenydd)***; (flag) ***cyhwfan***; (leaves) ***siffrwd***; (heart) ***crynu***
fly *enw* **cleren** *hon*, ***pryf*** *hwn*
fly *be* ***hedfan***, ***ehedeg***
flyer *enw* ***hedfanwr*** *hwn*, ***hedfanwraig*** *hon*
flying *enw* ***hedfan***
flyleaf *enw* ***tudalen rwymo*** *hon*
flyover *enw* ***pont***, ***pont-ffordd*** *hon*
foal *enw* ***ebol*** *hwn*, ***eboles*** *hon*
foam *enw* ***ewyn*** *hwn*
foam *be* ***ewynnu***
foaming *ans* ***ewynnog***
focus *enw* ***man canol***, ***ffocws*** *hwn*
lacking f~ ***ar chwâl***
they are the f~ of much discussion ***maent yn destun llawer o drafod***
to throw into sharp f~ ***dangos yn glir***
focus *be* ***canolbwyntio***, ***ffocysu***
fodder *enw* ***porthiant*** *hwn*
foe *enw* ***gelyn*** *hwn*
fog *enw* ***niwl*** *hwn*
foggy *ans* ***niwlog***
fogy *enw* ***cono*** *hwn*
foil *enw* ***ffoil*** *hwn*
foil *be* ***atal***, ***rhwystro***
fold *enw* ***plyg***, ***plygiad*** *hwn*; (sheep) ***corlan*** *hon*
fold *be* ***plygu***
folder *enw* ***plygydd*** *hwn*
foliage *enw* ***dail***, ***deiliach*** *hyn*
folio *enw* ***ffolio*** *hwn*
folk *enw* ***pobl***, ***gwerin*** *hon*

folklore *enw* ***llên gwerin*** *hon*
follow *be* ***dilyn***, ***canlyn***
follower *enw* ***dilynwr***, ***dilynydd*** *hwn*
following *ardd* ***yn dilyn***; ***o ganlyniad i***
  f~ the demonstration ***ar ôl y brotest***
  f~ the failure of ***oherwydd methiant***
  f~ this the pupils devised ***yna dyfeisiodd y disgyblion***
following *ans* ***dilynol***
  in the f~ manner ***fel hyn***; ***fel a ganlyn***
  the f~ main benefits resulted from the project ***dyma brif fanteision y prosiect***
  the f~ questions ***y cwestiynau isod***
follow-up *enw* ***dilyniant*** *hwn*
follow-up *ans* ***dilynol***; ***atodol***; ***ategol***
folly *enw* ***ffolineb***; (building) ***ffoledd*** *hwn*
foment *be* ***ennyn***
fond *ans* ***hoff***
  f~ memories ***atgofion melys/ cynnes*** *hyn*
fondle *be* ***anwylo***, ***anwesu***
fondness *enw* ***hoffter*** *hwn*
font *enw* ***bedyddfaen*** *hwn*; (typ.) ***ffont*** *hon*
food *enw* ***bwyd*** *hwn*
  f~ processor ***prosesydd bwyd*** *hwn*
foodstuffs *enw* ***bwydydd*** *hyn*
fool *enw* ***ffŵl***, ***hurtyn*** *hwn*
  more f~ me ***fel roeddwn i dwpa/ wiriona'***
fool *be* ***twyllo***
foolhardy *ans* ***byrbwyll***, ***rhyfygus***
foolish *ans* ***ffôl***, ***gwirion***
foolproof *ans* ***di-feth***
foot *enw* ***troed*** *hon*
foot-and-mouth disease *enw* ***clwyf y traed a'r genau*** *hwn*
football *enw* ***pêl-droed*** *hon*
footballer *enw* ***pêl-droediwr*** *hwn*
footbridge *enw* ***pompren*** *hon*
footfall *enw* ***cam*** *hwn*
footnote *enw* ***troednodyn*** *hwn*
footpath *enw* ***llwybr troed*** *hwn*
footprint *enw* ***ôl troed*** *hwn*
footstep *enw* ***cam*** *hwn*
fop *enw* ***ceiliog dandi*** *hwn*
for *ardd* ***am***, ***ar gyfer***, ***i***, ***dros***
for *cysyllt* ***gan***, ***canys***, ***oherwydd***
  f~ goodness sake ***er mwyn dyn***
forage *enw* ***porthiant*** *hwn*
foray *enw* ***cyrch***, ***ymosodiad*** *hwn*
forbearance *enw* ***goddefgarwch*** *hwn*
forbearing *ans* ***goddefgar***
forbid *be* ***gwahardd***
forbidden *ans* ***gwaharddedig***
forbidding *ans* ***anghynnes***, ***di-serch***
force *enw* ***grym*** *hwn*

through f~ of circumstances ***oherwydd yr amgylchiadau***
to join f~s with ***cydweithio â***
force *be* ***gorfodi***
forceful *ans* ***grymus***, ***egnïol***
forceps *enw* ***gefel (fain)*** *hon*
forcible *ans* ***trwy rym***
ford *enw* ***rhyd*** *hon*
fore *ans* ***blaen***
to the f~ ***ar flaen y gad***
forearm *enw* ***elin*** *hon*
forebode *be* ***argoeli***
foreboding *enw* ***argoel*** *hon*
forecast *enw* ***rhagolwg*** *hon*, ***rhagolygon*** *hyn*
forecast *be* ***darogan***, ***rhag-weld***
forefathers *enw* ***cyndeidiau*** *hyn*
forefinger *enw* ***bys blaen*** *hwn*
forego *be* ***aberthu***; ***rhoi'r gorau i***
foregoing *ans* ***blaenorol***
foregone *ans* ***rhagweladwy***, ***anochel***
foreground *enw* ***tu blaen***, ***blaendir*** *hwn*
forehead *enw* ***talcen*** *hwn*
foreign *ans* ***estron***
foreigner *enw* ***estron***, ***tramorwr*** *hwn*
foreman *enw* ***fforman*** *hwn*
foremost *ans* ***cyntaf***, ***blaenaf***; ***mwyaf blaenllaw***
first and f~ ***uwchlaw pob dim***
forename *enw* ***enw blaen*** *hwn*
forensic *ans* ***fforensig***
forerunner *enw* ***rhagflaenydd*** *hwn*
foresee *be* ***rhag-weld***
foreseeable *ans* ***rhagweladwy***
foresight *enw* ***rhagwelediad*** *hwn*
forest *enw* ***coedwig***, ***fforest*** *hon*
foretaste *enw* ***rhagflas*** *hwn*
foretell *be* ***darogan***, ***proffwydo***
forever *adf* ***am byth***; ***byth a beunydd***
forewarn *be* ***rhybuddio o flaen llaw***
foreword *enw* ***rhagair*** *hwn*
forfeit *be* ***fforffedu***; ***ildio***
forge *enw* ***gefail*** *hon*
forge *be* ***morthwylio***; ***creu***; (deceive) ***ffugio***
to f~ ahead ***bwrw ymlaen***
to f~ links with ***sefydlu cysylltiadau â***
forger *enw* ***ffugiwr*** *hwn*
forgery *enw* ***ffugiad*** *hwn*
forget *be* ***anghofio***
forgetful *ans* ***anghofus***
forget-me-not *enw* ***n'ad fi'n angof*** *hwn*
forgive *be* ***maddau***
forgiveness *enw* ***maddeuant*** *hwn*
forgiving *ans* ***maddeugar***
forgo *be* ***hepgor***
fork *enw* ***fforc***, ***fforch*** *hon*
fork *be* ***fforchio***
forked *ans* ***fforchog***
forkful *enw* ***fforchaid*** *hon*
forlorn *ans* ***diobaith***
form *enw* ***ffurf***; ***ffurflen*** *hon*; ***cyflwr***

f~s and precedents ***ffurfiau a chynseiliau*** *hyn*
f~ of speech ***ffordd o siarad*** *hon*
in/on f~ ***cael hwyl arni***
form *be* ***ffurfio***
formal *ans* ***ffurfiol***
formalize *be* ***ffurfioli***
formality *enw* ***ffurfioldeb*** *hwn*
format *enw* ***diwyg*** *hwn*
format *be* ***fformatio***
formation *enw* ***trefniant***, ***ffurfiant*** *hwn*
formative *ans* ***ffurfiannol***
former *ans* ***blaenorol***, ***cyn-***
formidable *ans* ***aruthrol***
formless *ans* ***annelwig***
formula *enw* ***fform[i]wla*** *hon*
formulate *be* ***llunio***; ***dyfeisio***
forsake *be* ***gadael***, ***cefnu ar***
forsaken *ans* ***gwrthodedig***
forseeable *ans* ***rhagweladwy***
for the f~ future ***am gryn amser eto***
fort *enw* ***caer*** *hon*
forte *enw* ***cryfder*** *hwn*
forthcoming *ans* ***ar ddod***, ***ar gyrraedd***; ***ar y gweill***; (forthright) ***di-flewyn ar dafod***
forthright *ans* ***di-flewyn ar dafod***
forthwith *adf* ***ar unwaith***, ***ar fyrder***, ***yn y fan a'r lle***
fortieth *ans* ***deugeinfed***
fortification *enw* ***atgyfnerthiad*** *hwn*
fortify *be* ***cryfhau***, ***atgyfnerthu***
fortitude *enw* ***gwroldeb*** *hwn*
fortnight *enw* ***pythefnos*** *hwn/hon*
fortress *enw* ***amddiffynfa***, ***caer*** *hon*
fortuitous *ans* ***trwy hap a damwain***
fortunate *ans* ***ffodus***
fortune *enw* ***ffawd*** *hon*; ***golud*** *hwn*
to pay a f~ for ***talu crocbris am***
forty *rhifol* ***deugain***
forum *enw* ***fforwm*** *hwn*
forward *ans* ***blaen***; ***digywilydd***
forward *ardd* ***ymlaen***
forward *enw* ***blaenwr*** *hwn*
forward-looking *ans* ***blaengar***
forward-thinking *ans* ***craff***; ***â gweledigaeth***
fossil *enw* ***ffosil*** *hwn*
fossilize *be* ***ffosileiddio***; ***ymgaregu***
foster *be* ***magu***, ***meithrin***
foster-child *enw* ***plentyn maeth*** *hwn*
foster-mother *enw* ***mamfaeth*** *hon*
foul *ans* (smell) ***aflan***, ***drewllyd***; (thoughts) ***ffiaidd***, ***mochynnaidd***; (language) ***brwnt***, ***anweddus***; (sport etc.) ***annheg***, ***brwnt***, ***budr***
a f~ deed ***anfadwaith*** *hwn*
f~ play ***chwarae brwnt*** *hwn*, ***camchwarae***
f~ throw ***camdafliad*** *hwn*
to fall f~ of the law ***torri'r gyfraith***
to fall f~ of someone ***pechu yn erbyn rhywun***

foul *be* ***baeddu***, ***difwyno***; (tangle) ***drysu***; (sport) ***chwarae'n frwnt etc., ffowlio***
found *be* ***sefydlu***, ***sylfaenu***
foundation *enw* ***sylfaen*** *hwn/hon*
f~ school ***ysgol sefydledig*** *hon*
f~ subject ***pwnc sylfaen*** *hwn*
founder *enw* ***sylfaenydd*** *hwn*
foundry *enw* ***ffowndri*** *hon*
fountain *enw* ***ffynnon*** *hon*
four *rhifol* ***pedwar*** *hwn*, ***pedair*** *hon*
fourfold *adf* ***yn bedwar cymaint***
fourteen *rhifol* ***pedwar ar ddeg*** *hwn*, ***pedair ar ddeg*** *hon*
fourteenth *ans* ***pedwerydd*** *hwn/* ***pedwaredd*** *hon* ***ar ddeg***
fourth *ans* ***pedwerydd*** *hwn*, ***pedwaredd*** *hon*
fowl(s) *enw* ***ffowlyn*** *hwn*, ***dofednod*** *hyn*
fox *enw* ***cadno***, ***llwynog*** *hwn*
foxgloves *enw* ***bysedd y cŵn*** *hyn*
foyer *enw* ***cyntedd*** *hwn*
fracas *enw* ***helynt*** *hon*, ***ffrwgwd*** *hwn*
fraction *enw* (math.) ***ffracsiwn*** *hwn*; ***mymryn (lleiaf)***
fractious *ans* (restless) ***rhwyfus***; (irritable) ***pigog***; (unruly) ***stranclyd***, ***afreolus***
fracture *enw* ***toriad*** *hwn*
fracture *be* ***torri***
fragile *ans* ***brau***, ***bregus***; ***eiddil***
fragility *enw* ***breuder***, ***eiddilwch*** *hwn*
fragment *enw* ***darn***, ***dernyn***, ***tamaid***, ***dryll*** *hwn*
fragment *be* ***darnio***, ***dryllio***
fragmentary *ans* ***darniog***, ***drylliedig***
fragmented *ans* ***tameidiog***
fragrance *enw* ***perarogl***, ***persawr*** *hwn*
fragrant *ans* ***persawrus***
frail *ans* ***brau***, ***bregus***; ***eiddil***, ***gwanllyd***, ***llesg***, ***musgrell***
frailty *enw* ***eiddilwch***, ***llesgedd*** *hwn*
frame *enw* ***ffrâm*** *hon*, ***fframwaith*** *hwn*
frame *be* ***fframio***; ***cynllwynio***, ***twyllo***
framework *enw* ***fframwaith*** *hwn*
franchise *enw* ***rhyddfraint***; ***masnachfraint*** *hon*
franchise *be* ***rhyddfreinio***, ***breinio***
franchised *ans* ***breiniol***
frank *ans* ***plaen***, ***agored***
frankincense *enw* ***thus*** *hwn*
frankness *enw* ***didwylledd*** *hwn*
frantic *ans* ***gwyllt***, ***gorffwyll***
fraternal *ans* ***brawdol***
fraternize *be* ***cyfeillachu***
fratricide *enw* ***brawdladdiad*** *hwn*
fraud *enw* ***twyll*** *hwn*
fraudulent *ans* ***twyllodrus***
fray *enw* ***ffrwgwd*** *hwn*
fray *be* ***treulio***; ***raflio***
freckle *enw* ***brycheuyn haul*** *hwn*, ***brychni haul*** *hyn*
free *ans* ***rhydd***; ***rhad ac am ddim***

free *be* ***rhyddhau***
freedom *enw* ***rhyddid*** *hwn*
freehold *enw* ***rhyddfraint*** *hon*
freelance *ans* ***ar ei liwt ei hun***
freely *adf* ***yn rhydd***
Freemasons *enw* ***Seiri Rhyddion*** *hyn*
Free-net *enw* ***rhadrwyd*** *hon*
free verse *enw* ***y wers rydd*** *hon*
freeware *enw* (computer) ***rhadwedd*** *hwn*
freewheel *be* ***hwylio mynd***
free will *enw* ***gwirfodd***
freeze *be* ***rhewi***
freezer *enw* ***rhewgell*** *hon*
freezing *ans* ***rhewllyd***, ***iasoer***
f~ point ***rhewbwynt*** *hwn*
freight *enw* ***cludiant*** *hwn*; ***llwyth*** *hwn*
freighter *enw* ***llong gludo*** *hon*
French fries *enw* ***sglodion tatws*** *hyn*
frenetic *ans* ***gorffwyll***, ***gwyllt***
frenzied *ans* ***gorffwyll***
frenzy *enw* ***gorffwylltra***, ***gwylltineb*** *hwn*
frequency *enw* ***amlder***; (radio) ***amledd*** *hwn*
frequent *ans* ***aml***, ***mynych***
frequent *be* ***mynychu***
fresco *enw* ***ffresgo*** *hwn*
fresh *ans* ***newydd***, ***croyw***, ***iach***
f~ air ***awyr iach*** *hon*
freshly *adf* ***o'r newydd***
freshness *enw* ***ffresni*** *hwn*
freshwater *ans* ***dŵr croyw***
fret *be* ***poeni***, ***pryderu***
fretful *ans* ***anniddig***, ***piwis***
friar *enw* ***brawd*** *hwn*
friction *enw* ***drwgdeimlad***; ***ffrithiant*** *hwn*
Friday *enw* ***Gwener*** *hwn*
fridge *enw* ***oergell*** *hon*
friend *enw* ***cyfaill*** *hwn*, ***cyfeilles*** *hon*
friendliness *enw* ***cyfeillgarwch*** *hwn*
friendly *ans* ***cyfeillgar***
friendship *enw* ***cyfeillgarwch*** *hwn*
frieze *enw* ***ffris*** *hwn*
fright *enw* ***ofn***, ***braw***, ***dychryn*** *hwn*
frighten *be* ***codi ofn***, ***dychryn***
frightened *ans* ***ofnus***, ***wedi cael ofn***
frightful *ans* ***dychrynllyd***
frigid *ans* ***rhewllyd***, ***oeraidd***
frill *enw* ***ffril*** *hwn*
fringe *enw* ***rhidens*** *hyn*; ***cwr*** *hwn*
frippery *enw* ***pethau ffrit*** *hyn*
frisky *ans* ***chwareus***
frivolity *enw* ***gwagedd***, ***lol*** *hwn*
frivolous *ans* ***gwamal***, ***penchwiban***
frizzy *ans* ***crychlyd***
frock *enw* ***ffrog*** *hon*
frog *enw* ***broga***, ***llyffant (melyn)*** *hwn*
frogspawn *enw* ***grifft*** *hwn*
frolic *be* ***prancio***
from *ardd* ***o***, ***oddi wrth***, ***oddi ar***
front *enw* ***blaen*** *hwn*

front *ans* ***ffrynt***
  f~ bench ***mainc flaen*** *hon*
  f~ door ***drws ffrynt*** *hwn*
  f~ page ***dalen flaen*** *hon*
frontier *enw* ***ffin*** *hon*, ***goror*** *hwn/hon*
front-wheel drive *enw* ***blaenyriant*** *hwn*
frost *enw* ***rhew***, ***barrug***, ***llwydrew*** *hwn*
frostbite *enw* ***ewinrhew*** *hwn*
frosty *ans* ***rhewllyd***, ***barugog***
froth *enw* ***ewyn*** *hwn*
froth *be* ***ewynnu***
frothy *ans* ***ewynnog***
frown *be* ***gwgu***
frozen *ans* ***wedi rhewi***
frugal *ans* ***cynnil***, ***darbodus***
fruit *enw* ***ffrwyth*** *hwn*
fruiterer *enw* ***gwerthwr ffrwythau*** *hwn*
fruitful *ans* ***ffrwythlon***
fruition *enw* ***dwyn ffrwyth***
fruitless *ans* ***diffrwyth***
frustrate *be* ***rhwystro***
frustrated *ans* ***rhwystredig***
frustration *enw* ***rhwystredigaeth*** *hon*
fry *be* ***ffrio***
frying pan *enw* ***padell ffrio*** *hon*
fuddled *ans* ***meddw***; ***cymysglyd***
fudge *enw* ***cyffug*** *hwn*; (mess) ***llanast***, ***gwaith carbwl*** *hwn*
fuel *enw* ***tanwydd*** *hwn*
fugitive *enw* ***ffoadur*** *hwn*
fugue *enw* ***ffiwg*** *hon*
fulcrum *enw* ***ffwlcrwm*** *hwn*
fulfil *be* ***cyflawni***, ***diwallu***
fulfilment *enw* ***cwblhau***; ***boddhad*** *hwn*
full *ans* ***llawn***, ***cyflawn***
fullback *enw* ***cefnwr*** *hwn*
full-cheeked *ans* ***bochog***
full moon *enw* ***lleuad lawn*** *hon*
fullness *enw* ***llawnder*** *hwn*
full stop *enw* ***atalnod llawn*** *hwn*
full-time *ans* ***llawn amser***
fully *adf* ***yn llawn***, ***yn hollol***
fulminate *be* ***taranu***
fulsome *ans* ***gormodol***, ***gwenieithus***, ***sebonllyd***
fumble *be* ***ymbalfalu***; ***dal yn lletchwith***
fume *be* ***mygu***; (person) ***berwi***, ***corddi***
fumes *enw* ***mwg***, ***tarth*** *hwn*
fumigate *be* ***mygdarthu***
fun *enw* ***hwyl*** *hon*, ***sbort*** *hwn/hon*
function *enw* ***swyddogaeth*** *hon*; ***achlysur***, ***derbyniad***; ***ffwythiant*** *hwn*
functional *ans* ***gweithrediadol***, ***gweithredol***
fund *enw* ***stôr***, ***cronfa*** *hon*
fund *be* ***ariannu***, ***cyllido***, ***noddi***
fundamental *ans* ***sylfaenol***
funds *enw* ***arian*** *hwn*
funeral *enw* ***angladd*** *hwn/hon*, ***cynhebrwng*** *hwn*
funereal *ans* ***angladdol***
fungus *enw* ***ffwng*** *hwn*

funnel *enw* ***twmffat***, ***twndis***; (ship) ***corn***, ***simnai*** *hwn*
funny *ans* ***doniol***, ***digrif***
fur *enw* ***ffwr*** *hwn*
furious *ans* ***cynddeiriog***, ***candryll***
furl *be* ***rhowlio***
furnace *enw* ***ffwrnais***, ***ffwrn*** *hon*
furnish *be* ***dodrefnu***; ***rhoi***
furniture *enw* ***dodrefn***, ***celfi*** *hyn*
furore *enw* ***cynnwrf*** *hwn*
furrow *enw* ***cwys*** *hon*
furrow *be* ***aredig***, ***torri cwys***
furry *ans* ***blewog***
further *ans* ***pellach***
  f~ education ***addysg bellach*** *hon*
further *adf* ***ymhellach***
further *be* ***hyrwyddo***
furtherance *enw* ***hyrwyddiad*** *hwn*
furthermore *adf* ***ar ben hynny***
furtive *ans* ***lladradaidd***, ***llechwraidd***
fury *enw* ***ffyrnigrwydd*** *hwn*, ***cynddaredd*** *hon*
furze *enw* ***eithin*** *hyn*
fuse *enw* ***ffiws*** *hon*
  f~ box ***blwch ffiwsiau*** *hwn*
fuse *be* ***ffiwsio***; ***ymdoddi***
fusion *enw* ***ymasiad*** *hwn*
fuss *enw* ***ffwdan*** *hon*
fuss *be* ***ffysan***, ***ffwdanu***
fussy *ans* ***ffwdanus***, ***trafferthus***
futile *ans* ***ofer***, ***seithug***
futility *enw* ***seithugrwydd*** *hwn*
future *enw* ***dyfodol*** *hwn*
fuzzy *ans* ***crychiog***; ***aneglur***

G

gabble *be* ***clebran***, ***rwdlian***
gable *enw* ***talcen (tŷ)*** *hwn*
gadget *enw* ***dyfais*** *hon*, ***teclyn*** *hwn*
Gaelic *enw* (language) ***Gaeleg*** *hon*
gaff *enw* ***tryfer*** *hon*
gag *enw* (in mouth) ***safnrhwym*** *hwn*; (joke) ***stori ddigri*** *hon*
gag *be* ***cau ceg, ffrwyno***
gaggle *enw* ***gyr*** *hwn*, ***haid*** *hon*
gaiety *enw* ***sirioldeb***, ***llonder*** *hwn*
gain *enw* ***ennill***; ***cynnydd*** *hwn*
  the greatest g~ ***y caffaeliad pennaf*** *hwn*
gain *be* ***ennill***, ***elwa***
  to g~ access ***sicrhau mynediad***
  to g~ attention ***dal sylw***
  to g~ insight ***dirnad***
  to g~ more experience ***magu mwy o hyder/brofiad***
  to g~ a reputation ***dod yn enwog am***
  to g~ respect ***ennyn parch***
gainful *ans* ***cyflogedig***
  g~ employment ***ennill bywoliaeth***
gait *enw* ***cerddediad***, ***osgo*** *hwn*
gala *enw* ***gŵyl*** *hon*
galaxy *enw* ***galaeth*** *hon*
gale *enw* ***tymestl*** *hon*
gall *enw* ***bustl*** *hwn*
gallant *ans* ***dewr***, ***gwrol***
gall bladder *enw* ***coden y bustl*** *hwn*
gallery *enw* ***oriel*** *hon*
gallivant *be* ***jolihoetio***
gallon *enw* ***galwyn*** *hwn*
gallop *enw* ***carlam*** *hwn*
gallop *be* ***carlamu***
galore *ans* ***digonedd***, ***llond gwlad***
galvanize *be* ***galfaneiddio***
gamble *enw* ***menter*** *hon*
gamble *be* ***gamblo***, ***hapchwarae***, ***mentro***
gambler *enw* ***gamblwr*** *hwn*
gambling *enw* ***hapchwarae***, ***gamblo***
gambol *be* ***prancio***
game *enw* ***gêm*** *hon*, ***chwarae*** *hwn*; ***anifeiliaid/adar hela*** *hyn*
game *ans* ***parod***, ***mentrus***
gander *enw* ***clacwydd*** *hwn*
gang *enw* ***haid*** *hon*, ***criw*** *hwn*
gangling *ans* ***heglog***
gangrene *enw* ***madredd*** *hwn*
gangway *enw* ***eil***, ***tramwyfa*** *hon*
gannet *enw* ***hugan*** *hon*
gap *enw* ***bwlch*** *hwn*, ***adwy*** *hon*
gaping *ans* ***cegrwth***
garage *enw* ***garej*** *hon*, ***modurdy*** *hwn*
garb *enw* ***gwisg*** *hon*
garbage *enw* ***sbwriel*** *hwn*
  g~ can ***bin sbwriel*** *hwn*

garble *be* ***llurgunio*****,** ***drysu*****,** ***cawlio***
garden *enw* ***gardd*** *hon*
gardener *enw* ***garddwr*** *hwn*, ***garddwraig*** *hon*
gardening *enw* ***garddio***
gargantuan *ans* ***anferthol***
gargle *be* ***garglo***
gargoyle *enw* ***gargoel*** *hwn*
garish *ans* ***gorliwgar, gorlachar***
garland *enw* ***torch o flodau*** *hwn*
garlic *enw* ***garlleg*** *hwn*
garment *enw* ***dilledyn*****,** ***pilyn*** *hwn*
garnish *be* ***addurno*****,** ***garnisio***
garret *enw* ***croglofft*** *hon*
garrison *enw* ***garsiwn*** *hwn*
garrotte *be* ***llindagu***
garrulous *ans* ***siaradus*****,** ***tafodrydd***
garter *enw* ***gardas:gardys*** *hon/hwn*
gas *enw* ***nwy*** *hwn*
g~ cylinder ***potel nwy*** *hon*
gaseous *ans* ***nwyol***
gash *enw* ***archoll*** *hon*
gash *be* ***torri***
gasp *enw* ***ebychiad*** *hwn*
gasp *be* ***ebychu***
gassy *ans* ***nwyol***
gastronomic *ans* ***gastronomegol***
gate *enw* ***clwyd*****,** ***llidiart*** *hon*; ***porth*** *hwn*
gateway *enw* ***porth, drws*** *hwn*, ***mynedfa*** *hon*
The centre is a g~ to ***Mae'r ganolfan yn agor y drws i***
gather *be* ***crynhoi*****,** ***ymgynnull***
gathering *enw* ***crynhoad*****,** ***cynulliad*****,** ***cyfarfod*** *hwn*
gauche *ans* ***lletchwith*****,** ***trwsgl***
gaudy *ans* ***gorliwgar***
gauge *enw* ***mesur*** *hwn*; ***medrydd*****,** ***mesurydd*** *hwn*
gauge *be* ***mesur*****,** ***cael amcan***; ***canfod hyd a lled***
gaunt *ans* ***esgyrnog*****,** ***main***
gauze *enw* ***meinwe*** *hwn*
gawk *be* ***edrych yn gegrwth***
gawp *be* ***edrych yn gegrwth***
gay *ans* ***hoenus, siriol***; (sexual) ***hoyw***
gaze *enw* ***trem*** *hon*
gaze *be* ***syllu***
gazelle *enw* ***gafrewig*** *hon*
gear *enw* (dress) ***gwisg*** *hon*, ***dillad*** *hyn*; (harness) ***gweddau*****,** ***harnais gwedd*** *hyn*; (goods/ utensils) ***offer*****,** ***taclau*** *hyn*; (mech. eng.) ***peirianwaith*****,** ***gêr*** *hyn*; (auto.) ***gêr*** *hon*
gearbox *enw* ***gerbocs*** *hwn*
geld *be* ***ysbaddu***
gem *enw* ***tlws*** *hwn*, ***gem*** *hon/hwn*
gender *enw* ***cenedl***; ***rhyw*** *hon*
g~ issues ***materion y ddau ryw***
gene *enw* ***genyn*** *hwn*
genealogical *ans* ***achyddol***
genealogy *enw* ***achyddiaeth*** *hon*
general *ans* ***cyffredinol***
general *enw* ***cadfridog*** *hwn*
generalization *enw* ***cyffredinoliad*** *hwn*

g

generalize *be* ***cyffredinoli***
generally *adf* ***ar y cyfan***, ***at ei gilydd***
generate *be* ***cynhyrchu***; ***creu***; ***generadu***; ***symbylu***; ***ennyn***; ***ysgogi***
generation *enw* (age) ***cenhedlaeth*** *hon*; (production) ***cynhyrchiad*** *hwn*
generator *enw* ***generadur***, ***cynhyrchydd*** *hwn*
generosity *enw* ***haelioni***, ***haelfrydedd*** *hwn*
generous *ans* ***hael***
genesis *enw* ***dechreuad*** *hwn*
genetics *enw* ***geneteg*** *hon*
genial *ans* ***hynaws***, ***siriol***
genitals *enw* ***organau cenhedlu*** *hyn*
genitive *ans* ***genidol***
genius *enw* ***athrylith*** *hon/hwn*
genre *enw* ***ffurf lenyddol*** *hon*
genteel *ans* ***syber***, ***bonheddig***
gentile *enw* ***cenedl-ddyn*** *hwn*
gentle *ans* ***addfwyn***, ***tirion***
  g~ persuasion ***darbwyllo'n gynnil***
gentleman *enw* ***bonheddwr***, ***gŵr bonheddig*** *hwn*
gentleness *enw* ***addfwynder*** *hwn*
gently *adf* ***yn dyner***, ***gan bwyll bach***
gentry *enw* ***bonedd***, ***crach*** *hwn*
genuflect *be* ***plygu glin***
genuine *ans* (authentic) ***dilys***; (person) ***cywir***, ***didwyll***
genus *enw* ***math*** *hwn*, ***rhywogaeth*** *hon*
geographer *enw* ***daearyddwr*** *hwn*, ***daearyddwraig*** *hon*
geography *enw* ***daearyddiaeth*** *hon*
geologist *enw* ***daearegydd*** *hwn*
geology *enw* ***daeareg*** *hon*
geometrical *ans* ***geometrig***
geometry *enw* ***geometreg*** *hon*
gerbil *enw* ***gerbil:jerbil*** *hwn*
germ *enw* ***bywyn***, ***egin***, ***hedyn*** *hwn;* (med.) ***germ*** *hwn*
German *enw* (language) ***Almaeneg*** *hon*
germane *ans* ***perthnasol***
germinate *be* ***egino***
gerrymander *be* ***ystumio ffiniau***
gesticulate *be* ***gwneud ystumiau***
gesture *enw* ***arwydd***, ***ystum*** *hwn*
get *be* (seek) ***mynd i gael/mofyn***; (acquire) ***cael***
  don't let it g~ to you ***paid â gadael iddo dy boeni***
  things will g~ better ***daw haul ar fryn***
  to be g~ting on for ***tynnu at***
  to g~ around (a problem) ***goresgyn***
  to g~ it right ***taro deuddeg***
  to g~ the attention of ***dal sylw***
  to g~ a message across ***cyfleu neges***

to g~ into the habit ***meithrin yr arfer***
to g~ someone started ***rhoi rhywun ar ben y ffordd***
geyser *enw* ***ffynnon boeth***, ***geiser*** *hon*
ghastliness *enw* ***hylltra***, ***hylltod***, ***erchylltra*** *hwn*
ghastly *ans* ***erchyll, ofnadwy, echryslon***
ghost *enw* ***ysbryd*** *hwn*
ghoul *enw* ***ellyll*** *hwn*
giant *enw* ***cawr*** *hwn*, **cawres** *hon*
gibber *be* ***rhefru***, ***baldorddi***
gibberish *enw* ***lol*** *hon*, ***dwli***, ***rwtsh*** *hwn*
gibbet *enw* ***crocbren*** *hon*
gibe *enw* ***gwawd*** *hwn*; ***ergyd*** *hon*
gibe *be* ***gwawdio***, ***gwatwar***
giddiness *enw* ***pendro*** *hon*
giddy *ans* ***chwil***, ***penfeddw***, ***penysgafn***
gift *enw* ***anrheg***, ***rhodd*** *hon*
gifted *ans* ***dawnus***, ***galluog***
gig *enw* (carriage) ***trap*** *hwn*; (boat) ***cwch bach***, ***bad*** (*hwn*); ***perfformiad*** *hwn*
gigantic *ans* ***cawraidd***, ***anferth***
giggle *be* ***piffian chwerthin***
gild *be* ***euro***, ***goreuro***
gill *enw* ***tagell*** *hon*
gilt *enw* ***eurwaith, eurad*** *hwn*
gimlet *enw* ***ebill*** *hwn/hon*
ginger *enw* ***sinsir*** *hwn*
ginger *ans* ***melyngoch, coch***
g~-haired person ***cochyn*** *hwn*, ***cochen*** *hon*
gingerly *ans* ***tringar***, ***gwyliadwrus***; ***gan bwyll***; ***fel iâr yn sengi ar farmor***
gipsy *enw* ***sipsi*** *hwn/hon*
giraffe *enw* ***jiráff*** *hwn*
gird *be* ***ymwregysu***
girder *enw* ***trawst*** *hwn*
girdle *enw* ***gwregys*** *hwn*
girl *enw* ***merch***, ***geneth*** *hon*
girlfriend *enw* ***cariad*** *hwn*
girth *enw* ***cengl*** *hon*; ***cylchfesur***; ***tewdra*** *hwn*
gist *enw* ***swm a sylwedd*** *hwn*
give *be* ***rhoi***
g~ up ***rhoi'r ffidil yn y to***
g~n ***o gael***; ***o gofio***
g~n that ***gan fod***
gizzard *enw* ***glasog*** *hon*
glacial *ans* ***rhewlifol***
glacier *enw* ***rhewlif*** *hwn*, ***afon iâ*** *hon*
glad *ans* ***balch***, ***llawen***; ***parod iawn***
gladden *be* ***bodloni***, ***sirioli***
glade *enw* ***llannerch*** *hwn/hon*
glamorous *ans* ***hudolus***, ***swynol***
glamour *enw* ***swyngyfaredd***, ***hudoliaeth*** *hon*
glance *enw* ***cipolwg*** *hwn/hon*
glance *be* ***bwrw cipolwg***
glare *enw* ***disgleirdeb*** *hwn*
glare *be* ***rhythu'n ddig***
glaring *ans* ***hollol amlwg***; ***yn rhythu***

g

glass *enw* ***gwydr***; (tumbler) ***gwydryn*** *hwn*
g~ ceiling ***grym anweledig*** *hwn*
glasses *enw* ***sbectol*** *hon*
glaze *enw* (shine) ***sglein*** *hwn/hon*; (ceramics) ***gwydredd*** *hwn*
glaze *be* ***sgleinio***; ***gwydro***; ***gosod gwydr mewn/ar***; (to dim, dull) ***pylu***
g~d eyes ***llygaid pŵl*** *hyn*
gleam *enw* ***llygedyn***, ***pelydryn*** *hwn*
gleam *be* ***tywynnu***
glean *be* ***lloffa***, ***cywain***
glee *enw* ***afiaith*** *hwn*, ***hoen*** *hon*
glen *enw* ***glyn*** *hwn*
glib *ans* ***tafodrydd***, ***slic***
glide *be* ***llithro***; ***gleidio***
glimmer *enw* ***llygedyn*** *hwn*
glimpse *enw* ***cip*** *hwn*, ***cipolwg*** *hwn/hon*
glimpse *be* ***cael cipolwg***
glint *enw* ***fflach*** *hwn*
glint *be* ***pefrio***
glisten *be* ***llewyrchu***, ***disgleirio***
glitter *be* ***disgleirio***, ***pelydru***
gloat *be* ***crechwenu***
global *ans* ***byd-eang***; ***cynhwysfawr***
globe *enw* ***cylch*** *hwn*, ***glob*** *hon*, ***y byd*** *hwn*
globular *ans* ***crwn, pellennaidd***
globule *enw* ***pelen***; (of fat) ***globwl*** *hwn;* (of water) ***diferyn*** *hwn*; (cawl) ***seren*** *hon*
gloom *enw* ***tywyllwch***, ***gwyll*** *hwn*; ***tristwch, anobaith*** *hwn*
g~ and doom ***gofid a gwae***
gloomy *ans* ***tywyll***; ***digalon***, ***diobaith***
glorify *be* ***mawrygu***
glorious *ans* ***gogoneddus***, ***godidog***
glory *enw* ***gogoniant*** *hwn*
gloss *enw* (shine) ***sglein*** *hwn/hon, **llewyrch*** *hwn*
glossary *enw* ***geirfa*** *hon*
glossy *ans* ***gloyw***
glove *enw* ***maneg*** *hon*
hand in g~ ***law yn llaw***
glow *enw* ***gwrid*** *hwn*, ***gwawr*** *hon*
glow *be* ***tywynnu***, ***cochi***
glower *be* ***cuchio***, ***gwgu***
glowing *ans* ***gwridog***
a g~ report ***adroddiad yn llawn canmoliaeth***
glucose *enw* ***glwcos*** *hwn*
glue *enw* ***glud*** *hwn*
glue *be* ***gludio:gludo***
glum *ans* ***digalon***, ***prudd***
glut *enw* ***gormodedd*** *hwn*
glutinous *ans* ***gludiog***
glutton *enw* ***bolgi*** *hwn*
glycerine *enw* ***glyserin*** *hwn*
gnarled *ans* ***cnotiog***
gnash *be* ***rhincian***, ***ysgyrnygu***
gnat *enw* ***gwybedyn*** *hwn*
gnaw *be* ***cnoi***
gnome *enw* ***dynan***, ***pwca*** *hwn*
go *be* ***mynd***

a number of things g~ing for it ***nifer o bethau o'i blaid***
all in one g~ ***i gyd gyda'i gilydd***
g~ for it ***ewch amdani***
to g~ ahead with ***bwrw ymlaen â***
to g~ deeper ***treiddio'n ddyfnach***
to g~ it alone ***mentro ar eich liwt eich hun***
to g~ out of fashion ***chwythu ei blwc***
to g~ out of your mind ***colli pwyll***
to g~ without saying ***go brin bod angen dweud***
to have a g~ ***mentro***

goad *enw* ***swmbwl*** *hwn*
goad *be* ***symbylu***, ***procio***
goal *enw* ***gôl*** *hon;* (objective) ***nod***, ***cyrchnod*** *hwn*
goalkeeper *enw* ***gôl-geidwad*** *hwn*
goat *enw* ***gafr*** *hon*
gobble *be* ***llowcio***
gobbledygook *enw* ***iaith aneglur***, ***ffiloreg*** *hon*
goblet *enw* ***ffiol*** *hon*
goblin *enw* ***coblyn*** *hwn*
god *enw* ***duw*** *hwn*
goddess *enw* ***duwies*** *hon*
godfather *enw* ***tad bedydd*** *hwn*
godless *ans* ***di-Dduw***
godlike *ans* ***fel duw***
godly *ans* ***duwiol***
godmother *enw* ***mam fedydd*** *hon*
godson *enw* ***mab bedydd*** *hwn*
goggles *enw* ***sbectol ddiogelwch*** *hon*
gold *enw* ***aur*** *hwn*
golden *ans* ***aur***, ***euraid***
goldfinch *enw* ***asgell aur*** *hon*, ***nico*** *hwn*
goldfish *enw* ***pysgodyn aur*** *hwn*
goldsmith *enw* ***eurych***, ***gof aur*** *hwn*
golf *enw* ***golff*** *hwn*
golfer *enw* ***golffiwr*** *hwn*, ***golffwraig*** *hon*
gondola *enw* ***gondola*** *hwn*
gong *enw* ***gong*** *hon*
good *ans* ***da***; ***graenus***; ***celfydd***
do g~ ***gwneud lles***
for g~ ***am byth***
g~ many ***cryn lawer***
g~ size ***o faint diogel***
in g~ faith ***yn gwbl ddiffuant***
the g~ the bad and the ugly ***y da***, ***y drwg a'r dychrynllyd***
to hold g~ for ***bod yn wir am***

goodbye *ebychiad* ***da bo***, ***hwyl***
good-looking *ans* ***golygus***
goodness *enw* ***daioni*** *hwn*
goods *enw* ***nwyddau*** *hyn*
goodwill *enw* ***ewyllys da*** *hwn*
goose *enw* ***gŵydd*** *hon*
gooseberry *enw* ***gwsberen*** *hon*
gooseflesh *enw* ***croen gŵydd*** *hwn*
gore *enw* ***gwaed*** *hwn*
gore *be* ***cornio***
gorge *enw* ***ceunant*** *hwn*

g

gorge *be* ***bwyta llond bol***, ***bwyta'ch gwala***
gorgeous *ans* ***gwych***, ***pert ofnadwy***
gorilla *enw* ***gorila*** *hwn*
gormless *ans* ***di-glem***
gorse *enw* ***eithinen*** *hon*
gory *ans* ***gwaedlyd***
gospel *enw* ***efengyl*** *hon*
gossamer *enw* ***gwawn*** *hwn*
gossip *enw* ***hen geg*** *hon*; ***clecs*** *hyn*
gossip *be* ***hel clecs***, ***cloncian***
gouge *enw* ***gaing gau*** *hon*
gouge *be* ***cafnu***
gourmand *enw* ***bolgi*** *hwn*
gout *enw* ***gowt*** *hwn*
govern *be* ***llywodraethu***
government *enw* ***llywodraeth*** *hon*
governor *enw* ***llywodraethwr*** *hwn*, ***llywodraethwraig*** *hon*
gown *enw* ***gŵn*** *hwn*
grab *be* ***cydio***, ***gafael***
  to g~ their attention ***hoelio eu sylw***
grace *enw* ***gosgeiddrwydd*** *hwn*; (prayer) ***bendith*** *hon*
grace *be* ***harddu***
graceful *ans* ***gosgeiddig***; ***cywrain***
graceless *ans* ***chwithig***
gradation *enw* ***graddoliad*** *hwn*
grade *enw* ***gradd***; ***graddfa*** *hon*
grade *be* ***graddio***, ***trefnu***; ***graddoli***
graded *ans* ***graddedig***
gradient *enw* ***graddiant*** *hwn*
gradual *ans* ***graddol***, ***cynyddol***
graduate *be* ***graddio***
graduates *enw* ***graddedigion*** *hyn*
graft *enw* ***impiad***, ***impyn*** *hwn*
graft *be* ***impio***
Grail *enw* ***Greal*** *hwn*
grain *enw* ***gronyn***; (texture) ***graen*** *hwn*
grain *be* ***graenu***
gram *enw* ***gram*** *hwn*
grammar *enw* ***gramadeg*** *hwn/hon*
grammatical *ans* ***gramadegol***
granary *enw* ***ysgubor*** *hon*
grand *ans* ***crand***, ***mawreddog***
  g~ total ***y cyfanswm terfynol*** *hwn*
grandad *enw* ***tad-cu***, ***taid*** *hwn*
grandchild *enw* ***ŵyr*** *hwn*, ***wyres*** *hon*
granddaughter *enw* ***wyres*** *hon*
grandeur *enw* ***gwychder***, ***mawredd*** *hwn*
grandfather *enw* ***tad-cu***, ***taid*** *hwn*
grandiose *ans* ***mawreddog***
grandma *enw* ***mam-gu***, ***nain*** *hon*
grandmother *enw* ***mam-gu***, ***nain*** *hon*
grand slam *enw* ***y gamp lawn*** *hon*
grandson *enw* ***ŵyr*** *hwn*
grandstand *enw* ***eisteddle***, ***prif safle*** *hwn*
granite *enw* ***gwenithfaen*** *hwn*
grant *enw* ***grant***, ***cymhorthdal*** *hwn*
grant *be* ***caniatáu***
granulate *be* ***gronynnu***
granule *enw* ***gronyn*** *hwn*
grapes *enw* ***grawnwin*** *hyn*

g

grapefruit *enw* ***grawnffrwyth*** *hwn*
graph *enw* ***graff*** *hwn*
graphic *ans* ***graffig***
grapple *be* ***ymgodymu***
grasp *be* ***cael gafael ar***
to g~ an opportunity ***achub cyfle***, ***bachu ar gyfle***
grass *enw* **porfa** *hon*, ***glaswellt*** *hwn*
grasshopper *enw* ***ceiliog y rhedyn***, ***sioncyn y gwair*** *hwn*
grassland *enw* ***tir glas***, ***glaswelltir*** *hwn*
grassy *ans* ***gwelltog***, ***glaswelltog***
grate *enw* ***grât*** *hwn/hon*
grate *be* ***crensian***, ***crafu***, ***rhygnu***, ***merwino***; ***gratio***
grateful *ans* ***diolchgar***
gratification *enw* ***boddhad*** *hwn*
to be a matter of g~ to ***mae'n destun balchder i***
gratify *be* ***boddhau***, ***rhyngu bodd***
gratifying *ans* ***braf***, ***boddhaus***; ***amheuthun***
gratis *adf* ***am ddim***
gratitude *enw* ***diolch***; ***diolchgarwch*** *hwn*
gratuitous *ans* ***di-alw-amdano***, ***direswm***
gratuity *enw* ***cildwrn*** *hwn*, ***rhodd*** *hon*
grave *enw* ***bedd*** *hwn*
grave *ans* ***difrifol***
gravel *enw* ***graean*** *hwn*, ***gro*** *hwn/hon*
graveyard *enw* ***mynwent*** *hon*
gravity *enw* (physics) ***disgyrchiant***; ***difrifoldeb***, ***dwyster*** *hwn*
gravy *enw* ***gwlych***, ***grefi*** *hwn*
graze *be* (feed) ***pori***; (scratch) ***crafu***
grease *enw* ***saim*** *hwn*
grease *be* ***iro***
greasy *ans* ***seimllyd***
great *ans* ***mawr***
a g~ time ***amser wrth eich bodd***
it's g~ ***mae'n braf/hwyl/wych***
she's g~ at writing ***mae ganddi ddawn ysgrifennu arbennig***
greatcoat *enw* ***cot fawr*** *hon*
greatness *enw* ***mawredd*** *hwn*
grebe *enw* ***gwyach*** *hon*
greed *enw* ***trachwant***, ***gwanc*** *hwn*
greedy *ans* ***barus***, ***gwancus***
green *ans* ***gwyrdd***; (growing things) ***glas***
greenery *enw* ***glesni*** *hwn*
greenhouse *enw* ***tŷ gwydr*** *hwn*
greenish *ans* ***gwyrddaidd***
greet *be* ***cyfarch***
greeting *enw* ***cyfarchiad*** *hwn*
gregarious *ans* ***hoff o gwmni***
grey *ans* ***llwyd***; ***di-liw***; ***digymeriad***
g~ mare ***caseg las*** *hon*
g~ hair ***gwallt gwyn/brith*** *hwn*
greyhound *enw* ***milgi*** *hwn*
greyish *ans* ***llwydaidd***
grid *enw* ***rhwyllwaith***; ***gratin*** *hwn*
griddle *enw* ***gradell*** *hon*
grief *enw* ***galar*** *hwn*

g

grievance *enw* ***cwyn*** *hon,* ***achwyniad*** *hwn*
to rake up old g~s ***codi hen grachod***
grieve *be* ***galaru***
grievous *ans* ***difrifol***
grill *enw* ***gridyll*** *hwn*
grill *be* ***grilio***
grim *ans* ***didrugaredd***, ***llym***
grimace *enw* ***ystum*** *hwn/hon,* ***cuwch*** *hwn*
grime *enw* ***baw***, ***parddu*** *hwn*
grin *enw* ***gwên*** *hon*
grin *be* ***gwenu***
grind *be* ***malu***, ***llifanu***, ***crensian***
grindstone *enw* ***carreg hogi*** *hon*
grip *enw* ***gafael*** *hon*
to come to g~s with ***cael gafael ar***
grip *be* ***gafael:gafaelyd***
gripping *ans* ***gafaelgar***
gristle *enw* ***gwythi*** *hyn*
grit *enw* ***graean*** *hwn*
grit *be* (teeth) ***rhygnu***
grizzle *be* ***cwyno***, ***conan***, ***gwenwyno***
grizzled *ans* ***brith***, ***broc***
groan *enw* ***ochenaid*** *hon,* ***griddfan*** *hwn*
groan *be* ***ochneidio***, ***griddfan***
grocer *enw* ***groser*** *hwn*
groggy *ans* ***sigledig***
groom *enw* ***gwas***, ***gwastrawd*** *hwn*
groom *be* (a horse) ***ysgrafellu***, ***gwastrodi***; (a person) ***tacluso***; (prepare) ***paratoi***
well g~ed ***trwsiadus***
groove *enw* ***rhigol*** *hon*
grope *be* ***ymbalfalu***
gross *be* ***ennill***
gross *ans* ***crynswth*** *hwn*
grotesque *ans* ***afluniaidd***
grotto *enw* ***ogof*** *hon*
ground *enw* ***daear***, ***sail*** *hon*
on the g~s that ***am fod***; ***oherwydd***
there are g~s for thinking ***mae yna le i gredu***
there is enough common g~ between ***mae digon yn gyffredin rhwng***
to get something off the g~ ***gosod ar waith***
ground *be* ***tirio***
ground floor *enw* ***llawr gwaelod*** *hwn*
groundless *ans* ***di-sail***
group *enw* ***twr***, ***dyrnaid***, ***grŵp*** *hwn*
group *be* ***casglu***
grouping *enw* ***grwpiad*** *hwn*
grouse *enw* ***grugiar*** *hon*
grouse *be* ***grwgnach***
grove *enw* ***llwyn*** *hwn*
grovel *be* ***ymgreinio***
grow *be* ***tyfu***
to g~ in complexity ***mynd yn fwyfwy cymhleth***
to g~ in understanding ***meithrin dealltwriaeth***

grower *enw* ***tyfwr*** *hwn*, ***tyfwraig*** *hon*
growl *be* ***chwyrnu***, ***arthio***
growth *enw* ***twf***, ***tyfiant*** *hwn*
g~ area ***maes twf*** *hwn*
grub *enw* ***cynrhonyn*** *hwn*
grubby *ans* ***brwnt***
grudge *enw* ***dig*** *hwn*, ***cynnen*** *hon*
grudging *ans* ***crintachlyd***
gruelling *ans* ***yn lladdfa***
gruesome *ans* ***erchyll***
gruff *ans* ***sarrug***
grumble *be* ***cwyno***, ***grwgnach***
grumpy *ans* ***piwis***; ***â chroen ei din ar ei dalcen***
grunt *be* ***rhochian***
guarantee *enw* ***gwarant*** *hon*
there's no g~ ***does dim sicrwydd***
guarantee *be* ***gwarantu***
guard *enw* ***gard:giard***, ***gwyliwr*** *hwn*
guard *be* ***gwarchod***
guardian *enw* ***gwarchodwr*** *hwn*, ***gwarchodwraig*** *hon*
guardianship *enw* ***gwarchodaeth*** *hon*
guard rail *enw* ***canllaw*** *hwn*
guerrilla *enw* ***herwheliwr*** *hwn*
g~ warfare ***herwryfela***
guess *enw* ***amcan***, ***dyfaliad*** *hwn*
it's anyone's g~ ***pwy a ŵyr***
guess *be* ***dyfalu***
guest *enw* ***gwestai*** *hwn*
guidance *enw* ***arweiniad***, ***cyfarwyddyd*** *hwn*
guide *enw* ***arweinydd***, ***tywysydd*** *hwn*
guide *be* ***arwain***, ***tywys***
guidebook *enw* ***arweinlyfr*** *hwn*
guideline *enw* ***canllaw*** *hwn*
guild *enw* ***urdd*** *hon*
guile *enw* ***dichell*** *hon*, ***twyll*** *hwn*
guileless *ans* ***gwirion***
guillemot *enw* ***gwylog*** *hon*
guillotine *enw* ***gilotîn*** *hwn*
guilt *enw* ***euogrwydd*** *hwn*
guilty *ans* ***euog***
guinea *enw* ***gini*** *hwn*
guinea pig *enw* ***llygoden gota*** *hon*
guise *enw* ***rhith*** *hwn*
in the g~ of ***fel petae***; ***cymryd arno***
guitar *enw* ***gitâr*** *hwn*
gulf *enw* ***gwlff*** *hwn*
gull *enw* ***gwylan*** *hon*
gullibility *enw* ***gwiriondeb***, ***diniweidrwydd*** *hwn*
gullible *ans* ***hygoelus***
gulp *enw* ***llwnc*** *hwn*
gulp *be* ***llyncu***, ***llowcio***
gum *enw* ***gwm*** *hwn*
gum *be* ***gludio***
gumption *enw* ***clem*** *hon*
gun *enw* ***dryll***, ***gwn*** *hwn*
gunfire *enw* ***saethu***, ***tanio*** *hwn*
gunpowder *enw* ***powdwr gwn*** *hwn*
gunshot *enw* ***ergyd gwn*** *hwn/hon*
gurgle *be* ***byrlymu***
gush *be* ***ffrydio***; ***parablu***
gust *enw* ***hwrdd***, ***cwthwm*** *hwn*

g

gusto *enw* ***awch***, ***afiaith*** *hwn*
gusty *ans* ***gwyntog***
gut *enw* ***perfedd*** *hwn*
gut *be* ***diberfeddu***
gutter *enw* ***cafn*** *hwn*, ***landar*** *hwn/hon*
  g~ politics ***budr-wleidydda***
guttural *ans* ***gyddfol***
guzzle *be* ***llowcio***
gymnasium *enw* ***campfa*** *hon*
gymnastics *enw* ***gymnasteg*** *hon*
gynaecologist *enw* ***gynecolegydd*** *hwn*
gyrate *be* ***cylchdroi***
gyroscope *enw* ***gyrosgop*** *hwn*

H

habit *enw* **arfer** *hwn/hon*, ***arferiad*** *hwn*
habitable *ans* ***y gellir byw ynddo***, ***cyfannedd***
habitat *enw* ***cynefin*** *hwn*
habitation *enw* ***annedd***, ***preswylfa*** *hon*
habitual *ans* ***arferol***, ***cyson***
they h~ly went ***arferent fynd***
habituate *be* ***cynefino***
hack *be* ***hacio***
hackle *enw* ***gwrychyn*** *hwn*
hackneyed *ans* ***ystrydebol***
hacksaw *enw* ***haclif*** *hon*
haddock *enw* ***corbenfras*** *hwn*
haemorrhage *enw* ***gwaedlif*** *hwn*
haemorrhoids *enw* ***clwy'r marchogion*** *hwn*
haft *enw* ***carn***, ***coes*** *hwn*
hag *enw* ***gwrach*** *hon*
haggard *ans* ***blinderus***
haggle *be* ***bargeinio***
hail *enw* ***cenllysg***, ***cesair*** *hyn*
hail *be* (greet) ***cyfarch***; ***bwrw cenllysg/cesair***
hair *enw* ***blewyn***; ***gwallt*** *hwn*
hairbrush *enw* ***brwsh gwallt*** *hwn*
haircut *enw* ***toriad gwallt*** *hwn*
hairless *ans* ***di-wallt***, ***moel***
hairstyle *enw* ***ffasiwn gwallt*** *hwn*
hairy *ans* ***blewog***, ***gwalltog***
hake *enw* ***cegddu*** *hon*
hale *ans* ***iach***, ***sionc***
half *enw* ***hanner*** *hwn*
to cut by h~ ***haneru***
halfbacks *enw* ***haneri*** *hyn*
half-baked *ans* ***hanner pan***
half-hearted *ans* ***llugoer***, ***claear***
half-hour *enw* ***hanner awr*** *hwn*
half-moon *enw* ***hanner lleuad*** *hwn*
halfpenny *enw* ***dimai*** *hon*
halfway *adf* ***hanner ffordd***
hall *enw* ***neuadd*** *hon*; ***cyntedd*** *hwn*
hallelujah *ebychiad* ***haleliwia***
hallmark *enw* ***dilysnod*** *hwn*; ***nodwedd amlycaf*** *hon*
hallow *be* ***cysegru***, ***sancteiddio***
Hallowe'en *enw* ***Calan Gaeaf*** *hwn*
hallucinate *be* ***gweld rhithiadau***
hallucination *enw* ***rhith*** *hwn*
halo *enw* ***corongylch*** *hwn*
halt *be* ***aros***, ***sefyll***
halter *enw* ***cebystr***, ***penffrwyn*** *hwn*
halting *ans* ***cloff***
ham *enw* ***cig mochyn*** *hwn*
hamlet *enw* ***pentrefan*** *hwn*
hammer *enw* ***morthwyl***, ***mwrthwl*** *hwn*
hammer *be* ***morthwylio***
to h~ home ***pwysleisio dro ar ôl tro***
hammock *enw* ***gwely crog*** *hwn*
hamper *enw* ***basged*** *hon*, ***cawell*** *hwn*
hamper *be* ***rhwystro***, ***atal***; ***amharu ar***

hamstring *enw* ***llinyn y gar*** *hwn*
hand *enw* ***llaw*** *hon*
  h~s of clock ***bysedd*** *hyn*
  the matter in h~ ***y mater dan sylw***
  the work is in h~ ***mae'r gwaith ar y gweill***
hand *be* ***estyn***
  to h~ in ***cyflwyno***
handbag *enw* ***bag llaw*** *hwn*
handbook *enw* ***llawlyfr*** *hwn*
handbrake *enw* ***brêc llaw*** *hwn*
handcuff *be* ***gefynnu***
handcuffs *enw* ***cyffion***, ***gefynnau*** *hyn*
handful *enw* ***llond llaw***, ***dyrnaid*** *hwn*
handicap *enw* ***anfantais*** *hon*
handicapped *ans* ***dan anfantais***
handicraft *enw* ***gwaith llaw*** *hwn*
handkerchief *enw* ***hances***, ***ffunen*** *hon*, ***macyn*** *hwn*
handle *enw* ***carn***, ***coes*** *hwn*, ***dolen*** *hon*
handle *be* ***bodio***, ***trafod***
handlebar *enw* ***corn*** *hwn*
handmaiden *enw* ***morwyn*** *hon*
handrail *enw* ***canllaw*** *hwn/hon*
handsaw *enw* ***llawlif*** *hon*
handshake *enw* ***ysgydwad llaw***
handsome *ans* ***golygus***, ***hardd***
  to pay h~ dividends ***talu ar ei ganfed***
handwriting *enw* ***ysgrifen***, ***llawysgrifen*** *hon*
handy *ans* ***hwylus***
  handy tip ***gair i gall***
handyman *enw* ***tasgmon*** *hwn*
hang *be* ***hongian***, ***crogi***
  h~ on! ***hanner munud!***
  to h~ out together ***cadw cwmni i'w gilydd***
  to h~ about ***tin-droi***
hang-glide *be* ***barcuta***
hanging *enw* ***crogi***
hangman *enw* ***crogwr*** *hwn*
hangover *enw* ***pen mawr*** *hwn*
hank *enw* ***cengl*** *hon*
hanker *be* ***hiraethu***
haphazard *ans* ***hap a damwain***; ***mympwyol***
hapless *ans* ***anffodus***
happen *be* ***digwydd***
happening *enw* ***digwyddiad*** *hwn*
happily *adf* ***yn hapus***
happiness *enw* ***hapusrwydd***, ***dedwyddwch*** *hwn*
happy *ans* ***hapus***, ***dedwydd***, ***llawen***
  to be h~ to ***bod yn ddigon parod i***
  to be h~ with ***ymfodloni***
  to make someone h~ ***codi calon***
happy-go-lucky *ans* ***jocôs***
harangue *be* ***rhoi pregeth***
harass *be* ***blino***, ***poeni***, ***aflonyddu***; ***bod ar gefn (rhywun)***
harbinger *enw* ***cennad*** *hwn/hon*
harbour *enw* ***porthladd*** *hwn*
  to h~ ideas ***coleddu syniadau***
hard *ans* ***anodd***, ***caled***; ***cadarn***
  a h~ sell ***gwerthu ymosodol***

h~ times ***dyddiau blin*** *hyn*
to be h~ done by ***cael cam***
to be h~ pressed ***bod dan bwysau***
to have a h~ time ***mynd drwy'r felin***
to take it h~ ***teimlo i'r byw***
harden *be* ***caledu***
hard-hearted *ans* ***calon galed***
hard-hitting *ans* ***di-flewyn ar dafod***
hardiness *enw* ***caledwch***, ***gwytnwch*** *hwn*
hardly *adf* ***prin***, ***o'r braidd***
hardness *enw* ***caledwch*** *hwn*
hardship *enw* ***caledi***, ***cynni*** *hwn*
hard up *ans* ***mae'n dynn/fain ar***
hardware *enw* ***caledwedd*** *hwn*
hardy *ans* ***caled***, ***gwydn***
hare *enw* ***ysgyfarnog*** *hon*
hark *ebychiad* ***erglyw!***
harlot *enw* ***putain*** *hon*
harm *enw* ***drwg***, ***niwed*** *hwn*
harm *be* ***niweidio***, ***gwneud drwg***
harmful *ans* ***niweidiol***
harmless *ans* ***diniwed***, ***diddrwg***
harmonious *ans* ***cytûn***
h~ relationship ***perthynas esmwyth*** *hon*
harmonize *be* ***cynganeddu***; ***cydweddu***
harmony *enw* ***harmoni*** *hwn*, ***cynghanedd*** *hon*
harness *enw* ***harnais*** *hwn*, ***gwedd*** *hon*
harp *enw* ***telyn*** *hon*
harp on *be* ***rhygnu ymlaen***
harpsichord *enw* ***harpsicord*** *hwn/hon*
harridan *enw* ***jadan:jaden*** *hon*
harrier *enw* ***boda tinwen*** *hwn*
harrow *enw* ***og:oged*** *hon*
harrowing *ans* ***dirdynnol***
harsh *ans* ***garw***, ***caled***
harshness *enw* ***gerwinder***, ***craster*** *hwn*
hart *enw* ***carw*** *hwn*
harvest *enw* ***cynhaeaf*** *hwn*
harvest *be* ***cynaeafu***
harvester *enw* ***medelwr***, ***cynaeafwr***; ***peiriant medi*** *hwn*
hassle *enw* ***ffwdan*** *hon*
haste *enw* **brys** *hwn*, ***hast*** *hon*
hasten *be* ***brysio***, ***cyflymu***
hasty *ans* ***brysiog***, ***byrbwyll***
hat *enw* ***het*** *hon*
hatch *be* ***deor***
hatchery *enw* ***deorfa*** *hon*
hatchet *enw* ***bwyell*** *hon*
hate *enw* ***casineb***, ***atgasedd*** *hwn*
hate *be* ***casáu***, ***ffieiddio***
hatred *enw* ***casineb***, ***atgasedd*** *hwn*
haughtiness *enw* ***rhodres***, ***trahauster*** *hwn*
haughty *ans* ***ffroenuchel***, ***trahaus***
haul *be* ***halio***, ***llusgo***
haulms *enw* ***gwrysg*** *hyn*
haunt *enw* ***cynefin*** *hwn*
haunt *be* (= frequent) ***mynychu (rhywle)***, ***byw a bod (yn***

rhywle); (of ghost) ***aflonyddu ar***, ***cerdded***
haunting *ans* ***adleisiol***, ***atgofus***, ***swynol***, ***hiraethus***; ***hunllefus***
have *be* ***bod gan***, ***meddu ar***
haven *enw* ***hafan*** *hon*
haversack *enw* ***bag cefn*** *hwn*, ***ysgrepan*** *hon*
havoc *enw* ***llanast*** *hwn*
hawk *enw* ***gwalch***, ***hebog*** *hwn*
haws *enw* ***criafol y moch*** *hyn*
hawthorn *enw* ***draenen wen*** *hon*
hay *enw* ***gwair*** *hwn*
hay fever *enw* ***clefyd y gwair*** *hwn*
haymaking *enw* ***lladd gwair***
haystack *enw* ***tas*** *hon*
hazard *enw* ***perygl*** *hwn*
hazard *be* ***mentro***
hazardous *ans* ***peryglus***
haze *enw* ***tarth***, ***tes*** *hwn*
hazel *enw* ***collen*** *hon*
hazelnuts *enw* ***cnau cyll*** *hyn*
hazy *ans* ***niwlog***, ***tesog***
he *rhag* ***ef***, ***fe***
head *enw* ***pen***; ***pennaeth*** *hwn*
h~ed paper ***papur swyddogol*** *hwn*
to compete h~ to ~h ***cystadlu'n uniongyrchol â***
head *be* (= lead) ***arwain***; (gardening) ***tocio***; (football) ***penio***
to h~ a list ***bod ar frig rhestr***
to h~ for ***bwrw (draw) am***
headache *enw* ***pen tost***, ***cur pen*** *hwn*
header *enw* ***peniad***; ***pennawd*** *hwn*
heading *enw* ***pennawd*** *hwn*
headland *enw* ***penrhyn*** *hwn*
headlight *enw* ***prif olau*** *hwn*, ***lamp flaen*** *hon*
headline *enw* ***pennawd*** *hwn*
headlong *adf* ***yn bendramwnwgl***; ***llwrw ei ben***
headmaster *enw* ***prifathro*** *hwn*
headmistress *enw* ***prifathrawes*** *hon*
headquarters *enw* ***pencadlys*** *hwn*
headship *enw* ***prifathrawiaeth*** *hon*
headstrong *ans* ***penstiff***, ***gwrthnysig***
head-waiter *enw* ***prif weinydd*** *hwn*, ***prif weinyddes*** *hon*
heady *ans* ***meddwol***, ***llesmeiriol***
heal *be* ***gwella***, ***iacháu***
health *enw* ***iechyd*** *hwn*
H~ and Safety at Work ***Iechyd a Diogelwch wrth Weithio/yn y Gweithle***
healthiness *enw* ***iechyd da*** *hwn*
healthy *ans* ***iach***, ***iachus***
heap *enw* ***pentwr*** *hwn*, ***tomen*** *hon*
heap *be* ***pentyrru***
hear *be* ***clywed***; (court) ***gwrando***
hearing *enw* ***clyw***; (court) ***gwrandawiad*** *hwn*
h~ defect ***diffyg ar y clyw***
hard of h~ ***yn drwm eich clyw***
hearken *be* ***gwrando***
hearsay *enw* ***sôn***, ***achlust*** *hwn*; (court) ***tystiolaeth ail-law*** *hon*

hearse *enw* ***hers*** *hon*
heart *enw* ***calon*** *hon*
  h~ attack ***trawiad ar y galon*** *hwn*
heartbeat *enw* ***curiad calon*** *hwn*
heartbreaking *ans* ***torcalonnus***
heartburn *enw* ***llosg cylla***, ***dŵr poeth*** *hwn*
hearten *be* ***calonogi***
heartfelt *ans* ***o lwyrfryd calon***
hearth *enw* ***aelwyd*** *hon*
heartland *enw* ***perfeddwlad*** *hon*
  Welsh h~ ***y Fro Gymraeg*** *hon*
heartless *ans* ***creulon***, ***didostur***
hearty *ans* ***calonnog***, ***twymgalon***
heat *enw* ***gwres*** *hwn*
heat *be* ***twymo***, ***cynhesu***, ***gwresogi***
heated *ans* ***brwd***; ***twym***, ***poeth***
heater *enw* ***gwresogydd*** *hwn*
heath *enw* ***rhos, gwaun*** *hon*
heathland *enw* ***rhostir*** *hwn*
heathen *enw* ***pagan*** *hwn*
heather *enw* ***grug*** *hwn*
heating *enw* ***gwres*** *hwn*
heatwave *enw* ***gwres mawr*** *hwn*
heave *be* ***codi***, ***gwthio i fyny***; (= haul) ***halio***; (= swell) ***ymchwyddo***, ***ymgodi***; (to be sick) ***chwydu***, ***cyfogi***
  to h~ a sigh ***ochneidio***, ***rhoi ochenaid***
heaven *enw* ***nefoedd***, ***nef*** *hon*
heavenly *ans* ***nefolaidd***
heaviness *enw* ***trymder*** *hwn*
heavy *ans* ***trwm***
  heavy demand ***galw mawr am***
heavyweight *ans* ***pwysau trwm***
Hebrew *enw* (language) ***Hebraeg*** *hon*
heckle *be* ***heclo***
heckler *enw* ***heclwr*** *hwn*
hectic *ans* ***fel ffair***, ***prysur ofnadwy***
hectare *enw* ***hectar*** *hwn*
hector *be* ***cega***
hectoring *enw* ***arthio***
hedge *enw* ***clawdd***, ***gwrych*** *hwn*
hedgehog *enw* ***draenog*** *hwn*
heed *be* ***talu sylw i***
  to h~ the advice of ***dilyn cyngor***
heedless *ans* ***di-hid:dihidio***
heel *enw* ***sawdl*** *hwn/hon*
hefty *ans* ***cadarn***, ***glew***, ***cryf***
  a h~ fine ***dirwy drom/sylweddol*** *hon*
hegemony *enw* ***penarglwyddiaeth***, ***tra-arglwyddiaeth*** *hon*
heifer *enw* ***anner*** *hon*
height *enw* ***taldra***, ***uchder*** *hwn;* ***uchafbwynt***, ***anterth*** *hwn*
heighten *be* ***codi'n uwch***
  to h~ awareness ***meithrin ymwybyddiaeth***
heinous *ans* ***ysgeler***, ***anfad***
heir *enw* ***etifedd***, ***aer*** *hwn*
helicopter *enw* ***hofrennydd*** *hwn*
helium *enw* ***heliwm*** *hwn*
hell *enw* ***uffern*** *hon*

through h~ and high water ***drwy ddŵr a thân***
hellish *ans* ***uffernol***
hello *ebychiad* ***sut ma'i?***, ***shwt ma'i?***
helmet *enw* ***helm***, ***helmed*** *hon*
help *enw* ***cymorth***, ***help*** *hwn*
help *be* ***cynorthwyo***, ***helpu***
helper *enw* ***cynorthwywr*** *hwn*
helpful *ans* ***o gymorth***, ***defnyddiol***
helpless *ans* ***diymgeledd***, ***diymadferth***
hem *enw* ***godre*** *hwn*
hem *be* ***hemio***
hemisphere *enw* ***hemisffer*** *hwn*
hemp *enw* ***cywarch*** *hwn*
hen *enw* ***iâr*** *hon*
hence *adf* ***felly***; ***dyna sy'n esbonio***; ***gan hynny***
henceforward *adf* ***mwyach***, ***o hyn ymlaen***
hen-house *enw* ***cwt ieir*** *hwn*
hepatitis *enw* ***llid yr afu*** *hwn*
her *rhag* (possessive) ***ei/ei – hi***; (indicative) ***hi***
herb *enw* ***llysieuyn*** *hwn*
herbal *ans* ***llysieuol***
herbalist *enw* ***meddyg llysiau***, ***perlysieuydd*** *hwn*
herbivore *enw* ***llysysydd*** *hwn*
herbs *enw* ***llysiau***, ***perlysiau*** *hyn*
herd *enw* ***buches*** *hon*, ***gyr*** *hwn*, ***haid*** *hon*
here *adf* ***yma***; ***dyma***
hereby *adf* ***drwy hyn***, ***gan hynny***
hereditary *ans* ***etifeddol***
heredity *enw* ***etifeddeg*** *hon*
herein *adf* ***yn hyn***
hereinafter *adf* ***wedi hyn***, ***o hyn ymlaen***
heresy *enw* ***heresi*** *hon*
hereupon *adf* ***ar hynny***
heritage *enw* ***etifeddiaeth***, ***treftadaeth*** *hon*
hermit *enw* ***meudwy*** *hwn*
hernia *enw* ***tor llengig*** *hwn*
hero *enw* ***arwr***, ***gwron*** *hwn*
heroic *ans* ***arwrol***
heroin *enw* ***heroin*** *hwn*
heroine *enw* ***arwres*** *hon*
heron *enw* ***crëyr***, ***crychydd*** *hwn*
herpes *enw* ***eryr*** *hwn*
herring *enw* ***pennog***, ***ysgadenyn*** *hwn*
hers *rhag* ***ei hun hi***
that's ~ ***hi piau hwnna***
herself *rhag* ***hi ei hun:hunan***
hesitant *ans* ***petrusgar***
hesitate *be* ***petruso***; ***cloffi rhwng dau feddwl***
hesitation *enw* ***petruster*** *hwn*
heterogeneous *ans* ***cymysgryw***, ***anghydryw***
heterosexual *ans* ***gwahanrywiol***
hew *be* ***naddu***, ***cymynu***
hexagon *enw* ***hecsagon*** *hwn*
heyday *enw* ***anterth*** *hwn*
hiatus *enw* ***bwlch*** *hwn*, ***adwy*** *hon*
hibernate *be* ***gaeafgysgu***
hiccup *enw* ***yr ig*** *hon*

hiccup *be* ***igian**, **mae'r ig arno***
hidden *ans* ***cudd**, **cuddiedig***
hide *enw* ***croen*** *hwn*; ***cuddfan*** *hwn/hon*
hide *be* ***cuddio**, **celu***
hideaway *enw* ***cuddfan*** *hwn/hon*
hideous *ans* ***erchyll**, **hyll***
hiding *enw* ***crasfa*** *hon*
hierarchy *enw* ***hierarchaeth*** *hon*
hieroglyph *enw* ***hieroglyff*** *hwn*
hi-fi *enw* ***hei-ffei*** *hwn*
higgledy-piggledy *adf* ***blith draphlith***
high *ans* ***uchel***
  h~ proportion ***cyfran fawr*** *hon*
  h~ quality ***graenus**; **disglair***
  h~-heeled shoes ***sgidiau sodlau main*** *hyn*
highbrow *ans* ***uchel-ael***
high court *enw* ***uchel lys*** *hwn*
higher *ans* ***uwch***
highland *enw* ***ucheldir*** *hwn*
highlight *enw* ***uchafbwynt*** *hwn*
highlight *be* ***uwcholeuo, amlygu**; **tanlinellu***
highlighter *enw* ***lliwoleuydd**, **lliwamlygydd*** *hwn*
high-minded *ans* ***mawrfrydig***
highness *enw* ***uchder**, **uchelder*** *hwn*
high priest *enw* ***archoffeiriad*** *hwn*
high-risk *ans* ***mentrus**; **peryglus***
high-spirited *ans* ***nwyfus***
high tide *enw* ***penllanw*** *hwn*
high treason *enw* ***teyrnfradwriaeth*** *hon*
highway *enw* ***ffordd fawr*** *hon*
highwayman *enw* ***lleidr pen-ffordd*** *hwn*
hike *be* ***heicio***
hilarious *ans* ***doniol iawn**, **digrif tu hwnt***
hilarity *enw* ***doniolwch*** *hwn*
hill *enw* ***bryn*** *hwn*, ***rhiw*** *hon*
hillock *enw* ***bryncyn*** *hwn*
hillside *enw* ***llechwedd**, **llethr*** *hon*
hilly *ans* ***mynyddig**, **bryniog***
hilt *enw* ***carn*** *hwn*
him *rhag* ***ef**, **fe**, **fo***
himself *rhag* ***ef ei hun:hunan***
hind *enw* ***elain*** *hon*
hinder *be* ***llesteirio**, **rhwystro***
hindrance *enw* ***rhwystr**, **llestair*** *hwn*
hindsight *enw* ***synnwyr trannoeth*** *hwn*
hinge *enw* ***colfach*** *hwn*
hint *enw* ***awgrym**, **tinc**; **gair o gyngor*** *hwn*
hint *be* ***lledawgrymu**; **taro'r post i'r pared glywed***
hip *enw* ***clun*** *hon*
hips *enw* (plants) ***egroes*** *hyn*
hire *be* ***llogi**, **cyflogi***
hirsute *ans* ***blewog***
his *rhag* (possessive) ***ef**, **o***
  that's h~ (emphatic) ***fe piau hwnna***
hiss *be* ***poeri**, **hisian***
historian *enw* ***hanesydd*** *hwn*
historic(al) *ans* ***hanesyddol***
history *enw* ***hanes*** *hwn*

h

hit *be* ***bwrw***, ***taro***
to h~ the headlines ***cipio'r penawdau***
hit-or-miss *ans* ***hap a damwain***
hitch-hike *be* ***bodio***, ***ffawdheglu***
hitherto *adf* ***hyd yn hyn***
hive *enw* ***cwch (gwenyn)*** *hwn*
a h~ of activity ***yn ferw gwyllt***
HMI *byrfodd* ***Arolygydd Ei Mawrhydi (AEM)***
hoard *enw* ***celc***, ***casgliad*** *hwn*
hoard *be* ***casglu***, ***cronni***
hoar frost *enw* ***barrug*** *hwn*
hoarse *ans* ***cryg:cryglyd***
hoarseness *enw* ***crygni*** *hwn*
hobble *enw* (limp) ***herc*** *hon*, ***cloffni*** *hwn*; (fetter) ***llyffethair*** *hon*
hobble *be* ***hercian***, ***cloffi***
hobby *enw* ***diddordeb*** *hwn*, ***hobi*** *hon*
hobgoblin *enw* ***pwca*** *hwn*
hockey *enw* ***hoci*** *hwn*
hod *enw* ***caseg fortar*** *hon*
hoe *enw* ***hof*** *hon*
hoe *be* ***hofio***, ***chwynnu***
hog *enw* ***twrch*** *hwn*
hog *be* ***meddiannu***, ***mynnu***
hog roast *enw* ***ffest mochyn*** *hwn*
hoist *enw* ***peiriant/teclyn codi*** *hwn*
hoist *be* ***codi***, ***halio***
hold *enw* ***howld*** *hon*
hold *be* ***dal***, ***gafael***; ***credu***, ***arddel***
they won't h~ it against you ***fyddan nhw ddim dicach***
to h~ information ***cadw gwybodaeth***
to h~ one's own ***dal fy (dy***, ***ei etc.) nhir***
to h~ out the possibility that ***cynnig y posibilrwydd***
to h~ true for ***bod yn wir am***
to put on h~ ***atal/gohirio dros dro***
hold-up *enw* ***lladrad arfog*** *hwn*; ***tagfa*** *hon*
holder *enw* ***deiliad*** *hwn*
hole *enw* ***twll*** *hwn*
holiday *enw* ***gŵyl*** *hon*
holiness *enw* ***sancteiddrwydd*** *hwn*
holistic *ans* ***cyfannol***
hollow *ans* ***gwag***, ***cau***; (of no substance) ***gwantan***
holly tree *enw* ***celynnen*** *hon*
holocaust *enw* ***galanas***, ***cyflafan*** *hon*, ***holocost*** *hwn*
holy *ans* ***sanctaidd***, ***cysegredig***
Holy Spirit *enw* ***yr Ysbryd Glân*** *hwn*
homage *enw* ***gwrogaeth*** *hon*
home *enw* ***cartref*** *hwn*, ***aelwyd*** *hon*
at h~ ***gartref***
going h~ ***mynd adref***
h~ area ***cynefin*** *hwn*; ***milltir sgwâr*** *hon*
to bring h~ to ***gwneud iddynt sylweddoli***
homeless *ans* ***digartref***
homelessness *enw* ***digartrefedd*** *hwn*, ***bod yn ddigartref***
homely *ans* ***cartrefol***
home ownership *enw* ***perchentyaeth*** *hon*

home rule *enw* ***ymreolaeth***; ***hunanlywodraeth*** *hon*
homesick *ans* ***hiraethus***
homesickness *enw* ***hiraeth*** *hwn*
homespun *ans* ***brethyn cartref***
homeward *adf* ***adref***
homework *enw* ***gwaith cartref*** *hwn*
homicide *enw* (crime) ***dynladdiad*** *hwn*; (person) ***dynleiddiad*** *hwn/hon*
homogeneous *ans* ***cydryw***
homosexual *enw* ***gwrywgydiwr*** *hwn*, ***lesbiad*** *hon*
homosexual *ans* ***cyfunrhywiol***, ***gwrywgydiol***, ***lesbiaidd***
honest *ans* ***gonest:onest***
honesty *enw* ***gonestrwydd: onestrwydd*** *hwn*
  in all h~ ***a bod yn gwbl onest***
honey *enw* ***mêl*** *hwn*
honeycomb *enw* ***crwybr***, ***dil mêl*** *hwn*
honeymoon *enw* ***mis mêl*** *hwn*
honeysuckle *enw* ***gwyddfid*** *hwn*
honorary *ans* ***mygedol***, ***anrhydeddus***
honour *enw* ***anrhydedd*** *hwn/hon*, ***bri*** *hwn*
  in h~ of ***o barch i***
honour *be* ***anrhydeddu***
  to h~ their commitments ***cadw (at) eu gair***
honourable *ans* ***anrhydeddus***
hood *enw* ***cwfl***, ***cwcwll*** *hwn*
hooded *ans* ***cycyllog***
hoodwink *be* ***twyllo***, ***camarwain***
hoof *enw* ***carn*** *hwn*
hook *enw* ***bach***, ***bachyn*** *hwn*
hook *be* ***bachu***
hooker *enw* ***bachwr*** *hwn*
hoop *enw* ***cylchyn***, ***cylch*** *hwn*
hoot *be* ***hwtian***
hooter *enw* ***corn*** *hwn*, ***hwter*** *hon*
hop *enw* ***herc*** *hwn*, ***naid fach*** *hon*
hop *be* ***hercian***
hope *enw* ***gobaith*** *hwn*
hope *be* ***gobeithio***
  h~ against h~ ***gobeithio yn groes i'r disgwyl***
hopeful *ans* ***gobeithiol***
hopeless *ans* ***anobeithiol***
  their situation is h~ ***mae hi ar ben arnynt***
horde *enw* ***haid*** *hon*
horizon *enw* ***gorwel*** *hwn*
horizontal *ans* ***llorweddol***
hormone *enw* ***hormon*** *hwn*
horn *enw* ***corn*** *hwn*
hornets *enw* ***cacwn*** *hyn*
horoscope *enw* ***horosgop*** *hwn*
horrendous *ans* ***dychrynllyd***
horrible *ans* ***ofnadwy***, ***erchyll***
horrific *ans* ***arswydus***, ***dychrynllyd***
horrify *be* ***brawychu***, ***arswydo***
horror *enw* ***arswyd***, ***dychryn*** *hwn*
horrors *enw* ***erchylltra*** *hwn*
horse *enw* ***ceffyl*** *hwn*
horse-block *enw* ***esgynfaen*** *hwn*
horse chestnut *enw* (tree) ***castanwydden*** *hon*

horsehair *enw* ***rhawn*** *hwn*
horseman *enw* ***marchog*** *hwn*
horsepower *enw* ***marchnerth*** *hwn*
horseshoe *enw* ***pedol*** *hon*
horse-trading *enw* ***bargeinio***
horsewoman *enw* ***marchoges*** *hon*
horticulture *enw* ***garddwriaeth*** *hon*
horticulturist *enw* ***garddwr*** *hwn*, ***garddwraig*** *hon*
hospice *enw* ***ysbyty, llety*** *hwn*; ***cartref, tŷ cysur*** *hwn*
hospitable *ans* ***croesawgar***
hospital *enw* ***ysbyty*** *hwn*
hospitality *enw* ***croeso***, ***lletygarwch*** *hwn*
host *enw* (large number) ***llu***, ***llond gwlad o***; ***gwesteiwr*** *hwn*
host *be* ***cynnal***; ***estyn croeso i***
hostage *enw* ***gwystl*** *hwn*
hostel *enw* ***neuadd breswyl*** *hon*
hostess *enw* ***gwesteiwraig*** *hon*
hostile *ans* ***gelyniaethus***
hostility *enw* ***gelyniaeth*** *hon*
hot *ans* ***twym***, ***poeth***
hotchpotch *enw* ***cawdel***, ***cawl*** *hwn*
hotel *enw* ***gwesty*** *hwn*
hotelier *enw* ***gwestywr*** *hwn*
hothead *enw* ***penboethyn*** *hwn*
hotline *enw* ***llinell arbennig*** *hon*
hotlink *enw* ***cyswllt cyflym*** *hwn*
hotplate *enw* ***plât poeth*** *hwn*
hot-water bottle *enw* ***jar***, ***potel ddŵr poeth*** *hon*
hound *enw* ***ci hela*** *hwn*
hour *enw* ***awr*** *hon*
hourglass *enw* ***awrwydr*** *hwn*
hourly *adf* ***o awr i awr***, ***wrth yr awr***
house *enw* ***tŷ*** *hwn*
house *be* ***lletya***, ***cartrefu***
houseboat *enw* ***cwch preswyl*** *hwn*
house-fly *enw* ***pry/pryf ffenest*** *hwn*
household *enw* ***teulu*** *hwn*
householder *enw* ***deiliad***, ***penteulu*** *hwn*
housekeeper *enw* ***gwraig cadw tŷ*** *hon*
house martin *enw* ***gwennol y bondo*** *hon*
House of Commons *enw* ***Tŷ'r Cyffredin*** *hwn*
House of Lords *enw* ***Tŷ'r Arglwyddi*** *hwn*
house owner *enw* ***perchen tŷ:perchennog tŷ*** *hwn*
house sparrow *enw* ***aderyn y to*** *hwn*
housewife *enw* ***gwraig tŷ*** *hon*
housework *enw* ***gwaith tŷ*** *hwn*
housing *enw* ***tai*** *hyn*
hovel *enw* ***hofel*** *hon*
hover *be* ***hofran***
hovercraft *enw* ***hofrenfad*** *hon*
how *adf* ***sut***, ***fel***
  h~ do you do? ***sut mae***? ***sut ydych chi?***
however *adf* ***sut bynnag***
  h~ well qualified ***er cystal eu cymwysterau***
  on h~ small a scale ***waeth pa mor fach bynnag***

h~ that may be ***sut/beth bynnag am hynny***, ***tae waeth am hynny***
howl *enw* ***gwaedd***, ***oernad*** *hon*
howl *be* ***udo***
hub *enw* ***both*** *hon*; ***craidd*** *hwn*
h~ site ***safle canolog*** *hwn*
hubbub *enw* ***dwndwr*** *hwn*
huddle *be* ***gwasgu at ei gilydd***
hue *enw* ***arlliw*** *hwn*, ***gwawr*** *hon*
huff *enw* ***pwd*** *hwn*
to feel h~ed ***pwdu***
huffy *ans* ***pwdlyd***
hug *enw* ***cofleidiad*** *hwn*
hug *be* ***cofleidio***
huge *ans* ***anferth:anferthol***
hull *enw* ***cragen llong*** *hon*
hum *be* ***mwmian:mwmial***, ***sïo:suo***
human *ans* ***dynol***
they are only h~ ***heb ei fai heb ei eni***
we are only h~ ***dim ond bodau meidrol ydym***
humane *ans* ***dyngarol***, ***tirion***, ***gwâr***
h~ killer ***lladdwr bi-boen*** *hwn*
humanist *enw* ***dyneiddiwr*** *hwn*
humanitarian *ans* ***dyngarol***
humanity *enw* ***dynoliaeth***, ***dynolryw*** *hon*
humanize *be* ***dynoli***
human resource management *enw* ***rheoli adnoddau dynol***
human resources *enw* ***adnoddau dynol*** *hyn*
human rights *enw* ***iawnderau/hawliau dynol*** *hyn*
humble *ans* ***diymhongar***, ***gostyngedig***
humbug *enw* ***twyll***, ***rhagrith*** *hwn*
humdrum *ans* ***undonog***, ***diflas***, ***di-fflach***
humid *ans* ***llaith***; (weather) ***mwll***, ***clòs***
humidity *enw* ***lleithder*** *hwn*
humiliate *be* ***bychanu***, ***torri crib***
humiliation *enw* ***gwarth***, ***cywilydd*** *hwn*
humility *enw* ***gostyngeiddrwydd***, ***gwyleidd-dra*** *hwn*
humorous *ans* ***doniol***
humour *enw* ***doniolwch***, ***hiwmor*** *hwn*; ***hwyliau*** *hyn*
hump *enw* ***crwbi:crwb*** *hwn*
hunch *enw* ***greddf*** *hon*; ***syniad*** *hwn*
hunchbacked *ans* ***cefngrwm***
hundred *rhifol* ***can***, ***cant***
hundreds *enw* ***cannoedd ar gannoedd*** *hyn*
hundredth *ans* ***canfed***
hundredweight *enw* ***cant*** *hwn*
hung *ans* ***crog***
hung parliament ***senedd grog*** *hon*
hunger *enw* ***chwant bwyd***, ***newyn*** *hwn*
hunger *be* ***newynu***
hungry *ans* ***newynog***, ***ar fy nghythlwng***

to be h~ for ***deisyfu***; ***dyheu am***
hunk *enw* ***cwlffyn*** *hwn*
hunt *enw* ***helfa*** *hon*
the h~ is on ***mae'r chwilio am -- wedi dechrau***
hunt *be* ***hela***
hunter *enw* ***heliwr*** *hwn*, ***helwraig*** *hon*; ***ceffyl hela*** *hwn*
huntsman *enw* ***heliwr*** *hwn*
hurdle *enw* ***clwyd*** *hon*
hurl *be* ***lluchio***, ***hyrddio***
hurricane *enw* ***corwynt*** *hwn*
hurry *enw* ***brys*** *hwn*, ***hast*** *hwn/hon*
there's no great h~ ***does dim byd mawr yn galw***
hurry *be* ***brysio***, ***prysuro***
hurt *enw* (= wound) ***dolur***, ***anaf***, ***briw*** *hwn*, ***gloes*** *hon*; (harm) ***drwg***, ***niwed*** *hwn*
hurt *be* ***brifo***, ***niweidio***, ***dolurio***, ***rhoi dolur***
hurtful *ans* ***niweidiol***, ***cas***
husband *enw* ***gŵr*** *hwn*
husbandry *enw* ***hwsmonaeth*** *hon*
hush *enw* ***distawrwydd***, ***tawelwch*** *hwn*
hush *be* ***distewi***
husk *enw* ***cibyn***, ***plisgyn*** *hwn*
husky *ans* ***bloesg***
hut *enw* ***caban***, ***cwt*** *hwn*
hutch *enw* ***cwb*** *hwn*
hybrid *ans* ***cymysgryw***
h~ worker ***gweithiwr amlbwrpas*** *hwn*
hydrant *enw* ***hydrant*** *hwn*
hydraulic *ans* ***hydrolig***
hydrobiology *enw* ***hydrobioleg*** *hon*
hydroelectric *ans* ***hydro-electrig, trydan dŵr***
hydrogen *enw* ***hydrogen*** *hwn*
hydrophobia *enw* ***y gynddaredd*** *hon*
hygiene *enw* ***hylendid***, ***glanweithdra*** *hwn*
hygienic *ans* ***hylan***
hymn *enw* ***emyn*** *hwn*
hymn-writer *enw* ***emynydd*** *hwn*, ***emynyddes*** *hon*
hyperactive *ans* ***gorfywiog***
hyperactivity *enw* ***gorfywiogrwydd*** *hwn*
hyperbole *enw* ***gormodiaith*** *hon*
hypercritical *ans* ***llawdrwm***
hypermarket *enw* ***archfarchnad*** *hon*
hyphen *enw* ***cysylltnod*** *hwn*
hypnotize *be* ***hypnoteiddio***
hypochondriac *enw* ***claf diglefyd*** *hwn*
hypocrisy *enw* ***rhagrith*** *hwn*
hypocritical *ans* ***rhagrithiol***, ***dauwynebog***
hypocrite *enw* ***rhagrithiwr*** *hwn*
hypothecate *be* ***neilltuo***
hypothesis *enw* ***damcaniaeth*** *hon*
hypothetical *ans* ***damcaniaethol***
hysterical *ans* ***hysteraidd***, ***gorffwyll***
hysterics *enw* ***sterics*** *hyn*

I

I *rhag* ***fi***, ***i***, ***mi***
I am *berf* ***wyf***, ***ydwyf***
ice *enw* ***iâ***, ***rhew*** *hwn*
  to cut no i~ with ***ni chafodd fawr o effaith ar***
Ice Age *enw* ***Oes yr Iâ*** *hon*
iceberg *enw* ***mynydd iâ*** *hwn*
ice cream *enw* ***hufen iâ*** *hwn*
ice hockey *enw* ***hoci iâ*** *hwn*
ice rink *enw* ***llawr sglefrio*** *hwn*
ice skating *enw* ***sglefrio***
icicle *enw* ***cloch iâ*** *hon*
icing *enw* ***eisin*** *hwn*
iconoclasm *enw* ***dryllio delwau***
icy *ans* ***rhewllyd***
idea *enw* ***syniad*** *hwn*
  a rough i~ ***bras amcan*** *hwn*
ideal *enw* ***delfryd*** *hwn*
ideal *ans* ***delfrydol***
identical *ans* ***unfath***
identification *enw* ***adnabyddiaeth*** *hon*; ***canfyddiad*** *hwn*
identify *be* (recognize) ***adnabod***, ***enwi***, ***arenwi***; (discover) ***canfod***
  to be i~ied in ***sydd i'w weld yn***
  to be i~ied with ***a gysylltir â***, ***i'w uniaethu â***
identity *enw* ***hunaniaeth*** *hon*
idiocy *enw* ***ynfydrwydd*** *hwn*
idiom *enw* ***priod-ddull*** *hwn*
idiosyncrasy *enw* ***mympwy***, ***hynodrwydd*** *hwn*
  i~ies of language ***teithi iaith*** *hyn*
idiot *enw* ***ynfytyn***, ***hurtyn*** *hwn*
idiotic *ans* ***ynfyd***, ***hurt***, ***twp***, ***gwirion***
idle *ans* ***didoreth***, ***segur***
  i~ chatter ***cleber wast*** *hwn*
  it's i~ to speculate ***di-fudd yw dyfalu***
idle *be* ***segura***
idleness *enw* ***segurdod*** *hwn*
idler *enw* ***diogyn*** *hwn*
idol *enw* ***eilun*** *hwn*, ***delw*** *hon*
idolize *be* ***addoli***, ***dotio ar***
idyllic *ans* ***paradwysaidd***
i.e. *byrfodd* ***h.y. (hynny yw)***
if *cysyllt* ***os***, ***pe***
igloo *enw* ***iglw*** *hwn*
ignite *be* ***cynnau***, ***tanio***
ignition *enw* ***taniad*** *hwn*
  i~ key ***allwedd danio*** *hon*
ignoble *ans* ***israddol***, ***taeogaidd***
ignominious *ans* ***gwarthus***, ***cywilyddus***
ignominy *enw* ***gwarth***, ***gwaradwydd*** *hwn*
ignoramus *enw* ***twpsyn*** *hwn*, ***twpsen*** *hon*
ignorance *enw* ***anwybodaeth*** *hon*
  to talk in i~ ***siarad ar/yn ei gyfer***
ignorant *ans* ***anwybodus***
ignore *be* ***anwybyddu***, ***diystyru***
ill *ans* ***tost***, ***sâl***
ill-advised *ans* ***annoeth***

ill-considered *ans* ***anystyriol***
ill-effect *enw* ***effaith niweidiol*** *hon*
illegal *ans* ***anghyfreithlon***
illegality *enw* ***anghyfreithlondeb*** *hwn*
illegible *ans* ***annarllenadwy***
illegitimacy *enw* ***anghyfreithlondeb*** *hwn*
illegitimate *ans* ***anghyfreithlon***
ill-health *enw* ***afiechyd*** *hwn*
illicit *ans* ***anghyfreithlon***
illiterate *ans* ***anllythrennog***
illness *enw* ***salwch***, ***afiechyd*** *hwn*
illogical *ans* ***afresymegol***
ill-treat *be* ***cam-drin***
illuminate *be* ***goleuo***, ***addurno***
illumination *enw* ***golau, lleufer*** *hwn*
illusion *enw* ***rhith*** *hwn*
illusory *ans* ***lledrithiol***
illustrate *be* ***darlunio***; ***cyfleu, egluro***, ***dangos***, ***enghreifftio***
illustration *enw* ***darlun*** *hwn* ***enghraifft*** *hon*
illustrator *enw* ***darlunydd*** *hwn*
illustrious *ans* ***disglair***, ***o fri***
image *enw* ***delw***, ***delwedd*** *hon*
imaginary *ans* ***dychmygol***
imagination *enw* ***dychymyg*** *hwn*
imaginative *ans* ***dychmygus***
imagine *be* ***dychmygu***
    fondly imagine ***credu'n ddiniwed***
imbalance *enw* ***anghydbwysedd*** *hwn*
imbecile *ans* ***ynfyd***, ***gwan ei feddwl***
imbibe *be* ***yfed***, ***drachtio***
imbroglio *enw* ***dryswch, cawl***, ***cawdel*** *hwn*
imbue *be* ***hydreiddio***; ***lliwio***
imitate *be* ***dynwared***, ***efelychu***
imitation *enw* ***dynwarediad***, ***efelychiad*** *hwn*
imitator *enw* ***dynwaredwr*** *hwn*
immaculate *ans* ***difrycheulyd***, ***fel pin mewn papur***
immaterial *ans* ***ansylweddol***, ***dibwys***
immature *ans* ***anaeddfed***
immeasurable *ans* ***anfesuradwy***, ***difesur***
immediate *ans* ***di-oed***, ***diymdroi***, ***syth***
    i~ needs ***anghenion cyfredol*** *hyn*
    in the i~ area ***yn y cyffiniau***
    in the i~ future ***cyn hir***
    put to i~ use ***defnyddio yn y man a'r lle***
    with i~ effect ***ar unwaith***
immemorial *ans* ***(ers) cyn cof***
immense *ans* ***anferth***, ***enfawr***
immerse *be* ***trochi***
immersion *enw* ***trochiad*** *hwn*
    i~ programme ***rhaglen drochi*** *hon*
    total i~ ***ymgolli'n llwyr***
immigrant *enw* ***mewnfudwr*** *hwn*, ***mewnfudwraig*** *hon*
immigrate *be* ***mewnfudo***

immigration *enw* ***mewnfudiad*** *hwn*
imminent *ans* ***ar ddigwydd***, ***agos***; ***cyn pen fawr o dro***
immobile *ans* ***llonydd, disymud***, ***diymod***
immobility *enw* ***llonyddwch***, ***disymudedd***, ***ansymudoldeb*** *hwn*
immoderate *ans* ***anghymedrol***
immodest *ans* ***anweddus***, ***aflednais***
immoral *ans* ***anfoesol***
immorality *enw* ***anfoesoldeb*** *hwn*
immortal *ans* ***anfarwol***
immortalize *be* ***anfarwoli***
immovable *ans* ***ansymudol***, ***diysgog***
immune *ans* ***rhydd***, ***diogel rhag***
immunity *enw* ***imwnedd*** *hwn*
immunize *be* ***imwneiddio***, ***gwrth-heintio***
immure *be* ***carcharu***
immutable *ans* ***digyfnewid***
imp *enw* ***coblyn***, ***cythraul*** *hwn*
impact *enw* ***effaith*** *hon*; ***trawiad*** *hwn*
impair *be* ***amharu ar***, ***andwyo***; ***gwanhau***
impairment *enw* ***nam***, ***diffyg*** *hwn*
impale *be* ***trywanu***
impalpable *ans* ***annheimladwy***
impart *be* ***rhoi***, ***cyfrannu***
to i~ information ***rhannu gwybodaeth***
impartial *ans* ***diduedd***
impartiality *enw* ***tegwch***, ***amhleidioldeb*** *hwn*
impasse *enw* ***lle amhosibl;*** (pol.) ***cyfwng*** *hwn*
impassioned *ans* ***teimladwy***; ***taer***
impassive *ans* ***didaro***, ***digyffro***
impatience *enw* ***diffyg amynedd*** *hwn*
impatient *ans* ***diamynedd***
impeach *be* ***uchelgyhuddo***
impeccable *ans* ***dilychwin***, ***di-fai***
impede *be* ***rhwystro***, ***atal***; ***amharu ar***
impel *be* ***ysgogi***
impending *ans* ***agos***, ***ar ddod***, ***ar fin digwydd***
impenetrable *ans* ***anhreiddiadwy***; (phys.) ***anhydraidd***
imperative *ans* ***gorchmynnol***; ***o'r pwys mwyaf***, ***hanfodol bwysig***
imperceptible *ans* ***anghanfyddadwy***
imperfect *ans* ***amherffaith***
imperfection *enw* ***amherffeithrwydd*** *hwn*
imperial *ans* ***imperialaidd***
imperious *ans* ***awdurdodol***, ***ffroenuchel***
impermanent *ans* ***dros dro***
impermeable *ans* ***anhydraidd***
impersonal *ans* ***amhersonol***
impersonate *be* ***dynwared***
impertinence *enw* ***digywilydd-dra*** *hwn*
impertinent *ans* ***digywilydd***

i

imperturbable *ans* ***digyffro***, ***difraw***
impetuosity *enw* ***gwylltineb***, ***byrbwylltra*** *hwn*
impetuous *ans* ***byrbwyll***
impetus *enw* ***ysgogiad*** *hwn*
impiety *enw* ***annuwioldeb*** *hwn*
impish *ans* ***direidus***
implacable *ans* ***anghymodlon***, ***di-droi'n-ôl***
implant *be* ***impio***, ***mewnblannu***
implement *enw* ***offeryn***, ***erfyn*** *hwn*
implement *be* ***gweithredu***
implicate *be* ***cysylltu rhywun â***
implication *enw* ***goblygiad*** *hwn*
implicit *ans* ***ymhlyg***
implied *ans* ***ymhlyg***, ***goblygedig***
implore *be* ***crefu***, ***deisyf***, ***erfyn***
imply *be* ***awgrymu***, ***golygu***
impolite *ans* ***anghwrtais***, ***anfoesgar***
import *be* ***mewnforio***
importance *enw* ***pwys***, ***pwysigrwydd*** *hwn*
important *ans* ***pwysig***
impose *be* ***gosod***; ***gorfodi***
imposing *ans* ***mawreddog***, ***urddasol***
imposition *enw* ***baich***, ***bwrn*** *hwn*
impossibility *enw* ***amhosibilrwydd*** *hwn*
impossible *ans* ***amhosibl***
impostor *enw* ***twyllwr*** *hwn*
impotence *enw* ***anallu***, ***diymadferthedd*** *hwn*; (med.) ***analluedd*** *hwn*
impotent *ans* ***diymadferth***, ***analluog***
impound *be* ***corlannu***; ***atafaelu***
impoverish *be* ***tlodi***
impoverishment *enw* ***tlodi***
impracticable *ans* ***anymarferol***
imprecise *ans* ***amhenodol***, ***heb fod yn fanwl***
impregnable *ans* ***anorchfygol***
impress *be* ***pwysleisio***, ***pwyso***
impression *enw* (effect on) ***argraff*** *hon*; (mark) ***ôl*** *hwn*, ***argraff*** *hon*; (publication) ***argraffiad*** *hwn*
impressionable *ans* ***hawdd gwneud argraff arno***
impressive *ans* ***trawiadol***
imprint *enw* ***argraffiad*** *hwn*
imprison *be* ***carcharu***
imprisonment *enw* ***carchariad*** *hwn*
improbability *enw* ***annhebygolrwydd*** *hwn*
improbable *ans* ***annhebygol***
impromptu *ans* ***difyfyr***, ***byrfyfyr***; (speech) ***o'r frest***
improper *ans* ***anghywir***; (indecent) ***anweddus***; (dance) ***afreolaidd***
impropriety *enw* (indecency) ***anwedduster*** *hwn*
improve *be* ***gwella***
improvement *enw* ***gwelliant*** *hwn*; (health) ***gwellhad*** *hwn*
improvise *be* ***cyfansoddi ar y pryd***
imprudent *ans* ***annoeth***
impudent *ans* ***digywilydd***, ***haerllug***

impulse *enw* ***ysgogiad*** *hwn*; ***mympwy*** *hon*
impulsive *ans* ***byrbwyll***
impunity *enw* (with impunity) ***yn ddi-gosb***, ***yn ddigerydd***
impure *ans* ***amhûr***
imputation *enw* ***priodoliad*** *hwn*
impute *be* ***priodoli***
in *ardd* ***yn***, ***mewn***
inability *enw* ***anallu*** *hwn*
inaccessible *ans* ***diarffordd***, ***anghysbell***, ***anghyraeddadwy***, ***anhygyrch***
inaccurate *ans* ***anghywir***, ***anfanwl***
inaction *enw* ***segurdod*** *hwn*
inactive *ans* ***diysgog***, ***segur***
inadequate *ans* ***annigonol***
inadmissible *ans* ***annerbyniol***
inadvertent *ans* ***diofal***, ***damweiniol***
inalienable *ans* ***diymwad***; ***anaralladwy***
inane *ans* ***hurt***, ***gwirion***
inanimate *ans* ***difywyd***
inapplicable *ans* ***anaddas***, ***anghymwys***
inarticulate *ans* ***aneglur***, ***bloesg***; ***anhuawdl***
inasmuch as *cysyllt* ***yn gymaint â***
inaudible *ans* ***anghlywadwy***, ***anhyglyw***
inaugurate *be* ***cychwyn***
inborn *ans* ***cynhenid***
incalculable *ans* ***anfesuradwy***, ***difesur***
incandescence *enw* ***tanbeidrwydd*** *hwn*
incandescent *ans* ***tanbaid***
incantation *enw* ***swyn*** *hwn*
incapable *ans* ***analluog***
incapacitate *be* ***analluogi***
incapacity *enw* ***anallu***, ***analluogrwydd*** *hwn*
incarcerate *be* ***carcharu***
incarnation *enw* ***ymgnawdoliad*** *hwn*
incautious *ans* ***difeddwl***, ***diofal***
incense *enw* ***arogldarth*** *hwn*
incense *be* ***cynddeiriogi***
incentive *enw* ***cymhelliad***, ***symbyliad*** *hwn*
I~ Allowance ***Lwfans Cymhelliant*** *hwn*
inception *enw* ***dechrau***, ***dechreuad***, ***cychwyn***, ***cychwyniad*** *hwn*
incessant *ans* ***di-baid***, ***di-dor***
incest *enw* ***llosgach*** *hwn*
inch *enw* ***modfedd*** *hon*
inchoate *ans* ***cychwynnol***
incidence *enw* ***trawiant***; ***amlder*** *hwn*
incident *enw* ***digwyddiad*** *hwn*
incidental *ans* ***achlysurol***
incidentally *adf* ***gyda llaw***
incinerate *be* ***llosgi***
incinerator *enw* ***llosgydd*** *hwn*
incisive *ans* ***miniog***, ***treiddgar***
incisor *enw* ***blaenddant*** *hwn*
incite *be* ***annog***, ***cymell***, ***cynhyrfu***

i

inclement *ans* ***garw***; ***didrugaredd***
inclination *enw* ***gogwydd*** *hwn*, ***tuedd*** *hon*
incline *enw* ***llethr*** *hwn/hon*, ***inclein*** *hwn/hon*, ***goleddf, rhipyn*** *hwn*
incline *be* ***gogwyddo***, ***tueddu***
include *be* ***cynnwys***
inclusive *ans* ***cynhwysol***; ***cynwysedig***
inclusiveness *enw* ***cynwysoldeb*** *hwn*
including *ardd* ***yn cynnwys***, ***gan gynnwys***
incognito *adf* ***yn anhysbys, yn ddirgel, heb yn wybod i neb***
incoherent *ans* ***digyswllt***, ***dryslyd***
income *enw* ***incwm*** *hwn*
incomer *enw* ***mewnfudwr*** *hwn*
incommensurate *ans* ***anghymesur***
incomparable *ans* ***anghymharol***, ***dihafal***; ***diguro***, ***heb ei ail***
incompatible *ans* ***anghymharus***, ***anghydnaws***
incompetence *enw* ***analluogrwydd***, ***anghymwysedd***, ***anfedrusrwydd*** *hwn*
incompetent *ans* ***anghymwys***, ***anobeithiol***, ***di-glem***
incomplete *ans* ***anghyflawn***, ***anorffenedig***
incomprehensible *ans* ***annealladwy***
inconceivable *ans* ***anhygoel***, ***y tu hwnt i amgyffred***
incongruity *enw* ***anghysondeb***, ***anghymarusrwydd*** *hwn*
incongruous *ans* ***anghyson***, ***anghymarus***
inconsequential *ans* ***dibwys***
inconsiderate *ans* ***difeddwl***, ***di-hid***
inconsistency *enw* ***anghysondeb*** *hwn*
inconsistent *ans* ***anghyson***
inconspicuous *ans* ***disylw***, ***anamlwg***
incontestable *ans* ***diymwad***
incontrovertible *ans* ***diamheuol***, ***diymwad***
inconvenience *enw* ***anghyfleustra***, ***anhwylustod*** *hwn*
inconvenient *ans* ***anghyfleus***
incorporate *be* ***corffori***, ***ymgorffori***
incorporation *enw* ***ymgorfforiad***, ***corfforiad*** *hwn*
incorrect *ans* ***anghywir***
incorruptible *ans* ***di-lwgr***; ***anllygradwy***
increase *enw* ***twf***, ***cynnydd*** *hwn*
increase *be* ***cynyddu***
increasing *ans* ***cynyddol***
incredible *ans* ***anghredadwy***, ***anhygoel***
incredulous *ans* ***anghrediniol***
increment *enw* ***cynnydd*** *hwn*; (of salary) ***ychwanegiad*** *hwn*
incremental *ans* ***cynyddol***; ***fesul tipyn***
incriminate *be* ***taflu bai ar***, ***cyhuddo***

incubate *be* ***deor***, ***gori***
inculcate *be* ***dysgu***, ***meithrin***
incumbent *enw* ***deilydd*** *hwn*
incumbent *ans* ***dyledus***, ***dyladwy***; ***gofynnol***
incur *be* ***achosi***
i~red by ***a ddaw yn sgil***
to i~ losses ***gwneud colledion***
to i~ expenses ***mynd i gostau***
incurable *ans* ***anwelladwy***, ***diwellhad***
incursion *enw* ***cyrch*** *hwn*
indebted *ans* ***dyledus***
indecent *ans* ***anweddus***, ***aflednais***
i~ haste ***ar ormod o frys***
indecipherable *ans* ***annarllenadwy***
indecision *enw* ***petruster***, ***amhendantrwydd*** *hwn*
indecisive *ans* ***petrus***, ***amhendant***
indecorous *ans* ***di-chwaeth***
indeed *adf* ***yn wir***
indefatigable *ans* ***diflino***, ***dyfal***
indefensible *ans* (of place) ***anamddiffynadwy***, ***anniffynadwy***; (conduct) ***diesgus***, ***digyfiawnhad***
indefinite *ans* ***amhendant***; ***di-ben-draw***
indelible *ans* ***annileadwy***
indemnify *be* ***gwarantu***; ***digolledu***
indemnity *enw* ***sicrhad***; ***digollediad*** *hwn*
indentation *enw* (= notch) ***rhic*** *hwn*; (= dent) ***tolc, pant*** *hwn*; (typing) ***cilosodiad*** *hwn*
independence *enw* ***annibyniaeth*** *hon*
independent *ans* ***annibynnol***
indestructible *ans* ***annistrywiadwy***
indeterminate *ans* ***amhenodol***, ***amheus***
index *enw* (alphabetical) ***mynegai*** *hwn*; (mathematical) ***indecs*** *hwn*
index *be* ***mynegeio***
Indian *enw* ***Indiad*** *hwn*
Indian *ans* ***Indiaidd***
I~ summer ***haf bach Mihangel*** *hwn*
indicate *be* ***dynodi***, ***mynegi***, ***nodi***, ***tynnu sylw***, ***dangos***
indication *enw* ***arwydd***; ***rhyw amcan*** *hwn*
indicative *ans* ***mynegol***
to be i~ of ***amlygu***
indict *be* ***cyhuddo***, ***ditio***
indictable *ans* ***ditiadwy***
indifference *enw* ***difrawder***, ***difaterwch*** *hwn*
indifferent *ans* ***difater***, ***dihidio***
of i~ quality ***o ansawdd digon cyffredin***
indigenous *ans* ***brodorol***, ***cynhenid***
indigent *ans* ***tlawd***, ***anghenus***
indigestion *enw* ***diffyg traul*** *hwn*
indignant *ans* ***dig***
indignation *enw* ***dicter***, ***digofaint*** *hwn*
indignity *enw* ***gwarth***, ***gwaradwydd*** *hwn*

indirect *ans* ***anuniongyrchol***
indiscernible *ans* ***anweladwy***
indiscreet *ans* ***annoeth***, ***tafodrydd***
indiscretion *enw* ***cam gwag***; ***datgeliad cyfrinach*** *hwn*
indispensable *ans* ***anhepgor***, ***anhepgorol***; ***rhaid wrth***
indisposed *ans* ***anhwylus***
indisputable *ans* ***diamheuol***; ***sicr ddigon***
indissoluble *ans* ***annatod***
indistinct *ans* ***aneglur***
indistinguishable *ans* ***diwahaniaeth***, ***yr un ffunud***
individual *enw* ***unigolyn*** *hwn*
individual *ans* ***unigol***
individuality *enw* ***hunaniaeth*** *hon*
indivisible *ans* ***diwahân***, ***anwahanadwy***
indolence *enw* ***diogi***, ***syrthni*** *hwn*
indolent *ans* ***dioglyd***, ***didoreth***
indomitable *ans* ***anorchfygol***, ***di-ildio***
indoors *adf* ***i mewn***, ***dan do***
indubitable *ans* ***diymwad***
induce *be* ***cymell***, ***darbwyllo***
inducement *enw* ***cymhelliad***, ***ysgogiad*** *hwn*
induction day *enw* ***diwrnod cynefino*** *hwn*
induction loop *enw* ***dolen anwythol*** *hon*
induction period *enw* ***cyfnod sefydlu*** *hwn*
induction programme *enw* ***rhaglen gynefino*** *hon*
induction year *enw* ***blwyddyn sefydlu*** *hon*
indulge *be* ***boddio***, ***maldodi***; ***ymbleseru***
to i~ in small talk ***clebran***
indulgence *enw* ***goddefgarwch***; ***ymfoddhad***, ***ymblesera*** *hwn*
indulgent *ans* ***goddefgar***; ***maldodus***
industrial *ans* ***diwydiannol***
industrialize *be* ***diwydiannu***
industrious *ans* ***diwyd***, ***gweithgar***
industry *enw* ***diwydiant***, ***gweithgarwch*** *hwn*
inebriate *be* ***meddwi***
inebriated *ans* ***meddw***
inedible *ans* ***anfwytadwy***
ineffable *ans* ***anhraethol***
ineffective *ans* ***aneffeithiol***
ineffectiveness *enw* ***aneffeithioldeb*** *hwn*
inefficiency *enw* ***aneffeithlonrwydd*** *hwn*
inefficient *ans* ***aneffeithlon***
ineligible *ans* ***anghymwys***
inept *ans* ***di-glem***, ***lletchwith***, ***di-sut***
inequality *enw* ***anghydraddoldeb***, ***anghyfartaledd*** *hwn*
inequitable *ans* ***annheg***, ***anghyfiawn***
ineradicable *ans* ***annileadwy***

inertia *enw* ***syrthni***, ***diffyg ynni***, ***diymadferthedd*** *hwn*
inescapable *ans* ***anochel***
inestimable *ans* ***difesur***, ***dirfawr***
inevitable *ans* ***anochel***, ***anorfod***; ***yn rhwym o***
inexact *ans* ***anfanwl***
inexcusable *ans* ***anesgusadwy***
inexhaustible *ans* ***dihysbydd***
inexpedient *ans* ***annoeth***, ***anaddas***
inexpensive *ans* ***rhad***
inexperienced *ans* ***dibrofiad***
inexplicable *ans* ***anesboniadwy***, ***astrus***
inexpressible *ans* ***anhraethol***
inextinguishable *ans* ***anniffoddadwy***
inextricable *ans* ***annatod***, ***annatodadwy***
infallible *ans* ***di-ffael***, ***di-feth***
infamous *ans* ***gwarthus***, ***cywilyddus***
infancy *enw* ***babandod*** *hwn*; ***dyddiau cynnar***
infant *enw* ***baban*** *hwn*
infantile *ans* ***babanaidd***, ***plentynnaidd***
infantry *enw* ***gwŷr traed*** *hyn*
infatuated *ans* ***wedi gwirioni***, ***wedi mopio***, ***wedi ffoli***
infect *be* ***heintio***
infection *enw* ***haint*** *hwn*
infectious *ans* ***heintus***
infelicitous *ans* ***amhriodol***
infer *be* ***casglu***; ***dirnad***
inference *enw* ***casgliad*** *hwn*
inferior *ans* ***israddol***; ***gwael***
inferiority *enw* ***israddoldeb*** *hwn*
  i~ complex ***cymhleth y taeog*** *hwn*
infernal *ans* ***uffernol***
infertile *ans* ***diffrwyth***
infest *be* ***bod yn fyw o***
infidel *enw* ***anghredadun*** *hwn*
infidelity *enw* ***anffyddlondeb*** *hwn*
infiltrate *be* ***ymdreiddio***
infinite *ans* ***annherfynol***
infinitive *enw* ***berfenw*** *hwn*
infinity *enw* ***anfeidroldeb***, ***annherfynoldeb*** *hwn*
infirm *ans* ***musgrell***, ***methedig***
infirmary *enw* ***ysbyty*** *hwn*
infirmity *enw* ***gwendid***, ***eiddilwch*** *hwn*
inflame *be* ***cynnau***; ***ennyn***, ***cynhyrfu***
inflamed *ans* ***llidiog:llidus***
inflammable *ans* ***hylosg***
inflammation *enw* ***llid***, ***enyniad*** *hwn*
inflammatory *ans* ***ymfflamychol***
inflatable *ans* ***pwmpiadwy***
inflate *be* ***chwythu gwynt i***
inflation *enw* ***chwyddiant*** *hwn*
inflexible *ans* ***anystwyth***, ***anhyblyg***; ***haearnaidd***
inflict *be* ***peri***, **achosi**
influence *enw* ***dylanwad*** *hwn*
influence *be* ***dylanwadu***

influential *ans* ***dylanwadol***
influenza *enw* ***ffliw*** *hon*
influx *enw* ***mewnlifiad*** *hwn*
inform *be* ***hysbysu***, ***rhoi gwybod i***
  to i~ our understanding of ***ychwanegu at ein dealltwriaeth o***
informal *ans* ***anffurfiol***
informality *enw* ***anffurfioldeb*** *hwn*
information *enw* ***gwybodaeth*** *hon*; (publicity) ***hysbysrwydd*** *hwn*
  bits of i~ ***gwybodaethau***
  I~ and Communication Technology ***Technoleg Gwybodaeth a Chyfathrebu***
  i~ dissemination ***lledaenu gwybodaeth***
  i~ exchange ***cyfnewid gwybodaeth***
  i~ handling ***trafod/trin gwybodaeth***
  i~ management ***rheoli gwybodaeth***
  i~ processing ***prosesu gwybodaeth***
  i~ retrieval ***adennill gwybodaeth***
informed *ans* ***gwybodus***
  i~ decision ***penderfyniad cytbwys*** *hwn*
infrastructure *enw* ***seilwaith*** *hwn*; ***strwythur sylfaenol*** *hwn*
infrequent *ans* ***anaml***, ***prin***
infringe *be* ***torri***, ***troseddu***, ***ymyrryd***, ***amharu ar***
infringement *enw* ***trosedd*** *hwn*
infuriate *be* ***cynddeiriogi***, ***codi gwrychyn***
ingenious *ans* ***dyfeisgar***
ingenuity *enw* ***dyfeisgarwch*** *hwn*
ingenuous *ans* ***diniwed***; **didwyll**
inglenook *enw* ***pentan*** *hwn*
inglorious *ans* ***distadl***; ***gwaradwyddus***
ingratiate *be* ***cynffonna***
ingratitude *enw* ***anniolchgarwch*** *hwn*
ingredient *enw* ***elfen*** *hon*; ***cynhwysyn*** *hwn*
inhabit *be* ***byw***, ***preswylio***
inhabitable *ans* ***preswyliadwy***, ***ffit i fyw***
inhabitants *enw* ***trigolion*** *hyn*
inhale *be* ***anadlu i mewn***
inharmonious *ans* ***aflafar***
inherent *ans* ***cynhenid***
  to be i~ in ***bod ynghlwm wrth***
inherit *be* ***etifeddu***
inheritance *enw* ***etifeddiaeth***, ***treftadaeth*** *hon*
inhibit *be* ***rhwystro***, ***atal***; ***cyfyngu ar***
inhibition *enw* (scientific/medical) ***ataliaeth*** *hon*; (shyness) ***swildod*** *hwn*
inhibitory injunction *enw* ***gwaharddeb*** *hon*
inhospitable *ans* ***digroeso***; ***llwm***
inhuman *ans* ***annynol***
inhumanity *enw* ***creulondeb*** *hwn*

inimical *ans* ***gelyniaethus***; ***yn groes i***
inimitable *ans* ***dihafal***, ***unigryw***
iniquity *enw* ***camwedd*** *hwn*
initial *enw* ***blaen lythyren*** *hon*
initial *be* ***llofnodi, arwyddo***
initial *ans* ***cychwynnol***, ***dechreuol***
initiate *be* ***cychwyn***, ***dechrau***; ***urddo***
initiation *enw* ***cychwyniad***; ***derbyniad*** *hwn*
initiative *enw* ***cam cyntaf*** *hwn*; (enterprise) ***menter*** *hon*
to take the i~ ***mentro ar ei ben ei hun***
inject *be* ***chwistrellu***
to i~ some pace ***cyflymu rhywfaint ar***
injection *enw* ***chwistrelliad*** *hwn*
injudicious *ans* ***annoeth***
injunction *enw* ***gorchymyn*** *hwn*, ***gwaharddeb*** *hon*
injure *be* ***anafu***, ***niweidio***
injurious *ans* ***niweidiol***
injury *enw* ***anaf***, ***niwed*** *hwn*
injustice *enw* ***anghyfiawnder***, ***cam*** *hwn*
ink *enw* ***inc*** *hwn*
inkling *enw* ***awgrym***; ***syniad*** *hwn*
inland *ans* ***mewndirol***
I~ Revenue ***Cyllid y Wlad*** *hwn*
inlet *enw* ***cilfach*** *hon*
inn *enw* ***tafarndy***, ***gwesty*** *hwn*
I~s of Court ***Lletyau'r Llysoedd*** *hyn*
innards *enw* ***perfeddion*** *hyn*
innate *ans* ***cynhenid***
inner *ans* ***mewnol***
innkeeper *enw* ***tafarnwr*** *hwn*, ***tafarnwraig*** *hon*
innocence *enw* ***diniweidrwydd***; ***dieuogrwydd*** *hwn*
innocent *ans* ***diniwed***; ***dieuog***
innocuous *ans* ***diniwed***, ***diddrwg***
innovate *be* ***arloesi***
innovation centre *enw* ***canolfan dulliau newydd*** *hon*
innovative *ans* ***arloesol***
innovator *enw* ***arloeswr*** *hwn*
innuendo *enw* ***ensyniad*** *hwn*
innumerable *ans* ***dirifedi***, ***aneirif***
inoculate *be* ***brechu***
inoffensive *ans* ***diniwed***, ***difalais***
inoperative *ans* ***segur***; ***di-rym***
inopportune *ans* ***anghyfleus***, ***annhymig***
inordinate *ans* ***gormodol***, ***afresymol***
input *enw* ***mewnbwn*** *hwn*
inquest *enw* ***cwest:cwêst*** *hwn*
inquietude *enw* ***pryder*** *hwn*
inquire *be* ***holi***, ***gofyn***
inquiry *enw* ***ymchwiliad***, ***ymholiad*** *hwn*
Inquisition *enw* ***Chwil-lys*** *hwn*
inquisitive *ans* ***chwilfrydig***, ***busneslyd***
inquisitorial *ans* ***chwilysol***, ***holgar***
insalubrious *ans* ***afiach***
insane *ans* ***gwallgof***, ***gorffwyll***

i

insanity *enw* ***gwallgofrwydd***, ***gorffwylltra*** *hwn*
insatiable *ans* ***anniwall***
inscribe *be* ***llythrennu***, ***arysgrifennu***
inscription *enw* ***arysgrif*** *hon*; ***cyflwyniad*** *hwn*
inscrutable *ans* ***annirnad***, ***difynegiant***
insect *enw* ***trychfilyn*** *hwn*
insecticide *enw* ***pryfleiddiad*** *hwn*
insecure *ans* ***llac***, ***ansicr***
i~ grasp of Welsh ***(rhai) bregus eu Cymraeg***
insecurity *enw* ***ansicrwydd*** *hwn*
inseminate *be* ***ffrwythloni***
insemination *enw* ***ffrwythloniad*** *hwn*
insensible *ans* ***anymwybodol***
insensitive *ans* ***ansensitif***, ***croendew***
inseparable *ans* ***anwahanadwy***
insert *be* ***gosod***, ***mewnosod***
insertion *enw* ***mewnosodiad*** *hwn*, ***ad-ddalen*** *hon*
in-service *ans* ***mewn swydd***
inset *be* ***mewnosod***
inside *enw* ***tu mewn:tu fewn*** *hwn*
inside *adf* ***y tu mewn i:y tu fewn i***
inside out *adf* ***y tu chwith allan***, ***tu mewn tu maes:tu fewn tu faes/fas***
insidious *ans* ***llechwraidd***; ***andwyol***; ***cyfrwys***
insight *enw* ***mewnwelediad*** *hwn*; ***cipolwg*** *hwn/hon*
to gain i~ ***amgyffred***
insignia *enw* ***arwyddlun***; ***bathodyn*** *hwn*; ***arfbais*** *hon*
insignificance *enw* ***dinodedd*** *hwn*
insignificant *ans* ***dinod***, ***distadl***
insincere *ans* ***ffuantus***
insinuate *be* ***ensynio***
insinuation *enw* ***ensyniad*** *hwn*
insipid *ans* ***diflas***, ***merfaidd***
insist *be* ***mynnu***
insistence *enw* ***taerineb*** *hwn*
insistent *ans* ***taer***, ***penderfynol***
insolence *enw* ***haerllugrwydd*** *hwn*
insolent *ans* ***haerllug***
insoluble *ans* ***annatrysadwy***; (in liquid) ***anhydawdd***
insomnia *enw* ***anhunedd*** *hwn*
insouciant *ans* ***di-hid***
inspect *be* ***archwilio***, ***arolygu***
inspection *enw* ***archwiliad***, ***arolygiad*** *hwn*
inspector *enw* ***arolygwr***, ***arolygydd*** *hwn*
inspectorate *enw* ***arolygiaeth*** *hon*
inspiration *enw* ***ysbrydoliaeth*** *hon*
inspire *be* ***ysbrydoli***
to i~ confidence ***ennyn hyder/ffydd***
inspired *ans* ***ysbrydoledig***
instability *enw* ***ansefydlogrwydd*** *hwn*
install *be* ***sefydlu***; ***gosod***

instalment *enw* ***rhan*** *hon*; ***rhandal***, ***rhandaliad*** *hwn*
instance *enw* ***enghraifft*** *hon*
in the first i~ ***yn gyntaf***
instant *enw* ***eiliad*** *hon/hwn*
instant *ans* ***parod***, ***di-oed***
instantly *adf* ***ar unwaith***, ***yn syth***
instead (of) *ardd* ***yn lle***
instep *enw* ***mwnwgl y troed*** *hwn*
instigate *be* ***symbylu***, ***ysgogi***; ***cychwyn***
instinct *enw* ***greddf*** *hon*
instinctive *ans* ***greddfol***
institute *be* ***sefydlu***, ***cychwyn***
to i~ proceedings ***dwyn achos***
institution *enw* ***sefydliad*** *hwn*
instruct *be* (teach) ***hyfforddi***; ***cyfarwyddo***
instruction *enw* ***hyfforddiant***; ***cyfarwyddyd*** *hwn*
instrument *enw* ***erfyn***, ***offeryn*** *hwn*
instrumental *ans* ***bod yn gyfrwng i wneud rhywbeth***; *(music)* ***offerynnol***
insubordinate *ans* ***gwrthryfelgar***
insubstantial *ans* ***ansylweddol***
insufferable *ans* ***annioddefol***
insufficiency *enw* ***diffyg***, ***prinder*** *hwn*
insufficient *ans* ***annigonol***, ***dim digon***
insular *ans* ***ynysig***
insulate *be* ***ynysu***, ***inswleiddio***
insulation *enw* ***ynysiad, inswleiddio*** *hwn*; (material) ***ynysydd***, ***inswleiddiwr*** *hwn*
insult *enw* ***sarhad*** *hwn*
insult *be* ***sarhau***; ***bwrw sen ar***
insulting *ans* ***sarhaus***
insuperable *ans* ***anorchfygol***
insurance *enw* ***yswiriant*** *hwn*
insure *be* ***yswirio***
insurgent *enw* ***gwrthryfelwr*** *hwn*
insurrection *enw* ***gwrthryfel***, ***terfysg*** *hwn*
intact *ans* ***cyfan***, ***cyflawn***
intangible *ans* ***anniffiniol, anghyffwrdd***
integer *enw* ***cyfanrif*** *hwn*
integral *ans* ***annatod***
integrate *be* ***cyfannu***, ***cymathu***, ***integreiddio***; ***cyd-blethu***
integrated *ans* (of children) ***integredig***; (of objects) ***cyfannol***
integration *enw* ***integreiddio***
integrity *enw* ***gonestrwydd***, ***unplygrwydd, cyfanrwydd*** *hwn*
intellect *enw* ***deall*** *hwn*
intellectual *ans* ***deallusol***, ***ymenyddol***
intelligence *enw* (mental ability) ***deallusrwydd***, ***crebwyll*** *hwn*; (information) ***gwybodaeth*** *hon*
intelligent *ans* ***deallus***, ***call***
intelligible *ans* ***dealladwy***
intemperate *ans* ***anghymedrol***
intend *be* ***bwriadu***, ***amcanu***
intense *ans* ***dwys***, ***angerddol***

i

i~ activity ***gweithgarwch mawr iawn*** *hwn*
intensify *be* ***dwysáu***; ***ffyrnigo***
intensive *ans* ***dwys***; ***manwl***
intention *enw* ***bwriad***, ***amcan*** *hwn*
intentional *ans* ***bwriadol***
interact *be* ***rhyngweithio***
interactive *ans* ***rhyngweithiol***
inter alia *adf* ***ymhlith pethau eraill***
intercede *be* ***eiriol***
intercept *be* ***rhyng-gipio***
intercessor *enw* ***cyfryngwr*** *hwn*
interchange *be* ***cyfnewid***
intercollegiate *ans* ***rhyng-golegol***
intercourse *enw* ***cyfathrach*** *hwn*
interdepartmental *ans* ***cydadrannol***
interdisciplinary *ans* ***rhyngddisgyblaethol***
interest *enw* ***diddordeb***; (financial) ***llog*** *hwn*
in the best i~ ***er lles***
in the i~ of brevity ***rhag afradu geiriau***
to pursue an i~ ***dilyn trywydd***
interest *be* ***diddori***; ***bod o ddiddordeb***; ***denu diddordeb***
interested party ***y sawl sydd â diddordeb/budd***
interest-free *ans* ***di-log***
interesting *ans* ***diddorol***
interfere *be* ***ymyrryd***; ***amharu ar***
interference *enw* ***ymyrraeth*** *hon*
interim *ans* ***dros dro***
interior *ans* ***y tu mewn:y tu fewn***
interject *be* ***ebychu***
interjection *enw* ***ebychiad*** *hwn*
interlace *be* ***plethu***
interlock *be* ***cyd-gloi***; ***cydieuo***
interlocutor *enw* ***cydsgwrsiwr***
interlocutory *ans* ***yng nghwrs achos***
interlude *enw* ***egwyl*** *hon*
intermediary *enw* ***canolwr***, ***cyfryngwr*** *hwn*
intermediate *ans* ***canolradd***
interminable *ans* ***di-ben-draw***, ***diddiwedd***
intermingle *be* ***cydgymysgu***
intermittent *ans* ***ysbeidiol***
intern *be* ***carcharu***
internal *ans* ***mewnol***
internalize *be* ***mewnoli***
international *ans* ***rhyngwladol***, ***cydwladol***
I~ Monetary Fund ***y Gronfa Ariannol Ryngwladol*** *hon*
Internet *enw* ***y Rhyngrwyd*** *hon*
interpersonal *ans* ***rhyngbersonol***
interplanetary *ans* ***rhyngblanedol***
interplay *be* ***cydadweithio***
interpret *be* ***dehongli***
interpretation *enw* ***dehongliad*** *hwn*
interpreter *enw* ***lladmerydd***, ***dehonglwr***, ***cyfieithydd*** *hwn*
interrelationship *enw* ***rhyngberthynas*** *hon*
interrogate *be* ***holi***
interrogation *enw* ***holiad***, ***holi*** *hwn*

interrogative *ans* ***gofynnol***
interrupt *be* ***ymyrryd***, ***torri ar draws***
interruption *enw* ***ymyriad***; ***toriad*** *hwn*
intersect *be* ***croestorri***
intersection *enw* (of roads) ***croesffordd*** *hon*; (math.) ***croestoriad*** *hwn*
interstice *enw* ***cyfwng*** *hwn*
intertwine *be* ***plethu***
interval *enw* ***egwyl*** *hon*; ***cyfwng*** *hwn*
at reasonable i~s ***yn weddol gyson***
intervene *be* ***ymyrryd***
intervention *enw* ***ymyrraeth*** *hon*
interview *enw* ***cyfweliad*** *hwn*
interview *be* ***cyfweld***
interviewer *enw* ***holwr***, ***cyfwelydd*** *hwn*
interweave *be* ***cydblethu***
intestine *enw* ***coluddyn*** *hwn*
intimacy *enw* ***agosatrwydd*** *hwn*
intimate *ans* ***agos iawn***
intimidate *be* ***dychryn***, ***bygwth***
into *ardd* ***i mewn i***
intolerable *ans* ***annioddefol***
intolerant *ans* ***anoddefgar***
intonation *enw* ***goslef***; ***cyweiriaeth*** *hon*
intoxicate *be* ***meddwi***
intoxication *enw* ***meddwdod*** *hwn*
intractable *ans* ***anhydrin***, ***anhywaith***, ***anystywallt***; ***dyrys iawn***
Intranet *enw* ***Mewnrwyd***, ***Cyfyngrwyd*** *hon*
intransigent *ans* ***cyndyn***, ***anhyblyg***
intransitive *ans* ***cyflawn***
intrepid *ans* ***eofn***, ***dewr***
intricacy *enw* ***cymhlethdod*** *hwn*
intricate *ans* ***cymhleth***, ***cywrain***
intrigue *enw* ***cynllwyn*** *hwn*
intrigue *be* ***cyfareddu***; ***ennyn chwilfrydedd/diddordeb***
intriguing *ans* ***cyfareddol***; ***gogleisiol***
intrinsic *ans* ***hanfodol***, ***cynhwynol***, ***cynhenid***
introduce *be* ***cyflwyno***
introduction *enw* ***cyflwyniad***; (music) ***rhagarweiniad*** *hwn*
introspective *ans* ***mewnsyllol***
introverted *ans* ***mewnblyg***
intrude *be* ***ymyrryd***
intruder *enw* ***tresmaswr*** *hwn*
intuition *enw* ***greddf*** *hon*
intuitive *ans* ***greddfol***
inundate *be* ***gorlifo***, ***boddi***
inure *be* ***cynefino***, ***ymgynefino***
invade *be* ***goresgyn***; ***tresmasu:tresbasu***
invader *enw* ***goresgynnydd***, ***tresmaswr:tresbaswr*** *hwn*
invalid *enw* ***claf***, ***methedig*** *hwn*
invalid *ans* ***annilys***

invalidate *be* ***dirymu***, ***annilysu***, ***tanseilio***
invalidity *enw* ***annilysrwydd***; (med.) ***anabledd*** *hwn*
invaluable *ans* ***amhrisiadwy***, ***hynod werthfawr***
invariable *ans* ***gwastad***, ***digyfnewid***
invasion *enw* ***goresgyniad*** *hwn*
invasive surgery *enw* ***llawdriniaeth fewndreiddiol*** *hon*
invent *be* ***dyfeisio***
invention *enw* ***dyfais*** *hon*
inventor *enw* ***dyfeisydd*** *hwn*
inventory *enw* ***rhestr*** *hon*
invert *be* ***troi wyneb i waered***; ***gwrthdroi***
invertebrate *enw* ***infertebrat*** *hwn*
invest *be* ***buddsoddi***; ***treulio (amser)***
investigate *be* ***ymchwilio***; ***chwilio a chwalu***
investigation *enw* ***ymchwiliad***; (med.) ***archwiliad*** *hwn*
investigator *enw* ***ymchwilydd*** *hwn*
investigatory *ans* ***ymchwiliadol***
investiture *enw* ***arwisgiad*** *hwn*
investment *enw* ***buddsoddiad*** *hwn*
inveterate *ans* ***rhonc***, ***ystyfnig***
invidious *ans* ***annymunol***; ***llechwraidd***; ***diddiolch***
invigilate *be* ***goruchwylio***
invigorate *be* ***bywiocáu***
invincible *ans* ***anorchfygol***
inviolable *ans* ***dihalog***; ***haearnaidd***
invisible *ans* ***anweledig***, ***anweladwy***
invitation *enw* ***gwahoddiad*** *hwn*
invite *be* ***gwahodd***
inviting *ans* ***gwahoddgar***, ***deniadol***, ***atyniadol***
invoice *enw* ***anfoneb*** *hon*
invoke *be* ***galw ar***
involuntary *ans* ***anfwriadol***, ***anwirfoddol***
involve *be* ***tynnu mewn***; ***golygu***; ***ymwneud â***
  the work i~s ***mae'r gwaith yn gofyn am***
  this i~s more than ***mae mwy i hyn na***
  this i~s the use of ***defnyddir***
involvement *enw* ***cysylltiad*** *hwn*, ***rhan*** *hon*, ***ymgyfraniad*** *hwn*
ion *enw* ***ïon*** *hwn*
ipso facto *adf* ***drwy'r ffaith ei hun***
irascible *ans* ***piwis***, ***pigog***
irate *ans* ***dig***, ***dicllon***, ***wedi gwylltio***
iris *enw* ***enfys y llygad*** *hon*, ***iris*** *hwn*
Irish *enw* (language) ***Gwyddeleg*** *hon*
Irish *ans* ***Gwyddelig***
Irishman *enw* ***Gwyddel*** *hwn*
Irishwoman *enw* ***Gwyddeles*** *hon*
irksome *ans* ***blin***, ***trafferthus***, ***llethol***
iron *enw* ***haearn*** *hwn*
iron *be* ***smwddio***

to i~ out fluctuations ***dileu amrywiadau***
ironic *ans* ***eironig***
irony *enw* ***eironi*** *hwn*
irradiate *be* ***arbelydru***
irrational *ans* ***afresymol***
irreconcilable *ans* ***anghymodadwy***, ***anghymodlon***
irrefutable *ans* ***anwadadwy***
irregular *ans* ***afreolaidd***
irregularity *enw* ***afreoleidd-dra*** *hwn*
irrelevant *ans* ***amherthnasol***
irremediable *ans* ***dirwymedi***, ***anwelladwy***
irreparable *ans* ***anadferadwy***, ***na ellir ei drwsio***
irrepressible *ans* ***diatal***
irreproachable *ans* ***difai***
irresistible *ans* ***anorchfygol***
irresolute *ans* ***petrus***
irresponsible *ans* ***anghyfrifol***
irreverence *enw* ***amarch*** *hwn*
irreversible *ans* ***diwrthdro***; ***di-droi'n-ôl***
irrevocable *ans* ***di-alw'n ôl***; ***di-droi'n ôl***
irrigate *be* ***dyfrhau***
irrigation *enw* ***dyfrhad*** *hwn*
irritability *enw* ***anniddigrwydd*** *hwn*
irritable *ans* ***piwis***, ***anniddig***
irritate *be* ***cythruddo***, ***pryfocio***; ***mynd dan groen***; ***cosi***
irritation *enw* ***dig***; ***poendod*** *hwn*
is *berf* ***mae***, ***oes***, ***sydd***
island *enw* ***ynys*** *hon*
isle *enw* ***ynys*** *hon*
isolate *be* ***ynysu***; ***datgysylltu (oddi wrth)***
isolation *enw* ***ynysiad***, ***arwahanrwydd***; ***diffyg cysylltiad*** *hwn*
issue *enw* ***rhifyn***; ***testun***, ***mater llosg*** *hwn*
this is not an i~ ***nid yw hwn yn codi***
to take i~ with ***anghytuno â***
issue *be* ***cyhoeddi***; ***rhoi***, ***dosbarthu***; ***codi***
isthmus *enw* ***culdir*** *hwn*
it *rhag* ***ef***; ***hi***; ***ei***
Italian *enw* ***Eidalwr*** *hwn*; (language) ***Eidaleg*** *hwn*
Italian *ans* ***Eidalaidd***
itch *be* ***cosi***; ***ysu***
item *enw* ***eitem*** *hon*
iterative *ans* ***ailadroddus***
itinerant *ans* ***crwydrol***, ***teithiol***
itinerary *enw* ***amserlen deithio*** *hon*
its *rhag* ***ei***
itself *rhag* ***ef/hi ei hun:hunan***
ivory *enw* ***ifori*** *hwn*
ivy *enw* ***iorwg***, ***eiddew*** *hwn*

J

jab *enw* ***prociad*** *hwn*
jab *be* ***procio***
jabber *be* ***clebran***, ***baldorddi***
jack *enw* ***jac***; (card) ***jac, cnaf***, ***gwalch*** *hwn*
every man j~ ***pob copa walltog***
jack *be* ***jacio***
jackdaw *enw* ***jac-y-do*** *hwn*
jacket *enw* ***siaced*** *hon*
jacket potatoes *enw* ***tatws trwy'u crwyn*** *hyn*
jackpot *enw* ***gwobr fawr*** *hon*
jaded *ans* ***wedi syrffedu ar***; ***blinedig***
jagged *ans* ***danheddog***
jaguar *enw* ***jagwar*** *hwn*
jail *enw* ***carchar*** *hwn*, ***dalfa*** *hon*
jailbird *enw* ***carcharor*** *hwn*
jailer *enw* ***ceidwad/swyddog carchar*** *hwn*
jam *enw* ***jam*** *hwn*
traffic j~ ***tagfa*** *hon*
jam *be* ***jamio***
j~ packed ***llawn dop***
jamboree *enw* ***jamborî*** *hwn*
janitor *enw* ***gofalwr***; ***porthor*** *hwn*
January *enw* ***Ionawr*** *hwn*
jar *enw* ***jar*** *hon*
jargon *enw* ***jargon*** *hwn/hon*
jaundice *enw* ***y clefyd melyn*** *hwn*
jaunt *enw* ***tro*** *hwn*
jaw *enw* ***gên*** *hon*
jay *enw* ***sgrech y coed*** *hon*
jazz *enw* ***jazz*** *hwn*
jealous *ans* ***eiddigeddus***, ***cenfigennus***
jealousy enw ***cenfigen*** *hon*, ***eiddigedd*** *hwn*
jeans *enw* ***jîns*** *hyn*
jeer *be* ***gwawdio***, ***gwatwar***
jell *be* ***ceulo***, ***caledu***
jelly *enw* ***jeli*** *hwn*
jellyfish *enw* ***slefren fôr*** *hon*
jeopardize *be* ***peryglu***; ***tanseilio***
jeopardy *enw* ***perygl*** *hwn*
to be in j~ ***bod yn y fantol***
jerk *enw* ***plwc*** *hwn*
jerky *ans* ***herciog***
jersey *enw* ***siersi*** *hon*
jest *enw* ***cellwair*** *hwn*
jest *be* ***cellweirio***
jester *enw* ***croesan***, ***cellweiriwr*** *hwn*
jet *enw* ***ffrwd***; ***jet*** *hon*; (mineral) ***muchudd*** *hwn*
jettison *be* ***gollwng***, ***taflu dros y bwrdd***
jetty *enw* ***glanfa*** *hon*
jewel *enw* ***gem*** *hon*, ***tlws*** *hwn*
the j~ in the crown ***y trysor pennaf (o'r holl drysorau)***
jeweller *enw* ***gemydd*** *hwn*
jewellery *enw* ***gemwaith*** *hwn*
Jewish *ans* ***Iddewig***
jib *enw* ***gwep***; ***hwyl flaenaf***; (of crane) ***braich*** *hon*

jib *be* ***nogio***, ***ystyfnigo***, ***jibio***
jiffy *enw* ***chwinciad*** *hwn*
jigsaw *enw* ***jig-so*** *hwn*
jingle *be* ***tincial***
jingle *enw* ***tincial***; ***rhigwm*** *hwn*
jink *be* ***ochr gamu***
jinx *enw* ***melltith*** *hon*, ***rhaib*** *hwn*
job *enw* ***gwaith*** *hwn*
  j~ specification ***manyleb swydd*** *hon*
  j~ description ***swydd-ddisgrifiad*** *hwn*
jockey *enw* ***joci*** *hwn*
jocular *ans* ***cellweirus***
jog *be* ***loncian***
join *be* ***cydio***, ***uno***; ***ymuno***
  to j~ forces ***dod ynghyd i***
joined up *ans* ***cydgysylltiedig***
joint *enw* ***cymal***; ***uniad***; (of meat) ***darn***, ***chwarthol*** *hwn*
joint *ans* ***cyd-***
  j~ and several liability ***atebolrwydd ar y cyd ac yn unigol***
  j~ committee ***cydbwyllgor*** *hwn*
  j~ finance ***cydgyllido***
  j~ funding ***cydariannu***
joke *enw* ***jôc*** *hon*
joke *be* ***jocan***
joker *enw* ***digrifwr*** *hwn*
jolly *ans* ***llawen***, ***llon***
jolt *enw* ***ysgydwad:ysgytwad*** *hwn*
jolting *ans* ***ysgytwol***
jostle *be* ***gwthio***
jot *enw* ***iot*** *hon*
jot *be* ***taro ar bapur***
journal *enw* ***papur newydd***; ***cylchgrawn*** *hwn*
journalese *enw* ***ieithwedd newyddiadura*** *hon*
journalism *enw* ***newyddiaduraeth*** *hon*; ***newyddiadura***
journalist *enw* ***newyddiadurwr*** *hwn*
journey *enw* ***taith*** *hon*
journey *be* ***teithio***
jovial *ans* ***llawen***
jowl *enw* ***cern***, ***gên*** *hon*
joy *enw* ***llawenydd*** *hwn*
  no j~ ***dim lwc***; ***yn ofer***
  the j~ of ***y wefr o***
joyful *ans* ***gorfoleddus***
joyless *enw* ***annifyr***, ***aflawen***
JP *byrfodd* ***YH (Ynad Heddwch)***
jubilant *ans* ***gorfoleddus***
jubilation *enw* ***gorfoledd*** *hwn*
jubilee *enw* ***jiwbilî*** *hon*
Judaism *enw* ***Iddewiaeth*** *hon*
judder *be* ***dirgrynu***
judge *enw* ***barnwr***, ***beirniad*** *hwn*
judge *be* ***barnu***
judgement *enw* ***barn*** *hon*
judicature *enw* ***barnweiniaeth*** *hon*
judicial *ans* ***cyfreithiol***, ***barnwrol***
  j~ enquiry ***ymchwiliad barnwrol*** *hwn*
  j~ review ***arolwg barnwrol***, ***adolygiad barnwrol*** *hwn*
judiciary *enw* ***barnwriaeth*** *hon*
judicious *ans* ***doeth***

judo *enw* ***jiwdo*** *hwn*
jug *enw* ***jwg*** *hwn/hon*
juggle *be* ***jyglo***
juice *enw* ***sudd*** *hwn*
juicy *ans* ***llawn sudd***
July *enw* ***Gorffennaf*** *hwn*
jumble *be* ***cymysgu***, ***drysu***
jumble sale *enw* ***ffair sborion*** *hon*
jump *enw* ***naid*** *hon*
jump *be* ***neidio***
jumper *enw* ***neidiwr*** *hwn*; ***siwmper*** *hon*
jumpy *ans* ***nerfus***, ***ofnus***
junction *enw* (of ways) ***cyffordd***, ***croesffordd*** *hon*; (of wires) ***cyswllt*** *hwn*
  j~ box ***blwch cyswllt*** *hwn*
juncture *enw* ***adeg*** *hon*
June *enw* ***Mehefin*** *hwn*
jungle *enw* ***jyngl*** *hon*; ***dryswch*** *hwn*
junior *ans* ***iau***
junk *enw* ***sothach***, ***sbwriel*** *hwn*
Jupiter *enw* ***Iau*** *hwn*
jurisdiction *enw* ***awdurdod*** *hwn*; ***awdurdodaeth*** *hon*
jurisprudence *enw* ***cyfreitheg*** *hon*
juror *enw* ***rheithiwr*** *hwn*
jury *enw* ***rheithgor*** *hwn*
just *ans* ***teg***, ***cyfiawn***
just *adf* ***yn union***, ***prin***
  j~ right ***taro deuddeg***
  j~ south of ***ychydig i'r de o***
  j~ suppose ***a bwrw am eiliad***
justice *enw* ***cyfiawnder*** *hwn*
  to do less than j~ ***gwneud cam â***
justifiable *ans* ***cyfiawn***; ***cyfiawnadwy***, ***digon teg***
justification *enw* ***cyfiawnhad*** *hwn*
justify *be* ***cyfiawnhau***
jute *enw* ***jiwt*** *hwn*
juvenile *ans* ***ifanc***; ***plentynnaidd***
juxtapose *be* ***cyfosod***
juxtaposition *enw* ***cyfosodiad*** *hwn*

K

kaleidoscope *enw* ***caleidosgop*** *hwn*
kangaroo *enw* ***cangarŵ*** *hwn*
karate *enw* ***karate*** *hwn*
kayak *enw* ***caiac*** *hwn*
keel *enw* ***cilbren*** *hwn*
  to bring back to an even k~ ***dod â phethau'n ôl i drefn***
keen *ans* ***craff***, ***brwd***
  a k~ sense of ***ymwybyddiaeth fyw o***
keen *be* ***dolefain***
keenness *enw* ***brwdfrydedd***; ***awch*** *hwn*
keep *enw* (castle) ***gorthwr*** *hwn*
keep *be* ***cadw***
  k~ at it ***dal ati***
  to k~ to ***glynu wrth***
  to k~ to a minimum ***cyfyngu cymaint â phosibl ar***
keeper *enw* ***ceidwad*** *hwn*
keeping *enw* ***gofal***, ***meddiant*** *hwn*
  in k~ with ***yn unol â***; ***yn cyd-fynd â***
keepsake *enw* ***cofrodd*** *hon*
ken *enw* ***dirnadaeth*** *hon*
kennel *enw* ***cwb***, ***cwt*** *hwn*
kerfuffle *enw* ***stŵr***, ***strach*** *hwn*
kernel *enw* ***cnewyllyn*** *hwn*
kestrel *enw* ***cudyll***, ***curyll*** *hwn*
kettle *enw* ***tegell*** *hwn*
key *enw* ***allwedd*** *hon*; (music) ***cywair*** *hwn*
key *ans* ***allweddol***
keyboard *enw* ***bysellfwrdd*** *hwn*, ***allweddell*** *hon*
keyhole *enw* ***twll y clo*** *hwn*
keynote *ans* ***prif (amcan)***
  k~ speech ***prif araith*** *hon*
key ring *enw* ***cylch allweddi*** *hwn*
key signature *enw* ***cyweirnod*** *hwn*
keystone *enw* ***maen clo*** *hwn*
kibbutz *enw* ***cibẃts*** *hwn*
kick *enw* ***cic*** *hon*
kick *be* ***cicio***
kid *enw* (goat) ***myn***; ***plentyn*** *hwn*
  my k~ brother ***fy mrawd bach***
kid *be* ***twyllo***; ***tynnu coes***
kidnap *be* ***herwgipio***
kidnapper *enw* ***herwgipiwr*** *hwn*
kidney *enw* ***aren*** *hon*
kidney beans *enw* ***ffa dringo*** *hyn*
kill *be* ***lladd***
killer *enw* ***lleiddiad***, ***lladdwr*** *hwn*
killing *enw* ***lladd*** *hwn*, ***lladdedigaeth*** *hon*
kiln *enw* ***odyn*** *hon*
kilo *enw* ***kilo*** *hwn*
kilogram *enw* ***kilogram*** *hwn*
kilometre *enw* ***kilometr*** *hwn*
kin *enw* ***tylwyth*** *hwn*
  kith and k~ ***câr a cheraint***
kind *enw* ***math*** *hwn/hon*
kind *ans* ***caredig***
kindergarten *enw* ***ysgol feithrin*** *hon*

k

kindle *be* ***cynnau***; ***ennyn***
kindliness *enw* ***caredigrwydd*** *hwn*
kindling *enw* ***tanwydd, cynnud*** *hwn*
kindly *ans* ***twymgalon***, ***hynaws***
kindness *enw* ***caredigrwydd*** *hwn*
kindred *enw* ***perthynas, carennydd*** *hwn*
kinetic *ans* ***cinetig***
king *enw* ***brenin*** *hwn*
kingdom *enw* ***teyrnas*** *hon*
kingfisher *enw* ***glas y dorlan*** *hwn*
kink *enw* ***plet***, ***plyg***, ***crych*** *hwn*
kinsfolk *enw (llu.)* ***perthnasau, tylwyth, ceraint***
kinsman *enw* ***câr, perthynas***
kinship *enw* ***carennydd*** *hwn*
kiosk *enw* ***ciosg*** *hwn*
kipper *enw* ***pennog coch***, ***ysgadenyn coch*** *hwn*
kirk *enw* ***eglwys***, ***llan*** *hon*
kiss *enw* ***cusan*** *hon/hwn*
kiss *be* ***cusanu***
kit *enw* ***pac***, ***gêr*** *hwn*, ***dillad*** *hyn*
kitchen *enw* ***cegin*** *hon*
kite *enw* ***barcud*** *hwn*
kitten *enw* ***cath fach*** *hon*
kittiwake *enw* ***gwylan goesddu*** *hon*
kitty *enw* ***cronfa*** *hon*, ***celc*** *hwn*
knack *enw* ***dawn*** *hon*
knave *enw* ***gwalch*** *hwn*
knead *be* ***tylino***
knee *enw* ***pen-glin*** *hwn*
kneecap *enw* ***padell pen-glin*** *hon*
kneel *be* ***penlinio***, ***penglinio***
knell *enw* ***cnul*** *hwn*
knickerbockers *enw* ***clos pen-glin*** *hwn*
knickers *enw* ***nicers*** *hyn*
knife *enw* ***cyllell*** *hon*
knight *enw* ***marchog*** *hwn*
knighthood *enw* ***urdd marchog*** *hon*
knit *be* ***gwau:gweu***
knitting *enw* ***gwau*** *hwn*
knob *enw* ***bwlyn***, ***dwrn*** *hwn*
knock *enw* ***cnoc***, ***ergyd*** *hon*
knock *be* ***curo***, ***taro***
knock on *be* ***taro('r bêl) ymlaen***
knock-on effect *enw* ***effaith ddilynol*** *hon*
knot *enw* ***cwlwm*** *hwn*
knot *be* ***clymu***
knotty *ans* ***cnotiog***
know *be* ***gwybod***, ***adnabod***
know-how *enw* ***gallu***, ***medr*** *hwn*; ***gwybodaeth a phrofiad ymarferol***
knowing *ans* ***ffel, cyfrwys***; ***ymwybodol***
knowing *enw* ***gwybod***
  there's no k~ ***does dim dal***
knowledge *enw* ***gwybodaeth***, ***adnabyddiaeth*** *hon*
  in the k~ that ***o wybod bod***
knowledgeable *ans* ***gwybodus***, ***hyddysg***
known *ans* ***gwybyddus***, ***hysbys***
  k~ as ***a elwir yn***
knuckle *enw* ***cwgn***, ***migwrn*** *hwn*

L

label *enw* ***label*** *hwn/hon*
label *be* ***labelu***
they cannot be l~ed criminals ***ni ellir eu galw'n droseddwyr***
laboratory *enw* ***labordy*** *hwn*
laborious *ans* ***llafurus***
labour *enw* ***llafur*** *hwn*
labour *be* ***llafurio***
laboured *ans* ***llafurus***
labourer *enw* ***labrwr***, ***gweithiwr*** *hwn*
laborious *ans* ***llafurus***
laburnum *enw* ***tresi aur*** *hyn*
labyrinth *enw* ***drysfa***, ***labrinth*** *hon*
lace *enw* (shoe) ***carrai***; ***les*** *hon*
lace (to make) *be* ***sideru***
lacerate *be* ***rhwygo***
lack *enw* ***diffyg*** *hwn*
l~ of concern ***dihidrwydd***
there is a serious l~ of ***nid oes hanner digon o***
lack *be* ***bod heb***
to l~ totally ***bod heb fymryn o***
lackadaisical *ans* ***didoreth***, ***diffaith***, ***di-hid***
lackey *enw* ***gwas bach*** *hwn*
lacklustre *ans* ***di-raen***, ***dilewyrch***
laconic *ans* ***cwta***, ***swta***
lad *enw* ***llanc*** *hwn*
bit of a l~ ***tipyn o dderyn/aderyn***
ladder *enw* ***ysgol*** *hon*
laden *ans* ***llwythog***
ladle *enw* ***lletwad*** *hon*
ladle *be* ***codi (cawl)***
lady *enw* ***boneddiges***; ***arglwyddes*** *hon*
ladybird *enw* ***buwch goch gota*** *hon*
lag *be* ***llusgo***
lagoon *enw* ***lagŵn***, ***morlyn*** *hwn*
lair *enw* ***gwâl***, ***ffau*** *hon*
laity *enw* ***lleygwyr*** *hyn*
lake *enw* ***llyn*** *hwn*
lamb *enw* ***oen*** *hwn*
lamb *be* ***wyna***
lambaste *be* ***lambastio***
lame *ans* ***cloff***
lament *enw* ***galarnad*** *hon*
lament *be* ***galaru***
lamentable *ans* ***truenus***
lamentation *enw* ***galarnad*** *hon*
laminate *be* ***lamineiddio***
lamp *enw* ***lamp***, ***llusern*** *hon*
lampoon *be* ***dychanu***
lamp-post *enw* ***postyn lamp*** *hwn*
lance *enw* ***gwaywffon*** *hon*
lancet *enw* ***fflaim*** *hon*
land *enw* ***tir*** *hwn*; ***gwlad*** *hon*
land *be* ***glanio***
landed *ans* ***tirfeddiannog, tiriog***
landfill *be* ***tirlenwi***
landform *enw* ***tirffurf*** *hwn*
landlord *enw* ***landlord*** *hwn*
landmark *enw* ***carreg derfyn*** *hon*; ***nod tir***, ***tirnod*** *hwn*; (= event) ***carreg filltir*** *hon*, ***trobwynt*** *hwn*
landscape *enw* ***tirwedd*** *hon*, ***tirlun*** *hwn*; (painting) ***tirlun*** *hwn*

l

landscaping *enw* ***tirlunio***
landslide *enw* ***tirlithriad*** *hwn*
lane *enw* ***lôn*** *hon*
language *enw* ***iaith***; ***ieithwedd*** *hon*
languid *ans* ***diegni***, ***didaro***
languish *be* ***nychu***, ***dihoeni***
languor *enw* ***syrthni*** *hwn*
lanky *ans* ***heglog***
lantern *enw* ***llusern*** *hon*
lap *be* ***llepian***, ***lapan***
  to l~ it up ***bydd yn fêl ar eu bysedd***
lapel *enw* ***llabed*** *hon/hwn*
lapidary *enw* ***gemydd*** *hwn*
lapse *enw* ***esgeulustra***, ***llithriad***; ***diffyg*** *hwn*
lapse *be* ***llithro***
  to l~ into English ***troi i'r Saesneg***
laptop computer *enw* ***gliniadur*** *hwn*
lapwing *enw* ***cornchwiglen*** *hon*
larceny *enw* ***lladrad*** *hwn*
larch *enw* ***llarwydden*** *hon*
lard *enw* ***bloneg***, ***lard*** *hwn*
larder *enw* ***pantri*** *hwn*
large *ans* ***mawr***, ***bras***
  the world at l~ ***y byd yn gyffredinol***
  to be at l~ ***bod â'u traed yn rhydd***
large print *enw* ***print bras*** *hwn*
large-scale *ans* ***helaeth***, ***ar raddfa fawr***
largesse *enw* ***haelioni*** *hwn*
lariat *enw* ***lasŵ*** *hwn*
lark *enw* ***ehedydd*** *hwn*
  for a l~ ***fel sbri***, ***o ran hwyl***
larva *enw* ***larfa*** *hwn/hon*
larvae *enw* ***cynrhon*** *hyn*
laryngitis *enw* ***dolur gwddf***; ***gwddwg tost*** *hwn*
larynx *enw* ***laryncs*** *hwn*
lascivious *ans* ***anllad***, ***trythyll***
laser *enw* ***laser*** *hwn*
lash *enw* ***llach*** *hon*
lash *be* ***chwipio***, ***leinio***
lass *enw* ***croten***, ***hogen***, ***lodes*** *hon*
lassitude *enw* ***llesgedd*** *hwn*
lasso *enw* ***lasŵ*** *hwn*
last *be* ***para***, ***parhau***
  the programme l~s 5 minutes ***5 munud yw hyd y rhaglen***
last *ans* ***diwethaf***, ***olaf***
  l~ minute ***munud olaf*** *hwn/hon*
  l~ resort ***mynd i'r pen***, ***os daw hi i'r pen***
lasting *ans* ***arhosol***; ***hirhoedlog***
latch *enw* ***clicied*** *hon*
  l~ on (attach) ***cydio yn***; (understand) **deall**
late *ans* ***hwyr***, ***diweddar***
latecomer *enw* ***hwyrddyfodiad*** *hwn*
latent *ans* ***cudd***, ***cêl***, ***ynghladd***
lateral *ans* ***ochrol***
latest *ans* ***diweddaraf***
lath *enw* ***dellten***, ***latsen*** *hon*
lathe *enw* ***turn*** *hon*
lather *enw* ***ewyn*** *hwn*, ***trochion*** *hyn*

Latin *enw* ***Lladin*** *hon*
latitude *enw* (geographical) ***lledred***; ***rhyddid*** *hwn*
latrine *enw* ***geudy*** *hwn*
lattice *enw* ***dellten*** *hon*
latticed *ans* ***rhwyllog***
latticework *enw* ***delltwaith***, ***rhwyllwaith*** *hwn*
laudable *ans* ***clodwiw***, ***canmoladwy***
laugh *enw* ***chwerthiniad*** *hwn*
laugh *be* ***chwerthin***
laughable *ans* ***chwerthinllyd***
laughing stock *enw* ***cyff gwawd*** *hwn*
laughter *enw* ***chwerthin***
launch *be* ***lansio***, ***gwthio cwch i'r dŵr***
laundress *enw* ***golchwraig*** *hon*
laundry *enw* ***golchdy*** *hwn*
laurel *enw* ***llawryf*** *hwn*
  to rest on their l~s ***pwyso ar eu rhwyfau***
lava *enw* ***lafa*** *hwn*
lavatory *enw* ***tŷ bach***, ***lle chwech*** *hwn*
lavender *enw* ***lafant*** *hwn*
lavish *ans* ***hael***
law *enw* ***deddf***, ***cyfraith*** *hon*
  l~ and justice ***cyfraith a chyfiawnder***
  l~ and order ***cyfraith a threfn***
lawful *ans* ***cyfreithlon***
lawless *ans* ***direol***, ***digyfraith***
lawlessness *enw* ***anhrefn*** *hon*
lawmaker *enw* ***deddfwr*** *hwn*
lawn *enw* ***lawnt*** *hon*
lawsuit *enw* ***achos cyfreithiol*** *hwn*
lawyer *enw* ***cyfreithiwr*** *hwn*, ***cyfreithwraig*** *hon*, ***twrnai*** *hwn*
lax *ans* ***llac***
laxative *enw* ***moddion gweithio*** *hwn/hyn*
lay *be* ***dodwy***; ***gosod***
  to l~ down criteria ***pennu meini prawf***
lay *ans* ***lleyg***
lay-by *enw* ***arhosfan*** *hwn/hon*
layer *enw* ***haen:haenen*** *hon*
layman *enw* ***lleygwr*** *hwn*
laze *be* ***diogi***, ***segura***
laziness *enw* ***diogi*** *hwn*
lazy *ans* ***diog***, ***dioglyd***
lead *enw* (metal) ***plwm*** *hwn*; (guidance) ***arweiniad*** *hwn*, ***esiampl*** *hon*; (= leash) ***tennyn*** *hwn*
  in the l~ ***ar y blaen***
lead *be* ***arwain***
  to l~ the way ***arloesi***, ***bod ar flaen y gad***
  to take the l~ ***cymryd yr awenau***
leader *enw* ***arweinydd***; ***ceffyl blaen*** *hwn*
leadership *enw* ***arweinyddiaeth*** *hon*, ***arweiniad*** *hwn*
leading *ans* ***blaenllaw***, ***arweiniol***
leaf *enw* ***deilen*** *hon*; (of book) ***dalen*** *hon*

l

to turn a new l~ ***troi dalen newydd***
leaflet *enw* ***taflen*** *hon*
leafy *ans* ***deiliog***
league *enw* ***cynghrair*** *hon/hwn*
not in the same l~ as ***does neb yn yr un cae ag ef***
to be in l~ with ***bod law yn llaw â***
leak *enw* ***gollyngiad*** *hwn*
leak *be* ***gollwng***
lean *be* ***pwyso***
lean *ans* ***main***
a l~ period ***cyfnod anodd*** *hwn*
l~ meat ***cig coch*** *hwn*
leap *enw* ***naid*** *hon*
leap *be* ***neidio***
learn *be* ***dysgu***
it is surprising to l~ ***syndod yw cael ar ddeall***
learned *ans* ***dysgedig***
learner *enw* ***dysgwr, disgybl o ddysgwr*** *hwn*
learning *enw* ***dysg*** *hon*
lease *enw* ***prydles*** *hon*
a new l~ of life ***adfywiad*** *hwn*
lease *be* ***prydlesu***
leash *enw* ***tennyn*** *hwn*
least *enw/ans/adf* ***lleiaf***
at the very l~ ***a dweud y lleiaf***
l~ said soonest mended ***taw piau hi***
they have not the l~ interest ***nid oes ganddynt rithyn o ddiddordeb***
leather *enw* ***lledr*** *hwn*
leave *enw* (permission) ***caniatâd*** *hwn*; (holiday) ***gwyliau*** *hyn*
l~ of absence ***cyfnod o absenoldeb***
to take l~ of their senses ***colli arnynt eu hunain***
leave *be* ***gadael***
leaven *enw* ***eples, lefain*** *hwn*
lecherous *ans* ***chwantus, blysig, anllad***
lecture *enw* ***darlith*** *hon*
lecture *be* ***darlithio***
lecturer *enw* ***darlithydd*** *hwn*
ledge *enw* ***sil*** *hwn/hon,* ***silff*** *hon*
ledger *enw* ***llyfr cyfrifon*** *hwn*
leech *enw* ***gelen*** *hon*
leek *enw* ***cenhinen*** *hon*
leer *be* ***cilwenu***
lees *enw* ***sorod*** *hyn*
leeway *enw* ***lle, rhyddid*** *hwn*
left *ans* ***chwith***
left-handed *ans* ***llaw chwith***
left luggage office *enw* ***storfa baciau*** *hon*
leftovers *enw* ***gweddillion*** *hyn*
leg *enw* ***coes*** *hon*
legacy *enw* ***cymynrodd, etifeddiaeth*** *hon*
legal *ans* ***cyfreithlon, cyfreithiol***
legality *enw* ***cyfreithlondeb*** *hwn*
legalize *be* ***cyfreithloni***
legation *enw* ***llysgenhadaeth*** *hon*
legend *enw* ***chwedl*** *hon*

footballing l~ ***arwr pêl-droed*** *hwn*
l~ in his lifetime ***cawr yn ei gyfnod***
living l~ ***cawr cyfoes*** *hwn*
legendary *ans* ***chwedlonol***
leggings *enw* ***bacsau*** *hyn*
legible *ans* ***darllenadwy***
legion *enw* ***lleng*** *hon*
legislate *be* ***deddfu***
legislation *enw* ***deddfwriaeth*** *hon*
to pass into l~ ***dod yn gyfraith gwlad***
legislative *ans* ***deddfwriaethol***
legislature *enw* ***corff deddfwriaethol*** *hwn*
legitimacy *enw* ***cyfreithlondeb*** *hwn*
legitimate *ans* ***cyfreithlon***, ***dilys***
legitimize *be* ***cyfreithloni***
leisure *enw* ***hamdden*** *hon*
at your l~ ***wrth eich pwysau***
leisurely *ans* ***hamddenol***
lemon *enw* ***lemon*** *hwn*
lemonade *enw* ***lemonêd*** *hwn*
lend *be* ***benthyca***
to l~ itself to ***mae'n ei gynnig ei hun***
length *enw* ***hyd*** *hwn*
a l~ of ***darn o***
at l~ ***yn faith***
discuss at l~ ***trafod yn fanwl***
lengthen *be* ***hwyhau***, ***estyn***, ***ymestyn***
lengthways *adf* ***ar ei hyd***
lengthy *ans* ***hir***
lenient *ans* ***tirion***, ***caredig***, ***llai llym***, ***trugarog***
lens *enw* ***lens*** *hon*
Lent *enw* ***y Grawys*** *hwn*
lentils *enw* ***ffacbys*** *hyn*
leopard *enw* ***llewpart*** *hwn*
leotard *enw* ***leotard*** *hwn/hon*
leprosy *enw* ***gwahanglwyf*** *hwn*
lesbian *enw* ***lesbiad*** *hon*
lesion *enw* ***anaf*** *hwn*
less *ans* ***llai***
lessen *be* ***lleihau***
lesser *ans* ***llai***, ***lleiaf***
lesson *enw* ***gwers*** *hon*
lest *cysyllt* ***rhag***, ***rhag ofn***
let *be* ***gadael***; ***gosod***; ***prydlesu***
l~ alone ***chwaethach***; ***heb sôn am***
l~ down ***siomi***
let's ***beth am***
lethal *ans* ***marwol***, ***angheuol***
lethargic *ans* ***cysglyd***, ***swrth***
lethargy *enw* ***syrthni*** *hwn*
letter *enw* ***llythyr*** *hwn*; ***llythyren*** *hon*
a red-l~ day ***dydd o lawen chwedl*** *hwn*
to the l~ ***i'r dim***
lettering *enw* ***llythrennu***
lettuce *enw* ***letysen*** *hon*
level *enw* ***lefel*** *hon*; (plain) ***gwastadedd*** *hwn*
level *ans* ***gwastad***
l~ headed ***pwyllog***, ***call***
level *be* ***gwastatáu***

l

levelness *enw* ***gwastatrwydd*** *hwn*
lever *enw* ***trosol*** *hwn*
  to act as a l~ ***bod yn gyfrwng***
leveret *enw* ***lefren*** *hon*
levity *enw* ***ysgafnder*** *hwn*
levy *enw* ***toll***, ***treth*** *hon*
levy *be* ***codi (treth)***
lewd *ans* ***anweddus***
lexicography *enw* ***geiriaduraeth*** *hon*, ***geiriadura***
liability *enw* ***atebolrwydd***, ***cyfrifoldeb***, ***ymrwymiad*** *hwn*; ***dyledion*** *hyn*
  he's a l~ ***mae'n fwrn***
liable *ans* ***atebol***; ***tueddol***
  to be l~ to ***yn agored i***
liaise *be* ***cysylltu***
liaison *enw* ***cysylltiad*** *hwn*
liar *enw* ***celwyddgi*** *hwn*
libel *enw* ***enllib*** *hwn*
libel *be* ***enllibio***
libellous *ans* ***enllibus***
liberal *enw* ***rhyddfrydwr*** *hwn*
liberal *ans* ***rhyddfrydig***, ***rhyddfrydol***; ***helaeth***; ***haelionus***
liberate *be* ***rhyddhau***
liberation *enw* ***rhyddhad*** *hwn*, ***gwaredigaeth*** *hon*
liberty *enw* ***rhyddid*** *hwn*
  to be at l~ ***bod â'u traed yn rhydd***
librarian *enw* ***llyfrgellydd*** *hwn*
library *enw* ***llyfrgell*** *hon*
licence *enw* ***trwydded*** *hon*
license *be* ***trwyddedu***
  l~d teachers ***athrawon trwyddedig*** *hyn*
lichen *enw* ***cen*** *hwn*
lick *be* ***llyfu***
lid *enw* ***caead***, ***clawr*** *hwn*
lie *enw* ***celwydd*** *hwn*
lie *be* ***dweud celwyddau***, ***rhaffu celwyddau***; ***gorwedd***
  to have a l~ in ***cysgu'n hwyr***
lieu *enw*
  in lieu of ***yn lle***
lieutenant *enw* ***is-gapten*** *hwn*
life *enw* ***bywyd*** *hwn*
  for the l~ of them ***yn eu byw***
  that's l~ ***fel 'na mae***
  the l~ and times of ***hanes bywyd***
lifeboat *enw* ***bad achub*** *hwn*
life jacket *enw* ***siaced achub*** *hon*
lifeless *ans* ***marw***, ***difywyd***
lifelong *ans* ***am oes***
  l~ learning ***dysgu gydol oes***
life sentence *enw* ***carchar am oes***
life-sized *ans* ***o faintioli llawn***
lifespan *enw* ***hoedl***, ***oes*** *hon*
lifetime *enw* ***bywyd*** *hwn*, ***oes*** *hon*
  early in its l~ ***yn fuan ar ôl ei sefydlu***
  during my l~ ***tra byddaf byw***
lift *be* ***codi***
  to l~ the conditions ***dileu'r amodau***
lift *enw* ***codiad*** *hwn*; (in a car) ***lifft***, ***pas*** *hwn/hon*; (= elevator) ***lifft*** *hon*
ligament *enw* ***gewyn***, ***giewyn***, ***tennyn*** *hwn*

light *enw* ***goleuni, golau*** *hwn*
according to their l~s ***fel y gwelant yn dda***
to bring to l~ ***amlygu***
to come to l~ ***dod i olau dydd***
to give the green l~ ***caniatáu***
light *ans* ***ysgafn; golau***
light *be* ***cynnau***
lighten *be* ***ysgafnhau; goleuo***
light-fingered *ans* ***â dwylo blewog***
light-hearted *ans* ***hwyliog***
lighthouse *enw* ***goleudy*** *hwn*
lighting *enw* ***goleuo, tanio***
lightning *enw* ***mellt*** *hyn*
light year *enw* ***blwyddyn oleuni*** *hon*
like *ans* ***tebyg i***
what's it l~ to ***sut beth yw***
like *ardd, adf* ***fel***
like *be* ***hoffi***
likelihood *enw* ***tebyg, tebygolrwydd*** *hwn*
likely *ans* ***tebygol, tebyg***
like-minded *ans* ***o gyffelyb fryd; llathen o'r un brethyn***
liken *be* ***tebygu, cymharu***
likeness *enw* ***tebygrwydd*** *hwn*
likewise *adf* ***hefyd, yn ogystal, yn yr un modd***
liking *enw* ***hoffter*** *hwn*
more to their l~ ***yn fwy at eu dant***
lilac *enw* ***lelog*** *hwn*
lily *enw* ***lili*** *hon*
limb *enw* ***aelod*** *hwn*; (of tree) ***cangen fawr*** *hon*
out on a l~ ***ar eich pen eich hun***
lime *enw* ***calch; leim*** *hwn*
limerick *enw* ***limrig*** *hwn/hon*
limestone *enw* ***carreg galch*** *hon*, ***calchfaen*** *hwn*
limit *enw* ***terfyn; cyfyngiad*** *hwn*
to push to the l~ ***gwthio hyd yr eithaf***
limit *be* ***cyfyngu***
limitation *enw* ***cyfyngiad*** *hwn*
limited *ans* ***cyfyngedig***
l~ in nature ***tlodaidd***
only a l~ amount ***dim ond hyn a hyn***
limitless *ans* ***diderfyn***
limp *enw* ***cloffni*** *hwn*, ***herc*** *hon*
limp *be* ***hercian***
limp *ans* ***llipa***
limpet *enw* ***llygad maharen*** *hwn*, ***brenigen*** *hon*
limpid *ans* ***tryloyw***
linctus *enw* ***moddion peswch*** *hwn*
linden *enw* ***palalwyfen*** *hon*
line *enw* ***llinell*** *hon*; ***llinyn*** *hwn*, ***lein*** *hon*
along the l~s that ***i'r perwyl bod***
in l~ with ***yn unol â***
l~ of argument ***trywydd dadl*** *hwn*
to be out of l~ with ***bod yn anghyson â***
to bring into l~ ***cysoni, cydymffurfio***

to stand in l~ ***sefyll mewn rhes***
hard l~s ***hen dro, trueni***
l~ manager ***rheolwr atebol*** *hwn*
lineage *enw* ***tras*** *hon*
linen *enw* ***lliain*** *hwn*
line-out *enw* (rugby) ***lein*** *hon*
liner *enw* ***llong fawr, leiner*** *hon*
linesman *enw* ***llumanwr*** *hwn*
linger *be* ***oedi, sefyllian***
linguist *enw* ***ieithydd*** *hwn*
linguistic *ans* ***ieithyddol***
linguistics *enw* ***ieitheg*** *hon*
liniment *enw* ***ennaint, eli*** *hwn*
lining *enw* ***leinin*** *hwn*
link *enw* ***dolen gyswllt*** *hon*; ***cysylltiad*** *hwn*
link *be* ***cyplysu, cydio, cysylltu***
linnet *enw* ***llinos*** *hon*
linseed *enw* ***had llin*** *hyn*
lint *enw* ***lint*** *hwn*
lion *enw* ***llew*** *hwn*
lip *enw* ***gwefus*** *hon*, ***min*** *hwn*; ***ymyl*** *hwn/hon*
lip-read *be* ***darllen gwefusau***
lip service *enw* ***geiriau teg*** *hyn*
lipstick *enw* ***minlliw*** *hwn*
liquefy *be* ***hylifo***
liqueur *enw* ***gwirod*** *hwn/hon*
liquid *enw* ***hylif*** *hwn*
liquidation *enw* ***diddymu***
liquidize *be* ***hylifo***
liquor *enw* ***gwirod*** *hwn/hon*
lisp *enw* ***tafod tew*** *hwn*
lisp *be* ***siarad â thafod tew***
list *enw* ***rhestr*** *hon*
list *be* ***rhestru***; (naut.) ***gogwyddo***
listen *be* ***gwrando***
listener *enw* ***gwrandawr*** *hwn*
listless *ans* ***di-ffrwt, llesg***
literacy *enw* ***llythrennedd*** *hon*
musical l~ ***llythrennedd gerddorol*** *hon*
literal *ans* ***llythrennol***
literary *ans* ***llenyddol***
literature *enw* ***llenyddiaeth*** *hon*
visual literature ***llunyddiaeth*** *hon*
litigant *enw* ***ymgyfreithiwr*** *hwn*
litigation *enw* ***cyfreithiad*** *hwn*; ***mynd i gyfraith, cyfreitha***
litigious *ans* ***ymgyfreithgar, cynhennus, cyfreithgar***
litre *enw* ***litr*** *hwn*
litter *enw* ***sbwriel*** *hwn*; (animals) ***tor, torllwyth*** *hon*
l~ed with mistakes ***yn frith o gamgymeriadau***
little *ans* ***bach, ychydig***
l~ or no ***odid ddim***
very l~ ***fawr o ddim***
live *be* ***byw***
countries and those who l~ in them ***gwledydd a'u trigolion***
how can you l~ with yourself? ***sut fedri di fyw yn dy groen?***
live *ans* ***byw***
livelihood *enw* ***bywoliaeth*** *hon*
liveliness *enw* ***bywiogrwydd*** *hwn*
lively *ans* ***bywiog, sionc***
to make more l~ ***bywiogi***

liver *enw* ***afu***, ***iau*** *hwn*
livery *enw* ***lifrai*** *hwn*
livid *ans* ***yn gandryll***
living *ans* ***byw***
  a l~ legend ***cawr yn ein cyfnod***
  l~ things ***creaduriaid*** *hyn*
living room *enw* ***ystafell fyw*** *hon*
lizard *enw* ***madfall***, ***genau-goeg*** *hon*
llama *enw* ***lama*** *hwn/hon*
load *enw* ***llwyth***, ***baich*** *hwn*
load *be* ***llwytho***
loaf *enw* ***torth*** *hon*
loaf *be* ***diogi***
loan *enw* ***benthyciad*** *hwn*
loan *be* ***benthyca***
loan-word *enw* ***gair benthyg*** *hwn*
loath *ans* ***amharod***, ***cyndyn***
loathe *be* ***casáu***
loathing *enw* ***atgasedd***, ***casineb*** *hwn*
loathsome *ans* ***anghynnes***
lobby *enw* ***porth***, ***cyntedd*** *hwn*; (political) ***lobi*** *hon*
lobby *be* ***lobïo***
lobster *enw* ***cimwch*** *hwn;* (female) ***sioden*** *hon*
lobster pot *enw* ***cawell cimwch*** *hwn*
local *ans* ***lleol***
locate *be* ***lleoli***; ***dod o hyd i***
location *enw* ***lleoliad*** *hwn*
lock *enw* ***clo***; (hair) ***cudyn*** *hwn*
  under l~ and key ***dan glo***
lock *be* ***cloi***
locked *ans* ***ar glo***, ***dan glo***
locker *enw* ***cwpwrdd bach*** *hwn*
lock forward *enw* ***clo*** *hwn*
lockjaw *enw* ***genglo*** *hwn*
locomotive *enw* ***injan drên*** *hon*
locust *enw* ***locust*** *hwn*
lodge *enw* (freemasons) ***cyfrinfa*** *hon*; (porter) ***porthdy*** *hwn*
lodge *be* ***lletya***; (an appeal) ***cyflwyno***
  to l~ a complaint ***achwyn***, ***gwneud cwyn***
lodgings *enw* ***llety*** *hwn*
lodger *enw* ***lletywr*** *hwn*, ***lletywraig*** *hon*
loft *enw* ***taflod*** *hon*
lofty *ans* ***tal***, ***uchel***
log *enw* ***boncyff***, ***plocyn*** *hwn*
log *be* ***cofnodi***
logbook *enw* ***llyfr lòg***, ***coflyfr*** *hwn*
loggerheads (at) *adf* ***yn benben***
logic *enw* ***rhesymeg*** *hon*
logical *ans* ***rhesymegol***
logistics *enw* ***logisteg*** *hon*
log off *be* (computer) ***cau***
log on *be* ***agor***
loin *enw* ***lwyn*** *hon*
loiter *be* ***loetran***, ***sefyllian***
loll *be* ***lled-orwedd***, ***gorweddian***, ***lolian***
lollipop *enw* ***lolipop*** *hwn*
lone *ans* ***unig***
loneliness *enw* ***unigrwydd***, ***unigedd*** *hwn*
lonely *ans* ***unig***

long *ans* ***hir***, ***maith***
a l~ way ***bellter ffordd***
for a l~ time ***ers tro byd***
l~ ago ***amser maith yn ôl***; ***ers talwm***; ***'slawer dydd***
l~ gone ***wedi hen fynd***
long *be* ***dyheu***, ***hiraethu (am)***
long-awaited *ans* ***hirddisgwyliedig***
long-established *ans* ***wedi hen ennill ei blwyf***
long-lived *ans* ***hirhoedlog***
longevity *enw* ***hirhoedledd*** *hwn*
longing *enw* ***dyhead***, ***hiraeth*** *hwn*
longitude *enw* ***hydred*** *hwn*
long-term *ans* ***hirdymor***, ***tymor hir***
long-winded *ans* ***hirwyntog***
loo *enw* ***tŷ bach***, ***lle chwech*** *hwn*
look *enw* ***golwg*** *hon*, ***edrychiad*** *hwn*
look *be* ***edrych***
and l~ out ***gwae***
l~ inside ***cymerwch gip***
to l~ after ***gwarchod***, ***gofalu am***
to l~ carefully ***craffu***
to l~ for ***chwilio am***
to l~ out for ***bod ar eich gwyliadwriaeth rhag***
to l~ to ***disgwyl i***
loom *enw* ***gwŷdd*** *hwn*
loom *be* ***ymddangos***, ***dod i'r amlwg***
loop *enw* ***dolen*** *hon*
loophole *enw* ***bwlch***, ***twll***, ***man gwan*** *hwn*, ***dihangfa*** *hon*
loose *ans* ***rhydd***; ***llaes***
loosen *be* ***rhyddhau***, **llaesu**
loot *enw* ***ysbail*** *hon*
loot *be* ***ysbeilio***
lop *be* ***tocio***
lope *be* ***brasgamu***
lopsided *ans* ***unochrog***
loquacious *ans* ***siaradus***, ***huawdl***
loquacity *enw* ***huodledd*** *hwn*
lord *enw* ***arglwydd*** *hwn*
lord *be* ***tra-arglwyddiaethu***
Lord Lieutenant *enw* ***Arglwydd Raglaw*** *hwn*
lorry *enw* ***lorri*** *hon*
lose *be* ***colli***
to l~one's temper ***gwylltio***
to l~ out ***bod ar eich colled***
loss *enw* ***colled*** *hon*
they are at a l~ to ***ni allant yn eu byw***
lost *ans* ***ar goll***
all is not l~ ***dyw hi ddim yn ddiwedd y byd***
lot *enw* ***coelbren*** *hwn*
a bad l~ ***cythraul mewn croen*** *hwn*
they are thoroughly happy with their l~ ***maent yn gwbwl hapus eu byd***
lot *rhag* ***llawer***
such a l~ ***cymaint***
l~s of ***mil a mwy***, ***llond cae***
to pay a l~ for ***talu crocbris am***
lotion *enw* ***hufen***, ***eli*** *hwn*
lottery *enw* ***lotri:loteri*** *hon/hwn*
National Lottery ***y Loteri Genedlaethol***

l

loud *ans* ***uchel***; ***uchel ei gloch***
loudspeaker *enw* ***uchelseinydd***, ***corn siarad*** *hwn*
lounge *enw* ***lolfa*** *hon*
lounge *be* ***gorweddian***, ***lolian***
louse *enw* ***lleuen*** *hon*
lout *enw* ***llabwst*** *hwn*
lovable *ans* ***hoffus***, ***serchus***, ***annwyl***
love *enw* ***cariad***, ***serch*** *hwn*; ***carwriaeth*** *hon*; (tennis) ***dim***
love *be* ***caru***, ***dwlu (ar)***
loveliness *enw* ***prydferthwch*** *hwn*
lovely *ans* ***hyfryd***, ***prydferth***
lover *enw* ***cariad***, ***carwr*** *hwn*
lovesick *ans* ***claf o gariad***
loving *ans* ***cariadus***, ***serchus***, ***annwyl***
low *ans* ***isel***
low *be* ***brefu***
lower *be* ***gostwng***; ***diraddio***
lower *ans* ***is***
lowland *enw* ***iseldir*** *hwn*
lowly *ans* ***gostyngedig***
low tide *enw* ***distyll***, ***trai*** *hwn*
loyal *ans* ***teyrngar***, ***ffyddlon***
loyalty *enw* ***teyrngarwch*** *hwn*
lubricate *be* ***iro***
lucid *ans* ***clir***, ***eglur***
luck *enw* ***lwc***, ***ffawd*** *hon*
luckless *ans* ***anlwcus***
lucky *ans* ***lwcus***, ***ffodus***
lucrative *ans* ***proffidiol***; ***talu'n dda***
ludic *ans* ***chwaraeol***
ludicrous *ans* ***chwerthinllyd***, ***hurt***
lug *be* ***llusgo***
luggage *enw* ***bagiau*** *hyn*
lugubrious *ans* ***prudd***
lukewarm *ans* ***claear***, ***llugoer***
lull *enw* ***gosteg*** *hwn/hon*
lull *be* ***gostegu***
lullaby *enw* ***hwiangerdd*** *hon*
luminous *ans* ***disglair***, ***golau***
lump *enw* ***lwmpyn***, ***talp*** *hwn*
lunacy *enw* ***gwallgofrwydd*** *hwn*
lunatic *enw* ***gwallgofddyn*** *hwn*
lunch *enw* ***cinio canol dydd*** *hwn* **packed l~** ***pecyn cinio/bwyd*** *hwn*
lunch *be* ***ciniawa***
lungs *enw* ***ysgyfaint*** *hyn*
lurch *be* ***gwegian***
lure *enw* ***abwydyn***, ***llith*** *hwn*
lure *be* ***denu***, ***llithio***
lurk *be* ***llechu***
lush *ans* ***toreithiog***, ***iraidd***
lust *enw* ***blys***, ***trachwant*** *hwn*
lust *be* ***chwennych***
lustre *enw* ***llewyrch*** *hwn*
lustrous *ans* ***gloyw***
lusty *ans* ***cryf***, ***lysti***
luxuriance *enw* ***helaethrwydd*** *hwn*, ***toreth*** *hon*
luxuriant *ans* ***toreithiog***
luxurious *ans* ***moethus***
luxury *enw* ***moethusrwydd*** *hwn*
lying *ans* ***celwyddog***
lyrical *ans* ***telynegol***
lyrics *enw* ***geiriau*** *hyn*

M

macabre *ans* **erchyll**, **angladdol**
macadamize *be* ***tarmacadameiddio***
macaroni *enw* ***macaroni*** *hwn*
mace *enw* (weapon) ***pastwn*** *hwn*; (ceremonial) ***brysgyll*** *hwn*
macerate *be* ***mwydo***; ***dihoeni***
machination *enw* ***cynllwyn*** *hwn*
machine *enw* ***peiriant*** *hwn*
machinery *enw* ***peirianwaith*** *hwn;* ***peiriannau*** *hyn*
mackerel *enw* ***macrell*** *hwn*
mackintosh *enw* ***cot law*** *hon*
mad *ans* ***gwallgof***, ***ynfyd***; (angry) ***crac***, ***blin***, ***cynddeiriog***
 he's m~ about cricket ***mae e'n dwlu ar griced***
madam *enw* ***madam***, ***meistres*** *hon*
madden *be* ***gwylltio***, ***cynddeiriogi***
madhouse *enw* ***gwallgofdy*** *hwn*
madman *enw* ***gwallgofddyn*** *hwn*
madness *enw* ***gwallgofrwydd*** *hwn*
magazine *enw* ***cylchgrawn*** *hwn*
maggot *enw* ***cynrhonyn*** *hwn*
Magi *enw* ***y Doethion*** *hyn*
magic *enw* ***hud a lledrith*** *hwn*
magical *ans* ***lledrithiol***
magician *enw* ***dewin***, ***consuriwr*** *hwn*
magisterial *ans* ***meistrolgar***
magistrate *enw* ***ustus*** *hwn*
magnanimity *enw* ***mawrfrydedd*** *hwn*
magnesium *enw* ***magnesiwm*** *hwn*
magnanimous *ans* ***mawrfrydig***, ***hael***
magnet *enw* ***magned*** *hwn*
magnetic *ans* ***magnetig***
magnetism *enw* **magnetedd** *hwn*; (study) ***magneteg*** *hon*
magnetize *be* ***magneteiddio***
magnification *enw* ***mwyhad***, ***chwyddiad*** *hwn*
magnificence *enw* ***gwychder***, ***ardderchowgrwydd*** *hwn*
magnificent *ans* ***gwych***, ***ardderchog***
magnify *be* ***chwyddo***, ***mwyhau***
magnitude *enw* ***maintioli*** *hwn*
magpie *enw* ***pioden*** *hon*
maid *enw* ***morwyn*** *hon*
 maid-of-all-work ***morwyn bob galw*** *hon*
maiden *enw* ***meinir***, ***rhiain***; ***gwyryf*** *hon*
mail *enw* ***post*** *hwn,* ***llythyron*** *hyn*
maim *be* ***clwyfo***, ***anffurfio***, ***llurgunio***
main *ans* ***prif***
 in the m~ ***gan mwyaf***, ***ar y cyfan***
mainland *enw* ***tir mawr*** *hwn*
main line *enw* ***lein fawr*** *hon*
main road *enw* ***priffordd***, ***ffordd fawr*** *hon*
mainstream *ans* ***cyffredinol***

m~ classes ***dosbarthiadau prif ffrwd*** *hyn*
maintain *be* ***cynnal***; ***maentumio***
to m~ a competitive edge ***cadw ar y blaen yn gystadleuol***
to m~ an awareness of ***bod yn gyson ymwybodol o***
to m~ good practice ***gweithredu arferion da***
maintenance *enw* ***cynhaliaeth*** *hon*; ***cynnal a chadw***
majestic *ans* ***urddasol***
majesty *enw* ***urddas***; ***mawrhydi*** *hwn*
major *enw* ***uchgapten*** *hwn*
major *ans* ***prif***, ***mwyaf***
majority *enw* ***mwyafrif*** *hwn*
make *be* ***gwneud***
to m~ clear ***datgan yn glir***
to m~ progress ***dod ymlaen***
to m~ up ***dyfeisio***, ***ffurfio***, ***llunio***, ***ymbincio***
to m~ up for ***gwneud iawn am***
to m~ good ***cywiro***
to m~ known ***lleisio***
to m~ one aware ***rhoi gwybod***
to m~ one's way ***ymlwybro***
to m~ someone happy ***codi calon***
to m~ the most of ***gwneud yn fawr o***
to m~ up lost work ***adennill y gwaith a gollwyd***
makeshift *ans* ***dros dro***
make-up *enw* ***colur*** *hwn*
maladministration *enw* ***camweinyddiad*** *hwn*, ***camweinyddu***
malady *enw* ***anhwylder***, ***clefyd*** *hwn*
malaise *enw* ***anniddigrwydd***, ***anhwylder*** *hwn*
malaria *enw* ***malaria***, ***y cryd*** *hwn*
malcontent *ans* ***anfoddog***, ***anfodlon***
male *enw* ***gwryw*** *hwn*
male *ans* ***gwryw***, ***gwrywaidd***
malefactor *enw* ***drwgweithredwr*** *hwn*
malevolence *enw* ***malais***, ***mileindra*** *hwn*
malevolent *ans* ***maleisus***, ***milain***
malfeasance *enw* ***drygwaith*** *hwn*
malfunction *enw* ***diffyg***, ***aflwydd*** *hwn*
malfunction *be* ***cau mynd***, ***pallu mynd***
malice *enw* ***malais*** *hwn*
malicious *ans* ***maleisus***
malign *ans* ***niweidiol***, ***milain***
malign *be* **pardduo**
malignant *ans* ***milain***; (med.) ***gwyllt***
malleable *ans* ***hydrin***, ***curadwy***
mallet *enw* ***gordd bren*** *hon*
malnutrition *enw* ***diffyg maeth*** *hwn*
malodorous *ans* ***drewllyd***
malpractice *enw* ***camymddygiad***, ***esgeulustod*** *hwn*; ***camweithredu***

m

malt *enw* ***brag*** *hwn*
maltreat *be* ***cam-drin***
mammal *enw* ***mamolyn*** *hwn*
mammoth *enw* ***mamoth*** *hwn*
man *enw* ***dyn***, ***gŵr*** *hwn*
to a m~ ***pob copa walltog***
to m~ a stand ***staffio stondin***
manacle *enw* ***gefyn*** *hwn*
manage *be* ***rheoli***; ***llwyddo***; ***ymdopi***; ***cael dau ben llinyn ynghyd***
manageable *ans* (person) ***hawdd ei drin***; (feasible) ***posibl***
management *enw* ***rheolaeth*** *hon*
manager *enw* ***rheolwr*** *hwn*, ***rheolwraig*** *hon*
managerial *ans* ***rheolaethol***
managing director *enw* ***rheolwr-gyfarwyddwr*** *hwn*
mandate *enw* ***mandad***, ***awdurdod*** *hwn*
mandated *ans* ***mandadedig***
mandatory *ans* ***gorfodol***
mane *enw* ***mwng*** *hwn*
manful *ans* ***gwrol***
mangle *be* ***rhwygo***, ***darnio***
manhandle *be* ***trafod â nerth bôn braich***; ***cam-drin***
mania *enw* ***gorffwylltra: gorffwylledd***; ***obsesiwn*** *hwn*
railway m~ ***clefyd y cledrau*** *hwn*
maniac *enw* ***gwallgofddyn*** *hwn*
manic *ans* ***manig***, ***lloerig***
manicure *be* ***trin (ewinedd/dwylo etc)***
manifest *ans* ***amlwg***
manifest *be* ***datguddio***; ***i'w gweld yn amlwg***
manifestation *enw* ***amlygiad***, ***ymddangosiad*** *hwn*
manifesto *enw* ***maniffesto*** *hwn*
manikin *enw* ***dynan*** *hwn*
manipulate *be* ***trafod***, ***trin***; ***defnyddio rhywun***
to m~ accounts ***ffugio cyfrifon***
to m~ funds ***camdrafod arian***
mankind *enw* ***dynolryw***, ***dynoliaeth*** *hon*
manliness *enw* ***gwroldeb***, ***dewrder*** *hwn*
manly *ans* ***gwrol***
man-made *ans* ***o waith llaw dyn***
manna *enw* ***manna*** *hwn*
manner *enw* ***ffordd*** *hon*, ***modd*** *hwn*
manoeuvrable *ans* ***hydrin***, ***symudadwy***
manoeuvre *enw* ***symudiad*** *hwn*
freedom of m~ ***rhyddid i weithredu***
manor *enw* ***maenor:maenol*** *hon*
manpower *enw* ***gweithlu*** *hwn*
manse *enw* ***mans*** *hwn*
manservant *enw* ***gwas*** *hwn*
mansion *enw* ***cwrt***, ***plas***, ***plasty*** *hwn*
manslaughter *enw* ***dynladdiad*** *hwn*
mantelpiece *enw* ***silff ben tân*** *hon*
mantle *enw* ***mantell*** *hon*

manual *enw* ***llawlyfr*** *hwn*
manual *ans* ***llaw***
m~ dexterity ***deheurwydd gyda'r dwylo***
manufacture *be* ***gweithgynhyrchu***
manufacturer *enw* ***gwneuthurwr***, ***cynhyrchwr*** *hwn*
manure *enw* ***gwrtaith*** *hwn*, ***tom/dom*** *hon*, ***tail*** *hwn*
manure *be* ***gwrteithio***
manuscript *enw* ***llawysgrif*** *hon*
many *ans* ***llawer***, ***llawer un***
how m~ ***(pa) faint***, ***(pa) sawl***
m~ and varied ***cant a mil***, ***llu***
m~ congratulations ***llongyfarchiadau mawr***
m~ thanks ***diolch o galon***
map *enw* ***map*** *hwn*
map *be* ***mapio***
maple *enw* ***masarnen*** *hon*
mar *be* ***difetha***, ***sbwylio***
marathon *enw* ***marathon*** *hwn*
maraud *be* ***ysbeilio***
marauders *enw* ***ysbeilwyr*** *hyn*
marble *enw* (rock) ***marmor*** *hwn*; ***marblen*** *hon*
March *enw* ***Mawrth*** *hwn*
march *enw* ***gorymdaith***; (music) ***ymdeithgan*** *hon*
march *be* ***gorymdeithio***
Marches *enw* ***y Gororau*** *hyn*
marchioness *enw* ***ardalyddes*** *hon*
mare *enw* ***caseg*** *hon*
margarine *enw* ***margarîn*** *hwn*
margin *enw* ***ymyl*** *hwn/hon*, ***godre*** *hwn*
the slenderest of m~s ***o drwch blewyn (yn unig)***
marginal *ans* ***ymylol***
marginalize *be* ***bwrw i'r ymylon***
marigold *enw* ***gold Mair*** *hwn*
marina *enw* ***marina*** *hwn/hon*
marine *ans* ***morol***
mariner *enw* ***morwr*** *hwn*
marionette *enw* ***pyped*** *hwn*
marital *ans* ***priodasol***
maritime *ans* ***arforol, glan môr***
mark *enw* ***marc***, ***nod*** *hwn*
mark *be* ***nodi***, ***marcio***
marked *ans* ***nodedig***, ***cryn***
to have a m~ effect on ***dylanwadu'n fawr ar***
to vary m~ly ***amrywio'n fawr***
market *enw* ***marchnad*** *hon*
a difficult m~ ***talcen caled*** *hwn*
marketable *ans* ***gwerthadwy***
marketing *enw* ***marchnata***
marksman *enw* ***saethwr*** *hwn*
marmalade *enw* ***marmalêd*** *hwn*
maroon *be* ***ynysu***
marquee *enw* ***pabell*** *hon*
marquis *enw* ***ardalydd*** *hwn*
marriage *enw* ***priodas*** *hon*
married *ans* ***priod***
marrow *enw* ***mêr*** *hwn*; (vegetable) ***pwmpen*** *hon*
marry *be* ***priodi***
Mars *enw* ***Mawrth*** *hwn*
marsh *enw* ***cors***, ***mignen*** *hon*

m

marshal *be* ***corlannu***
marshy *ans* ***cors[i]og***
marsupial *enw* ***bolgodog***, ***marswpial*** *hwn*
mart *enw* ***mart*** *hwn*, ***marchnad*** *hon*
martial *ans* ***milwrol***
martin *enw* ***gwennol*** *hon*
martyr *enw* ***merthyr*** *hwn*, ***merthyres*** *hon*
martyr *be* ***merthyru***
martyrdom *enw* ***merthyrdod*** *hwn*
marvel *enw* ***rhyfeddod*** *hwn*
marvel *be* ***rhyfeddu***
marvellous *ans* ***rhyfeddol***, ***anfarwol***
masculine *ans* ***gwryw***, ***gwrywaidd***
mash *enw* ***llith***; ***stwnsh*** *hwn*
mask *enw* ***mwgwd*** *hwn*
mask *be* ***mygydu***, ***cuddio***
mason *enw* ***saer maen***, ***masiwn*** *hwn*
mass *enw* (church) ***offeren*** *hon*; ***màs*** *hwn*
  m~ of detail ***pentwr o fanylion***
massacre *enw* ***cyflafan*** *hon*
massacre *be* ***lladd***
massage *be* ***tylino'r corff***
massive *ans* ***anferth***, ***enfawr***, ***aruthrol***
mast *enw* ***hwylbren***, ***mast*** *hwn*
master *enw* ***meistr*** *hwn*
master *be* ***meistroli***; ***bod yn feistr corn ar***
masterful *ans* ***meistrolgar***
masterpiece *enw* ***campwaith*** *hwn*, ***gorchest*** *hon*
mastery *enw* ***meistrolaeth*** *hon*
masticate *be* ***cnoi***
mat *enw* ***mat*** *hwn*
match *enw* ***matsien***; ***gêm***; ***cyfatebiaeth*** *hon*
match *be* ***cyfateb***; ***gweddu i***
  they cannot m~ ***ni allant gystadlu â***
  to m~ expectations ***bod cystal â'r disgwyl***
match-funding *enw* ***arian cyfatebol*** *hwn*
matchless *ans* ***digymar***, ***digyffelyb***, ***dihafal***
mate *enw* ***mêt***, ***partner*** *hwn*
mate *be* ***cyplu***
material *enw* ***defnydd***, ***deunydd*** *hwn*
material *ans* ***materol***; ***pwysig***, ***sylweddol***
maternal *ans* ***mamol***
maternity *enw* ***mamolaeth*** *hon*
maternity hospital *enw* ***ysbyty mamau*** *hwn*
mathematical *ans* ***mathemategol***
mathematics *enw* ***mathemateg*** *hon*
matins *enw* ***boreol weddi***; ***plygain*** *hwn*
matriarchal *ans* ***matriarchaidd***
matrimonial *ans* ***priodasol***
matrimony *enw* ***priodas*** *hon*
matron *enw* (hospital) ***metron*** *hon*

matt *ans* ***pŵl***
matted *ans* ***yn glymau***
matter *enw* ***sylwedd***, ***mater*** *hwn*
  a very m~ of fact way ***mewn ffordd ddigon swta***
  as a m~ of course ***fel rhan o'r drefn***
  it's all a m~ of money ***diwedd y gân yw'r geiniog***
  on the m~ of ***o ran***
matter *be* ***bod o bwys***, ***cyfrif***
mattock *enw* ***caib*** *hon*
mattress *enw* ***matres*** *hwn/hon*
mature *ans* ***aeddfed***
mature *be* ***aeddfedu***
maturity *enw* ***aeddfedrwydd*** *hwn*
maul *enw* ***sgarmes*** *hon*
maw *enw* ***cylla*** *hwn*
mawkish *ans* ***dagreuol***
maxim *enw* ***gwireb*** *hon*
maximize *be* ***cynyddu hyd yr eithaf***
maximum *enw* ***uchafswm***, ***uchafbwynt*** *hwn;* ***ar y mwyaf***
  the m~ advantage ***y budd pennaf*** *hwn*
  their m~ capacity ***hyd eithaf eu gallu***
  the m~ degree of ***cymaint â phosibl***
may *be* ***gallu***
  come what m~ ***doed a ddelo***
  they m~ as well go ***man a man iddynt fynd***
May *enw* ***Mai*** *hwn*
maybe *adf* ***efallai***
mayonnaise *enw* ***hufen salad*** *hwn*
mayor *enw* ***maer*** *hwn*, ***maeres*** *hon*
maypole *enw* ***bedwen Fai:bedwen haf*** *hon*
maze *enw* ***drysfa*** *hon*
me *rhag* ***fi***
mead *enw* ***medd*** *hwn*
meadow *enw* ***dôl*** *hon*
meagre *ans* ***prin***, ***tenau***
meal *enw* ***pryd*** *hwn*
  m~s on wheels ***pryd ar glud***
mean *ans* ***cybyddlyd***
mean *be* ***golygu***
  she m~s well ***mae ei chalon yn y lle iawn***
  this will m~ that ***felly***
  what it all m~s ***pwrpas y cyfan yw***
meander *be* ***ymddolennu***, ***dolennu***, ***ymdroelli***
meaning *enw* ***ystyr*** *hwn/hon*
meaningful *ans* ***ystyrlon***
meaningless *ans* ***diystyr***
meanness *enw* ***crintachrwydd***, ***cybydd-dod*** *hwn*
means *enw* ***modd*** *hwn*
  by all m~ ***ar bob cyfrif***
  by any m~ ***o bell ffordd***
  by this m~ ***fel hyn***
  to be a m~ to an end ***yn fodd i gyflawni diben***
  to confuse m~ and ends ***drysu modd a diben***
meantime *enw* ***cyfamser***

m

measles *enw* ***y frech goch*** *hon*
measurable *ans* ***mesuradwy***
measure *be* ***mesur***
it m~s 8 metres across ***mae'n 8 metr o led***
measure *enw* ***mesur*** *hwn*
a m~ of ***peth***, ***rhywfaint***; ***hyn a hyn o***
a simple m~ ***gweithred syml*** *hon*
in large m~ ***i raddau helaeth***
measureless *ans* ***anfesuradwy***
measurement *enw* ***mesur***, ***mesuriad*** *hwn*
meat *enw* ***cig*** *hwn*
scraps of m~ ***cigach*** *hyn*
meaty *ans* ***cigog***; (topic) ***swmpus, sylweddol***
mechanic *enw* ***mecanig, peiriannydd*** *hwn*
mechanical *ans* ***peirianyddol***, ***mecanyddol***
mechanism *enw* ***peirianwaith*** *hwn*
an effective m~ for ***ffordd effeithiol o***
mechatronics *enw* ***mecatroneg*** *hon*
medal *enw* ***medal*** *hon*, ***tlws*** *hwn*
meddle *be* ***busnesa***
media *enw* ***cyfryngau*** *hyn*
m~ studies ***astudio'r cyfryngau***
median *ans/enw* ***canol***, ***canolrif*** *hwn*
mediate *be* ***cyflafareddu***
mediator *enw* ***eiriolwr***, ***cyfryngydd*** *hwn*
medic *enw* ***meddyg*** *hwn*
medical *ans* ***meddygol***
medication *enw* ***meddyginiaeth*** *hon*
medicinal *ans* ***meddyginiaethol***
medicine *enw* ***meddyginiaeth*** *hon*, ***moddion*** *hyn*; (study) ***meddygaeth*** *hon*
medieval *ans* ***canoloesol***
mediocre *ans* ***gweddol***, ***cyffredin***
meditate *be* ***myfyrio***, ***synfyfyrio***
meditation *enw* ***myfyrdod*** *hwn*
meditative *ans* ***synfyfyriol***
medium *enw* ***canol***; (means) ***cyfrwng*** *hwn*
medium *ans* ***gweddol***, ***cymedrol***, ***canolig***
medium wave *enw* ***y donfedd ganol*** *hon*
medley *enw* (music) ***cadwyn*** *hon*
meek *ans* ***addfwyn***, ***gostyngedig***
meekness *enw* ***gostyngeiddrwydd***, ***addfwynder*** *hwn*
meet *be* ***cyfarfod***; (targets) ***cyrraedd***; (needs) ***ateb***
to make ends m~ ***cael dau ben llinyn ynghyd***
to fully m~ expectations ***mae hyn llawn cystal â'r disgwyl***
to m~ a challenge ***mynd i'r afael â sialens***
meeting *enw* ***cyfarfod*** *hwn*
megalith *enw* ***maen hir*** *hwn*
melancholy *enw* ***iselder ysbryd*** *hwn*

melancholy *ans* ***pruddglwyfus***
melée *enw* ***ysgarmes*** *hon*
mellifluous *ans* ***persain***
mellow *ans* ***aeddfed***, ***mwyn***
mellow *be* ***aeddfedu***
melodious *ans* ***melodaidd***, ***persain***
melody *enw* ***alaw*** *hon*
melon *enw* ***melon*** *hwn*
melt *be* ***toddi***, ***ymdoddi***
member *enw* ***aelod*** *hwn*
  M~ of Parliament ***Aelod Seneddol*** *hwn*
membership *enw* ***aelodaeth*** *hon*
  m~ form ***ffurflen ymaelodi*** *hon*
membrane *enw* ***pilen*** *hon*
memento *enw* ***cofrodd*** *hon*, ***swfenîr*** *hwn*
memoirs *enw* ***hunangofiant*** *hwn*
memorable *ans* ***cofiadwy***, ***bythgofiadwy***
memorandum *enw* ***memorandwm*** *hwn*
memorial *enw* ***cofeb*** *hon*
memorial *ans* ***coffa***
memorize *be* ***dysgu ar gof***
memory *enw* ***cof*** *hwn*
menace *enw* ***bygythiad*** *hwn*
menace *be* ***bygwth***
menacing *ans* ***bygythiol***
mend *be* ***cyweirio***, ***trwsio***
  on the m~ ***gwella***
mendacious *ans* ***celwyddog***
mendicant *enw* ***cardotyn*** *hwn*
menfolk *enw* ***gwŷr*** *hyn*
meningitis *enw* ***llid yr ymennydd*** *hwn*
menial *ans* ***isel***, ***gwasaidd***
menstruation *enw* ***mislif*** *hwn*
mensurable *ans* ***mesuradwy***
mental *ans* ***meddyliol***
mentality *enw* ***meddylfryd*** *hwn*
mention *be* ***crybwyll***, ***sôn***
mentor *enw* ***mentor*** *hwn*
mentoring *be* ***mentora***
menu *enw* ***bwydlen*** *hon*
mercantile *ans* ***masnachol***
mercenary *enw* ***milwr cyflog*** *hwn*
merchandise *enw* ***marsiandïaeth*** *hon*, ***nwyddau*** *hyn*
merchant *enw* ***masnachwr***, ***gwerthwr*** *hwn*; ***masnachwraig***, ***gwerthwraig*** *hon*
merciful *ans* ***trugarog***
mercifully *adf* ***trwy drugaredd***
merciless *ans* ***didrugaredd***; ***cignoeth***
mercury *enw* ***mercwri***, ***arian byw*** *hwn*
Mercury *enw* ***Mercher*** *hwn*
mercy *enw* ***trugaredd*** *hwn/hon*
mere *ans* ***dim ond***, ***yn unig***
meretricious *ans* ***ffuantus***
merge *be* ***cyfuno***; ***cyd-doddi***, ***uno***
merger *enw* ***cyfuniad*** *hwn*
meridian *enw* ***meridian*** *hwn*
merit *enw* ***haeddiant***, ***teilyngdod*** *hwn*
merit *be* ***haeddu***, ***teilyngu***
meritorious *ans* ***teilwng***

merlin *enw* ***cudyll bach*** *hwn*
mermaid *enw* ***môr-forwyn*** *hon*
merriment *enw* ***llawenydd**, **miri*** *hwn*
merry *ans* ***llawen**, **llon***
mesh *enw* ***rhwyll*** *hwn*, ***rhwyllwaith*** *hwn*
mesh *be* ***cydblethu***
mesmerize *be* ***mesmereiddio***
mess *enw* ***llanast*** *hwn*, ***smonach*** *hon*
message *enw* ***neges*** *hon*
messenger *enw* ***negesydd*** *hwn*
Messiah *enw* ***Meseia*** *hwn*
metabolism *enw* ***metabolaeth*** *hon*
metal *enw* ***metel*** *hwn*
metallic *ans* ***metelaidd***
metallurgy *enw* ***meteleg*** *hon*
metalwork *enw* ***gwaith metel*** *hwn*
metamorphosis *enw* ***trawsffurfiad*** *hwn*
metaphor *enw* ***trosiad*** *hwn*
meteor *enw* ***seren wib*** *hon*, ***meteor*** *hwn*
meteorological *ans* ***meteorolegol***
meteorology *enw* ***meteoroleg*** *hon*
meter *enw* ***mesurydd*** *hwn*
method *enw* ***dull*** *hwn*
methodical *ans* ***trefnus***
Methodist *ans* ***Methodistaidd***
methodology *enw* ***methodoleg*** *hon*
meticulous *ans* ***manwl gywir***
metre *enw* ***metr***; (poetry) ***mydr*** *hwn*
metric *ans* ***metrig***
metrical *ans* ***mydryddol***
metronome *enw* ***metronom*** *hwn*
metropolis *enw* ***prifddinas*** *hon*
metropolitan *ans* ***prifddinasol***
mettle *enw* ***rhuddin**, **ysbryd*** *hwn*
mettlesome *ans* ***nwyfus***
mew *be* ***mewian***
mews *enw* ***stryd bengaead*** *hon*
miasma *enw* ***drycsawr*** *hwn*
microbe *enw* ***microb*** *hwn*
microchip *enw* ***microsglodyn*** *hwn*
microelectronics *enw* ***microelectroneg*** *hon*
micrometer *enw* ***micromedr*** *hwn*
microphone *enw* ***microffon*** *hwn*
microprocessor *enw* ***microbrosesydd*** *hwn*
microscope *enw* ***microsgop*** *hwn*
to put under the m~ ***rhoi o dan y chwyddwydr***
microwave *enw* ***microdon*** *hon*
mid *ans* ***canol***
midday *enw* ***canol dydd*** *hwn*
midden *enw* ***tomen dail*** *hon*
middle *enw* ***canol*** *hwn*
middle *ans* ***canol***
middle-aged *ans* ***canol oed***
Middle Ages *enw* ***Canol Oesoedd**, **yr Oesoedd Canol*** *hyn*
middle class *enw* ***dosbarth canol*** *hwn*
middle ear *enw* ***clust ganol*** *hon*
Middle East *enw* ***Dwyrain Canol*** *hwn*

middling *ans* ***canolig***, ***gweddol***
midfield *ans* ***canol cae***
midnight *enw* ***hanner nos*** *hwn*
midriff *enw* ***canol*** *hwn*
Midsummer Day *enw* ***Gŵyl Ifan*** *hon*
midway *adf* ***hanner ffordd***
midwife *enw* ***bydwraig*** *hon*
mien *enw* ***golwg*** *hon*
miffed (to be) *be* ***gweld yn chwith***
might *enw* ***grym***, ***nerth*** *hwn*
might *be* ***efallai***
they m~ as well go ***man a man iddynt fynd***
mighty *ans* ***nerthol***, ***aruthrol fawr***
migrant *ans* ***mudol***
migrate *be* ***mudo***, ***ymfudo***
migration *enw* ***ymfudiad*** *hwn*
mild *ans* ***mwyn***, ***tyner***
mildew *enw* ***llwydni*** *hwn*
mildness *enw* ***mwynder***, ***tynerwch*** *hwn*
mile *enw* ***milltir*** *hon*
m~s better ***yn well o lawer***
mileage *enw* ***milltiroedd*** *hyn*
milestone *enw* ***carreg filltir*** *hon*
militant *ans* ***milwriaethus***
military *ans* ***milwrol***
militate *be* ***milwrio***
to m~ against ***gweithio yn erbyn***
milk *enw* ***llaeth***, ***llefrith*** *hwn*
milk *be* ***godro***
milky *ans* ***llaethog***
Milky Way *enw* ***y Llwybr Llaethog*** *hwn*
mill *enw* ***melin*** *hon*
mill *be* ***malu***, ***melino***
millennium *enw* ***milflwydd*** *hon*, ***mileniwm*** *hwn*
miller *enw* ***melinydd*** *hwn*
millimetre *enw* ***milimetr*** *hwn*
million *enw* ***miliwn*** *hon*
millionaire *enw* ***miliwnydd*** *hwn*
millionth *ans* ***miliynfed***
millstone *enw* ***maen melin*** *hwn*
mime *enw* ***meim*** *hon*
mime *be* ***meimio***
mimic *be* ***dynwared***
mimicry *enw* ***dynwarediad*** *hwn*
mince *be* ***briwo***, ***briwsioni***
without m~ing matters ***yn ddi-flewyn ar dafod***
mincemeat *enw* ***briwgig*** *hwn*
mind *enw* ***meddwl*** *hwn*
nobody in their right m~ ***neb call***
to speak one's m~ ***dweud yn blaen***; ***yn ddi-flewyn ar dafod***
mind *be* ***gwarchod***; ***malio***
mindful *ans* ***gofalus***
mindless *ans* ***difeddwl***
mine *rhag* ***eiddof fi, fy – i***
mine *enw* ***mwynglawdd*** *hwn*
mine *be* ***mwyngloddio***
miner *enw* ***glöwr***, ***mwynwr*** *hwn*
mineral *enw* ***mwyn*** *hwn*
mingle *be* ***cymysgu***
mingy *ans* ***cybyddlyd***, ***mên***, ***crintachlyd***
mini *enw* ***mini*** *hwn*

m

miniature *enw/ans* (art) ***miniatur*** *hwn*; ***bychan:bechan***
minim *enw* ***minim*** *hwn*
minimal *ans* ***odid ddim***
minimize *be* ***lleihau***
minimum *enw* ***isafbwynt***, ***lleiafswm*** *hwn*
to reduce to a m~ ***cyfyngu cymaint â phosibl***
with the m~ of delay ***yn ddioed***, ***yn ddiymdroi***
minion *enw* ***gwas bach*** *hwn*
minister *enw* ***gweinidog*** *hwn*
minister *be* ***bugeilio***, ***gweinidogaethu***
ministerial *ans* ***gweinidogol***, ***fel gweinidog***
ministry *enw* ***gweinyddiaeth*** *hon*; (church) ***gweinidogaeth*** *hon*
mink *enw* ***minc*** *hwn*
minnow *enw* ***silidón***, ***silcyn*** *hwn*
minor *enw* ***plentyn dan oed*** *hwn*
minor *ans* ***bach, mân, lleiaf***
m~ key ***cywair lleiaf/lleddf*** *hwn*
A m~ ***A leiaf***
minority *enw* ***lleiafrif*** *hwn*
minority *ans* ***lleiafrifol***
minstrel *enw* ***gŵr wrth gerdd*** *hwn*
mint *enw* (coins) ***bathdy***; (herb) ***mintys*** *hwn*
minus *ardd/enw* ***minws*** *hwn*
A m~ B ***tynnwch B o A***
minute *ans* ***mân***
minute *enw* ***munud*** *hon/hwn*; ***cofnod*** *hwn*
just a m~ ***hanner munud***
minute *be* ***cofnodi***
minutes *enw* ***cofnodion*** *hyn*
miracle *enw* ***gwyrth*** *hon*
miraculous *ans* ***gwyrthiol***
mirage *enw* ***rhith*** *hwn*
mire *enw* ***llaca*** *hwn*, ***cors*** *hon*
mirror *enw* ***drych*** *hwn*
mirror *be* ***bod yn ddrych o***; ***efelychu***
mirth *enw* ***digrifwch*** *hwn*, ***hwyl*** *hon*
misadventure *enw* ***anffawd*** *hon*
misapprehend *be* ***camddeall***
misappropriate *be* ***camddefnyddio***
misbehave *be* ***camymddwyn***
misbehaviour *enw* ***camymddygiad*** *hwn*
miscarriage *enw* (justice) ***camweinyddiad cyfiawnder***, ***erthyliad (naturiol)*** *hwn*
miscarry *be* ***erthylu('n naturiol)***
miscellaneous *ans* ***amrywiol***
miscellany *enw* ***amrywiaeth*** *hon*, ***cymysgwch***, ***cymysgedd*** *hwn*
mischance *enw* ***anlwc*** *hwn*
mischief *enw* ***drygioni***, ***drwg*** *hwn*
mischievous *ans* ***drygionus***, ***maleisus***
misconceive *be* ***camdybio***
misconception *enw* ***camdybiaeth*** *hon*, ***camsyniad*** *hwn*
misconduct *enw* ***camymddygiad***, ***camweinyddiad*** *hwn*

misconstrue *be* ***camddehongli***
miscount *be* ***camgyfrif***
miscreant *enw* ***drwgweithredwr*** *hwn*
misdeed *enw* ***trosedd***, ***camwedd*** *hwn*
misdeliver *be* ***camddosbarthu***
misdemeanour *enw* ***camymddygiad*** *hwn*
misdirect *be* ***camgyfeirio***
miser *enw* ***cybydd*** *hwn*
miserable *ans* ***diflas***, ***trist***, ***digalon***
misery *enw* ***diflastod***, ***trueni*** *hwn*
misfeasance *enw* ***camwaith***, ***camweithrediad*** *hwn*
misfortune *enw* ***anlwc*** *hwn*, ***anffawd*** *hon*
misgivings *enw* ***amheuon*** *hyn*
misgovern *be* ***camreoli***
misguided *ans* ***ffôl***, ***cyfeiliornus***
mishandle *be* ***camdrafod***; ***cam-drin***
mishap *enw* ***damwain*** *hon*
mishear *be* ***camglywed***
misinformation *enw* ***twyllwybodaeth*** *hon*
misinstruct *be* ***camgyfarwyddo***
misinterpret *be* ***camddehongli***
misjudge *be* ***camfarnu***
mislay *be* ***colli***
mislead *be* ***camarwain***
misleading *ans* ***camarweiniol***
a m~ impression ***camargraff*** *hwn/hon*
mismanage *be* ***camreoli***
mismanagement *enw* ***camreolaeth*** *hon*
mismatch *be* ***ieuo anghymarus***
misogynist *enw* ***casäwr gwragedd*** *hwn*
misprint *enw* ***gwall argraffu*** *hwn*
mispronunciation *enw* ***camynganiad*** *hwn*
misquote *be* ***camddyfynnu***
misread *be* ***camddarllen***
misrepresent *be* ***camliwio***; ***gwneud cam â***
misrepresentation *enw* ***camliwiad*** *hwn*
Miss *enw* ***Miss***, ***Y Foneddiges (Fng)*** *hon*
miss *be* ***methu***, ***colli***
to m~ someone ***gweld colli rhywun***; ***gweld eisiau***
to only just m~ ***bod ond y dim i***
missile *enw* ***taflegryn*** *hwn*
missing *ans* ***coll***, ***ar goll***
mission *enw* ***perwyl*** *hwn*, ***neges*** *hon*; ***cenhadaeth*** *hon*
missionary *enw* ***cenhadwr*** *hwn*, ***cenhades*** *hon*
misspell *be* ***camsillafu***
mist *enw* ***niwl***, ***tarth*** *hwn*
mistake *enw* ***camgymeriad*** *hwn*
mistake *be* ***camgymryd***
Mister *enw* ***Mister***, ***Y Bonwr (Br)*** *hwn*
mistime *be* ***camamseru***
mistletoe *enw* ***uchelwydd*** *hwn*
mistress *enw* ***meistres*** *hon*

mistrust *enw* ***drwgdybiaeth*** *hon*
mistrust *be* ***drwgdybio***
misty *ans* ***niwlog***
misunderstand *be* ***camddeall***
misunderstanding *enw* ***camddealltwriaeth*** *hon*
misuse *be* ***camddefnyddio***; ***cam-drin***
mite *enw* ***hatling*** *hon*; ***mymryn*** *hwn*; (arachnid) ***gwiddonyn, euddonyn*** *hwn*
mitigate *be* ***lliniaru***, ***lleddfu***
mitigating *ans* ***lliniarol***
mitigation *enw* ***lleddfiad***, ***lliniariad*** *hwn*
mix *be* ***cymysgu***
mixed *ans* ***cymysg***
mixer *enw* ***cymysgydd*** *hwn*
mixture *enw* ***cymysgedd*** *hwn/hon*
moan *enw* ***ochenaid*** *hon*; (grumble) ***cwyn*** *hon*
moan *be* ***ocheneidio***, ***griddfan***; ***cwyno***
moat *enw* ***ffos*** *hon*
mob *enw* ***ciwed***, ***haid*** *hon*
mobile *ans* ***symudol***
mobilize *be* ***cynnull***, ***byddino***
  to m~ resources ***rhoi adnoddau ar waith***
  to m~ the support of ***ennyn cefnogaeth***
mobility *enw* ***symudedd*** *hwn*
mock *be* ***gwatwar***, ***gwawdio***
  m~ examinations ***ffug arholiadau*** *hyn*
mockery *enw* ***gwatwar***, ***gwawd*** *hwn*
mode *enw* ***dull***, ***modd*** *hwn*
  m~ of thinking ***meddylfryd*** *hwn*
model *enw* ***model*** *hwn*
model *be* ***modelu***
moderate *ans* ***cymedrol***, ***rhesymol***; (middling) ***canolig, gweddol***, ***cyffredin***
moderate *be* ***cymedroli***; ***canoli***
moderation *enw* ***cymedroldeb*** *hwn*
modern *ans* ***modern***
  in the m~ world ***yn y byd sydd ohoni***
modernize *be* ***moderneiddio***, ***diweddaru***
modest *ans* ***diymhongar***
  a m~ increase ***rhywfaint o gynnydd***
  of m~ ability ***o allu cyffredin***
modesty *enw* ***gwyleidd-dra*** *hwn*
modicum *enw* ***mymryn*** *hwn*
modification *enw* ***newidiad***, ***addasiad*** *hwn*
modify *be* ***addasu***, ***cyfaddasu***, ***diwygio rhywfaint***
modulate *be* ***trawsgyweirio***
moist *ans* ***llaith***, ***gwlyb***
moisten *be* ***gwlychu***
moisture *enw* ***lleithder*** *hwn*
molar *enw* ***cilddant*** *hwn*
mole *enw* ***gwadd***, ***gwahadden*** *hon*
molecule *enw* ***molecwl*** *hwn*
molehill *enw* ***pridd y wadd*** *hwn*

molest *be* ***aflonyddu***, ***ymyrryd***
mollify *be* ***lliniaru***
mollusc *enw* ***molwsg*** *hwn*
molten *ans* ***tawdd***
moment *enw* ***moment*** *hon*
at that very m~ ***ar y gair***
at the m~ ***ar hyn o bryd***
for the m~ ***am y tro***
in a m~ ***mewn munud***
of any m~ ***o unrhyw bwys***
momentary *ans* ***dros dro***
momentous *ans* ***eithriadol o bwysig***
momentum *enw* ***momentwm*** *hwn*
monarch *enw* ***brenin***, ***teyrn*** *hwn*
monarchist *enw* ***brenhinwr*** *hwn*
monarchy *enw* ***brenhiniaeth*** *hon*
monastery *enw* ***mynachlog*** *hon*
monastic *ans* ***mynachaidd***
Monday *enw* ***Llun*** *hwn*
monetary *ans* ***ariannol***
money *enw* ***arian*** *hwn*
m~ talks ***diwedd y gân yw'r geiniog***
money-box *enw* ***cadw-mi-gei*** *hwn*
mongrel *ans* ***cymysgryw***
monitor *be* ***monitro***; ***cadw llygad barcud ar***
monk *enw* ***mynach*** *hwn*
monkey *enw* ***mwnci*** *hwn*
monochrome *ans* ***unlliw***
monoglot *ans* ***uniaith***
monologue *enw* ***ymson*** *hwn*
monopolize *be* ***monopoleiddio***
monopoly *enw* ***monopoli*** *hwn*
monotonous *ans* ***undonog***
monotony *enw* ***undonedd*** *hwn*
monster *enw* ***anghenfil*** *hwn*
monstrous *ans* ***anferthol***; ***gwarthus***
monsoon *enw* ***monsŵn*** *hwn*
month *enw* ***mis*** *hwn*
monthly *ans* ***misol***
monument *enw* ***cofeb*** *hon*
mood *enw* ***hwyl*** *hon*, ***tymer*** *hwn/hon*, ***ysbryd*** *hwn*
moon *enw* ***lleuad***, ***lloer*** *hon*
moon *be* ***tin-noethi***
moonlight *enw* ***golau lleuad*** *hwn*
moonlit *ans* ***goleu-leuad***, ***lloergan***
moor *enw* ***rhos***, ***gwaun*** *hon*; ***morfa*** *hwn*
moor *be* ***angori***
moorhen *enw* ***iâr fach y dŵr*** *hon*
moorland *enw* ***gweundir*** *hwn*
moral *ans* ***moesol***
morale *enw* ***hyder***, ***ysbryd***, ***morâl*** *hwn*
morality *enw* ***moesoldeb*** *hwn*
morals *enw* ***moesau*** *hyn*
morass *enw* ***mignen*** *hon*
moratorium *enw* ***moratoriwm*** *hwn*
morbid *ans* ***afiach***, ***morbid***
mordant *ans* ***deifiol***
more *ans* ***mwy***, ***ychwaneg***
moreover *adf* ***yn ogystal***, ***at hynny***
moribund *ans* ***marwaidd***
morning *enw* ***bore*** *hwn*
moron *enw* ***ynfytyn*** *hwn*
morose *ans* ***sarrug***

morsel *enw* ***tamaid bach*** *hwn*
mortal *enw* ***meidrolyn*** *hwn*
mortal *ans* ***meidrol***, ***marwol***
to be dealt a m~ blow ***taro yn ei dalcen***
mortality *enw* ***marwolaeth*** *hon*
mortally *adf* ***hyd at angau***, ***yn angheuol***
mortgage *enw* ***morgais*** *hwn*
mortgage *be* ***morgeisio***
mortuary *enw* ***marwdy***, ***corffdy*** *hwn*
mosque *enw* ***mosg*** *hwn*
moss *enw* ***mwsogl***, ***mwswm*** *hwn*
most *adf/ans* ***mwyaf***; ***hynod o***, ***tra/yn dra***
at m~ ***fan bellaf***
m~ of all ***yn bennaf oll***
to make the m~ of ***manteisio i'r eithaf***, ***gwneud y gorau o***
mote *enw* ***brycheuyn*** *hwn*
moth *enw* ***gwyfyn*** *hwn*
mother *enw* ***mam*** *hon*
M~'s Day ***Sul y Mamau*** *hwn*
motherhood *enw* ***mamolaeth*** *hon*, ***bod yn fam***
mother-in-law *enw* ***mam-yng-nghyfraith*** *hon*
motherly *ans* ***mamol***
mother tongue *enw* **mamiaith** *hon*
motif *enw* ***nodwedd***, ***motiff*** *hwn*
motion *enw* (movement) ***symudiad***; ***cynnig*** *hwn*
motionless *ans* ***disymud***, ***llonydd***
motivation *enw* ***ysgogiad***, ***cymhelliad*** *hwn*
motive *enw* ***cymhelliad*** *hwn*
motley *ans* ***brith***
motor *enw* ***motor*** *hwn*
m~ maintenance ***trwsio ceir***
motor vehicle *enw* ***modur***, ***cerbyd*** *hwn*
motor *ans* (med.) ***echddygol***
m~ defect ***diffyg/nam echddygol*** *hwn*
m~ skills ***sgiliau echddygol*** *hyn*
motorbike *enw* ***beic modur*** *hwn*
mottled *ans* ***brith***
motto *enw* ***arwyddair*** *hwn*
mould *enw* (fungus) ***llwydni:llwydi*** *hwn*; ***mowld*** *hwn*
to break the m~ ***torri tir newydd***
mould *be* ***mowldio***
moult *be* ***bwrw (blew***, ***plu***, ***croen)***
mound *enw* ***twmpath*** *hwn*
mount *enw* ***mynydd*** *hwn*
mount *be* ***dringo***, ***esgyn***
mountain *enw* ***mynydd*** *hwn*
mountain ash *enw* ***cerd[d]inen***, ***criafolen*** *hon*
mountaineer *enw* ***mynyddwr*** *hwn*, ***mynyddwraig*** *hon*
mountainous *ans* ***mynyddig***
mourn *be* ***galaru***
mournful *ans* ***galarus***, ***lleddf***
mourning *enw* ***galar*** *hwn*
mouse *enw* ***llygoden*** *hon*
moustache *enw* ***mwstas*** *hwn*
mouth *enw* ***ceg*** *hon*

mouth off *be* ***cega***
mouthful *enw* ***cegaid*** *hon*, ***llond ceg*** *hwn*
mouthpiece *enw* ***cetyn (ceg)***; (spokesman) ***llefarydd*** *hwn*
movable *ans* ***symudol***, ***symudadwy***
move *enw* ***symudiad*** *hwn*
  on the m~ ***ar y/eu ffordd***
move *be* ***symud***; (a motion) ***cynnig***
movement *enw* ***symudiad*** *hwn*
moving *ans* ***gwefreiddiol***, ***cyffrous***; ***yn cyffwrdd â'r galon***
mow *be* ***lladd***, ***torri***
MP *byrfodd* ***AS (Aelod Seneddol)***
mph *byrfodd* ***mya (milltir yr awr)***
Mrs *enw* ***Mrs, Y Fns (Foneddiges)*** *hon*
much *adf/ans* ***llawer***
  they don't think m~ of ***does ganddynt fawr o olwg ar***
  I thought as m~ ***dyna'r oeddwn i'n ei feddwl***
  to do m~ ***cyfrannu'n fawr at***
  to make too m~ of ***gwneud môr a mynydd o***
muck *enw* ***baw*** *hwn*
  to m~ in ***torchi llewys***
muck-spread *be* ***'sgwaru dom***
mucus *enw* ***llysnafedd*** *hwn*
mud *enw* ***llaid***, ***mwd*** *hwn*
muddle *enw* ***dryswch*** *hwn*
muddle *be* ***drysu***
muddy *ans* ***mwdlyd***
muff *be* ***methu***
muffle *be* (sound) ***lleihau***, ***lladd, mygu***
muffled *ans* ***aneglur, distaw***
mug *enw* ***mẁg*** *hwn*
muggy *ans* ***mwll***
mulberry *enw* ***morwydden*** *hon*
mule *enw* ***mul*** *hwn*
multicoloured *ans* ***amryliw***
multicultural *ans* ***amlddiwylliannol***
multidisciplinary *ans* ***amlddisgyblaethol***
multi-ethnic *ans* ***amlhiliol***
multifarious *ans* ***amryfal***
multilingual *ans* ***amlieithog***
multiparty *ans* ***amlbleidiol***
multiple *enw* ***lluosrif*** *hwn*
multiplication *enw* ***lluosi***
multiply *be* ***lluosi***
multi-purpose *ans* ***amlbwrpas***
multisensory *ans* ***amlsynhwyraidd***
multitude *enw* **lliaws** *hwn*, ***tyrfa*** *hon*
mumble *be* ***mwmian***, ***mwmial***
mummy *enw* ***mwmi*** *hwn*
munch *be* ***cnoi***
mundane *ans* ***cyffredin***, ***dinod***
  at a more m~ level ***ar lefel lai dyrchafedig***
municipal *ans* ***bwrdeistrefol***, ***trefol***
municipality *enw* ***bwrdeistref*** *hon*
mural *enw* ***murlun*** *hwn*
murder *enw* ***llofruddiaeth*** *hon*
murder *be* ***llofruddio***
murderer *enw* ***llofrudd*** *hwn*
murky *ans* ***tywyll***, ***lleidiog***

murmur *enw* ***murmur***, ***su*** *hwn*
murmur *be* ***sibrwd***, ***suo***
muscle *enw* ***cyhyr*** *hwn*
muscular *ans* ***cyhyrog***
muse *enw* ***awen*** *hon*
muse *be* ***pendroni***
museum *enw* ***amgueddfa*** *hon*
mushrooms *enw* ***madarch*** *hyn*
music *enw* ***cerddoriaeth*** *hon*
musical *ans* ***cerddorol***
musician *enw* ***cerddor*** *hwn*
mussel *enw* ***cragen las***, ***misglen*** *hon*
must *be* ***rhaid***, ***bod yn rhwym o***
mustard *enw* ***mwstard*** *hwn*
muster *be* ***crynhoi***
musty *ans* ***wedi llwydo***
mutate *be* ***newid***; (gram.) ***treiglo***
mutation *enw* ***newidiad***; (gram.) ***treiglad*** *hwn*
mute *ans* ***mud***
mutilate *be* ***llurgunio***, ***difrodi***
mutilation *enw* ***llurguniad*** *hwn*
mutiny *enw* ***gwrthryfel*** *hwn*
mutiny *be* ***gwrthryfela***
mutter *be* ***mwmian***, ***dweud dan eich anadl***
mutual *ans* ***eich gilydd***, ***y naill a'r llall***, ***cilyddol***
muzzy *ans* ***aneglur***
my *rhag* ***fy***
myopia *enw* ***golwg byr*** *hwn*
myriad *enw* ***myrdd*** *hwn*, ***llond gwlad o***
myrrh *enw* ***myrr*** *hwn*
myself *rhag* ***myfi fy hun***
mysterious *ans* ***rhyfedd***, ***dirgel***
mystery *enw* ***dirgelwch*** *hwn*
mystic *enw* ***cyfrinydd*** *hwn*
mystic *ans* ***cyfrin***
mystical *ans* ***cyfriniol***
mysticism *enw* ***cyfriniaeth*** *hon*
mystify *be* ***synnu***
mystique *enw* ***dirgelwch*** *hwn*
myth *enw* ***myth*** *hwn*
mythological *ans* ***mytholegol***
mythology *enw* ***mytholeg*** *hon*

N

nab *be* ***dal***, ***dala***
nadir *enw* ***isafbwynt*** *hwn*
nag *be* ***swnian***, ***cwyno***, ***cadw sŵn***
nail *enw* ***hoelen*** *hon*; ***ewin*** *hwn*
nail *be* ***hoelio***
nail-biting *ans* ***dirdynnol***
naïve *ans* ***diniwed***
naked *ans* ***noeth***
name *enw* ***enw*** *hwn*
name *be* ***enwi***
nameless *ans* ***dienw***
namely *adf* ***sef***
nanny goat *enw* ***gafr*** *hon*
nap *enw* ***cyntun*** *hwn*
nape *enw* ***gwar*** *hwn/hon*, ***gwegil*** *hwn*
napkin *enw* ***napcyn*** *hwn*
nappy *enw* ***cewyn***, ***clwt*** *hwn*
narcissus *enw* ***croeso'r gwanwyn*** *hwn*
narrate *be* ***adrodd***, ***traethu***
narrative *enw* ***traethiad***, ***naratif*** *hwn*
narrator *enw* ***adroddwr***, ***datgeinydd*** *hwn*
narrow *ans* ***cul***, ***main***
  narrow escape ***cael a chael***
narrow *be* ***culhau***, ***cyfyngu***
narrow-minded *ans* ***cul***
narrowness *enw* ***culni*** *hwn*
nasal *ans* ***trwynol***
nasty *ans* ***cas***, ***brwnt***
nation *enw* ***cenedl*** *hon*
national *ans* (of nation) ***cenedlaethol***; (of state) ***gwladol***
  N~ Assembly for Wales ***Cynulliad Cenedlaethol Cymru*** *hwn*
nationalism *enw* ***cenedlaetholdeb*** *hwn*
nationalist *enw* ***cenedlaetholwr*** *hwn*, ***cenedlaetholwraig*** *hon*
nationalist *ans* ***cenedlaetholgar***
nationality *enw* ***cenedligrwydd*** *hwn*
nationalize *be* ***cenedlaetholi***, ***gwladoli***
nationhood *enw* ***cenedligrwydd*** *hwn*
nationwide *ans* ***trwy Gymru/ Brydain gyfan***
native *enw* **brodor** *hwn*, ***brodores*** *hon*
native *ans* ***brodorol***
natter *be* ***rwdlan***, ***browlan***
natty *ans* ***sbriws***
natural *ans* ***naturiol***
naturalist *enw* ***naturiaethwr*** *hwn*, ***naturiaethwraig*** *hon*
nature *enw* ***natur***, ***anian*** *hon*
naughty *ans* ***drwg***
nausea *enw* ***cyfog*** *hwn*
nauseous *ans* ***cyfoglyd***
naval *ans* ***morol***, ***morwrol***
nave *enw* ***corff yr eglwys*** *hwn*
navel *enw* ***bogail*** *hwn*

n

navigate *be* ***mordwyo***; (the Internet) ***symud drwy'r testun***
navigation enw ***mordwyaeth*** hon
navigator *enw* ***llywiwr*** *hwn*
navy *enw* ***llynges*** *hon*
Nazi *enw* ***Natsi*** *hwn*
near *adf/ardd* ***yn agos***, ***bron***, ***ar gyfyl***
near *be* ***tynnu at***, ***agosáu at***
nearby *adf* ***gerllaw***, ***yn y cyffiniau***
nearly *adf* ***bron***
not n~ as good ***nid yw hanner cystal***
neat *ans* ***taclus***, ***twt***, ***pert***
nebula *enw* ***nifwl*** *hwn*
nebulous *ans* ***annelwig***, ***niwlog***
necessary *ans* ***angenrheidiol***
necessitate *be* ***gwneud yn angenrheidiol***, ***golygu bod rhaid***
necessity *enw* ***anghenraid***, ***rheidrwydd*** *hwn*
of n~ ***o raid***, ***gorfod***
neck *enw* ***gwddf*** *hwn*
necklace *enw* ***cadwyn am y gwddf*** *hon*
nectar *enw* ***neithdar*** *hwn*
need *enw* ***angen***, ***eisiau*** *hwn*
need *be* ***bod ag angen***
needle *enw* ***nodwydd*** *hon*
needless *ans* ***diachos***, ***afraid***, ***diangen***, ***di-alw-amdano***
needlewoman *enw* ***gwniadwraig*** *hon*
needlework *enw* ***gwniadwaith*** *hwn*
needy *ans* ***anghenus***
nefarious *ans* ***ysgeler***, ***anfad***
negate *be* ***negyddu***, ***dileu***, ***diddymu***
negation *enw* ***nacâd*** *hwn*
negative *enw* ***negydd*** *hwn*
negative *ans* ***negyddol***
neglect *enw* ***esgeulustra*** *hwn*
neglect *be* ***esgeuluso***
neglectful *ans* ***esgeulus***
negligence *enw* ***esgeulustod*** *hwn*
negligent *ans* ***esgeulus***
negligible *ans* ***bron dim***, ***heb fawr ddim***
negotiate *be* ***trafod***; ***sicrhau***; ***goresgyn***
to n~ a bend ***cymryd tro***
negotiation *enw* ***trafodaeth*** *hon*
neigh *be* ***gweryru***
neighbour *enw* ***cymydog*** *hwn*, ***cymdoges*** *hon*
neighbourhood *enw* ***bro***, ***cymdogaeth*** *hon*
neighbouring *ans* ***cyfagos***
neither *cysyllt* ***na:nac***
neon *enw* ***neon*** *hwn*
nephew *enw* ***nai*** *hwn*
nepotism *enw* ***nepotistiaeth*** *hon*
Neptune *enw* ***Neifion*** *hwn*
nerve *enw* ***nerf*** *hon/hwn*
nervous *ans* ***nerfus***, ***ar bigau drain***
nest *enw* ***nyth*** *hwn/hon*
nest *be* ***nythu***
nestle *be* ***cwtsio***, ***swatio***
net *enw* ***rhwyd*** *hon*

net *be* ***rhwydo***
netball *enw* ***pêl-rwyd*** *hon*
nethermost *ans* ***isaf***
nettle *enw* ***danhadlen*** *hon*
network *enw* ***rhwydwaith*** *hwn*
networking *enw* ***rhwydweithio***
neuter *be* ***sbaddu***
neutral *ans* ***niwtral***
neutrality *enw* ***niwtraliaeth*** *hon*
neutralize *be* ***niwtraleiddio***
neutron *enw* ***niwtron*** *hwn*
never *adf* ***byth***, ***erioed***, ***byth bythoedd***
nevertheless *adf* ***serch hynny***
new *ans* ***newydd***
  to be n~ to ***heb fod yn gyfarwydd â***
newborn *ans* ***newydd-anedig***
newcomer *enw* ***newydd-ddyfodiad*** *hwn*
new look *enw* ***newydd wedd*** *hon*
news *enw* ***newyddion*** *hyn*
newsletter *enw* ***cylchlythyr*** *hwn*
newspaper *enw* ***papur newydd*** *hwn*
newt *enw* ***madfall y dŵr*** *hwn*
New Year *enw* ***Blwyddyn Newydd*** *hon*
New Year's Day *enw* ***Dydd Calan*** *hwn*
New Year's Eve *enw* ***Nos Galan*** *hon*
next *ans* ***nesaf***, ***wedyn***
  n~ to no time ***mewn dim o dro***
nexus *enw* ***rhwydwaith*** *hwn*
nibble *be* ***deintio***, ***cnoi***
nice *ans* ***dymunol***, ***hyfryd***
niche *enw* ***cilfach*** *hon*, **safle** *hwn/hon*
nickname *enw* ***llysenw*** *hwn*
nickname *be* ***llysenwi***
nicotine *enw* ***nicotîn*** *hwn*
niece *enw* ***nith*** *hon*
niggardly *ans* ***tyn***, ***cybyddlyd***
niggle *be* ***hollti blew***; ***pryfocio***
nigh *adf* ***gerllaw***, ***ar ddigwydd***
night *enw* ***nos***, ***noson*** *hon*
  good n~ ***nos da***
nightclub *enw* ***clwb nos*** *hwn*
nightdress *enw* ***crys nos*** *hwn*, ***coban*** *hon*
nightingale *enw* ***eos*** *hon*
nightly *ans* ***nosol***
nightly *adf* ***beunos***
nightmare *enw* ***hunllef*** *hon*
nightshade *enw* ***codwarth du*** *hwn*
nil *enw* ***dim*** *hwn*; ***prin iawn***, ***bach iawn***
nimble *ans* ***chwim***, ***heini***, ***sionc***
nimbus *enw* (halo) ***corongylch*** *hwn*
nine *rhifol* ***naw***
nineteen *rhifol* ***pedwar*** *hwn/****pedair*** *hon* ***ar bymtheg***
nineteenth *ans* ***pedwerydd*** *hwn/* ***pedwaredd*** *hon* ***ar bymtheg***
ninetieth *ans* ***naw degfed***
ninety *rhifol* ***naw deg***
ninth *ans* ***nawfed***
nip *be* ***brathu***

n

nipple *enw* ***teth*** *hon*
nippy *ans* (cold) ***oer***; (fast) ***chwim***
nit *enw* ***nedden*** *hon*
nitrate *enw* ***nitrad*** *hwn*
nitrogen *enw* ***nitrogen*** *hwn*
nitwit *enw* ***hurtyn*** *hwn*
no *ans* ***dim***
no *adf* ***na***, ***ni***
nobility *enw* ***bonedd*** *hwn*
noble *ans* ***bonheddig***, ***urddasol***, ***dyrchafedig***
nobleman *enw* ***uchelwr*** *hwn*
nobody *rhag* ***neb***
nocturnal *ans* ***nosol***
nod *enw* ***amnaid*** *hon*
nod *be* ***amneidio***
node *enw* ***cwlwm*** *hwn*
nodule *enw* ***cnepyn*** *hwn*
noise *enw* ***sŵn***, ***twrw*** *hwn*
noisiness *enw* ***sŵn***, ***twrw*** *hwn*
noisy *ans* ***swnllyd***, ***uchel eu cloch***
nomad *enw* ***crwydryn*** *hwn*
nom de plume *enw* ***ffugenw*** *hwn*
nominal *ans* ***mewn enw***
nominate *be* ***enwebu***, ***cynnig enw***
nomination *enw* ***enwebiad*** *hwn*
nominator *enw* ***enwebydd*** *hwn*
nominee *enw* ***enwebai*** *hwn*
non-aligned *ans* ***anymochrol***
non-alignment *enw* ***anymochredd*** *hwn*
nonchalant *ans* ***didaro***
nonconformist *ans* ***anghydffurfiol***
Nonconformity *enw* ***Anghydffurfiaeth***, ***Ymneilltuaeth*** *hon*
non-confrontational *ans* ***di-wrthdaro***
Non-Departmental Public Body *enw* ***Corff Cyhoeddus Anadrannol*** *hwn*
non-discriminatory *ans* ***anwahaniaethol***
non-domestic rates *enw* ***trethi busnes*** *hyn*
none *rhag* ***dim un***
non-feasance *enw* ***anwaith***, ***gomeddiad*** *hwn*
non-fiction *enw* ***llyfrau ffeithiol*** *hyn*
nonentity *enw* ***neb o bwys*** *hwn*
nonetheless *adf* ***serch hynny***
nonplussed *ans* ***syn***, ***syfrdan***
  to be n~ ***cael eich bwrw oddi ar eich echel***
non-political *ans* ***amhleidiol***
non-responsive *ans* ***diymateb***
nonsense *enw* ***dwli*** *hwn*, ***lol*** *hon*, ***ffwlbri*** *hwn*
nonsensical *ans* ***gwirion***, ***hurt***
non sequitur ***nid yw'n dilyn***
non-standard *ans* ***ansafonol***
non-stop *ans* ***di-baid***, ***syth***
non-violent *ans* ***di-drais***
non-vocational *ans* ***analwedigaethol***
non-Welsh speaking *ans* ***di-Gymraeg***
nook *enw* ***cilfach*** *hon*

every n~ and cranny ***pob twll a chornel***
noon *enw* ***canol dydd***, ***hanner dydd*** *hwn*
no one *rhag* ***neb***
nor *cysyllt* ***na:nac***
norm *enw* ***norm*** *hwn*
normal *ans* ***arferol***, ***rheolaidd***
Norman *ans* ***Normanaidd***
north *enw* ***gogledd*** *hwn*
north-east *enw* ***gogledd-ddwyrain*** *hwn*
northern *ans* ***gogleddol***
north-west *enw* ***gogledd-orllewin*** *hwn*
nose *enw* ***trwyn*** *hwn*
nosey *ans* ***busneslyd***
nostalgia *enw* ***hiraeth*** *hwn*
nostril *enw* ***ffroen*** *hon*
not *adf* ***heb***, ***na:nad***, ***ni:nid***
notable *ans* ***nodedig***, ***hynod***
notch *enw* ***hac***, ***rhic*** *hwn*
note *enw* ***nodyn*** *hwn*
worthy of n~ ***yn haeddu sylw***
note *be* ***nodi***, ***sylwi ar***
notebook *enw* ***llyfr nodiadau*** *hwn*
nothing *enw* ***dim byd*** *hwn*
if n~ else ***yn un peth***
little or n~ ***fawr o ddim***
notice *enw* ***rhybudd***, ***hysbysiad*** *hwn*
at very short n~ ***heb fawr o rybudd***
notice *be* ***sylwi***
noticeable *ans* ***amlwg***, ***i'w weld***
notification *enw* ***hysbysiad*** *hwn*
notify *be* ***hysbysu***, ***rhoi gwybod***
notion *enw* ***syniad***, ***amcan*** *hwn*
notoriety *enw* ***enwogrwydd*** *hwn*; ***enw drwg*** *hwn*
notorious *ans* ***ag enw drwg***, ***diarhebol***
notwithstanding *ardd* ***er gwaethaf***
noun *enw* ***enw*** *hwn*
nourish *be* ***meithrin***
nourishment *enw* ***maeth*** *hwn*
novel *enw* ***nofel*** *hon*
novelty *enw* ***newyddbeth*** *hwn*
November *enw* ***Tachwedd*** *hwn*
novice *enw* ***newyddian*** *hwn/hon*, ***rhywun dibrofiad***
now *adf* ***yn awr***, ***heddiw***
for n~ ***am y tro***
from n~ on ***o hyn allan/ymlaen***
until n~ ***cyn hyn***, ***hyd yn hyn***, ***tan heddiw***
nowadays *adf* ***heddiw***, ***erbyn heddiw***, ***y dyddiau hyn***
nowhere *adf* ***yn unman***
they were n~ to be seen ***doedd dim sôn amdanynt***
to get n~ ***mynd i'r gwellt***
noxious *ans* ***niweidiol***, ***andwyol***
nuance *enw* ***arlliw*** *hwn*
nub *enw* (of question) ***craidd***, ***hanfod*** *hwn*
nuclear *ans* ***niwclear***
nude *ans* ***noeth***, ***noethlymun***
nudge *be* ***pwnio***
nudity *enw* ***noethni*** *hwn*

n

nuisance *enw* ***digon o farn***, ***poendod*** *hwn*
null and void *ans* ***di-rym***
nullity *enw* ***dirymedd*** *hwn*
numb *ans* ***dideimlad***
numb *be* ***merwino***, ***fferru***
number *enw* ***rhif*** *hwn*, ***nifer*** *hwn/hon*
number *be* ***cyfrif***, ***rhifo***
number crunching *enw* ***ymhél â ffigurau***
numbness *enw* ***merwindod***, ***diffyg teimlad*** *hwn*
numeracy *enw* ***rhifedd*** *hon*
numeral *enw* ***rhifol*** *hwn*; ***rhif***, ***rhifolyn*** *hwn*
numerical *ans* ***rhifol***
numerous *ans* ***niferus***, ***amryw byd o***
  on n~ occasions ***droeon***
nun *enw* ***lleian*** *hon*
nurse *enw* ***nyrs*** *hon/hwn*
nurse *be* ***nyrsio***
nursery *enw* ***meithrinfa*** *hon*
nursery rhyme *enw* ***hwiangerdd*** *hon*
nurture *be* ***meithrin***, ***magu***
nut *enw* ***cneuen*** *hon*
nutcracker *enw* ***gefel gnau*** *hon*
nutritious *ans* ***maethlon***
nutshell *enw* ***plisgyn***, ***masgl (cneuen)*** *hwn*
  in a n~ ***mewn gair***
nylon *enw* ***neilon*** *hwn*

O

oaf *enw* ***llabwst, llo*** *hwn*
oak *enw* ***derwen*** *hon*
oaken *ans* ***derw***
oar *enw* ***rhwyf*** *hon*
oarsman *enw* ***rhwyfwr*** *hwn*
oasis *enw* ***gwerddon*** *hon*
oatcake *enw* ***bara ceirch*** *hwn*
oath *enw* ***llw*** *hwn*
oatmeal *enw* ***blawd ceirch*** *hwn*
oats *enw* ***ceirch*** *hyn*
obdurate *ans* ***cyndyn***, ***ystyfnig***
obedience *enw* ***ufudd-dod*** *hwn*
obedient *ans* ***ufudd***
obeisance *enw* ***gwrogaeth*** *hon*
obese *ans* ***gordew***
obesity *enw* ***gordewdra*** *hwn*
obey *be* ***ufuddhau***
obfuscate *be* ***cawlio***, ***drysu***
obituary *enw* ***ysgrif goffa*** *hon*
 the o~ column ***colofn y marwolaethau*** *hon*
object *enw* ***gwrthrych*** *hwn*
object *be* ***gwrthwynebu***
objection *enw* ***gwrthwynebiad*** *hwn*
objectionable *ans* ***atgas***
objective *enw* ***nod*** *hwn/hon*
 with the o~ of ***gan geisio***
objective *ans* ***gwrthrychol***
objectivity *enw* ***gwrthrychedd*** *hwn*
objector *enw* ***gwrthwynebydd***, ***gwrthwynebwr*** *hwn*
obligation *enw* ***gorfodaeth*** *hon*, ***rheidrwydd*** *hwn*, ***rhwymedigaeth*** *hon*
obligatory *ans* ***gorfodol***
oblige *be* ***gorfodi***; ***gwneud tro da***
 to be o~d to ***bod rheidrwydd ar***
obliging *ans* ***cymwynasgar***
oblique *ans* ***lletraws***, ***ar osgo***
obliquely adf ***ar letraws***; (= indirectly) ***yn anuniongyrchol***
obliterate *be* ***dileu***
oblivion *enw* ***ebargofiant*** *hwn*
oblivious *ans* ***heb sylwi***
oblong *ans/enw* ***petryal***, ***hirsgwar*** (*hwn*)
obnoxious *ans* ***ffiaidd***
oboe *enw* ***obo*** *hwn*
obscene *ans* ***anweddus***, ***anllad***
obscenity *enw* ***anlladrwydd*** *hwn*
obscure *ans* ***aneglur***, ***tywyll***; ***di-nod***, ***di-sôn-amdanynt***
obscure *be* ***cuddio***, ***tywyllu***
obscurity *enw* ***dinodedd***, ***tywyllwch*** *hwn*
obsequious *ans* ***gwasaidd***
observant *ans* ***sylwgar***
observation *enw* ***sylw*** *hwn*
observatory *enw* ***arsyllfa*** *hon*
observe *be* ***cadw***, ***gwylio***, ***arsylwi***
 to o~ a principle ***parchu egwyddor***
observer *enw* ***sylwedydd*** *hwn*
obsession *enw* ***obsesiwn*** *hwn*
obsessive *ans* ***obsesiynol***

O

obsolete *ans* ***wedi hen ddarfod***, ***darfodedig***
obstacle *enw* ***rhwystr*** *hwn*
obstinate *ans* ***ystyfnig***, ***pengaled***
obstreperous *ans* ***cegog***
obstruct *be* ***rhwystro***, ***cau***
obstruction *enw* ***rhwystr*** *hwn*; ***tagfa*** *hon*
obtain *be* ***cael***, ***ennill***
obtainable *ans* ***ar gael***
obtrusive *ans* ***goramlwg***
obtuse *ans* ***twp***
o~ angle ***ongl aflem*** *hon*
obviate *be* ***cael gwared ar***
obvious *ans* ***amlwg***
to make o~ ***amlygu***
occasion *enw* ***achlysur*** *hwn*
occasion *be* ***achosi***
occasional *ans* ***achlysurol***, ***o dro i dro***
occult *ans* ***goruwchnaturiol***
occupant *enw* ***deiliad*** *hwn*
occupation *enw* (work) ***gwaith*** *hwn*, **swydd** *hon*; ***deiliadaeth*** *hon*; ***meddiannu***
occupy *be* ***meddiannu***
to o~ the attention of ***mynd â sylw/bryd***
occur *be* ***codi***, ***digwydd***, ***taro***
occurrence *enw* ***digwyddiad*** *hwn*
ocean *enw* ***cefnfor*** *hwn*
oceanic *ans* ***cefnforol***
o'clock *adf* ***o'r gloch***
October *enw* ***Hydref*** *hwn*
octopus *enw* ***octopws*** *hwn*
odd *ans* ***od***, ***rhyfedd***
the o~ one out ***yr un sy'n wahanol i'r lleill***
o~ number ***odrif*** *hwn*
oddness *enw* ***odrwydd*** *hwn*
odious *ans* ***ffiaidd***, ***anghynnes***
odium *enw* ***atgasedd*** *hwn*
odour *enw* ***aroglau***, ***oglau*** *hwn*
oesophagus *enw* ***pibell fwyd*** *hon*
of *ardd* ***o***
off *adf* ***ymaith***, ***i ffwrdd***
offbeat *ans* ***hynod***, ***gogleisiol***
offence *enw* ***trosedd*** *hwn/hon*; ***tramgwydd*** *hwn*
offend *be* ***pechu***, ***tramgwyddo***, ***digio***; ***troseddu***
they won't be o~ed ***ni fyddant dim dicach***
offender *enw* ***drwgweithredwr***, ***troseddwr*** *hwn*
offensive *ans* ***ymosodol***; ***sarhaus***, ***annymunol***
offer *enw* ***cynnig*** *hwn*
offer *be* ***cynnig***
offeree *enw* ***cynigai*** *hwn*
offeror *enw* ***cynigiwr*** *hwn*
offhand *ans* ***diserch***, ***surbwch***
office *enw* ***swyddfa***; ***swydd*** *hon*
through the good o~s of ***drwy garedigrwydd***
officer *enw* ***swyddog*** *hwn*
official *ans* ***swyddogol***
officiate *be* ***gweinyddu***, ***gweinidogaethu***; ***dyfarnu***
off-line *ans* ***all-lein***

offset *be* ***gwrthbwyso***, ***gwneud iawn yn rhannol***
offshore *ans* ***ar y môr***
offside (to be) *be* ***camsefyll***
offspring *enw* ***epil*** *hyn*, ***hil*** *hon*
off-the-shelf *ans* ***parod***
often *adf* ***yn aml***
ogle *be* ***llygadu***
oil *enw* ***olew*** *hwn*
oil *be* ***iro***
oil painting *enw* ***darlun olew*** *hwn*
oil tanker *enw* ***tancer olew*** *hwn/hon*
ointment *enw* ***eli*** *hwn*
O.K. *ebychiad* ***iawn! i'r dim!***
old *ans* ***hen***
  any o~ how ***rywsut rywfodd***
old age *enw* ***henaint*** *hwn*
old-fashioned *ans* ***henffasiwn***
  to become o~ ***chwythu eu plwc***
old hand *enw* ***hen law*** *hon*
old maid *enw* ***hen ferch*** *hon*
olive *enw* ***ffrwyth yr olewydd*** *hwn*
olive oil *enw* ***olew olewydd*** *hwn*
omelette *enw* ***omled*** *hwn/hon*
omen *enw* ***argoel*** *hon*
omission *enw* ***hepgoriad***, ***esgeulustod***, ***diffyg*** *hwn*
omit *be* ***gadael allan***, ***hepgor***
on *ardd* ***ar***
on *adf* ***ymlaen***
once *adf* ***unwaith***, ***ar un adeg***
  o~ in a lifetime ***unwaith mewn oes***
  o~ they have ***cyn gynted ag y byddant wedi***
  o~ understood ***o'u deall***
  too many things at o~ ***gormod o heyrn yn y tân***
one *rhifol* ***un***
  at any o~ time ***ar unrhyw adeg benodol***
  o~ day ***ryw ddydd***
  o~ member one vote ***un aelod un bleidlais***
  o~-off ***unigol***, ***un tro'n unig***
  o~ of the best ***gyda'r goreuon***
  o~-stop shop ***gwasanaeth cynhwysfawr*** *hwn*
  to o~ side ***i'r naill ochr***
onerous *ans* ***beichus***, ***trwm***
one-sided *ans* ***unochrog***
one-way *ans* ***unffordd***
ongoing *ans* ***parhaus***, ***yn parhau***
onion *enw* ***wynionyn*** *hwn*
  to know one's o~s ***gwybod be 'di be***
online *ans* ***ar-lein***
onlooker *enw* ***gwyliwr*** *hwn*
only *ans* ***unig***
only *adf* ***dim ond***, ***yn unig***
onset *enw* ***dyfodiad*** *hwn*
onus *enw* ***cyfrifoldeb*** *hwn*
opaque *ans* ***afloyw***, ***didraidd***
open *ans* ***agored***
open *be* ***agor***
opencast coal *enw* ***glo brig*** *hwn*
open-ended *ans* ***penagored***
opening *enw* ***agoriad*** *hwn*
open-minded *ans* ***â meddwl agored***

openness *enw* ***natur agored*** *hon*
opera *enw* ***opera*** *hon*
operate *be* ***gweithio***, ***gweithredu***
operation *enw* ***llawdriniaeth*** *hon*; ***gweithrediad*** *hwn*
operational *ans* ***gweithredol***
operator *enw* ***gweithiwr***, ***gweithredwr*** *hwn*
ophthalmologist *enw* ***offthalmolegydd*** *hwn*
opine *be* ***barnu***, ***tybio***
opinion *enw* ***barn*** *hon*
  opinion-formers ***pobl ddylanwadol eu barn***
opinion poll *enw* ***pôl piniwn***, ***arolwg barn*** *hwn*
opponent *enw* ***gwrthwynebydd*** *hwn*
opportune *ans* ***amserol***, ***cyfleus***
  an o~ time ***cyfle da i***
opportunity *enw* ***cyfle*** *hwn*
oppose *be* ***gwrthwynebu***
  as o~d to ***yn hytrach na***, ***o'i gymharu â***
opposing *ans* ***gwrthwynebus***
opposite *ans* ***cyferbyn***; ***gwrthwyneb***
  people of o~ sexes ***pobl o'r ddau ryw***
opposition *enw* ***gwrthwynebiad*** *hwn*
oppress *be* ***gormesu***
oppressive *ans* ***gormesol***
opt *be* ***dewis***
optician *enw* ***optegydd*** *hwn*
optimism *enw* ***optimistiaeth*** *hon*
optimist *enw* ***optimydd*** *hwn*
optimistic *ans* ***optimistaidd***, ***ffyddiog***
optimum *ans* ***gorau posibl***, ***mwyaf manteisiol***
option *enw* ***dewis*** *hwn*
optional *ans* ***dewisol***
opt out *be* ***eithrio***
opulent *ans* ***cyfoethog***, ***godidog***
or *cysyllt* ***neu***
oracy *enw* ***llafaredd*** *hon*
oral *ans* ***llafar***, ***geneuol***
orange *enw* ***oren*** *hon*
oration *enw* ***araith*** *hon*
orator *enw* ***areithiwr*** *hwn*
oratory *enw* ***areithyddiaeth*** *hon*
orbit *enw* ***cylchdro***, ***dalgylch*** *hwn*
orchard *enw* ***perllan*** *hon*
orchestra *enw* ***cerddorfa*** *hon*
orchid *enw* ***tegeirian*** *hwn*
ordain *be* ***ordeinio***
order *enw* ***gorchymyn*** *hwn*; ***trefn*** *hon*; ***archeb*** *hon*
  higher o~ skills ***uwch-fedrau*** *hyn*
  out of o~ ***ddim yn gweithio***; ***annerbyniol***
order *be* ***gorchymyn***; ***trefnu***; ***archebu***; ***gosod mewn trefn***
orderly *ans* ***trefnus***
ordinal *ans* ***trefnol***
ordinals *enw* ***trefnolion*** *hyn*
ordinary *ans* ***cyffredin***

Ordnance Survey *enw* ***yr Arolwg Ordnans*** *hwn*
ore *enw* ***mwyn*** *hwn*
organ *enw* ***organ*** *hon*
organic *ans* ***organaidd***
organism *enw* ***organedd*** *hwn*, ***organeb*** *hon*
organist *enw* ***organydd*** *hwn*
organization *enw* ***mudiad*** *hwn*; ***trefnu***
organizational *ans* ***trefniadaethol***
organize *be* ***trefnu***
organizer *enw* ***trefnydd*** *hwn*
Orient *enw* ***y Dwyrain*** *hwn*
oriental *ans* ***dwyreiniol***
orienteer *be* ***cyfeiriannu***
orifice *enw* ***twll*** *hwn*
origin *enw* ***dechreuad***, ***tarddiad***, ***gwraidd*** *hwn*
original *ans* ***gwreiddiol***
originality *enw* ***gwreiddioldeb*** *hwn*
originate *be* ***cychwyn***, ***tarddu***
ornament *enw* ***addurn*** *hwn*
ornate *ans* ***addurnedig***
orphan *ans* ***amddifad***
orphan *enw* ***plentyn amddifad*** *hwn*
orthodox *ans* ***uniongred***
orthography *enw* ***orgraff*** *hon*
oscillate *be* ***pendilio***
osprey *enw* ***gwalch y pysgod*** *hwn*
ossify *be* ***ymgaregu***
ostensibly *adf* ***yn ôl pob golwg***
ostentation *enw* ***rhodres*** *hwn*
ostrich *enw* ***estrys*** *hwn/hon*
other *ans/rhag* ***arall***, ***llall***, ***amgen***
  o~ than ***ac eithrio***, ***ar wahân i***
  some are better than o~s ***mae rhai yn well na'i gilydd***
  the o~ day ***pa ddydd***
  the o~ side of the hedge ***am y clawdd â***
  the o~ side of the world ***pen draw'r byd***
otherwise *adf* ***fel arall***
otter *enw* ***dyfrgi*** *hwn*
ounce *enw* ***owns*** *hon*
our *rhag* ***ein***
ourselves *rhag* ***ni ein hunain***
oust *be* ***disodli***
out *adf* ***allan***, ***maes***
  o~ of breath ***â'i gwynt yn ei dwrn***
  o~ of date ***ar ei hôl hi***, ***hen***
  o~ of hand ***dros ben llestri***
  o~ of order ***ddim yn gweithio***; ***annerbyniol***
  o~ of place ***amhriodol***, ***anaddas***
  o~ of reach ***y tu hwnt i gyrraedd***
out and out *ans* ***rhonc***
outburst *enw* ***ffrwydrad*** *hwn*
outcome *enw* ***canlyniad***, ***ffrwyth***; (of learning task) ***deilliant*** *hwn*
outcomes *enw* ***deilliannau*** *hyn*
outdistance *be* ***bod ymhell ar y blaen i***
outdo *be* ***rhagori ar***
outdoor *ans* ***awyr agored***, ***allanol***

O

outer *ans* ***allanol***
o~ space ***y gofod pell*** *hwn*
outfit *enw* ***dillad*** *hyn*
outgoing *ans* ***ymadawol***; ***rhadlon***; ***allblyg***
outhouse *enw* ***tŷ allan*** *hwn*
outlay *enw* ***gwariant*** *hwn*; ***traul*** *hon*
outline *enw* ***amlinelliad***, ***braslun*** *hwn*
outlive *be* ***goroesi***
outlook *enw* ***rhagolwg*** *hwn*
output *enw* ***allgynnyrch***, ***cynnyrch***; (of computer) ***allbwn*** *hwn*
outrage *enw* ***gwarth*** *hwn*
outrage *be* ***gwylltio***, ***cythruddo***
outreach *enw* ***allgymorth*** *hwn*
outright *adf* ***yn llwyr***, ***yn syth***
outright *ans* ***llwyr***
outset *enw* ***dechrau*** *hwn*
outside *enw/adf* ***tu allan***
outskirts *enw* ***cyrion*** *hyn*
outsource *be* ***contractio gwaith allan***
outspoken *ans* ***di-flewyn ar dafod***
outstanding *ans* ***nodedig***; ***heb eto ei gyflawni***
o~ problems ***problemau heb eu datrys***
o~ success ***llwyddiant ysgubol*** *hwn*
outstrip *be* ***trechu***
outward *ans* ***allanol***
outweigh *be* ***bod yn bwysicach na***
outwit *be* ***bod yn drech na***
oval *ans* ***hirgrwn***
ovary *enw* ***ofari*** *hwn/hon*
ovation *enw* ***cymeradwyaeth*** *hon*
oven *enw* ***ffwrn*** *hon*, ***popty*** *hwn*
over *ardd* ***uwch***, ***dros***, ***ar ben***
over *ans* ***gor-***, ***rhy***
overall *adf* ***at ei gilydd***, ***ar y cyfan***
overarching *ans* ***rhychwantol***
overbalance *be* ***cwympo drosodd***
overbearing *ans* ***trahaus***
overburden *be* ***gorlwytho***; ***gosod gormod o faich ar***
overcast *ans* ***cymylog***
overcharge *be* ***codi gormod***
overcoat *enw* ***cot fawr*** *hon*
overcome *be* ***goresgyn***, ***trechu***
overcrowding *be* ***gordyrru***
overdo *be* ***gorwneud***
overdraft *enw* ***gorddrafft*** *hwn*
overdue *ans* ***hwyr***, ***hen bryd***
overestimate *be* ***goramcangyfrif***
overflow *enw* ***gorlifiad*** *hwn*
o~ car park ***parc ceir wrth gefn***
overflow *be* ***gorlifo***
overhaul *enw* ***archwiliad*** *hwn*, ***atgyweirio***
overhead *ans* ***uwchben***
overhead projector *enw* ***uwchdaflunydd*** *hwn*
overheads *enw* ***gorbenion*** *hyn*
overland *ans* ***traws gwlad***
overlap *be* ***gorgyffwrdd***
overload *be* ***gorlwytho***

overlook *be* ***edrych dros***; ***esgeuluso***, ***colli golwg***
overnight *adf* ***dros nos***
overpower *be* ***trechu***
overpowering *ans* ***llethol***
overrate *be* ***gorbrisio***, ***gorganmol***
overrule *be* ***dyfarnu yn erbyn***, ***gwrthod***
overrun *be* ***heidio***, ***lledu***
overseas *adf* ***dramor***
oversee *be* ***goruchwylio***
overshadow *be* ***taflu cysgod***
oversight *enw* ***amryfusedd*** *hwn*
oversleep *be* ***cysgu'n hwyr***
overspend *be* ***gorwario***
overstate *be* ***gwneud gormod o***
overt *ans* ***agored***, ***amlwg***
overtake *be* ***goddiweddyd***, ***cael y blaen ar***
overthrow *be* ***dymchwel***
overtime *enw* ***goramser*** *hwn*, ***oriau ychwanegol*** *hyn*
overture *enw* ***agorawd*** *hon*
overturn *be* ***dymchwel***, ***moelyd***, ***gwyrdroi***
overview *enw* ***gorolwg*** *hwn*
overwhelm *be* ***llethu***, ***sathru***
overwhelming *ans* ***llethol***, ***anorthrech***
overwork *be* ***gorweithio***
owe *be* ***mae ar***
owing *ans* ***dyledus***
  o~ to ***oherwydd***
owl *enw* ***tylluan*** *hon*
own *be* ***meddu***, ***piau***
  to o~ up ***syrthio ar eich bai***, ***cyfaddef***
  my o~ house ***fy nhŷ fy hun***
  on my o~ ***ar fy mhen fy hun***
owner *enw* ***perchennog*** *hwn*
ox *enw* ***ych*** *hwn*
oxygen *enw* ***ocsygen*** *hwn*
oyster *enw* ***wystrysen*** *hon*
ozone *enw* ***osôn*** *hwn*

P

p *byrfodd* ***c*** **(ceiniog)**
p *byrfodd* ***t.*** **(tudalen)**
pace *enw* (step) ***cam***; (speed) ***cyflymdra:cyflymder*** *hwn*
to keep p~ with ***datblygu'r un mor gyflym***
to set the p~ ***bod ar flaen y gad***
pace *be* ***camu***
pacific *ans* ***heddychlon***, ***heddychol***
pacification *enw* ***taweliad***, ***llonyddiad*** *hwn*; ***tawelu***, ***llonyddu***
pacifist *enw* ***heddychwr*** *hwn*
pacify *be* ***tawelu***, ***gwastrodi***
pack *enw* ***pecyn*** *hwn*
p~ of lies ***tomen o gelwydd***; ***rhaffu celwyddau***
pack *be* ***pacio***
package *enw* ***pecyn*** *hwn*
packed lunch *enw* ***pecyn cinio/bwyd*** *hwn*
packet *enw* ***paced*** *hwn*
pact *enw* ***cyfamod***, ***cytundeb*** *hwn*
pad *enw* ***pad*** *hwn*
paddle *enw* ***padlen***, ***rhodl*** *hon*
paddle *be* ***padlo***
pagan *ans* ***paganaidd***
page *enw* ***tudalen*** *hwn/hon*; ***macwy*** *hwn*
pageant *enw* ***pasiant*** *hwn*
pageantry *enw* ***rhwysg*** *hwn*
pager *enw* ***galwr*** *hwn*
pail *enw* ***bwced*** *hwn/hon*
pain *enw* ***poen*** *hwn/hon*, ***dolur*** *hwn*
p~ or gain ***budd neu boen***
to be at p~s to ***gwneud eu gorau glas***
pain *be* ***brifo***
pained *ans* ***poenus***, ***pryderus***
painful *ans* ***poenus***
painless *ans* ***di-boen***
painstaking *ans* ***gofalus***, ***dyfal***
paint *enw* ***paent*** *hwn*
paint *be* ***peintio***
painter *enw* ***peintiwr*** *hwn*, ***peintwraig*** *hon*
painting *enw* ***peintiad***, ***llun*** *hwn*
pair *enw* ***pâr*** *hwn*
pairs ***deuoedd***
palomino *enw* ***ceffyl lliw llaeth a chwrw*** *hwn*
palace *enw* ***palas*** *hwn*
palatable *ans* ***blasus***, ***derbyniol***
palate *enw* ***taflod y genau*** *hon*
pale *ans* ***gwelw***, ***llwyd***, ***golau***
pale *be* ***gwelwi***
palette *enw* ***paled*** *hwn*
pallet *enw* ***gwely gwellt*** *hwn*
palliate *be* ***lleddfu***, ***llaesu***
pallid *ans* ***gwelw***, ***llwyd***
pallor *enw* ***gwelwder*** *hwn*
palm *enw* (hand) ***cledr y llaw*** *hwn*; (tree) ***palmwydden*** *hon*
Palm Sunday *enw* ***Sul y Blodau*** *hwn*
palpable *ans* ***cyffyrddadwy***; ***eglur***

palpitation *enw* ***dychlamiad y galon*** *hwn*
palsy *enw* ***parlys*** *hwn*
paltry *ans* ***pitw***, ***tila***
pampas *enw* ***paith*** *hwn*
pamper *be* ***mwytho***, ***maldodi***
pamphlet *enw* ***pamffledyn***, ***llyfryn*** *hwn*
pamphleteer *enw* ***pamffledwr*** *hwn*
pan *enw* ***padell*** *hon*
pan *be* ***rhidyllu***
panache *enw* ***steil*** *hwn*
pancake *enw* ***crempog***, ***ffroisen***, ***pancosen*** *hon*
pancreas *enw* ***cefndedyn*** *hwn*
pandemonium *enw* ***halibalŵ*** *hwn/hon*
pander *be* ***boddio***
pane *enw* ***cwarel***, ***paen*** *hwn*
panel *enw* ***panel*** *hwn*
pang *enw* ***gwayw*** *hon*
panic *be* ***gwylltio:gwylltu***
pansy *enw* ***pansi*** *hwn*
pant *be* ***dyhefod***, ***peuo***
panther *enw* ***panther*** *hwn*
pantomime *enw* ***pantomeim*** *hwn*
pantry *enw* ***pantri*** *hwn*
pants *enw* ***trôns*** *hyn*
papal *ans* ***pabaidd***
paper *enw* ***papur*** *hwn*
paper *be* ***papuro***
paperweight *enw* ***pwysau papur*** *hwn*
papier mâché *enw* ***mwydion papur*** *hyn*
par *enw* ***cyfartaledd*** *hwn*
par excellence *ans* ***tan gamp***
parable *enw* ***dameg*** *hon*
parachute *enw* ***parasiwt*** *hwn*
parade *enw* ***sioe***; ***gorymdaith*** *hon*
paradise *enw* ***paradwys*** *hon*
paradox *enw* ***paradocs*** *hwn*
paragraph *enw* ***paragraff*** *hwn*
parallel *enw* ***cyflin*** *hon*
parallel *ans* ***cyfochrog***
  a p~ document ***chwaer ddogfen*** *hon*
paralyse *be* ***parlysu***
paralysis *enw* ***parlys*** *hwn*
parameter *enw* ***ffin*** *hon*
paramount *ans* ***goruchaf***, ***pennaf***
paranoid *ans* ***paranoiaidd***
parapet *enw* ***rhagfur*** *hwn*
paraphrase *be* ***aralleirio***
parasite *enw* ***parasit*** *hwn*
parcel *enw* ***parsel*** *hwn*
  to be part and p~ ***rhan annatod***
parcel *be* ***parselu***
parch *be* ***crasu***, ***sychu***
parchment *enw* ***memrwn*** *hwn*
pardon *enw* ***maddeuant*** *hwn*
pardon *be* ***maddau***
pare *be* ***pilio***, ***plicio***
parenthesis *enw* ***sangiad*** *hwn*; ***cromfach*** *hon*
parent *enw* ***rhiant*** *hwn* (***rhieni*** *hyn*)
parish *enw* ***plwyf*** *hwn*
parishioners *enw* ***plwyfolion*** *hyn*
parity *enw* ***cydraddoldeb***, ***cyfartaledd*** *hwn*

p

p~ of esteem ***parch cyfartal***
park *enw* **parc** *hwn*
park *be* **parcio**
parking lot *enw* **maes parcio** *hwn*
parlance *enw* **iaith** *hon*
parliament *enw* **senedd** *hon*
parliamentary *ans* **seneddol**
parlour *enw* **cegin orau** *hon*
parlous *ans* **enbyd**
parochial *ans* **plwyfol**
p~ church council ***cyngor plwyf eglwysig*** *hwn*
parody *enw* **parodi** *hwn/hon*
parody *be* **parodïo**
paroxysm *enw* **pwl** *hwn*
parrot *enw* **parot** *hwn*
parry *be* **troi naill ochr**
parsimonious *ans* **cybyddlyd**
parsley *enw* **persli** *hwn*
parsnip *enw* **panasen** *hon*
parson *enw* **person**, **offeiriad** *hwn*
part *enw* **rhan** *hon*
for the most p~ ***gan mwyaf***, ***yn bennaf***
for their p~ ***o'u rhan hwy***
p~ and parcel ***rhan annatod***
part *be* **gwahanu**, **rhannu**, **gollwng gafael ar**
partake *be* **cyfranogi**; **cynnwys**
partial *ans* **rhannol**; **pleidiol**
participate *be* **cyfranogi**, **cymryd rhan**
participation *enw* **cyfranogiad** *hwn*
particle *enw* **gronyn**; (gram.) **geiryn** *hwn*
particular *ans* **arbennig**, **neilltuol**
parting *enw* **rhaniad, ymwahaniad** *hwn*
partisan *ans* **pleidiol**
partition *enw* **pared**, **palis** *hwn*; **rhaniad, dyraniad** *hwn*
partition *be* **rhannu**, **dyrannu**
partly *adf* **yn rhannol**
partner *enw* **cymar**, **partner** *hwn*
partnership *enw* **partneriaeth** *hon*
in p~ with ***law yn llaw â***
part of speech *enw* **rhan ymadrodd** *hon*
partridge *enw* **petrisen** *hon*
party *enw* **plaid** *hon*; **parti** *hwn*; **grŵp**, **cwmni** *hwn*
party political ***pleidiol-wleidyddol***
to be p~ to ***cyfrannu at***
pass *enw* **bwlch** *hwn*; (game) **pas** *hon*
pass *be* **pasio**, **caniatáu**; **mynd heibio**
to p~ on ***trosglwyddo***
passage *enw* **tramwyfa**, **rhodfa** *hon*
with the p~ of time ***ymhen hir a hwyr***
passenger *enw* **teithiwr** *hwn*, **teithwraig** *hon*
passer-by *enw* **un sy'n mynd heibio**
passing *ans* **mynd heibio**

p~ fancy ***ffansi'r funud***

passion *enw* ***angerdd*** *hwn*, ***nwyd*** *hwn/hon*

he has a p~ for walking ***cerdded yw ei ddiléit***, ***mae'n dwlu ar gerdded***

passionate *ans* ***angerddol***

passive *ans* ***goddefol***

passport *enw* ***trwydded deithio*** *hon*, ***pasport*** *hwn*

a p~ to ***allwedd i***, ***yn fodd i***

past *enw* ***gorffennol*** *hwn*

p~ master ***hen law***

past *ans* ***cynt***

past *ardd* ***wedi***

pasta *enw* ***pasta*** *hwn*

paste *enw* ***past*** *hwn*

paste *be* ***pastio***

pastern *enw* ***egwyd*** *hon*

pastime *enw* ***difyrrwch*** *hwn*

pastor *enw* ***bugail***, ***gweinidog*** *hwn*

pastoral *ans* ***bugeiliol***

pastry *enw* ***toes*** *hwn*

pasture *enw* ***porfa*** *hon*

pasty *enw* ***pastai*** *hon*

pat *enw* ***patiad*** *hwn*

pat *be* ***patio***; ***canmol (anifail)***

patch *enw* ***clwt***; ***darn (o dir)*** *hwn*

he's not a p~ on his father ***nid yw hanner cystal dyn â'i dad***

on his own p~ ***ar ei domen ei hun***

patch *be* ***clytio***, ***cyweirio***

patched *ans* ***clytiog***

patchwork *enw* ***clytwaith*** *hwn*

pate *enw* ***copa***, ***corun*** *hwn*

patella *enw* ***padell y pen-glin*** *hon*

patent *enw* ***breinlen*** *hon*, ***patent*** *hwn*

patent *be* ***rhoi patent ar***

patent *ans* ***amlwg***

paternal *ans* ***tadol***

paternity *enw* ***tadogaeth*** *hon*

path *enw* ***llwybr*** *hwn*

pathetic *ans* ***truenus***, ***pathetig***

pathology *enw* ***patholeg*** *hon*

patience *enw* ***amynedd*** *hwn/hon*

patient *enw* ***claf*** *hwn*

patient *ans* ***amyneddgar***

patois *enw* ***tafodiaith***; ***bratiaith***, ***llediaith*** *hon*

patriarch *enw* ***patriarch*** *hwn*

patriot *enw* ***gwladgarwr*** *hwn*

patrol *be* ***patrolio***

patron *enw* ***noddwr*** *hwn*, ***noddwraig*** *hon*

patronage *enw* ***nawdd*** *hwn*

patronize *be* ***noddi***; ***bod yn nawddoglyd***

patron saint *enw* ***nawddsant*** *hwn*

pattern *enw* ***patrwm*** *hwn*

patterned *ans* ***patrymog***

paucity *enw* ***prinder***, ***diffyg*** *hwn*

paunch *enw* ***bol*** *hwn*

pauper *enw* ***tlotyn*** *hwn*

pause *enw* ***saib*** *hwn*

pause *be* ***oedi***, ***gorffwys***

pave *be* ***palmantu***

to p~ the way for ***agor y drws i***, ***lledu'r ffordd i***

pavement *enw* ***palmant***, ***pafin*** *hwn*
pavilion *enw* ***pabell*** *hon*, ***pafiliwn*** *hwn*
paw *enw* ***pawen*** *hon*
paw *be* ***pawennu***
pawn *enw* (chess) ***gwerinwr*** *hwn*; ***gwystl*** *hwn*
pawn *be* ***gwystlo***
pawnbroker *enw* ***gwystlwr*** *hwn*
pay *enw* ***cyflog*** *hwn*
pay *be* ***talu***
  p~ as you earn ***talu wrth ennill***
  p~ heed to ***talu sylw i***
  p~ off ***dwyn ffrwyth***
pay back *be* ***ad-dalu***, ***talu nôl***; ***dial***
payable *ans* ***taladwy***, ***dyledus***
pay bargaining *enw* ***bargeinio am gyflog***
payee *enw* ***talai*** *hwn* (***taleion*** *hyn*)
paymaster *enw* ***tâl-feistr*** *hwn*
payment *enw* ***tâl*** *hwn*
pea *enw* ***pysen*** *hon*
peace *enw* ***heddwch*** *hwn*, ***tangnefedd*** *hwn/hon*
peaceful *ans* ***heddychol***, ***heddychlon***, ***distaw***
peacemaker *enw* ***heddychwr***, ***tangnefeddwr*** *hwn*; ***heddychwraig***, ***tangnefeddwraig*** *hon*
peaches *enw* ***eirin gwlanog*** *hyn*
peacock *enw* ***paun*** *hwn*
peak *enw* ***pig*** *hwn/hon*, ***brig***, ***copa*** *hwn*
  p~s and troughs ***llanw a thrai***; ***uchafbwyntiau ac isafbwyntiau***
peak *be* ***dod i anterth***, ***cyrraedd uchafbwynt***
peal *be* ***atseinio***
pear *enw* ***gellygen***, ***peren*** *hon*
pearl *enw* ***perl*** *hwn*
peasant *enw* ***gwladwr***, ***gwerinwr*** *hwn*
peat *enw* ***mawn*** *hwn*
pebble *enw* ***cerigyn*** *hwn* (***cerigos*** *hyn*)
peck *be* ***pigo***
peckish *ans* ***â chwant bwyd***
peculiar *ans* ***hynod***
  to be p~ to ***bod yn gyfyngedig i***
peculiarity *enw* ***hynodrwydd*** *hwn*; ***nodwedd*** *hon*
pecuniary *ans* ***ariannol***
pedagogy *enw* ***addysgeg*** *hon*
pedal *enw* ***pedal*** *hwn*
pedal *be* ***pedlo***
peddle *be* ***pedlera***
pedestrian *enw* ***cerddwr*** *hwn*
pedestrian *ans* ***ar draed***, ***pedestraidd***, ***di-sbonc***
pedigree *enw* ***ach***, ***llinach***, ***tras*** *hon*
pee *be* ***piso***
peel *enw* ***croen***, ***pil*** *hwn*
peel *be* ***crafu***, ***plicio***, ***tynnu ymaith***
peelings *enw* ***crafion***, ***creifion*** *hyn*
peep *be* ***sbecian***
peer *enw* ***cymar***; ***arglwydd*** *hwn*
peerage *enw* ***urdd yr arglwyddi*** *hon*; ***arglwyddiaeth*** *hon*

peerless *ans* ***digymar***
peers *enw* ***cyfoedion***; ***arglwyddi*** *hyn*
peevish *ans* ***piwis***, ***croes***, ***anfoddog***
peewit *enw* ***cornchwiglen*** *hon*
peg *enw* ***peg*** *hwn*
peg *be* ***pegio***
pejorative *ans* ***difrïol***
pellet *enw* ***pelen*** *hon*
pellucid *ans* ***clir***, ***tryloyw***
pelt *enw* ***croen*** *hwn*
pen *enw* ***pin ysgrifennu*** *hwn*; ***corlan*** *hon*
pen *be* ***ysgrifennu***; ***corlannu***
penalize *be* ***cosbi***
penalty *enw* ***cosb*** *hon*
penance *enw* ***penyd*** *hwn*
penchant *enw* ***hoffter*** *hwn*
pencil *enw* ***pensel*** *hon*:***pensil*** *hwn*
pending *ans* ***yn disgwyl***, ***ar y gweill***
pending *ardd* ***tan***, ***hyd nes***
pendulum *enw* ***pendil*** *hwn*
penetrate *be* ***treiddio***
penetrating *ans* ***treiddgar***
pen-friend *enw* ***ffrind post/ gohebol*** *hwn*
penguin *enw* ***pengwin*** *hwn*
penicillin *enw* ***penisilin*** *hwn*
peninsula *enw* ***gorynys*** *hon*, ***penrhyn*** *hwn*
penis *enw* ***cal:cala***, ***pidyn*** *hon*, ***penis*** *hwn*
penitent *ans* ***edifar***
penitentiary *enw* ***carchar*** *hwn*
penknife *enw* ***cyllell boced*** *hon*
penny *enw* ***ceiniog*** *hon*
pen-pal *enw* ***ffrind post/gohebol*** *hwn*
pen-portrait *enw* ***disgrifiad cryno*** *hwn*
pension *enw* ***pensiwn*** *hwn*
pension *be* ***pensiynu***
pensive *ans* ***meddylgar***
penult *enw* ***goben*** *hwn*
penultimate *ans* ***cynderfynol***, ***olaf ond un***
penury *enw* ***tlodi*** *hwn*
people *enw* ***pobl*** *hon/hyn*
people *be* ***poblogi***
pepper *enw* ***pupur*** *hwn*
pepper *be* ***pupro***
per annum *adf* ***y flwyddyn***
per capita *adf* ***y pen***
perceive *be* ***canfod***
  as p~d by ***ym marn***
  p~d benefit ***mantais amlwg*** *hon*
per cent *adf* ***y cant***
percentage *enw* ***canran*** *hon*
perceptible *ans* ***dirnadwy***, ***amlwg***
perception *enw* ***dirnadaeth*** *hon*
  a false p~ ***tybio ar gam***
perch *enw* ***clwyd*** *hon*; (fish) ***draenogiad*** *hwn*
percipient *ans* ***craff***
percolate *be* ***hidlo***
percolator *enw* ***percoladur*** *hwn*
percussion *enw* ***offerynnau taro*** *hyn*

p

perdition *enw* ***colledigaeth*** *hon*, ***difancoll*** *hwn*
peregrine falcon *enw* ***hebog tramor*** *hwn*
perennial *ans* ***lluosflwydd***
p~ problem ***problem oesol*** *hon*
perfect *be* ***perffeithio***, ***ymberffeithio***
perfect *ans* ***perffaith***, ***i'r dim***
perfection *enw* ***perffeithrwydd*** *hwn*
perfidy *enw* ***brad*** *hwn*
perforations *enw* ***tyllau*** *hyn*
perform *be* ***perfformio***, ***chwarae***, ***gweithredu***
performance *enw* ***perfformiad*** *hwn*
performer *enw* ***perfformiwr***, ***chwaraewr*** *hwn*, ***perfformwraig***, ***chwaraewraig*** *hon*
perfume *enw* ***persawr*** *hwn*
perfume *be* ***perarogli***
perfunctory *ans* ***swta***, ***diofal***
perhaps *adf* ***efallai***, ***hwyrach***, ***tybed***
peril *enw* ***perygl*** *hwn*
perilous *ans* ***peryglus***
perimeter *enw* ***perimedr***; ***terfyn allanol*** *hwn*
period *enw* ***cyfnod*** *hwn*; (physiol.) ***misglwyf***, ***mislif*** *hwn*
a considerable p~ of time ***cryn amser***
periodic *ans* ***cyfnodol***, ***achlysurol***
peripatetic *ans* ***teithiol***
peripheral *ans* ***ymylol***
periscope *enw* ***perisgop*** *hwn*
perish *be* ***marw***, ***trengi***
perishable *ans* ***darfodus***, ***byrhoedlog***
perjury *enw* ***anudon*** *hwn*
perk *enw* ***mantais*** *hon* (***mân fanteision*** *hyn*)
perk *be* **to p~ up** ***sirioli***, ***bywiocáu***; ***gwella***
perky *ans* ***sionc***, ***siriol***, ***talog***
permanent *ans* ***parhaol***
permeate *be* ***treiddio***, ***ymdreiddio***
they p~ all subjects ***maent yn codi ym mhob pwnc***
permissible *ans* ***caniataol***, ***goddefadwy***
permission *enw* ***caniatâd*** *hwn*
permissive *ans* ***goddefgar***
permit *enw* ***trwydded***, ***hawlen*** *hon*
permit *be* ***caniatáu***
if time p~s ***os bydd amser***
permutate *be* ***trynewid***
pernicious *ans* ***andwyol***, ***niweidiol***
peroration *enw* ***diweddglo***, ***perorasiwn*** *hwn*
perpendicular *ans* ***perpendicwlar***
per person *adf* ***y pen***
perpetrate *be* ***bod yn gyfrifol***, ***cyflawni***
perpetual *ans* ***parhaus***, ***diddiwedd***, ***di-baid***
a p~ source ***pwll diwaelod***
perpetuate *be* ***parhau***
perplex *be* ***drysu***, ***mwydro***

per se *adf* ***ynddo/ynddi'i hun***, ***fel y cyfryw***
persecute *be* ***erlid***
persecution *enw* ***erledigaeth*** *hon*
persevere *be* ***dyfalbarhau***, ***dal ati***
persist *be* ***dyfalbarhau***, ***dal ati***
persistence *enw* ***dyfalbarhad*** *hwn*
persistent *ans* ***dyfal***, ***cyson***
person *enw* ***rhywun*** *hwn*
personage *enw* ***rhywun pwysig*** *hwn*
personable *ans* ***golygus***
personal *ans* ***personol***
personalize *be* ***rhoi gwedd bersonol ar***
personality *enw* ***personoliaeth*** *hon*
personnel *enw* ***personél*** *hwn*
perspective *enw* ***persbectif*** *hwn*
a wider p~ ***ehangach gorwelion***
perspicacious *ans* ***craff***
perspiration *enw* ***chwys*** *hwn*
perspire *be* ***chwysu***
persuade *be* ***darbwyllo***, ***perswadio***, ***dwyn perswâd ar***
persuasion *enw* ***perswâd*** *hwn*
persuasive *ans* ***llawn perswâd, argyhoeddiadol***
p~ arguments ***dadleuon cryf*** *hyn*
pertain *be* ***perthyn (i)***, ***ymwneud â***
pertinent *ans* ***perthnasol***
perturb *be* ***aflonyddu***, ***tarfu***
peruse *be* ***darllen***, ***craffu ar***, ***bwrw golwg dros***
pervade *be* ***treiddio***
pervasive *ans* ***ymledol***
perverse *ans* ***gwrthnysig***, ***croes***
pessimist *enw* ***pesimist*** *hwn/hon*
pest *enw* ***pla***; ***poendod*** *hwn*
pester *be* ***plagio***, ***poeni***
pestilence *enw* ***pla*** *hwn*, ***haint*** *hwn/hon*
pet *enw* ***anifail anwes*** *hwn*
pet *be* ***anwesu***; ***anwylo***
petal *enw* ***petal*** *hwn*
petition *enw* ***deiseb*** *hon*
petition *be* ***deisebu***
petitioner *enw* ***deisebydd*** *hwn*
petrify *be* ***fferru (ag ofn)***, ***ymgaregu***
petticoat *enw* ***pais*** *hon*
pettiness *enw* ***bychander***, ***bychandra*** *hwn*
petty *ans* ***mân***, ***pitw***; ***hollti blew***
petulant *ans* ***pwdlyd***
pew *enw* ***côr*** *hwn*, ***sêt*** *hon*
pewter *enw* ***piwtar:piwter*** *hwn*
phantom *enw* ***drychiolaeth*** *hon*, ***ysbryd*** *hwn*
phantom *ans* ***lledrithiol***
Pharaoh *enw* ***Pharo*** *hwn*
pharmacist *enw* ***fferyllydd*** *hwn*
pharmacy *enw* (practice) ***fferylliaeth*** *hon*; (place) ***fferyllfa*** *hon*
phase *enw* ***cyfnod*** *hwn*
to be in p~ with ***mynd law yn llaw â***
phase in *be* ***graddol gyflwyno***
phase out *be* ***graddol ddiddymu***
pheasant *enw* ***ffesant*** *hwn*

p

phenomenal *ans* ***gwyrthiol***
phenomenon *enw* ***ffenomen*** *hon*, ***rhyfeddod*** *hwn*
philander *be* ***mercheta***
philanthropic *ans* ***dyngarol***
philology *enw* ***ieitheg*** *hon*
philosopher *enw* ***athronydd*** *hwn*
philosophical *ans* ***athronyddol***
philosophize *be* ***athronyddu***
philosophy *enw* ***athroniaeth*** *hon*
phlegm *enw* ***llysnafedd***, ***crachboer*** *hwn*
phlegmatic *ans* ***didaro***
phobia *enw* ***ffobia*** *hwn*
phoenix *enw* ***ffenics*** *hwn*
phone *enw* ***ffôn*** *hwn*
phone *be* ***ffonio***
phone call *enw* ***galwad ffôn***, ***caniad*** *hwn*
phoney *ans* ***ffug***
phonic *ans* ***ffonig***
photocall *enw* ***cyfle i dynnu lluniau***
photocopy *enw* ***llungopi*** *hwn*
photograph *enw* ***ffotograff*** *hwn*
photograph *be* ***tynnu llun***
photographer *enw* ***tynnwr lluniau***, ***ffotograffydd*** *hwn*
photography *enw* ***ffotograffiaeth*** *hon*
photosynthesis *enw* ***ffotosynthesis*** *hwn*
phrase *enw* ***ymadrodd*** *hwn*; (mus.) ***cymal*** *hwn*
phrase *be* ***mynegi***, ***geirio***
phrase-book *enw* ***llyfr ymadroddion*** *hwn*
phraseology *enw* ***ieithwedd*** *hon*
physical *ans* ***corfforol***
p~ strength ***nerth bôn braich***
physician *enw* ***meddyg*** *hwn*
physicist *enw* ***ffisegydd*** *hwn*
physics *enw* ***ffiseg*** *hon*
physiology *enw* ***ffisioleg*** *hon*
physiotherapy *enw* ***ffisiotherapi*** *hwn*
physique *enw* ***corffolaeth*** *hon*
pianist *enw* ***pianydd*** *hwn*
piano *enw* ***piano*** *hwn*
piccolo *enw* ***picolo*** *hwn*
pick *enw* (tool) ***caib*** *hon*; (choice) ***dewis***, ***detholiad*** *hwn*; (= best) ***y gorau*** *hwn*
pick *be* ***pigo***, ***dewis***
pickaxe *enw* ***picas*** *hon*
picket *be* ***picedu***
picnic *enw* ***picnic*** *hwn*
pictorial *ans* ***darluniadol***
picture *enw* ***llun***, ***darlun*** *hwn*
picture *be* ***darlunio***, ***portreadu***; ***dychmygu***
pictures *enw* (cinema) ***pictiwrs*** *hyn*
picturesque *ans* ***hardd***
pie *enw* ***pastai*** *hon*
p~ in the sky ***breuddwyd gwrach (wrth ei hewyllys)*** *hwn*
piebald *ans* ***brith***
piece *enw* ***darn*** *hwn*
in p~s ***yn deilchion***
to be of a p~ with ***cyd-fynd â***

to give a p~ of one's mind *rhoi llond pen i, rhoi pryd o dafod i*
to say their p~ *dweud eu dweud*
to tear to p~s *tynnu'n gareiau*
pied *ans* ***brith***
pierce *be* ***gwanu***, ***trywanu***
piercing *ans* ***treiddgar***
piety *enw* ***duwioldeb*** *hwn*
pig *enw* ***mochyn*** *hwn*
pigeon *enw* ***colomen*** *hon*
piggybacking *enw* ***arlwytho***
piggy bank *enw* ***cadw-mi-gei*** *hwn*
pigheaded *ans* ***ystyfnig, penstiff***
piglet *enw* ***mochyn bach*** *hwn*
pigment *enw* ***pigment*** *hwn*
pigsty *enw* ***twlc***, ***cwt mochyn*** *hwn*
pigtail *enw* ***pleth***, ***plethen*** *hon*
pike *enw* ***gwaywffon***, ***picell*** *hon*; (fish) ***penhwyad*** *hwn*
pile *enw* ***twmpath***, ***pentwr*** *hwn*
pile *be* ***pentyrru***
piles *enw* ***clwyf y marchogion*** *hwn*
pilfer *be* ***dwyn***, ***twgu***
pilgrim *enw* ***pererin*** *hwn*
pilgrimage *enw* ***pererindod*** *hwn/hon*
pill *enw* ***pilsen*** *hon*
pillar *enw* ***piler*** *hwn*, ***colofn*** *hon*
pillow *enw* ***clustog*** *hon*, ***gobennydd*** *hwn*
pilot *enw* ***peilot*** *hwn*
pilot *be* ***llywio***; ***rhagbrofi***
pimple *enw* ***ploryn*** *hwn*
pin *enw* ***pin*** *hwn*
pin *be* ***pinio***
to p~ back one's ears *moeli clustiau*
pinafore *enw* ***brat*** *hwn*, ***ffedog*** *hon*
pincers *enw* ***pinsiwrn*** *hwn*
pinch *be* ***pinsio***
pincushion *enw* ***pincas*** *hwn*
pine *enw* ***pinwydden*** *hon*
pine *be* ***hiraethu***
pineapple *enw* ***pinafal*** *hwn*
pine marten *enw* ***bele*** *hwn*
pink *ans* ***pinc***
pinnacle *enw* ***uchafbwynt*** *hwn*
pinprick *enw* ***pigiad pin*** *hwn*
pint *enw* ***peint*** *hwn*
pioneer *enw* ***arloeswr*** *hwn*, ***arloeswraig*** *hon*
pioneer *be* ***arloesi***, ***bod ar flaen y gad***
pious *ans* ***duwiol***
pip *enw* ***carreg*** *hon*
pipe *enw* ***pibell***, ***pib*** *hon*
pipeline *enw* ***piblin*** *hwn*; ***piblinell*** *hon*
to be in the p~ *ar y gweill*
piper *enw* ***pibydd*** *hwn*
pique *enw* ***pwd*** *hwn*, ***tymer ddrwg*** *hon*
piracy *enw* ***môr-ladrad*** *hwn*
pirate *enw* ***môr-leidr*** *hwn*
pistil *enw* ***pistil*** *hwn*
pistol *enw* ***pistol*** *hwn*
piston *enw* ***piston*** *hwn*
pit *enw* ***pwll***, ***pydew*** *hwn*
pitch *enw* (musical) ***traw*** *hwn*;

(sport) ***maes, cae*** *hwn*, (cricket) ***llain*** *hon*
pitcher *enw* ***piser*** *hwn*; ***stên*** *hon*
pitchfork *enw* ***picfforch***, ***picwarch*** *hon*
pitfall *enw* ***magl*** *hon*
pith *enw* ***bywyn*** *hwn*
pithy *ans* ***cryno, bachog***
pitiable *ans* ***truenus***, ***gresynus***
pitiful *ans* ***truenus***
pitiless *ans* ***didrugaredd***
pity *enw* ***tosturi***, ***trueni*** *hwn*
pity *be* ***tosturio wrth***
pivot *enw* ***colyn*** *hwn*
placard *enw* ***placard*** *hwn*
placate *be* ***tawelu***
place *enw* ***lle*** *hwn*
all over the p~ ***ar chwâl***
in p~ ***ar waith***, ***yn ei le***, ***ar gael***
p~ of worship ***addoldy*** *hwn*
place *be* ***lleoli***
placement *enw* ***lleoliad*** *hwn*
placid *ans* ***llonydd***, ***tawel***
plagiarism *enw* ***llên-ladrad*** *hwn*
plague *enw* ***pla*** *hwn*
plague *be* ***plagio***, ***poeni***
plaice *enw* ***lleden*** *hon*
plain *enw* ***gwastadedd*** *hwn*
plain *ans* ***plaen***, ***diaddurn***
plaintiff *enw* ***pleintydd*** *hwn*
plait *enw* ***pleth*** *hon*, ***plethyn*** *hwn*
plait *be* ***plethu***
plan *enw* ***cynllun*** *hwn*
plan *be* ***cynllunio***
plane *enw* ***plân*** *hwn*
plane *be* ***plaenio***, ***plamo***
planet *enw* ***planed*** *hon*
plane tree *enw* ***planwydden*** *hon*
plank *enw* ***astell***, ***ystyllen*** *hon*
planner *enw* ***cynlluniwr*** *hwn*
plant *enw* ***llysieuyn***, ***planhigyn*** *hwn*; ***peiriannau, offer*** *hyn*
plant *be* ***plannu***
plantation *enw* ***planhigfa*** *hon*
plaque *enw* ***plac*** *hwn*
plaster *enw* ***plastr*** *hwn*
plaster *be* ***plastro***
plastic *ans* ***plastig***
plate *enw* ***plât*** *hwn*
too much on their p~ ***gormod o heyrn yn y tân***
plateau *enw* ***llwyfandir*** *hwn*
platform *enw* ***platfform*** *hwn*
a p~ on which to build ***sylfaen i adeiladu arni***
computer p~ ***llwyfan cyfrifiadur*** *hwn*
platinum *enw* ***platinwm*** *hwn*
platitude *enw* ***ystrydeb*** *hon*
platter *enw* ***dysgl*** *hon*
plausible *ans* ***credadwy***
play *enw* ***drama*** *hon*
play *be* ***chwarae***
they have their part to p~ ***mae iddynt eu rhan***
to p~ down ***rhoi llai o bwys ar***
player *enw* ***chwaraewr*** *hwn*, ***chwaraewraig*** *hon*
a leading p~ ***ceffyl blaen*** *hwn*
playful *ans* ***chwareus***

playground *enw* ***buarth*** *hwn*, ***iard*** *hon*
playlet *enw* ***dramodig*** *hon*
playwright *enw* ***dramodydd*** *hwn*
plea *enw* ***deisyfiad*** *hwn*, ***apêl*** *hon*
plead *be* ***pledio***, ***erfyn***
pleasant *ans* ***hyfryd***, ***dymunol***
they were p~ly surprised ***cawsant eu siomi ar yr ochr orau***
please *be* ***rhyngu bodd***, ***plesio***
pleased *ans* ***bodlon***, ***balch***
pleasing *ans* ***difyr***, ***braf***, ***dymunol***
it is p~ to see ***da o beth yw cael gweld***
pleasure *enw* ***pleser***, ***mwynhad*** *hwn*
pleat *enw* ***pleten*** *hon*, ***plyg*** *hwn*
pleat *be* ***pletio***
plebiscite *enw* ***pleidlais gwlad*** *hon*
pledge *enw* ***ernes*** *hon*, ***addewid*** *hwn/hon*
pledge *be* ***addo***, ***gwystlo***
plenary *ans* ***llawn***, ***cyflawn***
plentiful *ans* ***helaeth***, ***toreithiog***, ***digon o***
plenty *enw* ***digon***, ***digonedd*** *hwn*
plethora *enw* ***myrdd***, ***gormodedd*** *hwn*
pleurisy *enw* ***llid pilen yr ysgyfaint*** *hwn*
pliable *ans* ***hyblyg***, ***ystwyth***
pliers *enw* ***gefelen*** *hon*
plod *be* ***ymlwybro***
plot *enw* ***llain*** *hon*; ***plot*** *hwn*; ***cynllwyn*** *hwn*
plot *be* ***plotio***; ***cynllwynio***
plough *enw* ***aradr*** *hwn/hon*
plough *be* ***aredig***
ploughman *enw* ***aradrwr*** *hwn*
ploughshare *enw* ***swch*** *hon*
plover *enw* ***cwtiad*** *hwn*
ploy *enw* ***ystryw***, ***dyfais*** *hon*
pluck *enw* ***dewrder***, ***plwc*** *hwn*
pluck *be* ***tynnu***, ***plycio***
plug *enw* ***plwg*** *hwn*
plug *be* ***plwgio***
plum *enw* ***eirinen*** *hon*
plumage *enw* ***plu*** *hyn*
plumb *ans* ***plwm***
plumb *be* ***plymio***
plumber *enw* ***plymer*** *hwn*
plume *enw* ***pluen*** *hon*
plummet *be* ***plymio***
plump *ans* ***llond eich croen***
plunder *be* ***anrheithio***, ***ysbeilio***
plunge *be* ***plymio***
pluperfect *ans* ***gorberffaith***
plural *ans* ***lluosog***
plus *enw* ***plws*** *hwn*
a p~ ***yn fantais ychwanegol***
plush *ans* ***moethus***
Pluto *enw* ***Plwton*** *hwn*
plutonium *enw* ***plwtoniwm*** *hwn*
plywood *enw* ***pren haenog*** *hwn*
pneumatic *ans* ***niwmatig***
pneumoconiosis *enw* ***clefyd y llwch*** *hwn*

p

pneumonia *enw* ***llid yr ysgyfaint***, ***niwmonia*** *hwn*
poach *be* ***potsio***, ***herwhela***
poacher *enw* ***potsiwr*** *hwn*
pocket *enw* ***poced*** *hon*
pocket *be* ***pocedu***
pockmark *enw* ***craith*** *hon*
podium *enw* ***podiwm*** *hwn*
poem *enw* ***cerdd*** *hon*
poet *enw* ***bardd*** *hwn*
poetical *ans* ***barddonol***
poetry *enw* ***barddoniaeth*** *hon*
poignant *ans* ***dwys***, ***ingol***
point *enw* ***pwynt*** *hwn*
  a talking p~ ***testun siarad*** *hwn*
  at some p~ ***rywbryd***
  at the p~ of death ***ar fin marw***
  at this p~ ***yma***, ***yn awr***
  the p~ has been made ***dywedwyd eisoes***
  the school in p~ ***yr ysgol dan sylw***
  to make a p~ of ***bwrw ati'n fwriadol***
  to the p~ ***i bwrpas***
  to the p~ where ***i'r graddau***
point *be* ***pwyntio***, ***cyfeirio***
  this p~s to ***mae hyn yn awgrymu***
pointed *ans* ***pigfain***; (remark) ***miniog***
pointless *ans* ***di-bwynt***, ***di-fudd***
poise *enw* ***ymarweddiad,urddas*** *hwn*
poison *enw* ***gwenwyn*** *hwn*
poison *be* ***gwenwyno***
poisonous *ans* ***gwenwynig***, ***gwenwynllyd***
poke *be* ***gwthio***, ***procio***
poker *enw* ***pocer***, ***procer*** *hwn*
poker-faced *ans* ***difynegiant***
polar bear *enw* ***arth wen*** *hon*
polarize *be* ***polareiddio***, ***pegynnu***
pole *enw* ***polyn***; ***pegwn*** *hwn*
Pole *enw* ***Pwyliad*** *hwn*
polecat *enw* ***ffwlbart*** *hwn*
police *enw* ***heddlu*** *hwn*
police *be* ***plismona***
policeman *enw* ***heddwas***, ***plismon*** *hwn*, ***plismones*** *hon*
police station *enw* ***swyddfa'r heddlu*** *hon*
policy *enw* ***polisi*** *hwn*
polish *enw* ***cwyr*** *hwn*; ***sglein*** *hwn/hon*; ***graen*** *hwn*
polish *be* ***gloywi***, ***caboli***
polished *ans* ***caboledig***, ***gloyw***
polite *ans* ***boneddigaidd***
politeness *enw* ***boneddigeiddrwydd*** *hwn*
political *ans* ***gwleidyddol***
  a p~ football ***cocyn hitio*** *hwn*
politician *enw* ***gwleidydd*** *hwn*
politicize *be* ***troi'n fater gwleidyddol***
politicking *be* ***gwleidydda***
politics *enw* ***gwleidyddiaeth*** *hon*
poll *enw* ***pôl*** *hwn*
pollen *enw* ***paill*** *hwn*
pollinate *be* ***peillio***

poll tax *enw* ***treth y pen*** *hon*
pollute *be* ***llygru***
pollution *enw* ***llygredd*** *hwn*
polyglot *ans* ***amlieithog***
polygon *enw* ***polygon*** *hwn*
polythene *enw* ***polythen*** *hwn*
pomegranate *enw* ***pomgranad*** *hwn*
pomp *enw* ***rhwysg*** *hwn*
pompous *ans* ***mawreddog***, ***rhwysgfawr***
pond *enw* ***pwll*** *hwn*
ponder *be* ***ystyried***, ***pendroni***
ponderous *ans* ***clogyrnaidd***
pontificate *be* ***doethinebu***
pony *enw* ***merlyn*** *hwn*, ***poni*** *hwn/hon*
pony-trekking *be* ***merlota***
poodle *enw* ***pŵdl*** *hwn*
pool *enw* ***pwll*** *hwn*
pool *be* ***crynhoi***
poor *ans* ***tlawd***; ***gwael***; ***truan***; (of language ability) ***coch***
poorhouse *enw* ***tloty*** *hwn*
pop *enw* ***pop*** *hwn*
  to p~ over ***pigo draw***
Pope *enw* ***Pab*** *hwn*
poplar *enw* ***poplysen*** *hon*
poppet *enw* ***pwt*** *hwn*
poppy *enw* ***pabi*** *hwn*
poppycock *enw* ***lol botes maip*** *hon*
populace *enw* ***poblogaeth*** *hon*
popular *ans* ***poblogaidd***; ***mae mynd mawr ar***
popularity *enw* ***poblogrwydd*** *hwn*
popularize *be* ***poblogeiddio***
populate *be* ***poblogi***
population *enw* ***poblogaeth*** *hon*
porch *enw* ***porth***, ***cyntedd*** *hwn*
pore *enw* ***mandwll*** *hwn*
pore *be* ***astudio'n fanwl***
pork *enw* ***porc***, ***cig mochyn*** *hwn*
porous *ans* ***hydraidd***
porpoise *enw* ***llamhidydd*** *hwn*
porridge *enw* ***uwd*** *hwn*
port *enw* ***porthladd*** *hwn*
portable *ans* ***cludadwy***
portal *enw* ***porth*** *hwn*
portend *be* ***argoeli***
portion *enw* ***rhan***, ***cyfran*** *hon*
portly *ans* ***llond ei groen***
portrait *enw* ***portread***, ***darlun*** *hwn*
portray *be* ***portreadu***, ***darlunio***, ***cyfleu***
portrayal *enw* ***portread*** *hwn*
pose *enw* ***ystum*** *hwn/hon*
pose *be* ***ystumio***; (problem) ***peri***; (question) ***codi***
poser *enw* ***pos*** *hwn*
position *enw* (of body) ***ystum*** *hwn/hon*; (location) ***safle*** *hwn/hon*, ***sefyllfa*** *hon*; (standpoint) ***safbwynt*** *hwn*
positive *ans* ***cadarnhaol***, ***pendant***
possess *be* ***meddu***, ***perchenogi***
possession *enw* ***meddiant*** *hwn*, ***perchenogaeth*** *hon*
possibility *enw* ***posibilrwydd*** *hwn*
  to allow for the p~ ***rhag ofn***

possible *ans* ***posibl***
made p~ by ***oherwydd***
post *enw* ***post*** *hwn*
post *be* ***postio***
postage stamp *enw* ***stamp post*** *hwn*
postcard *enw* ***cerdyn post*** *hwn*
postcode *enw* ***cod post*** *hwn*
poster *enw* ***poster*** *hwn*
posterior *enw* ***pen-ôl*** *hwn*
posthumous *ans* ***ar ôl marwolaeth***
postman *enw* ***postmon*** *hwn*
postmaster *enw* ***postfeistr*** *hwn*
postmistress *enw* ***postfeistres*** *hon*
Post Office *enw* ***Swyddfa'r Post***; (local) ***swyddfa bost*** hon, ***llythyrdy*** hwn
postpone *be* ***gohirio***
postulate *be* ***rhagdybio***
posture *enw* ***osgo*** *hwn*, ***ystum*** *hwn/hon*
posture *be* ***ymagweddu***, ***ymhonni***
posy *enw* ***pwysi***, ***tusw*** *hwn*
pot *enw* ***pot*** *hwn*
pot *be* ***potio***
potato *enw* ***pytaten***, ***taten***, ***tatysen*** *hon*
pot-bellied *ans* ***boliog***
potent *ans* ***grymus***, ***cryf***
potential *enw* ***potensial*** *hwn*
to attain/realise one's p~ ***gwireddu potensial***
potholer *enw* ***ogofwr*** *hwn*
potion *enw* ***dogn*** *hwn*
potter *enw* ***crochenydd*** *hwn*
pottery *enw* ***crochenwaith*** *hwn*
pouch *enw* ***cod*** *hon*, ***cwdyn*** *hwn*
poultry *enw* ***dofednod*** *hyn*
pounce *be* ***neidio***
pound *enw* ***punt*** *hon*; ***pwys*** *hwn*
pound *be* ***pwyo***, ***pwnio***
pour *be* ***arllwys***, ***tywallt***
pout *be* ***pwdu***, ***sorri***
poverty *enw* ***tlodi*** *hwn*
powder *enw* ***powdr:powdwr*** *hwn*
powder *be* ***powdro***
powdery *ans* ***fel powdr mân***
power *enw* ***gallu***, ***grym***, ***nerth***, ***pŵer*** *hwn*
p~ struggle ***ymgiprys am oruchafiaeth***
powerful *ans* ***grymus***
powerless *ans* ***di-rym***
practicable *ans* ***ymarferol***, ***posibl***
practical *ans* ***ymarferol***
to turn ideas into p~ reality ***gwireddu syniadau***
practicality *enw* ***ymarferoldeb*** *hwn*; ***camau ymarferol*** *hyn*
practice *enw* ***ymarfer***, ***arfer*** *hwn/hon*, ***ymarferiad*** *hwn*
good p~ ***arferion da*** *hyn*
in p~ ***mewn gwirionedd***
normal p~ ***y drefn arferol*** *hon*
to put into p~ ***gweithredu***
practitioner *enw* ***ymarferwr*** *hwn*
practise *be* ***ymarfer***, ***arfer***
pragmatic *ans* ***pragmataidd***
prairie *enw* ***paith*** *hwn*
praise *enw* ***canmoliaeth*** *hon*

praise *be* ***canmol***
praiseworthy *ans* ***canmoladwy***, ***clodwiw***
prance *be* ***prancio***
prank *enw* ***cast***, ***pranc*** *hwn*
prattle *be* ***clebran***, ***clepian***
prawn *enw* ***corgimwch*** *hwn*
pray *be* ***gweddïo***
prayer *enw* ***gweddi*** *hon*
preach *be* ***pregethu***
preacher *enw* ***pregethwr*** *hwn*
preamble *enw* ***rhagymadrodd*** *hwn*, ***rhaglith*** *hon*
precarious *ans* ***ansicr***, ***yn y fantol***
precaution *enw* ***gofal***, ***rhagofal*** *hwn*
  strict p~s ***camau trwyadl*** *hyn*
precede *be* ***rhagflaenu***
precedence *enw* ***blaenoriaeth*** *hon*
  for A to take p~ over B ***i A ddod o flaen B***
precedent *enw* ***cynsail*** *hwn/hon*
preceding *ans* ***blaenorol***
precept *enw* ***rheol*** *hon*; ***hawlio cyfran o'r dreth***
precinct *enw* ***canolfan siopa*** *hwn/hon*
precious *ans* ***gwerthfawr***
  your time is p~ ***mae'ch amser yn brin***
precipice *enw* ***dibyn***, ***clogwyn*** *hwn*
precipitate *be* ***ysgogi***, ***bwrw***
precipitate *ans* ***brysiog***, ***byrbwyll***
precipitous *ans* ***serth***
précis *enw* ***crynodeb*** *hwn*
precise *ans* ***manwl***, ***tra-chywir***
  at the p~ moment ***ar y gair***
precision *enw* ***manwl gywirdeb*** *hwn*
preclude *be* ***ddim yn caniatáu***
precocious *ans* ***henaidd***, ***hengall***
precognition *enw* ***rhagwelediad*** *hwn*
preconceive *be* ***rhagdybio***
preconception *enw* ***rhagdybiaeth*** *hon*
preconceptual *ans* ***cyn-gysyniadol***
precondition *enw* ***rhagamod*** *hwn*
precursor *enw* ***rhagflaenydd*** *hwn*
predator *enw* ***rheibiwr***, ***ysglyfaethwr*** *hwn*
predatory *ans* ***rheibus***, ***ysglyfaethus***
predecessor *enw* ***rhagflaenydd*** *hwn*
predetermined *ans* ***rhagbenodedig***
predicament *enw* ***helynt***, ***cawl***, ***picil*** *hwn*
predicate *enw* ***traethiad*** *hwn*
predicate *be* ***bod yn seiliedig ar***
predict *be* ***darogan***, ***proffwydo***
predictable *ans* ***rhagweladwy***
prediction *enw* ***proffwydoliaeth*** *hon*
predilection *enw* ***hoffter*** *hwn*
predominant *ans* ***mwyaf***, ***pennaf***
predominate *be* ***tra-arglwyddiaethu***
pre-eminent *ans* ***di-ail***, ***heb ei debyg***, ***dihafal***

p

pre-empt *be* ***achub y blaen***
pre-emptive *ans* ***rhagataliol***
p~-emptive strike ***rhagymosodiad*** *hwn*
preface *enw* ***rhagair*** *hwn*
prefect *enw* ***swyddog*** *hwn*
prefer *be* ***bod yn well gan***, ***ffafrio***; (charges) ***dwyn achos yn erbyn***
preferable *ans* ***gwell***, ***gwell byth***
preference *enw* ***ffafriaeth*** *hon*; ***dymuniad*** *hwn*
preferential *ans* ***ffafriol***
preferment *enw* ***dyrchafiad*** *hwn*
prefix *enw* ***rhagddodiad*** *hwn*
pregnancy *enw* ***beichiogrwydd*** *hwn*
pregnant *ans* ***beichiog***
prehistoric *ans* ***cynhanesyddol***
prejudge *be* ***rhagfarnu***
prejudice *enw* ***rhagfarn*** *hon*
prejudice *be* ***niweidio***, ***amharu ar***
prejudiced *ans* ***rhagfarnllyd***
prejudicial *ans* ***niweidiol***
prelim *enw* ***rhagbrawf*** *hwn*
preliminary *ans* ***rhagarweiniol***
prelude *enw* ***rhagarweiniad***, ***preliwd*** *hwn*
premature *ans* ***cynamserol***, ***annhymig***
premeditated *ans* ***bwriadol***
premier *enw* ***prif weinidog*** *hwn*
premier *ans* ***prif***
premise *enw* ***cynsail*** *hwn*, ***rhagdybiaeth*** *hon*
premises *enw* ***adeilad***, ***tŷ*** *hwn*
premium *enw* ***premiwm*** *hwn*
a p~ service ***gwasanaeth o'r radd flaenaf***
so-and-so is at a p~ ***mae galw mawr am***
premonition *enw* ***rhagrybudd*** *hwn*
preoccupied *ans* ***wedi ymgolli yn***; ***yn rhoi gormod o sylw i***
preparation *enw* ***paratoad*** *hwn*
preparatory *ans* ***rhagbaratoawl***; ***paratoadol***
p~ school ***ysgol baratoadol*** *hon*
prepare *be* ***paratoi***
preponderance *enw* ***mwyafrif*** *hwn*, ***toreth*** *hon*
preposition *enw* ***arddodiad*** *hwn*
prepossessing *ans* ***deniadol***
preposterous *ans* ***hurt***, ***chwerthinllyd***
prerequisite *enw* ***rhagofyniad*** *hwn*
prerogative *enw* ***hawl***, ***braint***, ***uchelfraint***, ***rhagorfraint*** *hon*
prerogative *ans* ***rhagorfreiniol***
Presbyterian *ans* ***Presbyteraidd***
pre-school child *enw* ***plentyn dan oed ysgol*** *hwn*
prescribe *be* ***rhagnodi***
prescription *enw* ***presgripsiwn*** *hwn*
prescriptive *ans* ***rhagnodol***; (opposite of 'descriptive') ***rhagsgrifiol***
presence *enw* ***presenoldeb*** *hwn*
to have sufficient p~ of mind

bod digon o gwmpas eich pethau

present *enw* ***anrheg***, ***rhodd*** *hon*

present *be* ***cyflwyno***

to p~ problems ***achosi/creu problemau***

present *ans* ***presennol***, ***sydd ohoni***

presentable *ans* ***cymeradwy***, ***taclus***

presenter *enw* ***cyflwynydd*** *hwn*

presentiment *enw* ***argoel*** *hon*

preservation *enw* ***cadwraeth*** *hon*

preservationist *enw* ***cadwraethwr*** *hwn*, ***cadwraethwraig*** *hon*

preserve *enw* ***cyffaith***, ***jam*** *hwn*; ***maes neilltuedig*** *hwn*

ability is not the p~ of the privileged few ***nid eiddo'r ychydig breintiedig yn unig yw gallu***

preserve *be* ***cadw***; ***cyffeithio***

preside *be* ***llywyddu***

presidency *enw* ***llywyddiaeth*** *hon*

president *enw* ***llywydd***, ***arlywydd*** *hwn*

presidential *ans* ***arlywyddol***

press *enw* ***gwasg*** *hon*

press *be* ***gwasgu***

hard p~ed ***dan bwysau***

to p~ ahead ***bwrw ymlaen***

pressure *enw* ***pwysau***, ***pwysedd***, ***gwasgedd*** *hwn*

prestige *enw* ***bri*** *hwn*

prestigious *ans* ***nodedig***, ***arbennig***

presumable *ans* ***tebygol***

presume *be* ***tybio***, ***rhagdybio***

presumption *enw* ***tybiaeth***, ***rhagdybiaeth*** *hon*; (impertinence) **hyfdra** *hwn*

presumptuous *ans* ***eofn***, ***hyf***, ***rhyfygus***

presuppose *be* ***rhagdybio***

pretentious *ans* ***ymhongar***

pretence *enw* ***esgus*** *hwn*

pretend *be* ***esgus***, ***cymryd arnoch***

preternatural *ans* ***goruwchnaturiol***

pre-test *enw* ***cynbrawf*** *hwn*

pre-test *be* ***cynbrofi***

pretext *enw* ***esgus*** *hwn*

under the p~ ***dan gochl***

pre-trial *be* ***cyndreialu***

pretty *ans* ***pert***, ***del***, ***tlws***

prevail *be* ***darbwyllo***; ***ennill y dydd***

prevalent *ans* ***cyffredin***, ***gan amlaf***

prevaricate *be* ***cloffi rhwng dau ateb***, ***osgoi ateb***; ***dweud celwydd***

prevent *be* ***rhwystro***, ***atal***

prevention *enw* ***rhwystrad***, ***ataliad*** *hwn*

preventative *ans* ***ataliol***

preview *be* ***gweld ymlaen llaw***

previous *ans* ***blaenorol***, ***cynt***

prevocational *ans* ***cynalwedigaethol***

prey *enw* ***ysglyfaeth*** *hon*

price *enw* ***pris*** *hwn*

price *be* ***prisio***

prick *enw* ***pigad***, ***pigiad*** *hwn*

prick *be* ***pigo***
prickly *ans* ***pigog***, ***croendenau***
pride *enw* ***balchder*** *hwn*
  to p~ oneself ***ymfalchïo***
  to take p~ in ***ymhyfrydu yn/mewn***
priest *enw* ***offeiriad*** *hwn*
priesthood *enw* ***offeiriadaeth*** *hon*
primacy *enw* ***blaenoriaeth*** *hon*, ***safle blaenllaw*** *hwn*
prima facie *adf* ***ar yr olwg gyntaf***
primarily *adf* ***yn bennaf***, ***yn fwy na dim***
primary *ans* (school) ***cynradd***; (basic) ***cychwynnol***, ***sylfaenol***
primary *enw* (election) ***rhagetholiad*** *hwn*
primate *enw* ***primat*** *hwn*
prime *enw* ***anterth*** *hwn*
prime *ans* ***prif***
  a p~ consideration ***ystyriaeth flaenllaw*** *hon*
  a p~ example ***enghraifft ragorol*** *hon*
primeval *ans* ***cynoesol***
primitive *ans* ***cyntefig***
  in p~ times ***yn oes yr arth a'r blaidd***
primrose *enw* ***briallen*** *hon*
prince *enw* ***tywysog*** *hwn*
princely *ans* ***tywysogaidd***
princess *enw* ***tywysoges*** *hon*
principal *enw* ***pennaeth*** *hwn*
principal *ans* ***prif***
principality *enw* ***tywysogaeth*** *hon*
principle *enw* ***egwyddor*** *hon*
principled *ans* ***egwyddorol***
print *enw* ***ôl***; ***print*** *hwn*
print *be* ***argraffu***
printer *enw* ***argraffwr***, ***argraffydd*** *hwn*
printout *enw* ***allbrint*** *hwn*
prior *enw* ***prior*** *hwn*
prior *ans* ***cynharach***, ***cynt***, ***ymlaen llaw***
prior (to) *adf* ***cyn***
prioritize *be* ***blaenoriaethu***
priority *enw* ***blaenoriaeth*** *hon*
priory *enw* ***priordy*** *hwn*
prism *enw* ***prism*** *hwn*
prison *enw* ***carchar*** *hwn*
prisoner *enw* ***carcharor*** *hwn*
pristine *ans* ***dilychwin***
privacy *enw* ***preifatrwydd*** *hwn*
private *ans* ***preifat***
privatize *be* ***preifateiddio***
privation *enw* ***cyni*** *hwn*
privilege *enw* ***braint*** *hon*
privileged *ans* ***breintiedig***
Privy Council *enw* ***y Cyfrin Gyngor*** *hwn*
Privy Councillor *enw* ***Cyfrin Gynghorydd*** *hwn*
prize *enw* ***gwobr*** *hon*
prize *be* ***gwerthfawrogi***
pro *ardd* ***o blaid***
proactive *ans* ***rhagweithiol***
probability *enw* ***tebyg***, ***tebygolrwydd*** *hwn*

probable *ans* ***tebygol***, ***tebyg***, ***siŵr o fod***
probation *enw* ***profiannaeth*** *hon*
probationary *ans* ***ar brawf***
probe *enw* ***chwiliedydd*** *hwn*
probe *be* ***chwilio***
probity *enw* ***gonestrwydd*** *hwn*
problem *enw* ***problem*** *hon*
problematical *ans* ***amheus***, ***problematig***, ***yn codi problemau***
proboscis *enw* ***duryn*** *hwn*
procedural *ans* ***trefniadol***
procedure *enw* ***trefn*** *hon*, ***gweithdrefniant*** *hwn*
proceed *be* ***mynd ymlaen***, ***mynd rhagddo***, ***bwrw ati***
proceedings *enw* ***trafodion*** *hyn*; (legal) ***achos*** *hwn*, ***gweithrediadau cyfreithiol*** *hyn*
process *enw* ***proses*** *hon*
to be in the p~ of ***bod wrthi***
process *be* ***prosesu***
procession *enw* ***gorymdaith*** *hon*
processor *enw* ***prosesydd*** *hwn*
proclaim *be* ***datgan***, ***cyhoeddi***
proclamation *enw* ***datganiad***, ***cyhoeddiad*** *hwn*
procrastinate *be* ***gohirio***, ***oedi***, ***llusgo traed***
procreate *be* ***cenhedlu***
procure *be* ***cael***, ***caffael***, ***sicrhau***
procurement *enw* ***caffaeliad*** *hwn*
prod *be* ***procio***
prodigal *ans* ***afradlon***
prodigious *ans* ***aruthrol***
prodigy *enw* ***rhyfeddod*** *hwn*
produce *enw* ***cynnyrch*** *hwn*
produce *be* ***cynhyrchu***, ***cyflwyno***, ***llunio***
producer *enw* ***cynhyrchydd*** *hwn*
product *enw* ***cynnyrch*** *hwn*, ***nwyddau*** *hyn*
production *enw* ***cynhyrchiad*** *hwn*
productive *ans* ***cynhyrchiol***
profane *ans* ***cableddus***
profess *be* ***proffesu***
profession *enw* ***galwedigaeth*** *hon*, ***proffesiwn*** *hwn*
professional *ans* ***proffesiynol***
professor *enw* ***athro*** *hwn*
proffer *be* ***cynnig***
proficiency *enw* ***gallu***, ***hyfedredd*** *hwn*
proficient *ans* ***hyddysg***; ***rhugl***
profile *enw* **amlinell** *hon*, ***proffil*** *hwn*
profile *be* ***amlinellu***, ***proffilio***
profit *enw* ***elw*** *hwn*
profit *be* ***elwa***
profitability *enw* ***proffidioldeb*** *hwn*
profitable *ans* ***proffidiol***, ***gwneud elw***, ***o fantais***
profligate *ans* ***afradlon***
pro forma *enw* ***ffurflen*** *hon*
profound *ans* ***dwfn***, ***dwys***
a p~ comment ***sylw treiddgar*** *hwn*
a p~ effect ***effaith aruthrol*** *hon*
p~ learning difficulties ***anawsterau dysgu difrifol*** *hyn*

p

to have a p~ belief ***credu o ddifrif calon***
profoundly *adf* ***yn ddwfn***
p~ deaf ***hollol fyddar***
profundity *enw* ***dyfnder*** *hwn*
profusion *enw* ***toreth*** *hon*
program(me) *enw* ***rhaglen*** *hon*
rolling p~ ***rhaglen dreigl*** *hon*
program *be* ***rhaglennu***
programmer *enw* ***rhaglennwr***, ***rhaglennydd*** *hwn*
progress *enw* ***hynt*** *hon*, ***cwrs*** *hwn*, ***cynnydd*** *hwn*
great p~ ***camau bras/breision*** *hyn*
in p~ ***ar y gweill***
p~ report ***adroddiad ar gynnydd***
to follow someone's p~ ***dilyn hynt a helynt***
progress *be* ***mynd yn eich blaen***
progression *enw* ***dilyniant***, ***symudiad*** *hwn*
progressive *ans* ***blaengar***; ***cynyddol***
prohibit *be* ***gwahardd***
prohibited *ans* ***gwaharddedig***
prohibitive *ans* ***llethol***, ***gormodol***
project *enw* ***cywaith***, ***prosiect*** *hwn*
project *be* (= plan) ***cynllunio***, ***bwriadu***; (= estimate) ***bwrw amcan***; (= throw) ***taflu***
to p~ pictures ***taflunio***
projected figures *enw* ***rhagamcanion*** *hyn*
projection *enw* ***tafluniad***; ***amcanestyniad*** *hwn*
projector *enw* ***taflunydd*** *hwn*
proletariat *enw* ***gwerin*** *hon*
proliferate *be* ***amlhau***, ***helaethu'n ddirfawr***
prolific *ans* ***toreithiog***
prologue *enw* ***prolog*** *hwn*
prolong *be* ***ymestyn, hwyhau***
promenade *enw* ***rhodfa*** *hon*
prominence *enw* ***amlygrwydd***, ***lle blaenllaw*** *hwn*
prominent *ans* ***amlwg***
promiscuity *enw* ***llacrwydd moesol***, ***anlladrwydd*** *hwn*
promise *enw* ***addewid*** *hwn/hon*
they fulfilled their p~s ***buont cystal â'u gair***
promise *be* ***addo***
Promised Land *enw* ***Gwlad yr Addewid*** *hon*
promising *ans* ***addawol***, ***argoeli'n dda***
promontory *enw* ***penrhyn*** *hwn*
promote *be* ***dyrchafu***; ***hyrwyddo***
promoter *enw* ***hyrwyddwr*** *hwn*
promotion *enw* ***dyrchafiad*** *hwn*
prompt *ans* ***prydlon***, ***diymdroi***
prompt *be* ***procio cof***
prone *ans* ***wyneb i waered***; ***chwannog***; ***yn agored i***
prong *enw* ***pig*** *hwn/hon*, ***fforch*** *hon*
pronoun *enw* ***rhagenw*** *hwn*
pronounce *be* ***datgan***; ***ynganu***
pronounced *ans* ***pendant***, ***amlwg***

to become more p~ ***bod yn fwyfwy felly***
pronouncement *enw* ***datganiad***, ***gosodiad*** *hwn*
pronunciation *enw* ***ynganiad***, ***cynaniad*** *hwn*
proof *enw* ***prawf*** *hwn*
prop *enw* ***prop*** *hwn*, ***ateg*** *hon*
prop *be* ***pwyso yn erbyn***
propaganda *enw* ***propaganda*** *hwn*
propagate *be* ***lluosi***
propel *be* ***gyrru***, ***gwthio ymlaen***
propeller *enw* ***sgriw yrru*** *hon*
propensity *enw* ***tuedd*** *hon*, ***tueddiad*** *hwn*
proper *ans* ***go iawn***, ***priodol***, ***dyladwy***
property *enw* ***eiddo*** *hwn*; (characteristic) ***priodoledd*** *hon*
prophecy *enw* ***proffwydoliaeth*** *hon*
prophesy *be* ***proffwydo***
prophet *enw* ***proffwyd*** *hwn*, ***proffwydes*** *hon*
propinquity *enw* ***agosrwydd*** *hwn*
proportion *enw* ***rhan***, ***cyfran*** *hon*
out of all p~ ***gwneud môr a mynydd allan o***
proportional *ans* ***cyfrannol***, ***cymesurol***
proportionate *ans* ***cymesur***
proposal *enw* ***cynnig*** *hwn*
propose *be* ***cynnig***
proposed *ans* ***arfaethedig***
proposer *enw* ***cynigydd*** *hwn*
proposition *enw* ***cynnig***, ***cynigiad*** *hwn*
proprietor *enw* ***perchen***, ***perchennog*** *hwn*
propriety *enw* ***priodoldeb*** *hwn*
pro rata *adf* ***yn ôl cyfrannedd***
prorogation *enw* ***gohiriad*** *hwn*
prorogue *be* ***gohirio***
proscribe *be* ***gwahardd***
proscribed *ans* ***gwaharddedig***
prose *enw* ***rhyddiaith*** *hon*
prosecute *be* ***erlyn***
prosecution *enw* ***erlyniad*** *hwn*
prosecutor *enw* ***erlynydd*** *hwn*
prosody *enw* ***mydryddiaeth*** *hon*
prospect *enw* ***rhagolwg*** *hwn*; **argoelion** *hyn*; (view) ***golygfa*** *hon*
prospect *be* ***chwilota***
prospective *ans* ***arfaethedig***, ***darpar***
prospectus *enw* ***prosbectws*** *hwn*
prosper *be* ***ffynnu***
prosperity *enw* ***ffyniant*** *hwn*
prosperous *ans* ***ffyniannus***, ***llewyrchus***
prostitute *enw* ***putain*** *hon*
prostrate *ans* ***ar ei hyd***
prostrate *be* ***ymgreinio***, ***ymostwng ar ei hyd***
protagonist *enw* ***prif gymeriad*** *hwn*
protect *be* ***amddiffyn***, ***gwarchod***, ***cysgodi***
protection *enw* ***amddiffyniad*** *hwn*

p

protective *ans* ***amddiffynnol***, ***gwarcheidiol***
protein *enw* ***protein*** *hwn*
protest *enw* ***gwrthdystiad*** *hwn*, ***protest*** *hon*
protest *be* ***gwrthdystio***, ***protestio***
Protestant *enw* ***Protestant*** *hwn*
protester *enw* ***gwrthdystiwr*** *hwn*, ***gwrthdystwraig*** *hon*
protocol *enw* ***protocol*** *hwn*
proton *enw* ***proton*** *hwn*
prototype *enw* ***cynddelw*** *hon*
protract *be* ***estyn***
protracted *ans* ***hir***
protraction *enw* ***estyniad*** *hwn*
protractor *enw* (geom.) ***onglydd*** *hwn*
protrusion *enw* ***gwrym*** *hwn*
proud *ans* ***balch***
prove *be* ***profi***
p~n ability ***maent wedi profi eu gallu***
proverb *enw* ***dihareb*** *hon*
provide *be* ***darparu***, ***rhoi***, ***cyflwyno***
providence *enw* ***rhagluniaeth*** *hon*
provident *ans* ***darbodus***
province *enw* ***talaith*** *hon*
provincial *ans* ***taleithiol***
provision *enw* ***darpariaeth*** *hon*
provisional *ans* ***dros dro***, ***amodol***
proviso *enw* ***amod*** *hwn/hon*
provocation *enw* ***cythrudd***, ***pryfociad*** *hwn*
provocative *ans* ***pryfoclyd***, ***dadleuol***
provoke *be* ***cythruddo***, ***pryfocio***, ***ennyn***, ***ysgogi***, ***tynnu blewyn o drwyn***
prow *enw* ***pen blaen*** *hwn*
prowess *enw* ***medrusrwydd*** *hwn*
prowl *be* ***prowlan***, ***llercian***
prowler *enw* ***llerciwr*** *hwn*
proximity *enw* ***agosrwydd*** *hwn*
to be in close p~ to ***bod yn ymyl***
proxy *enw* ***dirprwy*** *hwn/hon*
prudence *enw* ***pwyll***, ***gofal*** *hwn*
prudent *ans* ***darbodus***, ***gofalus***
prudish *ans* ***mursennaidd***
prune *be* ***tocio***, ***brigo***
prune *enw* ***eirinen sych*** *hon*
prurient *ans* ***trythyll***
pry *be* ***busnesa***
psalm *enw* ***salm*** *hon*
psalmist *enw* ***salmydd*** *hwn*
pseudonym *enw* ***ffugenw*** *hwn*
psyche *enw* ***seice*** *hwn*
psychiatric *ans* ***seiciatrig***, ***seiciatraidd***
psychiatrist *enw* ***seiciatrydd*** *hwn*
psychiatry *enw* ***seiciatreg*** *hon*
psychic *ans* ***seicig***
psychoanalyst *enw* ***seicdreiddiwr*** *hwn*
psychologist *enw* ***seicolegydd*** *hwn*
psychology *enw* ***seicoleg*** *hon*
pub *enw* ***tafarn*** *hwn/hon*
puberty *enw* ***oed aeddfedrwydd*** *hwn*

public *enw* ***y cyhoedd*** *hwn*
public *ans* ***cyhoeddus***
publican *enw* ***tafarnwr*** *hwn*, ***tafarnwraig*** *hon*
publication *enw* ***cyhoeddiad*** *hwn*
publicity *enw* ***cyhoeddusrwydd*** *hwn*
public school *enw* ***ysgol fonedd*** *hon*
publish *be* ***cyhoeddi***
publisher *enw* ***cyhoeddwr*** *hwn*
publishing *enw* ***cyhoeddi***
p~ house ***gwasg*** *hon*
pucker *be* ***crychu***
pudding *enw* ***pwdin*** *hwn*
puddle *enw* ***pwll*** *hwn*
puerile *ans* ***plentynnaidd***
puff *enw* ***chwa*** *hon*
puff *be* ***chwythu***, ***pwffian***
puffin *enw* ***pâl*** *hwn*
pull *enw* ***tynfa*** *hon*, ***plwc*** *hwn*
pull *be* ***tynnu***
pulley *enw* ***pwli*** *hwn*, ***chwerfan*** *hon*
pulp *enw* ***mwydion*** *hyn*
pulpit *enw* ***pulpud*** *hwn*
pulsate *be* ***curo***, ***dychlamu***
pulsating *ans* ***trydanol***, ***cyffrous***
pulse *enw* ***curiad y galon*** *hwn*
pulverize *be* ***malurio***
pump *enw* ***pwmp*** *hwn*
pump *be* ***pwmpio***
pump-prime *be* ***ysgogi***
pun *enw* ***gair mwys*** *hwn*
punch *enw* ***dyrnod*** *hwn/hon*; (tool) ***pwnsh*** *hwn*
punch *be* ***dyrnu***; ***pwnsio***
punctual *ans* ***prydlon***
punctuality *enw* ***prydlondeb*** *hwn*
punctuate *be* ***atalnodi***
punctuation *enw* ***atalnodiad***, ***atalnodi*** *hwn*
puncture *enw* ***twll*** *hwn*
pungent *ans* ***egr***, ***llym***
punish *be* ***cosbi***
punishment *enw* ***cosb*** *hon*
puny *ans* ***eiddil***, ***pitw***
pup *enw* ***cenau***, ***ci bach*** *hwn*
pupil *enw* ***disgybl*** *hwn*; ***cannwyll y llygad*** *hon*
puppet *enw* ***pyped*** *hwn*
puppy *enw* ***ci bach*** *hwn*
purchase *enw* ***pryniant*** *hwn*
purchase *be* ***prynu***
purchaser *enw* ***prynwr*** *hwn*, ***prynwraig*** *hon*
pure *ans* ***pur***
purgatory *enw* ***purdan*** *hwn*
purge *be* ***gweithio***
purification *be* ***puro***, ***pureiddio***
purify *be* ***puro***, ***pureiddio***
purist *enw* ***purydd*** *hwn*
purity *enw* ***purdeb*** *hwn*
purloin *be* ***lladrata***
purple *ans* ***porffor***
purport *be* ***proffesu***
purpose *enw* ***bwriad***, ***pwrpas***, ***diben*** *hwn*
purposeful *ans* ***pwrpasol***
purposeless *ans* ***dibwrpas***
purr *be* ***canu grwndi***

p

purse *enw* ***pwrs*** *hwn*, ***cod*** *hon*
pursuance *enw* ***cyflawniad*** *hwn*
in p~ of ***yn unol â***
pursue *be* ***ymlid***, ***dilyn***, ***bwrw ymlaen â***, ***cynnal***
pursuit *enw* ***ymlid*** *hwn*
purulent *ans* ***crawnllyd***
purview *enw* ***maes sylw*** *hwn*
pus *enw* ***crawn*** *hwn*
push *enw* ***gwthiad***, ***hwb*** *hwn*
push *be* ***gwthio***
to p~ it a bit ***ei mentro hi***
pusillanimous *ans* ***llwfr***
pustule *enw* ***ploryn*** *hwn*
put *be* ***rhoi***, ***gosod***
putrefy *be* ***madru***, ***pydru***
putrid *ans* ***mall***, ***pwdr***
putt *be* ***suddo***
putrefy *enw* ***pwti*** *hwn*
puzzle *enw* ***pos***, ***pysl*** *hwn*
puzzle *be* ***pendroni***
puzzling *ans* ***astrus***
pyjamas *enw* ***pyjamas*** *hyn*
pylon *enw* ***peilon*** *hwn*
pyramid *enw* ***pyramid*** *hwn*
pyre *enw* ***coelcerth*** *hwn*
python *enw* ***peithon*** *hwn*

Q

quack *enw* ***cwac***, ***doctor bôn clawdd*** *hwn*
quack *be* ***cwacian***, ***cwacio***
quad:quadrangle *enw* ***pedrongl*** *hwn/hon*, **petryal** *hwn*
quaff *be* ***drachtio***
quagmire *enw* ***cors***, ***mignen*** *hon*
quail *enw* ***sofliar*** *hon*
quaint *ans* ***od***, ***henffasiwn***
quake *be* ***dirgrynu***
Quaker *enw* ***Crynwr*** *hwn*
qualification *enw* ***cymhwyster*** *hwn*
qualified *ans* ***trwyddedig***, ***cymwysedig***
qualify *be* ***bod yn gymwys***; ***cymhwyso***, ***ymgymhwyso***; ***goleddfu***
qualitative *ans* ***ansoddol***
qualities *enw* ***ansoddau*** *hyn*
quality *enw* ***ansawdd*** *hwn/hon*, **safon** *hon*
  high q~ ***o safon***, ***graenus***
qualm *enw* ***pang***, ***petruster*** *hwn*,
quandary *enw* ***cyfyng-gyngor*** *hwn*, ***penbleth*** *hwn/hon*
quantify *be* ***mesur***, ***meintioli***
quantitative *ans* ***meintiol***
quantity *enw* ***maint***, ***swm*** *hwn*
quarantine *enw* ***cwarantin*** *hwn*
quarrel *enw* ***ffrae*** *hon*
quarrel *be* ***ffraeo***, ***cecru***
quarrelsome *ans* ***cecrus***
quarry *enw* ***chwarel***; ***ysglyfaeth*** *hon*
quarry *be* ***cloddio***
quart *enw* ***chwart*** *hwn*
quarter *enw* ***chwarter*** *hwn*
quarter *be* ***rhannu'n bedair***, ***chwarteru***
quarter-final *enw* (round) ***rownd gogynderfynol*** *hon*
quarterly *ans* ***chwarterol***
quartet *enw* ***pedwarawd*** *hwn*
quash *be* ***dileu***, ***gwastrodi***
quatercentenary *enw* ***pedwarcanmlwyddiant*** *hwn*
quaver *enw* ***cwafer*** *hwn*
quaver *be* ***cwafrio***
quay *enw* ***cei*** *hwn*
queasy *ans* ***clwc***
queen *enw* ***brenhines*** *hon*
queer *ans* ***rhyfedd***
quell *be* ***tawelu***, ***gostegu***
quench *be* ***diffodd***; ***torri***
querulous *ans* ***ceintachlyd***, ***cwynfanllyd***
query *enw* ***ymholiad*** *hwn*
query *be* ***holi***; ***amau***
quest *enw* ***cais*** *hwn*
  in their q~ to ***yn eu hymgais i***
question *enw* ***cwestiwn*** *hwn*
  in q~ ***hwnnw/honno/hynny***
  to be in q~ ***yn y fantol***
question *be* ***holi***, ***cwestiynu***; ***amau***

q

questionable *ans* ***amheus***
questioner *enw* ***holwr*** *hwn*, ***holwraig*** *hon*
question mark *enw* ***marc cwestiwn*** *hwn*
questionnaire *enw* ***holiadur*** *hwn*
queue *enw* ***ciw***, ***cwt*** *hwn*
queue *be* ***sefyll mewn rhes, ciwio***
quibble *be* ***hollti blew***
quick *enw* ***(y) byw*** *hwn*
quick *ans* ***cyflym***, ***buan***, ***parod***, ***awyddus***
quicken *be* ***cyflymu***
quicklime *enw* ***calch brwd*** *hwn*
quicksand *enw* ***traeth gwyllt***, ***traeth byw*** *hwn*
quicksilver *enw* ***arian byw*** *hwn*
quiescent *ans* ***llonydd***, ***tawel***
quiet *ans* ***tawel***, ***distaw***
quieten *be* ***tawelu***
quietness *enw* ***tawelwch***, ***distawrwydd*** *hwn*
quietude *enw* ***tawelwch***, ***distawrwydd*** *hwn*
quill *enw* ***cwilsen*** *hon*
quilt *enw* ***carthen*** *hon*, ***cwilt*** *hwn*
quince *enw* ***(afal cwins)***, ***cwins*** *hwn*
quintessence *enw* ***hanfod*** *hwn*
quintet *enw* ***pumawd*** *hwn*
quip *enw* ***ateb parod***, ***sylw bachog*** *hwn*
quip *be* ***cellwair***
quirk *enw* ***chwiw*** *hon*, ***cast*** *hwn*
quit *be* ***gadael***, ***rhoi'r gorau i***
quite *adf* ***yn hollol***
quiver *enw* ***cawell saethau*** *hwn*
quiver *be* ***crynu***
quiz *enw* ***cwis*** *hwn*, ***cystadleuaeth*** *hon*
quiz *be* ***holi***
quoit *enw* ***coeten*** *hon*
quoits *be* (to play) ***coetio***
quorum *enw* ***cworwm*** *hwn*
quota *enw* ***cwota*** *hwn*
quotation *enw* ***dyfyniad*** *hwn*
quote *be* ***dyfynnu***
to q~ ***chwedl***
quoth *berf* ***ebe***, ***medd***
quotient *enw* ***cyniferydd*** *hwn*

R

rabbi *enw* ***rabi*** *hwn*
rabbit *enw* ***cwningen*** *hon*
rabble *enw* ***ciwed*** *hon*
rabid *ans* ***cynddeiriog***
rabies *enw* ***y gynddaredd*** *hon*
race *enw* ***ras***; ***hil*** *hon*
race *be* ***rhedeg ras***, ***rasio***
to r~ through ***mynd drwy – fel y gwynt***
racetrack *enw* ***trac rasio*** *hwn*
racial *ans* ***hiliol***
r~ discrimination ***gwahaniaethu ar sail hil***
racism *enw* ***hiliaeth***, ***hilyddiaeth*** *hon*
rack *enw* ***rhesel*** *hon*
to go to r~ and ruin ***mynd i'r gwellt***
racket *enw* ***raced*** *hon*
raconteur *enw* ***storïwr*** *hwn*
raconteuse *enw* ***storïwraig*** *hon*
racy *ans* ***carlamus***
radar *enw* ***radar*** *hwn*
radiance *enw* ***gwawl***, **llewyrch** *hwn*
radiant *ans* ***pelydrol***, ***yn disgleirio***
radiate *be* ***tywynnu***, ***disgleirio***
radiation *enw* ***pelydriad*** *hwn*; ***ymbelydredd*** *hwn*
radiator *enw* ***rheiddiadur*** *hwn*
radical *ans* ***radicalaidd***
r~ reappraisal ***ailgloriannu trwyadl***
radicalism *enw* ***radicaliaeth*** *hon*
radio *enw* ***radio*** *hwn*
radioactive *ans* ***ymbelydrol***
radio-frequency *enw* ***radio-amledd*** *hwn*
radish *enw* ***rhuddygl*** *hwn*
radium *enw* ***radiwm*** *hwn*
radius *enw* ***radiws*** *hwn*
within a r~ of ***o fewn cylch/pellter o***
raffia *enw* ***raffia*** *hwn*
raffish *ans* ***afradlon***
raffle *enw* ***raffl*** *hon*
raffle *be* ***rafflo***
raft *enw* ***rafft*** *hon*
a whole r~ of ***llu o***
rafter *enw* ***dist***, ***trawst*** *hwn*
rag *enw* ***clwtyn***, ***cadach*** *hwn*
rage *enw* ***cynddaredd*** *hon*
rage *be* ***cynddeiriogi***
ragged *ans* ***carpiog***
raging *ans* ***gwyllt***, ***ffyrnig***
raid *enw* ***cyrch***, ***ymosodiad*** *hwn*
raid *be* ***dwyn cyrch ar***; ***ysbeilio***
raider *enw* ***ysbeiliwr*** *hwn*
rail *enw* ***canllaw***, ***cledren*** *hon*
rail *be* ***rhefru***
railway *enw* ***rheilffordd*** *hon*
r~ mania ***clefyd y cledrau*** *hwn*
raiment *enw* ***dillad*** *hyn*
rain *enw* ***glaw*** *hwn*
rain *be* ***bwrw glaw***, ***glawio***
rainbow *enw* ***enfys*** *hon*

r

raincoat *enw* ***cot law*** *hon*
raindrop *enw* ***diferyn***, ***defnyn o law*** *hwn*
rainfall *enw* ***glaw***, ***glawiad*** *hwn*
rainwater *enw* ***dŵr glaw*** *hwn*
rainy *ans* ***glawog***
raise *be* ***codi***
to r~ the awareness of ***cynyddu'r ymwybyddiaeth o***
to r~ the quality of ***gwella ansawdd***
raisin *enw* ***rhesinen*** *hon*
rake *enw* ***cribin*** *hwn*, ***rhaca*** *hwn/hon*; (slope) ***goleddfiad*** *hwn*
rake *be* ***cribinio***, ***rhacanu***
to r~ up an old grievance ***codi hen grach***
rally *enw* ***rali*** *hon*
ram *enw* ***hwrdd***, ***maharen*** *hwn*
ramble *be* ***crwydro***
rambling *ans* ***trofaus***, ***gwasgarog***
ramification *enw* ***cangheniad*** *hwn*
ramify *be* ***canghennu***, ***ymganghennu***
ramp *enw* ***esgynfa***; ***poncen*** *hon*
rampage *be* ***rhedeg yn wyllt***
rampant *ans* ***rhemp***
rampart *enw* ***rhagfur*** *hwn*
ram-raid *be* ***hyrddysbeilio***
ramshackle *ans* ***simsan***, ***sigledig***
ranch *enw* ***ransh*** *hon*
rancid *ans* ***sur***
rancour *enw* ***chwerwder***, ***gwenwyn*** *hwn*
random *ans* ***ar hap***, ***damweiniol***, ***hwnt ac yma***
randy *ans* ***chwantus***
range *enw* (extent) ***amrediad***, ***cylch***, ***ystod***; (tract of land) ***paith*** *hwn*; (mountains) ***cadwyn*** *hon*
rank *enw* ***rheng***, ***gradd*** *hon*, ***safle*** *hwn*
rank *be* ***trefnu***, ***graddoli***, ***gosod***
ransack *be* ***chwilota***; ***anrheithio***
ransom *enw* ***pridwerth*** *hwn*
rant *be* ***arthio***, ***rhefru***
rapacious *ans* ***rheibus***
rape *enw* ***trais*** *hwn*; (plant) ***erfinen yr ŷd*** *hon*
rape *be* ***treisio***
rapid *ans* ***cyflym***, ***buan***
rapidity *enw* ***cyflymdra***, ***buander*** *hwn*
rapist *enw* ***treisiwr*** *hwn*
rapscallion *enw* ***cnaf***, ***caridým*** *hwn*
rapt *ans* **wedi** ***ymgolli***
rapture *enw* ***perlewyg*** *hwn*
rare *ans* ***prin iawn***, ***anaml***
raring *ans* ***ar dân***, ***brwd***
r~ing to go ***yn dyheu/ar dân am gael mynd***
rarity *enw* ***prinder*** *hwn*
rascal *enw* ***gwalch*** *hwn*
rash *enw* ***brech*** *hon*
rash *ans* ***byrbwyll***, ***carlamus***
rashness *enw* ***byrbwylltra***, ***gwyllltineb*** *hwn*
rasp *enw* ***rhathell*** *hon*

rasp *be* ***rhygnu***
raspberries *enw* ***afan coch***, ***mafon*** *hyn*
rat *enw* ***llygoden Ffrengig***, ***llygoden fawr*** *hon*
rate *enw* ***cyfradd***, ***graddfa*** *hon*
rate *be* ***graddio***, ***ystyried***
how do you r~ your services? ***beth yw'ch barn am eich --?***
rather *adf* ***yn hytrach***; ***pur***, ***eithaf***
ratification *enw* ***cadarnhad*** *hwn*
ratify *be* ***cadarnhau***
ratio *enw* ***cymhareb*** *hon*
ration *enw* ***dogn*** *hwn/hon*
ration *be* ***dogni***
rational *ans* ***rhesymol***
rationalize *be* ***rhesymoli***; ***ad-drefnu***
rattle *enw* ***ratl*** *hon*
rattle *be* ***clecian***, ***clindarddach***
raucous *ans* ***croch***, ***aflafar***
ravage *be* ***difrodi***
to be r~d by ***wedi'i sigo gan***
rave *be* ***rafio***
raven *enw* ***cigfran*** *hon*
ravenous *ans* ***gwancus***
ravine *enw* ***ceunant*** *hwn*
raving mad *ans* ***cynddeiriog***
ravish *be* ***treisio***
ravishing *ans* ***cyfareddol***
raw *ans* ***amrwd***, ***crai***
r~ data ***data crai*** *hwn*
ray *enw* (light etc.) ***pelydryn*** *hwn*; (fish) ***cath fôr*** *hon*
raze *be* ***chwalu***
razor *enw* ***rasel*** *hon*
re *ardd* ***ynglŷn â***
reach *be* ***cyrraedd***, ***estyn***
to r~ a decision ***gwneud penderfyniad***
react *be* ***adweithio***, ***ymateb***
reaction *enw* ***adwaith***, ***ymateb*** *hwn*
reactionary *ans* ***adweithiol***
reactivate *be* ***ailgychwyn***, ***adfywio***
reactive *ans* ***adweithiol***, ***ymatebol***
read *be* ***darllen***
r~ all about it ***cewch wybod y cyfan yn***
readability *enw* ***darllenadwyedd***, ***rhwyddineb darllen*** *hwn*
readable *ans* ***darllenadwy***
reader *enw* ***darllenydd*** *hwn*
readily *adf* ***â chroeso***; ***yn hawdd***, ***yn rhwydd***
readiness *enw* ***parodrwydd*** *hwn*
in r~ for ***i baratoi ar gyfer***
reading *enw* ***darlleniad***, ***darllen*** *hwn*
readjust *be* ***ailaddasu***
ready *ans* ***parod***
reaffirm *be* ***ailgadarnhau***
reagent *enw* ***adweithydd*** *hwn*
real *ans* ***go iawn***, ***gwirioneddol***
r- anguish ***gofid calon*** *hwn*
r~ concern ***pryder dwfn*** *hwn*
a r~ drag ***poendod llwyr***, ***pen tost*** *hwn*
r~ evidence ***tystiolaeth bendant*** *hon*

r

r~ interest in ***diddordeb byw yn***
realign *be* ***aildrefnu***
realism *enw* ***realaeth*** *hon*
reality *enw* ***gwirionedd***, ***realiti*** *hwn*
in r~ ***yn y byd go iawn***
realization *enw* ***cyflawniad*** *hwn*; ***sylweddoli***
realize *be* ***sylweddoli***; ***cyflawni***
realm *enw* ***brenhiniaeth*** *hon*
in the r~ of ***ym maes***, ***ym myd***
reap *be* ***medi***
to r~ the benefit of ***maent ar eu hennill***; ***manteisio***
reaper *enw* ***medelwr*** *hwn*
reappear *be* ***ailymddangos***
reappraise *be* ***ailwerthuso***, ***adolygu***
rear *enw* ***y tu ôl*** *hwn*
rear *be* ***codi***
rearm *be* ***adarfogi***
rearrange *be* ***ad-drefnu***, ***aildrefnu***
reason *enw* ***rheswm*** *hwn*
it was for this r~ ***dyna pam***
reason *be* ***rhesymu***
reasonable *ans* ***rhesymol***
reasoning *enw* ***ymresymiad*** *hwn*
reassure *be* ***tawelu meddwl***, ***codi calon***
rebate *enw* ***ad-daliad*** *hwn*
rebel *enw* ***gwrthryfelwr*** *hwn*, ***gwrthryfelwraig*** *hon*, ***rebel*** *hwn*
rebel *be* ***gwrthryfela***
rebellion *enw* ***gwrthryfel*** *hwn*
rebellious *ans* ***gwrthryfelgar***
rebirth *enw* ***ailenedigaeth*** *hon*
rebound *be* ***adlamu***
rebuild *be* ***ailadeiladu***
to r~ confidence ***adfer ffydd***
rebuke *enw* ***cerydd*** *hwn*
rebuke *be* ***ceryddu***
rebut *be* ***gwrthbrofi***
recalcitrant *ans* ***gwrthnysig***
recall *be* ***galw i gof***, ***cofio***
recant *be* ***tynnu geiriau yn ôl***
recapture *be* ***adennill***, ***ailfeddiannu***
recast *be* ***ailwampio***, ***ail-lunio***
recede *be* ***cilio***
receipt *enw* ***derbynneb*** *hon*
receivable *ans* ***derbyniadwy***
receive *be* ***derbyn***
receiver *enw* ***derbynnydd*** *hwn*
to go into r~ship ***mynd i ddwylo'r derbynnydd***
recent *ans* ***diweddar***
receptacle *enw* ***llestr*** *hwn*
reception *enw* ***derbyniad*** *hwn*; ***derbynfa*** *hon*
receptionist *enw* ***derbynnydd*** *hwn*
recess *enw* ***gwyliau*** *hyn;* **encil** *hwn*
recession *enw* ***dirwasgiad*** *hwn*
recipe *enw* ***rysáit*** *hon;* **patrwm** *hwn*
recipient *enw* ***derbynnydd*** *hwn*
reciprocal *ans* ***o'r ddwy ochr***
recital *enw* ***datganiad*** *hwn*
recite *be* ***adrodd***
reckless *ans* ***dibris***, ***dienaid***
reckon *be* ***cyfrif***
reckoning *enw* ***cyfrif*** *hwn*

reclaim *be* ***adennill**, **adfer***
recline *be* ***gorwedd**, **gorweddian***
recluse *enw* ***meudwy*** *hwn*
recognize *be* (know) ***adnabod***; (accept) ***cydnabod***
to r~ the importance ***sylweddoli pa mor bwysig***
recognition *enw* ***cydnabyddiaeth*** *hon*
to gain r~ ***ennill eu plwyf***
to grow out of all r~ ***cynyddu'n aruthrol***
recoil *be* ***adlamu***
recollect *be* ***dwyn i gof**, **cofio***
recollection *enw* ***cof*** *hwn*
recommend *be* ***argymell***
recommendation *enw* ***argymhelliad*** *hwn*
recompense *enw* ***iawn**, **ad-daliad*** *hwn*
recompense *be* ***talu iawn***
reconcile *be* ***cymodi**, **cysoni***
reconciliation *enw* ***cymod*** *hwn*
reconsider *be* ***ailystyried***
record *enw* (written) ***cofnod***; (sound) ***record***; (best achievement) ***record*** *hon*
on r~ ***ar gof a chadw***
a r~ amount ***mwy nag erioed o'r blaen***
to place on r~ ***cofnodi***
record *be* ***cofnodi***; ***recordio***
recount *be* ***adrodd**, **traethu***; ***ailgyfrif***
recoup *be* ***adennill***
recourse *enw* (to have) ***troi at***
recover *be* ***ailddarganfod***; ***adennill***; ***adfer***; ***cael eu gwynt atynt***
recovery *enw* ***adferiad**, **gwellhad*** *hwn*
recreation *enw* ***adloniant*** *hwn*
recreational *ans* ***adloniadol***
recriminate *be* ***edliw**, **dannod***
recrimination *enw* ***edliwiad*** *hwn*
recruit *be* ***recriwtio***
rectangle *enw* ***hirsgwar**, **petryal*** *hwn*
rectification *enw* ***cywiriad*** *hwn*, ***unioni***
rectify *be* ***unioni**, **cywiro***
rectitude *enw* ***uniondeb*** *hwn*
rector *enw* ***rheithor*** *hwn*
rectory *enw* ***rheithordy*** *hwn*
recumbent *ans* ***ar eich gorwedd***
recuperate *be* ***adfer**, **dod atynt eu hunain***
recur *be* ***digwydd eto**, **ailddigwydd***
recurrence *enw* ***ail-ymddangosiad**, **ail-ddigwyddiad*** *hwn*
recurrent *ans* ***drosodd a thro***
r~ themes ***themâu sy'n codi droeon***
recycle *be* ***ailgylchu**, **ailgylchynu***
red *enw* ***coch*** *hwn*
red *ans* ***coch***
r~-letter day ***dydd o lawen chwedl*** *hwn*

Red Cross *enw* ***Croes Goch*** *hon*
redden *be* ***cochi***
redeem *be* ***adbrynu***; (debt) ***clirio***, ***ad-dalu***; ***cyfnewid***
Redeemer *enw* ***Gwaredwr*** *hwn*
redemption *enw* ***iachawdwriaeth*** *hon*
redhead *enw* ***cochyn*** *hwn*, ***cochen*** *hon*
red-hot *ans* ***eirias***
redness *enw* ***cochni*** *hwn*
redo *be* ***ail-wneud***
redouble *be* ***dwysáu***
redress *enw* ***iawn*** *hwn*; **camau cywiro** *hyn*
redress *be* ***unioni***
red tape *enw* ***biwrocratiaeth*** *hon*
reduce *be* ***lleihau***, ***gostwng***, ***cwtogi***
reduction *enw* ***lleihad***, ***gostyngiad*** *hwn*
redundancy *enw* ***colli swydd***, ***diswyddiad*** *hwn*
redundant *ans* ***diangen***, ***segur***
reed *enw* ***cawnen***, ***corsen*** *hon*
reef *enw* ***rîff*** *hon*
reek *be* ***drewi***
reel *enw* ***ril***, ***rilen*** *hon*
re-election *enw* ***ailetholiad*** *hwn*, *be* ***ailethol***
re-enter *be* ***dychwelyd***
re-establish *be* ***ailsefydlu***
refectory *enw* ***ffreutur*** *hwn*
refer *be* **cyfeirio**
referee *enw* ***dyfarnwr***; ***canolwr*** *hwn*
reference *enw* ***cyfeiriad***; ***tystlythyr*** *hwn*
  r~ books ***llyfrau cyfair*** *hyn*
referral *enw* ***cyfeireb*** *hon*
refill *be* ***ail-lenwi***
refine *be* ***puro***, ***coethi***, ***mireinio***, ***caboli***
refined *ans* ***coeth***; (pers.) ***diwylliedig***, ***chwaethus***
refinement *enw* ***coethder***, ***cywreinrwydd*** *hwn*
refinery *enw* ***purfa*** *hon*
reflate *be* ***ailchwyddo***
reflect *be* ***adlewyrchu***; ***myfyrio***, ***ystyried ymhellach***
reflection *enw* ***adlewyrchiad***; ***meddwl*** *hwn*
  on r~ ***o feddwl eto***
reflector *enw* ***adlewyrchydd*** *hwn*
reflex *enw* ***atgyrch*** *hwn*
reflexive *ans* ***atblygol***
reform *enw* ***diwygiad*** *hwn*
re-form *be* ***ailffurfio***
reform *be* ***diwygio***
reformer *enw* ***diwygiwr*** *hwn*
refract *be* ***plygu***
refrain *enw* ***byrdwn*** *hwn*, ***cytgan*** *hon*
refrain *be* ***ymatal***
  r~ from ***ymgadw rhag***
refresh *be* ***adfywio***
refreshing *ans* ***adfywiol***, ***amheuthun***

refreshments *enw* ***lluniaeth*** *hon*
refrigerate *be* ***rhewi***, ***oeri***
refrigerator *enw* ***cwpwrdd rhew*** *hwn*, **oergell** *hon*
refuge *enw* ***noddfa***, ***lloches*** *hon*
refugee *enw* ***ffoadur*** *hwn*
refulgent *ans* ***disglair***, ***llachar***
refund *enw* ***ad-daliad*** *hwn*
refund *be* ***ad-dalu***
refurbish *be* ***adnewyddu, gweddnewid***
refusal *enw* ***gwrthodiad*** *hwn*
refuse *enw* ***sbwriel:ysbwriel*** *hwn*
refuse *be* ***gwrthod***
refutable *ans* ***gwadadwy***
refute *be* ***gwrthbrofi***, ***gwrthod***
regain *be* ***adennill***, ***ailennill***
regal *ans* ***brenhinol***
regard *enw* ***golwg*** *hwn*
  high r~ ***uchel eu parch***
  to pay proper r~ to rules ***parchu rheolau***
regard *be* ***edrych ar***; **ystyried**
regarding *ardd* ***ynglŷn â***
regardless *adf* ***er hynny***, ***er gwaethaf pawb a phopeth***, ***waeth beth fo***
regards *enw* ***cofion*** *hyn*
regenerate *be* ***aileni***, ***adfywio***
regeneration *enw* ***adfywiad*** *hwn*
regime *enw* ***cyfundrefn*** *hon*
regiment *enw* ***catrawd*** *hon*
region *enw* ***rhanbarth*** *hwn*, ***ardal*** *hon*
  in the r~ of ***rhyw***, ***oddeutu***
regional *ans* ***rhanbarthol***
register *enw* ***cofrestr*** *hon*; (voice) ***cywair***
register *be* ***cofrestru***, ***cofnodi***, ***ymrestru***
registered *ans* ***cofrestredig***
registrable *ans* ***cofrestradwy***
registrar *enw* ***cofrestrydd*** *hwn*
registration *enw* ***cofrestriad*** *hwn*, *be* ***cofrestru***
registry *enw* ***cofrestrfa*** *hon*
regressive *ans* ***atchweliadol***
regret *enw* ***edifeirwch*** *hwn*
  with deep r~ ***gyda thristwch mawr***
regret *be* ***edifarhau***, ***difaru***
regrettable *ans* ***anffodus***, ***yn destun gofid***
regrettably *adf* ***ysywaeth***
regular *ans* ***cyson***, ***rheolaidd***
regularity *enw* ***cysondeb*** *hwn*
regulars *enw* ***ffyddloniaid*** *hyn*
regulate *be* ***rheoli***, ***rheoleiddio***
regulation *enw* ***rheol*** *hon*, ***rheoliad*** *hwn*
regulator *enw* ***rheolydd*** *hwn*
regulatory *ans* ***rheoleiddiol***, ***rheoliadol***
rehabilitate *be* ***adsefydlu***; ***ymaddasu***
rehabilitation *enw* ***ymaddasiad*** *hwn*
rehash *enw* ***cawl ail-dwym*** *hwn*
rehash *be* ***ailbobi***

r

rehearsal *enw* ***ymarfer***, ***rihyrsal*** *hwn/hon*
rehearse *be* ***ymarfer***
reign *enw* ***teyrnasiad*** *hwn*
reign *be* ***teyrnasu***
reimburse *be* ***ad-dalu***, ***digolledu***
reimbursement *enw* ***ad-daliad*** *hwn*
rein *enw* ***ffrwyn*** *hon*
  free r~ ***rhwydd hynt***
reindeer *enw* ***carw*** *hwn*
reinforce *be* ***atgyfnerthu***
reinstate *be* ***aildderbyn***, ***ailbenodi***
reintegrate *be* ***ailintegreiddio***
reiterate *be* ***ailadrodd***, ***ailbwysleisio***
reiteration *enw* ***ailadroddiad*** *hwn*
reject *be* ***gwrthod***, ***wfftio***
rejection *enw* ***gwrthodiad*** *hwn*
rejoice *be* ***gorfoleddu***, ***ymlawenhau***
rejoicing *enw* ***gorfoledd*** *hwn*
rejoinder *enw* ***ateb***, ***gwrthateb*** *hwn*
relapse *be* ***llithro'n ôl***, ***cwympo'n ôl***
relate *be* ***adrodd***; ***cydymdeimlo***; ***perthyn***
relation *enw* ***perthynas*** *hon*
  in r~ to ***ymwneud â***
relationship *enw* ***perthynas*** *hon*
relative *enw* ***perthynas*** *hwn/hon*
relative *ans* ***perthynol***
relatively *adf* ***cymharol***, ***gweddol***
relax *be* ***ymlacio***
relaxation *enw* ***ymlaciad*** *hwn*
relaxed *ans* (pers., body) ***wedi ymlacio***; (muscle) ***wedi llacio/llaesu***; (manner) ***diddig***, ***hamddenol***
relay *be* ***trosglwyddo***
  r~ race ***ras gyfnewid*** *hon*
release *be* ***rhyddhau***
relegate *be* (sport) ***gostwng***, ***diraddio***
relegation *enw* ***diraddiad*** *hwn*
relent *be* ***tosturio***, ***hanner maddau***
relentless *ans* ***didostur***, ***di-ildio***
relevance *enw* ***perthnasedd*** *hwn*
relevant *ans* ***perthnasol***
reliability *enw* ***dibynadwyaeth*** *hon*, ***dibynadwyedd*** *hwn*
reliable *ans* ***dibynadwy***, ***sicr***
reliance *enw* ***hyder*** *hwn*, ***ffydd*** *hon*
relic *enw* ***crair*** *hwn*
relief *enw* ***rhyddhad*** *hwn*
relieve *be* ***lleddfu***, ***rhyddhau***
religion *enw* ***crefydd*** *hon*
  minister of r~ ***gweinidog yr Efengyl*** *hwn*
religious *ans* ***crefyddol***
relinquish *be* ***gollwng***, ***rhoi'r gorau i***
relish *be* ***cael blas ar***
relive *be* ***ail-fyw***
relocate *be* ***adleoli***
reluctant *ans* ***anfodlon***
  r~ praise ***canmoliaeth grintach*** *hon*
rely *be* ***dibynnu***
remain *be* ***aros***
remainder *enw* ***gweddill***, ***rhelyw*** *hwn*

remains *enw* ***gweddillion*** *hyn*
remark *enw* ***sylw*** *hwn*
remark *be* ***gwneud sylw***, ***dweud***
remarkable *ans* ***hynod***, ***nodedig***, ***yn syndod***
remedial *ans* ***adferol***
  r~ class ***dosbarth adfer*** *hwn*
  r~ action ***camau cywiro*** *hyn*
remedy *enw* ***meddyginiaeth*** *hon*
remedy *be* ***gwella***
remember *be* ***cofio***
remembrance *enw* ***coffadwriaeth*** *hon*
remind *be* ***atgoffa***
reminisce *be* ***hel atgofion***
reminiscences *enw* ***atgofion*** *hyn*
remiss *ans* ***esgeulus***
remit *enw* ***cylch gwaith*** *hwn*
remnant *enw* ***gweddill*** *hwn*
remonstrate *be* ***protestio wrth***, ***dweud y drefn wrth***
remorse *enw* ***edifeirwch*** *hwn*
remote *ans* ***diarffordd***, ***anghysbell***
remoteness *enw* ***pellenigrwydd*** *hwn*
removable *ans* ***symudol***, ***symudadwy***
remove *be* ***symud ymaith***, ***dileu***
  at one r~ ***un cam i ffwrdd***
remunerate *be* ***talu***, ***gwobrwyo***
remuneration *enw* ***tâl*** *hwn*, ***cydnabyddiaeth*** *hon*
renaissance *enw* ***dadeni*** *hwn*
renew *be* ***adnewyddu***
renewal *enw* ***adnewyddiad*** *hwn*
renewed *ans* ***o'r newydd***
rennet *enw* ***cwyrdeb*** *hwn*
renounce *be* ***rhoi'r gorau i***
renovate *be* ***adnewyddu***
renown *enw* ***enwogrwydd*** *hwn*
rent *enw* ***rhent*** *hwn*
rent *be* ***gosod ar rent***
renunciation *be* ***ymwrthod***, ***ymwadu â***
reorganization *enw* ***ad-drefniant*** *hwn*
reorganize *be* ***ad-drefnu***
repair *enw* ***atgyweiriad*** *hwn*
repair *be* ***atgyweirio***, ***trwsio***
reparation *enw* ***iawndal*** *hwn*
repartee *enw* ***ateb parod*** *hwn*
repatriate *be* ***dychwelyd i'w wlad ei hun***
repay *be* ***ad-dalu***
repayment *enw* ***ad-daliad*** *hwn*
repeal *enw* ***diddymiad*** *hwn*
repeal *be* ***diddymu***
repealable *ans* ***diddymadwy***
repeat *enw* ***ailadroddiad*** *hwn*
repeat *be* ***ailadrodd***
repent *be* ***edifarhau***, ***edifaru***
repercussion *enw* ***sgil-effaith***, ***ôl-effaith*** *hon*
repetition *enw* ***ailadroddiad*** *hwn*
repetitious *ans* ***ailadroddus***, ***ailadroddllyd***
repetitive *ans* ***ailadroddus***
replace *be* ***ailosod***; ***amnewid***
replay *be* ***ailchwarae***
replenish *be* ***ail-lenwi***, ***adnewyddu***

r

replete *ans* ***llawn***, ***cyforiog***, ***yn frith***
replicate *be* ***ailadrodd***
reply *enw* ***ateb*** *hwn*
reply *be* ***ateb***
report *enw* ***adroddiad*** *hwn*
report *be* ***adrodd***, ***rhoi gwybod am***
reporter *enw* ***gohebydd*** *hwn*
repose *enw* ***gorffwys*** *hwn*
repository *enw* ***storfa*** *hon*
repossess *be* ***atafaelu***
reprehend *be* ***ceryddu***
reprehensible *ans* ***gresynus***, ***beius***
represent *be* ***cynrychioli***
representation *enw* ***portread***, ***darlun*** *hwn*; ***cynrychiolaeth*** *hon*
proportional r~ ***cynrychiolaeth gyfrannol*** *hon*
representative *enw* ***cynrychiolydd*** *hwn*
representative *ans* ***cynrychiadol***
repress *be* ***gwastrodi***; ***ffrwyno***; ***gormesu***
repression *enw* ***gormes*** *hwn/hon*, ***gorthrwm*** *hwn*
repressive *ans* ***gormesol***
reprieve *enw* (law) ***gohiriad*** *hwn*; (respite) ***oediad, seibiant*** *hwn*
reprimand *enw* ***cerydd*** *hwn*
reprimand *be* ***ceryddu***
reprint *enw* ***adargraffiad***, ***ailargraffiad*** *hwn*
reprint *be* ***adargraffu***
reprisal *enw* ***dial***, ***dialedd*** *hwn*
reproach *enw* ***cerydd*** *hwn*
reproach *be* ***ceryddu***, ***edliw***
reprobate *enw* ***adyn***, ***gwalch*** *hwn*
reproduce *be* ***atgynhyrchu***
reproduction *enw* ***atgynhyrchiad***, ***copi*** *hwn*
reprove *be* ***edliw***, ***ceryddu***
reptile *enw* ***ymlusgiad*** *hwn*
republic *enw* ***gweriniaeth*** *hon*
republican *ans* ***gweriniaethol***
repudiate *be* ***gwrthod arddel***, ***ymwrthod â***
repugnance *enw* ***gwrthuni*** *hwn*
repugnant *ans* ***gwrthun***
repulse *be* ***ôl-hyrddio***
repulsion *enw* ***ffieidd-dra*** *hwn*
repulsive *ans* ***ffiaidd***, ***atgas***
reputable *ans* ***safonol***
reputation *enw* ***enw***, ***bri*** *hwn*
to gain a r~ ***bod yn enwog am***
request *enw* ***cais*** *hwn*
request *be* ***gofyn am***, ***ceisio***
requiem *enw* ***offeren y meirw*** *hon*
require *be* ***gofyn***, ***mynnu***; (need) ***(bod, e.g. a oes) angen***
required *ans* ***gofynnol***
requirement *enw* ***angen***, ***gofyn/gofyniad*** *hwn*
requirements *enw* ***gofynion*** *hyn*
requisite *ans* ***gofynnol***, ***angenrheidiol***, ***dyladwy***
requite *be* ***ad-dalu***
rescind *be* ***diddymu***
rescue *be* ***achub***
research *enw* ***ymchwil*** *hon/hwn*

research *be* ***ymchwilio***
resemblance *enw* ***tebygrwydd*** *hwn*
resemble *be* ***bod yn debyg (i)***
resent *be* ***bod yn ddig***
resentful *ans* ***dal dig***
resentment *enw* ***dig***, ***dicter*** *hwn*
reservation *enw* ***gwarchodfa*** *hon*; ***amheuaeth*** *hon*
reserve *be* ***cadw***
reserve *enw* ***cronfa*** *hon*
reservoir *enw* ***cronfa*** *hon*
reshuffle *be* ***ad-drefnu***
reside *be* ***byw***
residence *enw* ***tŷ*** *hwn*, ***preswylfa*** *hon*
resident *enw* ***preswylydd*** *hwn*
  r~ since ***yno ers***
residuary *ans* ***gweddilliol***
residue *enw* ***gweddill*** *hwn*
resign *be* ***ymddiswyddo***
  r~ed to ***gorfod derbyn***
resignation *enw* ***ymddiswyddiad*** *hwn*
resilience *enw* ***gwytnwch*** *hwn*, ***gwrthod ildio***
resist *be* ***gwrthsefyll***
resistance *enw* ***gwrthsafiad*** *hwn*
resolute *ans* ***di-droi'n-ôl***, ***penderfynol***
resolution *enw* ***adduned*** *hon*; ***penderfyniad*** *hwn*; ***eglurder llun***
resolve *be* ***penderfynu***, ***torri (dadl)***, ***datrys***
resonant *ans* ***atseiniol***
resonate *be* ***atseinio***
resort *enw* ***cyrchfan*** *hwn*
  last r~ ***cam terfynol/eithaf*** *hwn*
resort *be* ***defnyddio***, ***troi at/i***
resound *be* ***diasbedain***
resource *enw* ***adnodd*** *hwn*, ***ffynhonnell*** *hon*
resourceful *ans* ***dyfeisgar***
resourcing *enw* ***darparu adnoddau***
respect *enw* ***parch*** *hwn*
  in other r~s ***fel arall***
  in r~ of ***o ran***
  in some r~s ***mewn rhai ffyrdd***
respect *be* ***parchu***
respectability *enw* ***parchusrwydd*** *hwn*
respectable *ans* ***parchus***
respectful *ans* ***llawn parch***
respecting *ardd* ***ynglŷn â***
respective *ans* ***priodol***, ***ei hun***
respectively *adf* ***yn y drefn honno***
respire *be* ***anadlu***
respite *enw* ***seibiant***, ***saib*** *hwn*
resplendent *ans* ***ysblennydd***
respond *be* ***ymateb***
respondent *enw* ***ymatebydd*** *hwn*
response *enw* ***ateb***, ***ymateb*** *hwn*
responsibility *enw* ***cyfrifoldeb*** *hwn*
  to take r~ ***arddel cyfrifoldeb***
responsible *ans* ***cyfrifol***
rest *enw* ***saib***, ***seibiant*** *hwn*
rest *be* ***gorffwys***
  their last r~ing place ***tŷ eu hir gartref***

restitution *enw* ***adferiad*** *hwn*, ***gwneud iawn am***
restive *ans* ***anhydrin***; ***aflonydd***
restoration *enw* ***adferiad*** *hwn*
restorative *ans* ***adferol***
restore *be* ***adfer***
restrain *be* ***ffrwyno***, ***dal yn ôl***; ***rhwystro***
restrict *be* ***cyfyngu***
restriction *enw* ***cyfyngiad*** *hwn*
restrictive *ans* ***cyfyngol***, ***rhwystrol***
restructure *be* ***ailstrwythuro***, ***aildrefnu***, ***ailwampio***
result *enw* ***canlyniad***, ***ffrwyth*** *hwn*
  to r~ in ***esgor ar***
resume *be* ***ailgychwyn***
résumé *enw* ***crynodeb*** *hwn*
resurface *be* (to return) ***ail-frigo***
resurgence *enw* ***adfywiad*** *hwn*
Resurrection *enw* ***Atgyfodiad*** *hwn*
resuscitate *be* ***dadebru***, ***adfywio***
retail *be* ***adwerthu***, ***mân-werthu***
retailer *enw* ***mân-werthwr*** *hwn*
retain *be* ***cadw***
retaliate *be* ***talu'r pwyth yn ôl***
retard *be* ***arafu***
retarded *ans* ***araf***
retch *be* ***gwag-gyfogi***, ***bwldagu***
rethink *be* ***ailfeddwl***, ***ailystyried***
reticence *enw* ***swildod*** *hwn*
retina *enw* ***rhwyden*** *hon*
retinue *enw* ***gosgordd*** *hon*
retire *be* ***ymddeol***
retired *ans* ***wedi ymddeol***
retirement *enw* ***ymddeoliad*** *hwn*
retort *enw* ***ateb parod*** *hwn*
retrace *be* ***olrhain***
retract *be* ***tynnu yn ôl***
retreat *be* ***cilio***, ***encilio***
retribution *enw* ***dial*** *hwn*, ***cosb*** *hon*
retrievable *ans* ***adferadwy***
retrieve *be* ***adennill***
  to r~ information from a text ***didoli gwybodaeth***
retrospective *ans* ***ôl-syllol***, ***ôl-weithredol***
return *enw* ***dychweliad***; ***elw***, ***canlyniad*** *hwn*
  by r~ ***gyda throad (y post)***
  in r~ ***yn gyfnewid***
return *be* ***dychwelyd***
returning officer *enw* ***swyddog canlyniadau*** *hwn*
reunion *enw* ***aduniad*** *hwn*
reunite *be* ***aduno***
revamp *be* ***ailwampio***
reveal *be* ***datgelu***, ***dinoethi***
revel in *be* ***ymhyfrydu***, ***bod yn fêl ar fysedd***
revelation *enw* ***datguddiad*** *hwn*
revelry *enw* ***rhialtwch*** *hwn*
revenge *enw* ***dial***, ***dialedd*** *hwn*
revengeful *ans* ***dialgar***
revenue *enw* ***cyllid***, ***incwm*** *hwn*
  r~ support grant ***grant cynnal incwm*** *hwn*
reverberate *be* ***atseinio***, ***diasbedain***
reverberation *enw* ***atsain*** *hon*, ***dirgryniad*** *hwn*

revere *be* ***parchu***
reverend *ans/enw* ***parchedig*** *hwn*; (title) **y Parchedig –**
reversal *enw* ***gwrthdroad*** *hwn*
reverse *enw* ***cefn***, ***gwrthwyneb*** *hwn*
the r~ is true ***fel arall y mae hi***
reverse *be* ***bacio***, ***gwrthdroi***
reversible *ans* ***cildroadwy***
reversion *enw* ***atchweliad*** *hwn*
revert *be* ***dychwelyd***
review *enw* ***adolygiad*** *hwn*
under r~ ***a arolygir***
review *be* ***adolygu***
reviewer *enw* ***adolygydd*** *hwn*
revile *be* ***difrïo***
revise *be* ***diwygio***, ***adolygu***
revision *enw* **adolygiad** *hwn*
revival *enw* ***adfywiad***, ***diwygiad*** *hwn*
revive *be* ***adfywio***, ***bywiogi***
revocable *ans* ***diddymadwy***
revocation *enw* ***diddymiad*** *hwn*
revoke *be* ***diddymu***
revolt *enw* ***gwrthryfel*** *hwn*
revolt *be* ***gwrthryfela***
it's r~ing ***mae'n troi arnaf***
revolution *enw* ***chwyldro*** *hwn*
revolutionary *ans* ***chwyldroadol***
revolve *be* ***cylchdroi***
revulsion *enw* ***ffieidd-dod*** *hwn*
reward *enw* ***gwobr*** *hon*
reward *be* ***gwobrwyo***
rewarding *ans* ***buddiol***
a r~ career ***gyrfa lewyrchus*** *hon*
reword *be* ***aralleirio***
rhetoric *enw* ***rhethreg*** *hon*
rhetorical *ans* ***rhethregol***
rheumatism *enw* ***gwynegon*** *hyn*, ***cryd cymalau*** *hwn*
rhinoceros *enw* ***rhinoseros*** *hwn*
rhombus *enw* ***rhombws*** *hwn*
rhubarb *enw* ***rhiwbob:riwbob*** *hwn*
rhyme *enw* ***odl*** *hon*
rhyme *be* ***odli***
rhythm *enw* ***rhythm*** *hwn*
rhythmical *ans* ***rhythmig***
rib *enw* ***asen*** *hon*
ribald *ans* ***masweddus***
ribbon *enw* ***rhuban*** *hwn*
rice *enw* ***reis*** *hwn*
rich *ans* ***cyfoethog***
richness *enw* ***cyfoeth*** *hwn*
rick *enw* ***helm***, ***tas*** *hon*
rickyard *enw* ***ydlan*** *hon*
rid *be* ***cael gwared***, ***gwaredu***
to get r~ of a cold ***bwrw annwyd***
riddle *enw* ***pos*** *hwn*
riddle *be* ***rhidyllu***
r~d with errors ***yn frith o wallau***
ride *be* ***marchogaeth***; ***teithio***
ride *enw* ***reid*** *hon*, ***tro*** *hwn*
rider *enw* (document) ***atodiad*** *hwn*
with the r~ that ***ar yr amod***
ridge *enw* ***trum***, ***crib*** *hon*, ***cefn*** *hwn*
ridicule *enw* ***gwawd***, ***gwatwar*** *hwn*
ridicule *be* ***gwawdio***, ***gwatwar***, ***wfftio***

r

ridiculous *ans* ***chwerthinllyd***, ***dwl***, ***gwirion***
rife *ans* ***rhemp***
riff-raff *enw* ***gwehilion*** *hyn*
rifle *enw* ***reiffl*** *hon*
rift *enw* ***rhwyg*** *hon*
rig *enw* ***llwyfan (olew)*** *hwn/hon*
rig *be* ***rigio***
right *enw* ***hawl*** *hon*
right *ans* ***cywir***; ***de***
  about r~ ***agos at eu lle***
  r~ and proper ***priodol***
  to be just r~ ***taro deuddeg***
  to be perfectly r~ ***bod yn llygad eu lle***
  the r~ hand ***y llaw dde*** *hon*
  on the* r~** ***ar y dde
right *adf* ***yn union***
  r~ at the beginning ***ar y dechrau'n deg***
righteous *ans* ***cyfiawn***
righteousness *enw* ***cyfiawnder*** *hwn*
rightful *ans* ***gwir***, ***haeddiannol***
rights *enw* ***hawliau***, ***iawnderau*** *hyn*
rigid *ans* ***anhyblyg***, ***caled***
rigidity *enw* ***diffyg hyblygrwydd*** *hwn*
rigmarole *enw* ***truth*** *hwn*
rigorous *ans* ***llym***, ***llwyr***, ***trylwyr***
rigour *enw* ***manylder***, ***trylwyredd*** *hwn*
rim *enw* ***ymyl*** *hwn/hon*
rime *enw* ***barrug***, ***llwydrew*** *hwn*
rime *be* ***barugo***, ***llwydrewi***
rind *enw* ***croen*** *hwn*; ***crofen*** *hon*
ring *enw* ***modrwy*** *hon*, ***cylch*** *hwn*
ring *be* ***canu***
ring binder *enw* ***ffeil fodrwy*** *hon*
ring-fence *be* ***rhoi cylch cadw am***
ringworm *enw* ***(y) darwden*** *hon*
rink *enw* ***llawr*** *hwn*
rinse *be* ***strelio***, ***rinsio***
riot *enw* ***terfysg*** *hwn*
  a r~ of colour ***môr o liwiau***
riotous *ans* ***terfysglyd***
rip *be* ***rhwygo***
ripe *ans* ***aeddfed***
  the time is r~ ***mae'n amser i***
ripen *be* ***aeddfedu***
ripple *enw* ***crychiad*** *hwn*
ripple *be* ***crychu***
rise *enw* ***codiad***, ***esgyniad*** *hwn*
  to give r~ to ***rhoi bod i***, ***arwain at***, ***esgor ar***
rise *be* ***esgyn***
risible *ans* ***chwerthinllyd***
rising *ans* ***sy'n codi***
risk *enw* ***perygl*** *hwn*, ***menter*** *hon*
risk *be* ***mentro***
risky *ans* ***peryglus***, ***mentrus***
rite *enw* ***defod*** *hon*
ritual *ans* ***defodol***
rival *enw* ***cystadleuydd*** *hwn*
rival *be* ***cystadlu â***
  that no other can r~ ***diguro***
rivalry *enw* ***cystadleuaeth*** *hon*
river *enw* ***afon*** *hon*
rivet *enw* ***rhybed*** *hwn*

rivet *be* ***rhybedu***
  r~ing ***eithriadol o ddiddorol***
road *enw* ***ffordd***, ***heol*** *hon*
  by r~ ***mewn car***, ***ar fws***
roadshow *enw* ***sioe deithiol*** *hon*
roam *be* ***crwydro***
roan *ans* ***broc***
roar *enw* ***rhu***, ***rhuad*** *hwn*
roar *be* ***rhuo***
roast *be* ***rhostio***
rob *be* ***dwyn***, ***lladrata***
robber *enw* ***lleidr*** *hwn*
robbery *enw* ***lladrad*** *hwn*
robin *enw* ***robin goch*** *hwn*
robot *enw* ***robot*** *hwn*
robust *ans* ***cryf***, ***cydnerth***, ***grymus***, ***cadarn***
robustness *enw* ***cryfder***, ***cadernid*** *hwn*
rock *enw* ***craig*** *hon*
rock *be* ***siglo***
rocket *enw* ***roced*** *hon*
rocket *be* ***saethu***
rocking chair *enw* ***cadair siglo*** *hon*
rocky *ans* ***creigiog***
rod *enw* ***rhoden*** *hon*
rodent *enw* ***cnofil*** *hwn*
roe *enw* ***gronell*** *hon*
rogue *enw* ***gwalch***, ***cnaf*** *hwn*
roister *be* ***cadw reiat***
role *enw* ***rhan*** *hon*
  lead r~ ***rhan y prif gymeriad***
  to play a leading r~ ***bod yn flaenllaw***
  r~ model ***esiampl*** *hon*
roll *enw* (paper etc.) ***rholyn*** *hwn*; ***cofrestr*** *hon*; (bread) ***cwgen*** *hon*
roll *be* ***treiglo***, ***rholio***
  roll on, roll off ***gyrru ymlaen***, ***ymaith***
roller *enw* ***rowl*** *hwn/hon*
roller-skate *be* ***sglefrholio***
Roman *enw* ***Rhufeiniad***, ***Rhufeiniwr*** *hwn*
Roman *ans* ***Rhufeinig***
romance *enw* ***rhamant*** *hon*
romantic *ans* ***rhamantaidd***, ***rhamantus***
romp *be* ***prancio***
roof *enw* ***to*** *hwn*
roof *be* ***toi***
rook *enw* ***ydfran*** *hon*
room *enw* ***ystafell*** *hon*; **gofod**, **lle** *hwn*
roost *be* ***clwydo***
roost *enw* ***clwyd*** *hon*
root *enw* ***gwraidd***, ***gwreiddyn*** *hwn*
  r~ causes ***achosion gwaelodol*** *hyn*
root *be* ***gwreiddio***
  r~ed to the spot ***sefyll yn stond***
rope *enw* ***rhaff*** *hon*
  on th r~s ***yn gwegian***
rose *enw* ***rhosyn*** *hwn*
rose-hips *enw* ***egroes*** *hyn*
rosemary *enw* ***rhosmari*** *hwn*
rostrum *enw* ***llwyfan*** *hwn/hon*
rot *enw* ***pydredd*** *hwn*

rot *be* ***pydru***
rotate *be* ***cylchdroi***
rotation *enw* ***cylchdro*** *hwn*
rotten *ans* ***pwdr***
rotund *ans* ***crwn***
rouge *enw* ***powdwr coch*** *hwn*
rough *ans* ***garw***, ***bras***
roughness *enw* ***garwedd***, ***gerwinder*** *hwn*
round *enw* ***tôn gron*** *hon*
round *ans* ***crwn***
round *adf* ***o gwmpas***
  all r~ ***ym mhob ffordd***, ***ym mhob man***
round *be* ***rowndio***
  to get r~ ***osgoi***, ***goresgyn***
  to r~ it all off ***i goroni'r cyfan***
roundabout *enw* ***ceffylau bach*** *hyn*; ***cylchfan*** *hwn/hon*
roundabout *ans* ***cwmpasog***
Roundhead *enw* ***Pengryniad*** *hwn*
roundness *enw* ***crynder*** *hwn*
round-up *enw* ***crynodeb*** *hwn/hon*
rouse *be* ***cynhyrfu***, ***deffro***
route *enw* ***ffordd*** *hon*
routine *enw* ***arfer*** *hwn/hon*, ***trefn arferol*** *hon*
rove *be* ***crwydro***
row *enw* ***ffrae*** *hon*, ***twrw*** *hwn*
row *enw* ***rhes*** *hon*
row *be* ***rhwyfo***
rowan *enw* ***cerd[d]inen***, ***criafolen*** *hon*
royal *ans* ***brenhinol***
royalty *enw* **brenhiniaeth** *hon*; ***breindal*** *hwn*
rub *be* ***rhwbio***
rubber *enw* ***rwber*** *hwn*
rubber-stamp *be* ***cymeradwyo***
rubbish *enw* ***sbwriel*** *hwn*
  rubbish ***lol botes maip***
rubble *enw* ***rwbel*** *hwn*
rubric *enw* ***pennawd***; ***cyfarwyddyd*** *hwn*
ruby *enw* ***rhuddem*** *hwn/hon*
ruck *enw* ***sgarmes*** *hon*
rudder *enw* ***llyw*** *hwn*
ruddiness *enw* ***gwrid***, ***cochni*** *hwn*
ruddy *ans* ***gwritgoch***
rude *ans* ***anghwrtais***
rudeness *enw* ***anghwrteisi***, ***haerllugrwydd*** *hwn*
rudimentary *ans* ***elfennol***
ruffian *enw* ***adyn***, ***dihiryn*** *hwn*
ruffle *be* ***crychu***, ***chwalu***, ***aflonyddu***
rug *enw* ***rỳg***, ***carthen*** *hon*
rugby *enw* ***rygbi*** *hwn*
rugged *ans* ***garw***, ***clogyrnog***
ruin *enw* ***adfail***, ***murddun*** *hwn*
  in r~s ***yn deilchion***
ruin *be* ***llwyr ddifetha***, ***distrywio***
ruinous *ans* ***dinistriol***, ***andwyol***; ***wedi mynd â'i ben iddo***
rule *enw* ***rheol*** *hon*
  r~s and regulations ***rheolau a rheoliadau*** *hyn*
rule *be* ***rheoli***, ***teyrnasu***
  to r~ out ***penderfynu peidio***

rumble *be* ***trystio***, ***rymblan***
to r~ on ***rhygnu ymlaen***
rumbustious *ans* ***llawn hwyl***
ruminate *be* ***cnoi cil***
rummage *be* ***chwilota***, ***twrio***
rumour *enw* ***si***, ***sôn*** *hwn;* ***si ym mrig y morwydd***
rumour has it ***yn ôl y sôn***
rump *enw* ***pedrain*** *hon,* ***pen ôl*** *hwn*
run *enw* ***rhediad*** *hwn*
in the long r~ ***yn y pen draw***
run *be* ***rhedeg***
to have r~ their course ***chwythu'u plwc***
to r~ with the fox and hunt with the hounds ***gweiddi hai efo'r cŵn a hwi gyda'r cadno***
rung *enw* ***ffon*** *hon,* ***gris*** *hwn*
runner *enw* ***rhedwr*** *hwn*
r~-up ***yr ail orau***
to do a r~ ***ei gwadnu hi***, ***cymryd y goes***
runway *enw* ***llwybr glanio*** *hwn*
rupture *enw* ***torllengig*** *hwn*
rural *ans* ***gwledig***
ruse *enw* ***ystryw*** *hwn/hon*
rush *enw* ***rhuthr*** *hwn*
rush *be* ***rhuthro***
russet *ans* ***cringoch***
rust *enw* ***rhwd*** *hwn*
rust *be* ***rhydu***
rustic *enw* ***gwerinwr***, ***gwladwr*** *hwn*
rustic *ans* ***gwladaidd***
rustle *be* ***siffrwd***
rusty *ans* ***rhydlyd***
rut *enw* ***rhigol***, ***rhych*** *hon*
ruthless *ans* ***didostur***, ***didrugaredd***
rye *enw* ***rhyg*** *hwn*

S

Sabbath *enw* ***Sabbath:Saboth*** *hwn*
sabbatical *ans* ***sabothol***
sac *enw* ***cwd*** *hwn*
sachet *enw* ***bag bychan*** *hwn*
sack *enw* ***sach*** *hwn/hon*
sack *be* ***diswyddo***
sackcloth *enw* ***sachliain*** *hwn*
  s~ and ashes ***sachliain a lludw***
sacrament *enw* ***sagrafen*** *hon*, ***y cymun*** *hwn*
sacred *ans* ***cysegredig***
sacrifice *enw* ***aberth*** *hwn/hon*
sacrifice *be* ***aberthu***
sacrilege *enw* ***halogiad*** *hwn*
sad *ans* ***trist***
  desperately s~ ***mwy trist na thristwch***
sadden *be* ***tristáu***
saddle *enw* ***cyfrwy*** *hwn*
saddle *be* ***cyfrwyo***
sadness *enw* ***tristwch*** *hwn*
safe *ans* ***diogel***
  better s~ than sorry ***gwell gofalu na difaru***
safeguard *enw* ***amddiffynfa*** *hon*; ***ffordd o sicrhau***
safeguard *be* ***diogelu***, ***gwarchod***
safety *enw* ***diogelwch*** *hwn*
safety belt *enw* ***gwregys diogelwch*** *hwn*
safety pin *enw* ***pin cau*** *hwn*
sag *be* ***sigo:ysigo***, ***pylu***
saga *enw* ***saga*** *hon*
sagacious *ans* ***craff***, ***hirben***
sage *enw* **saets** *hwn*; ***gŵr doeth*** *hwn*
sail *enw* ***hwyl*** *hon*
sail *be* ***hwylio***
sailor *enw* ***morwr*** *hwn*
saint *enw* ***sant*** *hwn*, ***santes*** *hon*
sake *enw* **(for the s~ of)** ***er mwyn***
salacious *ans* ***anllad***, ***trythyll***
salad *enw* ***salad*** *hwn*
salaried *ans* ***cyflogedig***
salary *enw* ***cyflog*** *hwn/hon*
  salaries and wages ***cyflogau wythnosol a misol*** *hyn*
sale *enw* ***arwerthiant*** *hwn*, ***sêl*** *hon*
saleable *ans* ***gwerthadwy***
salesman *enw* ***gwerthwr*** *hwn*
salient *ans* ***prif***, ***pwysicaf***, ***perthnasol***
saliva *enw* ***poer*** *hwn*
salmon *enw* ***eog*** *hwn*
saloon *enw* ***salŵn*** *hwn/hon*
salt *enw* ***halen*** *hwn*
salt *be* ***halltu***
salt cellar *enw* ***llestr halen*** *hwn*
salty *ans* ***hallt***
salubrious *ans* ***iachusol***
salubrity *enw* ***iachusrwydd*** *hwn*
salutary *ans* ***llesol***
salutation *enw* ***cyfarchiad*** *hwn*
salute *enw* ***saliwt*** *hon*
  this prize is a s~ to ***mae'r wobr hon yn gydnabyddiaeth o***

salute *be* ***saliwtio***
salvage *be* ***achub***, ***arbed***
salvation *enw* ***achubiaeth***, ***iachawdwriaeth*** *hon*
salve *enw* ***eli*** *hwn*
salver *enw* ***hambwrdd*** *hwn*
same *ans* ***yr un***
sameness *enw* ***unffurfiaeth*** *hon*
sample *enw* ***sampl***, ***enghraifft*** *hon*
sample *be* ***samplo:samplu***
sanatorium *enw* ***sanatoriwm*** *hwn*
sanctify *be* ***sancteiddio***, ***cysegru***
sanctimonious *ans* ***rhagrithiol***
sanction *be* ***cadarnhau***; ***caniatáu***
sanctions *enw* ***sancsiynau*** *hyn*
sanctity *enw* ***sancteiddrwydd*** *hwn*
sanctuary *enw* ***seintwar*** *hon*; ***cysegr*** *hwn*
sanctum *enw* ***cysegr sancteiddiolaf*** *hwn*
sand *enw* ***tywod*** *hwn*
sandal *enw* ***sandal*** *hon*
sand-dune *enw* ***twyn (tywod)***, ***tywyn*** *hwn*
sandpaper *enw* ***papur tywod*** *hwn*
sands *enw* ***traeth*** *hwn*
sandstone *enw* ***tywodfaen*** *hwn*
sandwich *enw* ***brechdan*** *hon*
s~ course ***cwrs rhyngosod***, ***rhyng-gwrs*** *hwn*
sandy *ans* ***tywodlyd***
sane *ans* ***call***
sanguine *ans* ***hyderus***
sanitary *ans* ***glanweithiol***
sanitation *enw* ***glanweithdra*** *hwn*
sanity *enw* ***pwyll***, ***callineb*** *hwn*
Santa Claus *enw* ***Siôn Corn*** *hwn*
sap *enw* ***nodd***, ***sudd*** *hwn*
sapling *enw* ***coeden ifanc*** *hon*
sapper *enw* ***cloddiwr*** *hwn*
sarcasm *enw* ***coegni*** *hwn*
sarcastic *ans* ***coeglyd***, ***crafog***, ***sarcastig***
sardine *enw* ***sardîn*** *hwn*
sardonic *ans* ***coeglyd***, ***glas (glaswenu)***
satchel *enw* ***bag ysgol*** *hwn*
sate *be* ***digoni***
satellite *enw* ***lloeren*** *hon*
satin *enw* ***sidan gloyw*** *hwn*
satiny *ans* ***sidanaidd***
satire *enw* ***dychan*** *hwn*
satirical *ans* ***dychanol***
satirize *be* ***dychanu***
satisfaction *enw* ***bodlonrwydd*** *hwn*
satisfactory *ans* ***boddhaol***
satisfy *be* ***bodloni***
saturate *be* ***trwytho***, ***mwydo***
Saturday *enw* ***Sadwrn*** *hwn*
Saturn *enw* ***Sadwrn*** *hwn*
sauce *enw* ***saws*** *hwn*
saucepan *enw* ***sosban*** *hon*
saucer *enw* ***soser*** *hon*
saucy *ans* ***beiddgar***, ***eofn***
saunter *be* ***mynd ling-di-long***, ***mynd o dow i dow***
sausage *enw* ***selsigen***, ***sosej*** *hon*
savage *enw* ***anwariad*** *hwn/hon*
savage *ans* ***anwaraidd***

S

savagery *enw* ***anwarineb*** *hwn*
save *be* ***achub***; ***cynilo***
s~ the day ***dod/camu i'r adwy***
saving *enw* (salvation) ***achubiaeth*** *hon*; (of expense) ***arbediad*** *hwn*
savings *enw* ***cynilion*** *hyn*
savings bank *enw* ***banc cynilo*** *hwn*
saviour *enw* ***gwaredwr*** *hwn*
savour *be* ***blasu***, ***sawru***
savoury *ans* ***sawrus***
saw *enw* ***llif*** *hon*
saw *be* ***llifio***
sawdust *enw* ***blawd/llwch llif*** *hwn*
say *be* ***dweud***
it is said that ***yn ôl y sôn/yr hanes***
that is to s~ ***hynny yw***
to have the final s~ ***bod â'r/cael y gair olaf***
to s~ much for ***yn glod i***
what would you s~ is? ***beth yn eich barn chi yw?***
saying *enw* ***dywediad*** *hwn*
scab *enw* ***crachen*** *hon*
scaffolding *enw* ***sgaffaldwaith*** *hwn*
scald *enw* ***llosgiad***, ***sgaldiad*** *hwn*
scald *be* ***sgaldian***, ***sgaldanu***
scale *enw* ***graddfa*** *hon*; ***cen*** *hwn*
the s~ of the problem ***maint y broblem***
scale *be* ***dringo***
scallywags *enw* ***tacle:taclau*** *hyn*
scalpel *enw* ***fflaim*** *hon*
scaly *ans* ***cennog***
scam *enw* ***twyll*** *hwn*
scamp *enw* ***cnaf*** *hwn*
scamper *be* ***rhedeg i ffwrdd***
scampi *enw* ***sgampi*** *hyn*
scan *be* ***sganio***; ***bras-ddarllen***
scandal *enw* ***sgandal***, ***gwarth*** *hon*
scandalize *be* ***pechu***
scandalous *ans* ***gwarthus***, ***cywilyddus***
scant *ans* ***prin***, ***fawr o***, ***ychydig o***
scantiness *enw* ***prinder*** *hwn*
scapegoat *enw* ***bwch dihangol*** *hwn*
scar *enw* ***craith*** *hon*
scarce *ans* ***prin***
scare *enw* ***dychryn***, ***braw*** *hwn*
scare *be* ***dychryn***, ***brawychu***
scarecrow *enw* ***bwgan brain*** *hwn*
scared *ans* ***wedi dychryn***
scarf *enw* ***sgarff*** *hon*
scarlet *enw* ***ysgarlad***, ***coch*** *hwn*
scary *ans* ***yn ddigon i godi ofn ar***
scathing *ans* ***deifiol***
scatter *be* ***chwalu***, ***gwasgaru***
scattered *ans* ***gwasgaredig***, ***ar chwâl***
scatty *ans* ***penchwiban***
scene *enw* ***golygfa*** *hon*, ***lleoliad*** *hwn*
a change of s~ ***newid byd***
scenery *enw* ***golygfeydd*** *hyn*
scenic *ans* ***golygfaol***
scent *enw* ***persawr***, ***sawr*** *hwn*
scent *be* ***synhwyro***, ***ogleuo***

sceptic *enw* ***amheuwr*** *hwn*
sceptic(al) *ans* ***sgeptig***, ***beirniadol***
sceptre *enw* ***teyrnwialen*** *hon*
schedule *enw* ***rhestr***, ***rhaglen***, ***atodlen*** *hon*
schedule *be* ***amserlennu***
scheme *enw* ***cynllun*** *hwn*
scheme *be* ***cynllwynio***
schism *enw* ***rhwyg*** *hon*
scholar *enw* ***disgybl***, ***ysgolhaig*** *hwn*
scholarly *ans* ***ysgolheigaidd***
school *enw* ***ysgol*** *hon*
 one s~ of thought ***barn un garfan***
schoolboy *enw* ***bachgen ysgol*** *hwn*
schoolgirl *enw* ***merch ysgol*** *hon*
schoolteacher *enw* ***athro ysgol*** *hwn*, ***athrawes ysgol*** *hon*
science *enw* ***gwyddoniaeth***; ***gwyddor*** *hon*
 the s~s ***y gwyddorau*** *hyn*
scientific *ans* ***gwyddonol***
scientist *enw* ***gwyddonydd*** *hwn*
scintillate *be* ***pefrio***, ***gwreichioni***
scissors *enw* ***siswrn*** *hwn*
scoff *be* ***gwawdio***, ***chwerthin am ben***
scold *be* ***dwrdio***, ***dweud y drefn***
scone *enw* ***sgon*** *hon*
scoop *enw* ***rhaw fach*** *hon*; (culinary) ***lletwad*** *hon*, ***sgŵp*** *hwn/hon*; (journ.) ***sgŵp*** *hwn/hon*
scoot *be* ***codi cynffon***, ***ei gloywi hi***
scope *enw* ***cwmpas***, ***maes***, ***cylch***, ***lle***, ***cyfle*** *hwn*
scorch *be* ***rhuddo***, ***deifio***
score *enw* ***sgôr*** *hon*
score *be* ***sgorio***
scorn *enw* ***dirmyg*** *hwn*
scorn *be* ***dirmygu***, ***gwawdio***
scornful *ans* ***dirmygus***
Scot *enw* ***Albanwr*** *hwn*, ***Albanes*** *hon*
scoundrel *enw* ***dihiryn*** *hwn*
scour *be* ***sgwrio:ysgwrio***; (search) ***chwilota***
scourge *be* ***fflangellu***
scout *enw* ***sgowt*** *hwn*
scowl *be* ***gwgu***, ***cuchio***
scramble *be* ***sgrialu***, ***sgramblo***
scrap *enw* ***darn***; ***sgrap*** *hwn*
scrap *be* ***dileu***, ***cael gwared ar***
scrapbook *enw* ***llyfr lloffion*** *hwn*
scrape *be* ***crafu***
scrappy *ans* ***bratiog***
scraps *enw* ***tameidiau***; ***gweddillion*** *hyn*
scratch *enw* ***crafiad*** *hwn*
 to create from s~ ***eu creu o'r cychwyn cyntaf***
 to come up to s~ ***cyrraedd y safon***
 to escape without a s~ ***dianc yn ddianaf/yn iach eich croen***
scratch *be* ***crafu***
scream *enw* ***sgrech*** *hon*
scream *be* ***sgrechian***
scree *enw* ***sgri***, ***marian*** *hwn*

S

screech *be* ***gwichian***
screen *enw* ***sgrin*** *hon*
screen *be* ***sgrinio***
screw *enw* ***sgriw*** *hon*
screw *be* ***sgriwio***
screwdriver *enw* ***sgriwdreifer*** *hwn*
scribble *enw* ***ysgrifen*** *hon*, ***sgribl*** *hwn*
scribble *be* ***sgriblan***
scribe *enw* ***ysgrifennydd***, ***cofnodwr*** *hwn*
scrimp *be* ***tolio***, ***cynilo***
script *enw* ***sgript*** *hon*
Scripture *enw* ***yr Ysgrythur*** *hon*
scrivener *enw* ***copïwr*** *hwn*
scroll *be* ***sgrolio***
scrotum *enw* ***cwd***, ***sgrotwm*** *hwn*
scrub *enw* ***prysgwydd*** *hyn*
scrub *be* ***sgwrio***
scruff *enw* ***gwar*** *hwn/hon*
scruffy *ans* ***blêr***, ***anniben***, ***diraen***
scrum *enw* ***sgrym*** *hon*
scrum-half *enw* ***mewnwr*** *hwn*
scrumptious *ans* ***amheuthun***, ***yn tynnu dŵr o'r dannedd***
scrunch *be* ***crychu***
scruple *enw* ***poen cydwybod*** *hon*
scrupulous *ans* ***gofalus***, ***manwl gywir***
  in s~ detail ***yn drylwyr o fanwl***
scrutineer *enw* ***archwiliwr*** *hwn*
scrutinize *be* ***archwilio***, ***craffu***, ***bwrw golwg dros***
scrutiny *enw* ***archwiliad*** *hwn*
  careful s~ ***edrych yn dra gofalus***
scuffle *enw* ***ysgarmes*** *hon*
scuffle *be* ***ymgiprys***
scull *enw* ***rhodl*** *hon*
scull *be* ***rhodli***
scullery *enw* ***cegin gefn*** *hon*
sculptor *enw* ***cerflunydd*** *hwn*
sculpture *enw* ***cerflun*** *hwn*
scum *enw* ***llysnafedd***, ***ewyn*** *hwn*
scurf *enw* ***cen*** *hwn*
scurrilous *ans* ***enllibus***
scurry *be* ***cythru***, ***rhuthro***
scurvy *enw* ***y llwg*** *hwn*
scythe *enw* ***pladur*** *hon*
scythe *be* ***pladuro***
sea *enw* ***môr*** *hwn*
  s~ change ***newid llwyr***
seafood *enw* ***bwyd môr*** *hwn*
seagull *enw* ***gwylan*** *hon*
seal *enw* (animal) ***morlo*** *hwn*; ***sêl*** *hon*
  s~ of approval ***cymeradwyaeth*** *hon*
seal *be* ***selio***
seam *enw* ***gwrym***; ***gwnïad*** *hwn*
seaman *enw* ***morwr*** *hwn*
seamless *ans* ***di-dor***
seamstress *enw* ***gwniadwraig*** *hon*
seamy *ans* ***salw***
sear *be* ***serio***
search *be* ***chwilio***
search engine *enw* ***chwiliadur***, ***chwilotydd*** *hwn*
searing *ans* ***deifiol***
seashell *enw* ***cragen fôr*** *hon*
seashore *enw* ***glan môr*** *hon*

seasickness *enw* ***salwch môr*** *hwn*
seaside *enw* ***glan môr*** *hon*
season *enw* ***tymor*** *hwn*
seasonable *ans* ***tymhorol***
seasoning *enw* ***sesnin*** *hwn*
seat *enw* ***sedd*** *hon*
seat *be* ***eistedd***
seaweed *enw* ***gwymon*** *hwn*
secluded *ans* ***o'r neilltu***
seclusion *enw* ***neilltuaeth*** *hon*
second *enw* ***eiliad*** *hwn/hon*
second *be* ***eilio***; ***secondio***
second *ans* ***ail***
  s~ to none ***diguro***, ***heb ei ail***
  without giving it a s~ thought ***heb feddwl dwywaith***
secondary *ans* (school) ***uwchradd***; (in order) ***eilaidd***
second class *ans* ***eilradd***
seconder *enw* ***eilydd*** *hwn*
second-hand *ans* ***ail-law***
secondment *enw* ***secondiad*** *hwn*
secrecy *enw* ***cyfrinachedd*** *hwn*
secret *enw* ***cyfrinach*** *hon*
  to make no s~ of ***peidio â cheisio celu'r ffaith***
secret *ans* ***cyfrinachol***
secretariat *enw* ***ysgrifenyddiaeth*** *hon*
secretary *enw* ***ysgrifennydd*** *hwn*, ***ysgrifenyddes*** *hon*
secrete *be* ***secretu***
secretive *ans* ***cyfrinachgar***; ***tawedog***
sect *enw* ***enwad*** *hwn*, ***sect*** *hon*
section *enw* ***rhan*** *hon*; (of department) ***adran***, ***is-adran*** *hon*; (biological) ***trychiad*** *hwn*
sector *enw* ***sector*** *hwn*
secular *ans* ***seciwlar***, ***lleyg***
secure *ans* ***diogel***, ***sicr***
secure *be* ***sicrhau***
  to s~ attention ***hoelio sylw***
security *enw* ***diogelwch*** *hwn*
sedative *enw* ***tawelydd*** *hwn*
sedate *be* ***lleddfu***, ***tawelu***
sediment *enw* ***gwaddod*** *hwn*
sedition *enw* ***anogaeth i fradwriaeth***
seduce *be* ***hudo***
seductive *ans* ***hudol***, ***hudolus***
sedulous *ans* ***dygn***, ***dyfal***
see *be* ***gweld***
  they were nowhere to be s~n ***doedd dim sôn amdanyn nhw***
  to s~ to it ***sicrhau***
seed *enw* ***hedyn***, ***had*** *hwn*
seed *be* ***hadu***
seek *be* ***ceisio***, ***chwilio (am)***
seem *be* ***ymddangos***
  it s~s unlikely ***go brin***
seeming *ans* ***ymddangosiadol***
seemliness *enw* ***gwedduster*** *hwn*
seemly *ans* ***gweddus***
seep *be* ***diferu***, ***ymollwng***
seer *enw* ***gweledydd*** *hwn*
see-saw *enw* ***si-so*** *hwn*
seethe *be* ***corddi***
  s~ing with excitement ***yn ferw gwyllt***

S

segment *enw* ***darn***, ***ewin*** *hwn*
segregate *be* ***gwahanu***
seize *be* ***cydio***, ***cipio***
to s~ the opportunity ***achub y cyfle***, ***bachu ar gyfle***
seizure *enw* ***atafaeliad***; (med.) ***trawiad*** *hwn*
seldom *adf* ***anaml***, ***prin***
select *be* ***dewis***, ***dethol***
select *ans* ***dethol***
selection *enw* ***detholiad*** *hwn*
self *enw* ***hunan*** *hwn*
self-appraisal ***hunanwerthuso***
self-confident *ans* ***hunanhyderus***
self-contained *ans* ***cyflawn ynddi ei hunan***
self-defeating *ans* ***yn drech na'i hunan***
self-defence *enw* ***hunanamddiffyn*** *hwn*
self-disciplined *ans* ***hunanddisgybledig***
self-employed *ans* ***hunangyflogedig***
self-explanatory *ans* ***digon hawdd ei ddeall***
self-government *enw* ***hunanlywodraeth*** *hon*
self-interest *enw* ***hunan-les*** *hwn*
selfish *ans* ***hunanol***
selfishness *enw* ***hunanoldeb*** *hwn*
selflessness *enw* ***anhunanoldeb*** *hwn*
self-portrait *enw* ***hunanbortread*** *hwn*
self-respect *enw* ***hunan-barch*** *hwn*
self-service *ans* ***gweini arnoch eich hun***
self-styled *ans* ***hunanhonedig***
self-sufficient *ans* ***hunangynhaliol***
self-taught *ans* ***hunanaddysgedig***
sell *be* ***gwerthu***
seller *enw* ***gwerthwr*** *hwn*, ***gwerthwraig*** *hon*
semantics *enw* ***semanteg*** *hon*
semblance *enw* ***llun*** *hwn*, ***golwg*** *hon*
semen *enw* ***hadlif*** *hwn*
semicircle *enw* ***hanner cylch*** *hwn*
semiconductor *enw* ***lled-ddargludydd*** *hwn*
semi-final *enw* ***rownd gynderfynol*** *hon*
senate *enw* ***senedd*** *hon*
senator *enw* ***seneddwr*** *hwn*, ***seneddwraig*** *hon*
send *be* ***anfon***
senescent *ans* ***yn heneiddio***
seneschal *enw* ***distain*** *hwn*
senile *ans* ***hen a musgrell***
senility *enw* ***musgrellni*** *hwn*
senior *ans* ***hŷn***, ***uwch***
sensation *enw* ***teimlad***, ***cynnwrf*** *hwn*
sensational *ans* ***cynhyrfus***, ***iasol***
sense *enw* ***synnwyr*** *hwn*
in a s~ ***ar ryw olwg***
it makes s~ to ***cam synhwyrol yw***

this is in no s~ a *nid yw hyn mewn unrhyw ffordd yn*
to lose their s~s *colli arnynt eu hunain*
to produce a s~ of movement *rhoi'r argraff fod pethau'n symud*
to see s~ *dod at eu coed*, *callio*
sense *be* ***synhwyro***
senseless *ans* ***disynnwyr*, *anymwybodol***
sensible *ans* ***synhwyrol***
to be s~ to *bod yn ymwybodol o*, *ymdeimlo â*
sensitive *ans* ***sensitif*, *teimladwy***
to be s~ to *ymdeimlo â*, *ymglywed â*
sensory *ans* ***synhwyraidd***
sensual *ans* ***nwydus***
sensuality *enw* ***trythyllwch*** *hwn*
sentence *enw* ***brawddeg***; (prison) ***dedfryd*** *hon*
sentiment *enw* ***teimlad*** *hwn*
to agree with the s~s *cytuno â'r sylwadau*
sentimental *ans* ***teimladwy***
sentinel *enw* ***gwarchodwr*** *hwn*
sentry *enw* ***gwyliwr*** *hwn*
separable *ans* ***gwahanadwy***
separate *be* ***gwahanu***
separate *ans* ***ar wahân***
separation *enw* ***gwahaniad*** *hwn*
September *enw* ***Medi*** *hwn*
septet *enw* ***seithawd*** *hwn/hon*
sepulchre *enw* ***beddrod*** *hwn*
sequel *enw* ***dilyniant*** *hwn*
sequence *enw* ***trefn*, *olyniaeth*** *hon*, ***dilyniant*** *hwn*
sequester *be* ***atafaelu***
serenade *enw* ***nosgan*, *serenâd*** *hon*
serenade *be* ***canu serenâd***
serene *ans* ***tawel*, *digyffro***
serenity *enw* ***tawelwch*** *hwn*
serf *enw* ***taeog*** *hwn*
sergeant *enw* ***rhingyll*** *hwn*
serial *enw* ***cyfres*** *hon*
s~ changes *ton ar ôl ton o newidiadau*
series *enw* ***cyfres*** *hon*
serious *ans* ***difrifol***
sermon *enw* ***pregeth*** *hon*
serpent *enw* ***sarff*** *hon*
serrated *ans* ***danheddog***
serum *enw* ***serwm*** *hwn*
servant *enw* ***gwas*** *hwn*
serve *be* ***gwasanaethu*, *bod yn fodd i***
to ~ an apprenticeship *bwrw prentisiaeth*
to s~ a probationary period *cwblhau cyfnod prawf*
to s~ a useful purpose *bod o fudd*
to s~ notice *hysbysu*
to s~ their purpose *ateb eu diben*, *gwneud eu gwaith*
to s~ them well *bod yn gaffaeliad*
service *enw* ***gwasanaeth*** *hwn*

to bring into s~ *rhoi ar waith*
serviceable *ans* ***defnyddiol***
servile *ans* ***gwasaidd***
servitude *enw* ***caethwasanaeth*** *hwn*
session *enw* ***sesiwn*** *hwn/hon*
set *enw* ***set*** *hon*
set *ans* ***sefydlog***
they are s~ to go ***maent ar fin mynd***
set *be* ***dodi***, ***gosod***, ***setio***; ***caledu***; (type) ***cysodi***
to s~ about ***bwrw ati***
to s~ aside ***rhoi o'r neilltu***
to s~ back ***amharu***, ***peri oedi***
to s~ free ***rhyddhau***
to s~ off ***ysgogi***, ***symbylu***, ***cychwyn***
to s~ out ***nodi***, ***darlunio***
to s~ out to ***ymroi i***
to s~ the ball rolling ***gwthio'r cwch i'r dŵr***
to s~ the pace ***bod ar flaen y gad***
setting *enw* ***gosodiad, lleoliad*** *hwn*; (of the sun) ***machlud*** *hwn*
settle *enw* (furniture) ***sgiw*** *hon*
settle *be* ***cartrefu***; ***torri dadl***
settled *ans* ***sefydlog***
settlement *enw* ***cytundeb***; ***anheddiad*** *hwn*
set-up *enw* ***sefyllfa***, ***trefn*** *hon*; ***cynllwyn***, ***trap*** *hwn*
seven *rhifol* ***saith***
seventeen *rhifol* ***dau/dwy ar bymtheg***
seventeenth *ans* ***ail ar bymtheg***
seventh *ans* ***seithfed***
seventieth *ans* ***saith degfed***
seventy *rhifol* ***saith deg***
sever *be* ***torri***, ***gwahanu***
several *ans* ***sawl (sawl un)***
severe *ans* ***caled***, ***llym***, ***difrifol***
severity *enw* ***llymder***, ***gerwinder*** *hwn*
sew *be* ***gwnïo***
sewage *enw* ***carthion*** *hyn*
sewer *enw* ***carthffos*** *hon*
sewerage *enw* ***carthffosiaeth*** *hon*
sex *enw* ***rhyw*** *hwn/hon*
sexist *ans* ***rhywiaethol***
sextant *enw* ***secstant*** *hwn*
sexual *ans* ***rhywiol***
shabby *ans* ***diraen***
shack *enw* ***cwt*** *hwn*
shackles *enw* ***hualau***, ***llyffetheiriau*** *hyn*
shackle *be* ***llyffetheirio***, ***caethiwo***
shade *enw* ***cysgod***; ***arlliw*** *hwn*
shade *be* ***cysgodi***
shaded *ans* ***lled dywyll***
shadow *enw* ***cysgod*** *hwn*
without a s~ of doubt ***heb ronyn/rithyn o amheuaeth***
shady *ans* ***cysgodol***
s~ character ***aderyn brith*** *hwn*
shaft *enw* ***coes***; ***siafft*** *hon*
shaggy *ans* ***blewog***
shake *be* ***ysgwyd***, ***siglo***

shaky *ans* ***crynedig***, ***simsan***
shallow *ans* ***bas***
sham *enw* ***twyll*** *hwn*
sham *be* ***ffugio***
shambles *enw* ***traed moch*** *hyn*, ***llanast*** *hwn*
shame *enw* ***cywilydd***, ***gwarth*** *hwn*
shame *be* ***codi cywilydd (ar)***
shamefaced *ans* ***penisel***
shameful *ans* ***cywilyddus***, ***gwarthus***
shameless *ans* ***digywilydd***
shamelessness *enw* ***digywilydd-dra*** *hwn*
shampoo *enw* ***siampŵ*** *hwn*
shank *enw* ***crimog***, ***gar*** *hon*
shanty *enw* ***cwt*** *hwn*; ***sianti fôr*** *hon*
shape *enw* ***siâp*** *hwn*, ***ffurf*** *hon*
shape *be* ***llunio***
shapely *ans* ***lluniaidd***, ***siapus***
share *enw* ***cyfran*** *hon*; ***cyfranddaliad*** *hwn*
share *be* ***rhannu***
  to s~ in the excitement ***profi tipyn o'r cyffro***
  to s~ the same values ***arddel yr un gwerthoedd***
  to s~ the view ***cydsynio â'r farn***
shark *enw* ***siarc*** *hwn*
sharp *ans* ***miniog***
  in s~ contrast to ***yn wahanol iawn i***
  s~er focus ***canolbwynt cliriach*** *hwn*
sharpen *be* ***hogi***, ***rhoi min ar***, ***miniogi***
  to s~ responses ***cyflymu ymateb***
sharpness *enw* ***awch***, ***min*** *hwn*
shatter *be* ***dryllio***
shave *be* ***eillio***
shaver *enw* ***rasel drydan*** *hon*
shawl *enw* ***siôl*** *hon*
she *rhag* ***hi***
sheaf *enw* ***ysgub*** *hon*
shear *be* ***cneifio***; ***torri***
shed *enw* ***cwt*** *hwn*, ***sièd*** *hon*
shed *be* ***cael gwared ar***
sheen *enw* ***llewyrch*** *hwn*
sheep *enw* ***dafad*** *hon*, ***defaid*** *hyn*
sheepdog *enw* ***ci defaid*** *hwn*
sheer *ans* ***serth***
sheet *enw* ***cynfas*** *hon*
shelf *enw* ***silff*** *hon*
shell *enw* ***cragen*** *hon*
shell *be* ***bombardio***; (fruit) ***plisgo***
shelter *enw* ***cysgodfan*** *hwn/hon*
shelter *be* ***cysgodi***
shenanigans *enw* ***ystryw*** *hon*, ***cast*** *hwn*
shepherd *enw* ***bugail*** *hwn*, ***bugeiles*** *hon*
sheriff *enw* ***siryf*** *hwn*
sherry *enw* ***sieri*** *hwn*
shibboleth *enw* ***siboleth*** *hwn*
shield *enw* ***tarian*** *hon*
shield *be* ***gwarchod***
shift *enw* ***newid*** *hwn*; ***sifft*** *hon*
shift *be* ***symud***, ***newid***

shiftless *ans* ***didoreth***
shifty *ans* ***llechwraidd***
shimmer *be* ***pelydru***, ***caneitio***
shine *be* ***disgleirio***, ***tywynnu***
shingle *enw* ***graean*** *hwn*, ***gro*** *hon*
shingles *enw* ***yr eryr*** *hwn*
shining *ans* ***disglair***, ***gloyw***
ship *enw* ***llong*** *hon*
shipment *enw* ***llwyth llong*** *hwn*
shipwreck *enw* ***llongddrylliad*** *hwn*
shipwright *enw* ***saer llongau*** *hwn*
shire *enw* ***sir*** *hon*
shirk *be* ***esgeuluso***
shirt *enw* ***crys*** *hwn*
shirty *ans* ***piwis***, ***blin***
shiver *be* ***crynu***, ***rhynnu***
shoal *enw* ***haig*** *hon*
shock *enw* ***ysgytwad*** *hwn*, ***sioc*** *hon*
  short, sharp s~ ***gwers gyflym ac effeithiol***
shock *be* ***rhoi ysgytwad***, ***syfrdanu***
shoddy *ans* ***bratiog***, ***tila***
shoe *enw* ***esgid*** *hon*
shoehorn *enw* ***siasbi*** *hwn*
shoelace *enw* ***carrai esgid*** *hon*
shoemaker *enw* ***crydd*** *hwn*
shoot *enw* ***eginyn***, ***blaguryn*** *hwn*
shoot *be* ***saethu***
  shot their bolt ***wedi chwythu'u plwc***
shop *enw* ***siop*** *hon*
  one-stop s~ solution ***ateb cyflawn***
shopkeeper *enw* ***siopwr***, ***dyn y siop*** *hwn*, ***siopwraig***, ***gwraig y siop*** *hon*
shopper *enw* ***siopwr*** *hwn*, ***siopwraig*** *hon*
shore *enw* ***glan*** *hon*
short *ans* ***byr***, ***cwta***
  at s~ notice ***ar fyr o dro***
  in s~ supply ***prin***, ***annigonol***
shortage *enw* ***prinder*** *hwn*
shortbread *enw* ***teisen Berffro*** *hon*
short-circuit *enw* ***cylched fer*** *hon*
shortcoming *enw* ***diffyg*** *hwn*
short cut *enw* ***llwybr llygad/tarw*** *hwn*
shorten *be* ***byrhau***, ***cwtogi***
shortfall *enw* ***diffyg*** *hwn*
shorthand *enw* ***llaw fer*** *hon*
short list *enw* ***rhestr fer*** *hon*
short-lived *ans* ***byrhoedlog***
short-sighted *ans* ***byr eich golwg***
short wave *enw* ***tonfedd fer*** *hon*
shot *enw* ***ergyd*** *hwn/hon*
shotgun *enw* ***dryll*** *hwn/hon*
shot-put *be* ***taflu'r maen***
shoulder *enw* ***ysgwydd*** *hon*
shoulder *be* ***ysgwyddo***
shout *enw* ***bloedd***, ***gwaedd*** *hon*
shout *be* ***bloeddio, gweiddi***
shove *enw* ***gwthiad*** *hwn*
shove *be* ***gwthio***
shovel *enw* ***rhaw*** *hon*
shovel *be* ***rhofio***
show *enw* ***arddangosfa***, ***sioe*** *hon*
show *be* ***dangos***

to s~ results ***dwyn ffrwyth***
shower *enw* ***cawod*** *hon*
show off *be* ***rhodresa***
shred *enw* ***rhecsyn***, ***darn*** *hwn*
shred *be* ***rhwygo***
shrew *enw* ***llŷg*** *hon*; (woman) ***cecren*** *hon*
shrewd *ans* ***craff***, ***hirben***
shriek *enw* ***sgrech*** *hon*
shriek *be* ***gwichian***, ***sgrechian***
shrill *ans* ***main***, ***treiddgar***
shrimp *enw* ***berdasen*** *hon*; ***berdysyn*** *hwn*
shrine *enw* ***man cysegredig*** *hwn*
shrink *be* ***crebachu***, ***mynd yn llai***, ***encilio***
shrivel *be* ***crebachu***, ***crychu***
shroud *enw* ***amdo*** *hwn*
shroud *be* ***amdoi***
shrub *enw* ***prysgwydden*** *hon*
shudder *enw* ***ias*** *hon*
shudder *be* ***crynu***
shun *be* ***gochel***, ***osgoi***
shut *be* ***cau***
s~ up ***bydd dawel***, ***byddwch yn dawel***
shutter *enw* ***caead*** *hwn*
shuttle *enw* ***gwennol*** *hon*
shuttlecock *enw* ***gwennol*** *hon*
shy *ans* ***swil***
shyness *enw* ***swildod*** *hwn*
sibilate *be* ***sisial***
sick *ans* ***sâl***, ***tost***
s~ joke ***jôc drist*** *hon*
s~ with worry ***poeni eich enaid***
sicken *be* ***clafychu***, ***gwneud yn sâl***
sickle *enw* ***cryman*** *hwn*
sickly *ans* ***gwanllyd***
sickness *enw* ***gwaeledd*** *hwn*
side *enw* ***ochr*** *hon*
the other s~ of ***am y – â***
the other s~ of the world ***pen draw'r byd***
side *be* ***ochri***
sideboard *enw* ***seld*** *hon*
sidestep *be* ***ochrgamu***
sidetrack *be* ***codi/dilyn sgwarnog***
siege *enw* ***gwarchae*** *hwn*
siesta *enw* ***cyntun*** *hwn*; ***hoi*** *hon*
sieve *enw* ***gogr***, ***rhidyll*** *hwn*
sieve *be* ***rhidyllu***
sift *be* ***gogrwn***, ***hidlo***; ***didoli***
sigh *enw* ***ochenaid*** *hon*
sigh *be* ***ochneidio***
sight *enw* (the faculty) ***golwg*** *hwn*; (appearance) ***golwg*** *hon*; (spectacle) ***golygfa*** *hon*
short-sightedness ***golwg byr*** *hwn*
out of s~ ***o'r golwg***
at first s~ ***ar yr olwg gyntaf***
sightseeing *enw* ***ymweld***
sign *enw* ***arwydd***, ***argoel*** *hwn*
s~s of wear and tear ***ôl traul***
sign *be* ***arwyddo***, ***llofnodi***, ***dynodi***
signal *enw* ***arwydd***; ***signal*** *hwn*
signature *enw* ***llofnod*** *hwn*
significance *enw* ***arwyddocâd*** *hwn*
significant *ans* ***arwyddocaol***

in a s~ number *mewn nifer da/dda*
s~ areas of *rhannau helaeth o*
s~ variation *cryn amrywiaeth*
signify *be* ***golygu***, ***dynodi***
to s~ their support for *datgan eu bod o blaid*
signpost *enw* ***arwyddbost*** *hwn*
silage *enw* ***silwair*** *hwn*
silence *enw* ***tawelwch***, ***distawrwydd*** *hwn*
silence *be* ***distewi***
silent *ans* ***distaw***, ***mud***
silhouette *enw* ***amlinell*** *hon*
silhouette *be* ***amlinellu***
silicon chip *enw* ***ysglodyn silicon*** *hwn*
silicosis *enw* ***clefyd y llwch/dwst*** *hwn*
silk *enw* ***sidan*** *hwn*
silken *ans* ***sidanaidd***
sill *enw* ***silff*** *hon*
silliness *enw* ***ffolineb***, ***hurtrwydd*** *hwn*
silly *ans* ***ffôl***, ***hurt***
silver *enw* ***arian*** *hwn*
silvery *ans* ***ariannaidd***
similar *ans* ***tebyg***, ***fel***
similarity *enw* ***tebygrwydd*** *hwn*
by their s~ to *gan debyced ydynt i*
simile *enw* ***cyffelybiaeth***, ***cymhariaeth*** *hon*
simmer *be* ***mudferwi***
simper *be* ***glaswenu***
simple *ans* ***syml***; ***gwirion***
simplicity *enw* ***symlrwydd***, ***diniweidrwydd*** *hwn*
simplification *enw* ***symleiddiad*** *hwn*
simplify *be* ***symleiddio***
simplistic *ans* ***gorsyml***
simulate *be* ***dynwared***
simulation *enw* ***dynwarediad*** *hwn*
simultaneous *ans* ***ar yr un pryd***, ***cydamserol***
sin *enw* ***pechod*** *hwn*
sin *be* ***pechu***
since *adf/ardd* ***ers***, ***er***
ever since *hyd heddiw*
since *cysyllt* (seeing as) ***gan fod***
sincere *ans* ***diffuant***, ***didwyll***
sincerely *adf* ***yn bur***
sincerity *enw* ***didwylledd***, ***diffuantrwydd*** *hwn*
sine die *adf* ***hyd ddiwrnod i'w bennu***
sinew *enw* ***gewyn***, ***giewyn*** *hwn*
sinful *ans* ***pechadurus***
sing *be* ***canu***
singe *be* ***deifio***, ***rhuddo***
singer *enw* ***canwr*** *hwn*, ***cantores*** *hon*
single *ans* ***sengl***
to be s~d out *cael sylw arbennig*
singly *adf* ***fesul un***; ***ar eich pen eich hun***
singular *ans* ***unigol***
sinister *ans* ***sinistr***, ***anfad***

sink *enw* ***sinc*** *hon*
sink *be* ***suddo***
sinless *ans* ***dibechod***
sinner *enw* ***pechadur*** *hwn*, ***pechadures*** *hon*
sinuous *ans* ***dolennog***, ***troellog***
sinus *enw* ***sinws*** *hwn*
sip *enw* ***llymaid*** *hwn*
sip *be* ***sipian***
siphon *enw* ***siffon:seiffon*** *hwn*
sir *enw* ***syr*** *hwn*
sissy *enw* ***cadi ffan*** *hwn*
sister *enw* ***chwaer*** *hon*
sister-in-law *enw* ***chwaer-yng-nghyfraith*** *hon*
sit *be* ***eistedd***
site *enw* ***safle*** *hwn*
sitter *enw* ***eisteddwr*** *hwn*; (sport) ***(rhywbeth) hawdd***
sitting *enw* ***eistedd***, ***eisteddiad*** *hwn*
sitting-room *enw* ***lolfa*** *hon*
situated *ans* ***wedi'i (l)leoli***
situation *enw* ***sefyllfa*** *hon*
six *rhifol* ***chwe:chwech***
sixteen *rhifol* ***un ar bymtheg***
sixteenth *ans* ***unfed ar bymtheg***
sixth *ans* ***chweched***
sixtieth *ans* ***trigeinfed***
sixty *rhifol* ***trigain***, ***chwe deg***
size *enw* ***maint***, ***maintioli*** *hwn*
sizeable *ans* ***sylweddol***
sizzle *be* ***sislan***
skate *enw* ***esgid sglefrio*** *hon*; (fish) ***cath fôr*** *hon*
skate *be* ***sglefrio***
skating rink *enw* ***llawr sglefrio*** *hwn*
skeleton *enw* ***sgerbwd*** *hwn*
sketch *enw* ***braslun*** *hwn*
sketch *be* ***braslunio***
skew *be* ***gogwyddo***
skewer *enw* ***gwäell*** *hon*
skewer *be* ***gwaëllu***
ski *enw* ***sgi*** *hon*
ski *be* ***sgio***
skid *enw* ***sglefriad*** *hwn*
skid *be* ***sglefrio***, ***sgidio***
skier *enw* ***sgïwr*** *hwn*
skilful *ans* ***medrus***, ***deheuig***
skill *enw* ***medr***, ***sgil*** *hwn*
  active and passive s~s ***medrau/sgiliau derbyn a defnyddio*** *hyn*
  higher order s~s ***uwch fedrau/sgiliau*** *hyn*
  manipulative s~s ***medrau/sgiliau trafod*** *hyn*
  productive s~s ***medrau/sgiliau cynhyrchu*** *hyn*
skim *be* ***sgimio***
  to s~ read ***cipddarllen***
skimpy *ans* ***prin***, ***cwta***
  s~ skirt ***sgert fain*** *hon*
skin *enw* ***croen*** *hwn*
skin *be* ***blingo***
skinny *ans* ***tenau***, ***esgyrnog***
skip *be* ***sgipio***
skirmish *enw* ***sgarmes*** *hon*
skirt *enw* ***sgert*** *hon*

skirt *be* ***mynd wrth odre***, ***mynd heibio i***
skit *enw* ***dychan*** *hwn*
skittish *ans* ***rhuslyd***; ***penchwiban***
skittles *enw* ***ceilys*** *hyn*
skulduggery *enw* ***misdimanars*** *hyn*
skulk *be* ***llechu***, ***stelcian***
skull *enw* ***penglog*** *hon*
skunk *enw* ***drewgi*** *hwn*
sky *enw* ***awyr*** *hon*
skylark *enw* ***ehedydd*** *hwn*
skylight *enw* ***ffenestr do*** *hon*
skyscraper *enw* ***nendwr*** *hwn*
slab *enw* ***slabyn*** *hwn*, ***slaben*** *hon*
slack *ans* ***llac***
slack(en) *be* ***llacio***, ***llaesu***, ***arafu***
slackness *enw* ***llacrwydd***, ***diogi*** *hwn*
slam *be* ***cau'n glep***
slander *enw* ***athrod*** *hwn*
slander *be* ***athrodi***
slanderous *ans* ***athrodus***
slang *enw* ***bratiaith*** *hon*
slant *enw* ***goleddf***, ***gogwydd*** *hwn*
slant *be* ***goleddfu***, ***gogwyddo***
slap *enw* ***slapen*** *hon*
slap *be* ***taro***, ***slapian***
slapdash *adf* ***rywsut-rywsut***
slash *enw* ***slaes*** *hon*
  forward s~ ***blaen slaes*** *hon*
slash *be* ***torri â chyllell***; ***gostwng yn sydyn ac yn sylweddol***
slate *enw* ***llechen*** *hon*; (rock) ***llechfaen*** *hwn*
slaughter *enw* ***lladdfa***, ***cyflafan*** *hon*
slaughter *be* ***lladd***
slave *enw* ***caethwas*** *hwn*, ***caethferch*** *hon*
slaver *be* ***driflan***
slavery *enw* ***caethwasiaeth*** *hwn*
slay *be* ***lladd***
sleazy *ans* ***llwgr***
sledge *enw* ***sled*** *hon*
sledgehammer *enw* ***gordd*** *hon*
sleek *ans* ***llyfn***
sleep *enw* ***cwsg*** *hwn*
sleep *be* ***cysgu***
sleeper *enw* ***cysgadur***, ***cysgwr*** *hwn*
sleepiness *enw* ***syrthni***, ***awydd cysgu*** *hwn*
sleepless *ans* ***digwsg***
sleepwalking *enw* ***cerdded yn eich cwsg***
sleepy *ans* ***cysglyd***
sleet *enw* ***eirlaw*** *hwn*
sleeve *enw* ***llawes*** *hon*
slender *ans* ***main***
  the s~est of margins ***o drwch blewyn***
slenderness *enw* ***meinder*** *hwn*
slew *be* ***gwyro***
slice *enw* ***tafell***, ***sleisen*** *hon*
slice *be* ***torri'n dafelli***
slick *ans* ***slic***
slide *enw* ***llithren*** *hon*; (photo.) ***tryloywder*** *hwn*
slide *be* ***llithro***

slight *enw* ***sarhad*** *hwn*
slight *ans* ***bychan***, ***eiddil***, ***prin***, ***mân***
slightness *enw* ***bychander***, ***eiddilwch*** *hwn*
slim *ans* ***main***
slim *be* ***colli pwysau***
slime *enw* ***llysnafedd*** *hwn*
slimy *ans* ***seimlyd:seimllyd***
sling *enw* ***ffon dafl*** *hon*
slink *be* ***llithro***, ***sleifio***
slip *enw* ***llithrad:llithriad*** *hwn*
slip *be* ***llithro***
slipper *enw* ***sliper***, ***llopan*** *hon*
slippery *ans* ***llithrig***
slit *enw* ***agen***, ***hollt*** *hon*
slit *be* ***hollti***, ***torri***
slither *be* ***sleifio***
sliver *enw* ***fflawen*** *hon*
slob *enw* ***llabwst*** *hwn*
slobber *be* ***glafoerio***
sloes *enw* ***eirin duon surion bach*** *hyn*
slog *be* ***slafio***
slogan *enw* ***arwyddair*** *hwn*, ***slogan*** *hwn/hon*
slope *enw* ***llechwedd*** *hon*
slope *be* ***goleddfu***
sloppy *ans* ***blêr***
sloth *enw* ***diogi*** *hwn*
slothful *ans* ***diog***
slouch *be* ***gwargrymu***
slovenliness *enw* ***blerwch***, ***annibendod*** *hwn*
slovenly *ans* ***blêr***, ***di-hid***, ***diolwg***
slow *ans* ***araf***
slow *be* ***arafu***
slowness *enw* ***arafwch*** *hwn*
slug *enw* ***gwlithen*** *hon*
sluggish *ans* ***dioglyd***, ***diegni***
sluice *enw* ***llifddor*** *hon*
slum *enw* ***slym*** *hon*
slumber *be* ***huno***
slump *enw* ***cwymp*** *hwn*
slump *be* ***syrthio***, ***cwympo***
slur *enw* ***sarhad*** *hwn*, ***sen*** *hon*
slur *be* ***llithro***, ***llusgo***
to **s~ one's words** ***siarad yn dew***
slush *enw* ***slwtsh*** *hwn*
sly *ans* ***slei***, ***dichellgar***
slyness *enw* ***cyfrwyster:cyfrwystra***, ***twyll*** *hwn*
smack *enw* ***clec*** *hon*
smack *be* ***taro***, ***curo***
smack of *be* ***sawru o***
small *ans* ***bach***, ***bychan***, ***mân***
small beer *enw* ***diod fain*** *hon*
small *enw* (of back) ***meingefn*** *hwn*
small coal *enw* ***glo mân*** *hwn*
smallholding *enw* ***tyddyn*** *hwn*
smallness *enw* ***bychander: bychandra*** *hwn*
smallpox *enw* ***y frech wen*** *hon*
smarmy *ans* ***seimlyd:seimllyd***
smart *ans* ***taclus***, ***twt***; ***call***
smart *be* ***llosgi***, ***pigo***, ***gwingo***
smart card *enw* ***cerdyn call/smart*** *hwn*: ***carden gall/smart*** *hon*
smartness *enw* ***craffter***, ***taclusrwydd*** *hwn*

smash *enw* ***gwrthdrawiad*** *hwn*
smash *be* ***malu***, ***malurio***
s~ed to smithereens ***yn chwilfriw***
smattering *enw* ***crap***, ***ychydig*** *hwn*
smear *be* ***iro***; ***difwyno***
smell *enw* ***oglau***, ***gwynt***, ***arogl*** *hwn*
bad s~ ***drewdod*** *hwn*
smell *be* ***arogli:arogleuo***, ***gwynto***; ***drewi***
to s~ burning ***clywed gwynt llosgi***
smelly *ans* ***drewllyd***
smelt *be* ***toddi***
smile *enw* ***gwên*** *hon*
to wear a broad s~ ***bod yn wên o glust i glust***
smile *be* ***gwenu***
smirk *be* ***glaswenu***
smite *be* ***taro***
smith *enw* ***gof*** *hwn*
smithereens *enw* ***teilchion*** *hyn*
smithy *enw* ***gefail*** *hon*
smoke *enw* ***mwg*** *hwn*
smoke *be* ***mygu***, ***ysmygu***
smoker *enw* ***ysmygwr*** *hwn*, ***ysmygwraig*** *hon*
smoky *ans* ***myglyd***
smooch *be* ***lapswchan***
smooth *ans* ***llyfn***; ***diffwdan***
smooth *be* ***llyfnhau***, ***llyfnu***
smoothness *enw* ***llyfnder*** *hwn*
smother *be* ***mogi:mygu***; ***gorchuddio***
smoulder *be* ***mudlosgi***
smudge *enw* ***ôl***, ***staen*** *hwn*
smudge *be* ***llychwino***, ***gadael ôl***
smug *ans* ***hunangyfiawn***
smuggle *be* ***smyglo***
smuggler *enw* ***smyglwr*** *hwn*
smut *enw* ***parddu*** *hwn*
smutty *ans* ***brwnt***, ***budr***
snack *enw* ***byrbryd*** *hwn*
snag *enw* ***rhwystr***, ***anhawster*** *hwn*
snail *enw* ***malwen***, ***malwoden*** *hon*
snake *enw* ***neidr*** *hon*
snake *be* ***dolennu***, ***nadreddu***
snap *enw* ***clec***, ***snap*** *hwn*
s~ decision ***penderfyniad sydyn*** *hwn*
snap *be* ***clecian***; ***torri'n glec***
snapdragon *enw* ***trwyn y llo*** *hwn*
snappy *ans* ***bachog***
snapshot *enw* ***cipolwg*** *hwn*
snare *enw* ***magl*** *hon*
snarl *be* ***ysgyrnygu***
snatch *be* ***cipio***
sneak *enw* ***llechgi***, ***snechgi*** *hwn*
sneaky *ans* ***llechwraidd***
sneer *be* ***glaswenu***
sneeze *be* ***tisian***
snide *ans* ***gwawdlyd***, ***coeglyd***
sniff *be* ***ffroeni***, ***sniffian***
snigger *be* ***glaswenu***, ***piffian chwerthin***
snipe *enw* ***gïach*** *hon*
snippet *enw* ***darn***, ***pwt*** *hwn*
snivel *be* ***snwffian***
snob *enw* ***hen drwyn***, ***snobyn*** *hwn*

snobbish *ans* ***crachaidd**,*
snobyddlyd
snooker *enw* ***snwcer*** *hwn*
snooze *enw* ***cyntun*** *hwn*
snore *be* ***chwyrnu***
snort *be* ***ffroeni***
snout *enw* ***trwyn*** *hwn*
snow *enw* ***eira*** *hwn*
snow *be* ***bwrw eira***
snowball *enw* ***pelen eira**, **caseg***
eira *hon*
snowdrift *enw* ***lluwch*** *hon*
snowdrop *enw* ***eirlys*** *hwn*, ***lili wen***
fach *hon*
snowflake *enw* ***pluen eira*** *hon*
snowman *enw* ***dyn eira*** *hwn*
snowplough *enw* ***swch eira*** *hon*
snowy *ans* ***o eira***
snub *ans* ***smwt***
snub *enw* ***sen*** *hon*, ***sarhad*** *hwn*
snuff *enw* ***snisin*** *hwn*
snuffle *be* ***snwffian***
snug *ans* ***diddos**, **clyd***
snuggle *be* ***cwtsio**, **swatio***
so *adf* ***felly**; **mor**, **cyn***
soak *be* ***mwydo**, **rhoi yng ngwlych***
to s~ in the atmosphere
ymgolli yn/ymglywed â
naws/awyrgylch
soap *enw* ***sebon*** *hwn*
soap *be* ***seboni***
soar *be* ***hedfan***
sob *enw* ***ochenaid*** *hon*
sob *be* ***beichio wylo/crïo***
sober *ans* ***sobr***
sobriety *enw* ***sobrwydd*** *hwn*
soccer *enw* ***pêl-droed*** *hon*
sociability *enw*
cymdeithasgarwch *hwn*
sociable *ans* ***cymdeithasgar***
social *ans* ***cymdeithasol***
socialism *enw* ***sosialaeth*** *hon*
socialist *enw* ***sosialydd*** *hwn*
socialize *be* ***cymdeithasu***
social worker *enw* ***gweithiwr***
cymdeithasol *hwn*
society *enw* ***cymdeithas*** *hon*
sociologist *enw* ***cymdeithasegydd***
hwn
sociology *enw* ***cymdeithaseg*** *hon*
sock *enw* ***hosan*** *hon*
socket *enw* ***soced*** *hwn/hon*
sod *enw* ***tywarchen*** *hon*; ***cythraul***
mewn croen**, **hen ddiawl *hwn*
sofa *enw* ***soffa*** *hon*
sofit *enw* ***bondo*** *hwn*
soft *ans* ***meddal**, **mwyn**, **tyner**,*
ysgafn
soften *be* ***meddalu**, **tyneru***
soft-hearted *ans* ***calon feddal**, **yn***
galon i gyd
softness *enw* ***meddalwch**,*
tynerwch *hwn*
software *enw* ***meddalwedd***
hwn/hon
soggy *ans* ***soeglyd***
soil *enw* ***pridd*** *hwn*
true children of the s~ ***hen ŷd y***
wlad
soil *be* ***baeddu**, **difwyno/dwyno***

S

sojourn *enw* ***arhosiad*** *hwn*
solace *enw* ***cysur***, ***solas*** *hwn*
solace *be* ***cysuro***
solar *ans* ***(o)'r haul***, ***heulol***, ***solar***
solder *enw* ***sodr:sodor*** *hwn*
solder *be* ***sodro***
soldier *enw* ***milwr*** *hwn*
sole *enw* ***gwadn*** *hwn/hon*
sole *ans* ***unig***, ***llwyr***
solecism *enw* ***gwall*** *hwn*
solemn *ans* ***difrifol***, ***dwys***
solemnity *enw* ***difrifoldeb*** *hwn*
sol-fa *enw* ***sol-ffa*** *hwn*
solicit *be* ***deisyf***, ***erfyn***
solicitor *enw* ***cyfreithiwr*** *hwn,* ***cyfreithwraig*** *hon*
solicitous *ans* ***gofalus***
solid *enw* ***solid*** *hwn*
solid *ans* ***cydnerth***, ***solet***, ***cadarn***
solidarity *enw* ***undod*** *hwn*
solidify *be* ***caledu***
solidity *enw* ***cadernid*** *hwn*
soliloquize *be* ***ymson***
soliloquy *enw* ***ymson*** *hwn*
solitary *ans* ***unig***, ***ar eich pen eich hun***
solitude *enw* ***unigedd*** *hwn*
solo *enw* ***unawd*** *hwn*
soloist *enw* ***unawdydd*** *hwn*
solstice *enw* ***heuldro*** *hwn*
soluble *ans* ***toddadwy***, ***hydawdd***
solution *enw* ***toddiant***; ***datrysiad*** *hwn*
solve *be* ***datrys***
solvency *enw* ***y gallu i dalu*** *hwn*
solvent *enw* ***toddydd*** *hwn*
solvent *ans* ***ag arian***, ***diddyled***
sombre *ans* ***tywyll***, ***prudd***
some *ans* ***peth***, ***rhyw***, ***rhai***
  at s~ length ***yn bur faith***
  s~ chance! ***gobaith caneri!***
  s~ party ***parti a hanner***
  to go s~ way to ***bod o ryw gymorth***
somebody *rhag* ***rhywun***
somehow *adf* ***r(h)ywsut***
somersault *enw* ***tin dros ben*** *hwn*
something *rhag* ***rhywbeth***
sometimes *adf* ***weithiau***, ***ambell waith***, ***o bryd i'w gilydd***
somewhat *adf* ***r(h)ywfaint***, ***braidd***
somewhere *adf* ***r(h)ywle***
somnolence *enw* ***syrthni*** *hwn*
somnolent *ans* ***cysglyd***, ***swrth***
son *enw* ***mab*** *hwn*
song *enw* ***cân*** *hon*
songbird *enw* ***telor*** *hwn*
son-in-law *enw* ***mab-yng-nghyfraith*** *hwn*
sonnet *enw* ***soned*** *hon*
sonorous *ans* ***soniarus***
soon *adf* ***cyn bo hir***, ***yn fuan***
soot *enw* ***parddu***, ***huddygl*** *hwn*
soothe *be* ***lliniaru***, ***lleddfu***
soothsayer *enw* ***dyn hysbys*** *hwn*
sophisticated *ans* ***soffistigedig***
sophistry *enw* ***twyllresymeg*** *hon*
soporific *ans* ***cysglyd***
sopping *ans* ***yn wlyb diferu***
soppy *ans* ***gwirion***

soprano *enw* ***soprano*** *hwn/hon*
sorcerer *enw* ***swynwr*** *hwn*
sorcery *enw* ***swyngyfaredd*** *hon*
sordid *ans* ***budr***, ***gwael***
sore *enw* ***briw***, ***dolur*** *hwn*
sore *ans* ***poenus***, ***tost***
sorely *adf* ***yn aruthrol***
 s~ in need ***â dwys angen***
 s~ missed ***bydd colled fawr ar eu hôl***
sorrow *enw* ***galar***, ***tristwch*** *hwn*
sorrow *be* ***gofidio***, ***tristáu***
sorrowful *ans* ***trist***, ***gofidus***
sorry *ans* ***edifar***
sort *enw* ***math*** *hwn*
sort *be* ***didoli***
sortie *enw* ***taith hedfan*** *hon*
soul *enw* ***enaid*** *hwn*
sound *enw* ***sŵn*** *hwn*
 s~ bite ***sylw bachog*** *hwn*
sound *be* ***seinio***, ***atseinio***
 to s~ off ***uchel eu cloch***
sound *ans* ***iach***, ***solet***
 s~ sense ***doeth o beth***
sounding board *enw* ***seinfwrdd*** *hwn*
 to act as a s~ b~ ***bod yn glust i wrando***
soundness *enw* ***sadrwydd*** *hwn*
soup *enw* ***cawl*** *hwn*
sour *ans* ***sur***
source *enw* ***ffynhonnell*** *hon*
sourpuss *enw* ***surbwch*** *hwn*
souse *be* ***trwytho***
south *enw* ***de*** *hwn*
southern *ans* ***deheuol***
southpaw *ans* ***llaw bwt***
southward(s) *adf* ***tua'r de***
souvenir *enw* ***swfenîr*** *hwn*
sovereign *enw* ***sofren***; ***brenhines*** *hon*, ***brenin*** *hwn*
sovereign *ans* ***goruchaf***
sovereignty *enw* ***sofraniaeth***, ***penarglwyddiaeth*** *hon*
sow *be* ***hau***
sow *enw* ***hwch*** *hon*
space *enw* ***gofod***, ***lle*** *hwn*
 s~ invaders ***goresgynwyr o'r gofod*** *hyn*
 watch this s~ ***rhagor yn fuan***
 within a short s~ of time ***yn fuan***
spacecraft *enw* ***llong ofod*** *hon*
spacious *ans* ***helaeth***, ***eang***
 s~ accommodation ***digonedd o le***
spade *enw* ***pâl***, ***rhaw*** *hon*
spadework *enw* ***gwaith caib a rhaw*** *hwn*
spaghetti *enw* ***sbageti*** *hwn*
span *enw* ***rhychwant*** *hwn*
 to have a short s~ ***para am gyfnod byr yn unig***
span *be* ***rhychwantu***, ***cynnwys***
spangle *be* ***serennu***
Spaniard *enw* ***Sbaenwr*** *hwn*
spanking *ans* ***sbon***
spanner *enw* ***sbaner*** *hwn/hon*
spare *be* ***arbed***, ***sbario***
spare *ans* ***cynnil***, ***prin***; ***dros ben***, ***sbâr***

S

sparing *ans* ***cynnil***, ***darbodus***
spark *enw* ***gwreichionen*** *hon*
spark *be* ***gwreichioni***
to s~ off ***ysgogi***, ***symbylu***
sparkle *enw* ***fflach*** *hon*
sparkle *be* ***pefrio***, ***serennu***
sparrow *enw* ***aderyn y to*** *hwn*
sparse *ans* ***tenau***, ***prin***
spasm *enw* ***pwl***, ***plwc*** *hwn*
spasmodic *ans* ***ysbeidiol***, ***bylchog***
spastic *ans* ***sbastig***
spate *enw* ***llifeiriant*** *hwn*
spatter *be* ***ysgeintio***, ***tasgu***
spawn *enw* ***sil***, ***grawn*** *hyn*, ***grifft*** *hwn*
spawn *be* ***esgor***, ***bwrw sil***
speak *be* ***siarad***, ***llefaru***
the figures s~ for themselves ***mae neges y ffigurau'n ddigon clir***
to s~ one's mind ***siarad yn ddi-flewyn ar dafod***
to s~ out ***dweud eu dweud***
speaker *enw* ***siaradwr*** *hwn*, ***siaradwraig*** *hon*, ***llefarydd*** *hwn*
spear *enw* ***gwaywffon*** *hon*
spear *be* ***trywanu***
special *ans* ***arbennig***
specialism *enw* ***arbenigedd*** *hwn*
specialist *enw* ***arbenigwr*** *hwn*
speciality *enw* ***arbenigedd*** *hwn*
specialized *ans* ***arbenigol***
species *enw* ***rhywogaeth*** *hon*
specific *ans* ***penodol***, ***pendant***, ***unswydd***
specification *enw* ***manyleb*** *hon*
job s~ ***manyleb swydd*** *hon*
specify *be* ***pennu***
specimen *enw* ***esiampl*** *hon*
specious *ans* ***twyllodrus***
speckle *be* ***britho***
spectacle *enw* ***golygfa*** *hon*
spectacles *enw* ***sbectol*** *hon*, ***gwydrau*** *hyn*
spectacular *ans* ***ysblennydd***, ***aruthrol***, ***godidog***
spectator *enw* ***gwyliwr*** *hwn*
spectre *enw* ***drychiolaeth*** *hon*, ***ysbryd*** *hwn*
spectrum *enw* ***sbectrwm*** *hwn*
speculate *be* ***damcaniaethu***; ***mentro***
speculation *enw* ***dyfaliad*** *hwn*, ***menter*** *hon*
speculative *ans* ***damcaniaethol***, ***mentrus***
speech *enw* (faculty) ***lleferydd*** *hwn*; (address) ***araith*** *hon*
s~ difficulty ***anhawster llefaru*** *hwn*
s~ impediment ***nam ar y lleferydd*** *hwn*
speed *enw* ***cyflymder***, ***buanedd*** *hwn*
speed *be* ***goryrru***
s~ up ***cyflymu***
speediness *enw* ***cyflymder***, ***cyflymdra*** *hwn*
speed limit *enw* ***cyfyngiad cyflymder*** *hwn*

speedy *ans* ***buan***
speleologist *enw* ***ogofwr*** *hwn*
spell *enw* ***swyn*** *hwn*
spell *be* ***sillafu***
spelling *enw* ***sillafiad*** *hwn*
spend *be* ***gwario***, ***treulio***
spent force ***wedi chwythu'i blwc***
sperm *enw* ***had***, ***sberm*** *hwn*
sphere *enw* ***sffêr*** *hwn/hon*, ***cronnell*** *hon*
spherical *ans* ***sfferaidd***
spice *enw* ***sbeis*** *hwn*
spicy *ans* ***sbeislyd***
spider *enw* ***corryn***, ***pryf copyn*** *hwn*
spike *enw* ***pigyn*** *hwn*
spill *be* ***colli***, ***sarnu***
spin *be* ***troelli***; ***nyddu***
spinach *enw* ***sbigoglys*** *hwn*
spinal *ans* ***y cefn***
spindle *enw* ***echel***, ***gwerthyd*** *hon*
spine *enw* ***asgwrn cefn*** *hwn*; (book) ***meingefn*** *hwn*
pay s~ ***colofn dâl*** *hon*
spineless *ans* ***di-asgwrn-cefn***
spinney *enw* ***gwig*** *hon*
spinster *enw* ***hen ferch*** *hon*
spiral *enw* ***troell*** *hon*
spire *enw* ***meindwr*** *hwn*
spirit *enw* ***ysbryd***, ***enaid*** *hwn*; (alcohol) ***gwirod*** *hwn/hon*
spirited *ans* ***bywiog***, ***nwyfus***
spiritless *ans* ***dieneiniad***, ***merfaidd***
spiritual *ans* ***ysbrydol***
spirituality *enw* ***ysbrydolrwydd*** *hwn*
spit *enw* ***poer*** *hwn*
spit *be* ***poeri***
spite *enw* ***sbeit*** *hwn*
in s~ of ***er gwaethaf***
spiteful *ans* ***mileinig***, ***milain***
spittle *enw* ***poer*** *hwn*
splash *be* ***tasgu***, ***sblasio***
splatter *be* ***tasgu***
splay *be* ***lledu***
spleen *enw* ***y ddueg*** *hon*
splendid *ans* ***ardderchog***, ***campus***
splendour *enw* ***gogoniant***, ***ysblander*** *hwn*
splice *be* ***plethu***
splinter *enw* ***ysgyren*** *hon*
splinter *be* ***torri'n ysgyrion***
split *enw* ***hollt*** *hon*
split *be* ***hollti***
spoil *enw* ***ysbail*** *hwn*
s~ heaps ***tomenni gwastraff*** *hyn*
spoil *be* ***difetha***
spoilsport *enw* ***surbwch*** *hwn*
spoke *enw* (of wheel) ***adain***, ***braich*** *hon*; (of ladder) ***ffon*** *hon*
spokesman *enw* ***llefarydd*** *hwn*
sponge *enw* ***sbwng*** *hwn*
sponsor *enw* ***noddwr*** *hwn*
sponsorship *enw* ***nawdd*** *hwn*
spontaneity *enw* ***natur ddigymell*** *hon*
spontaneous *ans* ***digymell***

S

s~ speech ***siarad o'r frest***
spool *enw* ***sbŵl*** *hwn*
spoon *enw* ***llwy*** *hon*
spoonful *enw* ***llwyaid*** *hon*
spoor *enw* ***ôl*** *hwn*
sporadic(al) *ans* ***ysbeidiol***, ***anfynych***, ***yn awr ac yn y man***
spore *enw* ***sbôr*** *hwn*
sport *enw* ***sbort*** *hwn/hon*; ***chwaraeon*** *hyn*
sportsman *enw* ***chwaraewr*** *hwn*
sportswoman *enw* ***chwaraewraig*** *hon*
spot *enw* ***man*** *hwn/hon*
spot *be* ***brychu***; ***gweld***
spotless *ans* ***dilychwin***, ***difrycheulyd***, ***fel pìn mewn papur***
spot on *ans* ***bod yn llygad eich lle***
spotted *ans* ***brych***
spouse *enw* ***priod*** *hwn/hon*
spout *enw* ***ffrwd*** *hon*; ***pig*** *hwn/hon*
spout *be* ***pistyllio***, ***ffrydio***
sprain *be* ***ysigo***
sprawl *be* ***gorweddian***
spray *enw* ***tusw*** *hwn*; ***ewyn*** *hwn*
spray *be* ***chwistrellu***
spread *be* ***taenu***, ***lledaenu***, ***gwasgaru***
sprig *enw* ***sbrigyn*** *hwn*
sprightly *ans* ***gwisgi***, ***hoenus***
spring *enw* ***gwanwyn*** *hwn*; (water) ***ffynnon*** *hon*; (device) ***sbring*** *hwn/hon*
no s~ chicken ***yn ei hoed a'i hamser***
spring *be* ***neidio***
to s~ from ***deillio o***
spring binder *enw* ***ffeil sbring*** *hon*
sprinkle *be* ***ysgeintio***
sprinkling *enw* ***taenelliad*** *hwn*
sprout *enw* ***eginyn***, ***blaguryn*** *hwn*
sprout *be* ***blaguro***
spruce *enw* ***pyrwydden*** *hon*
spruce *ans* ***twt***, ***destlus***
spry *ans* ***heini***, ***sionc***
spume *enw* ***ewyn***, ***distrych*** *hwn*
spur *enw* ***sbardun*** *hwn/hon*, **hwb** hwn
spur *be* ***sbarduno***
spurn *be* ***dirmygu***
sputter *be* ***ffrwtian***
spy *enw* ***ysbïwr*** *hwn*, ***ysbïwraig*** *hon*
spy *be* ***ysbïo***
squabble *enw* ***ffrae*** *hon*
squabble *be* ***ffraeo***
squad *enw* ***carfan*** *hon*
squadron *enw* ***sgwadron*** *hon/hwn*
squalid *ans* ***brwnt***, ***budr***
squall *enw* ***hwrdd (o wynt)***, ***chwythwm*** *hwn*
squalor *enw* ***budreddi***, ***aflendid*** *hwn*
squander *be* ***afradu***
square *enw* ***sgwâr*** *hon/hwn*
squash *enw* ***diod ffrwythau*** *hon*; (rackets) ***sboncen*** *hon*
squash *be* ***gwasgu***

squat *be* ***cyrcydu***
squeak *be* ***gwichian***
squeal *enw* ***gwich*** *hon*
squeeze *be* ***gwasgu***
squib *enw* ***sgwib*** *hwn/hon*
squint *enw* ***tro (yn y) llygad*** *hwn*
squint *be* ***ciledrych***
squint *ans* ***llygatgam***
squire *enw* ***sgweier***, ***yswain*** *hwn*
squirm *be* ***gwingo***
squirrel *enw* ***gwiwer*** *hon*
squirt *be* ***chwistrellu***
stab *be* ***trywanu***
stability *enw* ***sadrwydd***, ***sefydlogrwydd*** *hwn*
stable *enw* ***stabl*** *hon*
stable *ans* ***sefydlog***, ***sad***
stack *enw* ***pentwr*** *hwn*
stack *be* ***pentyrru***
staff *enw* **staff** *hwn*; (stick) ***ffon*** *hon*
stag *enw* ***bwch danas***, ***hydd*** *hwn*
stage *enw* (theatrical) ***llwyfan*** *hwn/hon*; (step) ***cam*** *hwn*
  at any s~ ***ar unrhyw adeg***
  at every s~ ***bob cam o'r ffordd***
  at the planning s~ ***ar y gweill***
  in s~s ***gam wrth gam***
  pupils at every s~ ***disgyblion o bob oed***
stage *be* ***llwyfannu***
stagecoach *enw* ***coets fawr*** *hon*
stagger *be* ***gwegian***, ***igam-ogamu***
staggering *ans* ***simsan***, ***ysgytwol***
stagnation *enw* ***marweidd-dra*** *hwn*
stagnate *be* ***troi'n ferddwr***
staid *ans* ***sobr***, ***sidêt***
stain *enw* ***staen*** *hwn*
stain *be* ***staenio***
stair *enw* ***gris*** *hwn/hon*
staircase *enw* ***grisiau*** *hyn*
stake *enw* ***polyn*** *hwn*
stakeholder *enw* ***budd-ddeiliad***; ***cyfranddeiliad*** *hwn*
stalactite *enw* ***stalactit*** *hwn*
stalagmite *enw* ***stalagmit*** *hwn*
stale *ans* ***hen***
stalk *enw* ***coes*** *hon*, ***coesyn*** *hwn*
stalk *be* ***stelcio***, ***llech-ddilyn***
stalker *enw* ***stelciwr*** *hwn*
stall *enw* ***côr*** *hwn*; ***stondin*** *hwn*
stall *be* ***tagu***
stamen *enw* ***brigeryn*** *hwn*
stamina *enw* ***dyfalbarhad*** *hwn*
stammer *enw* ***atal dweud*** *hwn*
stammer *be* ***bod ag atal dweud***, ***cecian***
stamp *enw* ***stamp*** *hwn*
  s~ of approval ***sêl bendith***
stamp *be* ***curo traed***, ***pystylad***
stampede *enw* ***rhuthr*** *hwn*
stance *enw* ***osgo***, ***safiad*** *hwn*
stand *enw* ***safiad***; (football) ***eisteddle*** *hwn*
stand *be* ***sefyll***; ***goddef***
  as things s~ ***y sefyllfa sydd ohoni***
  to s~ by a decision ***glynu wrth benderfyniad***
  to s~ comparison with ***dal cannwyll i***

to s~ down as ***ymddiswyddo o***
to s~ out ***rhagori***
to s~ up to examination ***dal dŵr***
standard *enw* ***safon***; ***baner*** *hon*
standard *ans* ***safonol***
standardize *be* ***safoni***
standing *ans* ***sefydlog***
standpoint *enw* ***safbwynt*** *hwn*
standstill *enw* ***safiad*** *hwn*
come to a s~ ***sefyll yn stond***
staple *enw* ***stwffwl*** *hwn*, ***stapal*** *hon*
staple *be* ***styffylu/stwfflo, staplo***
star *enw* ***seren*** *hon*
starch *enw* ***startsh*** *hwn*
stare *be* ***rhythu***, ***syllu***
stark *ans* ***moel***, ***noeth***
a s~ choice ***dewis clir*** *hwn*
in s~ contrast to ***yn dra gwahanol i***
starling *enw* ***drudwy*** *hwn*
starry *ans* ***serennog***, ***serog***
start *enw* ***dechreuad*** *hwn*; (fright) ***ofn*** *hwn*
start *be* ***cychwyn***, ***dechrau***; ***neidio***
to get them s~ed ***eu rhoi ar ben ffordd***
starter *enw* ***cychwynnwr***; ***man cychwyn***; ***cwrs cyntaf*** *hwn*
startle *be* ***dychryn***
starvation *enw* ***newyn*** *hwn*
starve *be* ***newynu***, ***llwgu***
state *enw* ***cyflwr*** *hwn*; ***gwladwriaeth*** *hon*
state *be* ***datgan***, ***enwi***
stateless *ans* ***diwladwriaeth***
stately *ans* ***urddasol***
statement *enw* ***datganiad***, ***gosodiad*** *hwn*
statesman *enw* ***gwladweinydd*** *hwn*
static *ans* ***statig***; ***sefydlog***
station *enw* ***gorsaf*** *hon*
stationary *ans* ***disymud***, ***yn eich unfan***
stationery *enw* ***papur ysgrifennu*** *hwn*
statistical *ans* ***ystadegol***
statistic *enw* ***ystadegyn*** *hwn*
statue *enw* ***cerflun*** *hwn*
stature *enw* ***corffolaeth*** *hon*, ***maintioli*** *hwn*
status *enw* ***statws*** *hwn*
statutory *ans* ***statudol***
staunch *ans* ***cadarn***
staunch *be* ***atal***
statute *enw* ***statud*** *hon*
stave *enw* ***erwydden*** *hon*
stay *be* ***aros***, ***sefyll***
steadfast *ans* ***cadarn***, ***disyflyd***
steadiness *enw* ***sadrwydd***, ***sefydlogrwydd*** *hwn*
steady *ans* ***sefydlog***, ***cyson***
steady *be* ***sefydlogi***
steak *enw* ***stêc***, ***stecen*** *hon*
steal *be* ***lladrata***, ***dwyn***
stealthy *ans* ***llechwraidd***, ***lladradaidd***
steam *enw* ***ager*** *hwn*

steam *be* ***mygu***
steam engine *enw* ***peiriant ager*** *hwn*
steed *enw* ***march*** *hwn*
steel *enw* ***dur*** *hwn*
steep *ans* ***serth***
steeple *enw* ***tŵr eglwys*** *hwn*
steepness *enw* ***serthrwydd*** *hwn*
steer *be* ***llywio***, ***cyfeirio***
steering wheel *enw* ***olwyn yrru/lywio***, ***llyw*** *hon*
stem *enw* ***coes*** *hon*
stem *be* ***atal***
stench *enw* ***drewdod*** *hwn*
stentorian *ans* ***byddarol***
step *enw* ***cam***, ***gris*** *hwn*
  before any s~s are taken ***cyn bwrw ati***
  a s~ change ***newid sylweddol*** *hwn*
  to be in s~ with ***cyd-fynd â***
  to take steps to ***mynd ati i***
step *be* ***camu***
stepbrother *enw* ***llysfrawd*** *hwn*
stepdaughter *enw* ***llysferch*** *hon*
stepfather *enw* ***llystad*** *hwn*
stepmother *enw* ***llysfam*** *hon*
stepsister *enw* ***llyschwaer*** *hon*
stepson *enw* ***llysfab*** *hwn*
stereotype *enw* ***ystrydeb*** *hon*
sterile *ans* ***diffrwyth, di-haint***
sterilize *be* ***steryllu***, ***diheintio***
sterling *ans* ***dilys***; ***sterling***
stern *ans* ***llym***, ***caled***
sternum *enw* ***cledr y ddwyfron*** *hon*
stertorous *ans* ***yn chwyrnu***
stethoscope *enw* ***corn meddyg*** *hwn*
stew *enw* ***stiw*** *hwn*
steward *enw* ***stiward*** *hwn*
stewardess *enw* ***stiwardes*** *hon*
stick *enw* ***ffon*** *hon*
stick *be* ***glynu***
  to s~ in their gullet ***bod yn dân ar eu croen***
sticker *enw* ***sticer*** *hwn*
sticky *ans* ***gludiog***
stiff *ans* ***anystwyth***, ***anhyblyg***
  s~ competition ***cystadlu brwd***
stiffen *be* ***caledu***, ***cyffio***
stiffness *enw* ***anystwythder***, ***stiffrwydd*** *hwn*
stifle *be* ***mygu***
stifling *ans* ***llethol***
stigmatize *be* ***stigmateiddio***
stile *enw* ***camfa***, ***sticill*** *hon*
stiletto shoes *enw* ***esgidiau sodlau main*** *hyn*
still *be* ***tawelu***
still *ans* ***llonydd***
still *adf* ***o hyd***
stillborn *ans* ***marw-anedig***
stillness *enw* ***llonyddwch*** *hwn*
stilted *ans* (of speech) ***clogyrnaidd***, ***afrwydd***
stimulant *enw* ***symbylydd*** *hwn*
stimulate *be* ***symbylu***, ***cyffroi***, ***ysgogi***
stimulus *enw* ***symbyliad*** *hwn*
sting *enw* ***pigiad***, ***brathiad*** *hwn*

sting *be* ***pigo***, ***brathu***
stinginess *enw* ***crintachrwydd*** *hwn*
stingy *ans* ***crintachlyd***, ***cybyddlyd***
stink *enw* ***drewdod*** *hwn*
stink *be* ***drewi*** *hwn*
stint *be* ***tolio***
stipulate *be* ***mynnu***; ***pennu***
stipulated *ans* ***penodedig***
stipulation *enw* ***amod*** *hwn/hon*
stir *be* ***troi***, ***corddi***
to s~ up a hornet's nest ***tynnu nyth cacwn am eich pen***
stirring *ans* ***cynhyrfus***
s~ speech ***araith danbaid*** *hon*
stirrup *enw* ***gwarthol*** *hon*
stitch *enw* ***pwyth*** *hwn*
stitch *be* ***pwytho***
stoat *enw* ***carlwm*** *hwn*
stock *enw* ***stoc***; ***cyff*** *hwn*
laughing s~ ***testun sbort***, ***cyff gwawd*** *hwn*
stock *be* ***stocio***
to take s~ ***pwyso a mesur***
stock exchange *enw* ***cyfnewidfa stoc*** *hon*
stockbroker *enw* ***brocer stoc*** *hwn*
stocking *enw* ***hosan*** *hon*
stocks *enw* ***cyffion*** *hyn*
stodge *enw* ***stwnsh*** *hwn*
stoical *ans* ***stoicaidd***
stoker *enw* ***taniwr*** *hwn*
stolid *ans* ***digyffro***
stomach *enw* ***stumog*** *hon*, ***cylla*** *hwn*
stomach *be* ***stumogi***, ***dioddef***, ***goddef***
stomp *be* ***pystylad***
stone *enw* ***carreg*** *hon*
stone *be* ***llabyddio***
Stone Age *enw* ***Oes y Cerrig*** *hon*
stonemason *enw* ***saer maen*** *hwn*
stony *ans* ***caregog***
s~ silence ***tawelwch llethol*** *hwn*
stool *enw* ***stôl*** *hon*
stoop *be* ***gwargrymu***, ***plygu***, ***cwmanu***
stop *be* ***aros***, ***atal***
to put a s~ to ***rhoi taw ar***
stopgap *enw* ***cam dros dro*** *hwn*
stoppage *enw* ***ataliad*** *hwn*
stopwatch *enw* ***atalwats*** *hon*
storage *enw* ***crynhoad*** *hwn*, ***storfa*** *hon*
store *enw* ***storfa*** *hon*
store *be* ***storio***
stork *enw* ***storc*** *hwn*
storm *enw* ***storm***, ***drycin*** *hon*
s~ in a teacup ***storom daranau***
stormy *ans* ***stormus***
story *enw* ***stori*** *hon*, ***hanes*** *hwn*
the s~ goes that ***yn ôl yr hanes***
story-teller *enw* ***storïwr***, ***cyfarwydd*** *hwn*
stout *ans* ***tew***; ***glew***
stoutness *enw* ***tewdra*** *hwn*
stove *enw* ***stôf*** *hon*
stow *be* ***rhoi i'w gadw***
straggle *be* ***llusgo mynd***
straight *ans* ***syth***, ***union***

straightaway *adf* ***ar unwaith***, ***yn union***
straighten *be* ***unioni***
straightforward *ans* ***uniongyrchol***
strain *enw* ***straen*** *hon*
to the s~s of ***i gyfeiliant***
strain *be* ***straenio***; ***hidlo***
strait *enw* ***culfor*** *hwn*
strand *enw* ***cainc*** *hon*; ***edefyn*** *hwn*; ***llinyn*** *hwn*; (beach) ***traethell*** *hon*, ***marian*** *hwn*
strange *ans* ***rhyfedd***
strangeness *enw* ***dieithrwch*** *hwn*
stranger *enw* ***dieithryn*** *hwn*
strangle *be* ***llindagu***, ***tagu***
strap *enw* ***strapen*** *hon*
strapping *ans* ***cydnerth***
stratagem *enw* ***ystryw*** *hwn/hon*
strategic *ans* ***strategol***
strategy *enw* ***strategaeth*** *hon*
straw *enw* ***gwellt*** *hwn*
strawberry *enw* ***mefusen*** *hon*
stray *be* ***crwydro***
to s~ from the point ***codi sgwarnog***
stray *ans* ***crwydrol***, ***ar grwydr***
streak *enw* ***strimyn*** *hwn*
streak *be* ***britho***; ***gwibio***
stream *enw* ***nant***, ***ffrwd*** *hon*; ***rhibidirês*** *hon*
on s~ ***ar waith***
stream *be* ***llifo***, ***ffrydio***
streamline *be* ***hwyluso***, ***ystwytho***
streamlined *ans* ***lliflin***
street *enw* ***stryd***, ***heol*** *hon*
strength *enw* ***nerth***, ***cryfder*** *hwn*
physical s~ ***nerth bôn braich*** *hwn*
strengthen *be* ***cryfhau***, ***atgyfnerthu***
strenuous *ans* ***egnïol***
stress *enw* ***pwysau*** *hwn*
a period of s~ and strain ***cyfnod o straen a thyndra***
stress *be* ***pwysleisio***
stretch *be* ***estyn***, ***ymestyn***
s~ your imagination ***rhowch rwydd hynt i'ch dychymyg***
stretcher *enw* ***cludwely*** *hwn*
strew *be* ***gwasgaru***
striated *ans* ***rhesog***, ***rhychedig***
strict *ans* ***llym***, ***caeth***
strictness *enw* ***llymder***, ***cywirdeb*** *hwn*
stricture *enw* ***cyfyngiad*** *hwn*
stride *enw* ***cam bras*** *hwn*
stride *be* ***brasgamu***
strident *ans* ***cras***, ***croch***
strife *enw* ***cynnen*** *hon*, ***ymryson*** *hwn*
strike *enw* (games) ***ergyd*** *hon*; (attack) ***ymosodiad, cyrch*** *hwn*; (industry) ***streic*** *hon*
strike *be* ***taro***, ***bwrw***
to s~ a balance ***sicrhau cydbwysedd***
striker *enw* ***streiciwr***; ***saethwr*** *hwn*
striking *ans* ***trawiadol***
string *enw* ***llinyn***, ***cortyn*** *hwn*; ***rhibidirês*** *hon*

stringent *ans* ***caeth***, ***llym***
strip *enw* ***stribed*** *hwn/hon*
strip *be* ***tynnu dillad***
stripe *enw* ***rhesen***, ***streipen*** *hon*
striped *ans* ***rhesog***
stripling *enw* ***llanc*** *hwn*
strive *be* ***ymdrechu***, ***ymlafnio***
stroke *enw* ***ergyd*** *hwn/hon*, ***trawiad*** *hwn*
stroke *be* ***canmol***, ***anwesu***
stroll *be* ***mynd am dro***
strong *ans* ***grymus***, ***cryf***, ***cadarn***
strongbox *enw* ***coffr cryf*** *hwn*
stronghold *enw* ***cadarnle*** *hwn*
strop *be* ***hogi***
structural *ans* ***adeileddol***, ***strwythurol***
structure *enw* ***adeiledd***, ***strwythur*** *hwn*
structured *ans* ***strwythuredig***
tightly s~ ***tyn ei [g]wead***
struggle *enw* ***ymdrech***, ***brwydr*** *hon*
an uphill s~ ***talcen caled*** *hwn*
struggle *be* ***strancio***, ***cael trafferth i***
strut *be* ***torsythu***
stub *enw* ***bonyn*** *hwn*
stubble *enw* ***bonion gwellt/blew***; ***sofl*** *hyn*
stubborn *ans* ***ystyfnig***, ***cyndyn***
stubbornness *enw* ***ystyfnigrwydd***, ***cyndynrwydd*** *hwn*
stubby *ans* ***byrdew***
stud *enw* ***styden*** *hon*
student *enw* ***myfyriwr*** *hwn*
studies *enw* ***astudiaethau***, ***efrydiau*** *hyn*
studio *enw* ***stiwdio*** *hon*
studious *ans* ***myfyrgar***
study *enw* ***astudiaeth*** *hon*
study *be* ***astudio***
stuff *enw* ***defnydd***, ***sylwedd*** *hwn*
stuff *be* ***stwffio***
stuffing *enw* ***stwffin*** *hwn*
stumble *be* ***baglu***
stump *enw* ***bôn***, ***bonyn*** *hwn*
stun *be* ***syfrdanu***, ***hurtio***; ***taro'n anymwybodol***
stunning *ans* ***syfrdanol***
stunt *enw* ***sbloet*** *hon*
stunt *be* ***crebachu***
stupefy *be* ***peri i gysgu***; ***syfrdanu***
stupendous *ans* ***aruthrol***
stupid *ans* ***twp***
stupidity *enw* ***twpdra*** *hwn*
stupor *enw* ***syrthni*** *hwn*
sturdiness *enw* ***cryfder***, ***cadernid*** *hwn*
sturdy *ans* ***cydnerth***, ***praff***
stutter *enw* ***atal (dweud)*** *hwn*
stutter *be* ***cecian***, ***cecial***
sty *enw* ***cwt (mochyn)***, ***twlc*** *hwn*; (eye) ***llefelyn*** *hwn*
style *enw* ***steil*** *hwn*, ***ffordd*** *hon*; (language) ***arddull***, ***ieithwedd*** *hon*
stylish *ans* ***cain***
stymie *be* ***atal***, ***llesteirio***
suave *ans* ***gwên-deg***

subconscious *enw* ***isymwybod*** *hwn*
subdivide *be* ***isrannu***
subdue *be* ***darostwng***, ***gostegu***
subject *enw* ***testun***, ***pwnc***; (gram.) ***goddrych*** *hwn*; (of king) ***deiliad*** *hwn*
subject *ans* ***darostyngedig***
s~ to ***ar yr amod***
subjective *ans* ***goddrychol***
sub judice *ans* ***dan ystyriaeth farnwrol***
subjugate *be* ***darostwng***
subjugation *enw* ***darostyngiad*** *hwn*
subjunctive *ans* ***dibynnol***
sublimate *be* ***sychdarthu***
sublime *ans* ***aruchel***, ***dyrchafedig***
from the s~ to the ridiculous ***o'r gwych i'r gwachul***
sublimity *enw* ***arucheledd*** *hwn*
submarine *enw* ***llong danfor*** *hon*
submerge *be* ***suddo***, ***ymsuddo***, ***boddi***
submission *enw* ***ymostyngiad***; ***cyflwyniad*** *hwn*
submissive *ans* ***ymostyngol***
submit *be* ***ymostwng***; (present) ***cyflwyno***, ***dadlau***
subordinate *ans* ***israddol***
subscribe *be* ***tanysgrifio***
subscriber *enw* ***tanysgrifiwr*** *hwn*
subscription *enw* ***tanysgrifiad*** *hwn*
subsequent *ans* ***dilynol***
subservient *ans* ***gwasaidd***
subside *be* ***suddo***, ***gostwng***
subsidence *enw* ***ymsuddiant*** *hwn*
subsidiarity *enw* ***is-reolaeth*** *hon*
subsidiary *ans* ***cynorthwyol***, ***atodol***
subsidize *be* ***sybsideiddio***
subsidy *enw* ***cymhorthdal*** *hwn*
subsist *be* ***dal i fyw***, ***bodoli***
subsistence *enw* ***cynhaliaeth*** *hon*
substance *enw* ***sylwedd*** *hwn*
substandard *ans* ***islaw'r safon, is-safonol***, ***eilradd***, ***gwael***
substantial *ans* ***sylweddol***
substantiate *be* ***cadarnhau***, ***profi***
substantive *ans* ***o bwys***, ***o sylwedd***
substitute *enw* ***eilydd*** *hwn*
substitute *be* ***eilyddio***, ***cyfnewid***, ***amnewid***
substitution *enw* ***cyfnewidiad*** *hwn*
subsume *be* ***llyncu***, ***plethu i***
subterfuge *enw* ***ystryw*** *hwn/hon*
subterranean *ans* ***tanddaearol***
subtitle *enw* ***is-deitl*** *hwn*
subtle *ans* ***cynnil***, ***cyfrwys***
subtlety *enw* ***cynildeb***, ***cywreinrwydd*** *hwn*
subtract *be* ***tynnu***
suburb *enw* ***maestref*** *hon*
suburban *ans* ***maestrefol***
subversive *ans* ***yn tanseilio***, ***chwyldroadol***
subvert *be* ***tanseilio***
succeed *be* ***llwyddo***; ***olynu***

S

success *enw* ***llwyddiant*** *hwn*
successful *ans* ***llwyddiannus***
to be s~ ***taro deuddeg***
succession *enw* ***olyniaeth*** *hon*
successive *ans* ***olynol***
successor *enw* ***olynydd*** *hwn*
succinct *ans* ***cryno***, ***byr***
succour *enw* ***ymgeledd*** *hwn*
succour *be* ***ymgeleddu***
succumb *be* ***ildio***
such *ans* ***cyfryw***, ***y fath***
suck *be* ***sugno***
suckle *be* ***sugno***
suction *enw* ***sugnedd*** *hwn*
sudden *ans* ***sydyn***, ***annisgwyl***, ***dirybudd***
suddenness *enw* ***sydynrwydd*** *hwn*
suds *enw* ***trochion*** *hyn*
sue *be* ***erlyn***, ***siwio***
suet *enw* ***siwed*** *hwn*, ***gweren*** *hon*
suffer *be* ***dioddef***
sufferer *enw* ***dioddefwr*** *hwn*
suffering *enw* ***dioddefaint*** *hwn*
suffice *be* ***bod yn ddigon***, ***digoni***
sufficient *ans* ***digon***
suffix *enw* ***olddodiad:ôl-ddodiad*** *hwn*
suffocate *be* ***mogi***, ***mygu***
suffocation *enw* ***mogfa*** *hon*
suffuse *be* ***ymledu***, ***bod yn gyforiog o***
sugar *enw* ***siwgr*** *hwn*
sugary *ans* ***siwgwraidd***
suggest *be* ***awgrymu***
suggestion *enw* ***awgrym*** *hwn*
suicidal *ans* ***hunanddinistriol***
suicide *enw* ***hunanladdiad*** *hwn*
suit *enw* ***siwt*** *hon*
to follow s~ ***gweithredu yn yr un modd***, ***dilyn yr un drefn***
suit *be* ***bod yn addas***, ***cydweddu***
suitable *ans* ***addas***, ***cymwys***, ***yn taro***
suitcase *enw* ***cês dillad*** *hwn*
suitor *enw* ***cariadfab*** *hwn*
sulky *ans* ***pwdlyd***
sullen *ans* ***sarrug***, ***swrth***
sultry *ans* ***mwll***
sum *enw* ***cyfanswm*** *hwn*
sum *be* ***mesur***, ***asesu***
to s~ up ***crynhoi***
summary *enw* ***crynodeb*** *hwn*
summer *enw* ***haf*** *hwn*
summit *enw* ***copa*** *hwn/hon*
summon *be* ***gwysio***
summons *enw* ***gwŷs*** *hon*
sumptuous *ans* ***moethus***
sun *enw* ***haul*** *hwn*
sunbathe *be* ***bolaheulo***, ***torheulo***
sunburn *enw* ***llosg haul*** *hwn*
Sunday *enw* ***dydd Sul*** *hwn*
sunder *be* ***gwahanu***
sundries *enw* ***mân bethau*** *hyn*
sundry *ans* ***amryw***, ***amrywiol***
all and s~ ***pawb a phobun***
sunflower *enw* ***blodyn yr haul*** *hwn*
sunny *ans* ***heulog***, ***tesog***
sunrise *enw* ***codiad haul*** *hwn*
sunset *enw* ***machlud haul*** *hwn*

sunshade *enw* ***cysgodlen*** *hon*
sunshine *enw* ***heulwen*** *hon*, ***golau haul*** *hwn*
sunstroke *enw* ***twymyn yr haul*** *hon*
suntan *enw* ***lliw haul*** *hwn*
super *ans* ***penigamp***, ***rhagorol***
superb *ans* ***gwych***
supercilious *ans* ***ffroenuchel***
superficial *ans* ***arwynebol***
superfluity *enw* ***toreth*** *hon*
superfluous *ans* ***dianghenraid***
superintend *be* ***arolygu***
superintendent *enw* ***arolygydd*** *hwn*
superior *ans* ***uwch***, ***uwchradd***
to be s~ to ***rhagori ar***
superiority *enw* ***rhagoriaeth*** *hon*
superlative *ans* ***rhagorol***, ***eithaf***
supermarket *enw* ***uwchfarchnad***, ***archfarchnad*** *hon*
supernatural *enw* ***y goruwchnaturiol*** *hwn*
supersede *be* ***disodli***, ***cymryd lle***
supersonic *ans* ***uwchsonig***
superstition *enw* ***ofergoel***; ***ofergoeliaeth*** *hon*
superstitious *ans* ***ofergoelus***
superstructure *enw* ***uwchstrwythur***, ***uwchfframwaith*** *hwn*
supervene *be* ***digwydd***, ***dilyn***
supervise *be* ***goruchwylio***, ***arolygu***
supervision *enw* ***goruchwyliaeth*** *hon*
supervisor *enw* ***goruchwyliwr***, ***arolygydd*** *hwn*
supine *ans* ***ar wastad eich cefn***
supper *enw* ***swper*** *hwn*
supplant *be* ***disodli***, ***cymryd lle***
supple *ans* ***ystwyth***, ***hydwyth***
supplement *enw* ***atodiad***, ***ychwanegiad*** *hwn*
supplementary *ans* ***atodol***, ***ychwanegol***
suppleness *enw* ***ystwythder***, ***hyblygrwydd*** *hwn*
supplicant *enw* ***deisyfwr*** *hwn*
supplicate *be* ***erfyn***, ***deisyf***
supplication *enw* ***erfyniad***, ***deisyfiad*** *hwn*
supplier *enw* ***cyflenwr*** *hwn*
supplies *enw* ***nwyddau***, ***cyflenwadau*** *hyn*
supply *enw* ***cyflenwad*** *hwn*, ***arlwy*** *hwn/hon*
in short s~ ***annigonol***
s~ teachers ***athrawon llanw/cyflenwi*** *hyn*
supply *be* ***cyflenwi***
support *enw* ***cefnogaeth***, ***cynhaliaeth*** *hon*
support *be* ***cynnal***
supportable *ans* ***cynaliadwy***
supporter *enw* ***cefnogwr*** *hwn*
suppose *be* ***tybio***, ***a bwrw***
supposition *enw* ***tybiaeth*** *hon*, ***dyfaliad*** *hwn*
suppositional *ans* ***dyfaliadol***
suppress *be* ***atal***, ***gostegu***

suppression *be* ***atal***, ***gostegu***
suppurate *be* ***crawni***, ***gori***
supremacy *enw* ***goruchafiaeth*** *hon*
supreme *ans* ***pennaf***, ***goruchaf***
supremo *enw* ***pennaeth*** *hwn*
surcharge *enw* ***tâl ychwanegol*** *hwn*
surcharge *be* ***codi ychwaneg***
sure *ans* ***sicr***
sureness *enw* ***sicrwydd*** *hwn*
surf *enw* ***ewyn*** *hwn*
surf *be* ***beistonna***; (the Internet) ***cribo***
surface *enw* ***wyneb*** *hwn*
surface *be* ***codi i'r wyneb***
a problem which has s~d ***problem sydd wedi codi'i phen***
surfboard *enw* ***astell feiston*** *hon*
surge *enw* ***ymchwydd***, ***dygyfor*** *hwn*
surgeon *enw* ***llawfeddyg*** *hwn*
surgery *enw* ***meddygfa***; ***triniaeth lawfeddygol***; ***cymhorthfa*** *hon*
surgical *ans* ***llawfeddygol***
surly *ans* ***sarrug***, ***swrth***
surmise *be* ***dyfalu***, ***tybio***
surmount *be* ***gorchfygu***, ***goresgyn***
surname *enw* ***cyfenw*** *hwn*
surpass *be* ***rhagori ar***
surplus *enw* ***gweddill*** *hwn*, ***gwarged*** *hwn/hon*
surprise *enw* ***peth annisgwyl***, ***syndod*** *hwn*
surprise *be* ***synnu***
surrender *be* ***ildio***
surreptitious *ans* ***llechwraidd***
surrogate *ans* ***dirprwyol***
surround *be* ***amgylchynu***
Cardiff and the s~ing region ***Caerdydd a'r cylch/cyffiniau***
s~ing areas ***ardaloedd cylchynol*** *hyn*
surroundings *enw* ***y byd o'u hamgylch*** *hwn*
surveillance *be* ***goruchwylio***, ***clustfeinio***
survey *enw* ***arolwg*** *hwn*
survey *be* ***cynnal arolwg***
survive *be* ***goroesi***
survivor *enw* ***goroeswr*** *hwn*
susceptibility *enw* ***chwanogrwydd***; ***teimlad*** *hwn*
susceptible *ans* ***tueddol***, ***chwannog***
suspect *enw* ***rhywun dan amheuaeth*** *hwn*
suspect *be* ***drwgdybio***, ***amau***
suspend *be* ***hongian***; ***diarddel***, ***atal***, ***rhoi o'r neilltu***
suspense *enw* ***gwewyr meddwl*** *hwn*
suspension *enw* (car) ***crogiant***, ***hongiad*** *hwn*
suspicion *enw* ***amheuaeth***, ***drwgdybiaeth*** *hon*
suspicious *ans* ***amheus***, ***drwgdybus***
sustain *be* ***cynnal***, ***ymgynnal***
sustainable *ans* ***cynaliadwy***

sustainability *enw* ***cynaladwyedd*** *hwn*
sustenance *enw* ***cynhaliaeth*** *hon,* ***arlwy*** *hwn/hon*
swaddle *be* ***lapio***
swagger *be* ***rhodresa***, ***torsythu***
swallow *enw* ***gwennol*** *hon*
swallow *be* ***llyncu***
swamp *enw* ***cors***, ***mignen***, ***gwern*** *hon*
swamp *be* ***boddi***
swap *be* ***cyfnewid***, ***ffeirio***
swarm *enw* ***haid*** *hon*
swarm *be* ***heidio***
swarthy *ans* ***pryd tywyll***
swath *enw* ***ystod***, ***gwanaf*** *hon*
swathe *be* ***lapio, rhwymo***
sway *be* ***gwegian***, ***siglo***
sway *enw* ***dylanwad*** *hwn*
 to hold s~ ***bod mewn grym***
swear *be* ***tyngu***, ***rhegi***
sweat *enw* ***chwys*** *hwn*
sweat *be* ***chwysu***
swede *enw* ***erfinen***, ***meipen***, ***rwden*** *hon*
sweep *be* ***ysgubo***
sweeping *ans* ***ysgubol***
 s~ views ***golygfeydd eang*** *hyn*
sweet *enw* ***losin***, ***da-da***, ***fferins*** *hyn*
sweet *ans* ***melys***
sweetbread *enw* ***cefndedyn*** *hwn*
sweeten *be* ***melysu***
sweetener *enw* ***melysydd*** *hwn*
sweetheart *enw* ***cariad*** *hwn*
sweetness *enw* ***melyster***, ***melystra*** *hwn*
 not all s~ and light ***ddim yn fêl i gyd***
swell *be* ***chwyddo***
swelling *enw* ***chwydd***; ***ymchwydd*** *hwn*
swelter *be* ***chwysu***
swerve *be* ***gwyro***
swift *ans* ***cyflym***, ***buan***
swiftness *enw* ***cyflymder***, ***cyflymdra*** *hwn*
swig *enw* ***dracht/tracht*** *hwn/hon*
swill *enw* ***golchion*** *hyn*
swim *be* ***nofio***
swimming pool *enw* ***pwll nofio*** *hwn*
swimsuit *enw* ***gwisg nofio*** *hon*
swindle *be* ***twyllo***
swine *enw* ***mochyn*** *hwn*
swing *enw* ***siglen*** *hon*
 s~s and roundabouts ***ennill ar y menyn***, ***colli ar y caws***
swing *be* ***siglo***
swirl *enw* ***chwyrlïad*** *hwn*
switch *enw* ***swits*** *hwn*
switch *be* ***newid***
 s~ off ***diffodd***
 s~ off completely ***colli pob diddordeb***
 s~ on ***troi ymlaen***, ***dechrau***
switchboard *enw* ***switsfwrdd*** *hwn*
swivel *be* ***troi ar ei echel***
swollen *ans* ***chwyddedig***
swoon *enw* ***llesmair*** *hwn*

S

swoon *be* ***llesmeirio***
swoop *be* ***disgyn***
swop *be* ***newid***
sword *enw* ***cleddyf*** *hwn*
swordsman *enw* ***cleddyfwr*** *hwn*
sycamore *enw* ***sycamorwydden*** *hon*
sycophant *enw* ***cynffonnwr*** *hwn*
syllabic *ans* ***sillafog***
syllable *enw* ***sillaf*** *hon*
syllabus *enw* ***maes llafur*** *hwn*
sylvan *ans* ***coediog***
symbol *enw* ***symbol*** *hwn*
symbolic(al) *ans* ***symbolaidd***
symbolize *be* ***symboleiddio***
symmetrical *ans* ***cymesur***
symmetry *enw* ***cymesuredd*** *hwn*
sympathetic *ans* ***llawn cydymdeimlad***
sympathize *be* ***cydymdeimlo***, ***bod yn gydnaws â***
sympathy *enw* ***cydymdeimlad*** *hwn*
symphony *enw* ***symffoni*** *hon*
symptom *enw* ***arwydd***, ***symptom*** *hwn*
synagogue *enw* ***synagog*** *hon*
synchronize *be* ***cydamseru***
syndrome *enw* ***syndrom*** *hwn*
synergy *enw* ***cyfegni*** *hwn*
synod *enw* ***synod*** *hwn/hon*
synonym *enw* ***cyfystyr*** *hwn*
synonymous *ans* ***cyfystyr***
synopsis *enw* ***crynodeb*** *hwn*
syntax *enw* ***cystrawen*** *hon*
synthesis *enw* ***cyfuniad***, ***cyfosodiad*** *hwn*
synthetic *ans* ***synthetig***
syringe *enw* ***chwistrell*** *hon*
system *enw* ***cyfundrefn***, ***system*** *hon*
systematic *ans* ***trwyadl***, ***systematig***
systematically *adf* ***gam wrth gam***, ***yn eu tro***, ***yn systematig***

T

tab *enw* ***llabed*** *hon*
tabby *ans* ***trilliw***
tabernacle *enw* ***tabernacl*** *hwn*
table *enw* ***bwrdd*** *hwn*, ***bord*** *hon*
table *be* ***cyflwyno***
tablecloth *enw* ***lliain bwrdd*** *hwn*
tablet *enw* ***tabled*** *hon*
table tennis *enw* ***tennis bwrdd*** *hwn*
taboo *enw* ***tabŵ*** *hwn*
tabular *ans* ***tablaidd***
tabulate *be* ***tablu***
tacit *ans* ***dealledig***
taciturn *ans* ***tawedog***, ***di-ddweud***
tack *enw* ***tac*** *hwn/hon*
  to change t~ ***torri cwys newydd***, ***newid cyfeiriad***
tack *be* ***tacio***
tackle *enw* ***gêr***, ***tacl*** *hwn*
tackle *be* ***taclo***, ***ymgodymu â***
  to t~ all aspects ***rhoi sylw i bob agwedd ar***
tact *enw* ***tact***, ***pwyll*** *hwn*
tactful *ans* ***diplomatig***, ***diplomataidd***, ***doeth***
tactical *ans* ***tactegol***
tactician *enw* ***tactegydd*** *hwn*
tactics *enw* ***tacteg*** *hon*
tactile *ans* ***cyffyrddol***
tadpole *enw* ***penbwl*** *hwn*
tag *enw* ***tag***, ***tocyn*** *hwn*
tail *enw* ***cynffon***, ***cwt*** *hon*
tailor *enw* ***teiliwr*** *hwn*
tailor *be* ***teilwra***
taint *be* ***llygru***, ***halogi***
tainted *ans* ***llygredig***, ***drwg***
take *be* ***cymryd***
  I was t~n by the portrayal ***fe'm swynwyd gan y portread***
  the idea has t~n off ***mae'r syniad wedi cydio***
  t~ note ***dalier sylw***
  to have what it t~s ***bod â'r doniau angenrheidiol***
  to t~ a long time ***cymryd hydoedd***
  to t~ charge ***cymryd yr awenau***
  to t~ every opportunity ***manteisio ar bob cyfle***
  to t~ leave of their senses ***colli arnynt eu hunain***
  to t~ on ***mynd i'r afael â***
  to t~ over the duties ***ymgymryd â'r cyfrifoldebau***
  to t~ the initiative ***mentro***
  to t~ the view ***bod o'r farn***
  to t~ their time ***mynd wrth eu pwysau***
  to t~ to their heels ***rhedeg nerth eu traed***
  to t~ up ***manteisio ar***
takeaway *enw* ***pryd parod*** *hwn*
taking *ans* ***atyniadol***
take-off *enw* ***esgyniad*** *hwn*
take over *be* ***cymryd drosodd***, ***cipio grym***

t

takings *enw* ***derbyniadau*** *hyn*
talc *enw* ***talc*** *hwn*
tale *enw* ***chwedl*** *hon*, ***hanes*** *hwn*
talent *enw* ***dawn***, ***talent*** *hon*
talented *ans* ***dawnus***, ***talentog***
talisman *enw* ***swyn*** *hwn*
talk *enw* ***sgwrs*** *hon*
  idle t~ ***malu awyr***
  small t~ ***mân siarad*** *hwn*
talk *be* ***siarad***
talkative *ans* ***siaradus***
tall *ans* ***tal***
tallboy *enw* ***cwpwrdd deuddarn*** *hwn*
tallow *enw* ***gwêr*** *hwn*
tally *be* ***cyfateb***
tally *enw* ***cyfrif*** *hwn*
  to keep a t~ of ***cofnodi nifer***
talons *enw* ***crafangau*** *hyn*
tame *ans* ***dof***
tame *be* ***dofi***, ***hyweddu***
tamper *be* ***ymyrryd â***
tan *enw* ***lliw haul*** *hwn*
tan *be* ***cael lliw haul***
tangible *ans* ***diriaethol***, ***go iawn***
tangle *be* ***drysu***
tank *enw* ***tanc*** *hwn*
tanker *enw* ***tancer*** *hwn/hon*
tannery *enw* ***tanerdy*** *hwn*
tantalize *be* ***tormentio***
tantamount *ans* ***cyfystyr***
tantrum *enw* ***strancio***
tap *enw* ***tap*** *hwn*
tap *be* ***tapio***
  to t~ into ***manteisio/tynnu ar***
tape *enw* ***tâp*** *hwn*
tape *be* ***tapio***
tape recorder *enw* ***recordydd tâp*** *hwn*
taper *be* ***meinhau***, ***mynd yn bigfain***
tapestry *enw* ***tapestri*** *hwn*
tapeworm *enw* ***llyngyren*** *hon*
tar *enw* ***tar*** *hwn*
tardy *ans* ***araf***, ***hwyrfrydig***; ***hwyr***
tares *enw* ***efrau*** *hyn*
target *enw* ***targed*** *hwn*
  on t~ ***yn unol â'r amodau***
target *be* ***targedu***
tariff *enw* ***toll*** *hon*
tarmac *be* ***tarmacadameiddio***, ***tarmacio***
tarn *enw* ***pwll***, ***llyn mynydd*** *hwn*
tarnish *be* ***pylu***
tarry *be* ***oedi***
tart *enw* ***tarten*** *hon*
tart *ans* ***sur***
tartan *ans* ***plod***, ***tartan***
task *enw* ***gorchwyl*** *hwn/hon*, ***gwaith*** *hwn*, ***tasg*** *hon*
  it's no easy t~ to ***nid ar chwarae bach y mae***
  t~ and finish ***gorchwyl a gorffen***
task force *enw* ***tasglu*** *hwn*
taste *enw* ***blas*** *hwn*, ***chwaeth*** *hon*
  t~r courses ***cyrsiau blasu*** *hyn*
  to their t~ ***at eu dant***
taste *be* ***blasu***
tasteful *ans* ***chwaethus***

tasteless *ans* ***di-chwaeth***; ***di-flas***
tasty *ans* ***blasus***
tattered *ans* ***carpiog***
in tatters ***yn gyrbibion ulw mân***
tattoo *enw* ***tatŵ*** *hwn*
taunt *enw* ***edliwiad*** *hwn*
taunt *be* ***edliw***, ***dannod***, ***gwawdio***
taut *ans* ***tyn***
tavern *enw* ***tafarn*** *hwn/hon*
tawdry *ans* ***tsiêp***
tawny *ans* ***llwydfelyn***, ***melyn***
tax *enw* ***treth*** *hon*
tax *be* ***trethu***, ***bod yn dreth ar***
taxable *ans* ***trethadwy***
taxation *enw* ***treth*** *hon*, ***trethiad*** *hwn*; ***codi trethi***
taxi *enw* ***tacsi*** *hwn*
taxpayer *enw* ***trethdalwr*** *hwn*
TB *byrfodd* (tuberculosis) ***y ddarfodedigaeth*** *hon*
tea *enw* ***te*** *hwn*
for all the t~ in China ***am bris yn y byd***
teach *be* ***dysgu***, ***addysgu***
teacher *enw* ***athro*** *hwn*, ***athrawes*** *hon*
teaching *enw* ***dysgeidiaeth*** *hon*
teacup *enw* ***cwpan te/de*** *hwn/hon*
team *enw* ***tîm*** *hwn*
teapot *enw* ***tebot*** *hwn*
tear *be* ***rhwygo***
tear *enw* ***rhwyg*** *hwn*
tear *enw* ***deigryn*** *hwn*
tearful *ans* ***dagreuol***
tease *be* ***poeni***, ***pryfocio***, ***tynnu coes***
teaspoon *enw* ***llwy de*** *hon*
teat *enw* ***teth*** *hon*
technical *ans* ***technegol***
technician *enw* ***technegydd*** *hwn*
technique *enw* ***techneg*** *hon*
technological *ans* ***technolegol***
technology *enw* ***technoleg*** *hon*
tedious *ans* ***diflas***
tedium *enw* ***diflastod***, ***undonedd***, ***syrffed*** *hwn*
teem *be* ***arllwys***; ***heigio***, ***bod yn frith o***
teenage *ans* ***yn eich arddegau***
teenager *enw* ***glaslanc*** *hwn*, ***glaslances*** *hon*
teeter *be* ***simsanu***
teethe *be* ***torri dannedd***
teetotalism *enw* ***dirwest*** *hwn/hon*
teetotaller *enw* ***llwyrymwrthodwr*** *hwn*
telecommunications *be* ***telathrebu***
teleconferencing *be* ***telegynadledda***
telepathy *enw* ***telepathi*** *hwn*
telephone *enw* ***ffôn*** *hwn*
t~ directory ***llyfr ffôn*** *hwn*
t~ number ***rhif ffôn*** *hwn*
telephone *be* ***ffonio***
telescope *enw* ***telesgop*** *hwn*
telescopic *ans* ***telesgopig***
teletext *enw* ***teletestun*** *hwn*
televise *be* ***teledu***
television *enw* ***teledu*** *hwn*

t

television set *enw* ***set deledu*** *hon*
telex *enw* ***telecs*** *hwn*
tell *be* ***dweud***, ***adrodd***
telling *ans* ***trawiadol***, ***deifiol***
temerity *enw* ***rhyfyg***, ***digywilydd-dra*** *hwn*
temper *enw* ***tymer***, ***natur*** *hon*
  to lose one's t~ ***gwylltio'n gacwn***
temper *be* ***tymheru***
temperament *enw* ***anian***, ***natur*** *hon*
temperance *enw* ***dirwest*** *hwn/hon*
temperate *ans* ***cymedrol***
temperature *enw* ***tymheredd***, ***gwres*** *hwn*
tempest *enw* ***tymestl*** *hon*
tempestuous *ans* ***tymhestlog***
temple *enw* ***teml***; (head) ***arlais*** *hon*
temporal *ans* ***tymhorol***
temporary *ans* ***dros dro***
tempt *be* ***temtio***
temptation *enw* ***temtasiwn*** *hwn/hon*
ten *rhifol* ***deg***
tenable *ans* ***cynaliadwy***, ***daliadwy***
tenacious *ans* ***dygn***, ***cyndyn***
tenacity *enw* ***dycnwch***, ***dyfalbarhad*** *hwn*
tenant *enw* ***deiliad***, ***tenant*** *hwn*
tend *be* ***gogwyddo***; ***tendio***
tendency *enw* ***tuedd*** *hon*
tender *ans* ***tyner***, ***brau***
tender *enw* ***cynnig***, ***tendr*** *hwn*
tender *be* ***tendro***
tender-hearted *ans* ***calon-feddal***
tendon *enw* ***gewyn***, ***giewyn*** *hwn*
tenet *enw* ***daliad*** *hwn*
  a central t~ ***elfen ganolog*** *hon*
tennis *enw* ***tennis*** *hwn*
tenor *enw* ***tenor*** *hwn*
tense *enw* ***amser*** *hwn*
tense *be* ***tynhau***
tense *ans* ***tyn***; ***dan straen***
tension *enw* ***tyndra*** *hwn*
tent *enw* ***pabell*** *hon*
tentacle *enw* ***tentacl*** *hwn*, ***hir grafangau*** *hyn*
tentative *ans* ***petrus***, ***petrusgar***
tenth *ans* ***degfed***
tenuous *ans* ***tenau***
  t~ connection ***cysylltiad brau*** *hwn*
tenure *enw* ***daliadaeth*** *hon*; ***dal swydd am***
tepid *ans* ***claear***, ***llugoer***
term *enw* ***tymor***; ***term*** *hwn*
termagant *enw* ***cecren*** *hon*
terminable *ans* ***terfynadwy***
terminal *enw* ***terfynell:terfynfa*** *hon*
terminal *ans* (final) ***terfynol***, ***angheuol***; (end of term) ***pen tymor***
terminate *be* ***terfynu***, ***dibennu***, ***rhoi diwedd ar***
termination *enw* ***terfyniad***, ***diwedd*** *hwn*
terms *enw* ***telerau***; ***termau*** *hyn*
  in similar t~ ***i'r un perwyl***
  in t~ of ***o ran***

t~s of reference ***cylch gorchwyl***
tern *enw* ***môr-wennol*** *hon*
terrace *enw* ***teras*** *hwn*
terrain *enw* ***tir*** *hwn*
terrestrial *ans* ***daearol***
terrible *ans* ***ofnadwy***
terrier *enw* ***daeargi*** *hwn*
terrific *ans* ***aruthrol***
terrify *be* ***dychryn***, ***brawychu***
territorial *ans* ***tiriogaethol***
territory *enw* ***tiriogaeth*** *hon*
terror *enw* ***arswyd***, ***braw*** *hwn*
terrorist *enw* ***terfysgwr*** *hwn*
terrorize *be* ***brawychu***, ***dychryn***
terse *ans* ***byr***, ***cryno***
tertiary *ans* ***trydyddol***
test *enw* ***prawf*** *hwn*
test *be* ***rhoi prawf ar***, ***profi***
testament *enw* ***ewyllys*** *hwn/hon*; ***testament*** *hwn*
testicle *enw* ***caill*** *hon*
testify *be* ***tystio***
testimonial *enw* ***geirda*** *hwn*; ***tysteb*** *hon*
testimony *enw* ***tystiolaeth*** *hon*
test tube *enw* ***tiwb prawf*** *hwn*
testy *ans* ***piwis***
tether *enw* ***tennyn*** *hwn*
text *enw* ***testun*** *hwn*
textbook *enw* ***gwerslyfr*** *hwn*
textual *ans* ***testunol***
texture *enw* ***gwead*** *hwn*
than *cysyllt* ***na:nag***
thank *be* ***diolch***
thankful *ans* ***diolchgar***
thankless *ans* ***di-ddiolch***
thanks *enw* ***diolch*** *hwn*; ***diolchiadau*** *hyn*
many t~ ***diolch o galon***
thanksgiving *enw* ***diolchgarwch*** *hwn*
that *rhag* ***hwnnw***, ***honno***, ***hynny***
that *cysyllt* ***bod***, ***mai***, ***taw***
thatch *enw* ***gwellt*** *hwn*
thaw *be* ***meirioli***, ***dadmer***, ***dadlaith***
theatre *enw* ***theatr*** *hon*
theatrical *ans* ***theatraidd***
theft *enw* ***lladrad*** *hwn*
their *rhag* ***eu***, ***'u (hwy, nhw)***
theirs *rhag* ***eiddynt hwy***, ***eu rhai nhw***
them *rhag* ***hwy***, ***nhw***
theme *enw* ***thema*** *hon*
themselves *rhag* ***eu hunain***
then *adf* ***yr adeg honno***, ***yna***
from t~ on ***o hynny allan***
t~ and now ***ddoe a heddiw***
theological *ans* ***diwinyddol***
theology *enw* ***diwinyddiaeth*** *hon*
theorem *enw* ***theorem*** *hon*
theoretic(al) *ans* ***damcaniaethol***
theorize *be* ***damcaniaethu***
theory *enw* ***damcaniaeth*** *hon*
therapist *enw* ***therapydd*** *hwn*
therapy *enw* ***triniaeth*** *hon*, ***therapi*** *hwn*
there *adf* ***acw***, ***yna***
t~ and then ***yn y fan a'r lle***
thereafter *adf* ***wedyn***, ***wedi hynny***

thereby *adf* ***gan hynny***; ***drwy hynny***
therefore *adf* ***felly***
thereupon *adf* ***ar hynny***
thermal *ans* ***thermol***
thermometer *enw* ***thermomedr*** *hwn*
thermonuclear *ans* ***thermoniwclear***
thesaurus *enw* ***thesawrws*** *hwn*
these *rhag* ***y rhai hyn***, ***y rhain***
thesis *enw* ***traethawd*** *hwn*
they *rhag* ***hwy***, ***nhw***
thick *ans* ***trwchus***, ***tew***
  through t~ and thin ***drwy'r chwith a'r chwerw***
thicken *be* ***tewhau***, ***tewychu***
thicket *enw* ***llwyn***, ***prysglwyn*** *hwn*
thickness *enw* ***trwch***, ***tewdra*** *hwn*
thickset *ans* ***cydnerth***
thief *enw* ***lleidr*** *hwn*
thigh *enw* ***clun***, ***morddwyd*** *hon*
thimble *enw* ***gwniadur*** *hwn/hon*
thin *ans* ***tenau***, ***main***
thin *be* ***teneuo***
thing *enw* ***peth*** *hwn*
  not a t~ ***dim byd o gwbl***
  t~s have changed ***daeth tro ar fyd***
  this is how t~s are ***dyna'r drefn***
think *be* ***meddwl***
  to t~ about ***ystyried***
  to t~ through ***meddwl yn ddwys***
thinker *enw* ***meddyliwr*** *hwn*
third *ans* ***trydydd*** *hwn*, ***trydedd*** *hon*
  one t~ ***traean*** *hwn*
thirst *enw* ***syched*** *hwn*
  a t~ for knowledge ***gwanc am wybodaeth***
thirsty *ans* ***sychedig***
thirteen *rhifol* ***tri ar ddeg*** *hwn*, ***tair ar ddeg*** *hon*
thirteenth *ans* ***trydydd ar ddeg*** *hwn*, ***trydedd ar ddeg*** *hon*
thirtieth *ans* ***degfed ar hugain***
thirty *rhifol* ***deg ar hugain***, ***tri deg***
this *rhag* ***hwn***, ***hon***, ***hyn***
thistle *enw* ***ysgallen*** *hon*
thistledown *enw* ***plu'r ysgall*** *hyn*
thorax *enw* ***thoracs*** *hwn*
thorn *enw* ***draenen*** *hon*
thorough *ans* ***trylwyr***, ***trwyadl***
thoroughbred *ans* ***o dras***
thoroughfare *enw* ***ffordd agored*** *hon*
those *rhag* ***y rhai yna, y rheina***; ***y rhai hynny***, ***y rheiny***
though *cysyllt* ***er***, ***pe:ped***
thought *enw* ***meddwl*** *hwn*; ***syniadaeth*** *hon*
thoughtful *ans* ***meddylgar***; ***ystyriol***
thoughtless *ans* ***difeddwl***, ***anystyriol***
thousand *rhifol* ***mil*** *hon*
thousandth *ans* ***milfed***
thrash *be* ***dyrnu***, ***colbio***
  to t~ it out ***mynd i blu***

thread *enw* ***edau*** *hon*, ***edefyn*** *hwn*
threat *enw* ***bygythiad*** *hwn*
threaten *be* ***bygwth***
three *rhifol* ***tri*** *hwn*, ***tair*** *hon*
threnody *enw* ***galarnad*** *hwn/hon*
thresh *be* ***dyrnu***
threshing machine *enw* ***dyrnwr*** *hwn*
threshold *enw* ***trothwy*** *hwn*
thrifty *ans* ***cynnil***, ***darbodus***
thrill *enw* ***gwefr***, ***ias*** *hon*
thrill *be* ***gwefreiddio***
thrive *be* ***ffynnu***
throat *enw* ***gwddf*** *hwn*
throaty *ans* ***gyddfol***
throb *enw* ***curiad*** *hwn*; (of pain) ***gwayw***, ***gwŷn*** *hwn*
throb *be* ***gwynio***; ***dyrnu***
throes *enw* ***gwewyr*** *hyn*
throne *enw* ***gorsedd*** *hon*
throng *enw* ***torf***, ***tyrfa*** *hon*
throng *be* ***tyrru, heidio***
throttle *enw* ***sbardun*** *hwn/hon*
throttle *be* ***tagu***, ***llindagu***
through *ardd* ***trwy:drwy***
through *adf* ***trwodd:drwodd***
  t~ and t~ ***o'i gorun i'w sawdl***
  to see the process t~ ***parhau â'r broses hyd y diwedd***
throughout *ardd* ***ledled***, ***trwy gydol***
throw *enw* ***tafliad*** *hwn*
throw *be* ***taflu***
thrush *enw* ***bronfraith*** *hon*
thrust *be* ***gwthio***
thrust *enw* ***gwthiad***; ***byrdwn*** *hwn*
thug *enw* ***llabwst***, ***dihiryn*** *hwn*
thumb *enw* ***bawd*** *hwn/hon*
thump *enw* ***ergyd***, ***cur*** *hwn/hon*
thump *be* ***colbio***, ***taro***
thunder *enw* ***taranau***, ***tyrfau*** *hyn*
thunder *be* ***taranu***
thunderbolt *enw* ***mellten, taranfollt***, ***llucheden*** *hon*
thunderclap *enw* ***taraniad*** *hwn*
thunderstorm *enw* ***storm o fellt a tharanau*** *hon*
Thursday *enw* ***dydd Iau*** *hwn*
thus *adf* ***fel hyn, felly***
thwart *be* ***atal***, ***llesteirio***
thyme *enw* ***teim*** *hwn*
tibia *enw* ***crimog*** *hon*
tic *enw* ***tic*** *hwn*
tick *enw* ***tipiad*** *hwn*; (insect) ***trogen*** *hon*
  in a t~ ***mewn chwinciad***
tick *be* ***tipian***
  what makes them t~? ***beth sydd yn eu hysgogi?***
ticket *enw* ***tocyn*** *hwn*
ticket office *enw* ***swyddfa docynnau*** *hon*
tickle *be* ***gogleisio***, ***cosi***
ticklish *ans* ***gogleisiol***
tidal wave *enw* ***ton lanw***, ***tswnami*** *hon*
tide *enw* ***llanw*** *hwn*
tidings *enw* ***newyddion*** *hyn*
tidy *ans* ***taclus***, ***trefnus***
tie *enw* ***tei*** *hwn/hon*

tie *be* ***clymu***
 to t~ in with ***cyd-fynd â***
tier *enw* ***rhes***, ***haen*** *hon*
tiered *ans* ***haenedig***
tiff *enw* ***cweryl*** *hwn*
tiger *enw* ***teigr*** *hwn*
tight *ans* ***tyn(n)***
 time is t~ ***mae amser yn brin***
tighten *be* ***tynhau***
tile *enw* ***teilsen*** *hon*
till *enw* ***til*** *hwn*
till *be* ***trin***, ***braenaru***
tiller *enw* ***llyw*** *hwn*
tilt *be* ***gogwyddo***, ***gwyro***
timber *enw* ***coed***, ***pren*** *hwn*
time *enw* ***amser***, ***amseriad***, ***pryd*** *hwn*; ***gwaith*** *hon*
time *be* ***amseru***
time lag *enw* ***oediad*** *hwn*, ***oedi***
timeless *ans* ***digyfnewid***, ***oesol***
timely *ans* ***amserol***
 a t~ word ***gair i gall***
timeshare *be* ***cyfranrannu***
timetable *enw* ***amserlen*** *hon*
time zone *enw* ***cylchfa amser*** *hon*
timid *ans* ***swil***, ***ofnus***
timidity *enw* ***swildod***, ***diffyg hyder*** *hwn*
timorous *ans* ***ofnus***
tin *enw* ***alcam***, ***tun*** *hwn*
tinge *enw* ***arlliw***, ***tinc*** *hwn*
tingle *be* ***gyrru ias trwy***
tinkle *be* ***tincial***
tint *enw* ***arlliw*** *hwn*, ***gwawr*** *hon*
tint *be* ***lliwio***
tinted *ans* ***wedi'i liwio/lliwio***
tiny *ans* ***bychan***, ***pitw***
tip *enw* ***blaen***; ***cildwrn***; ***tip*** *hwn*
 a handy t~ ***gair i gall***
tip *be* ***tipio***; ***cynnig cildwrn***
tipple *be* ***diota***
tiptoe *enw* ***blaen troed*** *hwn*
 on t~ ***ar flaenau'r traed***
tirade *enw* ***pregeth*** *hon*
tire *be* ***blino***, ***diffygio***
tireless *ans* ***diflino***
tiresome *ans* ***diflas***, ***syrffedus***
tissue *enw* ***meinwe*** *hon*
tit *enw* ***titw*** *hwn*; ***teth*** *hon*
 t~ for tat ***talu'r pwyth yn ôl***
titbit *enw* ***tamaid blasus*** *hwn*
tithe *enw* ***degwm*** *hwn*
titillate *be* ***goglais***
titivate *be* ***ymbincio***
title *enw* ***teitl*** *hwn*
titter *be* ***piffian chwerthin***
titular *ans* ***mewn enw***
titular saint *enw* ***nawddsant*** *hwn*
to *ardd* ***i***, ***at***, ***tua***, ***hyd***
toad *enw* ***llyffant dafadennog*** *hwn*
toadstool *enw* ***caws llyffant*** *hwn*
toast *enw* ***tost***; ***llwncdestun*** *hwn*
toast *be* ***crasu***; ***cynnig llwncdestun***
toaster *enw* ***tostiwr*** *hwn*
tobacco *enw* ***tybaco*** *hwn*
toboggan *enw* ***sled*** *hon*
today *adf/enw* ***heddiw***
 in t~'s world ***yn y byd sydd ohoni***

toe *enw* ***bys troed*** *hwn*
toffee *enw* ***cyflaith***, ***taffi*** *hwn*
together *adf* ***gyda'ch gilydd***, ***ynghyd***
toil *be* ***llafurio***
toilet *enw* ***tŷ bach***, ***toiled*** *hwn*
toilet paper *enw* ***papur tŷ bach*** *hwn*
toiletries *enw* ***pethau ymolchi*** *hyn*
token *enw* ***arwydd***; ***tocyn*** *hwn*
tolerable *ans* ***goddefadwy***, ***gweddol***
tolerance *enw* ***goddefgarwch***, ***goddefiant*** *hwn*
tolerant *ans* ***goddefgar***
tolerate *be* ***goddef***
toll *enw* ***toll*** *hon*
taking their t~ ***yn gadael eu hôl***
toll *be* ***canu cnul***
tomato *enw* ***tomato*** *hwn*
tomb *enw* ***bedd*** *hwn*
tombstone *enw* ***carreg fedd*** *hon*
tomcat *enw* ***gwrcath***, ***cwrcyn*** *hwn*
tomorrow *adf/enw* ***yfory***
ton *enw* ***tunnell*** *hon*
tone *enw* ***tôn***; (colour) ***gwawr*** *hon*
toneless *ans* ***di-liw***, ***diflas***
tongs *enw* ***gefel*** *hon*
tongue *enw* ***tafod*** *hwn*
t~-twister ***cwlwm tafod*** *hwn*
tonic *ans/enw* ***tonig*** *hwn*
tonight *adf/enw* ***heno***
tonsil *enw* ***tonsil*** *hwn*
too *adf* ***rhy***, ***gor-***; ***hefyd, yn ogystal***
tool *enw* ***arf***, ***erfyn***, ***offeryn*** *hwn*
tooth *enw* ***dant*** *hwn*
toothache *enw* ***y ddannoedd*** *hon*
toothbrush *enw* ***brws dannedd*** *hwn*
toothed *ans* ***danheddog***
toothpaste *enw* ***past dannedd*** *hwn*
toothpick *enw* ***pric dannedd*** *hwn*
top *enw* ***pen***, ***brig*** *hwn*
topic *enw* ***pwnc***, ***testun*** *hwn*
topical *ans* ***amserol***
topmost *ans* ***uchaf***
topographic(al) *ans* ***topograffaidd***
topography *enw* ***topograffeg*** *hon*
topple *be* ***cwympo***, ***disgyn***
top secret *ans* ***tra chyfrinachol***
tor *enw* ***twr*** *hwn,* ***moel*** *hon*
torch *enw* ***fflachlamp*** *hon*
torment *enw* ***artaith*** *hon*, ***cystudd*** *hwn*
torment *be* ***poenydio***
tornado *enw* ***corwynt*** *hwn*
torpedo *enw* ***torpido*** *hwn*
torpid *ans* ***marwaidd***
torrent *enw* ***cenllif***, ***llifeiriant*** *hwn*
torrid *ans* ***chwilboeth***, ***tanbaid***, ***nwydwyllt***
tortoise *enw* ***crwban*** *hwn*
tortoiseshell *ans* ***trilliw***
tortuous *ans* ***troellog***; ***trofaus***
torture *enw* ***artaith*** *hon*
torture *be* ***arteithio***
Tory *enw* ***Tori*** *hwn*
toss *be* ***taflu***
total *ans* ***holl***, ***cyfan***, ***llwyr***

t

total *enw* **cyfanswm** *hwn*
totally *adf* ***hollol***, ***yn llwyr***
to agree t~ ***cytuno i'r carn***
to become t~ confused ***drysu'n lân***
to fail t~ ***methu'n lân/deg â***
t~ lifeless ***yn farw gorn***
totalitarian *ans* ***totalitaraidd***
totality *enw* ***cyfanrwydd*** *hwn*
totter *be* ***gwegian***, ***simsanu***
touch *enw* ***cyffyrddiad*** *hwn*
touch *be* ***cyffwrdd***
there is no one to t~ him ***nid oes neb yn yr un cae ag ef***
touchdown *enw* ***glaniad*** *hwn*
touching *ans* ***teimladwy***
touchline *enw* ***ystlys*** *hwn/hon*
touchy *ans* ***croendenau***
tough *ans* ***gwydn***, ***caled***, ***grymus***
toughen *be* ***caledu***, ***cryfhau***
tour *enw* ***cylchdaith*** *hon*, ***tro*** *hwn*
tour *be* ***teithio, mynd ar daith***
tour de force *enw* ***campwaith*** *hwn*
tourism *enw* ***twristiaeth*** *hon*
tourist *enw* ***ymwelydd*** *hwn*
tournament *enw* ***twrnamaint*** *hwn*
tout *be* ***towtio***
tow *be* ***halio***, ***tynnu***
toward(s) *ardd* ***tua:tuag***, ***tuag at***, ***at***
towel *enw* ***lliain*** *hwn*
tower *enw* ***tŵr*** *hwn*
town *enw* ***tref*** *hon*
town hall *enw* ***neuadd y dref*** *hon*
township *enw* ***treflan***, ***trefgordd*** *hon*
tow rope *enw* ***rhaff halio*** *hon*
toxic *ans* ***gwenwynig***
toy *enw* ***tegan*** *hwn*
trace *enw* ***ôl***, ***arlliw*** *hwn*
trace *be* ***olrhain***, ***amlinellu***
tracery *enw* ***rhwyllwaith*** *hwn*
track *enw* ***trywydd*** *hwn*
track *be* ***dilyn trywydd***, ***cadw llygad ar***
tracksuit *enw* ***tracwisg*** *hon*
tract *enw* ***ehangder***; ***pamffledyn*** *hwn*
tractable *ans* ***hydrin***, ***hawdd ei drafod***
traction *enw* ***tyniant*** *hwn*
trade *enw* ***masnach***; ***crefft*** *hon*
trade *be* ***masnachu***
trademark *enw* ***nod masnach*** *hwn*
trader *enw* ***masnachwr*** *hwn*
trade(s) union *enw* **undeb llafur** *hwn*
trade unionist *enw* ***undebwr*** *hwn*
trading *ans* ***masnachol***
tradition *enw* ***traddodiad*** *hwn*
traditional *ans* ***traddodiadol***
traduce *be* ***difenwi***
traffic *enw* ***trafnidiaeth*** *hon*, ***traffig*** *hwn*
traffic jam *enw* ***tagfa*** *hon*
tragedy *enw* ***trasiedi*** *hon*
tragic *ans* ***alaethus***, ***trist***, ***mwy trist na thristwch***
trail *enw* ***ôl***, ***trywydd*** *hwn*
train *enw* ***trên*** *hwn*
set in train ***rhoi ar waith***

train *be* ***hyfforddi***, ***ymarfer***
trainee *enw* ***hyfforddai*** *hwn*
trainer *enw* ***hyfforddwr*** *hwn*
training *enw* ***hyfforddiant***, ***ymarfer*** *hwn*
traipse *be* ***llusgo***
trait *enw* ***nodwedd*** *hon*
traitor *enw* ***bradwr*** *hwn*
tramp *enw* ***sŵn traed***; ***trempyn*** *hwn*
tramp *be* ***cerdded yn drwm***
trample *be* ***sathru (ar)***, ***damsang (ar)***
trance *enw* ***llesmair*** *hwn*
tranquil *ans* ***tawel***, ***llonydd***
transact *be* ***trafod***, ***trin***, ***cyflawni***, ***gweithredu***
transactions *enw* ***trafodion*** *hyn*
transcend *be* ***codi uwchlaw***
transcendental *ans* ***trosgynnol***
transcribe *be* ***trawsgrifio***
transcript *enw* ***trawsgrifiad*** *hwn*, ***adysgrif*** *hon*
transcription *enw* ***adysgrif*** *hon*
transfer *enw* ***trosglwyddiad***, ***adleoliad*** *hwn*
transfer *be* ***trosglwyddo***, ***adleoli***
Transfiguration *enw* ***y Gweddnewidiad*** *hwn*
transfigure *be* ***gweddnewid***
transform *be* ***gweddnewid***, ***trawsnewid***
transformation *enw* ***trawsffurfiad***, ***trawsnewid*** *hwn*
transfusion *enw* ***trallwysiad*** *hwn*, ***trallwyso***
transgress *be* ***troseddu***, ***pechu***
transient *ans* ***dros dro***
transition *enw* ***trosglwyddiad***, ***trawsnewidiad*** *hwn*
transitional *ans* ***dros dro***, ***trawsnewidiol***, ***trosiannol***
transitive *ans* (verb) ***anghyflawn***
translate *be* ***cyfieithu***
translation *enw* ***cyfieithiad*** *hwn*
translator *enw* ***cyfieithydd*** *hwn*
transliterate *be* ***trawslythrennu***
transmission *enw* ***trosglwyddiad*** *hwn*, ***trosglwyddo***
transmit *be* ***anfon***, ***trosglwyddo***, ***cyflwyno***
transmitter *enw* ***trosglwyddydd***, ***trosglwyddwr*** *hwn*
transparency *enw* ***tryloywder*** *hwn*
transparent *ans* ***tryloyw***
transplant *be* ***trawsblannu***
transport *enw* ***cludiant*** *hwn*
transport *be* ***cludo***, ***mynd â***; (history) ***alltudio***
transportation *enw* (history) ***alltudiaeth*** *hon*
transpose *be* ***trawsgyweirio***
trap *enw* ***magl*** *hon*, ***trap*** *hwn*
  to avoid the t~ ***osgoi'r perygl***
trap *be* ***maglu***, ***dal***
trapeze *enw* ***trapîs*** *hwn*
trapezium *enw* ***trapesiwm*** *hwn*
trash *enw* ***sbwriel***, ***sothach*** *hwn*
travel *enw* ***taith*** *hon*
travel *be* ***teithio***

t

traveller *enw* ***teithiwr***; ***trafaeliwr*** *hwn*
traveller's cheque *enw* ***siec deithio*** *hon*
traverse *be* ***croesi***
travesty *enw* ***parodi***, ***camddarluniad*** *hwn*
trawl *be* ***treillio***
to t~ through ***chwilota mewn***
tray *enw* ***hambwrdd*** *hwn*
treacherous *ans* ***bradwrus***, ***dichellgar***
treachery *enw* ***brad*** *hwn*, ***bradwriaeth*** *hon*
treacle *enw* ***triagl***, ***triog*** *hwn*
tread *be* ***camu***, ***troedio***
treadle *enw* ***troedlath*** *hon*
treason *enw* ***bradwriaeth***, ***teyrnfradwriaeth*** *hon*
treasure *enw* ***trysor*** *hwn*
treasurer *enw* ***trysorydd*** *hwn*
treat *enw* ***peth amheuthun*** *hwn*
to look a t~ ***edrych yn bictiwr***
treat *be* ***trin***, ***trafod***
treatise *enw* ***traethawd*** *hwn*
treatment *enw* ***triniaeth*** *hon*
treaty *enw* ***cytundeb*** *hwn*
treble *be* ***treblu***
tree *enw* ***coeden*** *hon*
trek *enw* ***ymdaith*** *hon*
trek *be* ***ymdeithio***
tremble *be* ***crynu***
tremendous *ans* ***aruthrol***
tremor *enw* ***dirgryniad*** *hwn*
tremulous *ans* ***crynedig***
trench *enw* ***ffos***, ***rhych*** *hon*
trenchant *ans* ***cadarn***
trend *enw* ***tuedd*** *hon*, ***cyfeiriad*** *hwn*
trepidation *enw* ***ofn*** *hwn*
trespass *be* ***tresmasu***, ***ymyrryd â***
tresses *enw* ***tresi*** *hyn*
trial *enw* ***achos llys***, ***treial*** *hwn*
t~ and error ***cynnig a chynnig***
triangle *enw* ***triongl*** *hwn*
triangular *ans* ***trionglog***
tribal *ans* ***llwythol***
tribe *enw* ***llwyth*** *hwn*
tribulation *enw* ***trallod*** *hwn*
tribunal *enw* ***tribiwnlys*** *hwn*
tributary *enw* ***llednant***, ***isafon*** *hon*
tribute *enw* ***teyrnged*** *hon*, ***clod*** *hwn*
trick *enw* ***ystryw*** *hwn/hon*, ***tric*** *hwn*; ***camp*** *hon*
trick *be* ***twyllo***
trickery *enw* ***twyll***, ***ystryw*** *hwn/hon*
trickle *be* ***diferu***, ***treiglo***
tricky *ans* ***cyfrwys***; ***anodd***
trident *enw* ***tryfer*** *hon*
trifle *enw* ***peth dibwys***; ***treiffl*** *hwn*
trifling *ans* ***dibwys***, ***pitw***
trigger *enw* ***clicied*** *hon*
trigger *be* ***tanio***, ***cychwyn***, ***dechrau***
to t~ a reaction ***ysgogi***, ***arwain at***
trill *enw* ***tril*** *hwn*
trilogy *enw* ***triawd*** *hwn*
trim *ans* ***trwsiadus***, ***destlus***

trim *be* ***tocio***, ***twtio***
trimmings *enw* ***addurniadau*** *hyn*
Trinity *enw* ***Trindod*** *hon*
trio *enw* ***triawd*** *hwn*
trip *enw* ***gwibdaith*** *hon*
trip *be* ***baglu***
tripartite *ans* ***tridarn***
triple *be* ***treblu***
triple *ans* ***triphlyg***
triplicate *ans* ***triphlyg***
tripod *enw* ***trybedd*** *hon*
tripping *ans* ***gwisgi***
trite *ans* ***ystrydebol***
triumph *enw* ***buddugoliaeth*** *hon*
triumph *be* ***ennill buddugoliaeth***
triumphant *ans* ***buddugoliaethus***
trivia *enw* ***pethau dibwys*** *hyn*
trivial *ans* ***pitw***, ***dibwys***
triviality *enw* ***dinodedd***, ***distadledd*** *hwn*
trolley *enw* ***troli*** *hwn*
troop *enw* ***mintai*** *hon*, ***criw*** *hwn*
trophy *enw* ***tlws*** *hwn*
tropical *ans* ***trofannol***
trot *be* ***tuthian***
trot *enw* ***tuth*** *hwn*
  on the t~ ***y naill ar ôl y llall***
troubadour *enw* ***trwbadŵr*** *hwn*
trouble *enw* ***pryder***, ***gofid*** *hwn*; ***trafferth, anhawster, helynt*** *hwn*
trouble *be* ***poeni***; ***trafferthu***
troubleshooting *be* ***datrys problemau***
  a t~ approach ***ymagwedd ymarferol a blaengar***
troublesome *ans* ***trafferthus***
trough *enw* ***cafn*** *hwn*
trounce *be* ***cystwyo***, ***cledro***
trousers *enw* ***trywser:trywsus*** *hwn*
trout *enw* ***brithyll*** *hwn*
trowel *enw* ***trywel*** *hwn*
truancy *enw* ***triwantiaeth*** *hwn*
truant *ans* ***triwant***
truant *enw* ***triwant*** *hwn*
truce *enw* ***cadoediad*** *hwn*
truck *enw* ***tryc*** *hwn*
truck driver *enw* ***gyrrwr lorri*** *hwn*
truculent *ans* ***ffyrnig***, ***sarrug***
trudge *be* ***ymlwybro***
true *ans* ***gwir***, ***cywir***, ***gwir 'i wala***
  out of t~ ***heb fod yn hollol union***
  to ring t~ ***taro deuddeg***
truism *enw* ***gwireb*** *hon*
trump *enw* ***trwmp*** *hwn*
trump *be* ***trwmpo***
trumpet *enw* ***trwmped*** *hwn*
truncate *be* ***talfyrru***, ***tocio***, ***blaendorri***, ***torri ar***
trundle *be* ***treiglo***
trunk *enw* ***boncyff***; ***trwnc*** *hwn*
trust *enw* ***ymddiriedaeth***; ***ymddiriedolaeth*** *hon*
trust *be* ***ymddiried***
trustee *enw* ***ymddiriedolwr*** *hwn*
trustworthy *ans* ***dibynadwy***
trusty *ans* ***ffyddlon***, ***dibynadwy***
truth *enw* ***gwir***, ***gwirionedd*** *hwn*
truthful *ans* ***geirwir***, ***gonest***

t

truthfulness *enw* ***gwirionedd***, ***geirwiredd*** *hwn*
try *enw* ***cais*** *hwn*, ***ymgais*** *hwn/hon*
try *be* ***profi***, ***ceisio***
  keep t~ing ***daliwch ati***
  to t~ it on (with) ***trio'i lwc***
  to t~ out ***arbrofi gyda***
trying *ans* ***anodd***, ***yn dreth ar***
tryst *enw* ***oed*** *hwn*
tub *enw* ***twb***, ***twba*** *hwn*
tuba *enw* ***tiwba*** *hwn*
tube *enw* ***tiwb*** *hwn*
tuber *enw* ***cloronen*** *hon*; ***chwydd*** *hwn*
tuberculosis *enw* ***y ddarfodedigaeth*** *hon*
tuck *enw* ***twc*** *hwn*
tuck *be* ***twcio***
Tuesday *enw* ***dydd Mawrth*** *hwn*
tuft *enw* ***cudyn***, ***twffyn*** *hwn*
tug *enw* ***tyniad***, ***plwc*** *hwn*
tug *be* ***tynnu***, ***llusgo***
tuition *enw* ***hyfforddiant*** *hwn*
tulip *enw* ***tiwlip*** *hwn*
tumble *enw* ***codwm*** *hwn*
tumble *be* ***syrthio***, ***cwympo***, ***cael codwm***
tumbler *enw* ***gwydryn*** *hwn*
tumescent *ans* ***chwyddedig***
tumour *enw* ***tyfiant*** *hwn*
tumultuous *ans* ***cythryblus***; ***cynhyrfus***; (applause) ***byddarol***
tundra *enw* ***twndra*** *hwn*
tune *enw* ***alaw***, ***tôn*** *hon*
  in t~ ***mewn tiwn***; ***cywir ei draw/thraw***
tune *be* ***cyweirio***
tuneful *ans* ***persain***
tunnel *enw* ***twnnel*** *hwn*
turbid *ans* ***cymylog***, ***cymysglyd***
turbine *enw* ***tyrbin*** *hwn*
turbulence *enw* ***cynnwrf*** *hwn*
turbulent *ans* ***cythryblus***, ***aflonydd***
turf *enw* ***tywarchen*** *hon*
turgid *ans* ***chwyddedig***
turkey *enw* ***twrci*** *hwn*
turmoil *enw* ***berw***, ***cynnwrf*** *hwn*
turn *enw* ***tro***, ***troad*** *hwn*
  in t~ ***yn eu tro***
  U-t~ ***tro pedol***, ***newid meddwl yn llwyr***
turn *be* ***troi***
  to t~ around ***gweddnewid***, ***trawsnewid***; ***sicrhau tro ar fyd***
turning *enw* ***tro*** *hwn*
turnip *enw* ***erfinen*** *hon*
turnover *enw* ***trosiant*** *hwn*
turnpike *enw* ***tyrpeg*** *hwn*
turnstile *enw* ***giât dro*** *hon*
turpitude *enw* ***ysgelerder*** *hwn*
turquoise *ans* ***gwyrddlas***
turtle *enw* ***crwban y môr*** *hwn*
tusk *enw* ***ysgithr*** *hwn*
tussle *be* ***ymgiprys***
tussock *enw* ***twffyn*** *hwn*
tut *ebychiad* ***twt!***
tutor *enw* ***tiwtor*** *hwn*
tutor *be* ***tiwtora***

twaddle *enw* ***dwli*** *hwn*, ***lol*** *hon*
tweak *enw* ***pinsiad***, ***plyciad*** *hwn*
tweezers *enw* ***gefel*** *hon*
twelfth *ans* ***deuddegfed***
twelve *rhifol* ***deuddeg***
twentieth *ans* ***ugeinfed***
twenty *rhifol* ***ugain***
twice *adf* ***dwywaith***
twig *enw* ***brigyn*** *hwn*
twilight *enw* ***cyfnos***, ***gwyll*** *hwn*
twill *enw* ***brethyn caerog*** *hwn*
twin *enw* ***gefell*** *hwn/hon*
twine *be* ***cordeddu***, ***cyfrodeddu***
twinkle *be* ***pefrio***, ***serennu***
twirl *be* ***chwyrlïad*** *hwn*
twist *enw* (thread) ***edau*** *hon*; (hair) **plethen** *hon*; (tobacco) ***rholyn*** *hwn*; (turn) ***tro***, ***troad*** *hwn*; (warp in timber, twist in river) ***ystum*** *hwn*
twist *be* ***cyfrodeddu***; ***troi***
twit *enw* ***cnec***, ***hurtyn*** *hwn*
twitch *enw* ***plwc*** *hwn*
twitter *be* ***trydar***
two *rhifol* **dau** *hwn*, **dwy** *hon*
two-faced *ans* ***dauwynebog***
twofold *ans* ***deublyg***
two-timing *enw* ***chwarae'r ffon ddwybig***
tycoon *enw* ***teicŵn*** *hwn*
type *enw* ***math***; ***teip*** *hwn*
type *be* ***teipio***
typeface *enw* ***wyneb teip*** *hwn*
typewriter *enw* ***teipiadur*** *hwn*
typhoon *enw* ***corwynt*** *hwn*
typical *ans* ***nodweddiadol***
typist *enw* ***teipydd*** *hwn*, ***teipyddes*** *hon*
tyrannical *ans* ***gormesol***
tyrannize *be* ***gormesu***
tyranny *enw* ***gormes*** *hon*
tyrant *enw* ***teyrn***, ***gormeswr*** *hwn*
tyre *enw* ***teiar*** *hwn*

u

U

ubiquitous *ans* ***hollbresennol***, ***bondigrybwyll***
udder *enw* ***cadair*** *hon*, ***pwrs*** *hwn*
ugliness *enw* ***hagrwch*** *hwn*
ugly *ans* ***hyll***, ***hagr***, ***salw***
to make u~ ***hagru***
ulcer *enw* ***briw***, ***dolur*** *hwn*
ulterior *ans* ***cudd***
ultimate *ans* ***terfynol***, ***olaf***
ultimatum *enw* ***cynnig terfynol***, ***rhybudd olaf*** *hwn*
ultraviolet *ans* ***uwchfioled***
ultra vires *ans/adf* ***y tu hwnt i awdurdod***
umbilical cord *enw* ***llinyn bogail*** *hwn*
umbrella *enw* ***ambarél:ymbarél*** *hwn/hon*
under the u~ ***o dan fantell***
umpire *enw* ***dyfarnwr*** *hwn*
umpire *be* ***dyfarnu***
unabated *ans* ***di-ball***
unable *ans* ***analluog***, ***methu***
unacceptable *ans* ***annerbyniol***
unaccompanied *ans* ***digyfeiliant***; ***heb neb arall***
unaccomplished *ans* ***heb ei gyflawni***; ***di-ddawn***
unaccountable *ans* ***anesboniadwy***
unaccustomed *ans* ***anarferol***, ***anghyfarwydd***
unacknowledged *ans* ***anghydnabyddedig***
unadulterated *ans* ***pur***, ***digymysg***
unalloyed *ans* ***digymysg***
unaltered *ans* ***digyfnewid***
unambiguous *ans* ***diamwys***
unanimity *enw* ***unfrydedd*** *hwn*
unanimous *ans* ***unfrydol***
unanswerable *ans* ***anatebadwy***
unapproachable *ans* ***anhygyrch***, ***pell***
unarmed *ans* ***heb arfau***, ***anarfog***
unassuming *ans* ***dirodres***, ***diymhongar***
unattached *ans* ***heb fod ynghlwm***, ***digyswllt***
unattainable *ans* ***anghyraeddadwy***
unattended *ans* ***heb neb ar eu cyfyl***
unauthorized *ans* ***anawdurdodedig***
unavoidable *ans* ***anochel***, ***anorfod***
unaware *ans* ***anymwybodol***
unawares *adf* ***yn ddiarwybod***
unbalanced *ans* ***anghytbwys***
unbearable *ans* ***annioddefol***
unbeknown *ans* ***heb yn wybod***
unbelievable *ans* ***anghredadwy***, ***anhygoel***
unbiased *ans* ***diduedd***, ***cytbwys***
unbreakable *ans* ***anhydor***, ***na ellir mo'i dorri***
unbridled *ans* ***penrhydd***
unbroken *ans* ***di-dor***

unbutton *be* ***datod botymau***
uncalled for *ans* ***heb eisiau***, ***di-alw-amdano***
uncanny *ans* ***rhyfedd***
unceasing *ans* ***di-baid***, ***di-drai***
unceremonious *ans* ***diseremoni***, ***di-lol***
uncertain *ans* ***ansicr***
uncertainty *enw* ***ansicrwydd***, ***amhendantrwydd*** *hwn*
unchangeable *ans* ***digyfnewid***
uncharitable *ans* ***angharedig***, ***didostur***
unchecked *ans* ***diatal***, ***dilyffethair***; ***heb ei wirio***
uncivil *ans* ***anghwrtais***
uncivilized *ans* ***anwaraidd***
uncle *enw* ***ewythr*** *hwn*
unclean *ans* ***aflan***
unclear *ans* ***annelwig***, ***aneglur***
unclouded *ans* ***clir***, ***digwmwl***
uncomfortable *ans* ***anghyfforddus***, ***anghysurus***
uncommon *ans* ***anghyffredin***, ***anarferol***
uncomplaining *ans* ***dirwgnach***
uncompromising *ans* ***digyfaddawd***
unconcern *enw* ***difrawder***, ***dihidrwydd*** *hwn*
unconditional *ans* ***diamod***, ***diamodol***
unconscious *ans* ***anymwybodol***, ***diymwybod***
unconstitutional *ans* ***anghyfansoddiadol***
uncoordinated *ans* ***digyswllt***
uncork *be* ***tynnu corcyn***
uncouple *be* ***datgysylltu***, ***dadfachu***
uncouth *ans* ***aflednais***, ***anwaraidd***
uncover *be* ***dinoethi***, ***datguddio***
uncritical *ans* ***anfeirniadol***, ***llyncu yn ddihalen***
unctuous *ans* ***sebonllyd***, ***seimllyd***
uncultivated *ans* ***heb ei drin***; ***anniwylliedig***
undecided *ans* ***ansicr***, ***cloffi rhwng dau feddwl***
undeniable *ans* ***anwadadwy***, ***diymwad***
under *ardd* ***tan:dan***
under *adf* ***tanodd:danodd***
underachievement *enw* ***tangyflawniad*** *hwn*
underclothing *enw* ***dillad isaf*** *hyn*
undercover *ans* ***cudd***, ***cuddiedig***
undercurrent *enw* ***isgerrynt*** *hwn*
underdeveloped *ans* ***annatblygedig***, ***heb ei ddatblygu***
underestimate *be* ***tanbrisio***, ***tanamcanu***; ***methu â llawn sylweddoli***
underfund *be* ***tanariannu***
undergo *be* ***cael***
undergraduate *enw* ***myfyriwr*** *hwn*
underground *ans* ***tanddaearol***
undergrowth *enw* ***prysgwydd*** *hyn*

u

underhanded *ans* ***dichellgar***, ***twyllodrus***
underline *be* ***tanlinellu***
undermine *be* ***tanseilio***
underneath *adf* ***oddi tanodd***
underneath *ardd* ***tan***:***dan***
underpaid *ans* ***ar gyflog gwael***
underpin *be* ***bod yn sylfaen i***
underprivileged *ans* ***difreintiedig***
underside *enw* ***tu isaf*** *hwn*, ***tor*** *hon*
underspend *enw* ***tanwariant*** *hwn*
understand *be* ***deall***, ***dirnad***
understandable *ans* ***dealladwy***
understanding *enw* ***dealltwriaeth***, ***dirnadaeth*** *hon*
understate *be* ***peidio/methu â rhoi'r pwys dyladwy ar***
undertake *be* ***ymgymryd â***
undertaker *enw* ***ymgymerwr*** *hwn*
undertaking *enw* ***menter*** *hon*
undertone *enw* ***islais*** *hwn*
undervalue *be* ***tanbrisio***, ***ni pherchir digon ar***
underwater *ans* ***tanddwr***
underwear *enw* ***dillad isaf*** *hyn*
underwrite *be* ***gwarantu***
undeserved *ans* ***anhaeddiannol***
undesirable *ans* ***annymunol***
undetermined *ans* ***amhenodol***, ***amhendant***
undisciplined *ans* ***annisgybledig***
undisputed *ans* ***diamheuol***, ***diddadl***
undistinguished *ans* ***di-nod***, ***cyffredin***
undisturbed *ans* ***diymyrraeth***
undivided *ans* ***diwahân***
  u~ attention ***sylw llawn***; ***hoelio sylw***
undo *be* ***datod***, ***dadwneud***
undoing *enw* ***diwedd***, ***distryw*** *hwn*
undoubted *ans* ***diamau***, ***diamheuol***, ***diymwad***
undress *be* ***dadwisgo***, ***ymddihatru***
undue *ans* ***gormodol***, ***afraid***
unearthly *ans* ***annaearol***
uneasy *ans* ***anesmwyth***, ***anniddig***
uneducated *ans* ***annysgedig***
unemployed *ans* ***di-waith***, ***segur***
unemployment *enw* ***diweithdra*** *hwn*
unending *ans* ***diddiwedd***, ***diderfyn***
unenlightened *ans* ***anwybodus***
unequal *ans* ***anghyfartal***
unequalled *ans* ***digymar***, ***digyffelyb***
unequivocal *ans* ***diamwys***
unerring *ans* ***di-feth***
uneven *ans* ***anwastad***
uneventful *ans* ***diddigwyddiad***, ***digyffro***
unexpected *ans* ***annisgwyl***
unfailing *ans* ***di-feth***, ***di-ffael***
unfair *ans* ***anghyfiawn***, ***annheg***
unfairly *adf* ***yn annheg***
  to be treated u~ ***cael cam***
unfaithful *ans* ***anffyddlon***
unfaltering *ans* ***dibetrus***
unfashionable *ans* ***anffasiynol***
unfasten *be* ***datod***, ***agor***

unfathomable *ans* ***affwysol***
unfavourable *ans* ***anffafriol***
unfeeling *ans* ***dideimlad***, ***oeraidd***
unfettered *ans* ***dilyffethair***
u~ criticism ***beirniadaeth ddi-flewyn ar dafod*** *hon*
unfinished *ans* ***anorffenedig***
unfit *ans* ***anaddas***, ***anghymwys***; ***dim digon iach/heini***
unflinching *ans* ***di-syfl***
unfold *be* ***agor***; ***mynd rhagddo***
unforeseen *ans* ***annisgwyl***
unforgettable *ans* ***bythgofiadwy***, ***anfarwol***
unfortunate *ans* ***anffodus***
unfounded *ans* ***di-sail***
unfriendly *ans* ***digroeso***, ***anghyfeillgar***
ungainly *ans* ***afrosgo***
ungodly *ans* ***annuwiol***
ungrateful *ans* ***anniolchgar***
unguent *enw* ***ennaint*** *hwn*
unhappiness *enw* ***tristwch***, ***anhapusrwydd*** *hwn*
unhappy *ans* ***anhapus***, ***trist***
unhealthy *ans* ***afiach***
unheeding *ans* ***didaro***, ***dihidio***
unhook *be* ***dadfachu***
unhoped for *ans* ***annisgwyl***
unhurt *ans* ***dianaf***
unhypothecated *ans* ***heb ei neilltuo***
unicorn *enw* ***uncorn*** *hwn*
uniform *enw* ***lifrai*** *hwn*
school u~ ***gwisg ysgol*** *hon*
uniform *ans* ***unffurf***
uniformity *enw* ***unffurfiaeth*** *hon*
unify *be* ***uno***
unilateral *ans* ***unochrog***
unimaginable *ans* ***anhygoel***; ***y tu hwnt i'r dychymyg***
uninformed *ans* ***anwybodus***
uninhabitable *ans* ***yn amhosibl byw ynddo***
uninhabited *ans* ***anghyfannedd***
uninhibited *ans* ***dilyffethair***
uninjured *ans* ***dianaf***
uninspiring *ans* ***di-fflach***
unintelligible *ans* ***annealladwy***
unintentional *ans* ***anfwriadol***
uninterested *ans* ***difater***, ***di-hid***
uninterrupted *ans* ***di-dor***, ***di-baid***
uninviting *ans* ***digroeso***
union *enw* ***uniad***, ***undeb*** *hwn*
unique *ans* ***unigryw***
unison *enw* ***unsain*** *hon*
unit *enw* ***uned*** *hon*
unite *be* ***uno***
United Kingdom *enw* ***y Deyrnas Unedig*** *hon*
United Nations *enw* ***y Cenhedloedd Unedig*** *hyn*
unitize *be* ***unedeiddio***
unity *enw* ***undod*** *hwn*
universal *ans* ***byd-eang***
u~ truth ***gwirionedd oesol*** *hwn*
universe *enw* ***bydysawd*** *hwn*
university *enw* ***prifysgol*** *hon*
unjust *ans* ***anghyfiawn***, ***annheg***
unjustified *ans* ***di-sail***
unkempt *ans* ***anniben***, ***aflêr***

u

unknown *ans* ***anadnabyddus***, ***anhysbys***
unlawful *ans* ***anghyfreithlon***
unlawfulness *enw* ***anghyfreithlondeb*** *hwn*
unleash *be* ***gollwng***, ***rhyddhau***
unless *cysyllt* ***oni***, ***onid***
unlicensed *ans* ***annhrwyddedig***
unlikelihood *enw* ***annhebygolrwydd*** *hwn*
unlikely *ans* ***annhebygol***, ***go brin***
unlimited *ans* ***diderfyn***, ***di-ben-draw***
unload *be* ***dadlwytho***
unlock *be* ***datgloi***
unlucky *ans* ***anffodus***, ***anlwcus***
unmask *be* ***dinoethi***
unmerited *ans* ***anhaeddiannol***
unmistakable *ans* ***digamsyniol***
unmoved *ans* ***diysgog***, ***disyflyd***
unnatural *ans* ***annaturiol***
unnecessary *ans* ***dianghenraid***, ***afraid***
unnoticed *ans* ***disylw***
unobserved *ans* ***heb sylwi arno***
unobtrusive *ans* ***anymwthiol***
unoccupied *ans* ***gwag***
unoffending *ans* ***didramgwydd***
unofficial *ans* ***answyddogol***
unopposed *ans* ***diwrthwynebiad***
unpack *be* ***dadbacio***
unparalleled *ans* ***digyffelyb***, ***dihafal***
unpick *be* ***datbigo***; ***datbwytho***
u~ an argument ***mynd i'w blu***
unpleasant *ans* ***annymunol***
unpopular *ans* ***amhoblogaidd***
unprecedented *ans* ***heb gynsail***, ***digynsail***
unpredictable *ans* ***anwadal***, ***anrhagweladwy***
unprejudiced *ans* ***diragfarn***
unpretentious *ans* ***dirodres***, ***diymhongar***
unproductive *ans* ***diffrwyth***
unprofitable *ans* ***dielw***, ***di-fudd***
unprofessional *ans* ***amhroffesiynol***
unprompted *ans* ***digymell***
unpublished *ans* ***anghyhoeddedig***
unqualified *ans* ***anghymwys***; ***digymhwyster***; ***diamod***
unquestionable *ans* ***diamheuol***, ***does dim dwywaith***
unravel *be* ***datrys***
unreadable *ans* ***annarllenadwy***
unready *ans* ***amharod***; ***cyndyn***, ***anfodlon***
unreal *ans* ***afreal***
unreasonable *ans* ***afresymol***
unrelated *ans* ***digyswllt***
unrelenting *ans* ***diarbed***, ***di-ildio***
unreliable *ans* ***annibynadwy***, ***di-ddal***, ***chwit-chwat***, ***anwadal***
unremitting *ans* ***di-baid***, ***diflino***
unrequited *ans* ***heb ei gydnabod***
u~ love ***ymserchu diymateb***
unreserved *ans* ***heb ei gadw***
unrest *enw* ***aflonyddwch*** *hwn*
unrestricted *ans* ***di-rwystr***, ***dilyffethair***

unrewarding *ans* ***di-fudd***
unripe *ans* ***anaeddfed***
unrivalled *ans* ***dihafal***, ***diguro***
unroll *be* ***dadrolio***
unruly *ans* ***diwahardd***, ***diwardd***
unsafe *ans* ***anniogel***, ***peryglus***
unsatisfactory *ans* ***anfoddhaol***
unscrew *be* ***dadsgriwio***
unscrupulous *ans* ***diegwyddor***
unseasonable *ans* ***annhymhorol***
unseemly *ans* ***anweddus***
unsettled *ans* ***ansefydlog***
unshakeable *ans* ***diysgog***, ***disyflyd***
unsightly *ans* ***hagr***, ***hyll***
unsociable *ans* ***anghymdeithasol***
unsolicited *ans* ***digymell***, ***diwahoddiad***
unsound *ans* ***bregus***
unspeakable *ans* ***anhraethol***
unstable *ans* ***ansefydlog***, ***ansad***
unsteady *ans* ***simsan***
unswerving *ans* ***diwyro***
unsympathetic *ans* ***digydymdeimlad***; ***anghydnaws***
untamed *ans* ***anystywallt***, ***gwyllt***
untangle *be* ***datrys***
untapped *ans* ***dihysbydd***
untenable *ans* ***anghynaliadwy***
unthinkable *ans* ***y tu hwnt i amgyffred***
untidiness *enw* ***annibendod***, ***llanast*** *hwn*
untidy *ans* ***anniben***
untie *be* ***datod***
until *ardd/cysyllt* ***hyd***, ***nes***, ***tan***
u~ now ***hyd yn hyn***
untimely *ans* ***annhymig***, ***cynamserol***
untiring *ans* ***diflino***
untouched *ans* ***heb ei gyffwrdd***
untroubled *ans* ***dibryder***, ***digyffro***
untrue *ans* ***anghywir***, ***celwyddog***
untrustworthy *ans* ***annibynadwy***
untruth *enw* ***anwiredd*** *hwn*
unused *ans* ***heb ei ddefnyddio***
unusual *ans* ***anarferol***, ***anghyffredin***
unutterable *ans* ***anhraethol***
unveil *be* ***dadlennu***, ***dadorchuddio***
unversed *ans* ***dibrofiad***
unwelcoming *ans* ***digroeso***
unwell *ans* ***gwael***, ***anhwylus***
unwieldy *ans* ***anhylaw***
unwilling *ans* ***amharod***, ***anfodlon***
unwind *be* ***dadweindio***; ***datod***
unwise *ans* ***annoeth***
unwitting *ans* ***diarwybod***
unworkable *ans* ***anymarferol***
unworthy *ans* ***annheilwng***
unyielding *ans* ***di-ildio***
up *adf/ardd* ***i fyny***, ***lan***, ***i lan***
upbraid *be* ***ceryddu***
upbringing *enw* ***magwraeth*** *hon*
update *be* ***diweddaru***
upgrade *be* ***uwchraddio***
upheaval *enw* ***cyffro***, ***terfysg*** *hwn*
uphold *be* ***cynnal***, ***ategu***
upholstery *enw* ***clustogwaith*** *hwn*

u

upkeep *enw* ***cynhaliaeth*** *hon*
upon *ardd* ***ar***, ***ar warthaf***
upper *ans* ***uwch***, ***uchaf***
uppermost *ans* ***uchaf***
upright *ans* ***union***, ***unionsyth***
uprising *enw* ***terfysg***, ***gwrthryfel*** *hwn*
uproar *enw* ***trwst***, ***twrw*** *hwn*
uproot *be* ***dadwreiddio***
upset *be* ***troi***, ***dymchwelyd***
upset *enw* ***dymchweliad***; ***anhrefn***, ***dryswch*** *hwn*; ***siom*** *hwn/hon*, ***siomedigaeth*** *hon*, ***gofid*** *hwn*; ***strach*** hon
upshot *enw* ***canlyniad*** *hwn*
upside down *adf* ***wyneb i waered***
upskilling *enw* ***cynyddu a chaboli sgiliau***
upstairs *adf* ***lan lofft***, ***i fyny'r staer***
upstart *enw* ***ceiliog dandi*** *hwn*
up to date *ans* ***hollol gyfoes***
upturn *enw* ***ar i fyny***; ***cynnydd*** *hwn*
upturned *ans* ***wyneb i waered***
Uranus *enw* ***Wranws*** *hwn*
urban *ans* ***trefol***, ***dinesig***
urbane *ans* ***hynaws***, ***moesgar***
urchin *enw* ***crwt*** *hwn*
urge *enw* ***cymhelliad***, ***cynhyrfiad*** *hwn*
urge *be* ***annog***, ***cymell***
urgency *enw* ***brys*** *hwn*
urgent *ans* ***o frys***, ***brys***
urinate *be* ***gwneud dŵr***, ***piso***
urine *enw* ***troeth*** *hwn*
urn *enw* ***wrn*** *hwn*
us *rhag* ***ni***, ***ninnau***
usage *enw* ***defnydd*** *hwn*, ***triniaeth*** *hon*
use *be* ***defnyddio***
useful *ans* ***defnyddiol***
u~ hints ***gair i gall***
usefulness *enw* ***defnyddioldeb*** *hwn*
useless *ans* ***da i ddim***
uselessness *enw* ***anfuddioldeb*** *hwn*
user *enw* ***defnyddiwr*** *hwn*
u~-friendly ***hawdd ei ddefnyddio***
usher *enw* ***tywysydd*** *hwn*
usual *ans* ***arferol***, ***cyffredin***
usurp *be* ***camfeddiannu***
utensil *enw* ***llestr*** *hwn*
uterus *enw* ***croth*** *hon*
utilitarian *ans* ***ymarferol***
utility *enw* ***defnyddioldeb*** *hwn*
utilize *be* ***defnyddio***
utmost *ans* ***eithaf***
utter *be* ***llefaru***
utter *ans* ***llwyr***, ***hollol***, ***ulw***
utterance *enw* ***datganiad*** *hwn*
U-turn *enw* ***tro pedol*** *hwn*

V

vacancy *enw* ***swydd wag*** *hon*; **lle ar gael**
vacant *ans* ***gwag***
vacate *be* ***gadael***
vacation *enw* ***gwyliau*** *hyn*
vaccinate *be* ***brechu***
vaccination *enw* ***brechiad*** *hwn*
vaccine *enw* ***brechlyn*** *hwn*
vacillate *be* **anwadalu, simsanu**
vacuous *ans* ***gwag***
vacuum *enw* ***gwactod*** *hwn*
  in a v~ ***heb gyd-destun***
vagabond *enw* ***crwydryn, caridým*** *hwn*
vagina *enw* ***gwain*** *hon*, ***fagina*** *hwn*
vagrant *enw* ***crwydryn*** *hwn*
vague *ans* **annelwig, amhendant**
vain *ans* ***balch***, ***ofer***
vale *enw* ***dyffryn***, ***glyn*** *hwn*
valediction *enw* ***ffarwél*** *hwn/hon*, ***canu'n iach***
valentine *enw* ***folant*** *hon*
valiant *ans* ***dewr***
valid *ans* ***dilys***
validate *be* ***dilysu***
validator *enw* ***dilyswr*** *hwn*
validity *enw* ***dilysrwydd*** *hwn*
  of doubtful v~ ***amheus eu gwerth***
valley *enw* ***dyffryn***, ***cwm***, ***glyn*** *hwn*
valorize *be* ***sefydlu gwerth***
valour *enw* ***dewrder*** *hwn*
valuable *ans* ***gwerthfawr***
valuation *enw* ***prisiad*** *hwn*
value *enw* ***gwerth*** *hwn*
value *be* ***prisio***, ***gwerthfawrogi***, ***bod yn werthfawrogol o***
value added tax *enw* ***treth ar werth*** *hon*
valve *enw* ***falf*** *hon*
van *enw* ***fan*** *hon*
vandalism *enw* ***fandaliaeth*** *hon*
vandalize *be* ***fandaleiddio***
vanguard *enw* ***blaen y gad*** *hwn*
vanish *be* ***diflannu***
vanity *enw* ***gwagedd***, ***balchder*** *hwn*
vanquish *be* ***gorchfygu***, ***trechu***
vantage point *enw* ***llecyn manteisiol*** *hwn*
vaporize *be* ***anweddu***
vapour *enw* ***tarth*** *hwn*
variable *ans* ***amrywiol***, ***cyfnewidiol***
variable *enw* ***newidyn*** *hwn*
variation *enw* ***amrywiad*** *hwn*
varicose *ans* ***chwyddedig***
variety *enw* ***amrywiaeth*** *hwn/hon*
various *ans* ***gwahanol***, ***amryfal***
varnish *enw* ***farnais*** *hwn*
varnish *be* ***farneisio***
vary *be* ***amrywio***
vase *enw* ***llestr blodau*** *hwn*
vassal *enw* ***taeog***, ***deiliad*** *hwn*
vast *ans* ***anferth***, ***aruthrol***
vat *enw* ***cerwyn*** *hon*

V

vault *enw* ***cromen***, ***fowt*** *hon*
vault *be* ***neidio***
vaulted *ans* ***bwaog***, ***cromennog***
veer *be* ***gwyro***
vegetable *enw* ***llysieuyn*** *hwn*
vegetable *ans* ***llysieuol***
vegetarian *enw* ***llysieuwr: llysieuydd*** *hwn*
vegetate *be* ***pydru byw***
vegetation *enw* ***llystyfiant*** *hwn*
vehemence *enw* ***taerineb***, ***angerdd*** *hwn*
vehement *ans* ***chwyrn***, ***angerddol***
vehicle *enw* ***cerbyd*** *hwn*
veil *enw* ***llen*** *hon*
vein *enw* ***gwythïen*** *hon*
vellum *enw* ***memrwn*** *hwn*
velocity *enw* ***cyflymder:cyflymdra*** *hwn*
velvet *enw* ***melfed*** *hwn*
venal *ans* ***llygradwy***
vend *be* ***gwerthu***
vendetta *enw* ***galanas***; ***cynnen*** *hon*
vendor *enw* ***gwerthwr*** *hwn*
veneer *enw* ***argaen*** *hon*
venerable *ans* ***hybarch***
venerate *be* ***parchu***, ***anrhydeddu***
veneration *enw* ***parch*** *hwn*
venereal *ans* ***gwenerol***
vengeance *enw* ***dial***, ***dialedd*** *hwn*
venom *enw* ***gwenwyn*** *hwn*
venomous *ans* ***gwenwynig***
ventilate *be* ***awyru***, ***gwyntyllu***
ventilation *enw* ***awyriad*** *hwn*
ventriloquism *enw* ***tafleisiaeth*** *hon*, ***tafleisio***
venture *enw* ***menter*** *hon*
venture *be* ***mentro***
venue *enw* ***lleoliad***, ***man cyfarfod***, ***man perfformio*** *hwn*
Venus *enw* ***Gwener*** *hon*
verb *enw* ***berf*** *hon*
verbal *ans* ***llafar***, ***geiriol***
  v~ noun ***berfenw*** *hwn*
verbatim *adf* ***air am air***
verbiage *enw* ***gwag-siarad*** *hwn*
verbose *ans* ***amleiriog***
verdant *ans* ***gwyrddlas, tirf***
verdict *enw* ***dyfarniad*** *hwn*
verge *enw* ***ymyl*** *hwn*
  on the v~ of ***ar fin***
verifiable *ans* ***gwiriadwy***
verification *enw* ***gwiriad*** *hwn*
verify *be* ***gwirio***, ***cadarnhau***, ***dilysu***
verily *adf* ***yn bendifaddau***, ***yn wir***
vernacular *ans* ***cynhenid***, ***brodorol***
versatile *ans* ***amryddawn***
  this theme is so v~ ***mae'r thema mor benagored***
verse *enw* ***adnod*** *hon*; ***pennill*** *hwn*
version *enw* ***fersiwn*** *hwn/hon*
vers libre *enw* ***gwers rydd*** *hon*
versus *ardd* ***yn erbyn***
vertebrate *enw* ***fertebrat*** *hwn*
vertical *ans* ***unionsyth***; ***fertigol***
vertigo *enw* ***y bendro*** *hon*
verve *enw* ***bywyd*** *hwn*

very *adf* ***iawn***, ***dros ben***
vespers *enw* ***gosber*** *hwn*
vessel *enw* ***llestr*** *hwn*; ***llong*** *hon*, ***cwch*** *hwn*
vest *enw* ***fest*** *hon*
vested *ans* ***wedi ei ymddiried***
  the responsibility is v~ in ***mae'r cyfrifoldeb yn nwylo***
vested interest *enw* ***budd*** *hwn*
vestibule *enw* ***cyntedd*** *hwn*
vestige *enw* ***ôl***; ***rhithyn*** *hwn*
vet *be* ***gwirio***
veteran *ans* ***profiadol***
veterinarian *enw* ***milfeddyg*** *hwn*
veterinary *ans* ***milfeddygol***
veto *enw* ***pleidlais atal*** *hon*
vex *be* ***digio***, ***codi gwrychyn***; ***becso***
vexed *ans* ***dadleuol***
  v~ question ***cwestiwn anodd***, ***testun dadleuol*** *hwn*
via *ardd* ***trwy***, ***trwy law***
viable *ans* (of living organisms) ***hyfyw***; (workable) ***dichonadwy***; ***digon mawr***
viaduct *enw* ***traphont*** *hon*
vibrant *ans* ***ffyniannus***, ***bywiog***
vibrate *be* ***dirgrynu***; ***crynu***
vibration *enw* ***dirgryniad***; ***cryndod*** *hwn*
vicar *enw* ***ficer*** *hwn*
vice *enw* ***drygioni*** *hwn*, ***llygredigaeth*** *hon*
viceroy *enw* ***rhaglaw*** *hwn*
vice versa *adf* ***croesymgroes***, ***i'r gwrthwyneb***
vicinity *enw* ***cyffiniau*** *hyn*
vicious *ans* ***milain:mileinig***
vicissitude *enw* ***tro*** *hwn*; ***hynt a helynt***
victim *enw* ***ysglyfaeth*** *hon*
victor *enw* ***buddugwr***, ***gorchfygwr*** *hwn*
victorious *ans* ***buddugoliaethus***
victory *enw* ***buddugoliaeth***, ***goruchafiaeth*** *hon*
victuals *enw* ***bwyd*** *hwn*, ***lluniaeth*** *hon*
video *enw* ***fideo*** *hwn/hon*
videoconference *enw* ***fideogynhadledd*** *hon*
videoconferencing *be* ***fideogynadledda***
viewer *enw* ***gwyliwr*** *hwn*
vie *be* ***cystadlu***, ***ymgiprys***
view *enw* ***golygfa***, ***golwg*** *hon*
  in v~ of ***oherwydd***, ***yn wyneb***
  to come to a v~ ***ffurfio barn***
  to have a clear v~ of ***bod â darlun clir o***
  to make their v~s known ***dweud eu dweud***
view *be* ***gwylio***, ***bwrw golwg***
viewer *enw* ***gwyliwr*** *hwn*
vigil *enw* ***gwylnos*** *hon*
vigilance *enw* ***gwyliadwriaeth*** *hon*
vigilant *ans* ***gwyliadwrus***, ***effro***
vigorous *ans* ***egnïol***, ***heini***

vigour *enw* ***egni***, ***grym*** *hwn*
Viking *enw* ***Llychlynnwr*** *hwn*
vile *ans* ***ffiaidd***, ***brwnt***
village *enw* ***pentref*** *hwn*
villain *enw* ***dihiryn*** *hwn*
villein *enw* ***bilain*** *hwn*
vindicate *be* ***cyfiawnhau***, ***achub cam***, ***cadarnhau cywirdeb***
vindication *enw* ***cyfiawnhad*** *hwn*
vindictive *ans* ***dialgar***
vine *enw* ***gwinwydden*** *hon*
vinegar *enw* ***finegr*** *hwn*
vineyard *enw* ***gwinllan*** *hon*
violate *be* ***treisio***; ***torri***
violation *enw* ***toriad***, ***trais*** *hwn*
violence *enw* ***trais***, ***ffyrnigrwydd*** *hwn*
violent *ans* ***treisgar***, ***treisiol***
violet *enw* ***fioled*** *hon*, ***crinllys*** *hwn*
violin *enw* ***feiolin***, ***ffidl*** *hon*
viper *enw* ***gwiber*** *hon*
vire *be* ***trosglwyddo arian***
virement *enw* ***trosglwyddiad arian*** *hwn*
virgin *enw* ***gwyryf***, ***morwyn*** *hon*
virile *ans* ***egnïol***
virility *enw* ***gwrywdod***; ***egni*** *hwn*
virtual *ans* ***i bob pwrpas***; ***dichonadwy***
  v~ reality ***rhithwir*** *hwn*
virtue *enw* ***rhinwedd*** *hwn/hon*
virtuous *ans* ***rhinweddol***
virulent *ans* ***gwenwynig***; ***milain***
virus *enw* ***firws*** *hwn*
visa *enw* ***fisa*** *hon*
visage *enw* ***wynepryd*** *hwn*
vis-à-vis *ardd* ***ynglŷn â***
viscera *enw* ***ymysgaroedd*** *hyn*
viscount *enw* ***is-iarll*** *hwn*
viscous *ans* ***gludiog***
visibility *enw* ***amlygrwydd*** *hwn*, ***natur weladwy*** *hon*
visible *ans* ***gweladwy***, ***gweledig***
vision *enw* ***golwg*** *hwn*; ***gweledigaeth*** *hon*
visit *enw* ***ymweliad*** *hwn*
visit *be* ***ymweld â***
visitor *enw* ***ymwelydd*** *hwn*
visor *enw* ***miswrn*** *hwn*
visual *ans* ***gweledol***
visualize *be* ***dychmygu***
vital *ans* ***hanfodol***
vitality *enw* ***bywiogrwydd***, ***bywyd*** *hwn*
vitamin *enw* ***fitamin*** *hwn*
vitiate *be* ***nychu***, ***gwanhau***, ***gwneud drwg i***
vitriolic *ans* ***gwenwynllyd***
vivacious *ans* ***hoenus***, ***nwyfus***, ***llawn bywyd***
vivacity *enw* ***hoen*** *hon*, ***nwyf*** *hwn*
vivid *ans* ***llachar***, ***tanbaid***
vivisection *enw* ***bywddyraniad*** *hwn*
vixen *enw* ***cadnawes***, ***llwynoges*** *hon*
vocabulary *enw* ***geirfa*** *hon*
vocal *ans* ***llafar***, ***lleisiol***
  v~ opposition ***gwrthwynebu'n groch***

vocation *enw* ***galwedigaeth*** *hon*
vocational *ans* ***galwedigaethol***
vociferous *ans* ***uchel eich cloch***
vogue *enw* ***ffasiwn*** *hwn/hon*
voice *enw* ***llais*** *hwn*
voice *be* ***lleisio***
void *enw* ***gwagle***, ***gwacter*** *hwn*
void *ans* ***di-rym***
void *be* ***gwagio***
volatile *ans* ***gwamal***, ***anwadal***
volatility *enw* ***ansefydlogrwydd*** *hwn*
volcano *enw* ***llosgfynydd***, ***folcano*** *hwn*
vole *enw* ***llygoden bengron*** *hon*
volition *enw* ***ewyllys***, ***gwirfodd*** *hwn*
volt *enw* ***folt*** *hwn/hon*
voltage *enw* ***foltedd*** *hwn*
voluble *ans* ***huawdl***, ***siaradus***
volume *enw* ***uchder***, ***cyfaint*** *hwn*; (book) ***cyfrol*** *hon*
large v~s of useful information ***llond gwlad o wybodaeth ddefnyddiol***
the large v~ of answers ***y doreth o atebion***
voluntary *ans* ***gwirfoddol***
volunteer *enw* ***gwirfoddolwr*** *hwn*
voluptuous *ans* ***synhwyrus***, ***nwydus***, ***cnawdol***
vomit *be* ***cyfogi***, ***chwydu***
voracious *ans* ***gwancus***, ***barus***
vote *enw* ***pleidlais*** *hon*
vote *be* ***pleidleisio***
voter *enw* ***pleidleisiwr*** *hwn*, ***pleidleiswraig*** *hon*
vouch *be* ***dweud gair dros***
voucher *enw* ***taleb*** *hon*, ***tocyn*** *hwn*
vow *enw* ***adduned*** *hon*
vow *be* ***addunedu***
vowel *enw* ***llafariad*** *hon*
voyage *enw* ***mordaith*** *hon*
voyage *be* ***mordwyo***
voyager *enw* ***mordwywr*** *hwn*
vulgar *ans* ***di-chwaeth***; ***cyffredin***
vulnerability *enw* ***natur fregus*** *hon*
vulnerable *ans* ***hawdd eich clwyfo***, ***bregus***, ***diamddiffyn***
vulture *enw* ***fwltur*** *hwn*
vulva *enw* ***fwlfa*** *hwn*

W

wad *enw* ***wad*** *hwn/hon*, ***dyrnaid*** *hwn*
wadding *enw* ***wadin*** *hwn*
waddle *be* ***honcian cerdded***
wade *be* ***cerdded trwy ddŵr***, ***bracso***
wader *enw* ***rhydiwr*** *hwn*
wafer *enw* ***waffer***; ***afrlladen*** *hon*
waffle *be* ***gwag-siarad***, ***malu awyr***
wag *enw* ***aderyn*** *hwn*
wag *be* ***siglo***, ***ysgwyd***
wage *enw* ***cyflog*** *hwn*
w~s and salaries ***cyflogau misol ac wythnosol*** *hyn*
wager *enw* ***bet*** *hwn/hon*
wager *be* ***codi bet***, ***betio***
wages *enw* ***cyflog*** *hwn*
waggle *be* ***ysgwyd***
waggon *enw* ***wagen*** *hon*
wagtail *enw* ***sigl-i-gwt*** *hwn*, ***siglen*** *hon*
waif *enw* ***plentyn amddifad*** *hwn*
wail *enw* ***llef*** *hon*
wail *be* ***nadu***, ***llefain***
wainscot *enw* ***palis*** *hwn*
waist *enw* ***gwasg*** *hwn/hon*
waistcoat *enw* ***gwasgod*** *hon*
wait *enw* ***arhosiad*** *hwn*
wait *be* ***aros***
to w~ for ***disgwyl***
waiter *enw* ***gweinydd***, ***gwas*** *hwn*
waitress *enw* ***morwyn fwrdd*** *hon*
waive *be* ***hepgor***, ***rhoi o'r neilltu***
wake *enw* ***gwylnos***; ***dawns*** *hon*; ***ôl llong***
in the w~ of ***yn sgil***
walk *enw* ***tro*** *hwn*
every w~ of life ***ym mhob galwedigaeth***
walk *be* ***cerdded***
walker *enw* ***cerddwr*** *hwn*, ***cerddwraig*** *hon*
walking stick *enw* ***ffon*** *hon*
wall *enw* ***mur*** *hwn*
to drive them up the w~ ***eu gyrru'n benwan***
wallet *enw* ***waled*** *hon*
wallflowers *enw* ***blodau'r fagwyr*** *hyn*
wallop *be* ***cledro***
wallow *be* ***ymdrochi***, ***ymdrybaeddu***
wallpaper *enw* ***papur wal*** *hwn*
walnut *enw* ***cneuen Ffrengig*** *hon*
walnuts *enw* ***cnau Ffrengig*** *hyn*
walrus *enw* ***morlo ysgithrog***, ***morfarch*** *hwn*
wan *ans* ***gwelw***, ***llwyd***
wander *be* ***crwydro***
wanderer *enw* ***crwydryn*** *hwn*
wane *be* ***cilio***
want *enw* ***eisiau*** *hwn*
want *be* ***ymofyn***
wanton *ans* ***trythyll***, ***anllad***
war *enw* ***rhyfel*** *hwn*

to be in the w~s ***bod yn ei chanol hi***
warble *be* ***telori***
warbler *enw* ***telor*** *hwn*
ward *enw* ***ward*** *hwn*; ***etholaeth*** *hon*
warden *enw* ***warden***, ***ceidwad*** *hwn*
warder *enw* ***gwarcheidwad***, ***ceidwad*** *hwn*
wardrobe *enw* ***cwpwrdd dillad*** *hwn*
warehouse *enw* ***warws*** *hwn/hon*
warfare *enw* ***rhyfel*** *hwn*
wariness *enw* ***pwyll*** *hwn*, ***gwyliadwriaeth*** *hon*
warlike *ans* ***rhyfelgar***
warm *ans* ***cynnes***, ***twym***, ***gwresog***
warm *be* ***cynhesu***, ***twymo***, ***gwresogi***
warm-hearted *ans* ***twymgalon***
warmth *enw* ***gwres***, ***cynhesrwydd*** *hwn*
warn *be* ***rhybuddio***
warning *enw* ***rhybudd*** *hwn*
warp *be* ***camu***, ***ystumio***
warrant *enw* ***gwarant*** *hon*
warrant *be* ***peri***, ***haeddu***
warren *enw* ***cwningar*** *hon*
warrior *enw* ***rhyfelwr*** *hwn*
wart *enw* ***dafaden*** *hon*
wary *ans* ***gwyliadwrus***, ***gochelgar***
wash *be* ***golchi***, ***ymolchi***
washable *ans* ***golchadwy***
washbowl *enw* ***basn ymolchi*** *hwn*, ***powlen ymolchi*** *hon*
washerwoman *enw* ***golchwraig*** *hon*
washing *enw* ***golch***, ***golchiad*** *hwn*
washing machine *enw* ***peiriant golchi*** *hwn*
washing-up *enw* ***golchi llestri***
waspish *ans* ***pigog***, ***piwis***
wasps *enw* ***cacwn***, ***piffgwn*** *hyn*
wastage *enw* ***gwastraff*** *hwn*
waste *be* ***gwastraffu***
I was w~ing my breath ***waeth imi fod yn siarad â'r wal ddim***
waste *enw* ***gwastraff*** *hwn*
to go to w~ ***mynd yn ofer***
wasteful *ans* ***gwastraffus***
waster *enw* ***dyn ofer*** *hwn*
watch *enw* ***oriawr***; ***gwyliadwriaeth*** *hon*
watch *be* ***gwylio***
watchful *ans* ***gwyliadwrus***
to keep a w~ eye on ***cadw llygad barcud ar***
watchman *enw* ***gwyliwr*** *hwn*
watchnight *enw* ***gwylnos*** *hon*
water *enw* ***dŵr*** *hwn*
water *be* ***dyfrhau***, ***dyfrio***
water closet *enw* ***tŷ bach*** *hwn*
watercolour *enw* ***dyfrlliw*** *hwn*
watercress *enw* ***berwr dŵr*** *hwn*
waterfall *enw* ***rhaeadr*** *hon*
watering can *enw* ***can dyfrio*** *hwn*
watermark *enw* ***dyfrnod*** *hwn*
waterproof *ans* ***sy'n dal dŵr***, ***diddos***, ***dwrglos***

W

watershed *enw* ***cefndeuddwr*** *hwn*, ***gwahanfa ddŵr*** *hon*
watertight *ans* ***dwrglos***
waterwheel *enw* ***rhod ddŵr***, ***olwyn ddŵr*** *hon*
watery *ans* ***dyfrllyd***
watt *enw* ***wat*** *hwn*
wave *enw* ***ton*** *hon*
wave *be* ***chwifio***, ***codi llaw***
wavelength *enw* ***tonfedd*** *hon*
waver *be* ***gwamalu***, ***simsanu***
wavy *ans* ***tonnog***
wax *enw* ***cwyr***, ***gwêr*** *hwn*
way *enw* ***ffordd*** *hon*
  either w~ ***yn y naill achos neu'r llall***; ***beth bynnag a benderfynir***
  in a w~ ***ar ryw olwg***
  in many w~s ***ar lawer ystyr***
  in this w~ ***drwy hyn***; ***yn hyn o beth***
  one w~ or another ***rywsut rywfodd***
  to give w~ to ***cael eu disodli gan***
  to show the w~ ***gosod esiampl***
wayfarer *enw* ***fforddolyn*** *hwn*
wayward *ans* ***anwadal***; ***gwrthnysig***
we *rhag* ***ni***, ***ninnau***
weak *ans* ***gwan***, ***eiddil***
  w~ excuse ***esgus cloff*** *hwn*
weaken *be* ***gwanhau***
weakling *enw* ***llipryn*** *hwn*
weak-minded *ans* ***diniwed***, ***gwirion***
weakness *enw* ***gwendid*** *hwn*
weal *enw* ***gwrym*** *hwn*
wealth *enw* ***cyfoeth*** *hwn*
  a w~ of experience ***profiad helaeth*** *hwn*
wealthy *ans* ***cyfoethog***
  extremely w~ ***bod yn graig o arian***
wean *be* ***diddyfnu***
weapon *enw* ***arf*** *hwn*
wear *enw* ***traul*** *hon*
wear *be* ***gwisgo***, ***treulio***
  she's w~ing well ***mae cas cadw da arni***
  to w~ off ***pylu***, ***pallu***
weariness *enw* ***blinder***; ***diflastod*** *hwn*
wearisome *ans* ***blinderus***
weary *ans* ***blinedig***, ***wedi blino***
weasel *enw* ***gwenci*** *hon*
weather *enw* ***tywydd*** *hwn*
  to make heavy w~ ***gwneud môr a mynydd***
weather forecast *enw* ***rhagolygon y tywydd*** *hyn*
weathervane *enw* ***ceiliog gwynt*** *hwn*
weave *be* ***gwau***, ***gweu***; ***gwehyddu***
weaver *enw* ***gwehydd*** *hwn*
web *enw* ***gwe*** *hon*
webbed *ans* ***gweog***
wed *be* ***priodi***
wedding *enw* ***priodas*** *hon*
wedding ring *enw* ***modrwy briodas*** *hon*
wedge *enw* ***lletem*** *hon*

Wednesday *enw* ***dydd Mercher*** *hwn*
weed *be* ***chwynnu***
weedkiller *enw* ***chwynleiddiad***, ***chwynladdwr*** *hwn*
weeds *enw* ***chwyn*** *hyn*
week *enw* ***wythnos*** *hon*
weekday *enw* ***dydd/diwrnod gwaith*** *hwn*
weekend *enw* ***penwythnos*** *hwn*
weekend *be* ***bwrw'r Sul***
weekly *ans* ***wythnosol***
weep *be* ***wylo***
weft *enw* ***anwe*** *hon*
weigh *be* ***pwyso***
weight *enw* ***pwysau*** *hwn/hyn*
weighty *ans* ***trwm***, ***o bwys***
weir *enw* ***cored*** *hon*
weird *ans* ***rhyfedd***
welcome *enw* ***croeso*** *hwn*
welcome *be* ***croesawu***
weld *be* ***asio***, ***weldio***
welfare *enw* ***lles***, ***budd*** *hwn*
  w~ state ***y wladwriaeth les*** *hon*
welkin *enw* ***ffurfafen*** *hon*
well *enw* ***ffynnon*** *hon*
well *adf/ans* ***yn dda***; ***yn iach***
  schools would do w~ to ***buddiol fyddai i ysgolion***
  the work went w~ ***cafwyd hwyl ar y gwaith***
  to be w~ on the way to ***wedi cymryd camau bras***
  very w~ ***o'r gorau***
  work is w~ under way ***mae'r gwaith wedi hen ddechrau***
  you will know only too w~ ***fe wyddoch chi cystal â neb***
well-being *enw* ***lles*** *hwn*
well-bred *ans* ***o dras***
well-briefed *ans* ***hyddysg***
well-cared for *ans* ***â graen arni***
well-deserved *ans* ***haeddiannol***
well-disposed to *ans* ***bod yn bleidiol i***
well-equipped *ans* ***helaeth eu hoffer***
well-established *ans* ***hen***
well-fed *ans* ***porthiannus***
well-informed *ans* ***gwybodus***
wellingtons *enw* ***bwtsias*** *hyn*
well-intentioned *ans* ***llawn bwriadau da***
well-known *ans* ***adnabyddus***, ***cyfarwydd***
well-off *ans* ***cefnog***
well-positioned *ans* ***mewn sefyllfa dda***
well-presented *ans* ***graenus***
well-respected *ans* ***uchel eu parch***
Welsh *enw* (language) ***Cymraeg*** *hon*
Welsh *ans* ***Cymreig***
Welshman *enw* ***Cymro*** *hwn*
Welshness *enw* ***Cymreigrwydd***, ***Cymreictod*** *hwn*
Welshwoman *enw* ***Cymraes*** *hon*
welt *enw* ***gwrym*** *hwn*
welter *enw* ***toreth*** *hon*

W

wend *be* ***ymlwybro***
west *enw* ***gorllewin*** *hwn*
westerly *ans* ***gorllewinol***
western *ans* ***gorllewinol***
Westminster *enw* ***San Steffan***
wet *enw* ***gwlybaniaeth*** *hwn*
wet *be* ***gwlychu***
wet *ans* ***gwlyb***
wether *enw* ***mollt***, ***gwedder*** *hwn*
whale *enw* ***morfil*** *hwn*
wharf *enw* ***cei*** *hwn*, ***glanfa*** *hon*
what *rhag* ***beth***, ***pa beth***
whatever *rhag* ***beth bynnag***
whatsoever *ans* ***unrhyw***, ***o gwbl***
what-d'you-call *rhag* ***bechingalw***
wheat *enw* ***gwenith*** *hwn*
wheedle *be* ***perswadio***
wheel *enw* ***olwyn***, ***rhod*** *hon*
wheelbarrow *enw* ***berfa***, ***whilber*** *hon*
wheelchair *enw* ***cadair olwyn(ion)*** *hon*
wheelwright *enw* ***saer troliau*** *hwn*
wheeze *be* ***gwichian***
whelp *enw* ***cenau*** *hwn*
when *adf/cysyllt* ***pryd***, ***pan***
whenever *adf/cysyllt* ***bob tro***, ***pa bryd bynnag***
where *adf/cysyllt* ***ym mha le***, ***ble***; ***lle***
whereas *cysyllt* ***tra***, ***yn gymaint â***
whereby *cysyllt* ***trwy'r hwn/hon/hyn***
whereupon *cysyllt* ***gyda hyn/hynny***
wherever *adf/cysyllt* ***pa le bynnag***
wherewithal *enw* ***y modd*** *hwn*
whet *be* ***hogi***
whether *cysyllt* ***a***; ***p'un ai***
whetstone *enw* ***carreg hogi*** *hon*, ***hogfaen*** *hwn*
whey *enw* ***maidd*** *hwn*
which *ans/rhag* ***pa***
while *enw* ***ysbaid*** *hwn*
for a w~ ***ers tro***
while *cysyllt* ***tra***
whim *enw* ***mympwy*** *hwn*
whimper *be* ***griddfan***, ***nadu***
whimsical *ans* ***mympwyol***
whine *be* ***nadu***
whinny *be* ***gweryru***
whip *enw* ***chwip*** *hon*
whip *be* ***chwipio***
to w~ up ***cyffroi***
whippet *enw* ***ci cwrso***, ***corfilgi*** *hwn*
whirl *be* ***chwyrlïo***, ***troelli***
whirlpool *enw* ***trobwll*** *hwn*
whirlwind *enw* ***corwynt*** *hwn*
whirr *be* ***grwnial***, ***chwyrndroi***
whisk *be* ***ysgubo***; (food) ***curo***
whisker *enw* ***blewyn*** *hwn*
within a whisker ***o fewn y dim***
whisky *enw* ***chwisgi*** *hwn*
whisper *enw* ***sibrwd*** *hwn*
whisper *be* ***sibrwd***, ***sisial***
whist *enw* ***chwist*** *hwn*
whist-drive *enw* ***gyrfa chwist*** *hon*
whistle *enw* ***chwiban*** *hwn/hon*
whistle *be* ***chwibanu***

white *ans* ***gwyn***
white-hot *ans* ***eirias***, ***gwynias***
white lie *enw* ***celwydd golau*** *hwn*
whiten *be* ***gwynnu***
whiteness *enw* ***gwynder*** *hwn*
whitethroat *enw* (bird) ***llwydfron*** *hon*
whitewash *be* ***gwyngalchu***
whitlow *enw* ***ffelwm*** *hwn*, ***ewinor*** *hon*
Whit Monday *enw* ***Llungwyn*** *hwn*
Whit Sunday *enw* ***Sulgwyn*** *hwn*
whittle *be* ***naddu***; ***erydu***
whoever *rhag* ***pwy bynnag***
whole *ans* ***cyfan***, ***holl***
wholemeal *ans* ***grawn/gwenith cyflawn***
wholesale *be* ***cyfanwerthu***
whole-school *ans* ***ysgol-gyfan***
wholesome *ans* ***iachus***, ***iachusol***
wholly *adf* ***yn llwyr***
whoop *be* ***ubain***
whooping cough *enw* ***y pas*** *hwn*
whore *enw* ***putain***, ***hwren*** *hon*
whortleberries *enw* ***llus***, ***llusi duon bach*** *hyn*
why *adf* ***paham***, ***pam***
wick *enw* ***pabwyryn*** *hwn*
wicked *ans* ***drwg***, ***ysgeler***
wickedness *enw* ***drygioni*** *hwn*
wickerwork *enw* ***plethwaith*** *hwn*
wicket *enw* ***wiced*** *hon*
wide *ans* ***llydan***
wide awake *ans* ***effro***
widen *be* ***lledu***
widespread *ans* ***ar led***
widow *enw* ***gweddw***, ***gwraig weddw*** *hon*
widower *enw* ***gŵr gweddw*** *hwn*
widowhood *enw* ***gweddwdod*** *hwn*
width *enw* ***lled*** *hwn*
wield *be* ***trin***, ***trafod***
wife *enw* ***gwraig*** *hon*
wig *enw* ***gwallt gosod*** *hwn*
wild *ans* ***gwyllt***
wildlife *enw* ***bywyd gwyllt*** *hwn*
wilderness *enw* ***anial***, ***anialwch*** *hwn*
wildness *enw* ***gwylltineb*** *hwn*
wiles *enw* ***castiau*** *hyn*
wilful *ans* ***ystyfnig***; ***bwriadol***, ***bwriadus***
wilfulness *enw* ***ystyfnigrwydd*** *hwn*; ***natur fwriadol*** *hon*
will *enw* ***ewyllys*** *hwn/hon*
  goodwill ***ewyllys da***
willing *ans* ***parod***
will-o'-the-wisp *enw* ***Jac y lantar(n)*** *hwn*
willow *enw* ***helygen*** *hon*
will power *enw* ***grym ewyllys*** *hwn*
wilt *be* ***gwywo***
wily *ans* ***cyfrwys***, ***castiog***
win *be* ***ennill***
  to w~ through ***ennill y dydd***
wince *be* ***gwingo***
wind *enw* ***gwynt*** *hwn*
wind *be* ***dolennu***, ***dirwyn***, ***weindio***
winding *ans* ***dolennog***, ***troellog***
windmill *enw* ***melin wynt*** *hon*

W

window *enw* ***ffenestr*** *hon*
window-pane *enw* ***gwydr/paen ffenestr***, ***cwarel*** *hwn*
windpipe *enw* ***pibell wynt*** *hon*
windscreen *enw* ***ffenestr flaen*** *hon*
w~ wiper ***sychwr glaw*** *hwn*
wind up *be* ***dirwyn i ben***
windy *ans* ***gwyntog***
wine *enw* ***gwin*** *hwn*
wine cellar *enw* ***seler win*** *hon*
wing *enw* ***adain***, ***asgell*** *hon*
wing forward *enw* ***blaenasgellwr*** *hwn*
wink *enw* ***amrantiad***, ***chwinciad*** *hwn*
winner *enw* ***enillydd***, ***buddugwr*** *hwn*
winnings *enw* ***enillion*** *hyn*
winnow *be* ***nithio***
winter *enw* ***gaeaf*** *hwn*
winter *be* ***hendrefu***, ***gaeafu***
wintry *ans* ***gaeafol***
wipe *be* ***sychu***
wire *enw* ***gwifr***, ***gwifren*** *hon*
wireless *enw* ***radio*** *hon*
wiry *ans* ***gewynnog***
wisdom *enw* ***doethineb*** *hwn*
wise *ans* ***doeth***
wish *enw* ***awydd***, ***dymuniad*** *hwn*
wish *be* ***dymuno***
as many as you w~ ***faint a fynnoch***
wishful *ans* ***awyddus***
w~ thinking breuddwyd g***wrach*** *hwn*
wishy-washy *ans* ***merfaidd***, ***llipa***
wistful *ans* ***hiraethus***
wit *enw* ***ffraethineb***, ***arabedd*** *hwn*
to scare out of their w~s ***rhoi llond twll o ofn iddynt***
witch *enw* ***gwrach*** *hon*
witchcraft *enw* ***dewiniaeth***, ***swyngyfaredd*** *hon*
with *ardd* ***â:ag***, ***gyda:gydag***
withdraw *be* ***tynnu yn ôl***; ***encilio***
withdrawn *ans* ***tawedog***, ***tawedwst***, ***encilgar***
wither *be* ***gwywo***, ***crino***
withhold *be* ***dal yn ôl***, ***celu***, ***ymatal rhag***
within *adf/ardd* ***oddi mewn***, ***i mewn***, ***o fewn***, ***y tu fewn***, ***yn***
without *adf/ardd* ***heb***, ***y tu allan***
w~ doubt ***nid oes dwywaith***
withstand *be* ***gwrthsefyll***
witless *ans* ***hurt***
witness *be* ***tystio***
witticisms *enw* ***ffraethinebau*** *hyn*
wittingly *adf* ***yn fwriadol***
witty *ans* ***ffraeth***
wizard *enw* ***dewin*** *hwn*
wizened *ans* ***wedi crebachu***, ***crin***
woe *enw* ***gwae*** *hwn/hon*, ***trallod*** *hwn*
woebegone *ans* ***fel iâr ar y glaw***, ***trallodus***
woeful *ans* ***trist***, ***athrist***
wolf *enw* ***blaidd*** *hwn*
to cry w~ ***codi bwganod***
woman *enw* ***menyw***, ***gwraig*** *hon*

womanize *be* ***mercheta***
womanly *ans* ***benywaidd***
womb *enw* ***croth*** *hon*
wonder *enw* ***rhyfeddod*** *hwn*
wonder *be* ***rhyfeddu***, ***dyfalu***
wonderful *ans* ***rhagorol***, ***rhyfeddol***, ***anfarwol***
wondrous *ans* ***rhyfeddol***
woo *be* ***canlyn***
wood *enw* ***pren***, ***coed*** *hwn*; ***coedwig*** *hon*
woodbine *enw* ***gwyddfid*** *hwn*
woodcock *enw* ***cyffylog*** *hwn*
wooden *ans* ***pren***, ***o bren***
woodlouse *enw* ***gwrach y lludw***, ***gwrachen lludw***, ***mochyn y coed*** *hwn*
woodpecker *enw* ***cnocell y coed*** *hon*
wood pigeon *enw* ***ysguthan*** *hon*
woodwind *enw* ***chwythbrennau*** *hyn*
woodwork *enw* ***gwaith coed*** *hwn*
woof *enw* ***anwe*** *hon*
wool *enw* ***gwlân*** *hwn*
woollen *ans* ***gwlanog***
word *enw* ***gair*** *hwn*
  a w~ of caution ***gair i gall***
word *be* ***geirio***
wording *enw* ***geiriad*** *hwn*
word-processing *enw* ***prosesu geiriau***
work *enw* ***gwaith*** *hwn*
  a w~ of art ***campwaith*** *hwn*
  at w~ ***wrthi***
  to be hard at w~ ***bod wrthi'n ddyfal***
work *be* ***gweithio***
workable *ans* ***ymarferol***
worked up *ans* ***wedi cynhyrfu i gyd***
worker *enw* ***gweithiwr*** *hwn*
workforce *enw* ***gweithlu*** *hwn*
workhouse *enw* ***tloty*** *hwn*, ***wyrcws*** *hwn/hon*
workmanship *enw* ***saernïaeth*** *hon*, ***crefftwaith*** *hwn*
workshop *enw* ***gweithdy*** *hwn*
work-station *enw* ***gweithfan*** *hwn/hon*
world *enw* ***byd*** *hwn*
  w~-class ***o safon fyd-eang***
worldly *ans* ***bydol***
world-wide *ans* ***byd-eang***
worm *enw* ***abwydyn***, ***mwydyn***, ***pryf genwair*** *hwn*
wormwood *enw* ***wermwd lwyd*** *hon*
worn out *ans* ***wedi treulio***
worried *ans* ***pryderus***, ***gofidus***
worry *enw* ***pryder***, ***gofid*** *hwn*
worry *be* ***pryderu***, ***gofidio***
  to be w~ied sick ***becso'i enaid***
worrying *ans* ***pryderus***, ***gofidus***
worse *ans* ***gwaeth***
worsen *be* ***gwaethygu***, ***difrifoli***
worship *enw* ***addoliad*** *hwn*
worship *be* ***addoli***
worst *ans* ***gwaethaf***
  if it should come to the w~ ***petai'n mynd i'r pen***

W

worth *enw* ***gwerth*** *hwn*
worthily *adf* ***yn deilwng***
worthless *ans* ***diwerth***, ***da i ddim***
worthwhile *ans* ***buddiol, gwerth ei wneud***
worthy *ans* ***teilwng***
would-be *ans* ***darpar***
wound *enw* ***anaf***, ***clwyf*** *hwn*
wound *be* ***clwyfo***, ***anafu***
wow *be* ***cyfareddu***, ***swyno***
wraith *enw* ***drychiolaeth*** *hon*
wrangle *be* ***dadlau***, ***cweryla***
wrap *be* ***lapio***
wrasse *enw* ***gwrachen y môr*** *hon*
wrath *enw* ***dicter***, ***digofaint*** *hwn*
wreath *enw* ***torch*** *hon*
wreck *enw* (ship) ***llong ddrylliedig*** *hon*
wreck *be* ***dryllio***, ***malu***
wrecked *ans* ***drylliedig***
wren *enw* ***dryw (bach)*** *hwn*
wrench *enw* ***ysigiad*** *hwn*; (tool) ***tyndro*** *hwn*
wrench *be* ***rhwygo***
wrestle *be* ***ymaflyd codwm***
wretch *enw* ***truan*** *hwn*
wretched *ans* ***truenus***
wriggle *be* ***dolennu***, ***gwingo***
wrinkle *enw* ***crych*** *hwn*
wrinkle *be* ***crychu***
wrist *enw* ***arddwrn*** *hwn*
writ *enw* ***gwŷs***, ***gwrit*** *hon*
write *be* ***ysgrifennu***
writer *enw* ***ysgrifennwr***, ***awdur*** *hwn*
writhe *be* ***gwingo***
writing *enw* ***ysgrifen*** *hon*
wrong *enw* ***cam*** *hwn*
  to admit to being in the w~ ***syrthio ar ei fai***
wrong *ans* ***anghywir***
  it would be w~ to ***camgymeriad fyddai***
  something is very w~ ***mae rhywbeth mawr o'i le***
wrong *be* ***gwneud cam â***, ***cael cam***
wrongful *ans* ***ar gam***, ***anghyfiawn***
wrongly *adf* ***ar gam***
wrought iron *enw* ***haearn gyr*** *hwn*
wry *ans* ***mingam***

xenophobe *enw* ***un sy'n casáu estroniaid***

xenophobia *enw* ***senoffobia****;* ***ofn estroniaid*** *hwn*

xenophobic *ans* ***senoffobig****,* ***drwgdybus o estroniaid***

X-ray *enw* ***pelydr X*** *hwn*

xylophone *enw* ***seiloffon*** *hwn*

Y

yacht *enw* **cwch hwylio** *hwn*, **llong bleser** *hon*
yank *be* **plycio**
yap *be* ***clepian cyfarth***
yard *enw* ***buarth*** *hwn*, ***iard*** *hon*; (measurement) ***llathen*** *hon*
yarn *enw* ***edau*** *hon*; (story) ***chwedl*** *hon*
yawn *enw* ***dylyfiad gên*** *hwn*
yawn *be* ***dylyfu gên***, ***agor ceg***
year *enw* ***blwyddyn*** *hon*
  for y~s ***am flynyddoedd bwygilydd***
yearbook *enw* ***blwyddlyfr*** *hwn*
yearling *ans* ***blwydd***, ***blwydd oed***
yearly *ans* ***blynyddol***
yearn *be* ***dyheu***, ***hiraethu***
yearning *enw* ***hiraeth*** *hwn*, ***ysfa*** *hon*
yeast *enw* ***burum*** *hwn*
yell *enw* ***bloedd***, ***gwaedd*** *hon*
yell *be* ***gweiddi***, ***bloeddio***
yellow *ans* ***melyn*** (*hwn*), ***melen*** (*hon*)
yellowhammer *enw* ***bras melyn*** *hwn*, ***y benfelen*** *hon*
yelp *be* ***cyfarth***
yes *adf* ***do***, ***ie***, ***ydi***, ***ydyw***, ***oes***
yesterday *adf/enw* ***ddoe:doe***
yesteryear *enw* ***y llynedd*** *hon*; *adf* ***'slawer dydd***
yet *adf/cysyllt* ***eto***, ***er hynny***
yew *enw* ***ywen*** *hon*
yield *enw* ***cynnyrch*** *hwn*
yield *be* ***ildio***; ***cynhyrchu***
yobbo *enw* ***llabwst, iob*** *hwn*
yoghurt *enw* ***iogwrt*** *hwn*
yoke *enw* ***iau*** *hwn/hon*, ***gwedd*** *hon*
yokel *enw* ***creadur gwladaidd*** *hwn*
yolk *enw* ***melyn wy*** *hwn*
yonder *adf/ans* ***draw***, ***acw***
yore *enw* ***gynt***
you *rhag* ***ti:di***, ***chi:chwi***
young *ans* ***ifanc***, ***ieuanc***
youngster *enw* ***plentyn***, ***person ifanc*** *hwn*
your *ans* ***dy***, ***eich***
yours *rhag* ***eiddot ti***, ***eiddoch chi***
yourself *rhag* ***dy hun***, ***eich hunain***
youth *enw* ***ieuenctid***; ***llanc*** *hwn*
youthful *ans* ***ifanc***
yo-yo *enw* ***io-io*** *hwn*

Z

zeal *enw* ***brwdfrydedd*** *hwn*, ***sêl*** *hon*
zealot *enw* ***selogyn***, ***penboethyn*** *hwn*, ***penboethen*** *hon*
zealous *ans* ***brwd***, ***brwdfrydig***, ***taer***, ***penboeth***, ***selog***
zebra *enw* ***sebra*** *hwn*
  z~-crossing ***croesfan*** *hwn/hon*
zenith *enw* ***anterth***, ***entrych*** *hwn*
zephyr *enw* ***awel dyner*** *hon*
zero *enw* ***sero***, ***dim*** *hwn*
zest *enw* ***afiaith***, ***arddeliad*** *hwn*
zigzag *ans* ***igam-ogam***
zinc *enw* ***sinc*** *hwn*
zip *enw* (= energy) ***egni*** *hwn*; (fastener) ***sip***
  do up a z~ ***cau sip***
zodiac *enw* ***sidydd*** *hwn*
zone *enw* ***cylch***, ***parth*** *hwn*, ***cylchfa*** *hon*
  z~ off ***wedi'i gau***
zoo *enw* ***sw*** *hwn*
zoological *ans* ***sŵolegol***
zoologist *enw* ***sŵolegydd*** *hwn*
zoology *enw* ***sŵoleg*** *hon*
zoom *be* ***saethu***, ***gwibio***
  z~ in ***closio***, ***nesáu***
  z~ lens ***lens glosio*** *hon*

APPENDIX
Names of Countries

* Y ffurfiau a geir yn *Yr Atlas Cymraeg Newydd*

AFGHANISTAN **Affganistan; Afghanistan***
AFRICA **Affrica**
ALBANIA **Albania**
ALGERIA **Algeria**
ANGOLA **Angola**
ANTIGUA AND BARBUDA **Antigwa a Barbuda**
ARGENTINA **Ariannin**
ARMENIA **Armenia**
AUSTRALIA **Awstralia**
AUSTRIA **Awstria**
AZERBAIJAN **Azerbaijan**

BAHAMAS (THE) **Bahamas (y)**
BAHRAIN **Bahrain**
BANGLADESH **Bangladesh**
BARBADOS **Barbados**
BASQUE COUNTRY **Gwlad y Basg**
BAVARIA **Bafaria**
BELARUS **Belorwsia; Belarus***
BELGIUM **Gwlad Belg**
BELIZE **Belize**
BENIN **Benin**
BHUTAN **Bhwtan; Bhutan***
BOLIVIA **Bolifia; Bolivia***
BOSNIA-HERZEGOVINA **Bosnia a Hercegofina; Bosna-Hercegovina***
BOTSWANA **Botswana**
BRAZIL **Brasil**
BRITANNY **Llydaw**
BRUNEI **Brunei**
BULGARIA **Bwlgaria**
BURKINA FASO **Burkina**
BURMA **Burma**
BURUNDI **Burundi**

CAMBODIA **Cambodia**
CAMEROON **Camerŵn (y); Cameroun/Cameroon***
CANADA **Canada**
CAPE VERDE **Cabo Verde**
CATALONIA **Catalunya**
CENTRAL AFRICAN REPUBLIC **Gweriniaeth Canol Affrica**
CHAD **Tsiad; Tchad***
CHILE **Chile**
CHINA **Tsieina; China***
COLOMBIA **Colombia**
COMOROS **Comoro**
CONGO **Congo**
CORNWALL **Cernyw**
COSTA RICA **Costa Rica**
CROATIA **Croatia**
CUBA **Ciwba; Cuba***
CYPRUS **Cyprus**
CZECH REPUBLIC **Gweriniaeth Tsiec**

DENMARK **Denmarc**
DJIBOUTI **Djibouti**
DOMINICAN REPUBLIC **Gweriniaeth Dominica**

ECUADOR **Ecwador; Ecuador***
EGYPT **Aifft (yr)**
EL SALVADOR **El Salfador; El Salvador***
ENGLAND **Lloegr**
EQUATORIAL GUINEA **Guinea Gyhydeddol**
ERITREA **Eritrea**
ESTONIA **Estonia**
ETHIOPIA **Ethiopia**

FIJI **Ffiji; Fiji***
FINLAND **Ffindir (y)**
FRANCE **Ffrainc**
FRIESLAND **Ffryslân**

GABON **Gabon**
GAMBIA **Gambia**
GEORGIA **Georgia**
GERMANY **Almaen (yr)**
GHANA **Ghana**
GREECE **Gwlad Groeg:Groeg***
GREENLAND **Ynys Las (yr); Grønland***
GRENADA **Grenada**
GUATEMALA **Guatemala**
GUINEA **Guinée**
GUINEA-BISSEAU **Guiné-Bissau**
GUYANA **Guyana**

HAITI **Haiti**
HOLLAND **Iseldiroedd (yr)**
HONDURAS **Hondwras; Honduras***
HUNGARY **Hwngari**

ICELAND **Gwlad yr Iâ**
INDIA **India**
INDONESIA **Indonesia**
IRAN **Iran**
IRAQ **Irac; Iraq***
IRELAND **Iwerddon**
ISLE OF MAN **Ynys Manaw**
ISRAEL **Israel**
ITALY **Eidal (yr)**
IVORY COAST **Traeth Ifori (y); Côte d'Ivoire***

JAMAICA **Jamaica**
JAPAN **Japan**
JORDAN **Gwlad Iorddonen**

KAZAKHSTAN **Kazakstan**
KENYA **Cenia; Kenya***
KIRIBATI **Kiribati**
KUWAIT **Kuwait**
KYRGYZSTAN **Kyrgyzstan**

LAOS **Laos**
LAPPLAND **Lapdir**
LATVIA **Latfia; Latvia***
LEBANON **Libanus**
LESOTHO **Lesotho**
LIBERIA **Liberia**
LIBYA **Libia; Libya***
LIECHTENSTEIN **Liechtenstein**
LITHUANIA **Lithwania; Lithuania***

LUXEMBOURG **Lwcsembwrg; Luxembourg***

MACEDONIA **Macedonia**
MADAGASCAR **Madagascar**
MALAWI **Malawî**
MALAYSIA **Maleisia**; **Malaysia***
MALDIVES **Ynysoedd Maldif; Maldives***
MALI **Mali**
MALTA **Malta:Melita**
MAURITANIA **Mauritania**
MAURITIUS **Mawrisiws**; **Mauritius***
MEXICO **Mecsico**; **México***
MICRONESIA **Micronesia**
MOLDOVA **Moldofa:Moldafia**; **Moldova***
MONACO **Monaco**
MONGOLIA **Mongolia**
MOROCCO **Moroco**
MOZAMBIQUE **Mozambique; Moçambique***
MYANMAR **Myanmar**

NAMIBIA **Namibia**
NAURU **Nawrw**
NEPAL **Nepal**
NETHERLANDS (THE) **Iseldiroedd (yr)**
NEW ZEALAND **Seland Newydd**
NICARAGUA **Nicaragwa**; **Nicaragua***
NIGER **Niger**
NIGERIA **Nigeria**
NORTH KOREA **Gogledd Corea**; **Gogledd Korea***
NORWAY **Norwy**

OMAN **Oman**

PAKISTAN **Pacistan**
PANAMA **Panamá**
PAPUA NEW GUINEA **Papiwa Guinea Newydd**; **Papua* G~ N~**
PARAGUAY **Paragwâi; Paraguay***
PEOPLE'S REPUBLIC OF THE CONGO **Gweriniaeth Ddemocrataidd Congo**
PERU **Periw**
PHILIPPINES **Pilipinas**
POLAND **Gwlad Pwyl**
PORTUGAL **Portiwgal**

QATAR **Catar**; **Qatar***

REPUBLIC OF IRELAND **Gweriniaeth Iwerddon**
REPUBLIC OF SOUTH AFRICA **Gweriniaeth De Affrica**
ROMANIA **Rwmania**; **România***
RUSSIAN FEDERATION (THE) **Ffederasiwn Rwsia**
RWANDA **Rwanda**

SAMOA **Samoa**
SAN MARINO **San Marino**
SÃO TOMÉ AND PRÍNCIPE **São Tomé a Príncipe**
SAUDI ARABIA **Sawdi Arabia**; **Saudi Arabia***
SCANDINAVIA **Llychlyn**
SCOTLAND **Alban (yr)**

SÉNÉGAL **Senegal; Sénégal***
SEYCHELLES **Seychelles**
SIERRA LEONE **Sierra Leone**
SINGAPORE **Singapôr; Singapore***
SLOVAKIA **Slofacia**
SLOVENIA **Slofenia; Slovenija***
SOLOMON ISLANDS **Ynysoedd Solomon**
SOMALIA **Somalia**
SOUTH AFRICA **De Affrica**
SOUTH KOREA **De Corea; De Korea***
SPAIN **Sbaen**
SRI LANKA **Sri Lanca; Sri Lanka***
ST KITTS-NEVIS **Sant Kitts-Nevis**
ST LUCIA **Sant Lucia**
ST VINCENT AND THE GRENADINES **Sant Vincent a'r Grenadines**
SUDAN **Swdan (y); Sudan***
SURINAME **Swrinam; Suriname***
SWAZILAND **Gwlad Swasi; Gwlad Swazi***
SWEDEN **Sweden**
SWITZERLAND **Swistir (y)**
SYRIA **Syria**

TAIWAN **Taiwan**
TAJIKISTAN **Tajikistan**
TANZANIA **Tansanïa; Tanzania***
THAILAND **Gwlad Thai**
TOGO **Togo**
TONGA **Tonga**
TRINIDAD AND TOBAGO **Trinidad a Thobago; Trinidad a Tobago***
TUNISIA **Tiwnisia; Tunisia***
TURKEY **Twrci**
TURKMENISTAN **Tyrkmenistan; Turkmenistan***
TUVALU **Twfalw; Tuvalu***

UGANDA **Uganda**
UKRAINE **Wcráin; Ukrain***
UNITED ARAB EMIRATES **Emiradau Arabaidd Unedig**
UNITED KINGDOM (THE) **Deyrnas Unedig (y)**
UNITED STATES OF AMERICA (THE) **Unol Daleithiau America**
URUGUAY **Uruguay**
UZBEKISTAN **Wsbecistan; Uzbekistan***

VANUATU **Fanwatw; Vanuatu***
VENEZUELA **Feneswela; Venezuela***
VIETNAM **Fiet-nam; Viet Nam***

WALES **Cymru**

YEMEN **Yemen**
YUGOSLAVIA **Iwgoslafia**

ZAÏRE **Saïr**
ZAMBIA **Sambia; Zambia***
ZIMBABWE **Simbabwe; Zimbabwe***